Masque and Opera in England, 1656–1688

Masque and Opera in England, 1656–1688 presents a comprehensive study of the development of court masque and through-composed opera in England from the mid-1650s to the Revolution of 1688–89. In seeking to address the problem of generic categorization within a highly fragmentary corpus for which a limited amount of documentation survives, Andrew Walkling argues that our understanding of the distinctions between masque and opera must be premised upon a thorough knowledge of theatrical context and performance circumstances. Using extensive archival and literary evidence, detailed textual readings, rigorous tabular analysis, and meticulous collation of bibliographical and musical sources, this interdisciplinary study offers a host of new insights into a body of work that has long been of interest to musicologists, theatre historians, literary scholars, and historians of Restoration court and political culture, but which has hitherto been imperfectly understood.

A companion volume will explore the phenomenon of "dramatick opera" and its precursors on London's public stages between the early 1660s and the first decade of the eighteenth century.

Andrew R. Walkling is Associate Professor of Art History, English, and Theatre at Binghamton University (State University of New York, USA). He received his Ph.D. in British History from Cornell University, and has published widely on court culture and cultural production in Restoration England, and on the music of Henry Purcell.

Ashgate Interdisciplinary Studies in Opera
Series Editor
Roberta Montemorra Marvin, Institute for Italian Opera Studies,
University of Iowa, USA

The Ashgate Interdisciplinary Studies in Opera series provides a centralized and prominent forum for the presentation of cutting-edge scholarship that draws on numerous disciplinary approaches to a wide range of subjects associated with the creation, performance, and reception of opera (and related genres) in various historical and social contexts. There is great need for a broader approach to scholarship about opera. In recent years, the course of study has developed significantly, going beyond traditional musicological approaches to reflect new perspectives from literary criticism and comparative literature, cultural history, philosophy, art history, theatre history, gender studies, film studies, political science, philology, psychoanalysis, and medicine. The new brands of scholarship have allowed a more comprehensive interrogation of the complex nexus of means of artistic expression operative in opera, one that has meaningfully challenged prevalent historicist and formalist musical approaches. This series continues to move this important trend forward by including essay collections and monographs that reflect the ever-increasing interest in opera in non-musical contexts. Books in the series are linked by their emphasis on the study of a single genre—opera—yet are distinguished by their individualized and novel approaches by scholars from various disciplines/fields of inquiry. The remit of the series welcomes studies of seventeenth-century to contemporary opera from all geographical locations, including non-Western topics.

Recent titles in the series:

Opera as Soundtrack
Jeongwon Joe

Musicality in Theatre: Music as Model, Method and Metaphor in Theatre-Making
David Roesner

Postopera: Reinventing the Voice-Body
Jelena Novak

The Business of Opera
Anastasia Belina-Johnson and Derek B. Scott

Grétry's Operas and the French Public: From the Old Regime to Restoration
R.J. Arnold

Morality and Viennese Opera in the Age of Mozart and Beethoven
Martin Nedbal

Masque and Opera in England, 1656–1688

Andrew R. Walkling

LONDON AND NEW YORK

First published 2017
by Routledge
2 Park Square, Milton Park, Abingdon, Oxon OX14 4RN

and by Routledge
711 Third Avenue, New York, NY 10017

Routledge is an imprint of the Taylor & Francis Group, an informa business

© 2017 Andrew R. Walkling

The right of Andrew R. Walkling to be identified as author of this work
has been asserted by him in accordance with sections 77 and 78 of the
Copyright, Designs and Patents Act 1988.

All rights reserved. No part of this book may be reprinted or reproduced or
utilised in any form or by any electronic, mechanical, or other means, now
known or hereafter invented, including photocopying and recording, or in
any information storage or retrieval system, without permission in writing
from the publishers.

Trademark notice: Product or corporate names may be trademarks or
registered trademarks, and are used only for identification and explanation
without intent to infringe.

British Library Cataloguing-in-Publication Data
A catalogue record for this book is available from the British Library

Library of Congress Cataloging-in-Publication Data
Names: Walkling, Andrew R.
Title: Masque and opera in England, 1656–1688 / Andrew R. Walkling.
Description: Abingdon, Oxon; New York, NY: Routledge, 2017. |
Series: Ashgate interdisciplinary studies in opera | Includes bibliographical
references and index.
Identifiers: LCCN 2016011107 | ISBN 9781472446534
(hardback: alk. paper) | ISBN 9781315594217 (ebook)
Subjects: LCSH: Opera—England—17th century. | Masques with
music—17th century—History and criticism. | Masques, English—History
and criticism |
Classification: LCC ML1731.2 .W35 2017 | DDC 782.10942/09032—dc23
LC record available at http://lccn.loc.gov/2016011107

ISBN: 9781472446534 (hbk)
ISBN: 9781315594217 (ebk)

Bach musicological font developed by © Yo Tomita

Typeset in Times New Roman
by codeMantra

RUBECULÆ FILIO RUBECULÆ
MCMIII–MMII
AVO OPTIMO
FABULARUM AMATORI MUSICARUM OMNIUM
QUI ETIAM HAS
QUÆ INFRA EXPLICATÆ SUNT
DILIGEBAT
HOC OPUS DEDICATUM EST

Contents

List of figures, diagrams, and music examples	ix
List of tables	x
Acknowledgments	xi
Series editor's preface	xiv
Notes to the reader	xv
Introduction: Comparing apples and tomatoes: The problematics of Restoration masque and opera	1

PART I
"Their greatest gallantry imaginable": Masques, balls, and "recreational" acting at court — 25

1	Balls and the growth of Shrovetide entertainments	27
2	Youthful "recreational" theatrics, 1668–75	71
3	Masques and plays at court after 1675	112

PART II
"For such uses as the King shall direct": Through-composed opera, foreign musicians, and the Royall Academy of Musick — 141

4	Operatic experiments of the 1650s	143
5	Foreign musicians at the Restoration court, 1660–73	193
6	The Royall Academy of Musick, 1673–75	219
7	French musicians at court, 1675–89	264
8	Through-composed drama in the 1680s	291

viii *Contents*

Appendix A: Transcription of National Archives, London,
           AO1/2053/28, ff. 4ᵛ–5ʳ (costumes for
           1667 court ball)   309
Appendix B: Letters relating to Lord Sunderland's
           court ballet, 1686   311
Appendix C: Instrumental music associated with early
           operas and masques found in contemporary
           printed collections, 1662–c.1725   315

Select bibliography   319
Name index   333
Subject index   349
Works index   351

Figures, diagrams, and music examples

Figures

1.1 John Webb, design for Cockpit-in-Court Theatre, Whitehall Palace (originally constructed 1629–30), as remodeled in November 1660 (The Provost and Fellows of Worcester College, Oxford [Harris and Tait 4, detail])   37

4.1 Comparison of views of Rhodes from (a) von Breydenbach, *Peregrinationes in Terram Sanctam* (1486) (Wikimedia Commons [https://commons.wikimedia.org/wiki/File:Breydenbach_Rodis_ 1486.jpg]); (b) Camocio, *Isole famose porti* (1571–72) (By permission of the Folger Shakespeare Library [G1015 .C3 1574 Cage, pl. 69]); (c) Rosaccio, *Viaggio da Venetia, a Costantinopoli* (1598) (Houghton Library, Harvard University [Asia 9215.98*]); (d) Meisner/Kieser, *Thesaurus Philo-politicus* (1623/1638) (Wikimedia Commons [https://commons.wikimedia.org/wiki/File: Rodis_in_Orient_1638.jpg]); and (e) Webb, design for first scene from *The Siege of Rhodes* (1656) (© Devonshire Collection, Chatsworth. Reproduced by permission of Chatsworth Settlement Trustees)   169

4.2 Comparative details: Rhodes city wall, the coastline, and Mount Filerimos in three of John Webb's designs for *The Siege of Rhodes* (© Devonshire Collection, Chatsworth. Reproduced by permission of Chatsworth Settlement Trustees)   171

6.1 Anonymous engraved fold-out frontispiece from the *Ariane/Ariadne* programme libretti, showing a scene from the Prologue with Thames, Tiber, and Seine singing (Houghton Library, Harvard University [38576.42])   249

Diagrams

4.1 Stage configuration and coordination of scene changes in *The Siege of Rhodes*   174

Music examples

4.1 "Iantha," from *The Dancing Master*, ?1662   191

Tables

I.1	Comparison of theatrical works originally written for court performance, 1673–83	22
1.1	Balls at court, 1660–85, for which identities of some court participants are known	33
1.2	Non-dramatic balls and "masques" known to have been performed at court, 1660–88	40
1.3	Noble performers expected to appear in Lord Sunderland's court ballet, 15 February 1686	54
1.4	Comparison of Roger North's accounts of *The Queen's Masque* of 1671	67
2.1	Shrovetide/Lenten/Eastertide plays and masques at court, 1660–85, for which identities of some court participants are known	75
2.2	Noble/gentle performers in *Calisto*	97
2.3	Digest of work on stage and scenery for *Calisto*, November 1674–February 1675	104
4.1	Theatrical works known or believed to deploy through-composition or to contain substantial recitative passages, 1600–73	147
4.2	Generic features in (and performance venues for) the "operatic" productions of Davenant, compared with works by Flecknoe, Jordan, and Shirley, 1654–59	155
4.3	Musical, scenic, and plot structure in *The Siege of Rhodes*	165
4.4	Performers in the Duke's Company's "Solyman" plays, 1656–76	180
4.5	Instrumental music in the "operatic" productions of Sir William Davenant, 1656–59	187
4.6	Composers for the "operatic" productions of Sir William Davenant, 1656–59	192
5.1	Comparison of generic formulae in theatre patents and related documents of the 1660s	195
5.2	Gold chains and medals issued to Italian performers by Charles II, 1662–73	205
6.1	Church collections on king's brief for the Theatre Royal and neighboring properties, 1672–74	243
6.2	French dancers employed in *Ariane* and *Calisto*, 1674–75	259
7.1	Court payments to certain French musicians, 1668–89	274
7.2	Pastoral and domestic operatic episodes of the Sieur de Saint-Évremond, c.1678–1703	288

Acknowledgments

In looking retrospectively over an undertaking whose roots extend as far back as the early 1990s, it is not easy to summarize the numerous debts of gratitude that I have incurred. Many colleagues and friends have helped in ways large and small, by reading parts of the text, by engaging in conversations over particular points, or simply by expressing support for and interest in the project as it developed. Given the number and variety of those involved, I begin with a general apology to anyone who may inadvertently be left out: you know who you are, and every individual who has contributed to the collective venture of my growth as a scholar has my sincere thanks. It has been a long process, to be sure, but I have benefited from it in innumerable ways, and hope that I may someday be able to give back to others in a measure equal to what I have received.

Special appreciation is due to several esteemed colleagues who have supported my efforts over many years: Clive Holmes, who stood by me as I figured out my academic path; Neal Zaslaw, who opened numerous doors in the musicological world; Curtis Price, who consistently championed my work from its earliest stages; James Winn, who has been a steadfast and generous source of encouragement and advice over many years; and Ellen Harris, who not only read the manuscript of this book for Ashgate and provided valuable comments, but whose kindness and support have manifested themselves time and again. I would also like to thank Michael Burden, Peter Holman, and Robert Hume, each of whom stimulated in fundamental ways my developing interest in the field, as well as Linda Austern, Rebecca Herissone, Kathryn Lowerre, Robert Shay, Susan Shifrin, Robert Thompson, and Amanda Eubanks Winkler, who have offered friendship and support, as well as invaluable opportunities for intellectual conversation and debate. A number of other colleagues have provided guidance and feedback on specific matters—some so long ago that they may not even recall having done so: Andrew Ashbee, Christina Bashford, William Bulman, Hyeyun Chin, Beth Glixon, Frances Harris, Rebecca Harris-Warrick, Lynn Hulse, Claudia Kairoff, Jennifer Keith, David Lasocki, Peter Leech, Alan Luhring, Judith Mackerras, Carol Marsh, Mary Ann O'Donnell, Steven Plank, Judith Rock, Sandra Tuppen, and Bryan White all have my gratitude for their contributions.

Throughout the research and writing process, I have benefited from the kindness and professionalism of the librarians, archivists, and support staffs of The

xii *Acknowledgments*

National Archives, the British Library, the London Metropolitan Archives, and Westminster Abbey Library (London); the Bodleian Library and the Library of Worcester College (Oxford); the William Andrews Clark Memorial Library (Los Angeles, CA); the Folger Shakespeare Library (Washington, DC); the Department of Rare Books and Special Collections, Princeton University Library (Princeton, NJ); the New York Public Library, including the Library for the Performing Arts at Lincoln Center (New York, NY); the Irving S. Gilmore Music Library and the Beinecke Rare Book and Manuscript Library, Yale University (New Haven, CT); the Houghton Library, Harvard University (Cambridge, MA); and perhaps most notably Binghamton University Library, especially the hard-working staff of the Interlibrary Loan Department, who have always risen to the many challenges I have posed them.

I have received material support for travel to archives from several sources, including a long-ago Theodor E. Mommsen Travel Fellowship from the Department of History at Cornell University and, more recently, funds provided by the office of the Dean of Harpur College of Arts and Sciences, Binghamton University (generously bestowed by former dean Jean-Pierre Mileur) and grants from the Francis X. Newman Fund of the Department of English at Binghamton University. The earliest stages of writing this book were carried out at the William Andrews Clark Memorial Library during a one-month fellowship from the Center for Seventeenth- and Eighteenth-Century Studies at the University of California, Los Angeles. The cost of obtaining and licensing the images reproduced herein has been defrayed through a subvention from the AMS 75 PAYS Endowment of the American Musicological Society, funded in part by the National Endowment for the Humanities and the Andrew W. Mellon Foundation. A special note of thanks is due to my dear friends Andrew and Estelle Wilson, who have remained unstinting in their open-ended hospitality during my periodic research trips to London.

I am grateful to have found an intellectual home in the Binghamton University Departments of Art History, English, and Theatre, all three of which have warmly welcomed and supported my interdisciplinary endeavors. My many cherished colleagues are too numerous to name individually here, although I am especially grateful to John Tagg, Olivia Holmes, and Paul Schleuse, who have proven themselves, each in their own ways, indulgent friends and most agreeable interlocutors throughout the process.

This book, which underwent several changes of focus over the course of its gestation, might not have come to fruition were it not for the patient ministrations of Laura Macy at Ashgate, who recognized the project's potential and lent it her support at a critical stage. I am very much indebted to her, as well as to Roberta Marvin, who enthusiastically seconded her opinion; to Emma Gallon, who has expertly overseen the final production phase and who continues to lend her kind and attentive support to my efforts; and to Ellen Harris and the other (anonymous) external reader for Ashgate, both of whom offered valuable comments that helped me to sharpen the presentation of my arguments. Naturally, I take full responsibility for any errors, factual or editorial, that may arise.

Acknowledgments xiii

Finally, the success of this project—perhaps more than most—has hinged on the unwavering dedication and encouragement of my family. My son George endured my extended work weeks and other absences for so long that he has now reached an age where he can judge the results for himself; even if the subject is not precisely his cup of tea, I have no doubt that he will tackle it with his characteristic critical acumen. My parents, Robert and Julia Walkling, never ceased to believe in me; my mother merits special mention, both for reading much of the text in draft, and for serving as the conduit, not just for my oft-lamented protanomaly but also for those less tangible hereditary qualities bequeathed by my late grand-father. Throughout his near-century among us he offered an enduring model of intellectual vitality, and the dedication of this volume to his memory speaks for itself. Above all else, I cannot sufficiently express the depth of my gratitude to my beloved partner, Lakshmi Damayanthi. Without her devoted companionship and unflagging industry, her relentless cajoling, her indefatigable provision of suste-nance both physical and emotional, and her persistent willingness to read what-ever I put in front of her, this book might never have seen the light of day. Thank you, *mage wasthuwe*!

Series editor's preface

Ashgate Interdisciplinary Studies in Opera provides a centralized and prominent forum for the presentation of cutting-edge scholarship that draws on numerous disciplinary approaches on a wide range of subjects associated with the creation, performance, dissemination, and reception of opera and related genres in various historical and social contexts. The series includes topics from the seventeenth century to the present and from all geographical locations, including non-Western traditions.

In recent years, the field of opera studies has not only come into its own but has developed significantly, going beyond traditional musicological approaches to reflect new perspectives from literary criticism and comparative literature, cultural history, philosophy, art history, theater history, gender studies, film studies, political science, philology, psycho-analysis, and even medicine. The new brands of scholarship have allowed a more comprehensive and intensive interrogation of the complex nexus of means of artistic expression operative in opera, one that has meaningfully challenged prevalent historicist and formalist musical approaches. Today, interdisciplinary, or as some prefer cross-disciplinary, opera studies are receiving increasingly widespread attention, and the ways in which scholars, practitioners, and the public think about the artform known as opera continue to change and expand. *Ashgate Interdisciplinary Studies in Opera* seeks to move this important trend forward by including essay collections and monographs that reflect the ever-increasing interest in opera in non-musical contexts.

Roberta Montemorra Marvin
Series Editor

Notes to the reader

Like any focused academic investigation, the present study demands of its readers an understanding of certain technical matters that, while they may appear self-evident to the author and a small clutch of like-minded specialists, can give rise to confusion if they are not clearly articulated at the outset. My aim here is to offer explications of four fundamental practices upon which the discussion in this book relies, and of which the reader's awareness is vital to a proper appreciation and use of the book's arguments and findings. The first represents a standard caveat offered in many academic works examining aspects of early modern British history; the second deals with my particular concern for the treatment of primary sources (a justification for which appears in the Introduction, below), the third explains the referencing of certain administrative documents, and the fourth treats my approach to the citation of scholarly materials. Notwithstanding the present book's seemingly dense prose style, lengthy discursive footnotes, and complex tabular analyses, it has always been my intention to avoid gratuitously opaque language or technical jargon, and thus to foster a genuine appreciation on the reader's part for this topic that has so captivated me for such a long time.

Dating

From 5 October 1582 until 2 September 1752, a chronological span just shy of 170 years, the British Isles persisted in using the inaccurate Julian Calendar (first introduced in 45 BC by Julius Caesar), even as the major powers of Western Europe gradually adopted the reforms promulgated by Pope Gregory XIII in his bull *Inter gravissimas*. Thus, throughout the seventeenth century, English dates were ten days behind those of many of the country's Continental neighbors, including France, Spain, parts of Germany and the Low Countries, and much of Italy.[1] Diplomatic and other international correspondence frequently deployed

---

1 During the Restoration period, exceptions to this differential (*i.e.* Western European states whose calendars still matched that in use in the British Isles) included the Protestant regions of Germany and Switzerland, the northern provinces of the Netherlands, Tuscany, and all of Scandinavia. On 29 February 1700 (a date that did not exist on the Continent), Britain fell an additional day behind, even as several of the aforementioned states (Protestant Germany and Switzerland, the remaining Dutch provinces, and Denmark) were in the process of transitioning to the reformed calendar of their mostly Roman Catholic neighbors.

xvi *Notes to the reader*

a double-dating system, combining "Old Style" (Julian) and "New Style" (Gregorian) dates, *e.g.* "21/31 July" or "28 May/7 June." In instances where such documents are being cited, I reproduce this double-dating; however, when discussing events taking place in countries using the Gregorian Calendar, I simply give the New Style date, always specifying that fact in a parenthetical or footnoted remark. (An exception to this practice is in Tables 1.1, 2.1, and 2.2, where the dates of birth of those born overseas are recalculated into Old Style, with the recalculated date—or date and month, as appropriate—given in square brackets.) Finally, in any potentially confusing instances where English events are described in documents written by foreigners (*e.g.* those visiting from abroad) using New Style dating, the "correct" Old Style date of the event is given without comment in the text itself, with the discrepancy addressed in the notes.

The dating of English documents, and hence events, is further complicated by the fact that—despite widespread recognition of 1 January as "New Year's Day"—the English civil year officially began on 25 March (the Feast of the Annunciation, or "Lady Day"). As a result, certain kinds of documents, including court and other administrative records and some (but not all) printed books created or published between 1 January and 25 March may carry the previous year's date.[2] Unfortunately, however, the practice was by no means consistent in the later seventeenth century: while some scribes and printers scrupulously applied a dual-year date, *e.g.* "1662/3" or "1679/80," others have left us to guess whether they were adhering to the old system or conceding to the new—or indeed if a document with only a year on it was produced in a January–December year or a March–March year. In many instances, context or corroborating sources can resolve doubts, but this is not always the case, and historical scholarship on early modern Britain is littered with misdatings of documents and events that are the result of insufficient attention to the matter. I have therefore sought throughout the present book to be as thorough and accurate as possible in ascertaining the correct years of dated documents, or, barring that, to point out any uncertainties. In most instances, it has not been difficult to establish the correct year of an ambiguously dated document, and, reasoning that the old dual-year dating system is at best irrelevant and at worst confusing, I have silently modernized most such dates, implicitly regarding the year as beginning on 1 January. However, where direct quotations or dates of publication in bibliographical citations are concerned, and the year given is "incorrect" according to modern usage, I editorially restore the appropriate dual-year date in square brackets, *e.g.* "1659[/60]."

Transcription of primary sources

In keeping with this book's emphasis on the careful examination of primary sources, I have made every effort to present accurate, diplomatic transcriptions of seventeenth-century documents, both printed and manuscript. This includes reproducing typographical anomalies (*e.g.* stray italic characters) in the former,

---

2 Scotland, it should be noted, did not face this problem, having converted in 1600 to a civil year beginning on 1 January.

Notes to the reader   xvii

superscripts and abbreviation marks in the latter, and eccentric spelling and punctuation in all cases. My adherence to diplomatic principles extends even to a restrained signaling of ornamental capitals in some poetic and musical sources (*e.g.* "DEux ..."), although I have avoided the fussiness of typographical pseudo-facsimiles, for example silently modernizing all long-"s" and ligatured characters.[3] By the same token, while occasional occurrences of "dropped" and "turned" letters in printed sources have been corrected in square brackets, certain other by-products of the age of hand-set presswork, such as varying point sizes, swash capitals, font changes, and vagaries of spacing and kerning, are ignored, except in rare cases where they may be deemed to have textual significance.

Wherever possible, I have retranscribed documents from scratch rather than rely on published transcriptions. This process has frequently revealed inconsistencies (most of them subtle, but a few more glaring) between the originals and their modern "copies," and I hope that my efforts to provide reliable, fresh versions will be of service, even as I acknowledge the likelihood that future scholars will discover errors on my part as well. Perfection may be a goal, but it is seldom an outcome, and thus my primary intention is necessarily to model a process rather than to achieve anything like an impeccable result.

The notable exception to the aforementioned practice is in the rendering of seventeenth-century printed book titles in bibliographical references. This is a sticky issue for those who fancy themselves bibliographically discriminating and who recognize the value of the meticulous descriptive techniques codified by Fredson Bowers.[4] Notwithstanding my own admiration for Bowers, I have chosen in the present study to err on the side of simplicity, and to regularize the always-complicated typography of early modern title-pages into a form that largely follows modern conventions. This includes standardizing, at least to a degree, capitalization and punctuation, as well as shortening titles in most instances to a manageable length wherein only essential information is provided. I confess to a certain discomfort with this compromise, as it actually produces greater inconsistency by relying on case-by-case decisions about what to include or exclude, how to interpret display formats, etc. Among the many printed sources cited in this book, Restoration printed playbooks, with their characteristic two-part titling and their frequent identification of genre and performance circumstances—all set off by a hodgepodge of approaches to punctuation, capitalization, italicization, lineation, and spacing—provide an object lesson in the pitfalls of trying to bring a bibliographer's order to an inherently disorderly practice.[5] Ultimately, I ask readers'

---

3 A distinctive example of the schematic representation of decorative initial capitals can be found in Eugene Haun's quirky 1971 study, *But Hark! More Harmony* (cited in the Introduction, n. 10). Curiously, Haun seems to have restricted the practice to those passages in which he discusses the work of Richard Flecknoe: *cf.* pp. 26, 43–48, and 97–101 with p. 146.

4 Fredson Bowers, *Principles of Bibliographical Description* (Princeton: Princeton University Press, 1949; rpt. Winchester: St. Paul's Bibliographies, 1986–87; *idem* and New Castle, Delaware: Oak Knoll Press, 1994), esp. pp. 135–84.

5 Data on publishers given on the title-pages of seventeenth-century books is similarly inconsistent. Frequently, both printer and publisher/bookseller were listed (often using the formula "by [printer] for [bookseller]"); in most cases, I give only the name of the latter. However, when only a printer

xviii *Notes to the reader*

forgiveness for what looks like a lax approach to a difficult problem, even as I profess to have exercised tremendous care in every other aspect of the handling of primary sources.

Referencing of court and theatrical administrative records

Much of this book's argument is dependent upon a thorough scrutiny of manuscript documents, and many of those documents constitute official records produced by the royal court, treating administrative and financial matters relating to (among other things) the court musical establishment and the patent theatre companies. The vast majority of these records are held by The National Archives at Kew, London (known until 2003 as the Public Record Office), where they are ordinarily classed according to the government department by which they were originally produced. In the present book, citations preceded by the following abbreviations should be understood as referring to manuscripts found at this repository:

ADM	Records of the Admiralty
AO	Records of the Exchequer and Audit Department (Audit Office)
C	Records of Chancery
E	Records of the Exchequer
LC	Records of the Lord Chamberlain's Department
LS	Records of the Lord Steward's Department (Board of Green Cloth)
PC	Records of the Privy Council Office
PRO	Public Record Office: Gifts and Deposits[6]
SP	Records of the State Paper Office
T	Records of the Treasury
WORK	Records of the Ministry (*formerly* Office) of Works

---

is named, I supply that name, preceded by the preposition "by" to indicate the distinction. Where even less information appears, I use the abbreviations "n. p." ("no place," *i.e.* city of publication, listed) and "n. pub." ("no publisher" or printer listed). Where the first names of publishers (or printers) are abbreviated in a source, I expand them in brackets when possible.

6 This class of "extra-departmental" material includes a set of official financial documents generated during the tenure of Thomas Osborne, 1st Earl of Danby, as Lord Treasurer (1673–79) and retained by Danby upon his dismissal from office, according to contemporary custom. Most were placed on deposit in the Public Record Office in August 1929, where they are classed as PRO30/32/5–14 and 30–54 (a few are in the British Library, as Additional MSS 28074–77). Certain of these documents properly fall within established sequences of Treasury records, including T11, T27, T29, T33, T52–54, and T64, a fact that I have sought to indicate in the footnotes with the parenthetical designation "properly T ... ." In some instances, places in the numerical sequence of Treasury documents have been reserved (hence PRO30/32/39 = properly T11/4); in others, I have had to interpolate (hence PRO30/32/40 = properly T11/[7a]).

Notes to the reader xix

Thanks to the work of a number of extremely diligent scholars, certain types of documents, from The National Archives and elsewhere, have been thoroughly calendared, allowing much of the data they contain to be accessed from any good research library. Despite my concern to examine and retranscribe original sources wherever possible, I have sought to promote both accessibility and accountability by consistently providing parenthetical cross-references to the following four comprehensive calendars, taking care to note cases where information has been mis-cited, or where a relevant document is missing from the appropriate calendar. Each calendar is cited according to the short references listed below:

Ashbee — Andrew Ashbee, ed., *Records of English Court Music* (9 vols.: vols. 1–4: Snodland, Kent: Andrew Ashbee, 1986–91; vols. 5–9: Aldershot: Scolar Press, 1991–96) [*N.B.* vol. 1: 1660–1685; vol. 2: 1685–1714; vol. 3: 1625–1649; vol. 4: 1603–1625; vol. 5: 1625–1714; vol. 6: 1558–1603; vol. 7: 1485–1558; vol. 8: 1485–1714; vol. 9: index].

Calendar of State Papers, Domestic — John Bruce, William Douglas Hamilton, and Sophia Crawford Lomas, eds., *Calendar of State Papers, Domestic Series*, 1625–1649 (23 vols.: London: Her Majesty's Stationery Office, 1858–97); Mary Anne Everett Green, ed., *Calendar of State Papers, Domestic Series*, 1649–60 (13 vols.: London: Her Majesty's Stationery Office, 1875–86); Mary Anne Everett Green, F. H. Blackburne Daniell, and Francis Bickley, eds., *Calendar of State Papers, Domestic Series*, 1660–1685 (28 vols.: London: Longman, Green, Longman, & Roberts; Longman, Green, Longman, Roberts, and Green; Longmans, Green, Reader, and Dyer; Her/His Majesty's Stationery Office, 1860–1939); E. K. Timings, ed., *Calendar of State Papers Preserved in the Public Records Office*[,] *Domestic Series*, 1685–1689 (3 vols.: London: Her Majesty's Stationery Office, 1960–72); William John Hardy and Edward Bateson, eds., *Calendar of State Papers, Domestic Series*, 1689–1702 (11 vols.: London: Her/His Majesty's Stationery Office, 1895–1937) [*N.B.* volumes cited by date of coverage].

Calendar of Treasury Books — William A. Shaw, ed., *Calendar of Treasury Books* (8 vols. in 15: London: His Majesty's Stationery Office, 1904–23).

Register — Judith Milhous and Robert D. Hume, comps. and eds., *A Register of English Theatrical Documents 1660–1737* (2 vols.: Carbondale: Southern Illinois University Press, 1991) [*N.B.* items cited by catalogue number].

xx *Notes to the reader*

Citation of sources

The Selected Bibliography at the end of this volume lists printed primary and secondary sources deemed to be of central importance to the topic at hand and/or that occur multiple times in the footnotes. Within the footnotes themselves, full references are supplied only at a source's first appearance in each of the three sections of the book (the Introduction, Part I, and Part II); subsequently, abbreviated references (consisting of author's surname and, where necessary, an abbreviated title or title keyword) are given, but with cross-references provided where a substantial interval has elapsed since the initial full reference. The Selected Bibliography generally does not include printed primary and secondary sources that appear only in a single footnote; nor does it list any manuscript sources.

A few scholarly studies and editions of seventeenth-century texts are either so ubiquitous or so essential to the fabric of the present book that I have chosen to give their full citations here, rather than in the footnotes and bibliography. They are listed alphabetically according to the short reference used throughout:

Boswell	Eleanore Boswell (Murrie), *The Restoration Court Stage (1660–1702), With a Particular Account of the Production of* Calisto (Cambridge, MA: Harvard University Press, 1932; rpt. New York: Barnes & Noble, 1966).
Calendar of State Papers, Venetian	Rawdon Brown, G. Cavendish-Bentinck, Horatio F. Brown, and Allen B. Hinds, trans. and eds., *Calendar of State Papers and Manuscripts, Relating to English Affairs Existing in the Archives and Collections of Venice, and in Other Libraries of Northern Italy* (38 vols.: London: Her/His Majesty's Stationery Office, 1864–1947).
Evelyn, *Diary*	E. S. de Beer, ed., *The Diary of John Evelyn* (6 vols.: Oxford: Oxford University Press, 1955).
Holman, *Fiddlers*	Peter Holman, *Four and Twenty Fiddlers: The Violin at the English Court, 1540–1690* (Oxford: Clarendon Press, 1993).
Pepys, *Diary*	Robert Latham and William Matthews, eds., *The Diary of Samuel Pepys* (11 vols.: London: Bell & Hyman; Berkeley: University of California Press, 1970–83).
Stationers' Register	G. E. Briscoe Eyre, Charles Robert Rivington, and H. R. Plomer, eds., *A Transcript of the Registers of the Worshipful Company of Stationers: From 1640–1708 A. D.* (3 vols.: London: [the Bible Office of His Majesty's Printers for the Roxburghe Club], 1913–14; rpt. Gloucester, MA: Peter Smith, 1950, 1967).
Term Catalogues	Edward Arber, ed., *The Term Catalogues, 1668–1709 A.D.* (3 vols.: vol. 1: London: Aberdeen University Press for Professor Edward Arber, 1903; vols. 2–3: London: Guilford and Hart for Professor Edward Arber, 1905–6; rpt. New York: Johnson Reprint Corp., 1965).

Once again, this book's vaunted claim to thoroughness and consistency of approach is somewhat belied by one arbitrary set of omissions. Readers familiar with current conventions in musicology and early modern British bibliography may be surprised to learn that I have avoided referencing Donald Wing's *Short-Title Catalogue* of English-language books from the latter part of the seventeenth century[7] or the catalogues of early printed and manuscript musical sources produced by the Répertoire International des Sources Musicales (RISM) project,[8] and that I do not use the popular RISM system of library sigla.[9] All of these are useful tools: Wing, in particular, offers a potential solution to the problems of citation by title-page transcription discussed above. Yet this otherwise indispensable scholarly resource is peculiarly deficient with respect to certain kinds of musical materials, and even the RISM catalogues do not entirely fill that gap. More to the point, my reluctance to pepper my footnotes with Wing and RISM numbers and sigla is animated by a desire to avoid esoteric codes that demand cross-checking from readers whose concentration is already being tested by the book's substantial critical apparatus. Thus, the omission, however much it may run counter to my own scholarly instincts, is by design: notwithstanding its narrowness of focus or its undeniable technical complexities, the present study is intended above all to be enlightening and even pleasurable to its readers. As I frequently tell my students, genuine erudition results from a collaborative practice of investigation, in which those who are fortunate enough to be privy to a body of knowledge lead others on a mutually invigorating journey in which the process of discovery is as rewarding as, if not more so than, the final result. It is my hope that the exploration that follows goes some way toward embodying that principle.

---

7 Donald Wing, ed. (rev. and ed. by John J. Morrison, Carolyn W. Nelson, *et al.*), *Short-Title Catalogue of Books Printed in England, Scotland, Ireland, Wales, and British America and of English Books Printed in Other Countries 1641–1700* (4 vols.: second ed. [with vol. 1 rev.]; New York: Modern Language Association of America, 1982–98).

8 Karlheinz Schlager, Otto E. Albrecht, Ilse and Jürgen Kindermann, and Gertraut Haberkamp, eds., *Répertoire International des Sources Musicales, Series A/I: Einzeldrucke vor 1800* (15 [*i.e.* 14] vols.: Kassel: Bärenreiter-Verlag, 1971–2003), and François Lesure, ed., *Répertoire International des Sources Musicales, Series B/I: Recueils Imprimés XVIᵉ–XVIIᵉ Siècles, I[:] Liste Chronologique* (Munich: G. Henle Verlag, 1960).

9 See http://www.rism.info/en/sigla.html.

Introduction

Comparing apples and tomatoes: The problematics of Restoration masque and opera

"The purpose of the following pages is to trace the early development in England of what may be called the operatic principle." With these words, the musicologist Edward J. Dent opened his classic 1928 study *Foundations of English Opera*, a work that, for all the scholarship that has appeared subsequently, remains the seminal text for our understanding of large-scale English musical drama in the latter part of the seventeenth century.[1] It was Dent who laid out the essential terms of the discussion, and who delineated the basic generic limits of the English "operatic" form, and thus he who has influenced a century of scholarship on the intersection of the theatrical and the musical in England from the demise of the "classic" court masque after 1640 to the advent of Italian opera at the beginning of the eighteenth century. In *Foundations*, Dent set out to draw connections between the theatrical music of the Jacobean and Caroline courts and the efflorescence of public opera in the late-Stuart and Hanoverian period by tracing the often shifting and seemingly haphazard *mélange* of stylistic and generic approaches to musical drama that characterized the Restoration era and the years immediately thereafter, up to the death of Henry Purcell in 1695.

Dent's identification of an "operatic principle"—one that, he explains, "is neither the normal musical principle nor the normal dramatic principle"—is fundamental to the expository and interpretive thrust of his argument. Whereas literary and musicological scholarship have tended, in the modern era, to maintain their own distinct methodologies and objects of study, opera by its very nature has always demanded an interdisciplinary approach that is committed not just to the surmounting of conventional analytical categories and bodies of knowledge, but to a rigorous conceptual flexibility as well. This Dent achieves by opening up his definition of the "operatic" to encompass a wide variety of works whose deployment of music in a dramatic context ranges from the scrupulous "through-composition" with which the form has commonly been associated ever since the

---

1 Edward J. Dent, *Foundations of English Opera: A Study of Musical Drama in England During the Seventeenth Century* (Cambridge: Cambridge University Press, 1928; rpt. New York: Da Capo Press, 1965), vii. As Dent explains (p. ix), the book was "ready for press in 1915," but nonetheless benefited from further revisions in the dozen years that followed.

2   *Introduction*

earliest experiments of the Florentine *Camerata*, to the seemingly indiscriminate insertion of autonomous songs and musical episodes into primarily spoken plays. The boundaries of the category are thus shown to be both fungible and porous, a fact that complicates efforts at evaluation while at the same time allowing for the circumvention of such unhelpfully reductionist questions as what constituted the *first* English opera, or how the supposed English "resistance" to operatic form contributed to the circumstances under which Insular music would lag developmentally behind that of the Continent for centuries thereafter.

Foundations of English Opera represents a dual enterprise, at once archaeological and teleological in character. Dent gestures towards the former in his assertion that while "neither poets nor musicians have grasped it except spasmodically and intuitively," his operatic principle "underlies all their efforts, and the task of the historian only becomes more interesting as it becomes more difficult."[2] Dent's concern in this regard is to shine a light into the darker corners of English theatrical history and generic experimentation, noting that whereas "[a] writer who deals with opera from Gluck onwards may reasonably be expected to have at least seen on the stage most of the works that he mentions," in the case of the operatic output of seventeenth-century England (with the possible exception, he avers, of Nahum Tate and Henry Purcell's *Dido and Aeneas*), "[a] considerable effort of imagination is ... needed in reading such records as still remain."[3] *Foundations* therefore strives to reveal and evaluate the obscure textual and factual details appertaining to what can at best be described as an amorphous and highly fragmentary body of work—this despite the fact that Dent's book is extremely sparing with footnotes, and that it owes a significant debt to the archival work of earlier scholars, in particular W. H. Cummings, W. Barclay Squire, Henri Prunières, and W. J. Lawrence, as well as Dent's contemporary, Montague Summers. The status of *Foundations* as an essential work of scholarship thus derives not so much from the originality of its archival discoveries as from Dent's inspired synthesis of the materials unearthed by his predecessors and contemporaries as part of the first great age of modern historical documentation.

At the same time, Dent's book, as its title implies, offers a narrative whose historiographical orientation might best be described as Whiggish. This characterization can be amply illustrated by quoting Dent's other opening line, a more notorious salvo found not in his book's extra-paginated Preface but rather at the beginning of its first chapter: "The history of English Opera has been for the most part the record of three centuries of failure."[4] By presenting an argument whose underlying goal is to identify the seeds of "true" English opera, and by extension to seek some explanation for the supposedly belated germination of those seeds in an ungrateful British soil, Dent reinforces certain narrow and ultimately anachronistic modern cultural presuppositions about what kinds of musical drama merit

---

2 *Ibid.*, vii–viii.
3 *Ibid.*, viii–ix.
4 *Ibid.*, 1.

the designation "opera" and hence qualify as successes according to that exclusive definition. This bias is inadvertently betrayed by his invocation of *Dido and Aeneas*, a work well known to opera lovers—and, indeed, frequently held up as the pinnacle of English operatic achievement—but which, as recent scholarship has shown, is in fact one of the era's most anomalous and generically indeterminate creations. Despite superficial similarities, the basis of *Dido*'s appeal to modern opera-going audiences from Dent's time to ours actually bears little relation to the original circumstances or motivations behind the work's composition and putative first production. To the extent the mysterious *Dido and Aeneas* warrants consideration in the present study, it is only as a somewhat peripheral phenomenon whose existence serves as a foil for the evaluation of a corpus of works that are better documented and hence more readily susceptible to classification and analysis on the basis of context.

In the years since Dent penned his groundbreaking study, the conditions of scholarly investigation into the worlds of late-seventeenth-century British music and drama have undergone tremendous change. In terms of access to essential primary documentation, Dent would have had recourse to Henry Cart de Lafontaine's *The King's Musick* (1909)[5] and Allardyce Nicoll's *A History of Restoration Drama* (first published 1923),[6] as well as to much of the series of printed calendars of official documents held in the Public Record Office (now The National Archives) in London, the *Calendar of State Papers, Domestic* (1860–1939) and the *Calendar of Treasury Books* (1904–23).[7] Those of us working today, however, are considerably more fortunate. Restoration theatre studies took a great leap forward in 1960 with the publication of William Van Lennep's first volume of *The London Stage*: despite being now badly in need of an updated edition (and hence rarely cited in the present book as an authority in its own right), this work nevertheless provides an indispensable starting-point for any investigation into the London theatre world between the restoration of Charles II and the turn of the eighteenth century. Of even greater utility to the efforts of twenty-first-century scholars are two up-to-date calendars, Judith Milhous and Robert D. Hume's *A Register of English Theatrical Documents* (1991), a complement of sorts to *The London Stage*, and Andrew Ashbee's monumental *Records of English Court Music* series (1986–96), which builds upon and largely supersedes Lafontaine's old *King's Musick* volume. More recently, online databases of printed material, including Chadwyck-Healey's "Early English Books Online," Gale/Cengage's "Eighteenth-Century Collections Online," and the Bibliothèque Nationale de France's free "Gallica"

---

5 Henry Cart de Lafontaine, ed., *The King's Musick: A Transcript of Records Relating to Music and Musicians (1460–1700)* (London: Novello and Company, 1909).

6 Allardyce Nicoll, *A History of Restoration Drama, 1660–1700* (Cambridge: Cambridge University Press, 1923; rev. eds., 1928, 1940; rev. and reissued 1952 as vol. 1 of *A History of English Drama, 1660–1900* [7 vols.: Cambridge: Cambridge University Press], 1952–59, 1973; vol. 1 rpt. 1961, 1965, 1967, 1977, 2009).

7 For full references to these and other calendars and studies listed below, see the list of General Citations, p. xviii.

4   *Introduction*

service,[8] combined with the ongoing liberalization of self-service digital photography regulations at most major research libraries and archival repositories in the United Kingdom and the United States, have dramatically enhanced opportunities for scholars to access, with minimal fuss, a wide array of primary sources from the period.

The situation is rather different with respect to the scholarly edifice for which the aforementioned sources serve as a foundation. Dent narrowly missed the chance to avail himself of two important works of theatre history scholarship, Leslie Hotson's *The Commonwealth and Restoration Stage* (1928) and Eleanore Boswell (later Murrie)'s *The Restoration Court Stage* (1932), both of which (notwithstanding occasional errors) supply, alongside exhaustive documentation, crucial new insights into their respective subjects. With regard to the specific intersection of theatre and music, however, no post-Dentine study of consequence that was not primarily or exclusively concerned with Henry Purcell appeared in print during the next four decades.[9] Then, in the 1970s, there emerged three quite different but all essential works: Eugene Haun's *But Hark! More Harmony* (1971), a textual/historical study of Restoration opera libretti; Richard Luckett's article-length survey "Exotick but Rational Entertainments" (1977); and Curtis Price's wide-ranging *Music in the Restoration Theatre* (1979).[10] All three continue to garner attention and frequent citation, as does Judith Milhous's slightly later addition, "The Multimedia Spectacular on the Restoration Stage" (1984), which gives greater consideration to the performance/theatrical context.[11] Indeed, it can be argued that these four publications effectively constitute the latter-day corpus

---

8 "EEBO" and "ECCO" are both subscription-based, and thus in practice not available to all researchers. The same can be said of Gale's "17th and 18th Century Burney Collection Newspapers" and their extraordinary (but extremely unwieldy) "State Papers Online."

9 Two significant exceptions carved out by these stipulations include Alison Margaret Laurie, "Purcell's Stage Works" (2 vols.: Ph.D. dissertation, Cambridge University, 1962) and John M. Buttrey, "The Evolution of English Opera Between 1656 and 1695: A Re-investigation" (Ph.D. dissertation, Cambridge University, 1967). The former, as its title implies, is primarily concerned with Purcell; the latter pays special attention to the possible political implications of the operas and their texts. Mention should also be made of the influential if brief sketch provided in the first chapter of Eric Walter White, *The Rise of English Opera* ([New York]: Philosophical Library; London: John Lehmann, 1951; rpt. New York: Da Capo Press, 1972; revised as *A History of English Opera* [London: Faber and Faber, 1983]), and of the first part of Dennis Arundell's popularizing but nonetheless worthwhile *The Critic at the Opera* (London: Ernest Benn, 1957; rpt. New York: Da Capo Press, 1980).

10 Eugene Haun, *But Hark! More Harmony: The Libretti of Restoration Opera in English* (Ypsilanti: Eastern Michigan University Press, 1971); Richard Luckett, "Exotick but Rational Entertainments: The English Dramatick Operas," in Marie Axton and Raymond Williams, eds., *English Drama: Forms and Development: Essays in Honour of Muriel Clara Bradbrook* (Cambridge: Cambridge University Press, 1977), 123–41; Curtis A. Price, *Music in the Restoration Theatre* (Studies in Musicology, 4; Ann Arbor: UMI Research Press, 1979).

11 Judith Milhous, "The Multimedia Spectacular on the Restoration Stage," in Shirley Strum Kenny, ed., *British Theatre and the Other Arts, 1660–1800* (Washington: The Folger Shakespeare Library [Associated University Presses], 1984), 41–66.

Introduction 5

of scholarship on English "opera" from the 1650s to the 1690s: with the exception of a thought-provoking 1996 article by James Winn,[12] pretty much every subsequent effort to construct an overview of the subject has been fundamentally derivative in both substance and argument, relying largely on the conclusions outlined in these four studies and citing the same corpus of primary documents and more narrowly focused scholarly investigations referenced therein.

The overwhelming dearth of originality in accounts of large-scale Restoration musical drama since 1984 has generated more than just a critical impasse: more alarmingly, it has continued to feed a culture of superficiality, where the repetition of received opinions shades into a thoughtless recourse to unwarranted conclusions. Such patently false assertions as "Sir William Davenant produced three through-composed operas in the late 1650s," "Davenant's Duke's Company pioneered the use of theatrical spectacle in the 1660s, leaving the rival King's Company lagging behind," "the French opera *Ariane* was presented by the King's Company at Drury Lane in 1674," "in the wake of the 1673 Test Act, Charles II dismissed all of the foreign Roman Catholic musicians in his service," and "John Dryden and Louis Grabu's *Albion and Albanius* failed on the stage because of its poor critical reception"[13] stem not from any ambiguity in what the primary documents evince, but from a failure to actually read and consider those documents, presumably on the assumption that there is nothing new to be discovered and hence it is sufficient to rely upon the pronouncements of others rather than on the actual evidence. Moreover, while some frequently repeated statements ("the only original works created expressly with the intention of featuring on stage youthful courtiers whose identities are known to us are the court masques *Calisto* and *Venus and Adonis*"; "Nahum Tate and Henry Purcell's *Dido and Aeneas* was written for performance at a girls' boarding school") may only be categorized as *likely* to be untrue on the basis of our best scholarly guesses, there is still ample justification to regard them with strong suspicion, and to avoid reverting to inferences that have nothing more than a dubious longevity to recommend them. For all the value of Dent's pioneering efforts, and of the contributions of those who followed him a couple of generations later, they have for too long been conceded the final say.

The purpose of the present study, then, is to return to this well-trodden territory with a fresh eye, reexamining the evidence—both primary and secondary—and formulating new arguments and conjectures, all in an effort to tell the story of Restoration masque and opera in a way that combines familiar tropes with novel interpretations. The aim of my enterprise, which represents the first installment of a multi-part investigation, is to lend greater nuance and clarity to a subject that is essential to our understanding of both English music and English theatre/drama, as well as the history of the royal court and its milieu. Such an approach

---

12 James A. Winn, "Heroic Song: A Proposal for a Revised History of English Theater and Opera, 1656–1711," *Eighteenth-Century Studies* 30 (1996–97): 113–37.

13 All of the above (as well as the two below) are paraphrases of assertions found in multiple places in the critical literature.

6   Introduction

is dependent upon two fundamental principles. The first is interdisciplinarity: the methodology applied here, which can best be described as "historicist," incorporates tools and materials relevant to musicology, theatre history and theory, literary and art historical studies, administrative and political history, and the relatively new field of court studies. None of this should necessarily be surprising, or even novel, in a volume about masque and opera, and one presented as part of a series that is self-consciously conceived in interdisciplinary terms. Indeed, the aforementioned scholars—Dent, Haun, Luckett, Price, Milhous, and Winn—have each approached the subject from a different disciplinary standpoint. My own early training as a historian has certainly conditioned the methods and character of the study presented here. But no single discipline or methodology can adequately address on its own the history of the multifaceted endeavor that is opera, and I hope that a career spent trying to traverse (or at the very least evade) the traditional disciplinary boundaries of the academy has equipped me to offer some perspective on the subject that will be construed as new, and perhaps even thought-provoking.

The second principle has already been alluded to: namely, the need for a thoroughgoing return to and reassessment of the surviving primary sources—a sweeping category that encompasses everything from playtexts and libretti, to letters and diaries, to theatre and scene designs, to petitions and court cases, to the seventeenth-century equivalent of employee records and pay stubs. It is my contention that there is much to be gained from going back to basics, and thus I have sought wherever possible to consult the original manuscript and printed documents—if not in their physical form, then at least in facsimile—and have therefore chosen in most instances to cite these documents in my footnotes in preference to modern transcriptions or editions.[14] For the convenience of readers, cross-references to certain comprehensive printed calendars, especially Milhous and Hume's *Register*, Ashbee's *Records of English Court Music*, and the *Calendars* of *State Papers, Domestic* and of *Treasury Books*, are consistently provided. My hope is that as we all attain greater facility with these materials, and come to understand more clearly what they can (and cannot) tell us about the world of Restoration theatrical and musical production, further discoveries and conclusions will arise, additional myths will be dispelled, and the present study may even be relegated, like Dent's own book, to the status of a preliminary exploration.

None of the foregoing is meant to imply that any comprehensive reexamination of English masque and opera during the Restoration does not run up against a number of distinct problems, some of which may be insurmountable. The surviving source material is often woefully inadequate, particularly in the case of

---

14 Exceptions include the well-edited diaries of John Evelyn (1955) and Samuel Pepys (1970–83), the commonly cited transcripts of the Stationers' Company's *Registers* (1913–14) and *Term Catalogues* (1903–6), letters translated in the *Calendars of State Papers, Venetian* (1864–1947), and certain documents in private collections calendared in the *Reports* of the Royal Commission on Historical Manuscripts (1870–1976).

the all-important musical scores (among the numerous operatic works produced before 1690, only the second version of *Cupid and Death* [1659], *Venus and Adonis* [c.1683], and *Albion and Albanius* [1685] are preserved in their original, complete form), but also with respect to such things as theatrical company management practices, precise dates of performances, playhouse architecture, and personnel records for certain peripheral court appointees. In addition, the researcher confronts uncertainty as to the reliability of contemporary witnesses, difficulties of generic classification, and even questions about the relevance of the subject, particularly once Dent's teleology has been removed from the equation. With these issues taken into consideration, the two methodological foundations I have outlined assume even greater importance: the establishment of an interdisciplinary investigative framework and the turn to a rigorous engagement with primary sources become not simply means to an end, but justifications in their own right for embarking on the project. The value of the present work thus consists not so much in tracing any "operatic principle" as in charting a new course for the conduct of research into English cultural production at court and in the metropolis during the early modern era. In its effort to achieve this, my account is simultaneously empirical and interpretive, inscribing the arc of a broad historical narrative while maintaining a sharp focus on the particular and the incidental. Details are as crucial as is the wide view to the establishment of a clear understanding of past practices and phenomena, and too many scholars have been content to finesse the specifics, reckoning perhaps that the occasional oversimplification or misstated fact is of scant consequence to the larger argument. The present study, however, has demanded a more scrupulous approach, not only because the limited facts we have must be accurately read, understood, and interpreted if any reliable new information is to emerge, but also considering the multi-disciplinary audience to whom this book is addressed.

Perhaps nowhere are these concerns more clearly embodied than in this volume's tables. The presentation of information in tabular form offers a powerful tool for humanistic scholarship, efficiently digesting raw data in a way that promotes analysis and can ultimately reveal new insights. Tables and diagrams represent for me an essential component of the intellectual process, and there are many conclusions in this book that reflect behind-the-scenes tabular analysis that helped to sharpen my conclusions. But tables can also constitute product, and I have made an effort to include them here wherever I believe they will be helpful, not only for conveying the substance of my arguments, but as reference materials which readers can consult as needed. My tables may not draw the attention of a connoisseur like the great information design pioneer Edward Tufte, but they have been painstakingly crafted so as to reveal larger trends and patterns in response to a (prolonged) glance, while at the same time covering all necessary data points for the benefit of those who may wish to subject them to closer scrutiny. I have sought as much as possible to eliminate unnecessary embellishments—what Tufte calls "non-data ink"—from the tables, while still striving for the comprehensiveness of coverage that will maximize their utility to scholars at all levels of engagement.

8   *Introduction*

The tables are useful in revealing hitherto unseen patterns that can be demonstrated empirically, and I believe that this represents an important part of the present book's contribution. At the same time, I have not refrained from informed conjecture where I believe that such an approach can advance our thinking about the topic. My thoughts on such matters as the musical elements of *The Queen's Masque* of 1671, the activities of Louis Grabu at court from 1674–78, the identity of the central character in *Rare en Tout*, the courtly origins of Lee's *Mithridates*, and the possible performance context of *Venus and Adonis* represent ideas for which I have found provocative evidence and room for logical arguments, but not the definitive, unassailable proof that true empiricists might crave. Yet it is precisely because of the gaps in our knowledge, and the unlikelihood that such proof will ever emerge, that we should be encouraged to undertake educated, contextualized speculation that may help to add new dimensions to the story, in spite of the attendant risks. At the very least, I hope that my suggestions, hedged about as they must be with the necessary qualifications, will at least stimulate future efforts to understand better the world of Restoration musical theatre.

* * *

In order to proceed with our investigation, it is first necessary to identify and define as clearly as possible that investigation's object. The title of this book signals at the outset a dichotomy at the very least: "masque and opera," a pair of seemingly distinct but also overlapping categories that I have sometimes more glibly subsumed under the rubric "musical theatre" or, perhaps more precisely, "musical-theatrical entertainments." As readers will be well aware, neither masque nor opera can be described restrictively as a combination of music and theatre (let alone that narrower appellation, drama). With regard to masque, there are many characterizations that could be cited, although I still favor the relative economy of a formula I first advanced some years ago: a combination of "high and low drama, music, dance, [architecture,] ornate costumes, elaborate scenes and machines, high-flown philosophical rhetoric, structural and generic intricacy, and complex allegorical and political meaning."[15] The "classic" English court masque that grew to maturity between 1604 and 1640 had a very particular profile, consisting of a regicentric rhetoric couched in an entertainment focused on non-speaking courtly performers and largely devoid of conventional narrative structures. The masque was fundamentally declaratory rather than expository, existing outside of the Aristotelian strictures on "poetic" (*i.e.* dramatic) propriety, and drawing its authority from a Renaissance mythos of divinely ordained royal majesty and power. The lineage of opera is somewhat different: despite a similar courtly and intellectual pedigree, opera reflected a contrary effort not to cast off the classical conventions of drama but rather to heighten them, deploying music

---

15   Andrew R. Walkling, review of Andrew J. Sabol, ed., *A Score for* The Lords' Masque *by Thomas Campion, Renaissance Quarterly* 51 (1998), 1395–96, p. 1395.

Introduction   9

as a means to enhance dramatic "speech" by articulating the passions of onstage characters, thereby elevating the audience's response. Opera's use of expressive musical gestures, including its deployment of the new "technology" of recitative, sets it apart from the masque, where forms of tuneful air and speech-inflected declamation similarly coexist, but with an entirely different purpose, namely to craft a musical language whose character is ceremonial rather than emotive.

By the middle of the seventeenth century, however, both forms had undergone significant change. The masque as it had developed under the likes of Ben Jonson, and particularly through the creative efforts of Inigo Jones, ceased to exist after the outbreak of the English Civil War. Upon its return in the 1650s the form dropped much of its explicitly courtly rhetoric, moving instead into the realm of morality and employing a more conventional dialogic and hence dramatic idiom. Opera, originally a product of the Italian academies, transformed itself into a public, commercial venture in Venice at the end of the 1630s, although its further metamorphosis into an imperial art form in France during the late 1660s and early 1670s forms a part of the present story. With regard to these changes, the English experience is doubly problematic. When Charles II reclaimed his throne in 1660, conceptions of the masque had already completely changed (even as memories of the old features persisted), while opera—still regarded principally as an Italian phenomenon—remained as yet poorly understood, notwithstanding the pioneering efforts of Sir William Davenant. Hence, our employment of the terms "masque" and "opera" must acknowledge from the start an inherent degree of indeterminacy, an understanding that both designations sit uncomfortably in the late-seventeenth-century lexicon.

The uncertainty over how to define the "operatic" in this period stems in part from ambivalences regarding how musical drama should ideally be constituted. Commentators from across Europe had raised objections since opera's inauguration that sung dialogue, particularly in the mouths of everyday mortals, was unnatural and bizarre. As the expatriate poet and intellectual the Sieur de Saint-Évremond, put it,

> There is a ... thing in *Opera's* so contrary to nature that it offends my imagination; and that is the singing of the whole piece from beginning to end, as if the persons represented had ridiculously agreed to treat in Musick both the most common and most important affairs of their life. Is it to be imagined that a Master calls his Servant, or sends him of an errand, singing; that one friend imparts a secret to another, singing: that men deliberate in a Council, singing; that Orders in time of Battle are given singing; and that men are melodiously killed with Sword, Pike, and Musket?[16]

---

16 Charles de Marguetel de Saint-Denis, Seigneur de Saint-Évremond, "Upon Opera's. To the Duke of Buckingham," in *idem* (trans. Anon.), *Mixt Essays Upon Tragedies, Comedies, Italian Comedies, English Comedies, and Opera's* (London: Timothy Goodwin, 1685 [*Register*, no. 1262]; rpt. 1687), 20–21; unlike some other portions of the essay, this particular passage is repeated nearly

10   *Introduction*

The most acceptable solution in the eyes of Saint-Évremond and like-minded critics was the distancing of operatic subject matter from everyday life: regular folk warbling their way through quotidian activities looked ridiculous, but exceptions could be made for characters who transcended the bounds of that regularity, such as gods and goddesses, legendary heroes, magicians, and inhabitants of Arcadia. Indeed, the emotional intensification that musical setting provided actually helped to enhance, rather than debase, the mystical aura with which these operatic stories were surrounded. Such a logical workaround inevitably did not last, as can be seen in the humorous low characters of Venetian opera and ultimately in the rise of Neapolitan *opera buffa* at the beginning of the eighteenth century. But the principle of elevated, usually mythical, subject matter did manage to hold sway in the early Italian operas, in the French operas of Lully, and at other formative moments in the genre's history.

By contrast, English views of music in drama embody a certain cultural exceptionalism, born in part out of fundamental characteristics of the English language that have consistently bedeviled Anglophone poets and composers seeking to effect an ideal marriage between music and text.[17] The problem for English theorists and practitioners was twofold: first, how to construct an adequate style of declamatory musical text-setting that might function as an English version of the Italian *stilo recitativo*, thus enabling music to carry plot and dialogue forward; and second, whether English audiences, with their finely honed sense of poetic connoisseurship, would be willing to endure such an approach, even if it could be mastered. The issue of English dramatic recitative is addressed in detail in Part II of the present book; with respect to the tolerance of the theatre-going public for what is now somewhat awkwardly termed "through-composition," a new solution gradually presented itself in the shape of "dramatick opera," a form that I will be exploring in a separate, forthcoming study.

Whatever form it took, opera in England owed a considerable amount of inspiration to the masque, and it is important to keep in mind the fact that the masque's chief influence lies in the area of theatrical practice rather than of music *per se*, and hence any discussion of opera must consider this broader aspect. Haun's *But Hark! More Harmony* delineates the complicated legacy of masque

---

verbatim in another translation, *The Works of M^r de St. Evremont. In II. Volumes. Translated from the French* (London: Awnsham and John Churchill, 1700), 1: 522–23. For an entirely different rendition of the passage, see Ferrand Spence, *Miscellanea: or Various Discourses ... By the Sieur de Saint Euvremont* (London: Sam[uel] Holford, 1686), 44–46. See also Saint-Évremond's letter to Anne Hervart, 4 February [?1676] in René Ternois, ed., *Saint-Évremond: Lettres* (2 vols.: Paris: Marcel Didier, 1967–68), 1: 217–19, p. 218: "M. de Bukingan dit qu'il est serviteur des Opera tant qu'on y fera chanter: Hola, ho, Capitaine des Gardes, faites venir un tel; qu'est devenu cet autre? La Tragédie et la Comédie sont quasi tout en action comme le poëme, et quasi tout en récit; cela étant, il n'y a rien de si ridicule que de faire chanter en agissant, soit qu'on délibère dans un conseil, ou qu'on donne des ordres dans un combat, ou qu'on soit occupé à quelqu'autre fonction."

17   This quest forms the underlying theme of Ian Spink's excellent survey, *English Song: Dowland to Purcell* (London: B. T. Batsford, 1974; rpt. 1986).

Introduction 11

in the subsequent conceptualization of opera: not simply the "proper" masques of the court, nor even their adumbrations in the "interpolated masques" presented within the dramas of the commercial theatres, but also what W. J. Lawrence called the "substantive theatre masque," a free-standing entertainment independent of the courtly arena, but with certain masque-like qualities.[18] The plethora of aspects contained in this variety of masque-related forms—employment of music, scenic sophistication, pastoral and Olympian characters and themes, heightened poetic language, and even the upended world of the antimasque—reemerges in the opera to such an extent that the forms begin to parallel one another, with differences sometimes appearing to be more of emphasis than of fundamental character.[19] Opera and masque are not one and the same, but how they differ is more a matter of individual opinion than of some objective set of distinctions, and this ultimately leads to a kind of organic displacement as the former category progressively encroaches upon the territory of the latter during the decades surrounding the turn of the eighteenth century. Unlike the French, whose "academic" culture fostered the establishment of such strict generic categories as *ballet de cour*, *tragédie à machines*, *comédie-ballet*, *tragédie-ballet*, and *tragédie en musique*, the English seem to have preferred a slippery generic environment in which the exceptionalism noted above promoted a distinctive approach to musical drama without any concomitant clarification of generic definitions.

The problem of how opera and masque were defined and understood by the English is compounded by their inconsistent application of the terms in practice to individual works, thus further complicating efforts to determine precisely what is under investigation in any particular case. Davenant's *The Siege of Rhodes* (1656), often considered the first through-composed opera presented in England, is heralded in its prefatory puff entertainment (*The First Day's Entertainment at Rutland House*) as an opera,[20] and the term was picked up, seemingly at the playwright's own prompting, by two of Davenant's

---

18 William J. Lawrence, "The Origin of the Substantive Theatre Masque," in *idem*, *Pre-Restoration Stage Studies* (Cambridge, MA: Harvard University Press, 1927), 325–39.

19 See Jennifer McDonald's account of the crafting of Thomas Shadwell and Matthew Locke's *Psyche* of 1675: "Pastoral and sacrificial scenes and those derived from the masque and antimasque, were fused with the original play, transforming it, by means of their musical content, into the English 'Opera'" ("Matthew Locke's *The English Opera*, and the Theatre Music of Purcell," *Studies in Music* 15 [1981]: 62–75, p. 66).

20 Sir W[illiam] D[avenant], *The First Days Entertainment at Rutland-House, By Declamations and Musick: After the manner of the Ancients* (London: H[enry] Herringman, "1657" [but actually published November 1656: see Table 4.2 n. *]), sig. A4ʳ and pp. 12, 18, 36, 37, and 40; in referencing this work, I silently add the missing apostrophe to "*Days*"; the spelling "*Dayes*", used by Dent and others, derives from *The Works of Sʳ William Davenant Kᵗ* (London: Henry Herringman, 1673), section 1, p. 341. Note that a government report written sometime in early June 1656 called *The First Day's Entertainment* itself "Sʳ Will: Dauenants Opera": see SP18/128/108 (*Calendar of State Papers, Domestic 1655–56*: 396).

12   *Introduction*

contemporaries;[21] yet the published text contains no mention of that designation, and the entry made by Davenant's publisher in the Stationers' Company's *Register* describes the work as "a maske."[22] The dramatick operas *Psyche* (1675) and *Circe* (1677) are both labeled "A TRAGEDY" on their respective title pages, even though the composer Matthew Locke was at pains to define the former under the rubric "The English Opera,"[23] and an audience member at a performance of the latter described it as "rather an opera than a tragedie, in respect of ye variacen & ornament of the scenes and of ye musicall part of it."[24] The French court entertainment *Rare en Tout* (1677), a number of whose qualities are rather like those of the "LATE MASQUE AT COURT" *Calisto* (1675), calls itself "COMEDIE Meslée de MUSIQUE Et de BALETS," whereas a contemporary wrote to a friend referring to it as "a French opera."[25] Despite its status as the most prominent court masque of the Restoration, the famous *Calisto* suffers particularly in this regard: John Evelyn called it "a Comedie" when he attended a rehearsal on 15 December 1674 and "the *Pastoral*" when he returned a week later,[26] while an early newsletter report classified it confusingly as "a play and a opera,"[27] and a letter written months later, after the closure of the production, still designated it "the opera."[28] Add to these examples the problem of the through-composed *Venus and Adonis*, entitled "A Masque for ye entertainment

---

21 Letter from Abraham Cowley to an unknown correspondent, 3 April 1656: Princeton University Library, Taylor MSS, RTC01, Box 5, Folder 29, verso: "ye Opera"; letter from Davenant to Bulstrode Whitelocke, [?4] September 1656, printed in Bulstrode Whitelock[e], *Memorials of the English Affairs ... With Many Additions Never Before Printed* (London: J[acob] Tonson, 1732), 650: "*our Opera*." See also Whitelocke, *Memorials of the English Affairs* (London: Nathaniel Ponder, 1682), 639, and Ruth Spalding, ed., *The Diary of Bulstrode Whitelocke 1605–1675* (Records of Social and Economic History, New Series 13; Oxford: Oxford University Press for the British Academy, 1990), 449.

22 *Stationers' Register*, 2: 81 (entry of 27 August 1656).

23 See Matthew Locke, *The English Opera; or The Vocal Musick in Psyche, with the Instrumental Therein Intermix'd To which is Adjoyned The Instrumental Musick in the Tempest* (London: "by *T. Ratcliff,* and *N. Thompson* for the Author, and are to be Sold by *John Carr*," 1675).

24 Diary of Sir Edward Dering, Kent History and Library Centre, Maidstone, U275/A4, f. [189] (not seen), quoted in R. Jordan, "Some Restoration Playgoers," *Theatre Notebook* 35 (1981): 51–57, p. 51.

25 Letter of John Verney to Edmund Verney, 31 May 1677: Alfred J. Horwood, "The Manuscripts of Sir Harry Verney, Bart., at Claydon House, Co. Bucks.," in Historical Manuscripts Commission, *Seventh Report of the Royal Commission on Historical Manuscripts. Part I. Report and Appendix* (London: Her Majesty's Stationery Office, 1879), 433–509, p. 468.

26 Evelyn, *Diary*, 4: 49 and 51.

27 Newsletter sent to Sir Richard Bulstrode, 14 December 1674: Harry Ransom Humanities Center, University of Texas at Austin, PFORZ-MS-0675, p. 2 (see [Alphonse Wyatt Thibaudeau], ed., *The Collection of Autograph Letters and Historical Documents Formed by Alfred Morrison (Second Series, 1882–1893): The Bulstrode Papers, Volume I (1667–1675)* [1 vol. only; (London: Strangeways and Sons), 1897], 274).

28 Letter of Dr. William Denton to Sir Ralph Verney, 29 April 1675: "Manuscripts of ... Verney" (*op. cit.*), 492.

of ye King" in its principal manuscript score,[29] but "AN OPERA Perform'd before the KING. Afterwards at Mr. *JOSIAS PREIST's* Boarding School at *CHELSEY*" in the libretto for its subsequent presentation "By Young Gentlewomen,"[30] and the scale of the nominalist quandary becomes apparent. The advent of French opera in 1674 only muddied the waters further, importing a novel form associated with a term that had already begun to develop other, uniquely English, connotations. The resulting clash between terminology and expectations/understandings probably helped to fuel such oddities as John Evelyn's notorious diary entry of 5 January 1674 in which he reported that "I saw an *Italian Opera* in musique, the first that had ben in *England* of this kind."[31] Evelyn's perplexing observation will be addressed in Chapter 6, below, but it is worth noting here that some of the earliest appearances of the word "opera" in English[32] do refer explicitly to the Italian phenomenon, including those found in John Raymond's travelogue of 1648[33] and in Evelyn's own accounts of 1644–46 and 1652.[34] It is only in 1656, with the preparations for *The Siege of Rhodes*, that we first find the term being used to describe an English theatrical production, and as we have seen, that usage is by no means consistently deployed in

29 British Library, Add. MS 22100, f. 123^v.
30 Cambridge University Library, shelfmark Sel.2.123(6), p. 1; see the facsimile in Richard Luckett, "A New Source for 'Venus and Adonis'," *The Musical Times* 130 (1989): 76–79.
31 Evelyn, *Diary*, 4: 30.
32 We should note in passing the seventeenth-century English pronunciation of the word: "**op-peh-**ray," a rendering not too far removed from Nashville's "**op-**prie." The earliest clue is a couplet in the prologue to *The First Day's Entertainment at Rutland House* (sig. A4^r): "*Think this your passage, and the narrow way / To our Elisian Field, the* Opera." See also Davenant's "*EPITHA-LAMIUM. The morning after the* Marriage *of the Earl of* Barymore *with Mrs.* Martha Laurence" (written in November 1656) in *The Works of Sr William Davenant K^t*, section 1, p. 311: "And Poets, but they bear no sway; / And this, O costly *Opera!*"; Tho[mas] Pecke, *Parnassi Puerperium* (London: Tho[mas] Bassett, 1659), 180: "Your *Bonus Genius*, you this way display: / And to delight us, is your *Opera*"; and Edmund Gayton, *The Art of Longevity, or, A Diæteticall Institution* (London: "for the *Author*," 1659), 36: "For Playes are down, unless the puppet-play, / Sir *William's* lost, both *Oyle* and *Opera*."
33 Jo[hn] Raymond, *An Itinerary Contayning a Voyage, Made through Italy, in the Yeare 1646, and 1647* (London: Humphrey Moseley, 1648), 174: "A week after our arrive at *Sienna*, was an *Opera* represented on the new Theatre of *Prince Matthias*, with severall changes of Sceanes, as a Garden, Sea, Pallace, and other Machines, at which the *Italians* are spoke to be excellent."
34 Evelyn, *Diary*, 2: 202 (c.31 October 1644: "they sometimes recreate the People with publique Shews and Operas, as they call them"), 261 (19 November 1644: "a little before my Comming to the Citty, gave a Publique Opera (for so they call those Shews of that kind)"), 449 (June 1645: "we went to the Opera, which are Comedies [& other plays] represented in Recitative Music ..."); J[ohn] E[velyn], *The State of France, as it Stood in the IXth Yeer of this Present Monarch, Lewis XIIII* (London: G. Bedell and T. Collins, 1652), 111: "*streets* ... so incomparably fair and *uniform*, that you would imagine your self rather in some *Italian Opera*, where the diversity of *Scenes* surprise the beholder, then beleeve your self to be in a reall *Citie*." For other references to operas in the *Diary*, see 2: 388–89 (?1–3 May 1645 [possibly misplaced]), 474 (c. February 1646), and 503 (c. May 1646).

14   *Introduction*

this inaugural case.[35] If contemporaries were confused about how to wield the terms, those of us at a distance of several centuries must necessarily be even more so. Herein lies a basic predicament concerning that indispensable tool of modern scholarship, genre: not simply how a bewildering variety of generic tags were sometimes indiscriminately applied during this crucial developmental phase in the history of musical theatre, but, even more fundamentally, what to include in (or exclude from) the very category of the musical-theatrical. The dual quandaries of intra- and inter-generic distinction will, of course, never yield to any definitive solution, and thus it may be best left to the individual to determine which "expert" has fashioned the most accurate and comprehensive accounting of the musical-theatre genre as a whole and of the sub-generic distinctions within it.[36]

In the end, we can productively identify three variables relating to the application of the terms "masque" and "opera" to the theatrical circumstances of Restoration England: first, how contemporaries used them according to their own, indigenous understanding of the forms; second, how they applied them to foreign imports, whose characteristics were already established; and third, how we in the twenty-first century can most effectively deploy them as a basis for historical, generic, and textual analysis. The first two of these considerations necessarily condition the third, which is our principal concern here, and thus my goal is to treat the problem of contemporary nomenclature rather more lightly, with an eye chiefly to establishing categories that will assist us in our own investigations. To achieve this, however, we must at least inquire into the nature of the distinctions that may have motivated the generic choices of seventeenth-century practitioners and commentators, even if not always consistently. Among the myriad features and qualities of musical-theatrical entertainments that may have prompted

---

35 Neither of Davenant's previous proposals (of 1653 and early 1656) for the mounting of such productions invokes the word, leaving Abraham Cowley's letter of April 1656, cited in n. 21, above, as the earliest known application of the term in England to an explicitly non-Italian phenomenon. This determination excludes Richard Flecknoe's ambiguous usage in "*The Preface to the Reader*" prefixed to *Love's Dominion* (London: n. pub., 1654), sig. A4ʳ, where the theatre generally is described as "a Mirrour representing the Actions of men (and therefore by a better title than that of *Plays*, called *Actions* by some, and *Operaes*, or works, by others)."

36 For some lists and tabular examples, see Eric Walter White, comp., *A Register of First Performances of English Operas and Semi-Operas from the 16th Century to 1980* (London: The Society for Theatre Research, 1983; based on a list in *The Rise of English Opera*, Appendix A), esp. pp. 10–19; Robert D. Hume, "The Politics of Opera in Late Seventeenth-Century London," *Cambridge Opera Journal* 10 (1998): 15–43, p. 17 (Table 1); Michael Burden, "Aspects of Purcell's Operas," in *idem*, ed., *Henry Purcell's Operas: The Complete Texts* (Oxford: Oxford University Press, 2000), 3–27, p. 5 (Table 1); Todd S. Gilman, "London Theatre Music, 1660–1719," in Susan J. Owen, ed., *A Companion to Restoration Drama* (Oxford: Blackwell Publishers, 2001), 243–73, pp. 269–73 (Appendix); and my own "Court, Culture, and Politics in Restoration England: Charles II, James II, and the Performance of Baroque Monarchy" (2 vols.: Ph.D. dissertation, Cornell University, 1997), 1: 143–45 (Table 2.1). Each of these, it should be pointed out, contains one or more objective factual errors alongside the other, more subjective determinations that condition their differences of coverage and interpretation.

Introduction   15

contemporaries to categorize particular works in particular ways, we might consider the following "diagnostic" questions:

- Who were the performers ("occupational" or "recreational,"[37] and if both, what were their relationships to one another)?
- In what venue did the performance take place (at court or for a public, fee-paying audience)?
- Did the production incorporate scenic and—more importantly—machine technology?
- How many composers participated in the project (*i.e.* just one or a group)?
- What is the nature of the musical component (through-composed or intermingled with spoken passages)?
- If the work combines spoken and sung passages, how are the latter interpolated into the former (*e.g.* solely as *intermèdes* between acts, or at various points throughout the drama)?
- In what language was the work presented (usually English or French)?
- Is the work divided into acts, and if so, how many (usually 3 or 5)?
- Does the work begin with an allegorical/encomiastic prologue, addressing the monarch?
- Is the work's content primarily heroic or pastoral, and what is the role of the gods?
- Does the work have a comic (*i.e. lieto fine*) or a tragic ending?
- Is there a concluding grand entertainment, replete with songs and dances?
- What is the nature of the work's overall approach to allegorical meaning?[38]

Some of these questions address potential distinctions between masque and opera in the Restoration, while others are more useful for identifying certain characteristic features, particularly of the latter form—which includes the category of dramatick opera that I explore separately elsewhere. Yet no matter how one tries, it seems impossible to arrive at a consistent definition for either category. For example, is opera through-composed (*Ariane, Albion and Albanius*) or not (*Psyche, Circe*, etc.)? What about masque? (*Calisto* is not through-composed, but *Venus and Adonis* and *Dido and Aeneas* are.) Is a through-composed opera necessarily in a foreign language? (*Albion and Albanius* demonstrates otherwise, as do Davenant's experiments of the 1650s.) Is the allegorical, encomiastic prologue a characteristic of masques (*Calisto, Dido and Aeneas*) or of operas (the French *Ariane* and the mysterious anglicized version of the Italian *L'Erismena*, but also

---

37 I have adopted this distinction, in favor of the more conventional designations "professional" and "amateur," from Christopher Marsh, *Music and Society in Early Modern England* (Cambridge: Cambridge University Press, 2010); I am grateful to the anonymous press reader for suggesting this usage.

38 I am referring here to the distinction between "impressionistic" allegory and *roman à clef*, as discussed in my article "Politics and Theatrical Culture in Restoration England," *History Compass* 5.5 (August 2007), 1500–20, pp. 1506–10.

16   *Introduction*

John Dryden's very English "Arthur of Britain" project, and perhaps other similar creations of the 1680s?[39] Do English sung-and-spoken operas—*i.e.* dramatick operas—always close with an elaborate multi-part celebratory entertainment? (Most do; however Charles Davenant's *Circe* notably does not.) And how do we make sense of the tragic endings of *Venus and Adonis* and *Dido and Aeneas*, a feature that seems antithetical to everything the masque is supposed to be about?

The stated views of that leading author/playwright and nascent literary critic, the Restoration Poet Laureate John Dryden, are especially baffling in this regard: as Andrew Holland has aptly remarked, "Dryden's attitude to English music and to the new forms of stage-entertainment ... was curiously vacillating."[40] Leaving aside the incongruity of Dryden's antipathy toward "Scenes, Machines, and empty *Opera*'s" in 1674,[41] in his role as King's Patent Company shareholder, and his near-contemporaneous creation, as author, of the never-performed Miltonic adaptation *The State of Innocence, and Fall of Man: An Opera*, the Laureate's most frequently cited pronouncement on the nature of opera is itself something of an oddity. In 1685, in the Preface to *Albion and Albanius*, Dryden defined the form as follows:

> An *Opera* is a poetical Tale or Fiction, represented by Vocal and Instrumental Musick, adorn'd with Scenes, Machines and Dancing. The suppos'd Persons of this musical Drama, are generally supernatural, as Gods and Goddesses, and Heroes, which at least are descended from them, and are in due time, to be adopted into their Number. The Subject therefore being extended beyond the Limits of Humane Nature, admits of that sort of marvellous and surprizing conduct, which is rejected in other Plays. ... [T]he Expressions should be lofty, figurative and majestical: but the nature of an *Opera* denies the frequent use of those poetical Ornaments: for Vocal Musick, though it often admits a loftiness of sound: yet always exacts an harmonious sweetness; or to distinguish yet more justly, The recitative part of the *Opera* requires a more masculine Beauty of expression and sound: the other which (for want of a proper English Word) I must call, *The Songish Part*, must abound in the softness and variety of Numb'rs: its principal Intention, being to please the Hearing, rather than to gratify the understanding.[42]

This passage embodies a notable contrast between Dryden's thinking and that of most of his contemporaries, who unequivocally favored the mixed form we

---

39   The more generically ambiguous French works *Ballet et Musique* and *Rare en Tout* also have encomiastic prologues.

40   A. K. Holland, *Henry Purcell: The English Musical Tradition* (Harmondsworth: Penguin, 1932; rpt. 1948), 45.

41   John Dryden, "A Prologue spoken at the Opening of the New House, *Mar.* 26. 1674," in *Miscellany Poems ... By the most Eminent Hands* (London: Jacob Tonson, 1684), 286–89, p. 288.

42   John Dryden, *Albion and Albanius: an Opera. Perform'd at the Queens Theatre, in Dorset Garden* (London: for Jacob Tonson, 1685), sig. A2ʳ.

Introduction   17

now call dramatick opera: here, the principle of through-composition is implicitly accepted, and with it a hitherto neglected distinction between recitative—which (despite its musical character) is still capable of "admit[ting]" the "lofty, figurative and majestical" discourse favored by the poet—and aria ("*The Songish Part*"), in which music's "harmonious sweetness," competing with what Dryden elsewhere called "*the Harmony of words*,"[43] takes precedence over poetic sense. Flaunting his cosmopolitanism, Dryden defers not to English inclinations, but rather to the principles laid out by the form's true progenitors, arguing that "whosoever undertakes the writing of an *Opera* ... is oblig'd to imitate the Design of the *Italians*, who have not only invented, but brought to perfection, this sort of Dramatique Musical Entertainment" (sig. A2$^\text{v}$).

Yet while the precepts in Dryden's discourse may be sound, the stated definition is only selectively applicable to *Albion and Albanius* which, it has been argued, is actually the most masque-like of all Restoration theatrical entertainments.[44] Dryden's points about through-composition, the use of stage technology, and the presence of divinities and heroes (in the latter case an express compliment to Charles II and James II, who are represented onstage as the work's title characters) are indeed applicable, but in other ways—especially if we take into account its genesis, its structure and narrative, and its unique allegorical machinery—*Albion and Albanius* is an opera by fiat only. The choice even to create a through-composed public entertainment in English, the first such to appear in London since the end of the 1650s, seems to have grown out of the political and artistic circumstances of the moment—*i.e.* the "absolutist interval" of the mid-1680s, in which the Stuart monarchy sought to emulate the ruling style of a number of Continental states, in particular France—and so Dryden's project, and hence the principles he articulates, might be regarded as an aberration in the wider landscape of English musical theatre. Indeed, Dryden's ambivalence about the proper application of the term "opera" continued to reveal itself in the years that followed the appearance of *Albion and Albanius*. In 1690 he seems to have endorsed the idea that the dramatick opera *The Prophetess* (a.k.a. *Dioclesian*) should be considered an exemplar of the form, praising Henry Purcell's "happy and judic*ious* [*sic*] performances in the late *Opera*"[45]—this despite the fact that Dryden's ghostwritten

---

43 John Dryden, *Tyrannick Love, or the Royal Martyr* (London: H[enry] Herringman, 1670), sig. A4$^\text{r}$.

44 Paul Hammond, "Dryden's *Albion and Albanius*: The Apotheosis of Charles II," in David Lindley, ed., *The Court Masque* (The Revels Plays Companion Library; Manchester: Manchester University Press, 1984), 169–83. See also George Saintsbury, ed., *The Dramatic Works of John Dryden with a Life of the Author by Sir Walter Scott, Bart.* (8 vols.: Edinburgh: William Paterson, 1882), 7: 227: "It is not easy to see why Dryden should not have kept the ancient name of Masque for this piece,—a name which thoroughly fits it." I am less convinced by Eleanore Boswell's retort that "since Professor Saintsbury calls *Albion and Albanius* a masque, it may be equally well urged that *Calisto* is an opera: the structure is identical, but there is the fundamental difference that the masque was designed for amateurs, although they might, if necessary, be assisted by professionals" (*The Restoration Court Stage*, 110).

45 John Dryden, *Amphitryon; Or, The Two Socia's* (London: J[acob] Tonson and M. Tonson, 1690), sig. A3$^\text{r}$.

18   *Introduction*

Epistle Dedicatory to Purcell's published score of *Dioclesian* does not anywhere broach the term.[46] And the following year he came out with the much delayed and revised *King Arthur*, a work he had previously characterized as

> a Play, Of the Nature of the Tempest; which is, a Tragedy mix'd with *Opera*; or a *Drama* Written in blank Verse, adorn'd with Scenes, Machines, Songs and Dances: So that the Fable of it is all spoken and acted by the best of the Comedians; the other part of the entertainment to be perform'd by ... Singers and Dancers ... . It cannot properly be call'd a Play, because the action of it, is suppos'd to be conducted sometimes by supernatural means, or Magick; nor an *Opera* because the Story of it is not sung.[47]

Yet in the dedication prefixed to the 1691 playbook Dryden again temporizes, applying the contentious term in both senses: once to refer retrospectively to "the *Opera* of *Albion* and *Albanius*" and once to describe the present work as "this *Opera*."[48]

We might be forgiven for throwing up our hands in despair at such a terminological impasse. Indeed, in endeavoring to establish some test to ascertain whether a given work from the Restoration era should properly be considered a masque or an opera, one begins to feel a bit like the members of the Appeals Tribunal of H. M. Revenue and Customs, who in 1991 were tasked with deciding whether the baked confection known as a "Jaffa Cake" should be deemed a cake or a biscuit (cookie) for taxation purposes.[49] The commissioners mulled over a range of characteristics, including the word "cake" in the product's name; the ingredients, texture, and size of the object; the balance of individual components (sponge base, orange jam filling, chocolate coating); the method of packaging and marketing; the common method of consumption; and even what happens to the snack's consistency when it goes stale. In the end, the Jaffa Cake was ruled to be a cake (and hence not subject to a 17.5% [20% since 2011] value-added tax, a significant victory for manufacturer and consumers alike), but not without a rueful acknowledgement from the tribunal of the judgment's inherently arbitrary nature, particularly as regards the weight given to each of the factors enumerated above. The Jaffa Cake, it could be observed, is both a cake *and* a biscuit, a state of ambiguity that neither the law nor Her Majesty's Revenue were equipped to tolerate.

---

46 Henry Purcell, *The Vocal and Instrumental Musick of the Prophetess, or the History of Dioclesian* (London: "by *J. Heptinstall*, for the Author, and ... John Carr," 1691), sig. A2^{r-v}; see Roswell G. Ham, "Dryden's Dedication for *The Music of the Prophetesse*, 1691," *Publications of the Modern Language Association* 50 (1935): 1065–75.

47 *Albion and Albanius*, sig. (b)2^r.

48 John Dryden, *King Arthur: Or, The British Worthy. A Dramatick Opera* (London: Jacob Tonson, 1691), sigs. A1^r and A3^v.

49 *United Biscuits (UK) Ltd. v. The Commissioners of Customs and Excise*, LON/91/160 (VAT Decision 6344).

Introduction   19

While the Jaffa Cake may pose an especially delectable instance of the genre debate in practice, an even more illustrative example may be found in the frequently invoked argument over the proper means of distinguishing between fruits and vegetables. If a fruit should be considered, as one standard definition has it, "the usu[ally] edible reproductive body of a seed plant,"[50] where does that leave the cucumber, the eggplant/aubergine, the pepper, and the pea? If, on the other hand, fruits and vegetables are differentiated not according to their botanical qualities, but rather by their respective sweetness and savor, what are we to make of a sweet potato, maize, cassava, or even a carrot—to say nothing of the redoubtable plantain? Is a fruit somehow inherently juicy, whereas a vegetable is not? (Figs and tomatoes say otherwise.) Or does the determination have something to do with how we use it as an ingredient in recipes for more sophisticated delicacies such as soups or pies? (What then of, say, rhubarb?) Biologists since the time of Carl Linnaeus have struggled with the rigidities of the taxonomic system, where certain common or differentiating characteristics are necessarily emphasized at the expense of others, and so we might be forgiven for simply giving up entirely, surrendering our efforts at categorical nuance to the unforgiving precepts of an irrational subjectivity.

Yet with this inescapable principle once admitted, it is possible to turn for recourse to a remarkably illustrative solution, drawn (like the case of the Jaffa Cake) from the symbiotic realms of law and taxation. In 1892, the question we are considering came before the United States Supreme Court in the case of *Nix v. Hedden*, regarding a tariff levied by the Collector of the Port of New York on a shipment of imported tomatoes, which the plaintiff-in-error had unsuccessfully claimed should be classified as fruit and, hence, duty-free. In his opinion affirming the decision of the lower court, Justice Horace Gray argued that

> Botanically speaking, tomatoes are the fruit of a vine, just as are cucumbers, squashes, beans and peas. But in the common language of the people, whether sellers or consumers of provisions, all these are vegetables, which are grown in kitchen gardens, and which, whether eaten cooked or raw, are, like potatoes, carrots, parsnips, turnips, beets, cauliflower, cabbage, celery and lettuce, usually served at dinner in, with, or after the soup, fish or meats which constitute the principal part of the repast, and not, like fruits generally, as dessert.[51]

The rationale underlying the court's ruling is of particular relevance to our own generic dilemma: the determination of *Solanum lycopersicum*'s legally accepted status as a vegetable rather than a fruit is dependent not on any characteristic inherent to the object itself, but rather upon an external quality: its employment within

---

50 "Fruit" *n.* 1b (1), in *Webster's New Collegiate Dictionary* (Springfield, MA: G. and C. Merriam, 1975), 463.
51 *Nix v. Hedden*, 149 US 304 (37 L Ed 745).

20   *Introduction*

a socially defined context. A tomato is a vegetable because it is consumed in a particular way at a particular moment—those determiners having been established by means of a common usage whose arbitrariness is mitigated by its consensual, if ultimately circular, logical process. Herein lies the key to the masque/opera conundrum: if we consider use rather than content, the external as opposed to the internal, as a basis for discrimination, a workable solution to the problem begins to emerge. In Restoration England, a given free-standing musical-theatrical work, regardless of its particular features, can most readily be characterized as a masque if its performance takes place at court; conversely, when it appears on the public stage, it is an opera. Such an approach is not without its own inconsistencies, but it goes a long way toward resolving generic confusion on our part—and it has the added benefit of accounting for such anomalies as the contemporary reclassification of *Venus and Adonis* (and, by extension, *Dido and Aeneas*), or the seemingly capricious pronouncements of John Dryden. The esteemed late-nineteenth-century jurist Mr. Gray could be faulted for his lack of culinary adventurousness, but we cannot but admire his aptitude for severing Gordian knots.

The present study seeks to apply the logic adumbrated in *Nix v. Hedden* to a reconsideration of the nature and history of musical theatre in Restoration England—an undertaking I aim to continue in the separate exploration of dramatick opera that is to follow. The plethora of cultural and generic cross-currents that affected the development of musical-theatrical forms during this period demands an approach that is not simply chronological, but rather examines the individual strands of creative activity delineated in the first instance by the categories of "masque" and "opera," as defined principally by the qualities I have just outlined. Relying on my loose definition of masque as subsuming a variety of performances featuring courtly "recreational" performers, Part I explores a range of entertainments—some more overtly musical than others—associated with the courts of Charles II and James II. I begin, in Chapter 1, with an examination of court balls and related non-dramatic events, whose rise to prominence in the early years of the Restoration helped to effect the recovery of an older tradition of court entertainments associated with Shrovetide and the pre-Lenten season more generally. The chapter closes with a case study addressing a particular work whose textual components are lost to us, but which appears to have represented an intensification of the ball tradition at the beginning of the 1670s. This work, *The Queen's Masque*, also exemplifies the process by which it is possible to arrive at a partial understanding of the context and nature of such a production. Chapter 2 turns to a second phenomenon: the emergence of a much more novel tradition of court performances in which youthful members of the courtly elite prepared and presented spoken plays for the enjoyment of their elders. This tradition appears to have begun in the late 1660s with the coming of age of a new generation of young courtier-thespians, and it soon blossomed, through the injection of non-courtly "occupational" performers skilled in singing and character dancing, into what contemporaries came to dub "masque." The most notable exemplar of this development, and in many ways the high-water-mark of the form, was John Crowne and Nicholas Staggins's *Calisto* of 1675, which is here treated, like *The Queen's Masque*, as a more detailed case study at the end of the chapter. The case study, and hence the chapter, concludes with a return to more general questions about what the Restoration court sought to achieve by these productions, and how notions of courtly magnificence governed the ways in which they were conceived and mounted. Chapter 3 proceeds to the years after *Calisto*, seeking to understand how amateur court theatricals evolved in the aftermath of this grand entertainment. Both the productions themselves and the surviving corpus of documented facts about them are far more ephemeral than what *Calisto* provides, and hence it is necessary to engage in a good deal of informed speculation in order to make sense of their qualities and the place of each in the history of the genre. In two instances, I offer novel interpretations of works whose importance to our understanding of the development of amateur/"recreational" court performance has, I argue, been overlooked. I then turn to the 1680s and attempt to look afresh at the circumstances surrounding the production of one of the most well-preserved and yet most elusive examples of the Restoration court masque, John Blow's *Venus and Adonis*. The chapter closes with a brief consideration of possible reasons for the disappearance of court masque after the "Glorious Revolution": I argue that it was principally a demographic and generational shift, and only secondarily the change in political circumstances, that hastened the form's demise.

Throughout Part I, particularly in Chapters 2 and 3, the problem of imposing generic distinctions on the basis of inherent qualities is especially acute. While it is in no way my intention to imply that a work like Elkanah Settle and Matthew Locke's rhymed heroic tragedy *The Empress of Morocco* of 1673 should be considered a masque *per se*, I assert that its court provenance and the circumstances of its earliest performance give the work an affinity to the masque that is in fact considerably more germane than its oft-cited place in the supposed origin story of English dramatick opera.[52] Notwithstanding its famous musical "Masque of Orpheus," *The Empress of Morocco* is first and foremost a play, substantively no different from *The Indian Emperor*, *Horace*, and *The Faithful Shepherdess*, all of which were also presented by "recreational" performers at court during the late 1660s and early 1670s. *The Empress of Morocco*, however, can claim the added distinction of having been written for and premiered at court, rather than simply recycled from an earlier professional production. It thus belongs to a select group of works that includes *Calisto*, *Rare en Tout*, and *Venus and Adonis* (and probably also *Mithridates* and *Dido and Aeneas*), whose common origins as court entertainments dictate their consideration together as part of a single narrative, notwithstanding the diversity of their inherent qualities. The extraordinarily disparate nature of this group is illustrated in Table I.1, which poses most of the "diagnostic" questions enumerated above, along with some particulars of the diverse generic labels applied to each by contemporaries.[53]

---

52 It is, moreover, worth acknowledging the connections charted by Nancy Klein Maguire between the masque form and the heroic tragicomedies of the early Restoration period: see her *Regicide and Restoration: English Tragicomedy, 1660–1671* (Cambridge: Cambridge University Press, 1992), esp. chapter 3.

53 I have not included *Mithridates* or *Dido and Aeneas* in the table; most of their qualities, in any case, match those of *The Empress of Morocco* and *Venus and Adonis*, respectively.

Table I.1 Comparison of theatrical works originally written for court performance, 1673–83

QUALITIES	The Empress of Morocco	Calisto	Rare en Tout	Venus and Adonis
Date	1673 (?March/April)	1675 February–April	1677 29 May	c.1683 (?February)
Author	Settle	Crowne	La Roche	?Kingsmill
Dramatic type	tragedy	pastoral	comedy	pastoral
Designation	(play)	"masque"	"comedie"	"masque"
Alternative designation	—	"play & opera"	"opera"	"opera"
Known number of courtiers	?c.9[a]	c.20	1[b]	1[c]
Presence of professionals?	?yes[d]	yes	yes	yes
Venue	Hall Theatre	Hall Theatre	Hall Theatre	?Hall Theatre
Scene changes?[e]	yes	(yes)[f]	yes	no
Composer(s)?	1: Locke	1: Staggins	1: Paisible	1: Blow
Through-sung?	no	no	no	yes
Music/dance between acts?	no[g]	yes	yes	(yes)[h]
Language	English	English	French	English
Number of acts (excluding prologue)	5	5	3	3
Allegorical prologue?	no	yes	yes	(yes)[i]
Gods?	no	yes	no	yes
Comic or tragic ending	tragic	comic	comic	tragic
Concluding grand entertainment?	no	yes	yes	no

[a] Only 1 identified.

[b] Speculative.

[c] Plus "little cupids"?

[d] Possibly professional singers/dancers in Moorish dance scene (2.[ii]) and Masque of Orpheus (4.[iv])?

[e] *N.B.* machine effects in all four productions are extremely limited.

[f] One "full" scene change between Prologue and Act 1; other changes limited to upper-stage discoveries and possibly a moveable scenic object introduced onto the stage in Act 2

[g] Performance may have included standard "theatre suite" with act tunes.

[h] Dance(s) and act tune incorporated into the main action of the drama.

[i] Prologue not, strictly speaking, allegorical, but does address audience in courtly terms.

If the story of Restoration masque represents something of a hodgepodge, generically speaking, the history of opera during the same period poses its own set of challenges. Genre is less of a stumbling-block once we recognize the bases of the distinction between through-composed opera and dramatick opera: as I will argue in the sequel to this book, the origins of the latter form, which only emerged in the mid-1670s, are more closely bound up with the practices of the Restoration patent theatre companies than with developments in the musical arena. Yet having removed this complicating factor, we are left to confront the fractured and for the most part poorly documented history of the more explicitly musical form that remains. There are two principal issues that must be addressed in charting the history of through-composed opera in England prior to 1700: first, the severe limitations on the available evidence, which necessarily leaves many questions unanswered, and second, the need to understand the relationship between native exemplars of through-composed opera (such as *The Siege of Rhodes* and *Albion and Albanius*) and the growing foreign influences brought to bear on English musical theatre over the course of the Restoration period. In seeking to harmonize these two strands, I have taken a cue from John Dryden and his pre-Restoration forebears, Sir William Davenant and the much-maligned Richard Flecknoe, all of whom recognized not only the Italian origins of opera but also the importance of its two principal "technological" components: scenic spectacle and through-composition characterized by the use of the recitative style. At the same time, I am concerned to demonstrate the critical importance after 1660 of the Restoration court, its aspirations, practices, and political motives, in the creation of an operatic heritage, even if the actual fruits of that endeavor proved to be few and far between.

Drawing upon these considerations, Part II offers a parallel narrative to that presented in Part I, this time addressing the phenomenon of through-sung opera, both English and foreign, and the cultural and administrative forces that supported the sporadic efforts to introduce the form into England. Chapter 4 addresses the seminal experiments of the late 1650s, examining the early "operatic" projects of Davenant, Flecknoe, and others, with a particular emphasis on the two "technologies" mentioned above. Chapter 5 charts the move away from the nascent domestic operatic tradition after 1660, exploring the Restoration court's quest for the resources and personnel necessary to mount foreign musical extravaganzas— presentations that did not materialize, but whose prospects exerted a good deal of influence on the organization of Charles II's musical establishment. In Chapter 6, I explore the brief moment when these efforts finally did bear fruit in the creation of the shadowy "Royall Academy of Musick," which seems to have been at the center of a two-pronged effort to celebrate the court's new French and Italian connections occasioned by the remarriage of the king's brother and heir James, Duke of York, in late 1673, while simultaneously seeking to circumvent the restrictions on Roman Catholic royal servants dictated in the Test Act of the same year. The court-centered initiative of 1673–74 exerted a significant impact on the London musical and theatrical scene, embracing the recruitment of influential French

24   Introduction

musicians and dancers, the introduction of new operatic and balletic forms to both the court and the general public, and the flexing of royal muscle in matters relating to the status of the theatrical patent companies. Chapter 7 charts the aftermath of these developments, offering a new interpretation of the circumstances and activities of Charles II's French musicians in the years after 1674's operatic surge. Finally, Chapter 8 examines the revival of through-composed opera in the 1680s, focusing especially on the genesis and reception of Dryden and Grabu's *Albion and Albanius*, the only major musical-theatrical work of the Restoration era for which we possess that elusive trifecta of a comprehensive origin story, a substantive body of contemporary reaction, and a complete musical score. As in Part I, my narrative concludes with a projection into the post-Revolutionary era, inquiring briefly into the demise of through-composed opera after James II's reign, and its replacement with dramatick opera, that native form in which the employment of operatic "technologies" assumed a very different configuration.

As I hope the foregoing discussion has made clear, any attempt to bring unassailable clarity to the generic and documentary tangle that is English musical theatre between the mid-1650s and the beginning of the 1690s is pretty much doomed to failure. I readily acknowledge that the categories around which the present study is organized are subjective, and thus open to critique and revision. Chapter 4, for example, tells an important part of the story of through-composed opera in England, but is at the same time an outlier in a book whose principal concern is with the influence of the royal court on musical-theatrical innovation. I hope I have done a better job of explaining why, for example, *The Empress of Morocco* deserves primary consideration here rather than in my forthcoming exploration of dramatick opera, or why my seeming obsession with through-composition in Part II does not embrace *Venus and Adonis* or *Dido and Aeneas*. Such potential flaws are all to the good, of course: further debate about how best to understand and describe this material, as long as it is informed by a real engagement with the facts we have and by thoughtful analysis built upon those facts, is bound to yield new insights that will advance the field beyond the point of relative stasis at which it currently sits. If this book makes any claims to furthering the conversation, it is through the establishment of a foundation of empirical evidence upon which any future investigations of the field may find it convenient to rely. In the end, I hope that readers will join me in embracing the interpretive uncertainties that the subject entails and seek to draw their own conclusions about how best to put the evidentiary pieces together. Thanks in part to our ever-expanding access to primary source material, we are in a position to build in meaningful ways upon the seminal work undertaken by Edward Dent a century ago, even if the resulting edifice can only ever be provisional in character. The history of Restoration masque and opera is at once documentable and opaque, unified and divergent, and the chapters that follow attempt to embody those evident paradoxes. While I am in no position to offer apologies for the sometimes frustrating complexity of the subject matter, I hope that my effort to both illuminate and further vex our knowledge of these forms will contribute to a richer understanding of the works and their context.

Part I

"Their greatest gallantry imaginable"

Masques, balls, and "recreational" acting at court

1 Balls and the growth of Shrovetide entertainments

One of the defining characteristics of the pre-Civil War Stuart masque, a form that had itself grown out of the semi-theatrical masquerades and balls enjoyed by courtiers and their monarchs during the Tudor era, was the presence of courtly "recreational" performers on stage. Charles I and his queen Henrietta Maria famously assumed the mantle of masquers-in-chief in the grand productions of the 1630s, thereby putting the ultimate seal of approval on this type of activity. But an equally significant component of the form involved the participation of the court's most youthful denizens, as can be seen, for example, in the masques and "barriers" (masque-like displays of military prowess) created for Henry, Prince of Wales— who appeared in Ben Jonson's *Oberon, the Fairy Prince* in 1611, aged sixteen—and his surviving younger brother Charles—whose first masque performance was at the age of seventeen, in Jonson's *Pleasure Reconciled to Virtue* in 1618. With the latter man grown to adulthood and (seemingly) securely established on his throne, it was the turn of his own son and heir to lead a troupe of young compatriots onto a court stage. On 12 September 1636, at the tender age of six, the future Charles II took the lead role of Britomart (a possible echo of the female Knight of Chastity in Book III of Spenser's *The Faerie Queene*) in a masque-like entertainment at Richmond Palace.[1] While modest in comparison with the great Whitehall extravaganzas mounted by Inigo Jones, this anonymous piece not only marked the elevation of the young Charles to his rightful position as Prince of Wales, but also reinforced the place of children as legitimate performers in these types of court entertainments.

---

1   *The King and Qveenes Entertainement at Richmond. After Their Departvre from Oxford: In a Masque, presented by the most Illustrious Prince, Prince Charles Sept. 12. 1636* (Oxford: by Leonard Lichfield, 1636); for a typeset facsimile, see W. Bang and R. Brotanek, eds., *The King and Qveenes Entertainement at Richmond Nach der Q 1636 in Neudruck* (Materialien zur Kunde des älteren Englischen Dramas, ser. 1, vol. 2: Louvain: Uystpruyst; Leipzig: Harrassowitz, 1903; rpt. Vaduz: Kraus, 1965). For a discussion, see John H. Astington, "*The King and Queenes Entertainement at Richmond,*" *Records of Early English Drama Newsletter* 12/1 (1987): 12–18. The antimasque portion of this entertainment was reprinted as "*WILTSHIRE TOM,* An Entertainment at Court" in Francis Kirkman, *The Wits, or, Sport upon Sport*, part 2 (London: Francis Kirkman, 1673), 26–32; Charles Coleman's song "Did not you once, Lucinda, vow," which concluded the antimasque, resurfaced in 1684 in the third pageant of the annual Lord Mayor's Show: see Thomas Jordan, *London's Royal Triumph for the City's Royal Magistrate* (London: John and Henry Playford, 1684), 15.

28   *"Their greatest gallantry imaginable"*

Of course neither the young Prince of Wales nor his masque-loving parents had long to savor such diversions, given the advent of civil war and the ultimate collapse of the Stuart regime. But the young scion of the dynasty, in exile on the Continent from October 1651, did find occasional opportunities throughout his twenties to witness similar sorts of entertainments at the courts of his more fortunate royal and noble hosts. On 6 August 1653, while sojourning in Paris, Charles accompanied his younger brother, the Duke of Gloucester, to see a ballet performed for the court of his cousin Louis XIV at the Jesuit college of Louis-le-Grand in Paris.[2] And on 14 April 1654, Francesco Buti's comedy *Le Nozze di Peleo e di Teti*, with interpolated masque entries by the composer Carlo Caproli del Violino, was presented in Paris, with "the late Queen of *England*, the titular King of *Scotland* [*i.e.* Charles], and the titular Dukes of *York*, and *Glocester*" in attendance.[3] Indeed, Charles's younger brother James (aged twenty) was an active participant in the production, performing as one of "*twelve Fishers of Corrall*" alongside "The Duke of *Anjou* the Kings onely brother" and a number of other young French lords.[4] The text associated with James's appearance referred specifically to the plight of the English royal family:

> T'is not for me to fish for Corrall here,
> I to another Coast my course must steer,
> A fatall ground
> Which Seas surround.
> There I must fish upon an angry Main,
> More then two Crowns and Scepters to regain. (p. 8)

Charles and James's nine-year-old younger sister Henriette Anne (later Duchesse d'Orléans) also appeared in the performance, "*representing the muse* Erato, *which fell to her by lott*" (p. 2). Her text was similarly political, announcing that

---

2   Jean Loret, *La Muze Historique*, letter 4: 29 (9 August 1653); see J. Ravenel and Ed. V. de la Pelouze, eds., *La Muze Historique ou Recueil des Lettres en Vers Contenant les Nouvelles du Temps Écrites a son Altesse Mademoizelle de Longueville, Depuis Duchesse de Nemours (1650–1665)* (4 vols.: Paris: P. Jannet, 1857–78), 1: 395 (lines 105–68). I am grateful to Judith Rock for having brought this reference to my attention. All dates given in this paragraph are in "New Style," *i.e.* ten days ahead of those in England.

3   As reported in *The Weekly Intelligencer of the Common-VVealth* 332 (16–23 May 1654), 262. For discussions of this performance, see Per Bjurström, *Giacomo Torelli and Baroque Stage Design* (Uppsala Studies in the History of Art, New Series 2; Stockholm: Almqvist and Wiksell, 1961; 2nd ed., 1962), 160–75, and Susan Wiseman, *Drama and Politics in the English Civil War* (Cambridge: Cambridge University Press, 1998), 127–30. Two or three days later, Charles and his mother called upon the French king and his mother "at the *Louvre*, and after supper," were "entertained with a [*sic*] pleasure of a Mask" (*Weekly Intelligencer*, 263).

4   See James Howell's contemporeneous English translation of the work, *The Nvptialls of Peleus and Thetis. Consisting of a Mask and a Comedy,* [*F*]*or the The* [*sic*] *Great Royall Ball, Acted lately in Paris six times By The King* [*i.e.* Louis XIV] *in Person. The Duke of Anjou. The Duke of Yorke. with divers other Noble men. Also By The Princess Royall Henrette* [*sic*] *Marie. The Princess of Conty. The Dutchess of Roqvelaure. The Dutchess of Crequy. with many other Ladies of Honour* (London: Henry Herringman, 1654), 7.

My Innocent and young aspect,
Inspires both pitty and respect;
And he who loudly would complain
of *Princes* falls and *Peoples* raign,
Of angry starrs, and destiny,
Let him but cast his eyes on me. (p. 2)

While the English king-in-exile continued his politically driven peregrinations, departing Paris only three months after the performances of *Le Nozze* and setting up his court at Cologne, James remained in France, where he continued to attend balls and other entertainments.[5] In a letter to Charles dated 21 January 1656, Henry, Lord Jermyn noted in a postscript, "I send you the maske from Benserade. The duke of York can give you a good account of it; for he fayles it not at every dancing."[6] In 1658 (having relocated once again, this time to Bruges) the future monarch joined his siblings at the Antwerp lodgings of William Cavendish, Marquess (later Duke) of Newcastle on 27 February for a performance of a sumptuous masque prophesying Charles's imminent restoration.[7]

Given these activities, we might expect to see a spate of masques and other amateur theatrical entertainments at the English court once Charles II had regained his throne. Newcastle certainly did: his wide-ranging manuscript "advice" to the young monarch includes a section on "Your Majesties Devertisementes" in which he urges his former tutee to have regular masques ("Etalienes makes the Seanes beste, & all but your Majestie May have their Glorious Atier of Coper, which will Doe as well For two or three nightes, as silver, or Gold, & much Less charge") and balls (to which Charles should "Invite The young Ladyes, & give them a banquett, & Drinke their welcome with thankes").[8] Newcastle continues:

> I Should wish the firste time, That it is performed, to have all the Lordes, & their Ladyes, Sons, & Daughters, knights & gentle men, of qualety, & their Sons, & Daughters, Invited, to itt, & Every one to have ticketts From the Lord Chamberline for their Enterance, & the Lord Chamberline to bee very carefull, that none Else Enters, butt those that are Invited, to a voyd confution & Disorder[.]

---

5 See for example the report in *Mercurius Politicus* 297 (14–21 February 1656): 5970: "On the 16 the grand Balet, called Plyche [*sic*] or the Power of Love, was danced at the Louvre, in presence of the Queen, the Princesse of Orange, her brother the Titular Duke of York, their sister the little Princesse, Du[k]e *Francis* of Lorraine and his son Prince Ferdinand, with many other great Lords and Ladies."

6 *A Collection of the State Papers of John Thurloe, Esq.* (London: for the Executor of Fletcher Gyles, *et al.*, 1742), 1: 691.

7 See *Calendar of State Papers, Domestic* 1657–58: 296–97, 311 (Ashbee, 8: 135–36); unfortunately, no text for this production survives. I am grateful to Lynn Hulse for having originally provided me with this reference.

8 Bodleian Library, Oxford, Clarendon MS 109, transcribed in Thomas P. Slaughter, introd., *Ideology and Politics on the Eve of Restoration: Newcastle's Advice to Charles II* (Philadelphia: American Philosophical Society, 1984), 60.

30   *"Their greatest gallantry imaginable"*

A second performance of each masque should be set aside for "the Ins of courte, & non Else," and a third for "the Lord maior, Sheriffes, & all the Aldermen, with their wives, sons, & Daughters, with the principall merchants, & no other to come In."

Yet the evidence for such events in the earliest years of the Restoration is exceedingly scanty. For the most part, the new king had to be content with attending presentations sponsored by his subjects and mounted beyond the immediate confines of his court. Some of these entertainments incorporated theatrical elements, such as the public pageants put on by the City of London to celebrate his return to England in May 1660, his coronation in April 1661, and the arrival of his new queen, Catherine of Braganza in August 1662.[9] Others, while still theatrical, were more private: sometime in the spring or summer of 1660, Charles was entertained at Newcastle's residence in London with a masque-like entertainment written by the Marquess himself, praising Charles and mocking the French culture in vogue at court.[10] As early as April or May 1660, the cleric Anthony Sadler devised a somewhat overwrought "Sacred MASQUE ... FOR His saCRed Majesty" based on events from ancient Israel, although this was most likely never performed.[11] Still others consisted of danced entertainments, modeled on French *ballet de cour*, including one performed in 1660 under the auspices of Antoine de Bordeaux-Neufville, the French ambassador to England from 1654 until July 1660,[12] and one given on 3 January 1662 by the denizens of Lincoln's Inn, at which Charles and the Duke of York were in attendance.[13] But while this rather motley assemblage of works undoubtedly contained an array of masque-like elements, none can be considered courtly in a proper sense—indeed, in the case of the 1660 French ballet, it is unlikely that Charles II or members of his court attended this event, given the frosty relations between the king and the outgoing ambassador.[14]

---

9 John Tatham, *Londons Glory Represented by Time, Truth and Fame* (London: by William Godbid, 1660); John Ogilby, *The Relation of His Majestie's Entertainment* (London: by Tho[mas] Roycroft for Rich[ard] Marriott, 1661); *The Cities Loyalty Display'd* (London: n. pub., 1661); John Tatham, *Neptunes Address to His Most Sacred Majesty* (London: by William Godbid for Edward Powel, 1661); John Ogilby, *The Entertainment Of His Most Excellent Majestie* (London: by Tho[mas] Roycroft for John Ogilby, 1662); John Tatham, *Aqua Triumphalis* (London: by T. Childe and L. Parry for John Tatham, 1662).

10 Nottingham University Library, MS PwV23, ff. 4^r–12^r: see Lynn Hulse, "'The King's Entertainment' by the Duke of Newcastle," *Viator: Medieval and Renaissance Studies* 26 (1995), 355–405, which includes a diplomatic transcription of the text. I am grateful to Lynn Hulse for her generosity in discussing Newcastle's work with me.

11 [Anthony Sadler], *The Subjects Joy for The Kings Restoration, Cheerfully Made Known in A Sacred Masque: Gratefully Made Publique for His saCRed Majesty* (London: James Davis, 1660).

12 *Le Ballet de la Paix Dance en presence de Monseigneur le President de Bordeaux Ambassadeur Extraordinaire de Roy de France en Angleterre* (n. p.: n. pub., 1660).

13 Ενκυκλοχορεία*[,] or Vniversal Motion, Being Part of that Magnificent Entertainment by the Noble Prince, De la Grange, Lord Lieutenant of Lincolns Inn, Presented to the High and Mighty Charles II. Monarck of Great Brittain, France and Ireland* (London: n. pub., 1662). This event is mentioned in the contemporary diaries of both Samuel Pepys and John Evelyn: see Pepys, *Diary*, 3 (1662): 2 (3 January); Evelyn, *Diary*, 3: 307–8 (1 January), among numerous other sources (for which see *ibid.*, 307–8 n. 6). See also Folger Shakespeare Library, MS V.a.291, f. 144^r (Diary of John Ward, entry for 6 January).

14 See François Guizot, trans. Andrew R. Scoble, *Monk: or the Fall of the Republic and the Restoration of the Monarchy in England, in 1660* (London: Bell & Daldy, 1866), 240–56.

The growth of Shrovetide entertainments   31

During the first half of the 1660s, in fact, the court itself appears to have observed a strict distinction between drama and dance, with theatrical presentations offered by the professional actors of the King's and Duke of York's patent companies, usually at the Cockpit-in-Court, while courtly amateurs participated "recreationally" in non-dramatic balls in large rooms such as the Great Hall at Whitehall Palace. For the latter category, we are largely dependent upon the diary accounts of Samuel Pepys and John Evelyn, who frequently offer only the barest of glimpses, such as Evelyn's report of having witnessed a "greate Masque at Court" on 2 July 1663,[15] or Pepys's observation on 22 February 1664 that the Horse Guards had been ordered to guard "the hall (which there is a ball to be in tonight before the King)."[16] 1663 seems to have been a particularly busy year: the apparent surfeit of such entertainments may help to account for Evelyn's increasingly sketchy entries (10 January: "I saw a Ball daunced againe at Court by the *King, Duke & Ladys*, in greate pompe &c:"; 5 February: "at the greate ball at Court, where his Majestie, Queene &c daunced:"; and 19 August: "At night I saw the Ball at Court &c:"[17]). In one case, even the precise date is uncertain: on 7 March, Pepys heard news of a court ball "the other day" at which Charles II had pointedly snubbed Jane de Civelle, Baroness Gerard, for having revealed to the queen details of his relations with his mistress Barbara Villiers, Countess of Castlemaine.[18] Pepys—who expressed surprise at this development, noting that the lady's husband, Charles Gerard, Baron Gerard of Brandon (later 1st Earl of Macclesfield), was "a great favourite" of the king— only learned the information on 7 March, the Saturday after Ash Wednesday, although the ball would likely have occurred on or immediately before Shrove Tuesday, which fell on 3 March.[19]

In a couple of instances, the Restoration's two most inveterate diarists offer somewhat more information. On 31 December 1662, Pepys was taken by his colleague Thomas Povey to a ball "crammed with fine ladies, the greatest of the Court" at which he watched a number of prominent figures, including the king and the Duke of York, perform both French and English dances, "to my infinite content, it being the greatest pleasure I could wish now to see at Court."[20] And on 2 February 1665, Evelyn "Saw a fine Mask at Court perform'd by 6 Gent: & 6 Ladys

---

15 Evelyn, *Diary*, 3: 357.

16 Pepys, *Diary*, 5 (1664): 56.

17 Evelyn, *Diary*, 3: 350, 351–52, 360.

18 Pepys, *Diary*, 4 (1663): 68; see also Ronald Hutton, "Gerard, Charles, first earl of Macclesfield (*c*.1618–1694)," *Oxford Dictionary of National Biography*, Oxford University Press, 2004; online edition, January 2008 [http://www.oxforddnb.com/view/article/10550, accessed 4 January 2012].

19 Sandra Tuppen, "Shrove-Tide Dancing: Balls and Masques at Whitehall under Charles II," *The Court Historian* 15 (2010): 157–69, p. 159. Compare Pepys's use of the phrase "the other day" on 3 February 1665 (*Diary*, 6: 29; see n. 22, below), when in fact he means "yesterday"; by contrast, on 14 January 1668 he explicitly describes the performance of *The Indian Emperor* as "last night's work at Court" (*Diary*, 9: 23; see Chapter 2, n. 14, below).

20 Pepys, *Diary*, 3: 300–1.

32 *"Their greatest gallantry imaginable"*

surprizing his Majestie, it being Candlemas day,"[21] while the following day Pepys received a second-hand report that

> six women (my Lady Castlemayne and Duchesse of Monmouth being two of them) and six men (the Duke of Monmouth and Lord Aron and Monsieur Blanfort being three of them) in vizards, but most rich and antique dresses, did dance admirably and most gloriously.[22]

Yet another description of a court ball appears in the published journal of the French virtuoso Balthasar de Monconys, who visited England in May and June of 1663. On the 11th of May, Monconys and his companions

> fusmes à Oüital [Whitehall], où la Reyne eust vn petit bal en priué qui dura iusqu'à minuit: le Roy y vint au milieu du bal, dansa & prit la Reyne, qui prit M. le Duc de Cheureuse [?Francis Talbot, 11th Earl of Shrewsbury]: le Roy prit la second fois qu'il dansa Madame de Castelmene, puis s'en alla bientost aprés, & elle le suiuit incontinent; elle dansa sa coiffe de crespe sur la teste. L'on commença le bal par vn branle comme en France, & ensuite l'on dança des courantes & d'autres danses; le Duc d'York commença auec la Reyne. Quand elle ou le Roy dansoient, toutes les Dames demeuroient debout, & quand le Duc d'York dansoit, elles se leuoient seulement quand il commençoit, puis se rasseoient.[23]

All three of the foregoing examples are especially helpful in that they provide us with some details of who actually danced at these events. Table 1.1 offers a digest of the identities and ages (where known) of courtiers who performed in these and several other balls, mostly during the 1660s; the account by Pepys of a ball held in honor of the queen's birthday in 1666 is especially enlightening in this regard.[24]

We may catch a glimpse of yet another court entertainment from these early years in Anthony Hamilton's gossipy and semi-fictional *Memoirs of the Life of Count de Grammont*, first published in French in 1713. In chapter 7, Hamilton recounts the escapades of the Count, his future wife (and Hamilton's sister) Elizabeth, and others of the court circle in relation to "a noble Masquerade" devised by Queen Catherine of Braganza "where those whom she appointed to dance, were to represent different Nations."[25] According to Hamilton's report, in advance of the event "[t]he Queen sent Notes to such as were named, in which

---

21 Evelyn, *Diary*, 3: 397.
22 Pepys, *Diary*, 6 (1665): 29; Pepys describes the event as "a Masquerade before the King and Court the other day."
23 Balthasar de Monconys, *Iovrnal des Voyages de Monsievr de Monconys* (3 vols.: Lyon: Horace Boissat and George Remeus, 1665–66), 2: 24. The date given by Monconys is 21 May, New Style.
24 See Pepys, *Diary*, 7 (1666): 371–73.
25 Anthony Hamilton, trans. Abel Boyer, *Memoirs of the Life of Count de Grammont: Containing, in Particular, the Amorous Intrigues of the Court of England in the Reign of King Charles II* (London: J. Round *et al.*, 1714), 117; for the full account of the event, see pp. 116–31.

Table 1.1 Balls at court, 1660–85, for which identities of some court participants are known

DANCER	DATE OF BIRTH	31 Dec. 1662[A]	10 Jan. 1663[B]	5 Feb. 1663[C]	? Mar. 1663[D]	11 May 1663[E]	2 Feb. 1665[F]	15 Nov. 1666[G]	18 Feb. 1667[H]	29 May 1675[I]	15 Nov. 1676[J]	15 Nov. 1677[K]	15 Nov. 1684[L]
	DATE OF SHROVE TUESDAY:	3 Mar.					7 Feb.	[Queen Catherine's Birthday]	19 Feb.	[King's Birthday]	[Queen Catherine's Birthday]	[Queen Catherine's Birthday]	[Queen Catherine's Birthday]
Prince Rupert	[8] Dec. 1619							**46**					
?James Hamilton	?c.1620							**~46**					
Col. John Russell	?1620s							**~?**					
?Earl of Shrewsbury	c.1623					**~40**							
Duke of Buckingham	30 Jan. 1628							**38**					
Charles II	29 May 1630	32	32	32	32	32		36	36	45			
Countess of Arlington	1633							33					
Duke of York	14 Oct. 1633	29	29			29		33			41		
Earl of Ossory	8 Jul. 1634							32					
Baroness Gerard	c.1637				**~26**								
Duchess of York	12 Mar. 1637	25						29					
Duchess of Buckingham	30 Jul. 1638	24											
Queen Catherine	[15] Nov. 1638	24		24		24		28	28				
Earl of Arran	15 Jun. 1639						25						
Countess of Castlemaine	?Nov. 1640	22				22	24						
Marquis de Blanquefort	1641						~23						
?Winifred Wells	c.1642	~20											
Lady Essex Howard	1640s							~?					
Lord Douglas[a]	1646							~19					
?Mary Berkeley[b]	?after 1646							~?					
Earl of Rochester	10 Apr. 1647							19	19				
Frances Teresa Stuart[c]	8 Jul. 1647							19					
?Anne Temple	?c.1648							?~18					
Duke of Monmouth	[30 Mar.] 1649	13					15	17					
Thomas Felton	12 Oct. 1649								17				
Nell Gwyn	2 Feb. 1650								17				
William of Orange	[4] Nov. 1650											27	
Duchess of Monmouth	11 Feb. 1651	11					13	15					
Sir Edward Villiers[d]	?1655									~21			
Prince of Neuburg[e]	[9] Apr. 1658										17		
Mary of Modena	[25 Sep.] 1658										16		
Duchess of Norfolk[f]	1658/9												~26
Carey Fraser	c.1658									~18			
Princess Mary	30 Apr. 1662									13		15	
Princess Anne	6 Feb. 1665									10			
Duchess of Grafton	1667												~17
Lady Mary Tudor	?16 Oct. 1673												?11
Anne Charlotte De Vic	?	?											
Baroness Leijonbergh	?							?					
?Mr. Griffith	?							?					
Katherine Villiers	?												?
?Jane Fox	?												?
Countess of Pembroke[g]	?												?
AVERAGE AGE:		22¼				29⅖	20	28½	23⅖	23⅔			
MEDIAN AGE:		24	†	†	†	29	23	29	19	16½	†	†	†
MIDRANGE:		21½				31	19	30½	26½	27½			

N.B. For dancers in Lord Sunderland's court ballet of 15 February 1686, see Table 1.3.

Key:
† = statistically insignificant sample

Key to sources:
A Pepys, *Diary*, 3: 300–1; 4: 37.
B Evelyn, *Diary*, 3: 350.
C Evelyn, *Diary*, 3: 351–52.
D Pepys, *Diary*, 4: 68.
E Monconys, *Journal*, 2: 24.
F Pepys, *Diary*, 6: 29.
G Pepys, *Diary*, 7: 371–73.
H Evelyn, *Diary*, 3: 476; AO1/2053/28.
I Von Schwerin (ed. von Orlich), *Briefe*, 27.
J HMC *Rutland* 2: 32.
K Evelyn, *Diary*, 4: 123–24.
L HMC *Portland* 3: 383.

a James Douglas, 2nd Marquess of Douglas.
b "Lord George Barkeley's daughter."
c Later (1667) Duchess of Richmond (see Table 2.1).
d Later (1697) 1st Earl of Jersey.
e Johann Wilhelm II von Wittelsbach, later Duke of Jülich and Berg (1679) and Elector Palatine (1690).
f Formerly Lady Mary Mordaunt (see Table 2.1).
g Margaret Sawyer, married in July 1684 to Thomas Herbert, 8th Earl of Pembroke.

34   *"Their greatest gallantry imaginable"*

was marked the manner in which they were to dress themselves" (p. 119), and "[t]he Day of the Ball being come, the Court, more dazling than ever, display'd all its Magnificence at this Masquerade" (p. 126). He further recounts that

> [t]he Ball was not too well perform'd ... as long as they danc'd only grave Dances, and yet there were as good Dancers, and as beautiful Women in this Assembly, as can be found in the whole World: But as the Number was not great, they left *French*, and went to Country Dances. When those that were of the *Masquerade* had danc'd some of these, the *King* thought fit to produce his *Auxiliaries*, to give the others time to rest themselves: And so the *Queen's* and *Dutchess's* Maids of Honour danc'd with the Men who were of the Masquerade. (pp. 129–30)

Peter Holman has associated these events with *The Queen's Masque* of February 1671 (discussed below),[26] but the "Memoirs" of Gramont are focused exclusively on the early and mid-1660s, after which the Count returned to France with his English wife (who, in the story, is still the object of his early infatuation). Two central figures in Hamilton's recounting of this event are Elizabeth FitzGerald, Viscountess Muskerry and her husband Charles MacCarthy, Viscount Muskerry, who died on 3 June 1665 at the Battle of Lowestoft. Moreover, as one translator of the *Memoirs* has pointed out, another key player in the anecdote, Henrietta Maria Blagge (elder sister of Margaret Blagge, who later appeared in *Calisto*) married Sir Thomas Yarborough of Snaith, Yorkshire before March 1663, thereby providing a tentative *terminus ad quem* for the production in question[27]—assuming, of course, that it took place at all. Given that Catherine of Braganza had only been installed at Whitehall on 23 August 1662,[28] we are left with a relatively narrow window of opportunity for Hamilton's story. There is, it should be noted, no reason necessarily to connect it with the ball witnessed by Pepys on 31 December 1662, apart from the probably conventional shift from French to English dances (mentioned in the passage quoted below).

While communal dancing—including costumed "masquerades" like those just described—may have been plentiful enough in the early years of the Restoration, there seems to have been little inclination to proceed to the obvious next level, namely the kind of theatricalized courtly dance performance represented by the French *ballet de cour* and the English masque. In assessing the "Mask"/ "Masquerade" of 2 February 1665 described by Evelyn and Pepys, for example, Eleanore Boswell concludes that it was "surely the original masque pure and simple, a remarkable piece of what appears to be deliberate archaism, rather than a survival of the Caroline masque,"[29] and it may be noteworthy that all of

---

26 Holman, *Fiddlers*, 365–66.

27 Cyril Hughes Hartmann, *Memoirs of the Comte de Gramont by Anthony Hamilton. A New Translation by Peter Quennell with an Introduction and Commentary by Cyril Hughes Hartmann* (London: George Routledge and Sons, 1930), 372.

28 See Pepys, *Diary*, 3: 174–75.

29 Boswell, 137.

The growth of Shrovetide entertainments   35

our information about these earliest events comes from diaries and memoirs, no records of their occurrence appearing in court administrative documents. Indeed, in February 1663, only a few weeks before the ball at which he affronted Baroness Gerard, Charles II had written to his sister Henriette Anne in Paris, lamenting the lack of dramatic and terpsichorean skill on the part of prospective participants in such entertainments at his court:

> We had a designe to have had a masquerade heere, and had made no ill designe in the generall for it, but we were not able to goe through with it, not haveing one man heere that could make a tolerable entry.[30]

The king's pessimism, expressed nearly three years into his reign, helps to explain the dearth of genuine theatrical activities by courtly "recreational" performers at this time. Years of war and exile appear to have disrupted the normally lifelong process of training courtiers in the finer aspects of presentational dance and stage deportment, and this gap in the court's skill base must have had an effect on the ability to mount ballets and masques according to appropriate standards.

The court's dilemma was compounded by an additional consideration: at the time of Charles II's restoration to the throne, his palace at Whitehall lacked any appropriate venue for performances that might combine dancing and theatrics. Inigo Jones's famous Banqueting House of 1619–21 had ceased to function in this capacity as of 1635, a casualty of concerns that excessive candle-burning might deface the precious ceiling paintings commissioned by Charles I from Peter Paul Rubens.[31] In order to fill the resulting void, Jones oversaw in 1637 the construction

---

30 Letter of Charles II to Henriette Anne, Duchesse d'Orléans, 9 February 1663: Archives du Ministère des Affaires Étrangères, Paris, Mémoires et Documents: Angleterre 26, no. 13, transcribed in Julia Cartwright, *Madame: A Life of Henrietta, Daughter of Charles I. and Duchess of Orleans* (New York: Charles Scribner's Sons, 1894), 131–32, p. 132, and Cyril Hughes Hartmann, *Charles II and Madame* (London: William Heinemann, 1934), 68. Boswell (p. 136) quotes from the French translation of this letter printed in [Charles,] Comte de Baillon, *Henriette-Anne d'Angleterre[,] Duchesse d'Orléans[:] Sa Vie et sa Correspondance avec son Frère Charles II* (2nd ed., Paris: Perrin, 1887), 108–10. Charles's statement should be compared with that of the French ambassador, the Comte de Cominges, writing to Louis XIV only a few weeks earlier, on 25 January 1663 (New Style): "Le Balet est rompu manque de moyens; il n'y a personne qui sache danser, et moins encore pour le diriger, et former un sujet" (Archives du Ministère des Affaires Étrangères, Correspondance Politique: Angleterre 79); this passage is quoted in the anonymous review of Boswell's book in *The Times Literary Supplement* 1595 (25 August 1932): 591, but not, as the reviewer states, in J. J. Jusserand, *A French Ambassador at the Court of Charles the Second: Le Comte de Cominges From his Unpublished Correspondence* (New York: G. P. Putnam's Sons; London: T. Fisher Unwin, 1892), although neighboring passages can be found on pp. 196–97.

31 See Inigo Jones and Sir William Davenant, *Britannia Trivmphans: A Masque* (London: Thomas Walkley, 1637[/8]), sig. A2^r: "There being now past three yeers of Intermission, that the King and Queenes Majesties have not made Masques with shewes and Intermedij, by reason the roome where formerly they were presented, having the seeling since richly adorn'd with peeces of painting of great value, figuring the acts of King *Iames* of happy memory, and other inrichments: lest this might suffer by the smoake of many lights."

36   "Their greatest gallantry imaginable"

of "a new temporary roome of Timber, both for strength and capacitie of spectators,"[32] but this "Masquing Room," built over the course of only two months, was pulled down by Parliamentarian forces in 1645. The palace's stone Great Hall, which had occasionally been appropriated for performances under Charles I, still stood after 1660, but it was unavailable for grand productions due to its near-daily use as a refectory for the army of greater and lesser court servants whose appointments carried the right to "diet." Whitehall's only purpose-built performance venue was thus the Cockpit-in-Court, which had been converted by Jones in 1629–30 into a classical theatre, with a fixed Palladian *frons scenae* and tiers of amphitheatre-like seats ranged directly around the front of the stage (see Figure 1.1).[33] This space, designed to mimic the static scenic conditions of the pre-1642 public theatres, must have seemed decidedly old-fashioned after 1660, and would have quickly revealed itself as inadequate even for the straight plays put on by the public theatrical companies by royal command in the early years of the Restoration,[34] let alone for the dancing or scenic spectacle normally called for in court entertainments.

The solution to both problems seems to have emerged, albeit in a piecemeal fashion, as the by-product of an unrelated effort to streamline the court's operations. Beginning in December 1662 the Restoration court began to experiment with a series of retrenchment schemes designed to reduce the substantial expenditure on "diets" by eliminating unnecessary court positions and substituting a regular "boardwage" payment to cover the cost of meals for those who remained.[35] Although scholars have not hitherto drawn the connection,[36] it seems apparent that this effective privatization of court dining, which cast the great majority of the king's retainers onto the open market of London and Westminster inns and wholesale food purveyors, had the corollary benefit of freeing up a large interior space within the palace for alternative purposes. Thus, upon the suppression of diets for all lesser household servants, which took effect on 1 December 1662, we find a temporary stage being erected in the Great Hall, upon which plays appear to have been acted by the middle

---

32 *Ibid.*; see also Sir Balthazar Gerbier, *A Brief Discourse Concerning the Three Chief Principles of Magnificent Building* (London: n. pub., 1662), 40: "Neither can all great Rooms of Princely Palaces serve for this use, except they be after the Moddell of such as the Italians have built, as there is a good one at *Florence* in *Italy*, with conveyances for Smoak, and capacities for Ecchoes, which *Inigo Jones* (the late Surveyor) experimentally found at *Whitehall*, and by his built Banquetting House, so as having found his own fault, he was constrained to Build a Woodden House overthwart the Court of *Whitehall*."

33 Figure 1.1 shows a plan of the Cockpit-in-Court Theatre as refurbished by John Webb in November 1660: for a detailed discussion, see John Orrell, *The Theatres of Inigo Jones and John Webb* (Cambridge: Cambridge University Press, 1985), 90–112 (chapter 5).

34 For a list of plays performed at the Cockpit-in-Court between 1660 and 1664, see Boswell, 279–81.

35 Andrew Barclay, "Charles II's Failed Restoration: Administrative Reform Below Stairs, 1660–4," in Eveline Cruickshanks, ed., *The Stuart Courts* (Stroud: Sutton Publishing, 2000), 158–70.

36 See, however, the passing comment in Hugh Murray Baillie, "Etiquette and the Planning of the State Apartments in Baroque Palaces," *Archaeologia* 101 (1967): 169–99, p. 173.

The growth of Shrovetide entertainments 37

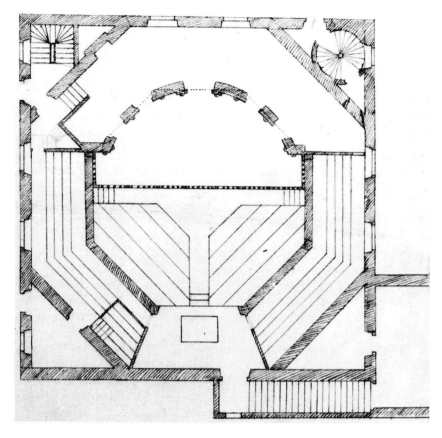

Figure 1.1 John Webb, design for Cockpit-in-Court Theatre, Whitehall Palace (originally constructed 1629–30), as remodeled in November 1660 (The Provost and Fellows of Worcester College, Oxford [Harris and Tait 4, detail])

of the month at the latest.[37] This stage was altered in January, February, and March 1663 and may have continued in use until September or October,[38] thereby potentially serving as the venue for the ball on or around Shrove Tuesday (3 March) mentioned by Pepys and the "greate Masque at Court" attended by Evelyn on 2 July (though perhaps not the "petit bal en priué" witnessed by Monconys

---

37 See Boswell, 25–27 and 242 (for the construction of and alterations to the stage) and 280–81 (for dates of plays that may have been acted there). The seemingly anomalous performance of Thomas Killigrew's *Claracilla* at the Cockpit-in-Court on 5 January 1663 may have been sponsored by the Duke and Duchess of York rather than the king (who did not attend): see Pepys, *Diary*, 4: 4–5.
38 On 5 October an unidentified play was performed at the Cockpit-in-Court (see Boswell, 281, citing LC5/61, p. 63). No order survives for the demolition of the Great Hall's temporary stage.

38   *"Their greatest gallantry imaginable"*

on 11 May). The rationale for the return to the old Cockpit-in-Court theatre in the autumn is not entirely clear, since practically all court diets (as well as boardwages) were suspended from Michaelmas 1663. However, the situation remained very much in flux[39] until October 1664, when a definitive plan was implemented that permanently stripped nearly all of Charles's servants, including the great officers of state, of their diets, granting boardwages in their stead. With this move, the Great Hall was at last free to be deployed as a permanent theatrical space, a function it was to retain with only brief abeyances until the destruction of Whitehall Palace by fire in January 1698.[40] The survival of designs by John Webb, both for the general fitting out of the stage and for scenes for a production of Roger Boyle, Earl of Orrery's play *Mustapha, the Son of Solyman the Magnificent*, offer an indication of the court's aspirations.[41] These drawings for both the plan and the elevation of the stage are endorsed "Plant [/uprights] of the sceanes for the Queens / Ballett in the Hall at Whitehall. / 1665. / To bee vsed also for masques & Playes. / 1. The Tragedy of Mustapha." There seems to be no documentation at all regarding the potentially interesting "Queens Ballett" explicitly referred to in the drawings, unless a "Compart seat or Throne for the Queen" constructed by the joiners as part of the refitting was a stage piece, as Eleanore Boswell suggests.[42] This production should not be conflated with the "fine Mask at Court" of 2 February 1665, performed before work on the new theatre had commenced, nor with the even earlier entertainment sponsored by Queen Catherine of Braganza, described in the *Memoirs of the Life of Count de Grammont* (see pp. 32–34, above). It is not clear whether this "Queens Ballett" was actually presented at all: at the end of June 1665 the court abandoned Whitehall on account of the plague, and it was more than a year before acting resumed in the "new" theatre.[43] In any event, Webb's drawings show, behind the proscenium (the design of which is given in another Webb drawing, probably from the same year), accommodation for four sets of wings and drops, a pair of shutters enclosing a rear space with three grooves for scenes of relieve and a stationary backdrop, and an upper discovery area with four tiers of seats labeled "Musick." The overall plan is undoubtedly modest in comparison with the great court theatres of France and Italy, but it demonstrates, alongside the crucial mention of a "ballett" and "masques," a clear design for the revival of spectacular theatrical productions at the English court: as John Orrell has observed, the choice of design features for the proscenium arch "indicates how completely Webb was captive to the old Caroline traditions of

---

39 In the summer of 1664, plans were laid for a resumption of some diets to take place as of Michaelmas, although these were abandoned at the eleventh hour (see Barclay, 64–65, citing LS13/33).

40 The best discussion of the history of the "Hall Theatre" can be found in Boswell, *passim*; for documents relating to the conversion of the Hall into a theatre in 1665, see pp. 243–45.

41 Devonshire Collection, Chatsworth; see Chapter 4 for further discussion of Orrery's play.

42 WORK5/7, f. 326[v] (*Register*, no. 302); see Boswell, 40.

43 Boswell (p. 44), however, thinks that it may have appeared in 1666, possibly between 18 and 29 October.

courtly magnificence."[44] Webb, who had served for many years as Inigo Jones's trusted deputy, certainly saw it this way, and understood the importance of his role in the process. In a petition of c.1668 supporting his claim to be named Surveyor General (a position that went instead to Christopher Wren), Webb pointed out to the king that "At Whitehall hee made yor Theater, and thereby discovered much of the Scenicall Art, wch to others then himselfe was before much unknowne."[45]

The Hall Theatre officially opened on 20 April 1665,[46] and its establishment as a permanent fixture at court proved a great boon for dramatic activity throughout the Restoration period. The London theatre companies and various traveling troupes regularly appeared to give command performances,[47] and as we shall see, a number of plays were presented by courtiers themselves, mostly in this venue as well. However, it made court balls somewhat more complicated to produce, as the carpenters of the Office of Works had to be deployed to joist and board over the floor of the theatre's pit, creating a five-foot-high platform flush with the front of the stage designed to enable dancing by all the courtiers in attendance—and then to disassemble the entire structure again after each event. This was initially done in an *ad hoc* manner each time it was required, although beginning around 1675 "a ready-made floor was always kept in the theatre, stored under the stage when not in use," and by the 1680s this kit included a special set of degrees and rails designed to run along the side walls of the theatre when the dance floor was being used.[48] The original inconveniences of the system do not seem to have prevented the presentation of balls at various times, however; indeed, certain periods witnessed bursts of activity, as can be seen in Table 1.2.

These included much of the first half of 1663 (before the construction of the theatre)[49] and the autumn and early winter months of 1666, 1685, and 1686. Of particular importance to the court calendar seems to have been a series of annual balls, mostly given in the mid-1670s, celebrating the birthday of Charles II's queen, Catherine of Braganza, on 15 November.[50] It is uncertain when this tradition began, or how consistently it was followed: Samuel Pepys provides an extensive accounting

---

44 Orrell, *Theatres*, 176; Orrell's very full discussion of the design of the Hall Theatre is on pp. 168–85 (chapter 10).

45 SP29/251/120. For a transcription, see John Bold, *John Webb: Architectural Theory and Practice in the Seventeenth Century* (Oxford: Clarendon Press, 1989), 182–83.

46 See Pepys, *Diary*, 6: 85: "This night, I am told, the first play is played in Whitehall=hall, which is now turned to a house of Playing." Previous editors of Pepys (Braybrooke [1825/1848–49], Bright [1875–79], Morley [1886], and Wheatley [1893–99]) give the interesting phrase "White Hall noon-hall" in place of "Whitehall=hall."

47 See Boswell's Appendix C (pp. 278–93) for a comprehensive list of known dramatic performances at court between 1660 and the end of the century.

48 Orrell, *Theatres*, 170–71.

49 See also letter of Samuel Boothhouse to Sir Richard Fanshawe, 12 April 1663, in Sophia Crawford Lomas, ed., *The Manuscripts of J. M. Heathcote, Esq., Conington Castle* (Norwich: Her Majesty's Stationery Office, 1899), 78, referring to "the Court entertainments, as balls and plays, which have been frequent this last winter."

50 The queen had been born in Portugal on 25 November 1638, a date reckoned as 15 November according to the Julian ("Old Style") calendar in use in England.

Table 1.2 Non-dramatic balls and "masques" known to have been performed at court, 1660–88

Year	Date	Specific Occasion (if known)	Location	References	Register, nos.
?1662–3	?		?	Memoirs of the Life of Count de Grammont, chap. 7	—
1662	31 December	Christmastide	?	Pepys, Diary, 3: 300–1	—
1663	10 January		?	Evelyn, Diary, 3: 350	—
	5 February	†	?	Evelyn, Diary, 3: 351–52	—
	>7 March	†? [Shrove Tuesday: 3 March]	?	Pepys, Diary, 4: 68	—
	11 May		?	Monconys, Journal, 2: 24	—
	2 July		?	Evelyn, Diary, 3: 357	—
	19 August		?	Evelyn, Diary, 3: 360	—
1664	22 February	†Shrove Monday	Hall	Pepys, Diary, 5: 56	—
1665	2 February	†Candlemas Day (Thursday before Shrove Tuesday)	?	Evelyn, Diary, 3: 397; Pepys, Diary, 6: 29	—
	? (or 1666?)[a]		Hall Theatre	Webb plan/elevation (Chatsworth); WORK5/7, f. 326^v	—; 302
1666	25 October	?birthday of queen's (late) mother[b]	Hall Theatre+	WORK5/9, f. 96^r; LC5/138, p. 74; Pepys, Diary, 7: 341	349; 350; —
	15 November	Catherine of Braganza's birthday	Hall Theatre+	WORK5/9, f. 108^v; Pepys, Diary, 7: 371–73	352; —
	? December		Hall Theatre+	WORK5/9, f. 120^v	361

Year	Date	Occasion	Venue	Sources	
1667	18 February	†Shrove Monday	Hall Theatre+	WORK5/9, f. 148ᵛ; AO1/2053/28; Evelyn, *Diary*, 3: 476	367; —; —
1671	15 November?	Catherine of Braganza's birthday	Hall Theatre	LC5/14, p. 61 rev.; LC5/64, f. 14ᵛ; LC9/109; LC9/273	653; 653; —; —
1672	4 January		Queen's Lodgings	Newsletter (*The Bulstrode Papers*, 1: 214)	
	19 February	†Shrove Monday	?Hall Theatre	Newsletter (*The Bulstrode Papers*, 1: 221)	
	15 November	Catherine of Braganza's birthday	Hall Theatre[+?]	LC5/64, f. 51ʳ; LS1/15 §*Annotacõne*, p. 2; LS13/171, p. 289; Evelyn, *Diary*, 3: 630	736; —; —; —
1673	15 November?	Catherine of Braganza's birthday	Hall Theatre	LC5/64, f. 79ᵛ	812
1675	29 May	Charles II's birthday	Hall Theatre+	LC5/141, p. 196; WORK5/25, f. 35ʳ; von Schwerin, xxvi, 27	919; 918; —
	15 November	Catherine of Braganza's birthday	Hall Theatre+	LC5/141, p. 288; WORK5/26, f. 94ʳ[; ?LC5/141, p. 346]	943; 941[; 958]
1676	8 February	†Shrove Tuesday	Hall Theatre	LS8/12, p. 18; WORK5/26, f. 124ʳ	—; 959
	15 November	Catherine of Braganza's birthday	Hall Theatre+	LC5/141, p. 471; WORK5/27, f. 93ʳ; Evelyn, *Diary*, 4: 101; HMC *Rutland* 2: 32	980; 979; —; —

(Continued)

Year	Date	Specific Occasion (if known)	Location	References	Register, nos.
1677	*15 November*	Catherine of Braganza's birthday	*Hall Theatre+*	WORK5/28, f. 80[r]; Evelyn, *Diary*, 4: 123–24; von Schwerin, 165, 166; Lake, "Diary," p. 9	1025; —; —; —
1681	15 November	Catherine of Braganza's birthday	*Hall Theatre*	Newsletter (Folger MS L.c.1148)	—
1683	14 February	†(Wednesday before Shrove Tuesday)	*Queen's Presence Chamber*	LS1/25; LS8/18; WORK5/35, f. 77[v]; WORK5/35, f. 85[r]	—; —; 1181; 1190
	17 February	†(Saturday before Shrove Tuesday)	*Hall Theatre+*	LC5/144, pp. 360, 364; WORK5/35, f. 85[r]	1191; 1190
	19 February	†Shrove Monday	*Hall Theatre[+?]*	LS1/25; LS8/18	—; —
1684	*15 November*	Catherine of Braganza's birthday	*Hall Theatre+*	LC5/145, p. 107; WORK5/38, f. 67[v]; Evelyn, *Diary*, 4: 395; Luttrell, *Relation*, 1: 320; HMC *Portland* 3: 383	1243; 1242; —; —; —
1685	? Jan./Feb.[c]	†? *[Shrove Tuesday: 3 March]*	*?Hall Theatre*	WORK5/38, f. 84[r]; LC5/145, p. 147	1248; —
	14 October	James II's birthday	*Hall Theatre+*	WORK5/39, f. 55[r]; LC5/201, p. 499; Evelyn, *Diary*, 4: 480	1264; 1266; —
	? November		*Hall Theatre+*	WORK5/39, f. 45[v]	1269
	? December		*Hall Theatre+*	WORK5/39, f. 35[v]	1272
1686	*15 February*	†Shrove Monday	*Dutchess of Portsmouth's Lodgings*	correspondence (see Appendix B)	—

	14 October[d]	James II's birthday	*Hall Theatre*+	WORK5/40, f. 44[r]; WORK5/40, f. 52[r]; LS1/30; Evelyn, *Diary*, 4: 526	1283; 1284; —; —
	? November		*Hall Theatre*+	WORK5/40, f. 60[v]	1287
	13 December		*Hall Theatre*+	WORK5/40, f. 67[r]; LS1/30	1292; —
1687	? January	*[Shrove Tuesday: 8 February]*	*Hall Theatre*+	WORK5/40, f. 75[r]	1296
1688	? January	*[Shrove Tuesday: 28 February]*	*Father Petre's Presence Chamber*	WORK5/41, f. 123[r]	1313

Key:

date ital. = some performers identified: see Tables 1.1 and 1.3

† = performed during Carnival season

+ = pit of Hall Theatre (approx. 1620 sq. ft.) joisted and boarded over at stage height to accommodate dancing

[a] "the Queens Ballett."

[b] Luísa Maria Francisca de Gusmão of Medina-Sidonia (3/13 October 1613–17/27 February 1666), former queen consort and regent of Portugal, mother of Catherine of Braganza: see Pepys ("a great Ball tonight at Court, being the Queenes birthday").

[c] Possibly not presented, owing to Charles II's death on 6 February.

[d] The first cited reference is dated September, but the court was at Windsor until 1 October.

44   *"Their greatest gallantry imaginable"*

of a ball in 1666,[51] whereas John Evelyn's reports of celebrations in 1668, 1674, and 1678 do not specifically mention any dancing on those occasions.[52] On the other hand, in 1672 Evelyn referred to "an extraordinary appearance of Gallantry & a Ball danced at Court,"[53] while administrative records from 1671, 1673, and 1675 suggest that balls were also held for the queen's birthday in those years, although no corroborating diary entries exist (conversely, the queen's birthday ball of 1681 is documented only in a newsletter report, and not in any court records).[54] Three of these balls are particularly well attested: in 1676, Evelyn wrote of "the famous Ball, daunced at Court on her Majesties *Birth-day*,"[55] and two letters from Grace, Lady Chaworth record the event—the latter recounting the aftermath of a duel that arose when William Cavendish, future Earl and 1st Duke of Devonshire, was reproved by a "Mr. Powre of Ireland one of our soldiers in France" for blocking the view of some women while standing "at the doore of the ball."[56] In 1677, Evelyn reported "a greate Ball at *Court*, where the Prince of *Orange* & his new *Princes* daunc'd," the recently wedded Princess Mary having "attir'd herselfe very richly with all her jewells";[57] ten days earlier, Mary's chaplain and tutor Dr. Edward Lake had estimated the value of the jewels presented to Mary by her new husband, William of Orange, at £40,000.[58] The 1684 festivities seem to have been especially elaborate, as Evelyn's uncharacteristically effusive account makes clear:

> Being the Queenes Birth-day, there was such fire works upon the Thames before White-hall, with pageants of Castles, Forts, & other devices of Gyrandolas, Serpents, The King & Queenes Armes & mottos, all represented in fire, as had not ben seene in any age remembred here: but that which was most remarkable was the several fires & skirmishes in the very water, which actualy moved a long way, burning under the water, & now and then appearing above

---

51 Pepys, *Diary*, 7: 371–73.

52 Evelyn, *Diary*, 3: 518 (1668: with fireworks), 4: 48 (1674: "the Court ... exceeding splendid, in Clothes & Jewells to the height of excesse"), and 4: 157 (1678: "I never saw the Court more brave").

53 Evelyn, *Diary*, 3: 630.

54 See references in Table 1.2; for further details of the 1681 ball, see n. 86, below.

55 Evelyn, *Diary*, 4: 101.

56 Grace, Lady Chaworth to Lord Roos, 16 and 23 November 1676, in H. C. Maxwell Lyte, *The Manuscripts of His Grace the Duke of Rutland, K. G., Preserved at Belvoir Castle. Vol. II* (Historical Manuscripts Commission, Twelfth Report, Appendix, Part V; London: Her Majesty's Stationery Office, 1889; hereafter cited as HMC *Rutland* 2), 31–32. For more on the former letter, see Chapter 2, n. 108, below.

57 Evelyn, *Diary*, 4: 123–24. See also letters of Otto von Schwerin the Younger to Elector Friedrich Wilhelm of Brandenburg, 13/23 and 16/26 November 1677, in Leopold von Orlich, ed., *Briefe aus England über die Zeit von 1674 bis 1678; in Gesandtschafts-Berichten des Ministers Otto von Schwerin des Jüngern an den Großen Kurfürsten Friedrich Wilhelm* (Berlin: G. Reimer, 1837), 165 and 166, and George Percy Elliott, ed., "Diary of Dr. Edward Lake, ... Chaplain and Tutor to the Princesses Mary and Anne, ... in the Years 1677–1678" (1846), in *The Camden Miscellany* 1 (Camden Society, 39; London: Camden Society, 1847), sig. [3]A1r–[3]D4v (pp. 1–32), p. 9.

58 "Diary of Dr. Edward Lake," 6.

The growth of Shrovetide entertainments   45

it, giving reports like Muskets & Cannon, with Granados, & innumerable other devices: It is said this sole Triumph cost 1500 pounds: which was concluded with a Ball, where all the young Ladys & Gallants daunced in the greate Hall: The Court had not ben seene so brave & rich in apparell since his Majesties restauration.[59]

There was certainly dancing on this occasion, as is evident from a letter of A. Stephens to Abigail Harley of 29 November 1684:

> The best dancers were the Duchesses of Norfolk and Grafton, Lady Mary Tudor, Mrs. Fox, and Villars the maid of honour, but Lady Pembroke was more taken notice of than any though in a contrary way than the former ladies, but she was the most assured young woman that I saw to perform no better, though it was as well as any expected.[60]

In contrast to the regular sequence of balls on 15 November, there is only one recorded instance of a ball being held on Charles II's birthday; this took place in 1675.[61]

Most of the events listed in Table 1.2 were probably not theatrical in any proper sense, although a few are of a more uncertain status, incorporating such elements as vocal music, professional dancers, or an unusually configured performance venue. For example, the Works accounts for the balls of 25 October 1666 and 15 November 1684 refer to the carpenters "mending & fitting the Ceanes" and "waiting in ye night vpon the stage and looking after the scenes," despite the fact that the floor of the pit was boarded over for dancing as usual.[62] The provisions supplied for the ball on the queen's birthday in 1672 included extra candles for the use of the "Sceen Keeper," John Bennett, which may indicate a dramatic component to this event, for which there is no certain record of the Hall Theatre's floor having been boarded over for dancing.[63] And in November 1675, the Master

---

59 Evelyn, *Diary*, 4: 395; compare Narcissus Luttrell, *A Brief Historical Relation of State Affairs* (6 vols.: Oxford: Oxford University Press, 1857), 1: 320: "in the evening were very fine fireworks on the water before Whitehall, which lasted for about two hours; and at night was a great ball at Whitehall, where the court appeared in much splendor and bravery."

60 Richard Ward, *The Manuscripts of his Grace the Duke of Portland, Preserved at Welbeck Abbey. Vol. III* (Historical Manuscripts Commission, Fourteenth Report, Appendix, Part II; London: Her Majesty's Stationery Office, 1894), 383. "Lady Pembroke" was Margaret Sawyer, daughter of the Attorney-General, Sir Robert Sawyer, recently (26 July) married to Thomas Herbert, who in 1683 had succeeded as 8th Earl of Pembroke.

61 See diary entry of Otto von Schwerin the Younger, 29 May/8 June 1675, and letter of von Schwerin to Elector Friedrich Wilhelm, 1/11 June 1675, both quoted in Orlich, ed., *Briefe aus England*, xxvi and 27.

62 WORK5/9, f. 96^r and WORK5/38, f. 67^v (*Register*, nos. 349 and 1242).

63 LS1/15 §*Annotacõne*, p. 2, discussed in Rob Jordan, "An Addendum to *The London Stage 1660–1700*," *Theatre Notebook* 47 (1993): 62–75, p. 68; see also LS13/171, p. 289 (mentioned in Boswell, 93). Jordan suggests that "since there is no provision for food for the performers or

46   *"Their greatest gallantry imaginable"*

of the Music Nicholas Staggins wrote out a fair copy of "Aires composed for ye Maske from ye fowle originall on score" and prepared parts of "the said musick for ye voyces, with ye instrumentall musick composed at ye same time."[64] It is impossible to determine whether this "Maske" might be equated with the ball performed on the queen's birthday that year, for which we would not normally expect vocal music. What is almost certain is that the reference is not to the music for *Calisto* performed seven to nine months earlier, since a warrant to pay Staggins for making copies of that music had already been issued in May.[65] Staggins was similarly involved nine years subsequently when, in late January 1685, he and ten members of the king's violins were ordered to "attend at his Majesty's Theatre Royal to practise music for a ball which is to be before his Majesty there."[66] Although the wording here is ambiguous, "his Majesty's Theatre Royal" is presumably meant as a reference to the Hall Theatre, located in the *royal* palace of Whitehall, rather than to the Drury Lane Theatre (which continued to be known as the "Theatre Royal" after the union of the King's and Duke's patent companies in November 1682):[67] sometime in January the carpenters made alterations to the Hall Theatre that included "making two desk boards for the Musick 8 fo^t long a peice, and setting vp two bearers for the Harpsicall,"[68] accommodations that would have suited precisely the group of instrumentalists mentioned in the order to the musicians. If these two documents are indeed related, it is worth noting that the alterations made in the Hall Theatre are not commensurate with the usual preparations for a ball, and hence there may have been a dramatic component to this event as well. Whether it ultimately occurred at all is another question, since the date of the order to the musicians, 26 January, came only a week before the onset of the convulsions that eventually resulted in Charles II's death on 6 February.

Throughout the early modern period in England, the winter months were traditionally set aside for the most lavish and high-profile court entertainments. In particular, these tended to appear during the seasons of Christmastide—from

---

for heating for the tireing rooms," any dramatic element may have been presented by court amateurs. Regarding the question of whether or not the pit was boarded over, see WORK5/19, f. 95^r (*Register*, no. 741), ordering payment to the carpenters for "taking downe the staige ouer ye pitt" in December. See also the warrant of 14 November for green baize to cover the stage and forms (LC5/64, f. 51^r [*Register*, no. 736]).

64 LC5/141, p. 346 (Ashbee, 1: 155–56), a warrant of 27 January 1676. For this particular task Staggins was assigned a total of £26 15s; the warrant includes additional payments for similar work done in other months for non-theatrical events.

65 See LC5/141, p. 197 (Ashbee, 1: 149–50): £10 for "writeing & pricking the tunes in the Maske, & for paper, pens & inke, etc." This money, part of a lump sum of £221 to be distributed by Staggins to certain of the musicians, was not actually paid until the following year: see PRO30/32/43 [properly "T52/5"], p. 51 and PRO30/32/46 [properly "T53/[0b]"], p. 290 (*Calendar of Treasury Books* 5: 123; Ashbee, 8: 223), dated 7 February 1676.

66 LC5/145, p. 147 (not in *Register*; see Ashbee, 1: 214), dated 26 January 1685.

67 Compare LC5/138, p. 259 (*Register*, no. 354), an order of 20 November 1666 for tin plates "for the Theatre Royall in Whitehall."

68 WORK5/38, f. 84^r (*Register*, no. 1248).

Christmas Day to Twelfth Night (5 January, the eve of the Feast of the Epiphany)—and Carnival—which formally began on Candlemas Day (2 February, the Feast of the Purification of the Virgin) and ended with Shrove Tuesday, the last day before the commencement of Lent. Because Shrove Tuesday was linked to the moveable feast of Easter (which followed it by forty-seven days), the period between Candlemas and the beginning of Lent could last as little as two or as long as thirty-seven days. Whatever its length, most of the Carnival entertainments given in the Restoration period were presented in or near Shrovetide, the three days immediately preceding Ash Wednesday. The Restoration undoubtedly witnessed an early and fairly robust revival of Shrovetide performances, which incorporated a particular tradition of presentations by courtly "recreational" performers that can be traced back to as early as 1663. This reemergent tradition increased in sophistication after the construction of the Hall Theatre, with the appearance of plays and masques, or in some instances of dance extravaganzas meant to serve as culminating events following a busy season of lesser balls and other performances put on by those in the court's orbit. Thus, the performance being prepared in late January 1685 was probably designed for presentation early in the Carnival season, perhaps to initiate an extended series of entertainments, given that Shrove Tuesday fell quite late that year, on 3 March. All this would, of course, have been cancelled after Charles II's death.[69] For the twenty-four Shrovetide seasons that fell within Charles II's reign, Sandra Tuppen has documented performances in or near Shrove Tuesday for at least fourteen and perhaps as many as eighteen of these years.[70] They consist of a mix of genres, including balls (listed here in Table 1.2), "recreational" plays and masques (calendared in Table 2.1), and professional plays given by the patent companies and French performers.[71] Not every year saw such an entertainment. In 1666, for example, most of Whitehall's denizens had decamped to Oxford to escape the ongoing outbreak of plague in London: as Daniel Defoe would later retrospectively observe, "All the Plays and Interludes, which after the Manner of the *French* Court, had been set up, and began to encrease among us, were forbid to Act."[72] In subsequent years the elaborate entertainments occasionally fell behind schedule and had to be performed in Lent or after Easter. But a fundamental pattern of Shrovetide revelry is nonetheless discernable, with "recreational" performances of various types constituting the dominant mode.

One of the most interesting such entertainments, from a documentary point of view, is that held on Shrove Monday (18 February) 1667. The editor of John Evelyn's *Diary* suggests that this "entertainment appears to have been a masque

---

69 Less certain is the purpose of the undated balls presented sometime in January during the last two years of James II's reign (see Table 1.2).

70 Tuppen, "Shrove-Tide Dancing," Tables 1 (p. 161) and 2 (p. 163).

71 These last are noted in Boswell's Appendix C.

72 Daniel Defoe, *A Journal of the Plague Year* (London: E. Nutt, J. Roberts, A. Dodd, and J. Graves, 1722), 35.

48 *"Their greatest gallantry imaginable"*

in the original sense, a masquerade,"[73] and indeed the carpenters were ordered to prepare the hall for dancing, as described above.[74] Evelyn's own entry, however, is unusually fulsome: the diarist reports that he "saw a magnificent Ball or Masque in the *Theater* at Court, where their Majesties & all the greate Lords & Ladies daunced infinitely gallant: the Men in their richly imbrodred, most becoming Vests."[75] The "Persian vest" had been introduced at court the previous Fall as a distinctively English answer to the perceived vanity of French fashion in everyday attire.[76] But the men's "most becoming Vests" worn for the Shrovetide ball were evidently far more elaborate, as can be seen in a document drawn up by the Master of the Robes some eleven years after the event. This supplementary account, submitted to clear an outstanding charge of £641 9s 6d for "Masquerading habits for dancing omitted in the year 1667,"[77] is transcribed in Appendix A. Besides revealing the significant expenditure lavished on the performance—and incidentally the names of three of the courtly participants, including the Earl of Rochester and Nell Gwyn (see Table 1.1)—it offers a wealth of interesting detail regarding both the costumes and, to some degree, the nature of the production itself. The 1667 entertainment may have been "a masquerade" in certain respects, but it appears to have included a distinctly theatrical element as well: notwithstanding Charles II's earlier complaint about "not having one man ... that could make a tolerable entry," we can see evidence among the costume bills not only of ostentatious courtly attire but also of quasi-dramatic character dances. In the case of the latter, at least six male dancing masters (and perhaps one female dancer) appear to have been employed: the bills list four "Habitts with other ffurniture for representing a Courtier[,] an English gent[leman,] a yeoman and a Plowman"; two "ffantasticke Habitts of blew Bayes. wth laced Capps & vizards," costumes for four "Scaramouches of blacke bayes with shoes," six "Roman Habitts of white Tinsell with blacke bugle Lace," and "Habitts for [six] Egiptian men and one Egiptian Woeman." As Appendix A reveals, the amounts expended on these "character" costumes were comparatively small: apart from the six Roman habits (which may have been worn by courtiers in any case[78]), the greatest single outlay

---

73 Evelyn, *Diary*, 3: 476, n. 2. Boswell (pp. 135–36) helpfully underscores the inexactitude with which contemporaries, particularly in these early years, deployed terms like "masque," "masquerade," "ball," and "ballet."

74 WORK5/9, f. 148[v] (*Register*, no. 367).

75 Evelyn, *Diary*, 3: 476.

76 See Esmond S. de Beer, "King Charles II's Own Fashion: An Episode in Anglo-French Relations 1666–1670," *Journal of the Warburg Institute* 2 (1938–39): 105–15 and Diana de Marly, "King Charles II's Own Fashion: The Theatrical Origins of the English Vest," *Journal of the Warburg and Courtauld Institutes* 37 (1974): 378–82. The official introduction of the vest had occurred on 14 October, the Duke of York's birthday.

77 Account for 29 September 1677–25 March 1678: AO1/2053/28, ff. 4[v]–5[r]; the very cursory notice of this document printed in the *Calendar of Treasury Books* 5: xxxiv does not do it justice.

78 The third of the named courtiers in the list, "M[r] ffelton" (*i.e.* Thomas Felton, a Page of Honour and, from 1671, Groom of the Bedchamber to Charles II and later, as 4th Baronet, Master and Comptroller of the Household under William III and Anne), was provided his own special costume,

The growth of Shrovetide entertainments   49

was the £14 3*s* spent on the four costumes for what must have been a parody of class relations (ranging from the "Courtier" to the "Plowman").[79] By contrast, a considerable expenditure was made on what appear to have been at least ten (and perhaps as many as twenty-six) costumes for individual courtiers: costs ranged from £11 18*s* 6*d* for "A Robe & doublet of Cloth of gold with other ffurniture" and £12 2*s* for "A Cherry colour sattin Vest and sarsnet breeches. the sleeues shamer'd w[th] [three] Rowes of Pearle. and other ffurniture"[80] to £66 5*s* 6*d* for "A scarlet Pudesoy[81] Coat shammerd with siluer and gold Lace," and an eye-popping £104 4*s* 6*d* for "A pinke Color Lutestring Coate wth Ringraves shamer'd all ouer with siluer Lace with other ffurniture,"[82] perhaps worn by Charles II himself. There is some evidence that the newly adopted vest, remarked upon by Evelyn, may have been a featured part of the show: five different entries in the account mention either "vest" or "wastcoate," and at least a couple of these entries seem to carry particular importance—they include £35 12*s* for four "vests & [four pair] of blew breeches wth other ffurniture" (the only uniformly costumed group of dancers in the account not associated with a character type); £50 5*s* 6*d* for "A Turcks Habitt wth a sky color vest [and?] a Coat of spotted Plush, the vest laced wth gold Lace and other ffurniture"; and what appears to have been a special expenditure of £10 7*s* for labor in "Makeing a purple Cloth suit embrodered[,] a fflannill wast coate, altring two Coates & Ringraves wth other ffurniture for M[is] Gwinn." Taken as a whole, the 1667 court entertainment looks very much like a full-scale French-style *ballet de cour*. Indeed, it may have required considerable rehearsal: a petition from Charles II's "Musitians in ordinary," possibly dating from this time, requests payment of a year's arrears in their salaries, "your Peticoners having all this Winter given their constant attendance morning and evening on this present Maske."[83]

---

consisting of "A Roman Roabe. Bases. breeches. & buskins"; he may thus have been the featured solo dancer of a Roman-themed entry, whose "chorus" may have been either "recreational" courtiers or "occupational" (*i.e.* professional) performers. Felton's attire cost £39 1*s*; the total spent on all the other six Roman habits was £52 10*s*. The account also lists "A Roman Habitt wth Scollops and other ffurniture" (at £18 4*s* 6*d*), which appears separately, and thus—particularly considering the ubiquity of Classical dress in early modern theatrical costume—may have been for a different entry.

79 The total expenditure for seventeen "character" costumes (*i.e.* excluding the six Roman habits) was a mere £41 15*s*.

80 "Sarsnet" or "sarcenet" is defined as "a thin silk, first used in the thirteenth century": see F. W. Fairholt, *Costume in England: A History of Dress to the End of the Eighteenth Century* (3rd ed., rev. by H. A. Dillon; 2 vols.: London: George Bell and Sons, 1885), 2: 357. The term "shammer'd," which appears frequently in these and other costume accounts of the period, is a corruption of the French *chamarrer*, meaning "to bedeck" or "adorn."

81 *I.e.* Paduasoy, "a smooth, strong silk [deriving] its name from Padua, the place of its first manufacture" (Fairholt, 2: 302).

82 A "ringrave" or "rhinegrave" consists of "full breeches, with bunches of ribands at the knee" (Fairholt, 2: 349); lutestring is "a very fine corded silk" (*ibid.*, 275).

83 SP29/441/32 and 33 (*Calendar of State Papers, Domestic* Addenda: 232–33; Ashbee, 8: 183); the second document is later than the first, since it refers to "the last masque" and includes Charles II's promise that a year's salary "should be paid forthwith."

50   *"Their greatest gallantry imaginable"*

The variety of types of Shrovetide entertainments over the years suggests an ongoing process of experimentation by the court throughout the Restoration period. In some years, these events appear to have been relatively modest, as for example in 1672 when "their Ma^tys were divertized at a Ball, in which the principall persons of quallity about Court bore their part, to their great satisfaccõn,"[84] and in 1676 when, according to the records of the Lord Steward and the Office of Works, there was a "Ball" and "danceing."[85] In neither case, we should note, is there any surviving record of the pit having been boarded over, as might normally be expected for such occasions.[86] In other years, the days leading up to and including Shrovetide may have seen a number of discrete events. This seems to have been the case in 1683 when the Lord Steward's records list supplies ordered for "several Balls in the Queens Presence Chamber & in the Hall," specifically identifying one given at the former location on Wednesday, 14 February and another at the latter on the 19th (Shrove Monday).[87] At the same time, documents from the Lord Chamberlain and the Office of Works appear to relate to a different event on Saturday the 17th, for which the pit was boarded over as usual;[88] one of these documents also mentions "removing all the Formes out of the Hall into the Q[ueen']s Presence [Chamber] and removing them back into the Hall and fitting and placing them there againe," most likely for the event on the 14th.[89] This sequence of balls—the first to appear after what looks to have been a five-year interruption in such activities contemporaneous with, and most likely

84 Newsletter sent to Sir Richard Bulstrode, 23 February 1672 (report for Shrove Monday, 19 February): Harry Ransom Humanities Center, University of Texas at Austin, PFORZ-MS-0613, p. 2 (see [Alphonse Wyatt Thibaudeau], ed., *The Collection of Autograph Letters and Historical Documents Formed by Alfred Morrison (Second Series, 1882–1893): The Bulstrode Papers, Volume I (1667–1675)* [1 vol. only: (London: Strangeways and Sons), 1897], 221).

85 LS8/12, p. 18; WORK5/26, f. 124^r (*Register*, no. 959); see Tuppen, "Shrove-Tide Dancing," 162.

86 Compare the event held on the queen's birthday in 1681, where the actors of the King's Company performed Nathaniel Lee's *The Rival Queens* in the Hall Theatre, "after wch was a ball & entteinm^t given to ye Co^lh" (Folger Shakespeare Library, MS L.c.1148). It should be pointed out that without the addition of the raised wooden floor usually deployed for balls, the Hall was not ideally suited for dancing, given that its real floor probably consisted of flagstones and/or tile.

87 The quoted passage is from LS8/18, while the two specific dates are given in LS1/25 §*Extraordinar*; see Tuppen, "Shrove-Tide Dancing," 162. For a reproduction of the page from LS1/25 relating to the Shrove Monday event, see Tuppen, 168; this document was first described in Jordan, "An Addendum to *The London Stage 1660–1700*" (see n. 63, above), 71, where it is incorrectly dated to 1682 rather than to 1682[/3]; Jordan observes that it is "the only [entry from the LS1 series] in which Dancing Masters and the use of Tireing rooms are mentioned."

88 LC5/144, p. 360 (warrant of 13 February to joist and board the pit for dancing "vpon Saterday next"; *Register*, no. 1191); LC5/144, p. 364 (warrant of 15 February for green baize "to be made ready for the dancing"; also mentioned under *Register*, no. 1191); WORK5/35, f. 85^r (account for joisting and boarding the pit "for a ball"; *Register*, no. 1190).

89 WORK5/35, f. 85^r; note that the previous month the carpenters had been employed in what may have been the preparatory work of "fitting and mending" the formes "for the Q^s Presence and carrying them into the Hall againe" (WORK5/35, f. 77^v [*Register*, no. 1181]).

a consequence of, the "Exclusion Crisis" of 1678–82[90]—may even have had a dramatic component: it has recently been speculated that it could have included a performance of the masque *Venus and Adonis*, to be discussed below. Whatever the case, it is evident that Shrovetide was the preferred time for the mounting of court entertainments that were particularly lavish or elaborate or, as we shall see presently, especially theatrical.

As Table 1.2 reveals, Charles's brother and successor seems to have shown a greater interest in holding court balls during his brief reign, particularly during the autumn months. For the most part no details have survived beyond the standard accountings of the carpenters' labor in modifying the Hall Theatre for the purpose, although an anonymous manuscript satire, believed to have been written in 1687 or early 1688, has the patent company actors complain that they have been rendered destitute because, among other things, "the Court has forsaken us for Masques & Balls."[91] Amongst this dearth of evidence, the Christmas and Carnival season of 1686—the first full season of James II's reign—provides an exceptional case, with courtly London virtually awash in balls and masquerades. The succession of grand events is difficult to reconstruct with absolute certainty: it may have begun as early as Saturday, 19 December 1685, with a ball hosted by Peregrine Osborne, Viscount Dumblane (eldest son of the Earl of Danby and future 2nd Duke of Leeds, who had danced in *Calisto* eleven years before, aged fifteen),[92] and although the royal couple's retreat for Christmastide was originally expected to bring a halt to such festivities,[93] by the end of the month "greete masquerades" were anticipated at the residences of a number of high-ranking courtiers.[94] A particularly well-attested example is a ball presented on Tuesday, 12 January by William Cavendish, 4th Earl (later 1st Duke) of Devonshire in his sumptuous rented accommodations at Montagu House in Bloomsbury, a building designed by Robert Hooke for Ralph Montagu, later Earl and Duke of Montagu. The house sported murals by the Italian allegorical painter Antonio Verrio and was described by John Evelyn as one "than

---

90 For what may be the single possible exception to this hiatus (which must, in any event, have been of quite limited scope), see n. 86, above.

91 Hugh MacDonald, ed., *A Journal from Parnassus* (London: Oxford University Press for P. J. Dobell, 1937), 55.

92 Letter of Bridget Noel to Katherine (*née* Noel) Manners, Countess of Rutland, 21 December 1685 (HMC *Rutland* 2: 98): "I was told there was a ball at my Lord Dumblain's of Saturday; how true it is I don't know. The Court removed a Saturday to Saint James where they continue till after Christmas."

93 Letter of Bridget Noel to the Countess of Rutland, 19 December 1685 (HMC *Rutland* 2: 98): "The King and Quen goes to San James tell after twell day [*i.e.* Epiphany], and I heare ther is to be noe more balls tell after that time."

94 Letter of Peregrine Bertie to Katherine Manners, Countess of Rutland, 26 December 1685 (HMC *Rutland* 2: 99): "Next week—they say—will bee very famous for the greete masquerades that are designed; my Lord Devonshire's will bee the first, the Duke of Somerset intends another, and my Lord Pembroke a third, besides these there will be a ball, if not a masque, at my Lord Sunderland's. The Venetian ambassadors designe to make two every weeke; they will have dancing and playing after the Venetian mode."

52 *"Their greatest gallantry imaginable"*

which for Painting & furniture, there was nothing more glorious in England."[95] As Bridget Noel reported to her sister Katherine, Countess of Rutland, sometime around 6 January, "All the town will be at the masquerade at Mountague House, and Lord Devensher desins none to be theare but people of qualety."[96] Peregrine Bertie, who had previously predicted an earlier date for the event,[97] corresponded with the Countess on the 9th, sending the news that

> My Lord Devonshire['s] masq which has been soe long talked of is now fixed to a day and will most certainly bee next Tuesday. There will be noe tickets, only one of the company must show his face and answer for the rest; for my owne part, I should not goe to it, were it not for the satisfaction of giving your Ladyship a relation of the glory and splendour of the entertainment which everybody says will be very noble.[98]

In the event, Bertie appears to have neglected his mission: writing two weeks later, he conceded,

> I am very sorry that I cannot oblige your Ladyshipp with a relation of the severall dresses att my Lord Devonshire's ball; the variety was so greate that it prevented my remembring any particular habit. If there should be another masque—as 'tis thought there will att the Duke of Summerset's—I will be sure to give your Ladyship an account of the fancied habits.[99]

By this time, however, Devonshire's triumph had been cruelly eclipsed: just a week after his celebrated ball, Montagu House burned to the ground. Responsibility for the catastrophe was difficult to pin down: in his same letter, Bertie reported that "they say the whole loss will fall to my Lord Montague, because fired by his servants; notwithstanding, my Lord Devonshire is obliged in a bond of 30,000*l.* to leave it as good as when hee tooke it." Within the larger social world, however, the celebrations went on: another highlight of the season was a performance of Lully and Quinault's opera *Cadmus et Hermione* by a French troupe at one of the public theatres on Thursday, 11 February, to be discussed in Chapter 8.

The season's most extraordinary event, however, fell on Monday, 15 February, the day before Shrove Tuesday. This was a "grate ball or masque att Court" (HMC *Rutland* 2: 102) put on by Robert Spencer, Earl of Sunderland, Lord President of the Privy Council, in the Whitehall apartments of the Duchess of Portsmouth. The entertainment, the preparations for and performance of which

---

95 Evelyn, *Diary*, 4: 497.

96 Letter of Bridget Noel to the Countess of Rutland, c.6 January 1686 (HMC *Rutland* 2: 100). Bridget added, "My brother John will be at all the masquerades."

97 Letter of Peregrine Bertie to the Countess of Rutland, 31 December 1685 (HMC *Rutland* 2: 100): "My Lord Devonshire's will not bee till some day next week."

98 Letter of Peregrine Bertie to the Countess of Rutland, 9 January 1686 (HMC *Rutland* 2: 101).

99 Letter of Peregrine Bertie to the Countess of Rutland, 23 January 1686 (HMC *Rutland* 2: 101–2).

The growth of Shrovetide entertainments   53

are described in a number of contemporary letters (see Appendix B for full references and transcriptions), was attended by King James and his queen, by James's younger daughter Princess Anne and her husband Prince George of Denmark, and by more than a dozen high-born ladies, as well as "noblemen, persons of quality, Ambassadors & forraign ministers" (Folger MS V.b.287 [5], p. 1). Although Lord and Lady Sunderland were the hosts, and the late king's mistress provided the venue, the guiding force seems to have been Queen Mary of Modena herself, who "prescribed" the masquers' costumes "by a picture sent to each of them" (BL Add. MS 28569, f. 60[r]). According to the queen's scheme, "[t]here was to be in all twelve couple, each woman after a severall country fashion, and the men to have the habits of the same country as their partners" (HMC *Rutland* 2: 102). This practice is strongly reminiscent of that described in Anthony Hamilton's *Memoirs of the Life of Count de Grammont* for the court ballet presumed to have taken place c.1662–63 (see pp. 32–34, above). Hamilton's work, published in 1713, is a literary, not a historical, document, and it is not impossible that this particular aspect of the 1686 ball may have inspired part of his description of the earlier entertainment. On the other hand, Hamilton was in Ireland in 1686, serving as governor of Limerick, and thus could not have been in attendance at the ball. It may simply be that assigning national "identities" to noble masquers by means of a note or picture sent from the queen was a conventional practice that recurred throughout the period—possibly also in the case of *The Queen's Masque* of 1671 (see below). In any event, what we know of the 1686 arrangement suggests that the performers were divided into four groups of three couples each, which can be roughly categorized as "Ancient," "European," "Oriental," and "Rural/Exotic" (see Table 1.3). We do not know the identities of all twenty-four of the "Mascaraders that danced,"[100] but Peregrine Bertie, writing early in February, names four couples—interestingly, one from each of the four groups I have identified—who were expected to perform.[101] Two of the male dancers had already hosted balls of their own: Viscount Dumblane on 19 December (noted above), and George Fitzroy, Duke of Northumberland (Charles II's youngest illegitimate son by Barbara Villiers, Countess of Castlemaine and Duchess of Cleveland) on 26 January at which, it was reported, "the company was but very ordinary."[102] Indeed, it is possible that some of the other young lords and gentlemen reported to have hosted balls during December and January were also participants in the entertainment of 15 February, which may have been intended as a kind of culminating event for the entire season. Those of

---

100 The phrase is from James Fraser's letter to Sir Robert Southwell (Folger MS V.b.287 [5], p. 1), which provides the most comprehensive list we have of the characters proposed by the queen.

101 Letter of Peregrine Bertie to the Countess of Rutland, 2 February 1686 (HMC *Rutland* 2: 102); see Table 1.3 for those named in Bertie's letter. John Povey, also writing to Sir Robert Southwell (BL Add. MS 28569, f. 60[v]), identifies an additional dancer, albeit not the part he took: Walter Bellew, son of Sir John Bellew, brought in at the last minute to fill "the place of the Lord Scarsdale who had strained his leg, against the time." (Lord Scarsdale was Robert Leke, formerly Baron Deincourt of Sutton, who had danced in *Calisto* in 1675.)

102 Letter of Peregrine Bertie to the Countess of Rutland, 28 January 1686 (HMC *Rutland* 2: 102).

Table 1.3 Noble performers expected to appear in Lord Sunderland's court ballet, 15 February 1686

	Role	Name	Relevant Relationship/Title	Date of Birth	Age on 15 Feb. 1686
Ancients	Greeks	Charles Montagu, 4th Earl of Manchester	son of Robert, 3rd Earl of Manchester later 1st Duke of Manchester	c.1656	~29
		Elizabeth Butler, Countess of Derby †	daughter of Thomas, 6th Earl of Ossory (son of 1st Duke of Ormonde) wife of William George Richard Stanley, 9th Earl of Derby	c.1660	~25
	Romans	?			
	Massilians	?			
Europeans	*Spaniards*[a]	*George Fitzroy, 1st Duke of Northumberland*	*illegitimate son of Charles II by Barbara Villiers* **[hosts ball, 26 January]**	*28 Dec. 1665*	*20*
		Isabella Bennet, Duchess of Grafton and 2nd Countess of Arlington ‡§	*daughter of Henry, 1st Earl of Arlington* *wife of Henry Fitzroy, 1st Duke of Grafton (illegitimate son of Charles II by Barbara Villiers)*	*1667*	*~18*
	Venetians	?			
	Poles	?			

Orientals	Moors ("Mauritanians")	Peregrine Osborne, Viscount Dumblane †	son of Thomas, 1st Earl of Danby later 2nd Duke of Leeds (etc.) **[hosts ball, 19 December]**	c. Dec. 1659	26
		?Jane Fox §	daughter of Sir Stephen Fox later (9 May 1686) wife of George Compton, 4th Earl of Northampton	?	?
	Turks	?			
	Hungarians	?			
Rural/Exotics	Shepherds	Edward Henry Lee, 1st Earl of Lichfield	son of Sir Francis Henry Lee, Bart. husband of Charlotte Fitzroy, illegitimate daughter of Charles II by Barbara Villiers	4 Feb. 1663	23
		Henrietta FitzJames, Baroness Waldegrave	illegitimate daughter of James II by Arabella Churchill wife of Henry Waldegrave, 1st Baron Waldegrave (created January 1686)	1667	~18
	Plain Country People	?			
	Peruvians	?			
	[UNIDENTIFIED ROLE][b]	Walter Bellew	son of Sir John Bellew, later (29 October 1686) 1st Baron Bellew of Duleek later 2nd Baron Bellew of Duleek	c.1664	~21

(*Continued*)

OTHERS REPORTEDLY HOSTING BALLS, DECEMBER– JANUARY	*Thomas Herbert, 8th Earl of Pembroke and 5th Earl of Montgomery*	**[?hosts ball, after 26 December]**	*c.1656*	*~30*
	George Berkeley, 1st Earl of Berkeley[c]	**[hosts ball, 29 December]**	*1626/7*	*~60*
	"Mr. Oldfield, Soho Square"	**[hosts ball, 30 December]**	*?*	*?*
	Robert Spencer, 2nd Earl of Sunderland	**[hosts ball, 31 December]**	*5 Sept. 1641*	*45*
	William Cavendish, 4th Earl (later 1st Duke) of Devonshire	**[hosts ball, 12 January]**	*25 Jan. 1640*	*47*
	Charles Seymour, 6th Duke of Somerset	**[?hosts ball, after 23 January]**	*13 Aug. 1662*	*23*
LADIES "EXCUSED" AS OF 2 FEBRUARY 1686	*Lady Anne Spencer*	*daughter of Robert Spencer, 2nd Earl of Sunderland later (?5 January 1687) wife of James Douglas/Hamilton, Earl of Arran (later 4th Duke of Hamilton)*	*24 June 1666*	*19*
	Anne Mason (later Brett), Viscountess Brandon	*daughter of Sir Richard Mason wife of Charles Gerard, Viscount Brandon (later 2nd Earl of Macclesfield)*	*1667/8*	*~18*

Key:

† = had appeared in *Calisto*, 1675 (see Table 2.2)

‡ = possibly had appeared in *Rare en Tout*, 1677 (see Table 2.1)

§ = had also danced in ball for Queen Catherine of Braganza's birthday (15 November), 1684 (see Table 1.1)

---

[a] Possibly did not perform, on account of the Duke of Grafton having recently committed manslaughter.

[b] Substituting for Robert Leke, 3rd Earl of Scarsdale (formerly Baron Deincourt of Sutton: see Table 2.2), following the latter's injury.

[c] Son, Charles Berkeley, Viscount Dursley (10th Baron Berkeley, 1689; 2nd Earl of Berkeley, 1698), born 8 April 1649.

The growth of Shrovetide entertainments   57

an appropriate age to participate in the 15 February ball included Thomas Herbert, Earl of Pembroke and Montgomery (aged approximately thirty), Charles Seymour, Duke of Somerset (aged twenty-three),[103] and perhaps "Mr. Oldfield [of] Soho Square" (age unknown).[104] Sunderland himself also seems to have held an earlier ball, on 31 December,[105] and it may be that the ball hosted by George Berkeley, Earl of Berkeley (aged approximately sixty) was in fact presented on behalf of the Earl's son Charles, Viscount Dursley (aged thirty-six).[106]

Originally planned for sometime early in the month,[107] Sunderland's ball had to be postponed when three of the female dancers withdrew for various reasons (HMC *Rutland* 2: 102). One later returned to the production, but there was an additional delay occasioned by a deadly duel on 2 February between Henry Fitzroy, Duke of Grafton (another son of Charles II and Barbara Villiers) and John Talbot, a brother of the Earl of Shrewsbury. Talbot was killed, and Grafton, whose wife Isabella Bennet was scheduled to dance with Grafton's brother Northumberland, had to go briefly into hiding until he received a pardon from his uncle the king. By 6 February it was reported that "[t]he greate ball att Court goes on still and others are sent to to dance in their places who desired to bee excused, and those who are prevented by the unfortunate quarrell between the Duke of Grafton and Mr. Talbot" (HMC *Rutland* 2: 103). One commentator even seems to have anticipated a performance on Monday the 8th (HMC *Rutland* 2: 106), but in the end the ball went forward a week later, possibly without the Duke of Northumberland and his sister-in-law, who were supposed to appear as Spaniards.[108] Remarking upon the seating arrangements at the supper, which he characterized as "very sumptuous and methodicall" (Folger MS V.b.287 [5], p. 1), James Fraser also described the strict system for admitting spectators to the event, according to which "none was permitted to come that had not a Ticket, and for every Ticket there was a place at the Ball, by wch means there was neither supernumerary persons nor places" (Folger MS V.b.287 [5], p. 2). Another commentator, John Povey, observed that as a result of this restriction the number of attendees was "fewer, than there are

---

103 For Pembroke and Somerset, see n. 94, above.

104 Letter of Peregrine Bertie to the Countess of Rutland, 31 December 1685 (HMC *Rutland* 2: 100): "Last night was a masque at Mr. Oldfield's in Soho Square, there was a great deale of very good company."

105 *Ibid.*: "To-night is one att my Lord Sunderland's, but the masque[r?]s will not bee entertained till after supper."

106 Letter of Peregrine Bertie to the Countess of Rutland, 1 January 1686 (HMC *Rutland* 2: 100): "my Lady Anne Littleton ... was that night [after the wedding of Lady Frances Knollys to the musician John Abell, Tuesday, 29 December] att my Lord Berkley's ball." Dursley was to become Baron Berkeley in 1689, and succeeded his father as Earl in 1698.

107 Letter of Peregrine Bertie to the Countess of Rutland, 28 January 1686 (HMC *Rutland* 2: 102; passage quoted in Appendix B).

108 James Fraser's letter to Sir Robert Southwell (see n. 100, above) enumerates only eleven couples, rather than the twelve mentioned both prospectively by Bertie and after the fact by John Povey (BL Add. MS 28569, f. 60^r). The ethnicity missing from Fraser's list is the Spaniards (one of the four groups named by Bertie, whose "Moores" are undoubtedly equivalent to Fraser's "mauritanian[s]").

58 *"Their greatest gallantry imaginable"*

generally Courtiers in the drawing-roome on a Sunday night" (BL Add. MS 28569, f. 60^r), noting the fact that Walter Bellew, the last-minute replacement for the Earl of Scarsdale (see n. 101, above), despite having spent £300 to equip himself for the ball, was unable to obtain a ticket even for his own mother, "and the Earl of Oxford, Lord Cornbury and others of less quality, found the like difficulty" (BL Add. MS 28569, f. 60^v). Ultimately, Povey's verdict on the whole experiment was mixed—"All was doubtless very splendid within, but not half so much talked off as others of less note: the reason of which is plaine" (BL Add. MS 28569, f. 60^v)—while Lord Grey went a step further, reportedly telling Peregrine Bertie that "it was not fine at all, and that everybody was displeased with it" (HMC *Rutland* 2: 104). Yet there was much to praise as well, in particular the glorious appearance of the performers: Povey assured his correspondent that "the least habit cost above a hundred pounds, and some above three hundred pounds, besides jewels of which Mrs Fox, and some others had above thirty thousand pounds value each" (BL Add. MS 28569, f. 60^r), while Fraser remarked, in a more general vein, that "if one were to have sought for diamonds or perles that night, no place in London could have afforded any but what was to be seen" at this "very noble and magnificent Ball" whose couples were "aray'd in all the glory & riches of the Indies" (Folger MS V.b.287 [5], p. 1). As in *Calisto*, the dancers were responsible for providing their own costumes, and this seems to have functioned not only as a broad vehicle for conspicuous consumption, but also as the basis for a certain degree of competition among the performers: Lady Lucy Bright confessed to the Countess of Rutland that "it pleased me to hear that the King said Lord Manchester was the best habitted and most gracefull dress off any" (HMC *Rutland* 2: 105). In the end, this much-anticipated but highly exclusive event had enough impact that, as one correspondent reported, "att Easter the Queen will have them all meet again in the great Hall where everybody may see them, for this, I hear, has disobliged very many people" (HMC *Rutland* 2: 105).[109]

While most of the court balls—both Shrovetide and otherwise—examined thus far were not strictly speaking dramatic events, several do show traces of some conventionally theatrical elements, whether in the use of scenic spectacle or other kinds of stagecraft, or in the appearance of professional ("occupational") performers alongside the "recreational" courtiers. Beginning in the late 1660s, however, a new class of recreational court entertainment emerged in the form of full-blown dramatic masques and plays. These works, which are also predominantly focused on the Carnival/Shrovetide season, constitute a similarly diverse group to the balls already discussed, both in terms of generic profile (to the extent that this can be determined) and in the amount of surviving documentary evidence. The majority were performed chiefly by children and adolescents, and will be explored in the next chapter; here, we will conclude by examining the single known case of a Restoration masque that featured adult courtly performers. Taken alongside the

---

109 The notion of an additional, post-Easter performance of a Shrovetide masque is not without precedent, as we will see in the case of *Calisto*. For an earlier example, see Ben Jonson's *The Masque of Augurs* (1622), which was performed on Twelfth Night (*i.e.* probably 5 January), and again on 5 or 6 May (the 5th being the second Sunday after Easter).

The growth of Shrovetide entertainments   59

court productions to be discussed in the chapters that follow, this rather elusive piece, with its more overtly dramatic character, brings us closer both to the historical traditions of the court masque and to the parallel developments in through-sung court opera that will be explored in Part II.

Case study: *The Queen's Masque* of 1671

After *Calisto* of 1675 (to be discussed in Chapter 2), the most extensively documented Shrovetide court performance of the Restoration is a work first presented on 20–21 February 1671 that has come to be known as *The Queen's Masque*. No text survives for this piece, and many of its features remain uncertain,[110] but it is possible to assemble some picture of the context and flavor of the work from the exceptional quantity of evidence left behind in both contemporary correspondence and official court records. *The Queen's Masque* appears to have formed part of a remarkably active calendar of court and court-related entertainments in this particular year: with Shrove Tuesday falling on the very late date of 7 March,[111] there was ample time for Carnival revels of various kinds. As early as 23 January, the French ambassador Charles Colbert, Marquis de Croissy, hosted the king and queen at a grand entertainment at his residence at York House, "where was great danceing and severall principall persons about the Towne in Maskerade."[112] This event was quickly followed by others at the Inns of Court, at which the king and queen were also present,[113] and spurred anticipation of even grander events to come. As one newsletter of 24 January reported,

> last night was a great Ball att the french Ambassadors where most of the Court were in Mascarade, on friday [*i.e.* 27 January] will be one at the temple, on Saturday at lincolnes Inn, and on Candlemas night a grand one at Court[.][114]

110 The title of the work is itself a modern coinage. Catherine of Braganza does seem to have been a leading light in the production, and Lady Mary Bertie reported as early as mid-January that "[t]he Queen is preparing a ball to bee danced in the greate Hall by herself and the Dutchesse of Buckingham, Richmond, Monmouth, Mrs. Berkeley, and Madame Kerrwell the French maid of honor. There are no men of quality but the Duke of Monmouth, all the rest are gentlemen" (letter of Lady Mary Bertie to Katherine Noel, 17 January 167[1]: HMC *Rutland* 2: 22). I use the title here for the sake of consistency, though it is singularly unhelpful, inviting confusion with the ephemeral "Queens Ballett" of 1665 or 1666, as well as the "noble Masquerade" of c.1662–63 described in the *Memoirs of the Life of Count de Grammont* (see pp. 38 and 32–34, above).

111 The only year in the latter half of the seventeenth century in which Shrove Tuesday fell on a later date was 1698 (8 March); by contrast, in 1668 Shrove Tuesday had occurred on 4 February, one day later than its earliest possible date (for which, in fact, there was no instance in seventeenth-century England).

112 Newsletter, 24 January 1671: SP29/287/110, p. 2 (see *Calendar of State Papers, Domestic* 1671: 43).

113 "Their Majesties and the Prince of Orange were present at the revels at the Temple on the 27th and at Lincoln's Inn on the 28th. Mr. Rich, Master of the Revels at Lincoln's Inn, has been knighted" ([digest of] newsletter, 31 January 1671: J. A. Bennett, *The Manuscripts of S. H. Le Fleming, Esq., of Rydal Hall* [Historical Manuscripts Commission, Twelfth Report, Appendix, Part VII; London: Her Majesty's Stationery Office, 1890; hereafter cited as HMC *Le Fleming*], 75).

114 Newsletter from John Starkey to Sir Willoughby Aston, Bart., 24 January 167[1]: British Library, Add. MS 36916, f. 207ʳ; this passage appears, without citation, in John Spurr, *England in the*

60   *"Their greatest gallantry imaginable"*

Despite the tremendous expectation this event engendered, its date seems to have been fluid. Candlemas (2 February) saw no sign of any performance, and two days later Lady Mary Bertie informed her friend Katherine Noel, the future Countess of Rutland, that "They say the greate ball is to be danced on Munday night," that is, 6 February.[115] This prediction, too, did not come to pass: only on the 9th did John Evelyn record having witnessed "the greate *Ball* danced by the *Queene* & greate Ladies at White hall Theater."[116] Yet this third date is itself problematic, as the 9th was the very day on which Anne Hyde, Duchess of York, gave birth to a daughter, hardly an appropriate moment for a performance of a masque. Evelyn's chronology for this retrospective portion of his diary is often suspect,[117] although it may just be that he attended a rehearsal, something he appears to have done again early in 1674 (possibly for *Ariane*; see Chapter 6) and in December of the same year (for *Calisto*). In any case, the Duchess of York's lying-in may have prompted the successive delays: the duchess was not well (by 31 March she would be dead from breast cancer[118]), and on 16 February plans were still sufficiently unclear that Lady Mary Bertie could report that "[h]ere is no newes but that the grand ballett is not to be danced till Shrove-Munday," that is, 6 March.[119] Those closer to the production seem to have known better, however: already on the 14th the Lord Chamberlain had ordered that the preparation of the queen's tiring room be completed "by Fridaye Night next," that is 17 February,[120] and on Monday the 20th the production finally appeared in all its glory. The official newsletters gushed with tidings of the event ("This Euening was danced over the grand Ballett at Whitehall, wherein the Court appeared ... in their greatest gallantry imaginable, & the time spent in Songs, the chiefest dances & Musick the Town could afford"[121]), and Lady Mary Bertie (who calls it "the grane ballett") identified seven of the

---

1670s: This Masquerading Age (Oxford: Blackwell Publishers, 2000), 110, where it is misdated to 4 January and "great" is given for "grand." See also the report of the Venetian ambassador Girolamo Alberti of 27 January (dated 6 February, New Style): "The Ambassador Colbert did not long delay the grand entertainment destined by him for the Court, and with extreme pomp he made royal provision of every luxury that France could produce. As the king and queen with some chosen persons of rank are preparing a grand ballet at the Court, the Spanish ambassador, moved by his own high spirit and by emulation, will not fail to follow the example" (*Calendar of State Papers, Venetian* 37 [1671–72]: 15).

115   Letter of Bertie to Noel, 4 February 167[1]: HMC *Rutland* 2: 22.
116   Evelyn, *Diary*, 3: 569–70.
117   See Arthur H. Scouten, "The Perils of Evelyn," *Restoration* 16 (1992): 126–28.
118   The child, Princess Catherine, did not survive much longer, expiring on 5 December.
119   Letter of Bertie to Noel, 16 February 167[1]: HMC *Rutland* 2: 22.
120   LC5/62, f. 121ʳ and LC5/63, p. 91 (see n. 139, below); specifically, this was an order for the installation of baize.
121   Newsletter sent to Sir Richard Bulstrode, 24 February 1671 (report for the 20th): Harry Ransom Center, PFORZ-MS-0576, pp. 1–2 (see [Thibaudeau], ed., *The Bulstrode Papers*, 1: 173); the word "appeared" is written twice, over the page break. Compare the similar but shortened version of this account found in HMC *Le Fleming*, 75, which is dated 21 February, and thus seems to describe the second night's performance: "This evening was danced the grand ballet at Whitehall. The Court appeared in their greatest gallantry."

The growth of Shrovetide entertainments   61

performers and reported that "[a]fter the ballet was over, several others danced, as the King, and Duke of Yorke, and Duke of Somerset, and Duke of Buckingham."[122] *The Queen's Masque* only appeared twice on the Whitehall stage, on the 20th and 21st of February, although a newsletter account from the 24th reported that "on Monday next [*i.e.* 27 February] its said they intend to performe it at the D[uke] of Ormonds. Where his Ma^ty & the whole Court intende to bee p^rsent,"[123] while another letter written the same day anticipates some sort of entertainment involving Barbara Villiers, formerly Countess of Castlemaine and now Duchess of Cleveland.[124] In the Hall Theatre, at least, the masquers were well looked after, enjoying bread, beer and wine (served in two dozen cups), fruit and confections, spices, meat, poultry, butter, and apples supplied by the Clerk of the Kitchen,[125] while other court functionaries attended upon them behind the scenes.[126]

There can be little doubt that the court regarded *The Queen's Masque* as an important—perhaps even a watershed—event. Significant attention was lavished on preparations in the Hall Theatre, and though not all of it was necessarily for

122 Letter of Bertie to Noel, 23 February 167[1]: HMC *Rutland* 2: 22–23. In another letter (see n. 110, above), Bertie listed the performers in the masque itself: "The Queen ... and the Dutchesse of Buckingham, Richmond, Monmouth, Mrs. Berkeley, ... Madame Kerrwell[, and] the Duke of Monmouth."

123 Newsletter sent to Sir Richard Bulstrode, 24 February 1671 (report for the 24th): Harry Ransom Center, PFORZ-MS-0576, p. 4 (see n. 121, above, and [Thibaudeau], ed., *The Bulstrode Papers*, 1: 174). The lodgings of James Butler, 1st Duke of Ormonde, were located on the "park side" of Whitehall Palace, just across King Street from the western end of the Privy Gallery and the northwest corner of the Privy Garden (see Simon Thurley, *The Whitehall Palace Plan of 1670* [London: London Topographical Society, 1998], 49–50). For the number and description of the rooms, originally configured for "Lady Ossory" (Ormonde's wife or daughter-in-law), see LC5/196, f. 5^v (surveyor's report, 1691: "5: Ground roomes, Kitchin, Larder, 5 upper roomes, :1: Clossett, 3:^d story 4 roomes 3: Garretts[;] in all 17"). How a production requiring an additional 1296 square feet of stage space beyond that normally available in the Hall Theatre and specially constructed accommodations for 2–3 musical ensembles would have translated to Ormonde's more modest three-story suite of rooms is not clear; perhaps this later performance focused exclusively on the music and eliminated some or all of the dancing. Alternatively, it may have taken place at Clarendon House, north of St. James's Palace, which Ormonde was renting at the time.

124 Letter of Richard Snesby to Gervase Holland, 24 February 1671: Nottingham University Library, MS Cl C 410 [not seen], quoted in Jordan, "An Addendum to *The London Stage 1660–1700*" [see n. 63, above], 65–66. The passage is somewhat confusing: "upon munday and Tuesday last there was Maskes att Whitehall & a third to be performed by the Dutches of Cleveland." Does this imply a third performance of *The Queen's Masque* to follow the two given in the Hall Theatre on the 20th and 21st (and thus possibly identical to the revival at the Duke of Ormonde's already noted), or is it meant to indicate that the duchess, who is not known to have danced in *The Queen's Masque*, intended to mount her own, separate entertainment, of which no record is known to survive?

125 LS8/7, ff. 161–63 and E351/1839 (not in *Register*; see Boswell, 93): "creditor" amounting to £165 18s 9d, February 1671, for "Expens[e]s magnæ Saltation' sive Grand Ballad pro iij^bus diebus Mens[i]s ffebruary 1670." Whether the three days mentioned in this document included the later performance on the 27th or a dress rehearsal before the 20th is uncertain.

126 WORK5/15, f. 138^r (*Register*, no. 600): warrant to mazerscourers, February 1671, for "attending in the Hall when ye Dancing was there" (one man for 2 nights and two men for 1 night [each?]).

62 *"Their greatest gallantry imaginable"*

this particular production, much would no doubt have been visible to those in attendance at the performances.[127] As early as the preceding November, the Hall underwent a general refurbishment, with the construction (and, seemingly, reconstruction) of a decorative false ceiling or "velarium,"[128] alterations to the carved figure of Fame surmounting the proscenium,[129] the re-covering of the stage with 100 yards of green baize,[130] and other minor repairs, such as the repointing of

127 The only documentation we have of any other production being put on in the Hall Theatre between October 1669 and November 1671 is John Evelyn's otherwise unsubstantiated remark that on the "next day" after the performance or rehearsal of *The Queen's Masque* that he witnessed on 9 February, "was acted there the famous Play, cald the Siege of *Granada* two days acted successively: there were indeede very glorious scenes & perspectives, the worke of Mr. *Streeter*, who well understands it" (Evelyn, *Diary*, 3: 569–70; see the table in Boswell, 284–85). Evelyn's remarks about Streeter's scenery could have been meant to apply to either show, or perhaps both; however, nowhere in Dryden's two-part heroic tragedy *The Conquest of Granada by the Spaniards* is there a call for a garden, a mill, or even clouds, for all of which Streeter was paid to paint in February (see n. 144, below). On the other hand, the more generic "boscage" included in a payment to Streeter from January might have been useful for a production of Dryden's play. It should be noted, however, that Evelyn's editor, E. S. de Beer, doubts the veracity of the diarist's account altogether (see *Diary* 3: 570 n. 1).

128 WORK5/15, f. 108ʳ (*Register*, no. 577): warrant to mazerscourers, November 1670, for "sweeping the Inside of yᵉ roofe of yᵉ Hall, & the Ceans & yᵉ walls there"; WORK5/15, f. 105ʳ (*Register*, no. 577): warrant to carpenters, November 1670, for construction of a scaffold to hold up the velarium and a second scaffold above the hung ceiling to serve as a walkway for the scenekeepers "to Goe rownd to hang vp yᵉ branches" (*i.e.* chandeliers), and for the placement of a doorway to provide access to the newly enclosed space (as well as the construction of an unrelated door for the private box assigned to the Surveyor General); WORK5/15, f. 115ᵛ (*Register*, no. 584): warrant to carpenters, December 1670, for "taking downe the Great Scaffold" and replacing it with two scaffolds to provide greater access for the scenekeepers, and constructing a 26-foot ladder, perhaps so as to avoid adding another door at the top of the wall. Payments were made in January 1671 to the mercer Phillip Lazenby for "fine skey Coloured Callico" and other materials for the velarium (WORK5/15, f. 130ʳ [*Register*, no. 593], total £20 9s, including a 3-shilling charge "ffor Carr[iage?]: at twice") and to Samuel Wells for £3 16s 2d "payd to seuerall taylers, for sewing the Cloth for the Ceiling in the Theater in whitehall and making knotts & other workes donne there by them in yᵉ months of nouember and december last" (WORK5/15, f. 129ʳ [*Register*, no. 593]). Robert Streeter was also paid 10s "ffor Colouring the Cord in yᵉ Ceiling" (WORK5/15, f. 130ʳ; see n. 129, below).

129 WORK5/15, f. 130ʳ (*Register*, no. 593): a general warrant for payment of £28 18s to Robert Streeter, January 1671, including £1 "ffor new painting the figure of fame and Altering the posture" and 10s "Payd by him to ye Joyner for new putting together the figure of fame," as well as for "Cutting all yᵉ bourds & naileing them" on the four pairs of scenic wings on the stage below. In Webb's original design for the proscenium from c.1665 (Devonshire Collection, Chatsworth), Fame is shown surmounting a broken segmental pediment upon which is superimposed an elaborated oval shield with the words "Hi sunt de pace triumphi / Bella dabunt alios" ("These are the triumphs of peace; others will wage wars"). She faces stage left, her wings spread, blowing on a long trumpet held in her left hand, while reaching out behind her with her right hand to touch the corner of the pediment.

130 LC5/62, f. 117ᵛ (*Register*, no. 578): warrant for 100 yards of baize to cover the stage, 1 November 1670; see also LC9/272, ff. 111ᵛ–12ʳ and LC9/381 (not in *Register*; see Boswell, 302), two copies of the upholsterer's bill covering labor for all baize work during the period from Michaelmas 1670–Lady Day 1671, including additional items cited below.

The growth of Shrovetide entertainments 63

windows and sealing up of drafts,[131] the laying of new matting,[132] and the purchase of a dozen tin sconces.[133] By December, the painter Robert Streeter had begun work on new scenery, painting the theatre's four pairs of wings with a sylvan "boscage" and providing a pair of back shutters which appear to have been finished not on site in the theatre, but at the artist's studio in Longacre.[134] In January a large thrust stage measuring approximately 27 x 36 feet was built over part of the pit, boarded in on the front and sides, and covered with baize to match the (considerably smaller) scenic space behind the proscenium arch.[135] February saw a burst of activity, with the carpenters in particular shouldering multiple tasks[136]: the thrust stage was enlarged, probably being extended into the pit by an additional 9 feet; special seating areas were created on the stage for at least two groups of musicians;[137] provisions were made for improved illumination of the

131 WORK5/15, f. 106^v (*Register*, no. 577) and WORK5/15, f. 117^r (*Register*, no. 584): warrants to plasterers, November and December 1670.
132 WORK5/15, f. 107^r (*Register*, no. 577) and WORK5/15, f. 117^r (*Register*, no. 584): warrants to matlayers, November and December 1670.
133 LC5/62, f. 117^r and LC5/63, p. 90 (*Register*, no. 579): warrant to Master of the Wardrobe, 2 November 1670. Six of the sconces were "to hang upp in the Theater," while the other six were "to Carrie about the Theatre."
134 WORK5/15, f. 115^v (see n. 128, above), including an order to the carpenters for "making a paire of large shutters in ye Ceans"; WORK5/15, f. 130^r (see n. 129, above), including payments to Streeter of £20 for painting the wings, £5 for painting the (unspecified) scene on the shutters, and £1 18s for providing 19 yards of primed cloth (presumably canvas) for the shutters; WORK5/15, f. 118^r (*Register*, no. 584): warrant to mazerscourers, December 1670, for "fetching the shutters for ye Ceans in ye hall from longacre." For the work done by the joiner on the four pairs of wings, see n. 129, above. Note also the lone payment of 1 shilling made in October 1670 to the London merchant and alderman Sir George Waterman for a piece of whipcord "for ye scenes in ye hall" (WORK5/15, f. 98^r [*Register*, no. 574]).
135 WORK5/15, f. 125^r (*Register*, no. 593): warrant to carpenters, January 1671, for constructing the new stage extension measuring "About 3 squares" (with a "square" consisting of 36 square yards or 324 square feet) and boarding up the sides with 90 feet of slit deal and inserting "a little dore there alsoe," presumably for access to the crawl space beneath; LC5/62, f. 119^v and LC5/63, p. 85 (*Register*, no. 597): warrant for strips of baize 3 yards wide and the length (*i.e.* 12 yards, technically the width) of the stage, 11 January 1671. There is also an undated bill (LC9/272, f. 94^r [not in *Register*; see Boswell, 302] for the half year from Michaelmas 1670–Lady Day 1671) for £5 3s 10d for 44½ yards of baize, which (assuming a bolt width of 3 yards) would seem to exceed that required for the covering of the stage by 8½ yards in length (*i.e.* 25½ square yards). Note also that LC9/272, ff. 111^v–12^r and LC9/381 (the bills for the upholsterers' labor, cited in n. 130, above) indicate that the thrust stage was covered over with baize twice, possibly in January (when the original 3-square extension was built) and then again in February (when a 1-square enlargement was added).
136 WORK5/15, f. 135^{r-v} (*Register*, no. 600): warrant, February 1671. This document is quoted in full in Boswell, 250, alongside others cited here.
137 "Cutting out part of the stage & fitting a place there for ye Queens musick, wth railes about it & bourded"; "Bourding wth slitt deale about ye Musick seate in ye Clowds Cont': about one square"; "Incloseing a roome for ye Italian musitions Cont': one square ½." The stated dimension of "one square" (*i.e.* 18 x 18 feet; see n. 135, above) for the "Musick seate in ye Clowds," which probably held members of Charles II's private music and/or band of twenty-four violins for the performance, suggests that this space was specially enlarged for the purpose: on Webb's 1665

64   *"Their greatest gallantry imaginable"*

performance space; a cloth ceiling was hung in the queen's tiring room; seating in the Hall itself was substantially altered; and rails with "flaps" were erected in neighboring rooms to maintain good order among the inevitable throngs of onlookers.[138] At the same time, the upholsterers lavished baize on the tiring rooms for the lady masquers[139] as well as the stage itself,[140] the Wardrobe provided richly upholstered chairs for the stage and chests for storing the musicians' elaborate uniforms,[141] several individuals and departments supplied materials for the stage lighting,[142] and other tradesmen carried out assorted minor duties.[143] Of

---

plans (which are not precisely to scale), this upper discovery space would appear to be approximately 18 feet wide (albeit obscured behind a 13-foot opening between the rear pair of wings), but Webb's markings confirm that its depth was no more than 8½ feet. The distinction between "ye Queens musick" and the "Italian musitions" is difficult to establish: from 1667, Catherine of Braganza's musical establishment, initially composed exclusively of Portuguese, incorporated the members of Charles II's band of Italian musicians as well (see Margaret Mabbett, "Italian Musicians in Restoration England (1660–90)," *Music and Letters* 67 [1986]: 237–47, p. 239, and Peter Leech, "Musicians in the Catholic Chapel of Catherine of Braganza, 1662–92," *Early Music* 29 [2001]: 570–87, p. 578).

138   As Lady Mary Bertie observed following her attendance at the first night's performance, "[i]t was so hard to get room that wee were forced to goe by four a clocke, though it did not begin till nine or ten" (letter of Bertie to Noel, 23 February 167[1]: HMC *Rutland* 2: 22).

139   LC5/62, f. 121^r and LC5/63, p. 91 (*Register*, no. 603): warrant, 14 February 1671; LC9/272, f. 98^v (not in *Register*; see Boswell, 302): undated bill (Michaelmas 1670–Lady Day 1671) for £11 0s 6d for 68 yards of baize for the queen's tiring room and 30 yards for the ladies' tiring room. If we consider the measurement given in the order to the carpenters (WORK5/15, f. 135^{r-v} [see n. 136, above]) to "lay ... Joysts for a Cloth Ceiling in ye Queens roome Cont' one square & ½," it is interesting to note that, supposing once again a 3-yard bolt width for baize (see n. 135, above), the 68 yards allotted for the queen's tiring room would yield 204 square yards of material, an amount nearly sufficient to cover four walls (or 2–3 walls and the ceiling and/or floor) of a single-cube room of precisely this dimension (1½ "squares," *i.e.* approximately 54 square yards, or 22 feet in height/width).

140   LC5/62, f. 121^v (*Register*, no. 605): warrant, 19 February 1671; LC9/272, f. 99^v (not in *Register*; see Boswell, 302): undated bill (Michaelmas 1670–Lady Day 1671) for £16 3s 5¼d for 143¾ yards of baize for stage, hangings, and forms.

141   LC5/63, p. 237 (*Register*, no. 604): warrant, 18 February 1671, for delivery of "six Turky worke charyes" and three trunks for "ye Indian Habitts for ye Musique." For more on the exotic outfits worn by Charles II's musicians, see Diana de Marly, "Musicians' Costumes in the Restoration Theatre," *Early Music* 5 (1977): 507–15.

142   WORK5/17, f. 23^r (*Register*, no. 616): payment of £6 2s 7d to John Wells, tinman, April 1671, for lighting accoutrements "made & deli^{ed}, for his Maties seruice in the Theater in Whitehall in ffeb: last"; WORK5/17, f. 38^r (*Register*, no. 629): payment of 7s 7d to Henry Glover, June 1671, for oil and wicks for the lamps. With reference to the first of these documents in particular, we can compare that part of the February order to the carpenters (WORK5/15, f. 135^{r-v} [see n. 136, above]) for "making a trough at ye foote of the stage for lights to stand in" and "making a place wth bourds for lights to stand on on both sides." See also LS8/7, ff. 161ff. and E351/1839 (see n. 125, above): "creditor" from the Clerk of the Kitchen, including charges for "inckle" (linen tape), cotton, wax, tallow lights, and torch staves for three nights at the time of the performances; given that the remainder of this creditor is for food provided for the masquers, however, these supplies may have been used backstage.

143   WORK5/15, f. 136^v (*Register*, no. 600): warrant to plasterers, February 1671; WORK5/15, f. 137^r (*Register*, no. 600): warrant to matlayers, February 1671.

The growth of Shrovetide entertainments 65

particular interest is the February warrant to pay Robert Streeter[144] for his work on what appear to be three scenic elements in the theatre: a pair of shutters showing a garden;[145] a backdrop (with a door inserted) depicting a mill;[146] and a set of upper cloud borders.[147] These details provide little to go on with regard to the actual dramatic character of the masque, but they do suggest the incorporation of a variety of scenes ranging from the rustic to the more grandly allegorical. The attire of the performers themselves must have been exceptionally splendid: Lady Mary Bertie recounted that they "were very richly [dressed] and danced very finely, and shifted their clothes three times,"[148] and a document of 14 March 1671 summarizing the amounts owed to various tradesmen by the Master of the Robes reveals a total charge for costumes of more than £2316.[149]

Given the wealth of documentation just surveyed, it is surprising how few traces of *The Queen's Masque* survive in the musical record. Peter Holman has identified what appears to be a six-movement suite for the production composed by John Banister, the former leader of the king's Twenty-Four Violins,[150] but only two songs,

144 WORK5/15, f. 144^r (*Register*, no. 600): warrant for payment of £17 1*s* to Streeter, February 1671. On 15 December 1671, a warrant was issued to pay Streeter the substantial sum of £83 "for worke about the Sceanes and Theatre at Whitehall" (T51/19, p. 27 [*Register*, no. 660; *Calendar of Treasury Books* 3: 1158]), but this may have had nothing to do with the performances of *The Queen's Masque* ten months earlier.

145 £6 "For painteing a paire of Shutters of a garden" and £2 "For 20 y^{r}ds of Cloath for ye said Shutters ready nailed vp and primed."

146 £4 "For paynting ye Scene of ye Mill" and 5*s* "For ye Joyners worke to make ye doo[r]e there in ye said Scene and for stuffe to doe it withall." The warrant to the carpenters of January 1671 (WORK5/15, f. 125^r [see n. 135, above]) includes "making a paire of back Ceanes in ye theater in whitehall."

147 £4 16*s* "For painting ye Clouds and seu'all Works done aboute them."

148 Letter of Bertie to Noel, 23 February 167[1]: HMC *Rutland* 2: 22.

149 SP44/25, ff. 195^v–96^r and SP44/26, f. 98^r (not in *Register*; see *Calendar of State Papers, Domestic* 1671: 132 [Ashbee, 8: 206]). The *Calendar of State Papers* gives a figure of £2316 1*s* 6*d*, but Boswell (p. 139) calculates the total as £2316 1*s* 2*d*. Boswell also speculates as to whether a bill from the royal tailor William Watts, dated 24 January 1672, for an elaborately laced coat and breeches with accessories "For Madam Carwel now Dutchesse of Portsmouth" in British Library, Add. MS 27588, f. 2 (not in *Register*) might also relate to *The Queen's Masque*, since the duchess, well on her way to becoming Charles II's new mistress, was one of the performers. Indeed, Lady Mary Bertie may have inadvertently described the wrong royal mistress when she wrote that "the Dutchesse of Cleveland was very fine in a riche petticoat and halfe shirte, and a short man's coat very richly laced, a perwig cravatt and a hat: her hat and maske was very rich" (letter of Bertie to Noel, 23 February 167[1]: HMC *Rutland* 2: 23). Cleveland (formerly Castlemaine) is not known to have performed in the masque, though she could well have been in attendance.

150 National Library of Scotland, MS 5777, ff. 41^v–42^r, 43^v–44^v (treble part only): see Holman, *Fiddlers*, 364–65. Holman also speculates that a pair of anonymous D-major dances ("The Queens Maske" and "Sarabrand") found in the keyboard collection *Musicks Hand-maid: New Lessons and Instructions for the Virginals or Harpsychord* (London: J[ohn] Playford, 1678), sigs. H1^v (no. 57) and H2^r (no. 58), may be associated with this work, although as we have already observed (n. 110, above), the title "The Queen's Masque" is by no means unique (and potentially not applicable at all) to the 1671 production. The manuscript containing Banister's suite is more helpful, clearly identifying the fifth movement as "Entry queens Ballett, 1671. whitthall" (f. 44^r).

66 *"Their greatest gallantry imaginable"*

both by Pelham Humfrey, are associated with the masque in contemporary publications. These songs, "I pass all my hours in a shady old grove" and "A lover I am and a lover I'll be," appear in the text-only verse collection *Westminster-Drollery* (printed in several editions between 1671 and 1674) as, respectively, *"The first Song in the Ball at Court"* and *"The second Song in the Masque at Court."*[151] As musical works, they are hardly distinguishable from any number of other dance-like triple-time strophic songs by such composers as Humfrey, John Banister, Robert Smith, and Alfonso Marsh that characterize English song style during the first decade and a half of the Restoration era. Neither could be considered "masque-like" in the way the songs of the 1630s composed for court entertainments have been described, and their texts—one somber, the other light-hearted—offer no hints as to the larger narrative design of the work. Such a dearth of evidence makes all the more tantalizing Lady Mary Bertie's observation that *The Queen's Masque* contained "fine musickes and excelent sing[ing] some new song[s] made [on] purpose for it."[152]

In fact, our best source of information regarding the musical and dramatic configuration of this entertainment is the trio of retrospective accounts written down by the musical enthusiast Roger North between c.1715 and the late 1720s, a half century and more after the event. These accounts, which vary slightly in detail, come from three versions of North's two-part manuscript treatise *The Musicall Grammarian*, the last of which is dated 1728. A side-by-side comparison of the texts enables us to learn a number of things about *The Queen's Masque* that we do not know from other sources, while at the same time providing some insight into North's process of revision (see Table 1.4).

As all three versions of North's account make clear, *The Queen's Masque* was conceived as a kind of *ballet des nations*, perhaps incorporating some sort of competition between the musical styles of various European countries. This apparently episodic structure—which could explain the multiple costume changes noted by Lady Mary Bertie—seems to have granted the English portion, with Humfrey's songs included therein, pride of place at the end (or "arrere," in North's more severe formulation) of the entertainment. Charles II's supposed preference for "I pass all my hours" (a detail not mentioned in the two earlier accounts) might be attributed to this intentional placement, although we should remember that the king was inclined to favor such rhythmically and harmonically simple tunes over the more dense and abstract foreign music that would have appealed to more musically sophisticated "others," presumably including North himself.[153]

---

151 *Westminster-Drollery. Or, A Choice Collection of the Newest Songs & Poems Both at Court and Theaters, By a Person of Quality* (London: H[enry] Brome, 1671 ["Never before publish'd"]; 1671 ["*With Additions*"; 3 separate issues]; 1672 ["*With Additions*"]; 1674 ["*The third Edition, with many more Additions*"]), 1–2. The songs were first printed with music in *Choice Songs and Ayres for One Voyce ... The First Book* (London: John Playford and John Ford, 1673), 15 and 12. See also British Library, Harley MS 3991, f. 155^r, where "I pass all my hours" is labeled "1st Song in ye Masque 1670" (*i.e.* 1671).

152 Letter of Bertie to Noel, 23 February 167[1]: HMC *Rutland* 2: 23. In another letter of 16 March, Bertie assured Noel that "I have sent you the songs that were in the ballet" (*ibid.*).

153 By the eighteenth century, an unsubstantiated tradition had developed that ascribed the text of "I pass all my hours" to Charles II himself: see Sir John Hawkins, *A General History of the Science*

The growth of Shrovetide entertainments 67

Table 1.4 Comparison of Roger North's accounts of *The Queen's Masque* of 1671

c.1715–20[a]	c.1726[b]	1728[c]
At court there was an essay after the fancy of K. Cha. 2. who ordered that ye masters of the severall nations in towne, should dress a peice of musick after the way of their severall countrys.	Once he took a fancy to have a sort of Opera in his theater at Whitehall; and the designe was, that every nation should shew upon ye stage a peice of their best musick, after the manner of their severall countrys.	Once the King had a fancy … for a comparison to hear the singers of the severall nations, …
This was performed on ye stage in ye Court theater. And there was Spaniards, Germans, Italian's, french, & English one after ye other, …	So there came Germanes, Spaniards Italians and french; the English brought up y^e 'rere. A peice of ye Italian consort I procured and as an example of the excellence of comon air in musick, I have added it ~~here~~ in score. I p^rsume Sig^r Babtista Draghe was ye composer of it.	German, Spanish, Italian, French, and English, performe upon the stage in Whitehall. The Itallians had that mentioned elswhere—Che dite che fatti, &c.
and it seemed a jest that the English was no better, then—I pass all my hours in a shady old Grove. &c. & a like single song or two more.	But ye English, who came with a few slight songs, as—I pass all my hours in a shady old grove,—A wife I doe hate for either she's fals or she's jealous—and ye like, after ye others made a poor appearance. And so proceeded ye court, in ye weighty affair of musick.	The English brought up the arrere under great disadvantage, with—I pass all my hours in a shady old grove, &c; … for tho the King chose that song as the best, others were not of his opinion.

[a] British Library, Add. MS 32536, f. 76^r ("An Essay of Musicall Ayre," c.1715–20); no published transcription.
[b] British Library, Add. MS 32533, f. 172^r–v ("Notes of Comparison between the Elder and later Musick and Somewhat Historicall of both," c.1726): transcribed in John Wilson, ed., *Roger North on Music: Being a Selection from his Essays written during the years c.1695–1728* (London: Novello, 1959), 300.
[c] Hereford Cathedral Library, MS R.11.xlii, f. 135^v ("Memoires of Musick being some historico-critticall collections of that subject," 1728): transcribed in Wilson, 350–51 and Mary Chan and Jamie C. Kassler, eds., *Roger North's The Musicall Grammarian 1728* (Cambridge: Cambridge University Press, 1990), 262.

North's own musical proclivities undoubtedly governed his particular interest in the Italian air "Amanti, che dite, che fate?," which he reproduced in full score at

---

and Practice of Music (5 vols.: London: T. Payne and Son, 1776), 4: 428 (Book IV, chapter 3) and 5: sig. 4R4^r (reference in the index). Hawkins prints the song ("said in an old copy to be written by king Cha. II" [5: 482])—as Appendix XXXII (5: 476–77).

68   *"Their greatest gallantry imaginable"*

the end of two of the manuscripts[154]—although his attribution of the work to the London-based Italian expatriate Giovanni Battista Draghi is incorrect. Draghi did indeed compose both Italian and English songs while in London,[155] but "Amanti, che dite" is in fact the concluding trio from Giacomo Carissimi's cantata *I Naviganti* ("Sciolto havean dall' alte sponde," c.1653) which, while it appears to have circulated widely in England, had no particular English provenance.[156] Perhaps most telling is North's cavalier treatment of the English songs. In the version of c.1726, he names two: the victorious "I pass all my hours in a shady old grove," and a second triple-time song by Humfrey, "A wife I do hate, for either she's false or she's jealous." This latter reference, however, may constitute an error on North's part. "A wife I do hate" was indeed current in 1671, but no contemporary evidence connects it with *The Queen's Masque*;[157] rather, it is known to have been performed in the King's Company's production of William Wycherley's *Love in a Wood*, which opened at Drury Lane later that spring, most likely during Lent.[158] It is entirely plausible that North, writing many decades after the event and conceivably relying on somewhat disordered notes, might confuse "A lover I am" and "A wife I do hate," both of which were composed by Humfrey around this time, albeit for different venues. Indeed, it may be noteworthy that North's 1728 text deftly glosses over the problem by mentioning only "I pass all my hours,"

---

154 Hereford Cathedral Library, MS R.11.xlii, ff. 144ᵛ–47ᵛ ("Sung at a muster of voices in the theater at White hall reign Charles 2"; for a transcription of the music, see John Wilson, ed., *Roger North on Music: Being a Selection from his Essays Written During the Years c.1695–1728* (London: Novello, 1959), 120–22 [partial only] and Mary Chan and Jamie C. Kassler, eds., *Roger North's The Musicall Grammarian 1728* [Cambridge: Cambridge University Press, 1990], 273–78). See also British Library, Add. MS 32533, where, despite North's claim that "I have added it here In score" (f. 172ʳ), it does not appear in the now-incomplete manuscript, apart from a three-bar excerpt given on f. 150ʳ.

155 See for example the two Italian songs "Occhi belli voi siete vezzosi" and "Oh' tiranna gelosia" by Draghi printed among similar works by the likes of Stradella, Cesti, Carissimi, and Rossi in Girolamo Pignani's collection *Scelta Di Canzonette Italiane de Piu Autori* (London: by A. Godbid and J[ohn] Playford, 1679), 61–63 and 73–77.

156 It may have been introduced into the 1671 performance by Vincenzo Albrici, the leader of the king's Italian Musicians: as Samuel Pepys learned from Giovanni Battista Draghi on 12 February 1667, "Jiacomo Charissimi is still alive at Rome, who was maister to Vincentio, who is one of the Italians the King hath here, and the chief composer of them" (Pepys, *Diary*, 8 [1667]: 56). See Wilson, ed., *Roger North*, 120–21 n. 27, speculating that the work's broader popularity in England may itself have derived from its performance as part of *The Queen's Masque*.

157 Its text is found near the texts of the other two songs in all but the third (1674) edition of *Westminster-Drollery*, as well as in other text-only collections—though, interestingly, it does not appear in the unusually compendious collection *The Theatre of Complements* of 1689. Its music was only first printed in the fifth part of *Choice Ayres* (1684).

158 See William Van Lennep, ed., *The London Stage[,] 1660–1800[:] A Calendar of Plays, Entertainments & Afterpieces Together with Casts, Box-Receipts and Contemporary Comment Compiled from the Playbills, Newspapers and Theatrical Diaries of the Period[,] Part 1: 1660–1700* (Carbondale: Southern Illinois University Press, 1965), 181.

The growth of Shrovetide entertainments   69

along with the pointedly vague "&c." Perhaps he had realized in the intervening couple of years that he could not be so certain which song was from the masque and which had appeared elsewhere. In any case, despite their greater harmonic simplicity as compared to Carissimi's richly polyphonic three-voice "Amanti, che dite, che fate?," the English songs were no less substantive in performance: none of the pieces (Italian and English alike) that we know to have been part of the masque would necessarily have required more than two or three minutes to sing, and this in itself might provide some insight into how *The Queen's Masque* may have been structured, and what other kinds of "German, Spanish, Italian, French, and English" music could have been included in the performance.[159]

Recently, Sandra Tuppen has observed that the manuscript copy of Banister's instrumental suite for *The Queen's Masque*, identified by Peter Holman, is seemingly interrupted *in medias res* by two dance movements from the French portion of Jean-Baptiste Lully's "Ballet des Nations," the grand closing entertainment of Molière's *comédie-ballet Le Bourgeois Gentilhomme*, first performed at Chambord for Louis XIV on 14 October 1670.[160] Tuppen shrewdly reasons that these movements may also have constituted a part of *The Queen's Masque*, with Lully's music being "borrowed, as a typical example of the French instrumental style, to represent France in the English work."[161] The episode from which they are drawn, originally the fifth *entrée* of Lully and Molière's concluding ballet (its final substantive episode, immediately prior to the work's brief closing chorus), is a duet for "DEux Musiciens Poitevins"[162] on the pleasures of love as symbolized by the singing of the nightingale. The *entrée* is in fact an integrated piece, with the two minuet tunes providing the entirety of the episode's musical material: each minuet in turn is successively danced by the two Poitevins and then repeated to a sung text—the first comprising individual solos (an haut-contre and a tenor) leading to a duet, the second performed as a duet throughout—and the *entrée* concludes with a reprise of both minuets, for which "Six autres François viennent apres vestus galament à la Poitevine, ... accompagnez de huit Flustes & de

---

159 Regarding the "German [and] Spanish" musicians mentioned by North, Holman (*Fiddlers*, 363) points out that there is no hard evidence for the appearance of ensembles representing these nationalities in the masque, or indeed that there were any such singers available in England at this time. As we have already seen (n. 137, above), the identities of the three ensembles mentioned in the Works documents are not altogether clear to begin with.

160 National Library of Scotland, MS 5777, ff. 42ᵛ–43ʳ; see n. 150, above. A separate tune at the bottom of f. 43ʳ is not from *Le Bourgeois Gentilhomme*, and thus appears to represent a continuation of the original music by Banister for *The Queen's Masque*.

161 Tuppen, "Shrove-Tide Dancing," 167.

162 Molière, *Le Bovrgeois Gentilhomme, Comedie-balet, faite a Chambort, Pour le Divertissement du Roy* (Paris: Pierre le Monnier, 1671), 163; see also the *livret* (containing only the texts of the musical selections) printed for the premiere performance: *Le Bovrgeois Gentil-Homme, Comedie-Ballet, Donné par le Roy à toute sa Cour dans le Chasteau de Chambort, au mois d'Octobre 1670* (Paris: Robert Ballard, 1670), 26.

70 *"Their greatest gallantry imaginable"*

Haut-bois, & dancent les Menuets."[163] The configuration of the episode in terms of structure and numbers of bars is thus as follows:

MINUET 1:
instrumental: ||: 8 :|| ||: 8 :|| ||: 8 :|| vocal: || : 8_{solo1} :|| ||: 8_{solo2} :|| ||: 8_{duet} :|| (*"Ah! qu'il fait beau dans ces bocages"*)

MINUET 2:
instrumental: ||: 8 :|| ||: 8 + 10 :|| vocal: || : 8_{duet} :|| ||: 8_{duet} + 10_{duet} :|| (*"Vois ma Climène, vois sous ce chêne"*)

MINUET 1+2:
instrumental: ||: 8 :|| ||: 8 :|| ||: 8 :|| instrumental: || : 8 :|| ||: 8 + 10 :||

The full episode, as performed at Chambord and subsequently in Paris, with all indicated repeats taken, thus contains precisely three hundred ¾ bars and, at a stately minuet tempo of ♩.= 45 beats per minute, should be slightly less than seven minutes in duration, and can be reduced to under four and a half minutes if the reprised pair of minuets at the end is eliminated. This would seem ideally proportioned for inclusion in *The Queen's Masque*, and I would therefore propose that Tuppen's suggestion can be taken a step further, and that the entire *entrée* from *Le Bourgeois Gentilhomme* may have been performed as a part of the Whitehall entertainment—a mere four and a half months, we should note, after its first appearance in France.[164] If this is true, it would offer further information on the nature of *The Queen's Masque*, and in any case suggests that, with careful decoding of the evidence, we may be able to learn still more about this elusive and curiously hybrid court production.

---

163 *Ibid.*, 164.

164 It is worth observing that three of the dancers and wind-players who are named in the 1670 *livret* (p. 28) as performing in the *entrée* at Chambord—Jean Favier and Adrien Merger de Saint-André (dancers), and [?Jean] Boutet (flute and oboe player)—would turn up in London in 1673–75, performing in such works as *Ballet et Musique*, *Ariane*, and *Calisto*. See Chapter 6, and Walkling, "Masque and Politics at the Restoration Court: John Crowne's *Calisto*" (see Chapter 2, n. 61, below), 34 and 36 (Table 2).

2   Youthful "recreational" theatrics, 1668–75

In certain respects, *The Queen's Masque* is a work that straddles the somewhat ill-defined boundary between the non- (or perhaps in some cases semi-) dramatic court balls already discussed and the much more explicitly theatrical plays and masques to be treated here. Of course, its ambiguous status is attributable in part to the lack of a surviving playtext and the resulting uncertainty about what the work actually looked like in performance. But whether or not it can properly be labeled "dramatic," *The Queen's Masque* has another important quality in common with its more strictly terpsichorean cousins, namely, that it featured adult performers. This characteristic, and the distinction it reveals between court balls and the more explicitly dramatic works we will now proceed to investigate, is significant. The balls were largely participatory entertainments, in which even the monarch and his immediate relations could be performers, as the undoubtedly inadequate accounting given in Table 1.1 demonstrates. Even balls such as those of 2 February 1665 and 15 February 1686 that appear to have been costumed and choreographed, and in which courtiers danced *for*, rather than *with*, the monarch, were intended to showcase the talents of those already fully integrated into the court society, who thus possessed some modicum of power or influence within that society. As can be seen from a cursory glance at Tables 1.1 and 1.3, nearly every performer whose identity is known to us was at least seventeen years old, and while most appear to have been in their twenties and early thirties,[1] a few (for example Prince Rupert, dancing on the queen's birthday in 1666) were considerably older than that. The very few exceptions to this trend are themselves noteworthy, in that they involve individuals who gained particular distinction as both dancers and actors on the court stage. James, Duke of Monmouth (Charles II's

---

1   In the case of the somewhat exceptional (because apparently costumed and choreographed) "fine Mask at Court" of February 1665, two of the three male performers identified by Pepys, "Lord Aron" (*i.e.* Richard Butler, 1st Earl of Arran) and "Monsieur Blanfort" (*i.e.* Louis de Duras, Marquis de Blanquefort, later 2nd Earl of Feversham) were in their early-to-mid-twenties at the time of the performance, as was Barbara Villiers, Countess of Castlemaine, who at age twenty-four was already the king's chief mistress and had borne four of the six children she was to conceive by him. (The fifth, George Fitzroy, later Earl and Duke of Northumberland, was born on 28 December 1665, and thus must have been conceived within two months of the performance.)

72 *"Their greatest gallantry imaginable"*

eldest and favorite illegitimate son) and his Duchess Anne, *suo jure* Countess of Buccleuch, are first recorded as dancing on 31 December 1662, when the duke was just thirteen and the duchess still only eleven. Throughout the 1660s, they remained the youngest (identified) dancers at several court balls, but also among those most commended for their skill,[2] and while the duchess's dancing career was prematurely cut short in May 1668, when she was seventeen, by a hip dislocation that rendered her permanently lame,[3] her husband, at the age of 25, appeared prominently (dancing, but not acting) in *Calisto* in 1675. Another youthful dancer was Princess Mary, eldest daughter of James, Duke of York, whose appearance (fifteen years old and newly married to William of Orange) at the queen's birthday ball in November 1677 followed not only her starring acting role in *Calisto* two and a half years earlier as well as an appearance in *The Faithful Shepherdess* five years before that (when she had not yet turned eight), but indeed many years of rigorous training in music and dancing.[4] As early as 2 April 1669, when Mary was still only six, Samuel Pepys saw her, "a little child in hanging sleeves, dance most finely, so as almost to ravish me, her airs were so good."[5]

Though barely teenagers when they began their careers as court dancers, the Duke and Duchess of Monmouth ultimately came to be at the forefront—and thus among the eldest—of a new generation of well-trained youthful courtly thespians whose activities would dominate the Shrovetide calendar beginning in the late 1660s. In *The Queen's Masque* of 1671, as in the balls of the previous decade, they were still the junior performers, despite by now having reached the ages of twenty-one and nineteen, respectively. This production saw the couple coming into their own as full-fledged members of the court,[6] on a par with others of the same

---

2 For example, by Pepys, who admired the Duchess of Monmouth's dancing (*Diary*, 3: 301) and acting (*Diary*, 9 [1668–69]: 23) alike.

3 See Pepys, *Diary*, 9: 191 and 201, and the entry of August 1668 in Charles II's Privy Purse accounts for £10 paid "To a Bone setter sent to the Duchess of Monmouth by Sr George Cartwright" (Bodleian Library, Malone MS 44, f. 108[r]: this eighteenth-century transcription of the Privy Purse accounts covers the period between February 1665 and June 1669 [ff. 100[r]–111[r]]).

4 See the successive editions of Edward Chamberlayne, *Angliæ Notitia: or The Present State of England* (London: John Martyn, 1669–79), which list both a "Dancing-Master" and a "Singing-Master" among the "Officers and Servants belonging to the Lady Mary." For more details on both Mary and her sister Anne's training in dance, music, and acting, see Walkling, "Professional Actors as Royal Drama Coaches, 1674–81" (see n. 77, below). A fourth, and more ambiguous, case of a youthful court dancer is Lady Mary Tudor, Charles II's daughter by the actress Mary Davis, who sang in *Venus and Adonis* c.1683 and danced at the queen's birthday ball in 1684 (see p. 45, above), supposedly aged eleven: there is, however, some question about the accuracy of Lady Mary's recorded date of birth, and she may in fact have been as old as sixteen at the time.

5 Pepys, *Diary*, 9: 507; "airs" is an editorial emendation for "ears" in Pepys's manuscript. Mary's instructor is believed to have been the musician Anthony Robert, a Frenchman who later sang in *Calisto* and, according to Pepys, "did heretofore teach the King and all the King's children, and the Queen-Mother herself, who doth still dance well." For more on Robert, see Chapter 6.

6 The Duchess of Monmouth seems to have appeared on stage in some capacity despite her inability to dance, and there is evidence that she maintained at least a peripheral involvement in other court theatrical entertainments at this time. Sometime in the early 1670s, Margaret Blagge (who later appeared in *Calisto*) recorded in her diary her resolution to "Go not to the *Dutchesse* of *Monmoth*, above once a Weeke, except we dresse to Rehearse; and then Cary a Book with me to read, when

Youthful "recreational" theatrics, 1668–75   73

age: while both Queen Catherine of Braganza and Mary, Duchess of Buckingham (daughter of Thomas, Lord Fairfax) were already in their early thirties, Frances Teresa Stuart, Duchess of Richmond and Lennox, was twenty-three and Louise de Kéroualle, the future Duchess of Portsmouth was, like the Duke of Monmouth, twenty-one. The average age of the identified performers in *The Queen's Masque* for whom we have definite birth dates[7] is thus between twenty-four and twenty-five, with the median age being twenty-two and the midrange twenty-five and a half. This squares with the figures for Lord Sunderland's court ballet of 1686,[8] and also to a substantial degree with those for several of the balls listed in Table 1.1. On the other hand, it can be contrasted with the statistics for the other "recreational" court plays and masques of the period. As is evident from Table 2.1, which offers a digest of all the known Shrovetide and Eastertide court dramatic productions of the Restoration, *The Queen's Masque* stands out as distinctively adult, and hence anomalous, whereas in the other dramatic entertainments of the 1660s and 1670s for which we have relevant information, both average and median ages are considerably lower, with only one performer certainly over the age of twenty-five, and one (the exceptional Princess Mary) as young as seven.

Besides leaving *The Queen's Masque* in an odd position, situated somewhere between the balls we have been discussing and a separate group of dramatic pieces in which music and choreography often figure only secondarily, this distinction regarding the age of the performers constitutes the first of several features that differentiate the productions of the Restoration court (at least one of which was explicitly designated a "masque") from the great theatrical extravaganzas of the early seventeenth century. Whereas the latter were chiefly allegorical and non-dramatic, relied heavily on spectacular machine technology, and allocated speaking and singing parts only to the professional "secondary" characters, leaving the courtiers free to dance (literally) for hours on end, the majority of Restoration "recreational" court theatrical performances consisted of spoken plays, presented with scene changes but few, if any, machine effects, and acted exclusively by children and young adults, who danced only occasionally, and may rarely have sung. Only in *Calisto* do we find definitive evidence of "occupational" performers appearing on stage alongside their social superiors, as would have been the case earlier in the century. But in this instance the professionals dominated the dancing and, with the

---

I don't Act" (John Evelyn, ed. Harriet Sampson, *The Life of Mrs. Godolphin* [London: Oxford University Press, 1939], 16). The rehearsals to which Blagge refers cannot have been for *The Queen's Masque*: as Sampson points out (p. 184), this entry, though undated in its surviving source, must have been written after the beginning of April 1671, when Blagge became a Maid of Honor to Queen Catherine of Braganza, who is mentioned later in the same passage.

7 "Mrs. Berkeley" was probably not Mary (*née* Bagot, 1645–79), wife of one Charles Berkeley, who had become Earl of Falmouth in March 1665, but rather Mary Berkeley (died 1719), daughter of George, Baron Berkeley (later 1st Earl of Berkeley; see also Chapter 1, n. 106, above), who subsequently became the wife of Ford, 3rd Baron Grey of Warke. Mary Berkeley's date of birth is not known, although it would have been after 1646, when her parents were married.

8 See Table 1.3: if we consider only the nine performers that we know were scheduled to appear as of early February, the average, median, and midrange ages are, respectively, nearly twenty-two (21⅞), twenty, and twenty-three and a half.

74   *"Their greatest gallantry imaginable"*

(much younger) courtiers declaiming all of the spoken lines, were left to express themselves—vocally, at least—exclusively through the medium of song.

Documentation survives, to a greater or lesser degree, for six or seven such productions organized during the decade between 1668 and 1678.[9] The former year saw two in rapid succession, beginning with John Dryden's *The Indian Emperor* on 13 January. A sequel to Sir Robert Howard's *The Indian Queen*, *The Indian Emperor* had been premiered in April 1665 by the King's Company, and was already well known to London audiences.[10] The court performance was recorded in an official newsletter, which announced that "This Evening is repeated in the great Hall by some persons of quality the Indian Empe[r]. but the Company is made very private, soe as few attempt to gett in."[11] Two of the "persons of quality" were the Duke and Duchess of Monmouth, now aged eighteen and sixteen, and the identities of two other performers, Captain Charles O'Brien[12] and Henrietta-Maria Cornwallis,[13] are known from an account by Samuel Pepys, who was informed the following day that

> the ladies and Duke of Monmouth and others acted *The Indian Emperour*—wherein ... not any woman but Duchess of Monmouth and Mrs. Cornwallis did anything like, but like fools and sticks; but that these two did do most extraordinary well—that not any man did any thing well but Captain Obryan, who spoke and did well; but above all things, did dance most incomparably[.][14]

---

9 This accounting is almost certainly incomplete. See for example the "meditation" written by Lady Elizabeth Livingston, a Maid of Honor to the queen, observing that "my time was Waisted in dressing, in danceing, in seing, and in Acting of Play's[,] In Hunting, in musick, in all sorts of deuertions" (Bodleian Library, MS Rawlinson D. 78, pp. 178–79: see Douglas G. Greene, ed., *The Meditations of Lady Elizabeth Delaval Written Between 1662 and 1671* [Surtees Society, 190: Gateshead: Northumberland Press, 1978], 123). The entry, which seems to refer generically to the years of Livingston's tenure at court in the mid-1660s, was written on the second Sunday of Lent in either 1667 (*i.e.* 3 March) or 1668 (*i.e.* 16 February); the calculation of the specific date depends on what Livingston, who was born in October 1649, meant by the phrase "*in my 18th yeare*" in the heading to this section (p. 175). See also an earlier entry in the same volume, under the title "Meditations writ When I was 18 yeare's Old and a halph" (p. 158): "Many an houer haue I robed my selfe off rest, to waist Them in dancing, in play, in reading unprofitable Books, and such foleish deuertions ..." (p. 159).

10 The play's only song, "Ah, fading joy" from Act 4, scene 3, was set by Pelham Humfrey, and appears in the first part of *Choice Ayres*, the second edition of 1675, pp. 70–71, and the "Newly Re-printed" (*i.e.* third) edition of 1676, pp. 66–67.

11 Newsletter sent to Sir Richard Bulstrode, 16 January 1668 (report for Monday the 13th): Harry Ransom Center, PFORZ-MS-0445, p. 3 (see [Thibaudeau], ed., *The Bulstrode Papers*, 1: 19, which erroneously gives "foure" for "some").

12 O'Brien is believed to have been the second son of Murrough O'Brien, 1st Earl of Inchiquin, and was born sometime before 1657, the year in which he was kidnapped by agents employed by his father in an unsuccessful attempt to raise the boy as a Roman Catholic. The young Captain appears later to have served under the command of the Duke of Monmouth, and was killed at the Siege of Maastricht in June 1673.

13 Daughter of Charles, Baron Cornwallis of Eye; in 1688, her brother (also Charles, Baron Cornwallis) became the Duchess of Monmouth's second husband.

14 Pepys, *Diary*, 9: 23–24. Earlier editions of Pepys (see Chapter 1, n. 46, above) give "stocks" for "sticks."

Table 2.1 Shrovetide/Lenten/Eastertide plays and masques at court, 1660–85, for which identities of some court participants are known

			The Indian Emperor[A]	Horace[B] *	The Faithful Shepherdess[C]	The Queen's Masque[D]	The Empress of Morocco[E]	Calisto[F] †	Rare en Tout[G]	?Mithridates[H] ‡	?Venus and Adonis[I]
PERFORMANCE:											
LOCATION:			Hall Theatre	Hall Theatre	St. James's Palace (?Guard Chamber)	Hall Theatre	Hall Theatre	Hall Theatre	Hall Theatre	Lord Chamberlain's	?
DATE:			13 Jan. 1668	4 Feb. 1668	6 Apr. 1670[a]	20–21 Feb. 1671	? Mar./Apr. 1673[b]	22 Feb. 1675[c]	29 May 1677	8 Feb. 1678[d]	?1683
DATE OF SHROVE TUESDAY:			4 Feb.		15 Feb.	7 Mar.	11 Feb.	16 Feb.	[King's Birthday]	12 Feb.	20 Feb.
PERFORMER	**DATE OF BIRTH**	**AUTHOR(S) FIRST PUBLIC PERFORMANCE:**	John Dryden — April 1665	Katherine Philips/Sir John Denham — January 1669	John Fletcher (first perf'd c.1608) — June 1663	— —	Elkanah Settle — July 1673	John Crowne —	Anne de La Roche-Guilhen —	Nathaniel Lee — ?March 1678	?Anne Kingsmill et al. — [17 April 1684][e]
Duchess of Buckingham	30 Jul. 1638	§				32					
Queen Catherine	[15] Nov.1638	§				32					
Countess of Castlemaine	?Nov. 1640	§		27							
?Mary Berkeley	?after 1646	§				20–24?					
Duchess of Richmond	8 Jul. 1647	§				23					
Duke of Monmouth	[30 Mar.]1649	§	18			21	25				
Duchess of Portsmouth	Sep. 1649					21					
Thomas Felton	12 Oct. 1649	§		18							
Duchess of Monmouth	11 Feb. 1651	§	16	16	*Hip permanently dislocated, May 1668*	19					
Mary Davis	c.1651							[~23]			~31
Frances Apsley	1653									~24	
Henrietta-Maria Cornwallis	1655		~13	~13							

(Continued)

Performer	Date		11–26?	11–26?		14–16?	Killed at siege of Maastricht, June 1673		
Lady Elizabeth Howard	after 1655								
Capt. Charles O'Brien	before 1657	‖							
Lady Mary Mordaunt	1658/9	‖		~11		~16	~16		
Carey Fraser	c.1658	‖				~16	~16		
Princess Mary	30 Apr. 1662	‖		7		12	12		Married, moved to The Hague, November 1677
Princess Anne	6 Feb. 1665	‖				10		13	
?Duchess of Grafton	1667	‖						~9	
Lady Mary Tudor	?16 Oct. 1673	‖							?9

Key:

§ = performer also known to have danced in court ball(s), 1662–67 (see Table 1.1)

‖ = performer also known to have danced in court ball(s), 1675–86 (see Tables 1.1 and 1.3)

* Other identified performers in *Horace*: Henry Savile; Sir Greville Verney; Edward Griffin; James Hamilton; Thomas Howard.

† For other identified performers in *Calisto*, see Table 2.2.

‡ Possible other performers in *Mithridates*: Isabella Apsley, Lady Wentworth; Mary Cornwallis.

Key to sources identifying performers:

A Pepys, *Diary*, 9: 23–24.

B Manuscript cast lists in Harvard University (Houghton Library) and Trinity College, Dublin copies of *Horace* (1667 ed.); "Prologue *to* Horace, *spoken by the Dutchess of Munmouth, at Court*," in *Covent Garden Drolery* (London: James Magnes, 1672), 80–81, and "*Prologue to* Horace, *spoken by the Dutchess of Munmouth at Court*," in *Covent Garden Drolery ... The Second Impression, with Additions* (London: James Magnes, 1672), 80–81.

C Diary of Richard Boyle, Earl of Burlington (Chatsworth), vol. 5; "Epilogue, *spoken by the Lady Mary Mordont, before the King and Queen, at Court, to the faithfull Shepheardess*," in *Covent Garden Drolery*, 86, and "Epilogue *spoken by the Lady Mary Mordant, before the King and Queen, at Court, to the faithfull Shepheardess*," in *Covent Garden Drolery ... The Second Impression, with Additions*, 86.

[D] H. C. Maxwell Lyte, *The Manuscripts of His Grace the Duke of Rutland, K. G., Preserved at Belvoir Castle. Vol. II* (Historical Manuscripts Commission, Twelfth Report, Appendix, Part V; London: Her Majesty's Stationery Office, 1889), 22 (letter from Lady Mary Bertie to Katherine Noel [later Katherine Manners, Countess of Rutland], 17 January 1671).

[E] "*The first* Prologue *at Court, spoken by the Lady* ELIZABETH HOWARD" and "*The second* Prologue *at Court, spoken by the Lady* ELIZABETH HOWARD," in Elkanah Settle, *The Empress of Morocco. A Tragedy* (London: William Cademan, 1673), sigs. *A3*[r], *A3*[r–v]; "*A Prologue spoken at Court to the Emperess of* Morocco," "*Spoken by the Lady* Elizabeth Howard," and "*Another Prologue spoke at Court to the Emperess of* Morocco," in *A Collection of Poems Written upon several Occasions By several Persons* (London: Tho[mas] Collins, John Ford, and Will[iam] Cademan, 1673), "178" [*recte* 168]–"179" [*recte* 169], 170–171, and "182" [*recte* 172]–174.

[F] John Crowne, *Calisto: Or, The Chast Nimph. The Late Masque at Court* (London: James Magnes and Richard Bentley, 1675), sig. b3[v]–b4[r].

[G] Identification speculative (see discussion below).

[H] Identification speculative, based upon court documents and correspondence (see discussion below).

[I] British Library, Add. MS 22100, ff. 124[r] and 129[r].

---

[a] Date of Easter: 3 April.

[b] Date of Easter: 30 March.

[c] Plus additional performances through at least 28 April; date of Easter: 4 April.

[d] Performed again at Holyrood Palace, Edinburgh, 15–24 November 1681, to celebrate Catherine of Braganza's birthday.

[e] At Josias Priest's boarding school, Chelsea.

78   *"Their greatest gallantry imaginable"*

Plans for the production may have been laid as early as the fall of 1667, since the first published edition of the play, which appeared in that year, contains a dedication to the Duchess of Monmouth dated 12 October.[15] Pepys's informant, Elizabeth Pearse, additionally provided the noteworthy fact that "she did sit near the players of the Dukes House," suggesting that the professional acting companies may have had a hand in helping the young courtiers to mount the performance. Curiously, the court presentation was followed within just over a week by a professional revival of the play by the King's Company at the Bridges Street Theatre, which Charles II and Catherine of Braganza attended.[16] Whatever connections may have existed in this instance, *The Indian Emperor* seems to have remained a staple of amateur theatrical endeavors: the play was mounted by the ephemeral "Duchess of Portsmouth's Company" sometime before 1675,[17] and productions by children continued to be given into the eighteenth century.[18]

Within slightly more than three weeks of the *Indian Emperor* production, the court witnessed yet another "recreational" performance of a play, this time on Shrove Tuesday itself (4 February). Katherine Philips's translation of Pierre Corneille's *Horace*, which had been left unfinished upon the poetess's death in

---

15 John Dryden, *The Indian Emperour, or, The Conquest of Mexico by the Spaniards. Being the Sequel of the Indian Queen* (London: H[enry] Herringman, 1667), sig. A2^r–A3^v.

16 LC5/139, p. 129 and LC5/12, p. 17. These (partially duplicate) lists give the date of the performance as 22 January (a Wednesday); Van Lennep, ed., *The London Stage* (1: 128) inexplicably dates the performance to Monday the 20th.

17 The company seems to have brought in the King's Company actors Martin Powell and John Coysh to lead an otherwise mostly inexperienced cast: see Kenneth M. Cameron, "The Monmouth and Portsmouth Troupes," *Theatre Notebook* 17 (1962–63): 89–94. The only evidence for this production hitherto recognized comes from the prologue (spoken by Powell) and epilogue (spoken by "*a Girl*") printed in Thomas Duffett, *New Poems, Songs, Prologues and Epilogues* (London: Nicholas Woolfe, 1676)/"P. W.," *New Songs, and Poems, A-la-mode both at Covrt, and Theaters, Now Extant* (idem, 1677), 89–93. However, a deposition in the (1677?) case *Rex v. Browne* refers to the information of one Thomas Nichols, a journeyman apothecary and "a worthless fellow," who asserted that the defendant (Browne, who was Clerk of the Coopers' Company) had committed seditious libel against the king by, among other things, composing a poem entitled "A Dialogue of the Two Horses." In response, Browne presented evidence that "this said Nichols was of lewd life and conversation, and had turned player, and acted on the stage, particularly in *The Indian Emperor*, and had repeated this dialogue between the Two Horses to his Master Comedians, as a proof of his parts and memory, but (it seems) was hiss'd off the stage, and thereupon had been heard to say that he now intended to live by his wits, and get an acquaintance with merchants and citizens' wives, and be maintained by the strength of his back" (British Library, Harley MS 5903, ff. 123^r–130^v, f. 128^r; see James Winston's nineteenth-century transcription of the relevant portions of this document in Folger Shakespeare Library, MS Y.d.23 [1950]).

18 See for example the private performance held in the spring of 1732, at the home of John Conduitt, Master of the Mint, in St. George's Street, Hanover Square, with three youthful members of the royal family in attendance—an event memorialized in William Hogarth's painting "A Performance of *The Indian Emperor or The Conquest of Mexico by the Spaniards*" (1732–35; private collection). Of less certain status is the "PROLOGUE To a play entituled, *The Indian Empress* [sic]. A TRAGEDY *acted by some young Ladyes at* Green-wich" in P[atrick] K[er], *Flosculum Poeticum* (London: Benjamin Billingsley, 1684), 58–59 (followed by an "EPILOGUE," p. 60).

Youthful "recreational" theatrics, 1668–75   79

1664 and was subsequently completed by Sir John Denham, had not hitherto appeared on the public stage.[19] The court performance was thus a significant event, unlike the "very private" presentation of *The Indian Emperor* in January (albeit still as exclusive as any court masque from the time of Charles II's predecessors). One newsletter account reported that

> This night there is a play Acted at Court by the Dutchess of Monmouth Countess of Castlemain and others. [T]he Countess is adornd with Jewells to the Value of 200000$^\text{li}$. the Crowne Jewells being taken from the tower for her. [T]here are none but the Nobility admitted to see it. The play is Madam Phillips' translation of Corneiles Horace, finished by S$^\text{r}$ John Denham[.][20]

Two manuscript cast lists in contemporary printed copies of the play provide the names of ten performers (see Table 2.1),[21] including the three whom Pepys (who never mentions the *Horace* production) had heard praised for their dancing in *The Indian Emperor*.[22] The Duchess of Monmouth, who played the role of Sabina, was later credited with speaking the prologue (although, as Peter Beal points out, it appears to have been written for delivery by a man),[23] and the epilogue was

---

19 For an excellent treatment of this production, see Peter Beal, *In Praise of Scribes: Manuscripts and their Makers in Seventeenth-Century England* (Oxford: Clarendon Press, 1998), 179–91. As Beal points out (p. 180), Denham's translation of the concluding scenes appears to have been produced with an eye toward readying the play for performance, possibly at the instigation of the Duchess of Monmouth.

20 Newsletter from John Starkey to Sir Willoughby Aston, Bart., 4 February 166[8]: British Library, Add. MS 36916, f. 62$^\text{r}$. Later in 1668, the Florentine visitor Lorenzo Magalotti recorded that Philips's translation of *Horace* "was represented at court this year; Madam Castlemaine, among others, acted in it": see W. E. Knowles Middleton, ed. and trans., *Lorenzo Magalotti at the Court of Charles II: His* Relazione d'Inghilterra *of 1668* (Waterloo, Ont.: Wilfrid Laurier University Press, 1980), 144.

21 Harvard University, Houghton Library, fEC65 .P5397 667p and Trinity College, Dublin, Old Library, V.ee.4, p. [68] *bis* (sig. Aaaa1$^\text{v}$); both are reproduced in Beal, 183. The two lists disagree slightly as to the roles taken by three of the male performers: James Hamilton, Lord Paisley, played either Valerius or Horace; Edward Griffin (later 1st Baron Griffin of Braybrooke) played either Horace or Curtius; and the aforementioned Captain O'Brien played either Curtius or Valerius. The Duke of Monmouth did not appear, having departed the day after the performance of *The Indian Emperor* for a sojourn at the French court: see the newsletter sent to Sir Richard Bulstrode, 16 January 1668: Harry Ransom Center, PFORZ-MS-0445, p. 1 (see [Thibaudeau], ed., *The Bulstrode Papers*, 1: 19).

22 See also the report of the Swedish ambassador, Count Dona, in a letter of 8 February 1668: "Den ledze týzdagz wardt een sköön *Comedie l'Horace* spehladt af nögre persohner uthi Hôfwet, som *Mad$^\text{e}$ la Duchesse de Montmouth, Mad$^\text{es}$ Castelmaine & Cornewallis* och förnehme Mong persohner, till Kongenz och heela Hôfwetz störste *Contentement* och Nöye" (British Library, Sloane MS 1974, f. 8$^\text{v}$, quoted in Ethel Seaton, *Literary Relations of England and Scandinavia in the Seventeenth Century* [Oxford: Clarendon Press, 1935; rpt. New York: Benjamin Blom, 1972], 337–38).

23 See "Prologue *to* Horace, *spoken by the Dutches of* Munmouth, *at Court*," in *Covent Garden Drolery* and "*Prologue to* Horace, *spoken by the Dutchess of* Munmouth *at Court*," in *Covent Garden Drolery ... The Second Impression, with Additions* (London: James Magnes, 1672), 80–81 (for a discussion of the editions and states of this poetic miscellany, see Paul Hammond, "The

80   *"Their greatest gallantry imaginable"*

delivered by Henry Savile in the part of King Tullus.[24] But it was the presence of Barbara Villiers, Countess of Castlemaine, who performed the part of Camilla, that particularly fascinated contemporary commentators.[25] Lady Castlemaine had featured prominently in the "fine Mask at Court" in February 1665; now, three years later, she was at the height of her power and influence with the king, as witnessed by the extraordinary embellishment of her costume noted above. Indeed, this feature emerges in all of the accounts of the production: Thomas Rugge recorded in his "Diurnal" a "great Mask at Court, where the Countess of Castlmaine [*sic*] Apeared in a dress of dimonds & preteious stones,"[26] while John Evelyn reported that "The excessive galantry of the Ladies was infinite, Those especialy on that [___] Castlemaine esteemed at 40000 pounds & more: & far out shining the Queene &c."[27] Evelyn's estimate of £40,000 for the value of the jewels worn by Lady Castlemaine is considerably less than the £200,000 posited in the newsletter already quoted, but the effect was the same in the public consciousness: a scurrilous broadside attack on the king's mistress, printed the following April, satirically quotes the duchess as announcing that

> on *Shrove-Tuesday* last, Splendidly did we appear upon the Theatre at W. H. being to amazement wonderfully deck'd with Jewels and Diamonds, which the (abhorred and to be undone) Subjects of this Kingdom have payed for.[28]

Now aged twenty-seven, Castlemaine appears to have been the senior member of what was otherwise a relatively young cast: the Duchess of Monmouth, for

---

Prologue and Epilogue to Dryden's Marriage A-la-Mode and the Problem of Covent Garden Drolery," *Papers of the Bibliographical Society of America* 81 [1987]: 155–72). Lines 13–20 of the prologue are quoted in Gerard Langbaine, *An Account of the English Dramatick Poets* (Oxford: for George West and Henry Clements, 1691), 404–5 and in Sir Thomas Pope Blount, *De Re Poetica: or, Remarks upon Poetry* (London: R[ichard] Bentl[e]y, 1694), 170. In the former source, it is said to have been spoken by "the Duke of *Monmouth*," which, as Beal points out (p. 185), is impossible, since the duke had left England some three weeks earlier. A manuscript copy of the prologue appears at the end of the Trinity College copy of the printed play cited above (n. 21), and is reproduced in Beal, 186.

24 See Beal, 188–89 (where the two known manuscript copies of the epilogue are reproduced).

25 When *Horace* appeared on the public stage the following year (see below), one commentator described it as "a new play, which wase neuer acted, but by the Lady Castlemaine" (letter of Elizabeth Cottington to Herbert Aston, 16 January 1669: British Library, Add. MS 36452, f. 83ʳ).

26 British Library, Add. MS 10117, f. 218ᵛ.

27 Evelyn, *Diary*, 3: 505. The pregnant blank space left by Evelyn probably marks the diarist's self-censorship of an opprobrious term for the king's mistress, of whom Evelyn was not enamored. As Ethel Seaton points out (*Literary Relations*, 338 n. 1), Boswell erroneously identifies 4 February as Ash Wednesday (p. 137), and is therefore confused by Evelyn's reference (Evelyn, we should note, records receiving Communion on 2 February, a Sunday, and moreover explicitly labels the 5th as Ash Wednesday: see *Diary*, 3: 505–6).

28 *The Gracious Answer of the most Illustrious Lady of Pleasure, the Countess of Castlem—— To the Poor-Whores Petition* ("*Given at our Closset in Kingstreet Westminster, Die Veneris* April 24, 1668").

example, was sixteen, and Mrs. Cornwallis about thirteen.[29] However, the production may also have included adult "occupational" performers, since the account given by Evelyn (who seems to have gained admittance to the performance in spite of the professed exclusion of non-noble courtiers) describes it as "the Trajedie of *Horace* (written by the virtuous *Mrs. Philips*) acted before their *Majesties*: 'twixt each act a Masque & *Antique*: daunced." The published copies of the play provide no details of these *intermèdes*, but the work was similarly treated when it appeared in January 1669 at Bridges Street: Samuel Pepys attended the show on the 19th, describing it as "a silly Tragedy; but [the comedian John] Lacy hath made a farce of several dances, between each act, one,"[30] while John Evelyn's wife Mary wrote disapprovingly to a friend of the production, "with a farce and dances between every act, composed by Lacy and played by him and Nell [Gwyn]," as an example of "the strange veneration paid to the ruins of ancient structures, greater than the entire edifices ever could pretend to" in contemporary London society.[31] Philips and Denham's translation was, of course, based on a French original, but the insertion of *intermèdes*, both at court and in the public theatre, is a noteworthy development, and one that anticipates the structure of *Calisto* seven years later.

The presumed success of *The Indian Emperor* and *Horace* in 1668 appears to have resulted in further "recreational" performances by the children of the court, although in most subsequent cases less information has survived. On 6 April 1670, according to a contemporary newsletter, "their Majesties were diverted with a comedy acted at St. James's by the little young ladies of the Court, who appeared extraordinarily glorious and covered with jewels."[32] Although the decision to mount the performance at St. James's Palace rather than at Whitehall suggests a largely private event,[33] it was probably identical with the presentation of John Fletcher's *The Faithful Shepherdess* recorded by Richard Boyle, 1st Earl of Burlington, in his diary for 2 April: "I saw Lady Mary, daughter of the Duke

---

29 The average age of the six cast members whose dates of birth are known with some accuracy, including Henry Savile (b. 1642), Sir Greville Verney (b. 1649) and Thomas Felton (b. 12 October 1649), was nineteen and a half. The dates of birth of O'Brien (after c.1641 and before 1657), Edward Griffin (before 1651), James Hamilton, and Thomas Howard are not known.

30 Pepys, *Diary*, 9: 420; Pepys further observes that "his words are but silly, and invention not extraordinary as to the dances; only some Dutchmen come out of the mouth and tail of a Hamburgh sow." Charles II attended performances on the 16th and the 21st (the latter with the queen): see LC5/12, p. 17. For a full speculative list of performances of the play at this time, see Van Lennep, ed., *The London Stage*, 1: 153–54.

31 Letter of Mrs. Evelyn to Mr. Terryll [*i.e.* Tyrrell], 10 February 1669: British Library, Add. MS 78438, f. 9 (transcribed in William Bray, ed., *Diary and Correspondence of John Evelyn, F.R.S.* [London: George Routledge and Sons; New York: E. P. Dutton and Co., 1906], 734).

32 HMC *Le Fleming* (see Chapter 1, n. 113, above), 70; *cf.* the nearly identical report in the newsletter sent to Sir Richard Bulstrode, 8 April 1670 (report for the 7th): Harry Ransom Center, PFORZ-MS-0538, p. 3 (see [Thibaudeau], ed., *The Bulstrode Papers*, 1: 135): "The last euening their Ma[ties] were diverted at S[t] Jameses by a Comedy acted by the little young Ladyes of the Court who appeared extraordinary glorious, and covered with Jewells."

33 The performance may have been in the Guard Chamber at St. James's: see Boswell, 59. It is also noteworthy that the performance took place three days after Easter, rather than in Shrovetide.

82   *"Their greatest gallantry imaginable"*

of York, and many young ladies act the Faithful Shepherdess very finely."[34] This may have represented the theatrical debut of Princess Mary (the future Queen Mary II), who was not quite eight years old at the time.[35] Mary is believed to have taken the role of the chaste priestess Clorin, whose name she later adopted in her intimate correspondence with her friend Frances Apsley.[36] The only other performer we can identify is Lady Mary Mordaunt, the approximately eleven-year-old daughter of the 2nd Earl of Peterborough, and future Duchess of Norfolk, who delivered the epilogue.[37] Fletcher's play, which was first performed c.1608, probably by the

34 Diary of Richard Boyle, 1st Earl of Burlington (Devonshire Collection, Chatsworth), vol. 5 (not seen). Van Lennep, ed., *The London Stage*, 1: 169, speculates that the date may be in error (2 April was Holy Saturday), though the Earl could have witnessed a rehearsal rather than the actual performance.

35 See James A. Winn, "John Dryden, Court Theatricals, and the 'Epilogue to the faithfull Shepheard-ess'," *Restoration* 32/2 (Fall 2008): 45–54, pp. 46 and 52 n. 7. There is no evidence to support Boswell's claim (p. 130) that Mary's younger sister Anne, then just five years old, appeared in the production; indeed, as Winn points out (p. 51 n. 5), Anne was in France at the time, receiving medical treatment for problems with her eyes.

36 See British Library, MS Loan 57/69, *passim*, transcribed in Benjamin Bathurst, ed., *Letters of Two Queens* (London: R. Holden, 1924). In turn, Mary referred to Apsley as "my dearest dear husband" and "Aurelia." The origin of either of these pet names is uncertain. Clorin has just buried her only lover as *The Faithful Shepherdess* begins, yet Mary seems to associate her "husband" reference explicitly with that character when, on 17 December 1677, shortly after her marriage to William of Orange, she writes a letter to Apsley, signing herself "Mary Clorin" and adding the postscript "you se tho I have another husban I keep the name of my frist" (MS Loan 57/69, f. 156^r [Bathurst, 84]; see also the letter of 11 January ?1678, which she signs both "Marie Clorin" [f. 71^v; Bathurst, 86] and, in what appears to be a postscript or doodle, written in a different hand, "Mary Oreng" [f. 72^r]). Complicating the matter is the fact that there is no Aurelia in *The Faithful Shepherdess* at all. Characters named Aurelia do, however, appear in several other plays known to have been performed in London during the 1660s, including Abraham Cowley's *The Guardian/ Cutter of Coleman Street* (1661, 1668, 1669), James Shirley's *The Changes* (1662, 1663, 1667, 1668), Sir George Etherege's *The Comical Revenge, or Love in a Tub* (1664, 1665, 1666, 1667, 1668, 1669), and John Dryden's *An Evening's Love* (1668, 1669). Several others, while not performed, were available in print, including Philip Massinger's *The Maid of Honour* (1632), Massinger and John Fletcher's *The Prophetess* (1647), Thomas Rawlins's *The Rebellion* (1640, 1652), the anonymous *The Ghost, or The Woman Wears the Breeches* (1653), and Lodowick Carlell's *The Fool Would be a Favorite* (1657). There is also an Aurelia in Part 2 of Madeleine de Scudéry's romance novel *Ibrahim, or The Illustrious Bassa* (English translation by Henry Cogan published in 1652 and 1674). Although her writing left a great deal to be desired, Mary appears to have been an avid reader of plays, and one who retained passages for subsequent quotation: see BL MS Loan 57/69, ff. 182^r and 169^r (Bathurst, 54 and 51), in which Mary quotes from Nathaniel Lee's *Sophonisba* (1676) and, as James Winn has shown ("John Dryden, Court Theatricals, and the 'Epilogue to the faithfull Shepheardess'," 47 and 52 n. 15), *The Indian Emperor*. The latter is, of course, of particular interest, given the court production of January 1668.

37 See "Epilogue, *spoken by the Lady* Mary Mordont, *before the King and Queen, at Court, to the faithfull Shepheardess*," in *Covent Garden Drolery*, 86, and "Epilogue *spoken by the Lady* Mary Mordant, *before the King and Queen, at Court, to the faithfull Shepheardess*," in *Covent Garden Drolery ... The Second Impression, with Additions*, 86. In "John Dryden, Court Theatricals, and the 'Epilogue to the faithfull Shepheardess'," James Winn proposes that the epilogue be considered as the work of the recently appointed Poet Laureate, John Dryden; a related case is the "*EPILOGUE intended to have been spoken by the Lady* Henr[ietta] Mar[ia] Wentworth *when* Calisto *was acted*

Youthful "recreational" theatrics, 1668–75 83

Children of the Blackfriars, and was given its earliest Restoration production by the King's Company in June 1663 (with subsequent performances in October 1668 and February 1669),[38] was well chosen as a dramatic vehicle for the youthful performers of Charles II's court. As would later be the case in *Calisto* (and, to a certain extent, in *Venus and Adonis*), it presented an idyllic pastoral setting tempered by outbursts of lewd behavior and sexualized violence that are ultimately contained, by means of magical or divine authority, for the greater good of the community. In both *The Faithful Shepherdess* and *Calisto*, dramatic tension and humor are introduced through ill-intentioned antagonists who resort to shape-shifting disguises in order to pursue their sexual desires: Amaryllis magically takes on the appearance of Amoret in order to seduce Perigot; Jupiter seeks to ravish Calisto while posing as Diana. Ultimately, however, a new serenity and rectitude emerge from the disorder: in *Calisto*, the wronged nymphs are vindicated and (notwithstanding Jupiter's initial promise to "crown 'em stars"[39]) are preserved on Earth to "*oblige a Throne* [and] *grace some Fav'rite Crown*" (p. [82]), while in *The Faithful Shepherdess* Clorin, having cured the wounded and reformed the incontinent, admonishes the Priest of Pan to look after his charges, urging him among other things to

> banish all complements, but single truth
> from every tongue, and every Shepherds heart,
> let them still use perswading, but no Art[.][40]

One difference between the two works is noteworthy: as James Yoch has pointed out, *The Faithful Shepherdess* concludes not with a grand entertainment, but rather with a modestly restrained and decorous scene whose "quietly personal dimensions ... show the value of simplicity, which daringly reverses the splendid

---

at Court," printed in *Miscellany Poems* (London: Jacob Tonson, 1684), 327–28, which is also generally believed to be by Dryden: see James Anderson Winn, *John Dryden and His World* (New Haven: Yale University Press, 1987), 271–72 and 585 n. 47.

38 See Pepys, *Diary*, 4: 182 and 9: 326–27, 329, and 459. In the earliest performance Pepys attended, on 13 June 1663, he had noted that the play's popularity was "only for the Scenes sake, which is very fine endeed, and worth seeing"; he subsequently attended the play on 10, 12, and 14 October 1668, primarily to "hear the French Eunuch sing," but then on 26 February 1669 remarked upon the "empty house, there not being, as I could tell the people, so many as to make up above 10*l* in the whole house," while at the same time observing that "the music is the better, by how much the House the emptier." In the King's Company performances, the part of Amoret may have been played by Margaret Hughes, subsequently the mistress of Charles II's cousin Prince Rupert: see Richard Flecknoe's epigram "*To Mrs. Margaret Hewes*" in his *Epigrams. of all Sorts, Made at Several Times, on Several Occasions* (London: for the Author, 1671), 56: "you did get / So great a fame by Acting *Amouret*, / As ever after 'twas enough to say / *Hewes* had a part in't to commend the play."

39 John Crowne, *Calisto* (see n. 62, below), 79. For the possible identity of the "French Eunuch," see p. 204 n. 37, below.

40 John Fletcher, *The Faithfull Shepherdesse ... The Fifth Edition* (London: G. Bedell and T. Collins, 1665), 69. This vision of a restored innocence characterized by integrity and authenticity can be contrasted with the rather more cynical depiction of manipulative language and behavior in *Venus and Adonis*, where the characters' actions ultimately lead to a tragic, rather than a comic, outcome.

84   *"Their greatest gallantry imaginable"*

effects aimed for in the operatic ensembles that conclude continental models" of pastoral tragicomedy.[41] Such an ending would seem well suited to a performance put on (unlike the extravagant *Calisto* five years later) in the relatively unadorned and private space of St. James's.

Despite the numerous Restoration performances of *The Faithful Shepherdess*, both in the public theatres and at court, the work's textual history in this period is far from clear. The 1665 "Fifth Edition" of the play does not differ substantially from that published at the time of the work's premiere more than half a century earlier, and thus it tells us little about stagecraft or musical conventions used in the play after 1660. Pepys's account (see n. 38, above) informs us that a "French Eunuch" was employed to sing in the production in October 1668, and his comment the following February suggests that music was an important component of Fletcher's play.[42] The printed text includes four songs: in the first act the shepherds *"sing in praise of Pan"* (p. 5) as part of their purifying ceremony and, later on, a *carpe diem* song punctuates the lascivious shepherdess Cloe's successive meetings with two of her potential lovers; in the third act, the God of the River offers succor to Amoret if she will become his partner, and in the fifth, the pastoral concludes with another song honoring Pan and acknowledging his protection of the shepherds' community. Music survives for only one of these songs, the third-act "Do not fear to put thy feet naked in the river sweet," sung by the God of the River: the setting, by John Wilson, was first printed in 1659, and probably dates from the 1634 court performance.[43] It is therefore likely that new settings of the other three texts, or perhaps entirely new songs, had to be created when the play was revived in 1663. In fact, three songs by Matthew Locke, all published in the 1667 collection *Catch that Catch Can: or the Musical Companion*, could possibly have been written for performance in *The Faithful Shepherdess*. All are set in three parts; in terms of tone and subject matter they seem to be unique

---

41 James J. Yoch, "The Renaissance Dramatization of Temperance: The Italian Revival of Tragicomedy and *The Faithful Shepherdess*," in Nancy Klein Maguire, ed., *Renaissance Tragicomedy: Explorations in Genre and Politics* (New York: AMS Press, 1987), 115–38, p. 132.

42 For another musical element, probably associated with a prewar performance of the play, see Sir William Davenant's dialogue between a priest and a nymph *"Sung as a Prologue when the faithful Shepherdess was Presented,"* in *The Works of Sr William Davenant K^t* (London: Henry Herringman, 1673), section 1, p. 305.

43 *Select Ayres and Dialogues For One, Two, and Three Voyces* (London: John Playford, 1659; rpt. as the first part of *The Treasury of Musick*, 1669), 98; see also John Wilson, *Cheerfull Ayres or Ballads First Composed for one Single Voice and Since Set for Three Voices* (Oxford: Ric[hard] Davis, 1660), Cantus Primus, pp. 24–25; Cantus Secundus/Bassus, p. 16. This set of three partbooks appears actually to have been published in 1659: see George Thomason's annotation "Septemb: 20 ... 1659" on the British Library's copy (shelfmark K.2.a.2). The title of the latter collection helps to explain why this solo song for the God of the River appears in a three-part setting in both publications.

Youthful "recreational" theatrics, 1668–75   85

in Locke's canon, and no information is known concerning their origins.[44] The songs are "To Pan, great Pan! to thee we sing," "Hail, hail, ye hallow'd Numens of this place," and "Cloris, it is not in our pow'r to say how long our Love will last."[45] The first two could have been sung in the first and last acts, while "Cloris, it is not in our pow'r," a strophic song in four stanzas celebrating inconstancy in love, would work well as a replacement for Fletcher's original song ("Come, shepherds, come") in the latter part of Act 1. The substitutions being proposed here are by no means a perfect fit: in particular, "To Pan, great Pan" concludes with a cryptic reference to "that best man of War, / *Bryaxis* that found, / how to heal our deep wound, / with such Art there appears not a Scar," which seems to have nothing to do with the plot of *The Faithful Shepherdess* or its themes of love. On the other hand, the play itself is singularly unclear about why the shepherds and shepherdesses are celebrating a "holy festival / in honour of our great god" (p. 4) at this particular moment in the drama, and if Locke had indeed been commissioned to prepare new songs for the 1663 revival, the adulatory reference to the otherwise unidentified "*Bryaxis*" might have been intended as a compliment to the recently restored Charles II.[46] While these points are entirely speculative, they could provide some fleeting insight into how *The Faithful Shepherdess* was presented, not only on the public stage during the 1660s, but at St. James's in 1670 as well.[47]

In 1672 or early 1673, the court appears to have witnessed another "recreational" production, this time of a newly written (and far more dramatically intense) play, Elkanah Settle's *The Empress of Morocco*. This controversial piece, which spawned its own minor literary war between the playwright and a group of detractors thought to have included John Dryden, John Crowne, and Thomas

---

44 All other three-part songs ascribed to Locke are associated with identifiable performance works or are drinking songs.

45 *Catch that Catch Can: or the Musical Companion* (London: J[ohn] Playford, 1667), 168–70, 171–73, and 194–95. The last of these also appears in A. B., *Synopsis of Vocal Musick* (London: Dorman Newman, 1680), 74–75 (printing the text of the first two stanzas only).

46 Given its military overtones, the song's reference is presumably not to the Greek sculptor of the fourth century B.C. who worked on the Mausoleum at Halicarnassos.

47 The supposed court performance of *The Faithful Shepherdess* listed in Van Lennep, ed., *The London Stage*, 1: 60 under 6 January 1663 is almost certainly a ghost: see Montague Summers, ed., *Covent Garden Drollery* (London: The Fortune Press, 1927), 121, who miscites the date given for a performance "acted before their Majesties at *Sommerset House* on *Twelfth-Night*, 1633[/4]" in Langbaine, *An Account of the English Dramatick Poets*, 208. For a discussion of Summers's error, see G. Thorn-Drury, ed., *Covent Garden Drollery: A Miscellany of 1672* (London: P. J. and A. E. Dobell, 1928), 146–47. The court performance of 1634 was presented in the cast-off costumes created for Queen Henrietta Maria's performance of *The Shepherds' Paradise* the previous year, and "The scenes were fitted ... and made, by Mr. Inigo Jones, in the great chamber": see N. W. Bawcutt, ed., *The Control and Censorship of Caroline Drama: The Records of Sir Henry Herbert, Master of the Revels 1623–73* (Oxford: Clarendon Press, 1996), 186 (no. 280).

86　*"Their greatest gallantry imaginable"*

Shadwell,[48] is famous primarily for having been published with a series of five engraved images by William Dolle that purport to represent scenes from the play's production at the new Dorset Garden Theatre, which premiered in early July 1673.[49] The earlier court performance is more elusive: we have no certain date, although Eleanore Boswell has noted orders for the construction of a limited amount of scenery in March 1673 (painted by Robert Streeter) and for five carpenters to attend at performances in the Hall Theatre for six nights in April.[50] We only know of the existence of this production at all from a very limited body of sources, none of which involve diary entries or other contemporary comment. In his dedication of the play to Henry Howard, then Earl of Norwich, Settle asserts that Howard had "*bred it up amongst Princes, presenting it in a* Court-Theatre, *and by persons of such Birth and Honour, that they borrow'd no Greatness from the Characters they acted.*"[51] In addition, several prologues intended for delivery at court were printed in the 1673 playbook and in a contemporary miscellany.[52] Finally, three early-eighteenth-century advertisements for revivals of the play state that it had been "acted several times at Court by Persons of Great Quality, for the Entertainment of his late Majesty K. Charles II."[53] The advertisements are sufficiently removed in time that they could equally reflect a genuine historical tradition or simply a reading (similar to our own) of the other materials, all of which would have been readily accessible at the time. Yet there may indeed have been multiple court performances, since the playbook and miscellany provide as many as four separate court prologues for the play. At least three of these were

---

48　For facsimile texts of *The Empress of Morocco* and the ripostes it generated, see Maximillian E. Novak, intro., *The Empress of Morocco and Its Critics* (Augustan Reprint Society, Special Publications 3; Los Angeles: William Andrews Clark Memorial Library, 1968).

49　Elkanah Settle, *The Empress of Morocco. A Tragedy. With Sculptures. As it is Acted at the Duke's Theatre* (London: William Cademan, 1673). The playbook also includes a fold-out frontispiece engraved by William Sherwin that provides the earliest image we have of Dorset Garden's exterior riverfront façade. Charles II attended a performance of the play at Dorset Garden on 3 July: see LC5/141, p. 216 and Houghton Library, Harvard University, fMS Thr 57 (4) (*Register*, no. 924).

50　Boswell, 132–33 and 152–53, citing entries in WORK5/19 (quoted on p. 251) and WORK5/21 (calendared on p. 272). In 1673, Shrove Tuesday fell on 11 February; the production of *The Empress of Morocco* may have occurred after Easter (30 March), like that of *The Faithful Shepherdess* in 1670 (see n. 33, above).

51　Settle, *The Empress of Morocco*, sig. A2ᵛ. While on his diplomatic mission to Morocco at the beginning of the decade, Howard had held the title of Baron Howard of Castle Rising; he became Earl of Norwich in 1672, and in 1677 he succeeded his brother to the multiple titles of Earl of Arundel, Earl of Surrey, Earl of Norfolk, and (6th) Duke of Norfolk.

52　"*The first* Prologue *at Court, spoken by the Lady* ELIZABETH HOWARD" (written by the Earl of Mulgrave) and "*The second* Prologue *at Court, spoken by the Lady* ELIZABETH HOWARD" (written by the Earl of Rochester), in Settle, *The Empress of Morocco*, sigs. A3ʳ, A3ʳ⁻ᵛ; "*A Prologue spoken at Court to the Emperess of* Morocco," "*Spoken by the Lady* Elizabeth Howard," and "*Another Prologue spoke at Court to the Emperess of* Morocco," in *A Collection of Poems Written upon Several Occasions By Several Persons* (London: Tho[mas] Collins, John Ford, and Will[iam] Cademan, 1673), "178" [*recte* 168]–"179" [*recte* 169], 170–171, and "182" [*recte* 172]–174.

53　*The Post Man* "393" (19–21 August 1701), *The Daily Courant* 717 (2 August 1704), and *The Daily Courant* 728 (15 August 1704); the quotation is from the last of these sources.

Youthful "recreational" theatrics, 1668–75   87

"*Spoken by the Lady* Elizabeth Howard,"[54] the daughter of the dedicatee, who was at the time between fourteen and sixteen years old.[55]

The Empress of Morocco, whose story is based on information gathered during Howard's embassy to North Africa between June 1669 and October 1670,[56] is exceptional in a number of respects. Besides the Dolle engravings already mentioned, as well as the extraordinary controversy the play generated, the production included a wealth of scenic embellishment and featured Matthew Locke's seminal "Masque of Orpheus" in Act 4 scene [iv], which Curtis Price has described as "[t]he most skillful use of a masque to advance a plot" in Restoration drama.[57] But in spite of its bombastic language and convoluted intrigues, its impressive visual palette, and its innovative deployment of music, *The Empress of Morocco* emerges under close scrutiny as a work created first and foremost for the court and its "recreational" players. Besides Locke's through-sung masque, the play contains only one other song (the strophic "No music like that which loyalty sings" in 2.[ii], performed with a dance for which no music is known to survive), and the remaining non-scenic spectacle is limited to trumpet fanfares, the discharging of guns, "*a shower of Hail*" that opens Act 4 scene ii, and possibly the emergence of masquer-devils through a trap door in the Masque of Orpheus. While scholars have tended to link *The Empress of Morocco* with contemporary Dorset Garden spectaculars, Settle's play is in fact noteworthy for a complete absence of flyings and other spectacular machine effects, presumably in deference to the limited capabilities of the Hall Theatre, its original performance venue.[58]

---

54 The third item in *A Collection of Poems*, which does not mention Lady Elizabeth, is identical to the second prologue (by Rochester) printed in the *Empress of Morocco* playbook, which does. The second item in *A Collection of Poems* is not labeled as a prologue or epilogue—nor, indeed, is it explicitly associated with Settle's play, although the connection appears to be implied. Yet its status remains unclear: it seems to describe itself as "a flattering Prologue" in line 7, but in the previous line it has the play's youthful performers "Reflect[ing] on all they may have anger'd here," as if the play has already concluded.

55 No other performer in this production has been identified, although it is possible that the cast may have included Princess Mary and Lady Mary Mordaunt, both of whom had first acted in *The Faithful Shepherdess* in 1670 and later appeared in *Calisto* in 1675, and Margaret Blagge, who complained in an undated diary entry written sometime after April 1671 about having to attend unspecified rehearsals at the Duchess of Monmouth's lodgings (see n. 6, above).

56 William J. Bulman, "Publicity and Popery on the Restoration Stage: Elkanah Settle's *The Empress of Morocco* in Context," *Journal of British Studies* 51 (2012): 308–39. I am grateful to William Bulman for providing me with a copy of this article prior to its publication.

57 Curtis A. Price, *Music in the Restoration Theatre* (Studies in Musicology, 4; Ann Arbor: UMI Research Press, 1979), 30–31. Locke's music, which survives in Christ Church, Oxford, Mus. 692, ff. 1–5, is edited in Michael Tilmouth, transcr. and ed., *Matthew Locke: Dramatic Music with the Music by Humfrey, Banister, Reggio and Hart for "The Tempest"* (Musica Britannica 51; London: Stainer and Bell, 1986), 1–16.

58 The fourth Dolle engraving does show devils hovering in the air and coming up through traps in the stage, and the order to the carpenters of March 1673 calls for "Cutting out a way in the stage for a trapp dore" in the Hall Theatre (WORK5/19, f. 125ʳ and WORK5/21, f. 28ʳ [*Register*, nos. 764 and 772]; there is also a payment of 5*s* to the blacksmith William Beach for "ij new large plate spring boults for a trapp doare on yᵉ Stage in yᵉ Theater" in WORK5/21, f. 30ᵛ). The flying effect

88   *"Their greatest gallantry imaginable"*

Rather, the work's spectacular component inheres almost entirely in the scenes, the one element that, as we know from John Webb's drawings, the Hall Theatre was capable of handling.[59] Elkanah Settle's achievement was to create a work for the court that made the best use of the limited resources available at Whitehall, and that managed to translate well to Dorset Garden despite its failure adequately to exploit that theatre's superior technology. Given that the 1673 playbook, whose title page trumpets the production "As it is Acted at the Duke's Theatre," nonetheless takes note of the work's court provenance, we might imagine that the preparation of the lavish engravings—presumably a costly affair—must have received some sponsorship from the court itself, even if it is the Dorset Garden proscenium (and exterior façade) that figure prominently in the illustrations. The spectacle of Settle's play is perforce all about the scenery, and such publicity would, in an appropriately indirect fashion, have displayed the court and its theatrical endeavors to best advantage.   ·

Case study: *Calisto*

The efforts of the Restoration court to mount theatrical performances—particularly those acted by children and teenagers—beginning in the late 1660s may be said to have reached their apogee in the 1675 production of *Calisto*, a work whose extensive (and unprecedented) wealth of surviving documentation has been explored in detail, both by Eleanore Boswell in 1932[60] and by myself in 1996.[61] Prominently described on the title page of its printed playbook as "the late Masque at Court,"[62] *Calisto* represents the coming together of several generic and performative strands: the longstanding Stuart tradition of court masque; the more recent run of recreational, child-centered plays; and a number of quite new concepts adopted from French operatic and musical-theatrical practice.[63] At its core, *Calisto* is a

---

    may have been added when the production was mounted at Dorset Garden; in any case neither is at all essential to the play's action.

59 In March 1673, Robert Streeter was paid a total of £6 11*s* 8*d* for painting a backcloth, consisting of 50 yards of material, "like rusticke stone worke" and for procuring and painting an "Arch and ... cross peece of stoneworke" on an additional 17½ yards of cloth (WORK5/17).

60 Boswell, *passim*, esp. pp. 177–227 and 303–43.

61 Andrew R. Walkling, "Masque and Politics at the Restoration Court: John Crowne's *Calisto*," *Early Music* 24 (1996): 27–62.

62 John Crowne, *Calisto: Or, The Chaste Nimph. The Late Masque at Court, As it was frequently Presented there, By several Persons of Great Quality. With the Prologue, and the Songs Betwixt the Acts* (London: James Magnes and Richard Bentley, 1675). The playbook was advertised in the Term Catalogue for Michaelmas 1675: see *Term Catalogues*, 1: 218. Subsequent advertisements for the playbook continue to emphasize the special qualities of the production: see for example the "*Catalogue of some PLAYS Printed for* J. Magnes *and* R. Bentley" appended (p. [68]: sig. K2ᵛ) to Thomas D'Urfey, *Squire Oldsapp: Or, the Night-Adventurers* (London: James Magnes and Richard Bentley, 1679), which touts *Calisto* as "A Masque, acted at Court by the Lady *Mary*, the Lady *Anne*, and many other Persons of the greatest Quality in *England*."

63 For an evocative treatment of *Calisto* focusing on the unwilling participation of Margaret Blagge, former Maid of Honor to the Queen, see Frances Harris, *Transformations of Love: The Friendship*

Youthful "recreational" theatrics, 1668–75   91

practice associated with French *tragédie en musique* of apportioning the creation of text and music to a single author/composer pair, rather than the larger collaborative group employed in other musical-theatrical extravaganzas of the time, such as the contemporary dramatick operas *The Tempest* and *Psyche*.[68] The resulting creative empowerment of the artistic team, a phenomenon famously manifest in the collaborations of Jean-Baptiste Lully and Philippe Quinault, seems to have freed up both playwright and composer to explore approaches to achieving an overarching dramatic unity in their novel, generically experimental English piece. In particular, Crowne seems to have drawn inspiration from Molière and Lully's 1668 *George Dandin/Le Grand Divertissement Royal de Versailles*, in which the usual series of discrete inter-act *divertissements* was, just as in *Calisto*, replaced with a continuous pastoral story-line that progressed from *intermède* to *intermède*, paralleling the ongoing dramatic development of the main spoken play.[69] Even Staggins contrived to introduce his own element of thematic unity, reprising the tune of the fourth *intermède*'s choral song "[O] joy, shepherds, joy: Diana's disgrac'd" for the masque's celebratory valediction, "All pleasure[s] but love from our hearts we'll be chasing."[70]

This is not to say that *Calisto* was entirely French-influenced: indeed, significant elements of the earlier English court masque tradition can be found, effectively belying Crowne's professed lack of understanding of "the *Prologue* and *Songs*, the Nature of which I was wholly a stranger to, having never seen any thing of the kind" (sig. a1ᵛ). While his claim of never having *seen* such things in performance might be taken at face value, it is very likely that Crowne would have read the texts of at least some court masques of the early seventeenth century, since both the prologue and the final *intermède* show marked structural and

---

Sadie, ed., *The New Grove Dictionary of Music and Musicians* [London: Macmillan, 1980], 18: 55; the connection is, however, eliminated from the article on Staggins in the 2nd ed. [*idem*, 2001], 24: 258), would comprise the bulk of the instrumental music required for the through-composed Prologue. The only lacunae are the "several Sarabrands" which were danced by "the Princesses and the other Ladies ... with Castanets" (*Calisto*, sig. a4ᵛ), for which Holman posits "improvised pieces played by the guitars?." A possible source of these sarabands might be the second edition of *Apollo's Banquet*, published in 1678: the second section of this instrumental collection, entitled "The Tunes of the usual *French-Dances* at COURT and DANCING-SCHOOLS" begins with "AN *Entry*" followed by seven sarabands in various keys (only one of these movements had appeared in the first edition of *Apollo's Banquet* [1670], while subsequent extant editions of the collection progressively eliminate most of the sarabands). There is no certain evidence that any of these movements have any relation to the *Calisto* prologue (nor that the "*Entry*" is in any way associated with either *Calisto* or any of the sarabands), but the appearance of such a large number of sarabands in this collection published only three years after the *Calisto* performances is itself an interesting phenomenon. For a comprehensive list of Restoration theatrical entertainments in which sarabands are called for, see Price, *Music in the Restoration Theatre*, 36 and 257 n. 73.

68 This phenomenon is noted in Walkling, "Masque and Politics," 52.

69 Tuppen, "Shrove-Tide Dancing," 166.

70 See British Library, Add. MS 19759, f. 18ᵛ. Frances Harris (*Transformations of Love*, 230) misrepresents Peter Holman's argument when (citing *Fiddlers*, 371) she characterizes Staggins's music as "thin textured and short-winded, some of it scarcely adequate for public performance."

92   *"Their greatest gallantry imaginable"*

narrative affinities to the earlier form. Echoes of the "classic" masque form were not entirely unprecedented among the court entertainments of the Restoration: *The Indian Emperor*, *Horace*, and *The Faithful Shepherdess* all had some masque-like qualities, for example in the epideictic rhetoric of their prologues and epilogues, and in the performance of a culminating dance and/or song just prior to the end of each play. But *Calisto* mimics much more closely the tenor and the ethos of the early-Stuart masque. This can be seen particularly in the allegorical prologue. The curtain rises to the sound of "lamenting Voices ... on both sides of the Theatre" crying "Fly, Fly, Help, Oh! Help, or we dye" (sig. a4^r). These *"complainings,"* wafted over to the English shore from a Europe wracked by turmoil, strike fear in the heart of the Nymph of the River Thames (sung by the actress and onetime royal mistress Mary ["Moll"] Davis), who seeks solace from the figures of Peace and Plenty and allegorical personifications of the four continents. Their offerings of loyalty and gifts are punctuated by the appearance of the masque's noble and gentle performers as "Shepherds and Nymphs, Dancing round the *Thames*" and her attendants. At this point, the *"Genius of England"* (sung by the composer and Gentleman of the Chapel William Turner) awakens and reassures his lover Thames: the city of London, here allegorized as "Augusta," may be discomfited by the condition of Europe, but these are not England's problems (*"this sweet Isle no Monster can invade"* [sig. b1^r]), and in any case *"the mild power of this happy place"* (that is, Charles II) has sent *"Two Heroes of his own Celestial Race"* to triumph over sea and land *"And make the Nymphs in safety dwell."* These heroes then appear in succession: "one Crown'd with a Naval Crown" (sig. b1^v) representing the Duke of York as (until recently) Lord High Admiral, and "one Crown'd with a Mural Crown" representing the Duke of Monmouth, who had distinguished himself assisting French forces at the siege of Maastricht in the spring of 1673.[71] Both warriors are praised in a triumphal chorus, and the Genius of England welcomes them *"to my blest abode"* as "A Temple of Fame appears" (sig. b2^r). The Genius then invites the company to depart in order to pay tribute to *"our Divinity,"* the king, but then suddenly espies both Charles and his queen in the audience (*"But stay! what wonder does my spirit seize? / See! here are both the great Divinities"*), and subsequently leads the assembly in honoring the monarchs with a song and "An Entry of Rural Gods and Nymphs."

The affinities between this structure and that of the early-seventeenth-century masque are striking: while *Calisto* presents no antimasque apart from the offstage "lamenting Voices" at the beginning, the episodic series of character appearances that follows conforms closely to the Jonsonian pattern, in which dramatic tension (such as it is) is established through third-person reports of innocents in peril, then resolved through the intervention of the king, thereby allowing the innocents to appear in the guise of the masquers, posing silently on stage as they are lauded,

---

71 See Harris, *Transformations of Love*, 215, for a discussion of the extraordinary reenactment of the Maastricht siege organized by Monmouth at Windsor Castle in August 1674, which Harris aptly characterizes as "a theatrical spectacle."

Youthful "recreational" theatrics, 1668–75   93

along with the royal personage who has effected their salvation, by the assembled allegorical and divine characters. The main differences in *Calisto* are that the masquers are not the innocents-in-peril, but rather the heroes sent by Charles to preserve them,[72] and that the king's commission of these heroes is—his godlike persona notwithstanding—the product of earthly, rather than any divine, authority. Interestingly, the "Hero of the Sea" was personated on stage not by the Duke of York himself, but by one Colonel Orpe, who would later (1684) become a Lieutenant in the Horse Guards. By contrast, the "Hero of the Land" was in fact played by the Duke of Monmouth (who had already appeared on stage earlier in the prologue, dancing a minuet after the "several Sarabrands" performed by "the Princesses and the other Ladies" for Thames), thus restoring the older convention of presenting royal/noble masquers on stage under self-referential allegorical personae. Finally, given that this presentation is not a free-standing masque, but rather the prologue to the play-with-*intermèdes* that follows, Crowne was obliged to insert a brief transitional episode consisting of a song and "An Entry of Carpenters" (sig. b2^v), in place of the traditional *aubade* and withdrawal of the masquers after the measures and revels (which are themselves conspicuously lacking here). This slightly incongruous—but, for those familiar with the quotidian operation of the Hall Theatre, wryly clever—episode is performed "When the Prologue is done, and all gone off the Stage" (sig. b2^r), perhaps in front of the curtain while the stage was reset with the pastoral scene designated for the remainder of the show.

An additional echo of the older masque tradition can be seen in the final *intermède* of *Calisto*, when the newly married shepherds happen upon "two *African* Women" (p. 80) who declare themselves to have been "*lately ... as fair, / As your Shepherdesses are.*" Their black skin is the fault of Phaeton, who "*powr'd whole streams / Of melting beams, / Red, and glowing hot upon us*" when he fell from the sky while driving the chariot of the Sun, so that they are now obliged to "*range the World around, / To see if our lost Beauty can be found.*"[73] The solution to their wanderings, however, is at hand: "a third *African* woman" enters to inform them that "*our Beauty's found*" in the red and white complexions of the two nymphs Calisto and Nyphe, who are about to be stellified and who enter—now silently, like conventional masquers—"under a Canopy, supported by *Africans*" (p. 81) as the god-filled empyrean opens above them. For this scene, the playwright must have drawn inspiration from Ben Jonson's *Masque of Blackness* of 1605. Like Crowne, on whom the idea of including Africans was imposed from on high, Jonson had

---

72 Curiously, given the service provided by both York (in the Third Anglo-Dutch Naval War) and Monmouth (in the simultaneous French invasion of the Low Countries), the implied aggressors here ("*Some Gyants*," as the Genius of England describes them [sig. b1^r]) would seem to be the beleaguered Dutch, rather than the forces of Louis XIV.

73 The depradations caused by Phaeton's fall form a background to the masque's main story: see for example p. 5, where Jupiter tells Mercury, "Thou know'st what ills of late were done, / In Heav'n and Earth, by *Phœbus* Frantick Son: / I from high Heav'n descending to survey / The half-burnt World, and with a God-like care / All ruin'd places to repair, / Came here to view my lov'd *Arcadia*."

94   *"Their greatest gallantry imaginable"*

similarly deployed this theme to characterize the ladies in his masque "because it was her majesty's will to have them blackamores at first."[74] Jonson's work features as its masquers twelve noble "Daughters of Niger," who have mistakenly been led to believe that they were once "as fair / As other dames" until Phaeton's "heedless flames were hurled / About the globe" (p. 53; lines 138–39, 137–38). As a result, they traverse the world in search of a remedy that will come only when they reach England, "where bright Sol ... / ... doth never rise or set, / But in his journey passeth by, / And leaves that climate of the sky / To comfort of a greater light [*i.e.* James I], / Who forms all beauty with his sight" (p. 54; lines 165–70). In order that the transformation they desire may be effected, they are guided to England by a vision and, having attained their object, must at each full moon bathe their bodies in "that purer brine / And wholesome dew called rosmarine" (p. 59; lines 314–15) and wash their limbs in sea-foam, subsequently returning after a year to dry their faces "in the beams of yond' bright sun" (p. 60; line 324), *i.e.* in the presence of King James, in order to complete their epidermal cure.[75] Interestingly, however, *Calisto* reverses the dynamic of racial change and reconciliation established in *The Masque of Blackness*. Whereas Jonson's Daughters of Niger suffer under a misapprehension, unaware that they have always been dark-skinned and that, moreover, "in their black the perfect'st beauty grows" (p. 52; line 119), Crowne's Africans were indeed white in appearance prior to Phaeton's fall, and thus have been genuinely affected by that very recent event. Yet where Jonson's "Ethiops" are afforded a "cure" for the blackness that had always been theirs, the lately darkened Africans of *Calisto*, by contrast, gracefully accept their new appearance as a permanent change, reasoning that, given the exalted circumstances of the light-complexioned Calisto and Nyphe,

> *... instead of what we sought,*
> *Our Black with us must fair be thought.*
>
> ...
>
> *No Losers we shall prove,*
> *By parting with our Red and White;*
> *If black will serve the turn of Love;*
> *For Beauty's made for Loves delight.* (p. 81)

This more stoical attitude emphasizes the special status of the two paler nymphs—and by extension of their royal alter-egos Mary and Anne—underscoring not only their standing within the social hierarchy but also their well-maintained chastity, both in the drama, whose story Crowne had to alter from its original source in

---

74 Stephen Orgel, ed., *Ben Jonson: The Complete Masques* (New Haven: Yale University Press, 1969), 48 (lines 18–19).

75 Ultimately the nymphs are waylaid by an envious Night and only reappear after three years, in Jonson's *Masque of Beauty* of 1608 (actually delayed because of the wedding masques *Hymenaei* and *The Lord Hay's Masque* performed during Shrovetide in 1606 and 1607).

Youthful "recreational" theatrics, 1668–75   95

order to prevent Calisto being actually raped, and in the lascivious world of the Restoration court.[76]

The youth of the courtly performers in *Calisto* is a significant factor, of course, and reminds us that, for all its status as a vehicle for generic innovation, the 1675 masque continued many of the traditions that we have observed in the works presented during the preceding seven years. Chief among these was the use of children as performers. We are fortunate to have a full cast list of the royal, noble, and gentle masquers, and most of the names can be identified with a fair degree of certainty, which, in turn, allows us to offer rough estimates of the average ages of the masquers. Table 2.2 provides at least approximate ages for eleven of the twelve women and five of the nine men, with the average age of the former being just over 14 and that of the latter nearly 21.

We can also arrive at a somewhat more accurate figure for the seven women who took speaking roles in the masque: the average age of this group (which includes both Princess Anne, the youngest member of the entire cast, and Margaret Blagge, one of the oldest) is about 14½. With youth, of course, came inexperience. At least two of the female performers (Lady Mary Mordaunt and Princess Mary) had already honed their thespian skills in *The Faithful Shepherdess* five years earlier—and may, for all we know, have appeared in *The Empress of Morocco* as well (see n. 55, above)—and there is a tradition, first recorded in the eighteenth century, that the famous actor and Duke's Company manager Thomas Betterton "instructed the noble Actors, and supplied the part of Prompter, and Mrs Betterton gave lessons to the young Princesses."[77] Even

---

76 We might well sympathize with Crowne, who appears to have struggled with the difficult task of forging a middle way between the explicitness characteristic of the Restoration court and the inhibition appropriate to the public display of pre-adolescent heiresses to the throne. This dilemma is reflected in the fact that his initial draft of the script seems to have been insufficiently innocuous: "I did a little fail in my first attempt; my Arrows (though as fine as I could then in haste turn 'em) yet were too course for a Court. I often pared 'em, and much difficulty I found to make 'em thin enough to pass through nice and delicate Ears, without wounding 'em, an Art which with much pains in this Emendation I attained" (sig. a2ʳ). The paradoxical intermingling of chastity and sexual license, both on- and offstage in the performances of *Calisto* and in its Restoration courtly milieu, have provided ample fodder for readings of the masque inflected by questions of sexuality and gender: see Carol Barash, *English Women's Poetry, 1649–1714: Politics, Community, and Linguistic Authority* (Oxford: Clarendon Press, 1996), 46–50; Harriette Andreadis, *Sappho in Early Modern England: Female Same-Sex Literary Erotics, 1550–1714* (Chicago: University of Chicago Press, 2001), 151–76 (chapter 5); Valerie Traub, *The Renaissance of Lesbianism in Early Modern England* (Cambridge: Cambridge University Press, 2002), 253–57; and Matthew Jenkinson, *Culture and Politics at the Court of Charles II, 1660–1685* (Woodbridge: The Boydell Press, 2010), 107–33 (chapter 4). For preliminary versions of the latter two discussions, see Traub, "The Perversion of 'Lesbian' Desire," *History Workshop Journal* 41 (Spring 1996): 23–49, and Jenkinson, "John Crowne, the Restoration Court, and the 'Understanding' of *Calisto*," *The Court Historian* 15 (2010): 145–55.

77 Henry Brougham *et al.*, comp., *Biographia Britannica: or, the Lives of the Most Eminent Persons Who have Flourished in Great Britain and Ireland, From the Earliest Ages, Down to the Present Times* (6 vols.: London: W. Innys *et al.*, 1747–66), 2 (1748): 772. This anecdote seems to have

96 *"Their greatest gallantry imaginable"*

so, the preparation of *Calisto* seems to have been plagued with delays. Crowne notes in his Preface that the masque's premiere occurred "some Months after the time first decreed, but that hapned from the discretion of those on whom the Dancing and Musical parts depended, who found it required time to do any thing in Perfection" (sig. a1ᵛ), and newsletter reports in mid-December 1674 variously announced planned performances on New Year's Day[78] and Epiphany.[79] Ultimately, the show did not go on until February,[80] and even then the intended premiere on Shrove Tuesday (16 February) had to be postponed to the following Monday (22 February, during Lent) because, as the Venetian ambassador cryptically remarked, "they could not get ready in time."[81] Whether this was on account of the lengthy spoken play performed by the "recreational" courtiers or the musical sections presented by the "occupational" singers, dancers, and instrumentalists is not clear: Crowne's more general assignment of blame to "those on whom the Dancing and Musical parts depended" could be nothing more than a tactful diversion intended to cover up for the (entirely understandable) problem of getting polished performances out of courtly ladies as young as ten, the supposed exertions of Mr. and Mrs. Betterton notwithstanding.[82] Certainly, rehearsals must have been plentiful enough: an order of 28 November 1674

---

been first written down by the antiquarian William Oldys, sometime before 1724: see Andrew R. Walkling, "Professional Actors as Royal Drama Coaches, 1674–81" (in progress).

78 Newsletter sent to Sir Richard Bulstrode, 14 December 1674: Harry Ransom Center, PFORZ-MS-0675, p. 2 (see [Thibaudeau], ed., *The Bulstrode Papers*, 1: 274): "The first of Janary [*sic*] yᵉ yoong Princes and Nobility are to divert theire Maᵗʸᵉ and Court, wᵗʰ a Play & a Opera in wᶜʰ yᵉ splendʳ of yᵉ English monarchy will be seen."

79 Newsletter sent to Sir Richard Newdigate, 15 December 1674: Folger Shakespeare Library, MS L.c.120: "On Twelfe day the Principallest abᵗ yᵉ Court divert their Maᵗʸˢ wᵗʰ a Play & Opera wherein yᵉ Splendor & Grandeur of the English Monarchy will bee seene."

80 Mary of Modena, the (relatively) new Duchess of York, had given birth to a child on 9 January—a fact that I failed to note in "Masque and Politics," 29—which may have occasioned the postponement from Epiphany to Shrovetide.

81 *Calendar of State Papers, Venetian* 38 (1673–75): 371; see the discussion in Walkling, "Masque and Politics," 29–30.

82 On 16 February, the date of the intended premiere, Arthur Annesley, 1st Earl of Anglesey, recorded in his diary that in "yᵉ afternoon" he "went to the maske at court to see my daughter Decies dance &c[;] it lasted till past one at night[.] I did dutyes after" (British Library, Add. MS 40860, f. 84ʳ). Anglesey's "daughter Decies" was Catherine Fitzgerald, married in 1673 to the Earl's eight-year-old grandson, John Power, Viscount Decies (later 2nd Earl of Tyrone). Given the seemingly unequivocal statement of the Venetian ambassador quoted above, it seems as if this marathon session may have been another rehearsal; if so, its extraordinary length suggests just how unprepared the production must have been at that point. Anglesey, who appears to have had little interest in the theatre, most likely did not stay for long, hence his ability to carry out his customary "dutyes" as Lord Privy Seal after witnessing the dancing. Later, on 25 March, while the revised version of *Calisto* was in rehearsals for its second run, Catherine fled from her child groom with the connivance of the Earl of Ossory, prompting Anglesey to denounce her as "false bold ungratefull daughter Decies" (f. 85ʳ; entries not transcribed in the relevant Historical Manuscripts Commission Report [*Fitzherbert*: see p. 240 n. 81, below], which dismisses them [p. 278] as "of little interest").

Table 2.2 Noble/gentle performers in *Calisto*

Name	Marital Status, 1675	Relevant Relationship/Title	Relationships of Blood & Marriage	Previously Discussed	Date of Birth	Age on 22 Feb. 1675
Princess Mary	S^A	daughter of James, Duke of York later Princess of Orange and Queen Mary II	α	∞	30 Apr. 1662	12
Princess Anne	S^B	daughter of James, Duke of York later Queen Anne	α	∞	6 Feb. 1665	10
Lady Henrietta Maria Wentworth, 6th Baroness Wentworth	S^C	daughter of Thomas, 5th Baron Wentworth (son of Earl of Cleveland)	[αβ]	ML	11 Aug. 1660	14
Anne (Palmer) Fitzroy, Countess of Sussex	M^1	illegitimate daughter of Charles II by Barbara Villiers	α	ML	1661	~13
Lady Mary Mordaunt	S^D	daughter of Henry, 2nd Earl of Peterborough later 7th Duchess of Norfolk	β	ML	1658/9	~16
Margaret Blagge	S^E	daughter of Col. Thomas Blagge		∞	2 Aug. 1652	22
Sarah Jenyns	S^F	daughter of Richard Jenyns later 1st Duchess of Marlborough		ML	5 Jun. 1660	14
Elizabeth Butler, Countess of Derby	M^2	daughter of Thomas, 6th Earl of Ossory (son of 1st Duke of Ormonde)		ML	c. 1660	~14
Henriette Kéroualle, Countess of Pembroke and Montgomery	M^3	daughter of Guillaume de Penancoët, Sieur de Kéroualle (sister of Duchess of Portsmouth)	γ	ML	1650	~24
Lady Catherine (Osborne) Herbert	M^4	daughter (4th) of Thomas, 1st Earl of Danby	γ	+	?c. 1662	?~12
Catherine Fitzgerald	M^5	daughter of Sir John Fitzgerald of Dromana later Viscountess Grandison of Limerick		B	Aug. 1660	14
Carey Fraser	S^G	daughter of Sir Alexander Fraser, Bart. (Chief Physician to Charles II) later 3rd Countess of Peterborough	β	ML	c. 1658	~16

(Continued)

Name	Marital Status, 1675	Relevant Relationship/Title	Relationships of Blood & Marriage	Previously Discussed	Date of Birth	Age on 22 Feb. 1675
James (Crofts) Scott, Duke of Monmouth	M[6]	illegitimate son of Charles II by Lucy Walter/Barlow	α	ML	[30 Mar.] 1649	25
Peregrine Osborne, Viscount Dumblane	S[H]	son (2nd) of Thomas, 1st Earl of Danby later 2nd Duke of Leeds (etc.)	γ	ML	c. Dec. 1659	15
Robert Leke, Baron Deincourt of Sutton	M[7]	son of Nicholas, 2nd Earl of Scarsdale later 3nd Earl of Scarsdale		ML	9 Mar. 1654	20
John Trevor	?	son of Sir John Trevor (Secretary of State)		ML	before 1657	~19
Mr. (Col.) Orpe		(Lieutenant of the Horse Guards, 1684)		W	?	?
Mr. Lane		?relative of Jane Lane, Lady Fisher		ML	?	?
Mr. Leonard		?		–	?	?
William Fanshaw	S[I]	(Master of Requests, 1679)	α′	W	c. 1650	~25
?[Mr. Stafford]				–	?	?

N.B. For roles played and other documentary information, see Walkling, "Masque and Politics at the Restoration Court," 33 (Table 1).

Key:

∞ = identified/discussed in multiple sources
ML = identified/discussed in James Maidment and W. H. Logan, *The Dramatic Works of John Crowne. With Prefatory Memoir and Notes* (4 vols.: Edinburgh: William Paterson; London: H. Sotheran & Co., 1873–74), 1: 327–40
B = identified in Boswell, *The Restoration Court Stage*, 196 (*N.B.* Boswell's identification of Lady Katherine Herbert is incorrect.)
W = identified in Walkling, "Masque and Politics at the Restoration Court," 37
+ = new identification
– = still not adequately identified

Key to blood/marriage relationships:

α (Stuart):   Princess Mary   James Scott, Duke of Monmouth*   <HALF-SIBLINGS>   *Mary Walter* = (1676) William Fanshaw
               [SIBLINGS]   <COUSINS>   [HALF-SIBLINGS]
               Princess Anne   Anne Fitzroy, Countess of Sussex
                                                                        *MONOGAMOUS LOVER of Henrietta Wentworth

β (Mordaunt):   Lady Mary Mordaunt   <COUSINS>   *Charles Mordaunt, later 3rd Earl of Peterborough*** = Carey Fraser
                                                                        **SECOND COUSIN of Henrietta Wentworth

γ **(Herbert/Osborne):**   Henriette Kéroualle = *Philip Herbert, 7th Earl of Pembroke and Montgomery*   \<COUSINS\>   *James Herbert* = Lady Catherine Osborne

                                                                                                                                    [SIBLINGS]

                                                                                                                         Peregrine Osborne, Viscount Dumblane

---

[1] Married (16 May 1674) to Thomas Lennard, 15th Baron Dacre and 1st Earl of Sussex.

[2] Married (10 July 1673) to William George Richard Stanley, 9th Earl of Derby.

[3] Married (17 December 1674) to Philip Herbert, 7th Earl of Pembroke and Montgomery.

[4] Married (1 July 1674) to James Herbert of Tythorpe House, Kingsey, Buckinghamshire (grandson of 4th Earl of Pembroke and Montgomery).

[5] Married (20 May 1673) to John Power, Viscount Decies (age 8; son of 1st Earl of Tyrone); marriage later voided. 25 March 1676, married Edward Villiers (son of 4th Viscount Grandison).

[6] Married (20 April 1663) to Anne Scott, Countess of Buccleuch.

[7] Married (c.11 February 1672) to Mary Lewes of Ledstone, Yorkshire.

[A] 4 November 1677, married William, Prince of Orange, later William III.

[B] 28 July 1683, married George, Prince of Denmark, later Duke of Cumberland.

[C] Never married; 1680, became permanent mistress of the Duke of Monmouth.

[D] 8 August 1677, married Henry Howard, later 7th Duke of Norfolk (*etc.*).

[E] 16 May 1675, married Sidney Godolphin, subsequently 1st Earl of Godolphin.

[F] 1 October 1678, married John Churchill, later 1st Duke of Marlborough.

[G] c. 1678, married Charles Mordaunt, later 3rd Earl of Peterborough.

[H] 25 April 1682, married Bridget Hyde of Allruy, Hertfordshire.

[I] 9 September 1675, married Mary Walters (half sister of Duke of Monmouth).

100 *"Their greatest gallantry imaginable"*

anticipates practicing in the Hall Theatre every Tuesday, Thursday, and Saturday throughout December, and this likely continued into January and February.[83] John Evelyn is known to have attended rehearsals on two Tuesdays in December, the 15th and the 22nd,[84] while a later rehearsal on 2 February (also a Tuesday) was witnessed by the king, the queen, and the Duke of York;[85] indeed, Crowne himself described the production as being

> followed at innumerable Rehearsals and all the Representations by throngs of Persons of the greatest Quality, and designed for the Pleasures and Divertisements of Their Majesties, and Royal Highnesses, and accordingly very often Graced with Their Presences[.][86]

After the belated premiere on 22 February, there seems to have been another performance sometime before 9 March, the date on which Charles II departed for Newmarket.[87] However, these were not deemed satisfactory, at least by the author,[88] and the text was subjected to a wholesale revision in the weeks that followed, with new performances of the masque taking place in April, after Easter. These included one on the 22nd[89] (at which the unseemly behavior of Henry

---

83 LC5/141, pp. 74 and 551 (*Register*, no. 880), ordering "fires in panns betweene ye sceenes and in y^e pitt by reason the Duke of Yorkes Children wilbe there." Writing in defense of his later revisions to the text, Crowne suggests that audiences had grown "weary" of the earlier version of the masque "at the 20*th* or 30*th* [representation], for near so often it had been Rehearsed and Acted" (sig. $a2^v$). The period from 28 November to 13 February is eleven weeks, and would thus have included 34 possible rehearsal days, according to the Tuesday/Thursday/Saturday scheme outlined in the document cited above.

84 Evelyn, *Diary*, 4: 49–51.

85 Harry Ransom Center, PFORZ-MS-0681, p. 3 (see [Thibaudeau], ed., *The Bulstrode Papers*, 1: 277): "On Wed. night after Councell theire Ma^{tyes} & Royall Highnesses were p^rsent at the Rehearsall of the Great Maske, wch will be publiquely acted on Tuesday 7 night next, by wch time her Royall Highness will be able to be p^rsent being already thankes be to God in pritty Good health" (*The Bulstrode Papers* gives "Royal Highnesse" for the manuscript's "Royall Highnesses," which would seem in any case to be incorrect, since the Duchess of York was then recovering from childbirth); see also Folger Shakespeare Library, MS L.c.142. As I noted in "Masque and Politics," 55–56 n. 21 (citing LC5/141, p. 55), there appears to have been a dress rehearsal on Monday, 15 February.

86 *Calisto*, sig. $a1^r$. Crowne's account is echoed by Langbaine (*An Account of the English Dramatick Poets*, 92), who describes the masque as "writ at the Command of her present Majesty" (*i.e.* Mary II).

87 Crowne refers to revisions (see below) being carried out "between the second and third Representation" (sig. $a2^{r-v}$); for more on the evidence for performances, see Walkling, "Masque and Politics," 30.

88 *Calisto*, sig. $a2^r$: "in the womb it was squeez'd, and hinder'd of its due growth by intolerable strait lacings; and lastly, forced on an immature and hasty birth; by all which inconveniences, it was impossible it should prove otherwise than a weak, lean, ricketty, deformed piece, and as such (notwithstanding the kindness it received from others,) it was looked on by me; and accordingly I was impatient till I had strangled it, and in the room produced something less imperfect."

89 Diary entry of Otto von Schwerin the Younger, quoted in von Orlich, ed., *Briefe aus England* (see Chapter 1, n. 57, above), xxvi: "Den 2. Mai [*i.e.* 22 April, Old Style] Abends wurde auf dem Schlosse ein Ballet und eine Komödie von des Herzogs von York Töchtern gespielt, der sämmtliche Gesandten beiwohnten."

Hyde, 2nd Earl of Clarendon, resulted in the Earl's dismissal from his position as Chamberlain to the Queen[90]), another on the 23rd,[91] and probably yet another on the 28th.[92] Crowne's six-month respite between the composition of the original masque in August or September and the revisions of March–April seems to have allowed him a chance to rethink some of the spoken dialogue: having originally employed an irregular Pindaric format "as the readiest and quickest for one that was in haste ... where the Poet is not bound to wait the leisure of a stubborn syllable to Rime, but to take the Rime where he can catch it, without any more trouble" (sig. a3^r), he subsequently devoted his energies to setting the revised text in more regular heroic couplets, whose greater difficulty in the composition was offset by their "more Majestick, Lofty and Musical" qualities. Judging from the disposition of these varying styles through the surviving text, it would appear that Crowne rewrote nearly the entire spoken portion of the masque for the April performances: with the exception of the first scene of Act 1 (pp. 1–6), the overwhelming bulk of *Calisto* as printed in the 1675 playbook is in heroic couplets,[93] a fact that could well comport with Margaret Blagge's complaint, made sometime between February and April, that "the alterations are many, the ladys not disposed

90 Letter of John Verney to Sir Ralph Verney, 25 April 1675: Alfred J. Horwood, "The Manuscripts of Sir Harry Verney, Bart., at Claydon House, Co. Bucks.," in Historical Manuscripts Commission, *Seventh Report of the Royal Commission on Historical Manuscripts. Part I. Report and Appendix* (London: Her Majesty's Stationery Office, 1879), 433–509 (hereafter cited as HMC *Verney*), p. 464: "The King on Saturday night sent for the keys from the Earl of Clarendon—'tis said the reason is, that last Thursday a play was acted at court, and after orders given that no more should be let in, his lordship came to the door, which the guard refused to open, tho' he told them who he was, on which he broke it open and struck a yeoman of the guard. Some say a chamberlain was never before turned out for beating a yeoman of the guard. There are three lords competitors for the office, Sunderland, Sussex, and Cornwallis"; *ibid.*, 492: letter of Dr. William Denton to Sir Ralph Verney, 29 April 1675: "Your friend Clarendon has lost his key. The pretence was that he struck one of the guard at the setting in unto the opera, but other reasons are guessed. ... Clarendon's key is not yet disposed of, it is said that it is between Sunderland and Sussex." I was not aware of these documents when I published "Masque and Politics" in 1996; the former letter is quoted in Van Lennep, ed., *The London Stage*, 1: 231, but is not there connected with *Calisto*, an association that the latter document would seem to make explicit, given its use of the unusual term "opera." On the other hand, as I noted in "Masque and Politics," 30, the new costumes for the April revival were supposedly not ready until the 23rd (see Boswell, 182).

91 Letter of Otto von Schwerin the Younger to Elector Friedrich Wilhelm of Brandenburg, 23 April/3 May 1675, in von Orlich, ed., *Briefe aus England*, 21: "Aus diesen Ursachen ist selbigen Tages kein Rath gehalten worden, und vermuthlich wird solches heute abermals nicht geschehen, weil der König wieder im Parlament gesessen und gegen 4 Uhr die Kutsche bestellt, um in die Komödie zu fahren."

92 See Walkling, "Masque and Politics," 30. At least two singing roles were reassigned for the later performances: see *ibid.*, 38 and 41.

93 Additional Pindaric passages appear in 1.ii (pp. 6 and 8), 1."v" (*recte* iii) (pp. 9 [two lines only], 10, and 12), Act 2 (pp. 14–15, 16–17, and 19), and Act 3 (pp. 26, 28, 30, 32, 36 [one line only], and 38). Acts 4 and 5 are entirely in heroic couplets (apart from one pentameter ABAB quatrain on p. 68). With respect to the Prologue and *intermèdes*, the text printed in the playbook matches that in the programme libretto (see n. 120, below), although we cannot be certain at which set of performances the libretto was distributed.

102 *"Their greatest gallantry imaginable"*

to act som of them."[94] Why Charles II would have acceded to the playwright's inclination to (in Crowne's words) "strangle" the earlier version of his masque "and in the room produce[] something less imperfect" is uncertain. Surely the king's chief concern was to present a courtly spectacle, and the post-Easter revival of *Calisto* did not inevitably require a wholesale rewriting of the text (accompanied by a heavy burden of additional rehearsals for the masquers), however much its author might have wished "not only to repair my own Reputation, but to give some refreshment to the Audiences, who would have been weary of a better Play at the second or third Representation" (sig. a2^v). Crowne's claim of agency in this matter seems to run counter to the more typically abject stance he articulates throughout most of the playbook's introductory commentary, and would thus appear to preclude the possibility of express royal displeasure with the earlier version's content or poetic form. Whatever the case may be, the court (the young lady actresses excepted) seems to have welcomed a further opportunity to showcase both its talent pool and its opulence, and therefore encouraged the retooled April performances to go forward.

While *Calisto*'s novelties are legion, the masque nonetheless offers an opportunity to understand more fully the interests and concerns of Charles II's court as they relate to the sponsorship of "recreational" theatricals, in particular those performed by children, during the first decade and a half of the Restoration era. As the foregoing examples demonstrate, the presentation of court masques and plays in the late 1660s and early 1670s was less about the articulation of defined ideological messages, as had been the case in the earlier Stuart period, than it was concerned with a projection of royal magnificence through spectacle. Certainly, some ideological elements can be found: the unabashed triumph of Pelham Humfrey's English song in *The Queen's Masque*, for example, or the more subtle exploration of the relationship between theatricality and royal power that is evident in *The Empress of Morocco*.[95] *Calisto* is also a potentially rich field for political interpretation, given its courtly context and its highly sexualized themes. But it is the spectacular qualities of these masques and plays—a function not so much of text as of performance—that come most unambiguously to the fore when we examine them as a group. Only in the case of *Calisto*, we should note, was a court performance of this kind memorialized in a publicly available printed text, something akin to those retrospectively configured masque libretti that were a regular phenomenon during the earlier part of the century, with their lists of the masquers' names (Crowne ostentatiously produces just such a list on sigs. b3^r–b4^v) and descriptions of the astounding stage effects. The latter feature is,

---

94 British Library, Add. MS 78307, f. 60^r (formerly Evelyn Papers, no. 1744; see Walkling, "Masque and Politics," 30 and 56 n. 25).

95 See Andrew R. Walkling, "The Apotheosis of Absolutism and the Interrupted Masque: Theater, Music, and Monarchy in Restoration England," in Julia Marciari Alexander and Catharine MacLeod, eds., *Politics, Transgression, and Representation at the Court of Charles II* (New Haven: Yale University Press, 2007), 193–231, esp. pp. 197–205.

of course, absent from the *Calisto* playbook, since that aspect of the spectacle was prominently lacking from all Restoration-era performances put on at the poorly equipped Hall Theatre. The playbook seems to call for only two basic scenic locales: that of the Prologue (a pair of shutters and side wings showing "ye Prosspect of Somersett House and ye Thames"[96]), and the generalized rural "ARCADIA" (sig. b4^v) in which all of the main play and the *intermèdes* are set.[97] Only one other scene-related stage direction is given in the playbook: the second *intermède* is said to take place "*near the Vale, whither the Winds carryed* Calisto" (p. 24), later described by the chorus as "*this inchanted Grove*" (p. 25). But there is no indication that an actual change of scenery was effected here: rather, it may have involved the introduction of a moveable (possibly three-dimensional) object, within which Calisto could be imprisoned by the "*Winds*" at Jupiter's command (p. 23), and which could then have been wheeled partway off the stage, allowing the *intermède* immediately following to occur "*near*" it. Aside from this rather low-tech effect, the only visually spectacular moments in the masque are accomplished by the opening of an upper discovery space: at the climax of the Prologue "A Temple of Fame appears" (sig. b2^r), and in the final *intermède*, the same space is opened to reveal the "Heav'n ... fill'd with Gods and Goddesses" (p. 81), and "*Jupiter* ... descend[s] out of the Heaven" (p. [82]) to deliver the Epilogue.[98] In actuality, *Calisto* seems to have presented a bit more scenic variation than the playbook suggests: the entries in an "Extraordinary Account" of payments to carpenters and to the painter Robert Streeter give a number of interesting details about the preparations for the production (see Table 2.3).[99]

In this document, we learn that besides the Somerset (here called "Denmark") House scene, Streeter painted a scene of "boscage" of slightly narrower dimensions, and that there was in addition an "arbour" scene (which apparently did

---

96 LC5/141, p. 551 (*Register*, no. 892), the general warrant to the Office of Works for alterations to the Hall Theatre. The dating of this document, 25 January 1675, is problematic, given that some of the work ordered therein appears already to have been completed in November and December: see Table 2.3, and n. 114, below.

97 The scenic divisions of the first act (the only act to have any such divisions) appear to be French scenes, requiring no change of locale, and the transition to each *intermède* simply involves the entrance of the singing pastoral characters after the speaking actors have left the stage.

98 In Act 3, a group of "*Airy Spirits*" enter and "*seize* Juno" (p. 36) at Jupiter's behest, but this does not seem to have involved any flying or other spectacular effects. We might compare the moment in the operatic version of *The Tempest* (1674), Act 4, scene 3, where Prospero "*stamps, and many Spirits appear*," who then usher the Courtier characters to their assigned prisons in caves at the rear of the stage: see *The Tempest, Or the Enchanted Island* (London: Henry Herringman, 1674), 66.

99 WORK5/24, ff. 408–20 (*Register*, no. 873) and E351/3288. See the more detailed discussion of the *Calisto* scenery in Boswell, 208–14. Streeter, a versatile artist, was also one of London's most respected decorative painters: for a catalogue of his known and attributed works, both extant and lost, see the anonymous "Editorial" article "Robert Streater," *Burlington Magazine* 84 (1944): 2–12; this article does not, however, consider the court theatrical records in its efforts to establish a comprehensive inventory of Streeter's output. Information specifically on Streeter's decorative work can be found in Edward Croft-Murray, *Decorative Painting in England, 1537–1837* (2 vols.: London: Country Life, 1962), 1: 226–27.

Table 2.3 Digest of work on stage and scenery for *Calisto*, November 1674–February 1675

A. Stage (CARPENTERS)

  1. floor

N   • boards taken up, planed, relaid

  2. enlargement

N   • enlarged 1 yard into pit; front end boarded

  3. trap door

N   • new door and frame installed

B. Scenes (CARPENTERS; RICHARD RIDER, *master carpenter*; ROBERT STREETER, *serjeant painter*)

  1. proscenium arch *(see below, under "wings")*

N   • CARPENTERS: scaffold built for taking arch down for enlargement

JF   • STREETER: painting addition to arch; repairs [£5]

  2. wings {**"To widen the whole stage by drawing Back the side sceenes & altering the frames & Gro[o]ves accordingly"**}

N   • CARPENTERS: scenes taken down and reduced; grooves shortened

JF   • STREETER: cleaning wall between wings, painting color (twice), painting boscage [£3]

  3. shutters

N   • CARPENTERS: height(?) raised

D   • CARPENTERS: new floor built beside shutters for drawing them back [50']

JF   • CARPENTERS: grooves built above and below for "Denmark" House and arbor; scenes installed

JF   • CARPENTERS: *lighting*: backs lined for putting up lights

    a. Somerset/"Denmark" House {**"To make a new paire & releiues rep^rsentinge ye Prosspect of Somersett House & ye Thames"**}

JF   • RIDER: main frame [14' 9" x 15']; pr. side frames [14' 9" x 4' ea.]

JF   • STREETER: painting scene [£12]

    b. arbor

JF   • CARPENTERS: edges cut (?on front main frame)

JF   • RIDER: main frame (front) [14' x 15']; main frame (back) [14' 9" x 15']; pr. side frames (back) [14' 9" x 4' ea.]

    c. boscage {**"To make a new paire of shutters of Boscage"**}

JF   • RIDER: main frame [13' x 15']; pr. side frames [13' x 4' ea.]

JF   • STREETER: painting scene [£10]

  4. clouds {**"To alter all the Cloudes aboue suiteable to the same by heightheninge them and ading to them"; "To make an openinge for a Heaven aboue with all the sceenes of Cloudes & shutter of Cloudes necessary"; "To make Seates for ye Goddesses & diverse Releiues proper for that rep^rsentacõn"**}

N   • CARPENTERS: clouds taken down; boarding behind

D   • CARPENTERS: hanging "circular clouds"; installing pr. shutters with new grooves

D   • CARPENTERS: stairs into clouds installed [8 steps]

JF   • CARPENTERS: edges cut

JF   • CARPENTERS: "circular seats" for goddesses installed

JF   • CARPENTERS: relieves installed

JF   • CARPENTERS: *lighting*: degrees built behind back clouds for setting lights

JF   • CARPENTERS: *lighting*: sconces and candlesticks nailed to backs

JF   • RIDER: main frame [13' x 15']; pr. side frames [13' x 4' ea.]

(Continued)

JF	• STREETER: painting 139 yards [£17 7s 6d]
JF	• STREETER: painting clouds in front of seats [*]

    5. upper discovery space

      a. Temple of Fame {"**To make a Temple in the Cloudes with sceenes of Varnished silke & places for lights for ye same**"}

JF	• CARPENTERS: *lighting*: boarding at rear for mounting of sconces and candlesticks
JF	• RIDER: main frame [11' 6" x 7' 6"]; pr. open side frames [11' 6" x 3' ea.]; pr. side frames [11' 6" x 3' ea.]; pr. side frames [13' x 4' ea.]; pr. side frames [13' x 4' ea.]
JF	• STREETER: painting scene [£5]

      b. glory

JF	• CARPENTERS: *lighting*: frame with degrees built for lights behind
JF	• RIDER: open back frame [11' 6" x 7' 6"]; frame for taffeta [3' 6" x 3' 6"]
JF	• STREETER: providing taffeta [12s]

    6. miscellaneous scenery

      a. flowery bank[a]

JF	• CARPENTERS: edges cut
JF	• STREETER: painting scene [*]

      b. peacock[b]; eagle[c]; vine[d]

JF	• STREETER: painting scene [*]

C. Accommodations for Music (CARPENTERS)

    1. band

N	• music seats dismantled; 2 floors laid; new floor with several degrees

    2. kettledrum

JF	• frame built [4']

---

* Total for five items (clouds; flowery bank; peacock; eagle; vine): £3.

Key:
Sources: WORK5/24, ff. 408–20 ("Extraordinary Account"):
N = account for November
D = account for December
JF = account for January–February
{} = quotation from LC5/141, p. 551 (Lord Chamberlain's warrant to the Office of Works, dated 24 January 1675)
(*N.B.* see Boswell, *The Restoration Court Stage*, 236 and 252–55 for transcriptions.)

---

[a] ?Moveable scene representing "*the Vale, whither the Winds carryed* Calisto" (Act 2).
[b] ?Moveable chariot for Juno.
[c] ?Moveable chariot for Jupiter.
[d] ?Canopy for Calisto and Nyphe (fifth *intermède*).

not require Streeter's attention), consisting of the usual back frame and pair of side frames—the same size as the Denmark House scene—as well as a cut-out front frame. A good deal of work was done on the clouds, and a relatively simple "glory" was created for the appearance of heaven at the end. Of greater interest is the Temple of Fame from the Prologue, which seems to have entailed a complex perspective effect requiring a main frame 11½ feet high by 7½ feet wide, plus

106 *"Their greatest gallantry imaginable"*

two pairs of side frames of the same height, each piece being 3 feet wide, plus two more pairs of side frames measuring 13 feet by 4 feet per piece. Because no actors appeared in the Temple (unlike in the heaven later on), it may have been possible to create an impressive visual effect using a deep perspective to simulate a supposedly vast structure. Alongside these scenic creations, John Webb's proscenium arch was widened, with Streeter painting the inserted section and making repairs to the decade-old structure, and the artist also decorated several smaller items, including a "flory banke" (possibly the moveable vale, discussed above), for which the carpenters created a specially cut edge; a peacock (possibly a wheeled chariot for Juno); an eagle (the same for Jupiter, perhaps to be used at the beginning of the Epilogue); and a "Vine" (perhaps the "Canopy, supported by *Africans*" [p. 81] under which Calisto and Nyphe are paraded in the fifth *intermède*). None of these can have been especially complicated, since the artist was paid only £3 for all four items plus some additional work on a small piece of cloud scenery.[100] Finally, the account shows that the stage was equipped with "a new Dore & frame in ye floore of ye said stage for ye sinkeing vnderneath ye same," apparently replacing or supplementing the trap created in the spring of 1673, possibly for *The Empress of Morocco* (see n. 58, above), although the use of such a device is nowhere indicated in the *Calisto* playbook.[101]

Yet even when these spectacular elements are taken into account, it is evident that large parts of the masque went by without any scene changes or machine effects whatsoever. Indeed, the amount of spectacle in *Calisto* is considerably more limited than that in the much vaunted *Empress of Morocco* production of two years before which, as we have noted, was itself subject to quite strict limitations. How, then, did *Calisto* and its predecessor entertainments contrive to offer an experience of spectacle to their audiences? The answer can be found not so much in the plays' verbal and musical rhetoric, or even in their staging, but in the physical presence of the performers themselves. In exploring the 1675 production, Eleanore Boswell has called the costumes "undeniably the greatest glory of *Calisto*," and estimates their total cost at over £5000.[102] Only some £2700 of this amount can be documented using the extant household accounts: nearly all of the most elaborately dressed performers appear to have provided their own habits, and thus we have no certain record of the costumes' materials or appearance.[103]

---

100 It should be noted that Streeter was not in the best of health during the preparations for *Calisto*: on 20 January 1675 John Evelyn recounts that, after having visited and prayed with his friend Margaret Blagge, he went "to see Mr. *Streeter* that excellent Painter of Perspective &c: & *Landscip*, to comfort, & encourage him to be cut for the stone, with which that honest man was exceedingly afflicted" (Evelyn, *Diary*, 4: 51–52).

101 In February 1679, the carpenters were paid for "altering a trapp doore, in the middle of the stage, and makeing it good againe as it was" (WORK5/30, f. 116^r [*Register*, no. 1073]).

102 Boswell, 214; her discussion of the costumes in on pp. 214–19.

103 This includes all but one of the twelve courtly ladies in the production, as well as the former royal mistress Mary Davis (who sang the parts of Thames and the shepherdess Sylvia). By contrast, the court expended £176 17s 11½d of its own money to deck out six of the eight(?) gentlemen as

Our one useful piece of evidence is the attire of Margaret Blagge, who, alone among the court ladies, was insufficiently well endowed to supply a rich garment of her own. Blagge's Diana costume cost the court £247 12s 2d for the fabric, plus £8 for its construction by the royal tailor John Allan, as well as £25 for her rich feathered headdress and £3 18s for a quiver, bow, and arrows.[104] But even more stunning was the extraordinary lapidary wealth with which the young lady was decked. John Evelyn took particular note of this feature when he attended rehearsals in December: on the 15th (the same day that Blagge's costume was first delivered from the Great Wardrobe for her use[105]) he remarked that the ladies "were all covered with *Jewels*,"[106] and a week later he recounted that Blagge

> had about her neere 20000 pounds worth of *Jewells*, of which one she lost, borrowed of the Countesse of Suffolck, worth about 80 pounds, which the *Duke* [of York] made good; & indeede the presse of people was so greate, that it was a wonder she lost no more."[107]

Certainly, Evelyn's estimate of £20,000 for the value of the jewels on his young friend's costume seems excessive, but when we consider that she was only one of twelve courtly ladies in the production, we can begin to appreciate the visual magnificence to which the audience was treated. Of course, sartorial splendor had always been an important element of court masques from their earliest beginnings in the Tudor period, but it is instructive to note how frequently this feature was remarked upon by Restoration commentators when they spoke of the entertainments we have been discussing (some of which, in point of fact, were not properly masques at all), and even of some of the non-dramatic balls.[108] As we have

---

"Roman Combatants" in the Prologue (LC9/274, pp. 254, 255, 259, 261, 270, 271, 273, and 293; see Boswell, 321).

104 LC9/274, pp. 241 (gold brocade), 242 (lace), 252 (imported Spanish lace), 272 (quiver/bow/ arrows), 289 (tailor's bill), and 293 (feathers); see Boswell, 323–24. Blagge may also have played the (singing) role of the Third African Woman in the fifth *intermède*: see Walkling, "Masque and Politics," 45; this costume was considerably cheaper at £13 (LC9/274, pp. 252, 269, and 272; see Boswell, 335). In *The Life of Mrs. Godolphin* (ed. Sampson, p. 55; see n. 6, above), John Evelyn records that "I have a particular Accompt still by me, of the Rich *Aparell* & *Robes* she had on her, amounting (besids the *Pearles*, & Precious-stones) to above 300ᵗᵇ."

105 See Walkling, "Masque and Politics," 43–44 (Table 3).

106 Evelyn, *Diary*, 4: 50.

107 Evelyn, *Diary*, 4: 51. Compare Evelyn's account of this incident in his *Life of Mrs. Godolphin* (ed. Sampson, p. 55): "a Disaster there hapn'd which Extreamely Concern'd her, and that was the losse of a *Diamond* of Considerable Value, which had ben lent her by the *Countesse* of *Suffolck*: The stage was imediately Swep't, and dilligent search made to find it; but without Successe: So as probably, it had ben taken from her, as she was often inviron'd, with that infinite Crowde, which 'tis impossible to avoid upon Such Occasions: But, the losse was soone repaird; for his R. *Highnesse* (Understanding, the trouble she was in,) generously Sent her wherewith to make my Lady *Suffolck* a present of as good a Jewel."

108 A year and a half after *Calisto*, in November 1676, Grace, Lady Chaworth reported in a letter to her brother that "the clothes last night at the Queenes birth-night ball was infinite rich, espeicially

108 *"Their greatest gallantry imaginable"*

already observed, actual estimates of the value of jewels in particular, including the wildly disparate figures of £200,000 and £40,000 for Lady Castlemaine in *Horace*, Evelyn's £20,000 for Margaret Blagge in *Calisto*,[109] and the £30,000 worn by Mrs. (?Jane) Fox at Lord Sunderland's court ballet in 1686 are probably too subjective to be taken seriously,[110] but such phrases as "most rich and antique dresses" (Pepys: the "fine Mask at Court," 1665), "infinitely gallant ... in their richly imbrodred, most becoming Vests" (Evelyn: the "magnificent Ball or Masque," 1667), "[t]he excessive galantry of the Ladies was infinite" (Evelyn: *Horace*, 1668), "to amazement wonderfully deck'd with Jewels and Diamonds" (*The Gracious Answer ... To the Poor-Whores Petition: Horace*), "extraordinarily glorious and covered with jewels" (newsletter: *The Faithful Shepherdess*, 1670), "their greatest gallantry imaginable" (newsletter: *The Queen's Masque*, 1671), "infinite rich" (Lady Chaworth: Catherine of Braganza's birthday ball, 1676), "not ... seene so brave & rich in apparell since his Majesties restauration" (John Evelyn: Catherine of Braganza's birthday ball, 1684), or "aray'd in all the glory & riches of the Indies" (James Fraser: Lord Sunderland's court ballet, 1686)[111] nonetheless help to convey, however imperfectly, a sense of the visual feast that these court performances offered.[112]

The display of jewels and other ornaments on the Whitehall stage as a means of advertising the luxury of the Restoration court would undoubtedly have been an effective strategy even in instances where, as with *The Indian Emperor* in 1668, "the Company is made very private, soe as few attempt to gett in."[113] In part,

---

M[is] Phraser [*i.e.* Carey Fraser, who had appeared in *Calisto*] who put downe all for a gowne black velvet imbroydered with all sorts of slips inbost worke of gold and silver and peticote one broad ermine and gold lace all over ... they say cost 800*l*" (HMC *Rutland* 2: 32: see Chapter 1, n. 56, above).

109 It is worth observing that the lost jewel said to be worth £80, and for which "dilligent search" was made, constituted only 1/250 of the full value estimated by Evelyn for all of Margaret Blagge's lapidary adornments.

110 See pp. 79–80, 107, and 313 (Appendix B). Compare also Edward Lake's estimate of £40,000 for the value of the jewels given by William of Orange to Princess Mary upon their wedding and worn by the latter a few days later at the ball on 15 November 1677 (see p. 44). As Peter Beal points out (*In Praise of Scribes*, 187 n. 106), the crown jewels, which supposedly formed part of Lady Castlemaine's attire in *Horace*, had cost in their entirety no more than about £22,000 (and perhaps only half as much) when they were created in 1661.

111 See Chapter 1, nn. 22 and 75; this chapter, nn. 27, 28, and 32; Chapter 1, n. 121; this chapter, n. 108; and Chapter 1, n. 59, above, and Appendix B. Only for the court performances of *The Indian Emperor* and *The Empress of Morocco*—among the least well-documented productions in any case—do we have no such statements.

112 See Richard Flecknoe's poem "*On Mistress* Stuarts *dancing in* Whitehall, *all shining with Jewels*," first published in Flecknoe's *Epigrams of All Sorts* (London: for the Author, 1669), 26–27. Frances Teresa Stuart is known to have danced, probably wearing jewels given her by Charles II, at the ball on 15 November 1666 (see Table 1.1), about four and a half months before she eloped and became Duchess of Richmond and Lennox.

113 Harry Ransom Center, PFORZ-MS-0445, p. 3 (see [Thibaudeau], ed., *The Bulstrode Papers*, 1: 19).

Youthful "recreational" theatrics, 1668–75   109

this was due to the publicity surrounding such events, which would have been effective enough that those unable to attend might be overawed simply by the hyperbolic descriptions of the finery. But in most instances it was in the court's interest to encourage large crowds of (socially suitable) witnesses to actually view the splendor with their own eyes. We can see this in the case of *Calisto*, where the early preparations included having the carpenters add two solidly constructed galleries to the sides of the Hall Theatre, each 36 feet long by 4½ feet wide and containing two rows of benches,[114] and set up railings and partitions outside the theatre to keep the anticipated crowd under control.[115] Yet the grand performances appear always to have been limited in number—for *Calisto*, we know certainly of only four: two during Lent (prior to 9 March) and two of the revised version, after Easter. To compensate for this possibly intentional dearth of formal presentations, the court opened rehearsals to the public—hence Crowne's statement that audiences could have seen *Calisto* as many as 20 or 30 times (see n. 83, above). Indeed, this occurred quite early in the production process, when the show would have appeared in a very unpolished and fragmentary form. The design seems to have been to create a second tier, so to speak, of staged extravagance whose purpose was almost certainly not dramatic entertainment as such, but rather the display of lavishly costumed noble bodies—which also incidentally helped to foster anticipation for the eventual finished product. Such spectacles may have been open to any curious onlookers who happened to be passing through Whitehall at the time, and only rarely were they recorded for posterity, for example in John Evelyn's uniquely voluminous reminiscences, or more publicly in the newsletters when the royal entourage chose to drop by. Read alongside Crowne's more general—albeit admittedly self-serving—report of "throngs of Persons of the greatest Quality" following "innumerable Rehearsals and all the Representations," Evelyn's remarks regarding the "greate ... presse of people" and "that infinite Crowde, which 'tis impossible to avoid upon Such Occasions" (see n. 107, above) offer some glimpse of the goings-on at the *Calisto* rehearsals,

114 These galleries were to be "on each side ranginge with the Gallery at ye End" (LC5/141, p. 551). See WORK5/24 (Extraordinary Account, December; see n. 99, above): masons: "cutting several̶l̶ holes in ye stone wa̶l̶l̶s of ye Theatre for ye fastening of ye trusses ... to supporte ye new galleryes there"; carpenters: "frameing & putting vp 8 trusses of timber for ye supporteing ye galleries on each side ye pitt & makeing ye said galleries each 36 fo^{te} long 4 fo^{te} & a halfe wide & boarding vp ye foresides thereof & vnderneath ye degrees, makeing two degrees for seates in ye said galleryes at ye whole length of ye galleries[;] takeing down ye boarding of three windowes behind ye galleries for ye fastening of ye timber worke of ye said trusses and putting in 5 peeces of timber into ye Iambs of ye said windowes." See also the order to the plasterers in the same month for "plaistering with lime and haire ye slitt Deale lineing behind ye degrees in ye new gallery made in ye theater" (WORK5/24, f. 114^v [*Register*, no. 882]).

115 See for example the order of April 1675 to the carpenters for "putting up a boarded fence in ye passage to Whitehall bridge before ye Theater dore 25 foo^t in length, putting up railes with flapps to them att ye Staire head going to ye Kings Guard Chamber & in ye guard Chamber & att ye Theatree [*sic*] dore next ye guard Chamber to keepe ye people from Crowding into ye Theatre" (WORK5/25, f. 26^r [*Register*, no. 915]).

110 *"Their greatest gallantry imaginable"*

and would likely be applicable to rehearsals for the other court entertainments we have been discussing.[116] In the case of *Calisto*, we should recall that the rehearsal of 15 December was probably the first in which the ladies were in costume. The donning of full masquing attire so early in the rehearsal process may have been driven in part by the need to clarify gesture and blocking in such bulky garments, especially given the Hall Theatre's relatively constricted acting space, but it also speaks to the court's desire to attract admiring bystanders, even if this involved the considerable risk of exposing thousands of pounds worth of jewels to potential loss or theft, as Margaret Blagge's experience on the 22nd demonstrates. How the young lady fared on the numerous subsequent rehearsal days in January, February, and April, we do not know, nor what mishaps might have befallen her fellow performers, who may have worn only their own, rather than borrowed, jewelry and thus could perhaps afford to be more casual about such things. Yet through it all, the court's propagandistic purposes were undoubtedly being served.[117]

Calisto represents a high point of the Restoration masquing tradition, as attested to by the enormous amount of interest, publicity, and expense surrounding its appearance, to say nothing of the unusually thorough documentation that survives.[118] None of the recreational courtly entertainments presented before or after 1675 left such a substantial impression on either the public consciousness or the archival record. This must be at least partly attributable to the fact that in combining a dramatic production presented by youthful courtly actors with a music-and-dance spectacular created exclusively for court performance and mounted with great fanfare, Crowne and Staggins's masque brings together elements from both of the strands of court entertainment we have been exploring. In this respect, it can be regarded as a kind of culmination of all that had preceded it, and, moreover, as a work that engages in a certain degree of generic and performative experimentation. But *Calisto*'s exceptional qualities do not end there. It is, in fact, a highly complex generic hybrid, blending the practices of earlier Restoration court theatricals with the more far-flung conventions of English court masque and French *comédie-* and *tragédie-ballet*. Such features as the pastoral rhetoric, the sung allegorical prologue, the amount of musical elaboration throughout, the

---

116 Note that Evelyn also seems to have witnessed a rehearsal for *The Queen's Masque* on 9 February 1671 (Evelyn, *Diary*, 3: 569–70; see p. 60, above), and perhaps one for *Ballet et Musique* or *Ariane* on 5 January 1674 (see pp. 234–36, below). For the possibility that the Earl of Burlington saw a rehearsal of *The Faithful Shepherdess* on 2 April 1670, four days before it was formally presented to the king and queen, see n. 34, above.

117 According to Evelyn, Blagge was only too eager to shed her "Rich *Aparell* & *Robes* ... of all which she im̄ediatly dispoil'd, & stript herself of, so soon as ever she could get cleare of the *Stage*" (*The Life of Mrs. Godolphin* [ed. Sampson], 55).

118 The verdict ultimately pronounced by Harris (*Transformations of Love*, 230) seems unnecessarily harsh: "For all its huge expense the project was sleazy and makeshift from the first. With no one capable of recreating the elaborate stage machinery of the earlier court theatre, the spectacle depended entirely on the costumes and scenery."

nature of the dancing, the extraordinary size of the cast and orchestra,[119] and even the issuance of both a retrospective printed playbook and a programme libretto for use at performances[120] reveal the influence of new ideas about the nature and purpose of court-sponsored musical-theatrical entertainments that were emerging in England during the mid-1670s. The novel form from which *Calisto* derived these elements was through-sung, balletic, performed by (adult) "occupational" singers and dancers, and, perhaps above all, overtly and unabashedly French. Indeed, French ballet and opera had already taken a primary place at court by the time *Calisto* was presented in 1675, and their influence can be observed not only in this work, but in other masque-like presentations of the later 1670s and the 1680s. These French entertainments at least partially supplanted the courtly productions of the first decade and a half of Charles II's reign, but their generic and performative distinctiveness from the "recreational" balls, plays, and masques that we are exploring here dictates that they be considered in Part II, where they will emerge as part of a separate, if parallel, strand in the development of musical theatre during the Restoration period.

119 See Walkling, "Masque and Politics," esp. Tables 2 and 5. Among other tasks, the carpenters were ordered "To enclose the front of the pitt next the stage for the musick the whole breadth of ye house" (LC5/141, p. 551), creating an orchestra pit some 39½ feet wide, assuming the measurements given in John Webb's 1665 plan can be relied upon.

120 John Crowne, *The Prologue to Calistho, with the Chorus's Between the Acts* (London: n. pub., 1675).

3 Masques and plays at court after 1675

With its glorious display, its multitude of performers, and its prominence on the London social scene, *Calisto* certainly represents the high-water mark of theatrical splendor at the Restoration court. Subsequent entertainments were invariably mounted on a smaller scale, and hence at considerably reduced cost to the perpetually cash-strapped Charles II. This did not mean, however, that *Calisto* had no lasting impact on court theatrical productions going forward. Even with all its superficial splendor stripped away, Crowne and Staggins's masque had helped to solidify two important principles. First, it had demonstrated the value to the court of placing its youngest members on the stage not simply as an exercise meant to instill poise and deportment, but rather explicitly for public consumption—and hence augmented as necessary by trained "occupational" performers whose presence would inevitably enhance production values. Second, it established a protocol for generic experimentation that was to have near-term consequences and that would also extend into the next decade. Even without recourse to a bottomless purse, the court would be able to seek out new opportunities for self-promotion by means of theatrical performances that transcended conventional norms, and hence had the potential to keep audiences interested.

Both of these principles emerge in the first court production known to have been mounted after *Calisto*: a three-act French comedy entitled *Rare en Tout*, with a libretto by the Huguenot expatriate novelist Anne de La Roche-Guilhen[1] and

---

1 Anne de La Roche-Guilhen, *Rare en Tout: Comedie Meslée de Musique Et de Balets Representée devant Sa Majesté Sur le Theatre Royal De Whitehall* ("Londres": Jacques Magnes and Richard Bentley, 1677); modern editions are in Perry Gethner, ed., *Femmes dramaturges en France (1650–1750)* (Biblio 17, no. 79; Paris: Biblio 17, 1993), 127–80, and by Juliette Cherbuliez in Aurore Evain, Perry Gethner, and Henriette Goldwyn, eds., *Théâtre de Femmes de l'Ancien Régime*, vol. 2, *XVIIe Siècle* (La Cité des Dames; Saint-Étienne: Publications de l'Université de Saint-Étienne, 2008) 467–529. An English translation of the former edition is in Perry Gethner, ed., *The Lunatic Lover and Other Plays by French Women of the 17th and 18th Centuries* (Portsmouth, NH: Heinemann, 1994), 89–138. The work is briefly discussed in W. J. Lawrence, "Rare en Tout, 1677; and James Paisible," *The Musical Antiquary* 2 (1910–11): 57–58 and Spire Pitou, "A Forgotten Play: La Roche-Guilhen's 'Rare en tout' (1677)," *Modern Language Notes* 72 (1957): 357–59 (which, however, contains a number of errors). For consideration of La Roche's biography and works, see Alexandre Calame, *Anne de La Roche-Guilhen: Romancière Huguenote 1644–1707*

Masques and plays at court after 1675 113

music by the French wind player Jacques Paisible (whose career we will explore further in Chapter 7). *Rare en Tout* was presented as part of Charles II's 1677 birthday celebration, and hence more than two years after *Calisto*. It is nowhere near as well documented as the earlier work: an order survives for the preparation of the Hall Theatre,[2] and among the Lord Steward's records is a creditor for the supply of provisions "pro le Ball Menss Maij 1677."[3] The most frequently cited document is an order dated 22 May for "Musitians to attend y[e] ffrench Comœdie," in which the Lord Chamberlain Henry Bennet, 1st Earl of Arlington, commands Matthew Locke ("officiat[ing]" for the Master of the Music Nicholas Staggins, who was traveling abroad at the time) to ensure that

> all his Ma[ties] Musitian [*sic*] doe attend to[e] practice in y[e] Theater at Whitehall at such tymes as Madame Le Roch [& Mr Paisible *interlined*] shall appoynt for y[e] practicenig [*sic*] of such Musick as is to be in y[e] ffrench Comedy to be acted before his Ma[tie] on y[e] Nyne & twentieth of May instant[.][4]

The employment of "all his Ma[ties] Musitian[s]," coupled with Arlington's stern injunction to Locke to "giue notice unto them that they fayle not hereof," testifies to the event's perceived importance. On the other hand, the stated plan to perform the work on Charles II's actual birthday (Tuesday the 29th) appears to have hit a snag, since both of the surviving reports of the occasion appear to indicate a one-day postponement: on 31 May, the French ambassador Honoré Courtin informed Simon Arnauld, Seigneur de Pomponne, the French Secrétaire d'État pour les Affaires Étrangères, "C'estoit avant *hier* le jour de la naissance du Roy de la Grande Bretagne. … On eut le soir une petite comédie françoise à Withal avec des entrées de ballet et des récits,"[5] and John Verney, writing to his brother Edmund on the same day, pointedly noted that "On *Wednesday* his Majesty's birth night was some gallantry at Whitehall, where was acted a French opera."[6] W. J. Lawrence, considering only Verney's statement, speculates that this might represent an error,[7] but such postponements were not altogether uncommon, as we have already seen

---

(Études de Philologie et d'Histoire, 24; Geneva: Droz, 1972); Moses Hardin, *Modern Techniques in a Seventeenth-Century Writer: Anne de la Roche-Guilhen* (Bern: Peter Lang, 1997); and Amelia Sanz, "Anne de la Roche-Guilhem, 'Rare en Tout'," in Jean Delisle, ed., *Portraits de Traductrices* (Ottawa: Presses de l'Université d'Ottawa; Artois: Artois Presses Université, 2002), 55–85.

2 LC5/142, p. 40 (28 May 1677: *Register*, no. 1013).

3 LS8/13, ff. [143][r]–[148][r] (May 1677: not in *Register*; see Boswell, 94); see also the deleted account on ff. [70][r]–[74][v]. Items delivered include bread, beer and wine, wax and tallow candles, and charcoal.

4 LC5/142, p. 38 (22 May 1677: *Register*, no. 1010; Ashbee, 1: 171–72).

5 Archives du Ministère des Affaires Étrangères, Paris, Correspondance Politique: Angleterre 123, f. 266[v] (dated 10 June, New Style), quoted in René Ternois, ed., *Saint-Évremond: Lettres* (2 vols.: Paris: Marcel Didier, 1967–68), 2: 194 n. 3 (my emphasis).

6 HMC *Verney* (see Chapter 2, n. 90, above), 469 (my emphasis).

7 W. J. Lawrence, "Early French Players in England," in *idem*, *The Elizabethan Playhouse and Other Studies* (2 vols.: Stratford-upon-Avon: Shakespeare Head Press, 1912–13; rpt. New York: Russell & Russell, 1963), 1: 125–56, p. 147.

114   *"Their greatest gallantry imaginable"*

in the various (often much longer) delays that plagued *The Queen's Masque* in 1671, *Calisto* in 1675, and Lord Sunderland's court ballet in 1684.

Despite John Verney's description of it as an "opera," *Rare en Tout* is in fact a curious generic amalgam whose features are indebted to the *comédie-ballet* form, in which a spoken play is embellished with both occasional diegetic songs and more complex inter-act *divertissements* that are sometimes also diegetically introduced.[8] The first and second acts of *Rare en Tout* are followed by grand entertainments of singing and dancing, presented for the *"Chanteuse Angloise"* Isabelle by her respective suitors, the French singer Tirsis and the Gascon adventurer Rare en Tout.[9] Moreover, each suitor interacts with Isabelle in song during the main play: the otherwise invisible Tirsis shares a pair of stanzas with her in Act 1, and Rare en Tout engages the lady in a kind of singing contest, involving two French songs and two unspecified *"air*[s] *Anglois"* (p. 21), that forms what Perry Gethner calls "le centre de la pièce"[10] and seals, at least for a time, the characters' mutual attraction. In certain respects, *Rare en Tout* adheres to the generic and organizational formulae laid out in *Calisto*. Like the 1675 masque, it emanates from a two-person creative team and focuses the bulk of its musical material in an allegorical prologue and a series of *intermèdes*, culminating in a grand concluding pastoral entertainment. Both works, moreover, incorporate masque-like elements, such as the acknowledgement of the king's physical presence by the allegorized characters in the prologue[11] and the inclusion, in tandem with the final sung celebration, of a spoken epilogue (here *"l'amour fait un Discours aux dames"* in the audience[12]). On the other hand, *Rare en Tout* departs from the *Calisto* model in significant ways. It offers not a mythological pastoral, but rather a kind of parlor comedy, incorporating ultimately superfluous romantic elements.[13] Furthermore, the balance of music and speech in the opening and concluding episodes is oddly configured: in the prologue, the epideictic dialogue between Europe and Thames—a

---

8   Gethner, ed., *Femmes dramaturges*, 132.

9   In the first instance, an entertainment of singing tritons and nereids and dancing fishermen (pp. 14–16), we learn earlier from Isabelle's maid Finette that "On regalle Madame au bord de la Thamise: / D'instruments concertez avec de belles voix, / Ensuite nous verrons au son de six hautbois, / Dancer quelques pescheurs sur un air agréable, / Cela n'a-t-il pas l'air d'une feste admirable" (p. 9). The second *intermède*, of lovers (pp. 27–29), is given in *"la maison de rare en tout qui donne a sa maitresse le divertissement d'un concert fort agreable, & d'une entrée de matassins"* (p. 27).

10   Gethner, ed., *Femmes dramaturges*, 133. As Pitou observes (p. 359), "The third act contains no singing, Rare-en-tout's callous nature leaving no room for harmony."

11   *Rare en Tout*, sig. A4[r]: La Thamise informs L'Europe, "Je vois qu'il porte icy ses pas, / La fortune te favorise, / Déja de [s]on aspect tu me parois surprise, / Quand tu le verras mieux que ne sera ce pas."

12   *Ibid.*, 39–40; this speech, *"qui sert d'Epilogue,"* comes before rather than after the final sung portion of the work.

13   They are superfluous in the sense that Rare en Tout eventually loses his beloved when she overhears him admitting to Climène that "Je suis presentement amoureux d'Isabelle; / Mais je pouray changer pour une autre plus belle, / Et selon que l'amour guidera mes regards, / Mes Victimes pourront courir quelques hazards" (p. 32). See Gethner's exploration of Rare en Tout as an exemplar of the *"petit-maître"* (*i.e.* fop) character type (*Femmes dramaturges*, 131–32).

Masques and plays at court after 1675 115

component that, according to the convention prevailing in both England and France, would normally have been sung—appears here to have been spoken, while the final *intermède* commences with l'Amour's epilogue-like address to the ladies before the music resumes in order to allow a group of shepherds, shepherdesses, and satyrs to "*finisse[z] la Comedie par des Chants & des Dances.*" Finally, it must be remembered that La Roche and Paisible's work is on a considerably smaller scale than its precursor,[14] is dominated by professional performers rather than court amateurs, and is actually spoken/sung in French.

It is hard to say with certainty who would have performed the onstage parts in *Rare en Tout*. The main speaking cast is quite small, requiring only three principal actors (the males Rare en Tout and his servant La Treille, and the female servant Finette). A further two women may have been needed to share the minor roles of Europe, Thames, l'Amour, and the jilted "*Chanteuse Françoise*" Climène (who delivers only a single speech at the beginning of Act 3, and never actually sings anything[15]). In fact, an unidentified French acting troupe seems to have been in England at the time: in February the Office of Works was ordered to prepare the Hall Theatre "as the ffrench Comœdians shall desire you for theire Accomodation,"[16] and not long afterwards the epilogue to the Dorset Garden play *The French Conjurer* has the farcical title character Monsieur (performed by Anthony Leigh) satirically proclaim that "*De Wit, de Sense, de Fame, and de Renown, / Be in de* French *Troop at toder end o'Town,*"[17] *i.e.* at Whitehall. Yet while a few of these French actors may have been pressed into service for the one-off court event for the king's birthday, the remainder of the performers in *Rare en Tout* would likely have been drawn from other sources. With the exception of the title character—who as we have observed, performs two solo songs, one in French and one in English—a strict distinction between actors and singers prevails in the production. The musical portions of the prologue and *intermèdes*

---

14 Act 1, scene 1 consists of a lengthy expository monologue by Rare en Tout's servant La Treille, a feature perhaps meant to compensate for the work's compacted three-act structure.

15 Having observed (*Femmes dramaturges*, 133) that "Climène fut le nom de guerre d'un des sopranos français les plus renommés de l'époque, Mlle Brigogne," Gethner goes on to point out, rather unhelpfully, that "nous ne savons pas si Mlle Brigogne joua le rôle de Climène, qui semblerait lui avoir convenu" (p. 135).

16 LC5/141, p. 528 (5 February 1677: *Register*, no. 995).

17 T[homas] P[orter], *The French Conjurer. A Comedy. As it is Acted At the Duke of York's Theatre* (London: L. Curtis, 1678), [47]; for a brief discussion, see Lawrence, "Early French Players," 146–47. The playbook was licensed for publication on 2 August 1677, and the performance is tentatively dated to June in Van Lennep, ed., *The London Stage* (1: 257–58), but Judith Milhous and Robert D. Hume ("Dating Play Premières from Publication Data, 1660–1700," *Harvard Library Bulletin* 22 [1974]: 374–405, p. 387) point out that the epilogue reference would have been relevant any time after the February order to the Office of Works. The epilogue contrasts the Duke's Company's outlay of "*Ten thousand pound*" to build Dorset Garden seven years earlier with the visiting French who, "*Like true Knight Erran, scorn so long a stay; / Act but a veek or fortnight, and away,*" although the actual length of the traveling company's sojourn would seem, by the scanty evidence, to have been somewhat longer than this couplet suggests.

116 *"Their greatest gallantry imaginable"*

would have required, besides the considerable instrumental forces of Charles II's musical establishment, a minimum of five professional singers (three men and two women[18]) able to present a range of solo and ensemble work, as well as a group of dancers who could have been either courtiers or professionals.

This leaves the two singing characters from the main drama for our consideration. Tirsis, whose part is fleeting, could easily have been performed by one of the male singers seen in the prologue and *intermèdes*. Isabelle, however, is a bit more problematic: as the play's principal love interest, who appears in all three acts and is meant to witness both the first and second *intermèdes*, she could not have been personated by one of the female singers inventoried above. In any event, her role is oddly configured, presenting her more as a kind of icon than as a dramatic character, a largely distant object of extravagant worship by both Rare en Tout and (by implication) the play's audience. Her sole responsibility is to perform three courtly songs—two in French and one in English—and to react in various ways to her suitors' speeches and actions,[19] all the while uttering not a single spoken line and maintaining a somewhat haughty but fundamentally passive demeanor in relation to the histrionic grandiloquence of her onstage companions, including even the minor character Climène. Despite being wooed for a time by the capricious Rare en Tout, Isabelle ultimately maintains an unsullied chastity—even doing so in a non-confrontational (and hence non-theatrical) manner by communicating her rejection of the faithless devotee through her servant Finette. Indeed, her strikingly masque-inflected part looks for all the world like something written to be performed by a courtier—probably a young woman of "quality" whose portrayal of the play's "*Chanteuse Angloise*" was intended to combine a personal display of courtly refinement and skill (albeit without dancing, as far as we can tell) with a broader compliment to Charles II's developing Anglo-French tastes. Thus, while it was certainly not a full-fledged production by a cast of courtly "recreational" performers such as those we have examined thus far, *Rare en Tout* might nonetheless be understood as a masque-like showcase for a single courtier, a kind of attenuated successor to the much more extravagant *Calisto* of two years earlier.

If we are seeking a possible candidate for the role of the French play's musically expressive but otherwise poised and unattainable beauty, Isabelle, we can

---

18 The prologue requires three "voix" of unidentified gender, singing solos and as a trio; the first *intermède* presents three (male) tritons and two (female) nereids; the second *intermède* has three "Hommes" and two "Femmes," who would seem to incorporate "Un Amant" (p. 27) and "Un autre Amant" (p. 28); the final *intermède* is a bit more diversified, containing for certain two shepherds, one shepherdess, and one satyr, but possibly dividing the shepherdess parts among two singers. The opening stage direction for the final *intermède* (p. 40) refers to "*Des Bergers des Bergeres & des Satires*" who "*paroissent des deux costez du Theatre*," but any additional satyrs were probably dancers. All of this is assuming that in every instance "Le Chœur" simply consists of the soloists singing together as an ensemble.

19 See for example pp. 7 ("*Isabelle regarde dédaigneusement Rare en tout, & s'esloigne de luy sans parler*") and 32 ("*Pandant que Rare-en-tout parle, Isabelle l'écoute & témoigne par ses actions, le mepris qu'elle a pour luy elle se retire ensuitte*").

hardly do better than the character's namesake and the dedicatee of La Roche's printed playbook, the nine- or ten-year-old Isabella Bennet, Duchess of Grafton. The daughter of Lord Chamberlain Arlington and child-bride of Henry Fitzroy, second son of Charles II and Barbara Villiers, Isabella was already an accomplished young lady who reputedly lived up to La Roche's praise of her as *"distinguer d'une maniere surprenante dans un age ou l'on est ordinairement inconnu au monde."*[20] In 1672, at her first marriage to Fitzroy[21] at the tender age of four or five, John Evelyn had described Isabella as "a Sweete Child, if ever there was any" and, at the couple's "remarriage" in 1679, he would call her "this sweetest, hopfullest, most beautifull child, & most vertuous too."[22] In May 1677 the duchess would have been approximately the same age as Princess Anne when she played Nyphe in *Calisto* in 1675 and (more uncertainly) as that of Lady Mary Tudor as Cupid in *Venus and Adonis* in c.1683. Although casting a prepubescent girl in the role of love interest to a lewd Gascon might strike us as more than a bit untoward, such a move really differs little in its essential character from the more ample bawdry of *Calisto*; both productions are, in any case, at pains to draw a bright line between chastity in peril and chastity actually violated.

It perhaps stands to reason that the Earl of Arlington might have sought to present a court entertainment built around his only child and heir (Isabella, already a duchess by marriage, would succeed her father as *suo jure* Countess of Arlington in 1685), who had been too young to appear in *Calisto*, despite the exalted social standing she had already attained by that time. As a committed Francophile, the Earl would presumably have favored the distinctive format of *Rare en Tout*,[23] and he appears to have entrusted the organization of the production to his friend the French expatriate Charles de Marguetel de Saint-Denis, Seigneur de Saint-Évremond, as is noted in Ambassador Courtin's report of the event.[24] Saint-Évremond, in turn,

---

20 *Rare en Tout*, sig. A2^r.

21 At the time of the marriage, Fitzroy was created Earl of Euston; he would become Duke of Grafton in 1675.

22 Evelyn, *Diary*, 3: 622 (1 August 1672); 4: 184 (6 November 1679); *cf.* La Roche's dedication (*Rare en Tout*, sig. A2^v): "l'on découvre en vous tout ce qui peut charmer, / La beauté, la douceur, l'esprit, la connoissance, / Et vous n'avez rien de l'enfance." The always-opinioned Evelyn goes on to lament the match between Charles's dissolute son and this young lady "who if my augurie deceave me not, will in few yeares be such a paragon, as were fit to make the Wife of the greatest Prince in Europe" (*cf.* the *Diary*, 4: 119 [10 September 1677], where he similarly characterizes her as "worthy for her beauty & vertue of the greatest Prince in Christendom"). As we have seen in Chapter 1, Isabella subsequently appeared in Catherine of Braganza's birthday ball on 15 November 1684 (see Table 1.1)—where one observer counted her among "The best dancers" (see p. 45, above)—and she was scheduled to perform in Lord Sunderland's court ballet on 15 February 1686 (see Table 1.3), but had to withdraw after her husband murdered the Earl of Shrewsbury's brother John Talbot in a duel.

23 For a good discussion of Arlington's cultural activities and priorities, see Helen Jacobsen, "Luxury Consumption, Cultural Politics, and the Career of the Earl of Arlington, 1660–1685," *Historical Journal* 52 (2009): 295–317.

24 "Tout cela tombe sur St. Evremont qui en paroissoit le directeur" (see n. 30, below). For a discussion of the relationship between Arlington and Saint-Évremond, see Quentin M. Hope, *Saint-Evremond and His Friends* (Geneva: Droz, 1999), 255–57.

118   *"Their greatest gallantry imaginable"*

may have been responsible for the choice of La Roche and Paisible as librettist and composer: as we shall see in Chapter 7, Paisible and Saint-Évremond remained active collaborators throughout the 1680s and 1690s, and La Roche was also a member of their circle, which formed in the mid-1670s around Hortense Mancini, Duchess Mazarin. La Roche, indeed, may have arrived in England in Mazarin's train in December 1675,[25] and she was evidently well known to Saint-Évremond, who twice mentions her in letters he wrote to Charlotte Beverweerd in the summer of 1677,[26] and who also refers to her in passing in his poem "Les Avantages de l'Angleterre."[27] Indeed the two writers had a good deal in common: both, despite their long residences in London, seem never to have mastered the English language, and they shared an association with the Paris bookseller Claude Barbin, who began publishing Saint-Évremond's works (without authorization) in 1670 and, between 1674 and 1683, would serve as La Roche's French publisher as well. Charlotte Beverweerd, we should note, was the Earl of Arlington's sister-in-law, and hence young Isabella's aunt, and her familiarity with La Roche may have been a result of the latter's own connection to Isabella, whom she is said to have served as governess.[28] This last connection, which neatly completes the quadrilateral relationship between La Roche, her patron and colleague Saint-Évremond, his friend Lord Chamberlain Arlington, and Arlington's accomplished daughter, enables us to imagine *Rare en Tout* as a very particular cultural and propagandistic project, "presented" to the king on his birthday by one of his leading court servants, while at the same time featuring that servant's precocious child, who also happened to be married, at least on paper, to one of the monarch's offspring. In order to cement her reputation as a budding courtier in her own right, Isabella would have been groomed, perhaps by La Roche herself, to show off her musical skills in both English and French, and to display a mastery of the latter tongue sufficient to enable her to interact effectively with the play's imported performers. Such an

---

25 Gethner, *Femmes dramaturges*, 129.

26 Pierre Des Maizeaux and Israel Silvestre, eds., *Oeuvres Meslées de M[r]. de Saint-Evremond, Publiées sur les Manuscrits de l'Auteur* (2 vols: London: Jacob Tonson, 1705), 2: 233 and 235; see Ternois, ed., *Saint-Évremond: Lettres*, 1: 307 and 312.

27 Des Maizeaux and Silvestre, eds., *Oeuvres Meslées*, 2: 649.

28 In a marginal note in *Oeuvres Meslées*, 2: 233, Pierre Des Maizeaux explains that "*Mademoiselle de La Roche Guilhen étoit alors auprès de la fille unique du Comte d'*Arlington, *mariée ensuite au duc de* Grafton." The precise chronology of this relationship is uncertain: La Roche's statement in her dedication of *Rare en Tout* to Isabella (sig. A2[r]) that "Je n'ay connu l'éclat de vos jeunes beautez, / Que d'une assez grande distance; ... *Mais Madame, quoy que je n'aye veu vostre aymable personne que dans une foule qui ne me laissoit rien de particulier, elle n'a pas fait moins d'impression sur mon cœur*" could be no more than a rhetorical nicety, or it might indicate that the closer relationship between the two hinted at by Des Maizeaux lay in the future. In any event, Isabella herself eventually became a full-fledged member of the Mazarin circle: her name is mentioned, for example, in Saint-Évremond's *Scene de Bassette* of c.1692 (see Table 7.2, below). La Roche appears to have left England in 1679, when she was issued a pass to travel to "parts beyond seas" (8 August: SP44/51, p. 283 [*Calendar of State Papers, Domestic 1679–80*: 351]), but she was permanently back in London after 1686, following Louis XIV's revocation of the Edict of Nantes.

accomplishment would likely have been easily achieved, given her parents' own linguistic and cultural cosmopolitanism.[29]

In the end, it appears that the producers' ambitions were not entirely realized, as both of the surviving notices of *Rare en Tout* imply that the play was not well received. Courtin expressed his opinion that "La Comédie estoit détestable, et la Musique ne valoit pas mieux. Tout cela tombe sur St. Evremont qui en paroissoit le directeur. Il fait ce qu'il peut pour se défendre de cette qualité."[30] John Verney was only slightly more generous, calling the work

> most pitifully done, so ill that the King was aweary on't, and some say it was not well contrived to entertain the English gentry, who came that night in honour to their King, with a lamentable ill-acted French play, when our English actors so much surpass; however, the dances and voices was pretty well performed.[31]

Courtin and Verney would probably have begun from different points as regards their basic attitudes toward the performance of French drama in England, and thus the unanimity of their condemnation implies that *Rare en Tout* may really have been poorly executed. How much the failure would have rubbed off on the work's promoters (including, if my surmise is correct, Arlington and his daughter) is debatable, although Courtin's remark that Saint-Évremond "peut pour se défendre" his association with the production—and perhaps the fact that *Rare en Tout* is never mentioned in Saint-Évremond's own voluminous writings—hints at the chastening effect of such a mishandled opportunity. The subsequent impact of the play is effectively nil: Saint-Évremond appears to have retreated into his own private, domestic operatic experiments;[32] Paisible and La Roche continued to build their respective careers, but neither ever wrote another such work for the court; and, as we shall see presently, Arlington may have found other outlets for pleasing his royal master with court theatrical entertainments. In any event, the experiment in lighthearted French semi-musical drama was not repeated, and were it not for the publication of the text—whether as a programme libretto for distribution at

---

29 According to John Evelyn, writing on 10 September 1677, Arlington possessed "the Latine French & Spanish tongues in perfection" (*Diary*, 4: 118). Isabella's mother, Isabella van Nassau-Beverweerd, was Dutch, and a daughter of Lodewijk van Nassau-Beverweerd, an illegitimate son of the late Stadholder Maurice, Prince of Orange.

30 Archives du Ministère des Affaires Étrangères, Correspondance Politique: Angleterre 123, ff. 266^v–67^r. Courtin's correspondent, Pomponne, replied with some surprise: "C'est la premiere fois que M. de St. Evremont ayt mal reussy a une chose qu'il a entreprise; aussy crois-je qu'il ne s'estoit guere appliqué cy devant à regler une comédie" (Archives du Ministère des Affaires Étrangères, Correspondance Politique: Angleterre 123B, f. 136^v).

31 HMC *Verney*, 469.

32 See Chapter 7, below, and Susan Shifrin and Andrew R. Walkling, "'Idylle en Musique': Performative Hybridity and the Duchess Mazarin as Visual, Textual, and Musical Icon," in Susan Shifrin, ed., *"The Wandering Life I Led": Essays on Hortense Mancini, Duchess Mazarin and Early Modern Women's Border-Crossings* (Newcastle upon Tyne: Cambridge Scholars Publishing, 2009), 48–99.

120   *"Their greatest gallantry imaginable"*

the performance or as a retrospective souvenir of the event is not certain—*Rare en Tout* itself might indeed have ended up as what Spire Pitou later dubbed it: "A Forgotten Play."[33]

* * *

The Restoration court's shift in the mid-1670s to new types of theatrical entertainment, heralded by the advent of French opera and ballet to be discussed in Chapter 6 and reflected in the unusual features of such works as *Calisto* and *Rare en Tout*, did not entirely displace the older forms. As we have seen, court balls continued to be mounted, particularly in celebration of the queen's birthday (15 November), and there is evidence that "recreational" theatrical presentations also persisted. Hard facts are difficult to come by, and hence much of what can be said remains speculative, but it appears that the performances were largely private, and perhaps more modest in terms of production values than the ostentatious presentations of the preceding several years. One such performance seems to stand out as especially influential: in a number of familiar letters written by the teenaged Princess Anne to her friend Frances Apsley, Anne refers to Apsley as "Semandra" and to herself as "Ziphares."[34] Semandra and Ziphares are the ill-starred lovers in Nathaniel Lee's tragedy *Mithridates, King of Pontus*, and it is likely that the two young court ladies had appeared together in a production of this play, with Anne in the cross-dressed role of the hero.[35] Such a prospect is made all the more likely by Anne's further references in a pair of letters to "my honourd Mothere faire Monima" (Monima being the spurned wife of Ziphares's father Mithridates, and hence the young prince's stepmother), and to "my Brothere" (most likely referring to Ziphares's wicked half-sibling Pharnaces, since Princess Anne had no actual brother of her own at this time).[36] James Winn believes that the

33 None of Paisible's music is known to survive, although Silas Wollston has recently suggested that the fifteen-movement suite in Yale University, MS Filmer 7, ff. 66^v–69^r "might conceivably relate to *Rare en tout*": see "New Light on Purcell's Early Overtures," *Early Music* 37 (2009): 647–55, p. 655 n. 35. The 52-page playbook, we should note, appears to have been produced in a hurry: its publishers Magnes and Bentley evidently used two distinct compositors, possibly working in separate shops, since the typographical style changes markedly at the beginning of signature D. Inconsistencies between the two halves can be found in the rendering of act and scene headings in numbers rather than words, the reduced use of leading between individual speeches, and the printing of speech prefixes in Italic rather than Roman type. Perhaps most notably, the spelling of the title character's name changes from "Rare en Tout" to "Rare-en-Tout."

34 British Library, MS Loan 57/71, *passim*, transcribed in Bathurst, ed., *Letters of Two Queens* (see Chapter 2, n. 36, above); the first such letter—written not to Frances but rather to her mother, Lady Apsley—is on f. 33^r (from Windsor, dated "June ye 18th" ?1679; see Bathurst, 102–3). Frances, who was Anne's senior by twelve years, was also the person addressed by Anne's sister, Princess Mary, as "husband" and "Aurelia" (discussed in Chapter 2).

35 See James Anderson Winn's excellent discussion of *Mithridates* in *Queen Anne: Patroness of Arts* (Oxford: Oxford University Press, 2014), 63–69. I am grateful to Professor Winn for sharing with me the results of his work in progress.

36 British Library, MS Loan 57/71, ff. 69$^{r–v}$ (3 October 1679) and 41^r (12 May ?1680); see Bathurst, 111–12 and 114–15. Bathurst suggests that "Monima" may be Frances's sister Isabella Apsley,

Masques and plays at court after 1675   121

ladies' performance of this play took place sometime in 1679, probably between the beginning of March, when Anne's father and stepmother, the Duke and Duchess of York, went into exile in Brussels, and late August, when Anne and her three-year-old half-sister Isabella left London to join them.[37] Winn notes that the first letter in which Anne refers to Frances Apsley as "Semandra" is dated 18 June, probably in 1679, and he further suggests that Anne's stepmother Mary of Modena, had she been present at the time of the production, would have frowned upon the princess's performing a male part.[38] The court production would thus have postdated by more than a year the public premiere of the play by the King's Company, which *The London Stage* places sometime in February 1678, an estimate based on the printed playbook's licensing date of 28 March of that year.[39]

This logic, however, is by no means definitive, and it is entirely possible that the court performance of *Mithridates* actually predated that on the public stage. To begin with, Ziphares is hardly an objectionable role: he is the undoubted hero of Lee's play, whose passionate devotion to his beloved is matched only by unswerving loyalty to his tyrannical father—a part ideally suited to an up-and-coming royal thespian like Anne. Moreover, the letter of 18 June ?1679 is in fact the earliest surviving letter from the princess, and does nothing to prove that she had not already been addressing Frances Apsley as "Semandra" for a considerable time. The practice certainly proved durable: as Benjamin Bathurst observes, "the use of these names was continued until after the marriage of Frances; that is to say, for some seven or eight years."[40] We also need to consider two hints dropped by Nathaniel Lee himself in the 1678 *Mithridates* playbook. Midway through his lengthy dedication of the play to Charles Sackville, 6th Earl of Dorset, Lee suddenly veers off course, beseeching his dedicatee to bestow "a greater Honour ... and so important, *I* cannot name it without apprehension: *Mithridates* being in your hands, desires to be laid at the Feet of the Queen."[41] Queen Catherine of Braganza, Lee declares,

> has been pleas'd to grace him [*i.e.* Mithridates, a synecdoche for the play] with her Presence, and promis'd it again with such particular praises ... that shou'd he not express his Gratitude almost to adoration, he wou'd deserve another Fate, when he is next represented, than what he has hitherto receiv'd.

Lady Wentworth; for Pharnaces, James Winn (*Queen Anne*, 657 n. 45) proposes Mary Cornwallis. It should be noted that "my Brothere" appears to be physically present with Anne when she mentions her to Frances Apsley from Brussels (3 October 1679), and is either with Anne at Windsor (12 May ?1680) or has recently departed from thence.

37 Winn, "'Epilogue to the faithfull Shepheardess'," 51 n. 3 and *Queen Anne*, 657 n. 45.

38 Winn, *Queen Anne*, 658 n. 47.

39 Van Lennep, ed., *The London Stage*, 1: 267. The publication was advertised in the Term Catalogue printed in June 1678: see *Term Catalogues*, 1: 320.

40 Bathurst, 42; the last letters from Anne in which these names appear are thought to be from the summer of 1686: see Bathurst, 195–96.

41 Nathaniel Lee, *Mithridates, King of Pontus* (London: James Magnes and Rich[ard] Bentley, 1678), sig. A3^r.

122 *"Their greatest gallantry imaginable"*

Lee's remark is of considerable interest: not only does it reveal that the queen has witnessed the play (a fact not otherwise known from documentary evidence), but that she intends to show her favor by doing so again. Of course, Queen Catherine could have attended a performance at Drury Lane when *Mithridates* first opened there—this is impossible to determine, unfortunately, since no records survive of royal payments to the King's Company between 5 May 1677 and the company's dissolution in April–May 1682. But attendance at plays by members of the royal family did not usually merit notice in printed playbooks, and there is reason to suspect that Lee is referring to a special event, such as a court performance that could have occurred prior to the work's public premiere. A second clue that could be taken to support this theory can be found in Lee's prologue to the play. Following the usual attacks on the critics in the pit, the prologue concludes by turning to the theme of beauty:

> *To Beauty our last Vows, like yours, are made:*
> *Beauty, which still adorns the op'ning List,*
> *Which* Cæsar's *Heart vouchsafes not to resist:*
> *To that alone devoted is this day;*
> *For, by the Poet, I was bid to say,*
> *In the first draught, 'twas meant the* Ladies Play. (p. [79][42])

Passing over the sly reference, in the third line quoted above, to Charles II's notorious susceptibility to feminine charms, we can take particular notice of the wording of the final two lines, with their puzzling reference to the play's *"first draught."* These lines, spoken by one of the actors, are at pains to emphasize Lee's agency (*"by the Poet, I was bid to say"*), while their typographical configuration on the printed page draws our attention to the phrase "Ladies Play." One interpretation of the passage could be that, in spite of the play's relentlessly morbid subject matter, it was originally written to appeal in particular to the female members of the audience, through its depiction of the lovers Semandra and Ziphares. Indeed, in his dedication, Lee tells the Earl of Dorset that "When *I* design'd to draw [Ziphares] for the Ladies, endearing, soft, and passionately loving, *I* thought on you, and found the way to Charm 'em."[43] But the playwright's designation of *Mithridates*, in its first draft, as *"the* Ladies['] play" might also be intended to refer to the work's possible origin as a vehicle for the young lady actors of the court. The play, we should note, could well have been written with such performers in mind: despite its dark mood, the unrepentant wickedness of its Iago-like villains, and its

---

42 Sig. L4ʳ, but in some copies inserted between sigs. A and B. There are in fact two states of this leaf: see Fredson Bowers, "The Prologue to Nathaniel Lee's 'Mithridates', 1678," *Papers of the Bibliographical Society of America* 44 (1950): 173–75.

43 *Ibid.* Lee continues: "And 'tis most certain, he who obliges those Fair Criticks to be of his Party, has the surest Cards that ever Poet plaid: *I* cannot but own the Honours they have done me, and entreat your Lordship to secure 'em my Friends."

Masques and plays at court after 1675 123

somewhat prurient focus on the title character's ravishment of the beautiful and chaste Semandra, *Mithridates* is almost a kind of academic drama, whose focus is more on grand oratory than on action *per se*, and whose appeal lies neither in gruesome onstage bloodlettings nor in labyrinthine plot twists, but rather in the intricately expressed emotions—the aspirations, desires, and suffering—of the characters. For all its tragic qualities, *Mithridates* is actually not far removed, in terms of its structure, rhetoric, and emotional profile, from a pastoral such as *The Faithful Shepherdess*.

It is therefore necessary to consider the possibility that *Mithridates*, in some earlier "*first draught*," was originally created for a court performance by Princess Anne and her friends—perhaps with a smaller cast and a simplified structure,[44] and without significant scenic and musical elaboration.[45] Such a possibility would place the performance not in 1679, but rather in late 1677 or early 1678, during the Christmas/Carnival season, and in advance of the Drury Lane production that is believed to have appeared in February or March. Unlike *Calisto*, it would have been a low-profile event, probably not mounted in the Hall Theatre: *The London Stage* suggests that the performance took place "at St. James's Palace or at Sir Allen Apsley's house in St. James's Square."[46] I would propose, rather, that *Mithridates* may have been the play performed on 8 February 1678, the Friday before Shrove Tuesday, in the Whitehall lodgings of the Lord Chamberlain, the Earl of Arlington.[47] Five costumes were ordered for

44 In the playbook (sig. A3ᵛ), Lee suggests that those who object to his insertion of brief battle/crowd scenes at the beginning of Acts 3 and 5 "may for their satisfaction leave 'em out, and the Play will be entire." This advice appears to have been at least partly followed in the 1695 manuscript copy of the play associated with the English College at Douai in France (Bibliothèque Publique, Douai, MS 787; see A. L. McLeod, "The Douai MS. of Lee's 'Mithridates'," *Notes and Queries* 205 [n. s., 7, 1960]: 69–70), where Act 5, scene 1 is missing. The removal of these two scenes (3.i: "*The Field*"; 5.i: unspecified outdoor scene) effectively eliminates the need for scene changes throughout the play, despite the playbook's explicit directions in some cases (1.i: "*The outer-part of the Temple of the Sun*"; 3.ii: "*The Palace-Garden*"), and the implied locales in others (such as 4.i, which takes place in an unspecified sequence of bedchambers, first Mithridates's, then Ziphares's).

45 Cues in Act 1 for "The sacred Musick" (p. 5) and an "*Entertainment*" in which "*An Image of Victory descends with two Crowns in her hands*" (p. 9) before crashing spectacularly onto the stage, and in Act 3 for "*Ziphares's Triumph*," consisting of "*a Street full of Pageants*" in which some people "*dance before him, while the Priests sing*" (p. 37) could have been inserted by Lee for the public production, subsequent to his "*first draught*." The one identified song in *Mithridates*, Louis Grabu's "One night while all the village slept," with words supplied by Sir Carr Scrope, is an interpolation that has no real bearing on the plot, being sung by the servant Ismenes to soothe the distraught Ziphares "into a slumber" (p. 55) in Act 4.

46 Van Lennep, ed., *The London Stage*, 1: 267. This source's estimate as to the date encompasses the entire range of possibilities we have been discussing: "between January 1677/8 and August 1679."

47 It is not certain which of Arlington's apartments at Whitehall was pressed into service for this event: in his official capacity as Lord Chamberlain, he would have occupied a suite of rooms situated in an extension of the Privy Gallery range at the south side of the Pebble Court, slightly east of the Banqueting House, labeled "O" on the Whitehall Palace plan of 1670 (in which it is assigned to the then Lord Chamberlain, Edward Montagu, 2nd Earl of Manchester). However, his wife

124   *"Their greatest gallantry imaginable"*

the production,[48] and a rudimentary two-foot-high stage measuring 19 feet by 12 feet was erected, with a 7½-foot-high rail at the rear "for to hang a hanging vppon for y[e] Actors to goe behind."[49] While the scant documentary record is devoid of evidence regarding what play was presented (the costume bill simply calls it "the Mask"), or who appeared in it, *Mithridates*, starring Princess Anne and Frances Apsley, would seem a good fit. The performance, falling only two days after Anne's thirteenth birthday and slightly more than two months following her sister Mary's departure for Holland, would have highlighted the princess's coming into her own as a court actress, representing a significant step up from her 1675 stage debut as the second-fiddle Nyphe in *Calisto*.

Whether or not they are indeed one and the same, either *Mithridates* or the 1678 near-Shrovetide performance might be associated with another theatrical text, Edmund Waller's "Prologue to the Lady Actors," printed posthumously in 1690.[50] Waller's eighteen-line prologue is clearly designed for a "recreational" performance before the king by young actresses. It begins,

> AMaze us not with that Majestic Frown,
> But lay aside the greatness of your Crown.
> For your diversion here we act in Jest;

and contrasts the position of the ladies—whose boldness on the stage is "less careful" than their "more serious, and more wise" demeanor in everyday life—with that of professional actors, who "on the Stage shew all their skill, / And after do as Love and Fortune will." The theme of the young ladies' divergent circumstances on- and offstage is further explored when the prologue describes them "feign[ing] warm Lovers, tho our Breasts be cold" and urges the audience to overlook any flaws in the performance, focusing instead on how well the erstwhile thespians "act ... the parts, to which we're born," as opposed to those they have temporarily assumed for this production. The rhetoric of Waller's brief text is precisely in line

---

Isabella (*née* Beverweerd) had her own suite along the Thames foreshore (labeled "f" on the plan) next to the queen's residence, and Arlington appears to have had new lodgings fitted up in April 1670 in that same area of the palace, possibly either in or adjacent to those of his Countess: see Thurley, *The Whitehall Palace Plan of 1670* (see Chapter 1, n. 123, above), 32. The performance most likely did *not* take place in "The Lord Arlingtons Office" at the eastern end of the Privy Gallery (labeled "V" on the plan), which Arlington held while Secretary of State and probably relinquished upon becoming Lord Chamberlain in September 1674.

48 LC5/65, f. 42[r] (stamped foliation 66[r]); LC5/143, p. 32 (*Register*, no. 1043); LC9/115; LC9/275, ff 167[v]–168[v]. The tailor, Monsieur Charles Cabin, had worked on the costumes for *Calisto*; see J. D. C., "Christmas at the Court of Charles the Second," *Notes and Queries* 18 (2nd ser., no. 6, 1858): 517–20.

49 WORK5/29, f. 120[r] (*Register*, no. 1042). See also the carpenters' account for December 1677, which included "lengthening the degrees in y[e] Lord Chamberlaines and Lord Treasurers lodgs 3 fo[t] ½ long[r] then they were before" (WORK5/28, f. 88[r] [*Register*, no. 1035]).

50 Edmund Waller, *The Second Part of Mr. Waller's Poems* (London: Tho[mas] Bennet, 1690), 53–54; the poem also appears (shorter by two lines and with a few minor variants) in Edmund Waller, *The Maid's Tragedy Altered. With some other Pieces* (London: Jacob Tonson, 1690), 50–51.

Masques and plays at court after 1675   125

with that of the prologues and epilogues associated with *Horace*, *The Faithful Shepherdess*, *The Empress of Morocco*, and *Calisto*, and thus, whether or not it was intended for the court performance of *Mithridates* and/or for delivery at the "masque" or play presented under the Lord Chamberlain's auspices in early 1678,[51] it certainly contributes to the body of evidence regarding performances of this type at the Restoration court.

Princess Anne's stage career probably encompassed more than just the London productions of *Calisto* and *Mithridates* already discussed; indeed, she would ultimately enjoy comparatively greater opportunities for participating in recreational theatrical endeavors at court than had her elder sister. Mary's acting career, which appears to have begun with *The Faithful Shepherdess* in 1670 (performed just shy of her eighth birthday), definitively ended with her marriage to William of Orange on 4 November 1677, at the age of fifteen and a half. Anne, on the other hand, had already turned ten when *Calisto* was first presented, but, in contrast to Mary, did not wed until 28 July 1683, by which time she was nearly eighteen and a half, thus leaving a period of some eight and a half years in which she was free to engage in such youthful courtly diversions. She is even reported to have received elocution lessons from the actress Elizabeth Barry, a consequence of Charles II finding himself "pleased with the natural sweetness of her voice."[52] Moreover, during this period Anne developed a strong bond with her young stepmother Mary of Modena, Duchess of York, who appears to have had a special interest in the performance of plays, on a small scale, by members of her entourage. As early as the summer of 1675, writing from Windsor to a friend, the duchess had reported that

> we go every night ethiere by watter or by land, or a walking or a fisching, or sometimes to contre gentelmens houses where we dance and play at little plays, and cary our one super and supe in the garden or in the field.[53]

By October 1679, in exile in Brussels, and with Princesses Anne and Isabella in attendance, Mary appears to have sponsored a "recreational" production of Sir George Etherege's comedy *The Man of Mode*, a play Etherege had dedicated to the duchess when it was published in 1676, and for which Sir Carr Scrope

---

51 An alternative explanation is that Waller's prologue could have been written for the 1670 performance of *The Faithful Shepherdess* at St. James's, which was also acted only by young ladies and is known to have been attended by both the king and the queen. The only poetic text unambiguously connected with that recreational production is an epilogue (see Chapter 2, n. 37, above).

52 See Winn, *Queen Anne*, 63 and 658 n. 46 and Walkling, "Professional Actors as Royal Drama Coaches, 1674–81" (see Chapter 2, n. 77, above). Barry was a member of the Duke's Company, and thus would have had no connection with the King's Company's public performances of *Mithridates*, which starred Elizabeth Boutell as Semandra and Mary Corbet as Monima (see the cast list printed in the *Mithridates* playbook, p. [80]).

53 Letter of Mary of Modena, Duchess of York to Susanna Armyne, Baroness Belasyse of Osgodby, 19 July 1675, transcribed in Margaret R. Toynbee, "A Further Note on an Early Correspondence of Queen Mary of Modena," *Notes and Queries* 193 (1948): 292–95, p. 293.

126   *"Their greatest gallantry imaginable"*

(who also contributed the words for the song in *Mithridates*) had written the original prologue and probably one of the song texts. Anne, who may have been involved, reported on 3 October that "the play is practisde to night,"[54] although it is uncertain whether it was ever actually performed, since the entire household left Brussels for The Hague just three days later, and then returned suddenly to England a few days after that. By the end of November, however, the duke and duchess were in Edinburgh (minus Anne and Isabella, who remained in London), and on 16 January 1680, Mary wrote to her friend Lady Belasyse that "my maids are going to act another play, tis to be Aurenzeb."[55] Whether the phrase *"another play"* (my emphasis) refers back to the Fall production of *The Man of Mode* in Brussels or implies that some further play performances had already taken place in Edinburgh is uncertain, but the plans to present John Dryden's *Aurengzebe* (1675) may also have come to naught, since the duke and duchess were summoned back to court before the end of the month, and departed for London on the 28th.

Such performances as there were, both in Brussels and in Edinburgh, must necessarily have been modest in scope. The York household was, at least initially, quite small in exile, consisting of only "un fort petit nombre de domestiques" when the couple first set out in March 1679, although by the following June the seeming permanence of their banishment led to "My lord Peterborough and his Lady ... coming over with my Lady Bellasis and many others, which will make a full court here."[56] Even after October 1680, when the duke returned to Edinburgh for what would become a year-and-a-half stint as Charles II's Lord High Commissioner in Scotland, lodging his family in Holyrood Palace and thereby establishing a quasi-royal court in that kingdom for the first time in thirty years, matters were probably not much changed. There is, in fact, no record of any theatrical performances in Edinburgh during the ensuing year. However, in July 1681, Princess Anne again journeyed out of England to be with her parents,[57]

---

54 Letter of Princess Anne to Frances Apsley, 3 October 1679 (British Library, MS Loan 57/71, f. 69ʳ; see Bathurst, ed., *Letters of Two Queens*, 111–12, p. 112). Catherine Watts, one of the duchess's Maids of Honor, played the role of Lady Townley, although Anne remarked that the role "I beleeve wont much become her."

55 Letter of Duchess of York to Baroness Belasyse, 16 January 1680, transcribed in Toynbee, "A Further Note," 294.

56 Letters of Paul Barillon d'Amoncourt, Marquis de Branges (French ambassador in London) to Louis XIV, 13 March 1679 (New Style) and Sir Richard Bulstrode to Sir Leoline Jenkins, 26 June 1679, quoted in Margaret R. Toynbee, "An Early Correspondence of Queen Mary of Modena," *Notes and Queries* 188 (January–June 1945): 90–94, 112–18, and 135–40, pp. 116 and 117. See also SP44/51, p. 267 (3 July 1679: *Calendar of State Papers, Domestic 1679–80*: 348): pass to Brussels for "Henry, Earl of Peterborough, and Penelope, his wife, with 20 menservants and 11 womenservants"; and SP104/51, p. 283 (7 August 1679: *Calendar of State Papers, Domestic 1679–80*: 213 [quoted, with some inaccuracies, in Toynbee, 118]): "Pass for Dame Susanna Belasyse of the Bed Chamber to the Duchess of York with William Fortrey and Trevor Fortrey, his sister, Anne Wentworth and Charles Crachrode with their 12 servants and with their wearing apparel and 1,300 *oz.* of plate to pass into Flanders." Anne and Isabella arrived later in August.

57 Anne left London on 13 July and arrived in Scotland on the 19th. This time she was not accompanied by Princess Isabella, who had died at the age of 4½ on 2 March 1681, while her mother was in exile.

Masques and plays at court after 1675   127

and on Tuesday, 15 November, according to the chronicler Sir John Lauder, the birthday of Queen Catherine of Braganza was commemorated at Holyrood with a new performance of *Mithridates*,[58] "before ther Royall Hynesses, &c., wheirin Ladie Anne, the duke's daughter, and the Ladies of Honor ware the onlie actors."[59] This time, Anne (now aged sixteen) is said to have taken the role of the heroine Semandra, and to have received coaching from the Dublin-based actor Joseph Ashbury, who happened to be in Edinburgh on tour.[60] In a letter written on 26 November to his niece the Countess of Lichfield, the Duke of York reported that

> my daughter acted on thursday last [*i.e.* the 24th], for the third and last tyme hir play, there were five of them that did their parts very well, and they were very well drest, so that they made a very fine show, and such a one as had not been seen in this country before[.][61]

Several interesting points emerge from this account. First, given that, according to the duke, no such production had previously been seen in Scotland, this particular show must have been more public than the (supposed) *Aurengzebe* performance of January 1680, and hence more like those London presentations with which we are by now familiar. Second, the play was acted not once, but three times; this is the only "recreational" court theatrical production of the period besides *The Queen's Masque* and *Calisto* for which we have unequivocal evidence of multiple performances

---

58 Note Queen Catherine's special association with this play, emphasized by Lee in his dedication to the 1678 edition already discussed. In London, where Catherine was actually present in 1681, the occasion was celebrated with a performance of another play by Lee, *The Rival Queens*, acted by the King's Company at court (see the documents cited in Van Lennep, ed., *The London Stage*, 1: 303). *Mithridates* had itself been revived on the London stage sometime in mid-October 1681, only a month before the amateur performance in Edinburgh (see *ibid.*, 1: 301–2); the play was subsequently seen again by Mary of Modena (now queen) on 4 February 1686, this time in a performance by the United Company at either Drury Lane or Dorset Garden, in which Cardell Goodman (who had appeared as Pharnaces in 1678) is thought to have played Ziphares (see letter of Peregrine Bertie to the Countess of Rutland, 6 February 1686 in HMC *Rutland* 2: 104).

59 Sir John Lauder (later Lord Fountainhall), ed. Adam Urquhart and David Laing, *Historical Observes of Memorable Occurrents in Church and State from October 1680 to April 1686* (Bannatyne Club, no. 66: Edinburgh: Thomas Constable, 1840), 51. Lauder, who calls *Mithridates* "a comedy," reveals his prejudices when he continues, "Not only the canonists, both Protestant and Popish, but the very Heathen Roman lawyers, declared all scenicks and stage players infamous, and will scarce admit them to the sacrament of the Lord's Supper."

60 Ashbury's company had arrived in Scotland in July. See William Van Lennep, "The Smock Alley Players of Dublin," *ELH* 13 (1946): 216–22, p. 220. As Van Lennep points out (n. 12), the details of the story are somewhat uncertain, particularly since Ashbury is not named by either of the contemporary commentators, Sir John Lauder and the Duke of York. For more on this anecdote, see Walkling, "Professional Actors as Royal Drama Coaches, 1674–81."

61 Letter of James, Duke of York to Charlotte Fitzroy, Countess of Lichfield, 26 November "1682" [*recte* 1681]: Folger Shakespeare Library, MS X.c.90, no. 2, p. 2 (transcribed in Harold Arthur, Viscount Dillon, "Some Familiar Letters of Charles II. and James Duke of York Addressed to their Daughter and Niece, the Countess of Litchfield [*sic*]," *Archaeologia* 58 [1902–3]: 153–88, p. 162).

128 *"Their greatest gallantry imaginable"*

(as opposed to mere open rehearsals).[62] Finally, James confirms Lauder's statement that Lee's play was presented by only five performers—according to Lauder, Anne and her stepmother's four Maids of Honor.[63] It is not clear how the extant version of the play could have been performed by a cast of five: even if every supernumerary were excised and the wicked characters Pharnaces, Pelopidas, and Andravar distilled down to one figure, six actors would be required to support the basic plot. Perhaps, under pressure of limited personnel, the less essential role of Monima (which we can be fairly sure was acted in the earlier London production) was dispensed with, or it may be that a drastically truncated version of the play eliminated Semandra's aged father, Archelaus. It is worth noting that the unidentified production of 8 February 1678 in the Lord Chamberlain's lodgings at Whitehall, which I have suggested may have been *Mithridates*, involved the ordering of only five costumes from the tailor.[64] In any event, the small-cast version of Lee's play necessitated by any such performance, whether at Whitehall or at Holyrood, may be identifiable with the playwright's elusive *"first draught."*

* * *

Whatever the actual circumstances surrounding the London court production of *Mithridates*, which was clearly intended as a private, low-profile event incorporating only minimal music or dancing, there is evidence that the court also had in mind, at least initially, the continuation of more substantive masque performances in the aftermath of *Calisto*. A document prepared sometime around 1675 containing "An Estimate of the charge of the Ordinary Provisions to be made by the Master of the Great Wardrobe for his Maties Service yearly" includes anticipated expenditures for "Furnishing the Theater of Whitehall for Maskes Play's and Dances,"[65] and an imprest of £1000 issued to the Lord Chamberlain's secretary Richard Coling on 9 November 1674, while *Calisto* was still in rehearsal, was intended "to be employed towards the Expences of Masques to be hereafter p^rsented before his Matie from tyme to tyme."[66] However, the astronomical cost of *Calisto* may have forced a lowering of expectations with regard to the scope and extravagance of such productions, and in any case the field was becoming considerably more

---

62 Note, however, the strong possibility that *The Empress of Morocco* also received multiple performances, as evidenced by the sequence of distinct prologues, discussed in Chapter 2, above.

63 Probably Catherine Sedley, Catherine Watts, Frances Walsingham, and Catherine Fraser, as identified in Edward Chamberlayne, *Angliæ Notitia ... The Fourteenth Edition* (London: R. Littlebury, R. Scott, and G. Wells, 1682; see also Chapter 2, n. 4, above), 245.

64 See n. 48, above. This, of course, does not necessarily mean that only five performers participated in this production: as the example of *Calisto* demonstrates, it is possible that high-ranking performers (such as Anne) would have provided their own costumes.

65 Folger Shakespeare Library, MS X.d.76, ff. 2^r and 6^v. The specific cost is unspecified, but the item is listed among "The Extraordinary Provisions" for which the Wardrobe estimated annual expenditures of £10,000.

66 LC5/141, pp. 50, 550 (*Register*, no. 875).

diversified. With the advent of French through-composed opera and ballet in 1673–74 (a phenomenon that will be explored in Chapter 6), a new outlet had been established for channeling the court's creative energies with respect to encomiastic drama and, as we shall see, the differing circumstances of these productions spurred efforts to establish new procedures and parallel personnel structures to promote and support the performance of these novel works. Yet at the same time, the traditional court musical establishment, so prominently on display in *Calisto*, continued to play a role. As we have noted, Nicholas Staggins appears to have composed and arranged music in November 1675 for an unidentified entertainment described as "ye Maske."[67] Moreover, in the winter of 1676 Staggins was sent on an extended trip to "France … Italy, & other Forrin Parts," most likely to study operatic practices, from which he returned more than two years later, probably in June 1678.[68] By this time, Matthew Locke—who appears to have been fulfilling some of Staggins's duties—had died, and Louis Grabu—who, as we will see in Chapter 7, may also have been acting on his official successor's behalf—had left the orbit of the court, and Staggins seems henceforward to have associated himself with John Blow, the Organist and Master of the Children of the Chapel Royal. Sometime in the early 1680s, Staggins and Blow were together appointed to the place of Composer for the Violins in Ordinary, a position that had been held jointly by Pelham Humfrey and Thomas Purcell from 1672, and by Purcell alone after Humfrey's death in July 1674.[69] Blow and Staggins first occupied the position without fee from 1680 or 1681,[70] and in August 1682, upon Thomas Purcell's decease, received a grant of the place with a salary of £200 per annum from the Exchequer "for life and to the longer liver of them," the same shared arrangement that had previously been made for Humfrey and Purcell a decade earlier.[71]

---

67 See Chapter 1, nn. 64 and 65, above. On the other hand, the arresting designation "Master of the Masques" applied to Staggins in the *Calendar of Treasury Books* entry for the £221 *Calisto* payment of 7 February 1676 is actually a transcription error (5: 123, unfortunately repeated in Ashbee, 8: 223) for "Master of the Music": see the errata listing at *ibid.*, 5: 1685.

68 See the discussion in Chapter 7. Interestingly, the violinist and composer John Banister also received permission, on 23 May 1679, "to travel beyond the seas, and to be absent from his attendance by the space of six months, or longer if his occasions shall require" (LC5/143, p. 334 [Ashbee, 1: 185]); a pass for that travel was issued on 28 July 1679 (SP44/51, p. 277 [*Calendar of State Papers, Domestic* 1679–80: 350; Ashbee, 8: 235]). However, this may have been related to his position as music master to Princess Anne (see the 1677 establishment book of James, Duke of York: British Library, Add. MS 18958, f. 8^v [Ashbee, 2: 121]), who left England on 20 August to join the Duke and Duchess of York in Brussels. Whether or not Banister actually made the trip is uncertain, as he died in London on 3 October.

69 For Humfrey and Purcell's appointment (succeeding George Hudson), see LC5/14, p. 107 (10 January 1672: Ashbee, 1: 111).

70 The post was "to come in ordinary with fee upon the death, surrender, or other avoidance of Thomas Purcell." For this warrant (dated simply "1680–1"), see LC5/144, p. 63 (Ashbee, 1: 194).

71 LC5/144, p. 233 (10 August 1682: Ashbee, 1: 201) and SO3/18, f. 160^v (October 1682: Ashbee, 5: 81). A second position of Composer for the Violins had been held by Matthew Locke, who was succeeded upon his death (1677) by Henry Purcell; see Holman, *Fiddlers*, 440–41. The Private

130 *"Their greatest gallantry imaginable"*

Just when Staggins and Blow assumed their new official duties as composers for the court, the political and cultural upheaval associated with the "Exclusion Crisis" of 1678–82 was subsiding, and the two men appear to have sought to take advantage of a renewed interest in court musical, and possibly theatrical, entertainments. The clearest evidence for this is the frequently cited "Petition of John Bleau & Nicholas Staggins praying his Maj^ties Royall Grant & License for the erecting an ~~such~~ Academy or Opera of Musick, & performing or causing to be performed therein their Musicall compositions," submitted sometime in the spring of 1683.[72] The petition itself does not survive; what we have is a "reference" of the petition, dated 4 April 1683, to Lord Chamberlain Arlington, who was instructed to report "what his Maj^ty may fitly do in it for the Pet^rs gratification." It is not clear precisely what Charles II was agreeing to support: the phrase "Academy or Opera of Musick" has been read as referring to some sort of institution, perhaps a putative successor to the "Royall Academy of Musick" of the 1670s. But "Academy" and "Opera" remained somewhat vague terms at the time, and could equally have been meant to designate a physical space, whose "erect[ion]" in an architectural sense would have accommodated the performance of musical works "therein." Blow and Staggins's project might, therefore, be related to an undated document laying out a proposal for "A large Musick=roome, with conveniences about it, Propos'd to be erected at Whitehal where it wilbe an ornament, and of speciall use to his Ma^ts servants in that Science, And for communicacōn therein with all other lovers of Musick, homebred & Strangers."[73] This bifolium paper, a fair-copy draft designed for the appending of signatures by "Welwishing virtuoso's, and Masters & Sons of Musick ... that from their cheerfulnes & number the freinds of this laudable designe may take courage to proceede effectually upon it," offers details of a 40′ by 30′ "Grand chamber ... arched, and windowed, seeld, and deale wainscoted layd in oyle, as shalbe most proper for a harmonical structure, with floores, vaults & cavities suitable and usefull," along with ancillary rooms including "a habitacōn for the guardian of the whole." A system of governance consisting of "certain By-lawes to be framed by the Trustees" is promised, and there is said to be a quite substantial fund of £4000 to support the project, "wch his Ma^ty we presume wilbe gracōusly pleased to allow of, and wch otherwise is like to dye

---

Music had its own composer position, which was held in succession from the Restoration by Henry Lawes (d. 1662), Charles Coleman (d. 1664), and Henry Cooke, who seems to have combined it with the position of Master of the Children of the Chapel Royal. On Cooke's death (1672), these two positions passed together, first to Humfrey and then to Blow, both of whom ultimately held them in conjunction with the jointly held composing position in the Violins. For Blow's appointment to this position of "composer in his Majesty's private musick for voices in ordinary," see LC5/140, p. 510 (23 July 1674: Ashbee, 1: 140); LC5/141, p. 168 (27 April 1675: Ashbee, 1: 149).

72 SP44/55, p. 248 (*Calendar of State Papers, Domestic* January–June 1683: 158). In the original document, the word "an" is written above "such," which appears to have been deleted. A facsimile of this document can be found in Bruce Wood and Andrew Pinnock, "'Unscarr'd by turning times'?: The dating of Purcell's Dido and Aeneas," *Early Music* 20 (1992): 372–90, p. 387.

73 SP29/443/51 (*Calendar of State Papers, Domestic* Addenda: 506; Ashbee, 8: 340 [but not seen by Ashbee]); the document, endorsed "found with papers of 1671," is now dated "c.1680."

without benefit at all to Him." The proposal expresses the hope that the king "may please to graunt the place for it in one of the out-courts, where it will not preiudice any building, storeplace, or passage." A marginal note at the top, opposite the phrase "Musick=roome," adds the alternative designation "Musick-Colledge." There is no indication of what kinds of musical works might be performed, or whether the building would also be a place of instruction, along the lines of John Banister's "Academy" of 1672–79, discussed by Peter Holman.[74] The space was clearly designed for medium-sized entertainments: the "Grand chamber" would have been about one-third the size of the Hall Theatre, but quadruple that of the approximately 20′ by 15′ "Kings Musick house" shown on the 1670 "Fisher" plan of Whitehall Palace, which was in any case probably only intended for rehearsals and storage of instruments.[75] There is, in fact, no explicit discussion in the document of how the royal musicians themselves might benefit from this innovation, but the request to locate the new structure within the confines of Whitehall Palace must have presupposed their participation in the organization's activities. In any event, despite the large sum of money earmarked for the project, and the presumed royal approbation offered to the lost Blow/Staggins petition of 1683, no such project seems to have come to fruition. James II may have put a stop to it as part of the economies he instituted upon assuming the throne, or, as Bruce Wood and Andrew Pinnock have suggested, Blow may have lost interest after the death of his wife in childbirth in October 1683 significantly augmented the composer's non-musical responsibilities.[76] Either way, it may be noteworthy that in the closing months of Charles II's reign, Francis Gwyn, a Groom of the Bedchamber, had sought and received permission to reconstruct his lodging in the Scotland Yard precinct of Whitehall Palace and "thereon to build a room for the King's musicians more convenient and larger than and in place of the little shed which they at present have ... in which they do use to hang up their instruments and is capable of no other use."[77]

There is, however, one relatively modest court work written around this time that could have been intended for performance in the proposed "Musick=roome"/"Colledge"/"Academy or Opera": Blow's *Venus and Adonis* (whose librettist, James Winn has suggested, may have been Anne Kingsmill, subsequently Anne Finch, later Countess of Winchilsea, a Maid of Honor to Mary of Modena between 1682 and 1684[78]). The precise date of its composition is uncertain, and thus its relationship to the project just discussed cannot be

---

74 Holman, *Fiddlers*, 349–52.

75 See Thurley, *The Whitehall Palace Plan of 1670*. In November 1675, the space had been repaired by the Office of Works, who had also "erected One roome over it for the use of the Master of his Ma[ties] Musick" (LC5/141, p. 286 [Ashbee, 1: 153]).

76 Wood and Pinnock, "'Unscarr'd by turning times'? ...," 388.

77 T4/2, pp. 78–79 (1 September 1684: *Calendar of Treasury Books* 7: 1317; Ashbee, 8: 258). The Lord Chamberlain endorsed Gwyn's request on 5 December: LC5/145, p. 121 (Ashbee, 1: 213).

78 James A. Winn, "'A Versifying Maid of Honour': Anne Finch and the Libretto for *Venus and Adonis*," *Review of English Studies* n. s., 59 (2008): 67–85.

132 *"Their greatest gallantry imaginable"*

definitively ascertained; all we know about the work's purpose is summed up in the descriptive title "A Masque for ye entertainment of ye King" attached to the earliest surviving manuscript score.[79] As a dramatic piece, *Venus* is exceptionally unassuming and technically straightforward: its demands in terms of scenery and props are minimal, and thus it would seem well suited to a performance in a small-scale, non-theatrical space—something analogous to those used in 1670 and 1678 for the spoken plays *The Faithful Shepherdess* and (possibly) *Mithridates*. On the other hand, it has recently been proposed that *Venus and Adonis* be identified with the Shrovetide entertainment of 19 February 1683, performed in the Hall Theatre.[80] Given that the projected "Musick=roome" had not yet been built at this time (and never would be), it is certainly possible that Blow's diminutive operatic piece was a kind of testing of the waters, perhaps offered as a one-off performance in the larger venue in order to show, concurrently with the submission of the petition, how much might be accomplished using the lesser resources of the hoped-for space. Whatever the case, 1683 makes reasonably good sense as a date for this work, although the actual timing and location of the performance must remain a matter for speculation.

Blow's piece is known not from any court documents or contemporary commentary, but rather from a series of musical and textual sources. The earliest of these sources, which provides the "masque" designation already cited, also appears to identify two of the performers: at the respective first appearances in the score of the characters Cupid and Venus, an unknown hand has copied into the manuscript the names "Lady Mary Tudor" and "Mrs Davys."[81] "Mrs Davys" is undoubtedly Mary Davis, known as "Moll," who had served as an actress and sometime singer/dancer with the Duke's Company beginning in 1662. Davis left the stage in 1668 to become a mistress of Charles II, returning briefly to the boards in 1675 to sing the parts of Thames and the shepherdess Sylvia in *Calisto*.[82] Lady Mary Tudor, said to have been born on 16 October 1673, was the product of Moll Davis's affair with the king. The only other reliable facts we have about *Venus* relate to its subsequent appearance as "AN OPERA Perform'd ... By Young Gentlewomen" at the boarding school run by the dancing master Josias Priest and his wife Frances, located outside London in the Chelsea mansion formerly owned by Sir Arthur Gorges.[83] The performance took place on 17 April 1684, accord-

---

79 British Library, Add. MS 22100, f. 123^v.

80 Tuppen, "Shrove-Tide Dancing" (see Chapter 1, n. 19, above), 168–69. The documentation for this entertainment is discussed in Chapter 1, n. 87, above.

81 British Library, Add. MS 22100, ff. 124^r and 129^r.

82 See Walkling, "Masque and Politics," 38. Davis is believed to have performed the role of Ariel in performances of *The Tempest* during the 1660s. There is no evidence that she appeared as Venus in *Psyche* in 1675, as Jennifer McDonald claims in "Matthew Locke's The English Opera, and the Theatre Music of Purcell," *Studies in Music* 15 (1981): 62–75, p. 65.

83 Gorges, who died in October 1661, was son of the Jacobean poet and civil servant of the same name, and became the third husband of Mary Bayning (d. 1672), the mother of Barbara Villiers, Countess of Castlemaine and Duchess of Cleveland. The house was being used as a young ladies' boarding school as early as 1676, when it was under the control of the court musicians Jeffery

Masques and plays at court after 1675   133

ing to a note scrawled on the front of the unique copy of the eight-page printed programme libretto by John Verney, whose niece attended the school.[84] Since the libretto explicitly describes the work as having been "Perform'd before the KING. Afterwards at Mr. *JOSIAS PREIST*'s Boarding School," we can establish April 1684 as a *terminus ad quem* for the date of the original court performance. But no further information about either production has so far come to light.

Venus and Adonis is a difficult piece to categorize. In certain respects it appears to fall more properly into the class of material to be treated in Part II—for example on account of its through-composition and its exhibition of French musical influences. But as we have seen, it is also explicitly designated "A Masque" and, like other productions from *The Indian Emperor* to *Mithridates*, it appears to have featured court-associated figures prominently among its performers; hence, it demands at least some consideration within the courtly "recreational" tradition that we have been exploring thus far.[85] Perhaps the most common fallacy committed by scholars has been to focus too much on comparisons between *Venus and Adonis* and *Calisto*. To be sure, these two "masques" have several features in common: both are based on Ovidian myths and comprise pastoral settings and characters; both make extensive use of music and dance; both rely on French practices in composition and scoring;[86] and both are original pieces written explicitly for performance at court and not intended (unlike, say, *The Empress of Morocco* and perhaps *Mithridates*) to be resurrected subsequently on the public stage. But *Calisto* is an

---

Banister and James Hart: see Thomas Duffett, *Beauties Triumph; A Masque. Presented by the Scholars of Mr. Jeffery Banister, And Mr. James Hart, At their New Boarding-School for Young Ladies and Gentlewomen, kept in that House which was formerly Sir Arthur Gorges, At Chelsey* (London: n. pub., 1676). The Priests took over the management of the school in the autumn of 1680, announcing in the *London Gazette* (1567 [22–25 November 1680], verso), that "JOsias Priest, Dancing-Master, that kept a Boarding-School for Gentlewomen in *Liecester* [*sic*] *Fields*, is removed to the great School-House at *Chelsey*, which was Mr. *Portmans*, where he did Teach, there will continue the same Masters, and others, to the Improvement of the said School." A 1685 document reproduced by Jennifer Thorp suggests that Hart, at least, may have continued to teach at the school under Priest's directorship: see Thorp, "Dance in Late 17th-Century London: Priestly Muddles," *Early Music* 26 (1998): 198–210, p. 203 (illus. 2).

84   Cambridge University Library, shelfmark Sel.2.123. The entire libretto appears in reduced facsimile in Richard Luckett, "A New Source for 'Venus and Adonis'," *The Musical Times* 130 (1989): 76–79. At the bottom of p. 2, Verney also identifies the young ladies who took the three leading roles:

"M[r] Priest's Daughter Acted Adonis
M[ris] Baker a Dutch young Gentlewom[n] Acted Venus
M[ris] ffeltham Acted Cupid."

For the third name, Luckett reads "Helsham."

85   Moll Davis, of course, was originally a professional actress; however, her position as an ex-royal mistress (and mother of one of the king's illegitimate offspring) complicates her status, to the extent that we can regard her as a kind of court figure by the early 1680s. Even in *Calisto*, Davis appears to have been treated differently from the other "occupational" singers, for example with regard to the provision of her costume: see Walkling, "Masque and Politics," 38 and 61 n. 96.

86   See Holman, *Fiddlers*, 371–75.

134 *"Their greatest gallantry imaginable"*

extravagantly public work for which extensive documentation survives, whereas *Venus* shares with a number of the other, more obscure productions of the period a degree of intimacy, a sort of inward-looking courtliness, that eschews the assertive epideictic rhetoric of *Calisto*, or *Rare en Tout*, or the through-composed operatic entertainments to be explored in Chapters 6 and 8. In certain respects, *Venus and Adonis* incorporates features of all its courtly predecessors, combining the tragic arc of political/heroic plays like *The Indian Emperor*, *Horace*, *The Empress of Morocco*, and *Mithridates* with the pastoralism of *The Faithful Shepherdess* and *Calisto*, while introducing its own innovations, including through-composition and a curious non-encomiastic prologue that includes a satirical jab at the audience more characteristic of the spoken prologues and epilogues common in the public theatres. Ultimately, perhaps, this "Masque for ye entertainment of ye King" must simply be regarded as *sui generis*. On the other hand, such distinctions (as also the fundamental difference in the nature of the source material) should not blind us to the undeniable continuities in performance circumstances between the "recreational" court dramas of the 1660s and 1670s and *Venus and Adonis* in the succeeding decade. It is true that, following the five-year hiatus in the production of balls, masques, and plays at court that coincided with the political crisis over Exclusion, the form underwent significant generic change.[87] But the essential features persist, and thus it is incumbent upon us to understand *Venus* as integral to the tradition of courtly "recreational" theatrical entertainments in the Restoration.

What, then, are the implications of our examination of *Venus and Adonis* as part of the larger context of Restoration court theatrical productions? In the first place, it bears observing that what we lack in historical documentation is amply made up for by a wealth of performance material, which has, perhaps paradoxically, allowed scholars to pursue a line of analysis largely unattainable even in the case of so apparently transparent and well documented a work as *Calisto*, the music for which survives only in a fragmentary state.[88] But perhaps the most intriguing consequence of situating *Venus and Adonis* within the courtly tradition emerges from the acknowledgement of how much we do *not* know about when, where, how, and why it was performed, coupled with a recognition that this absence of documentation represents not an extreme instance, but rather an incremental and hence intermediate position with respect to those other works that also suffer, to a lesser degree, from the haphazardness of surviving evidence. Throughout the foregoing discussion, I have sought to assemble the widely scattered documentation that enables us to establish, however provisionally, a composite picture of

---

87 After the 1681 presentation of *Mithridates* in Edinburgh, all evidence for the production of straight plays by court "recreational" performers ceases, suggesting that through-sung masques like *Venus* may have been intended to fill the resultant gap. (For one possible exception, see n. 102, below.)

88 Indeed, whereas the text and the music of *Venus and Adonis* have come down to us complete, nearly every other Restoration court work in which music forms a significant component presents some defective state of survival, ranging from "reconstructable" (*The Faithful Shepherdess*, *The Empress of Morocco*) to fragmentary (*The Queen's Masque*, *Calisto*) to simply "lost" (the vast majority of the through-composed works to be examined in Part II).

recreational theatrical activities at the Restoration court. In the majority of cases such evidence is meager or even circumstantial: a passing entry in a diary, a comment in a letter, a published prologue or epilogue, a manuscript cast list. In most instances, the official court records are insufficiently specific, or silent altogether. Such a state of affairs obliges us, despite a few well-documented examples (*The Queen's Masque, Calisto*), to accustom ourselves to amounts of empirical data ranging from limited (*The Indian Emperor, Horace, The Faithful Shepherdess*) to minimal (*The Empress of Morocco, Mithridates*) to virtually nonexistent (*Venus and Adonis*). The variable quality of this documentation should not necessarily surprise us: we have observed that several of these entertainments were intentionally kept private, and some were produced on a quite modest scale. Keeping this in mind, it would be unwise to conclude that the productions surveyed thus far, all of which have left at least a trace of their court provenance, constitute the totality of such events. Indeed, such a corollary is inescapable, as *Venus and Adonis*, absent its plentiful textual sources, demonstrates. While the supposition that *Venus* was presented in the Hall Theatre on Shrove Monday 1683 may be correct, it is important to remember that it is no more than a guess, based upon the presence of "professional dancers and musicians and warm dressing rooms" and "the same sorts of quantities of bread, beer and wine [as] supplied for the professional cast of *Calisto* and [Rochester's] *Valentinian*."[89] No contemporary narrative or administrative document so much as mentions *Venus*, and apart from the one manuscript's identification of Moll Davis and Lady Mary Tudor as performers, none of the work's textual sources provides any tangible details concerning the presumed court premiere.[90] Surely, then, there must be additional cases in which these two infelicitous variables—lack of historical documentation and dearth of performance materials—actually coincide, with results that can prove debilitating to our efforts at recovery and understanding. We may never know what other works may have been performed at, or even written exclusively for, the court, but whose traces in the historical record have utterly disappeared. Only an exceptionally rare conjunction of scattered and ephemeral scraps of data—a single surviving copy of a printed text distributed at a subsequent non-courtly revival, an adaptive reuse incorporated without acknowledgement into a public stage performance, unattributed excerpts reproduced in contemporary miscellanies or songbooks, a manuscript score copied from a now-lost original by an interested antiquarian many decades after the event—and the ability of scholars to exercise creative inference, informed by a thorough grasp of the relevant context, upon these evidentiary shreds can offer the opportunity to add, however tentatively, some new piece to this history that the intervening centuries have so successfully obscured.

---

89 Tuppen, "Shrove-Tide Dancing," 169.

90 The same manuscript (British Library, Add. MS 22100) that identifies Davis and her daughter also indicates some problem with respect to the dance known as "Cupid's Entry," intended to be performed at the end of the Prologue: here, the original scribe, John Walter, has displaced the dance to the first page (f. 123^r), preceding the overture, and marked it "A Dance in ye prolouge: wch was ommitted."

136 *"Their greatest gallantry imaginable"*

Such conditions may be instructive with regard to one particularly celebrated—and problematic—case: Nahum Tate and Henry Purcell's *Dido and Aeneas*. The extraordinarily murky circumstances surrounding this most famous of Restoration musical-theatrical works are well known, and it is not my intention to rehearse them in detail here.[91] But recent debates over the possibility of a court origin for this mysterious composition—a possibility suggested by the revelation of more than simply formal similarities between *Dido* and *Venus and Adonis*[92]—might be enriched by considering the factors I have just outlined. To the extent that *Venus* represents a generic experiment that builds in innovative ways upon the conventions of court plays and masques from the 1670s, *Dido* can be understood as greatly expanding the implications and scope of that same experimental process. Tate and Purcell appropriate significant elements of the earlier work, including its through-composed structure, its French stylistic features, and its tragic *dénouement*. Yet at the same time, they extend these earlier developments to a considerable degree, displacing the pastoral mode in favor of the epic, vastly increasing the role of dance by distributing it throughout the entire work,[93] and once again devising a generically novel prologue—this time cast in the more familiar political/allegorical vein, but embodying an intricacy of both rhetoric and structure that strangely occludes its celebratory intentions. Viewed within the context of Restoration "recreational" court drama, such qualities—in fact, the very aspects of *Dido and Aeneas* that scholars have had the most difficulty explaining—may begin to make more sense, even if we cannot know for certain what motivated Tate and Purcell's particular choices.

An emphasis on performative continuity in the court theatrical tradition, as opposed to the differences underscored by generic, structural, and stylistic analysis, allows us to ask additional questions about *Dido and Aeneas*. Could it, for example, have served as another vehicle for the vocal (and dance) talents of Moll Davis and her royal daughter? The voice ranges of the characters Venus and Dido are effectively a match, as are those of Cupid and Belinda.[94] Uncertainty persists about the likely date for a supposed court performance of *Dido*, but if it occurred around 1687, as I have proposed, Lady Mary Tudor would have been

---

91 My own best effort at surveying the developing state of knowledge and opinion regarding the date, circumstances, and purpose of *Dido* (as well as its supposed political implications) can be found in Andrew R. Walkling, "Politics, Occasions and Texts," in Rebecca Herissone, ed., *The Ashgate Research Companion to Henry Purcell* (Aldershot: Ashgate, 2012), 201–67, pp. 222–24 *et seq.*; however, see also in particular my response to a communication from Curtis Price in *Journal of the American Musicological Society* 64 (2011): 268–74.

92 The essential development was Richard Luckett's discovery (see n. 84, above) of the 1684 boarding-school libretto (and hence performance) of *Venus*, which is closely analogous to the more famous libretto (and performance, now believed to have occurred in 1688) of *Dido*, the unique copy of which is in the Royal College of Music, London, shelfmark D144.

93 See Andrew R. Walkling, "The Masque of Actaeon and the Antimasque of Mercury: Dance, Dramatic Structure, and Tragic Exposition in *Dido and Aeneas*," *Journal of the American Musicological Society* 63 (2010), 191–242, pp. 200–7 *et seq.*

94 Wood and Pinnock, "'Unscarr'd by turning times'?," 384 (Table 1). Note that this is *not* the case with Adonis (a baritone) and Aeneas (a bass), whose ranges only overlap by a semitone.

Masques and plays at court after 1675   137

some four years older, and no doubt ready to take on the more mature role of Dido's confidante. We might also speculate as to the role of the French wind player Jacques Paisible in either or both productions: *Venus* explicitly requires "flutes" (*i.e.* French recorders) in its scoring, and Peter Holman has suggested that, as in *Calisto*, the same players may also have wielded oboes, if only to double the violins.[95] *Dido* (whose musical sources are, of course, far less authoritative) makes no mention of wind instruments, but could just as easily have deployed them as part of the orchestral texture.[96] As the leading performer on French wind instruments at the Restoration court—he was formally sworn of James II's musical establishment in 1685 but, as we shall see in Chapter 7, probably also had a significant, if less public, court position during the preceding reign—Paisible may well have been involved in both *Venus* and *Dido*. Of particular interest in this regard is the fact that, sometime after 4 December 1686, he and Moll Davis were married.[97] The couple could have become acquainted through any number of court channels, musical or otherwise, but the possibility of a "production romance" as the germ of their relationship is certainly an intriguing one.[98] All of these questions, of course, depend upon a tenuous chain of speculation, and must therefore be regarded in that light; however, speculation is perforce the lifeblood of all contextual (and even a good portion of the interpretive) scholarship on *Dido*, and it is thus all the more vital that we seek to understand how this notable work may have emerged out of a developing Restoration court theatrical tradition—one, moreover, that is almost certainly more far-reaching than the surviving evidence might appear to suggest.

One feature of both *Venus and Adonis* and *Dido and Aeneas* that has often received attention is that, alongside their status as *sui generis* works, they also represent an unexpected dead end in the development of English musical drama. The intimately dimensioned, through-composed tragic chamber opera did not subsequently become a staple of either court or public stage, and it was only in the first decade of the eighteenth century that English audiences came to appreciate the qualities of through-sung drama via large-scale Italian opera, rather than any native form. It is significant that the seeming disappearance of the short-lived indigenous style coincides with the "Glorious Revolution" and the consequent shift in

---

95 Holman, *Fiddlers*, 374.

96 Holman, on the other hand, rather perversely speculates that the use of wind instruments in *Venus* "may be a sign that it was conceived for larger forces than ... *Dido and Aeneas*, which seems to have been written just for strings" (*ibid.*).

97 George J. Armytage, ed., *Allegations for Marriage Licences Issued by the Vicar-General of the Archbishop of Canterbury, July 1679 to June 1687* (Harleian Society, 30; London: [Harleian Society], 1890), 256. For contemporary comment on the marriage, see John Harold Wilson, *All the King's Ladies: Actresses of the Restoration* (Chicago: University of Chicago Press, 1958; rpt. Chicago: Midway Reprints, 1974), 141. Less than a year later, on 16 August 1687, Lady Mary Tudor was wedded to Edward, Viscount Radcliffe (later 2nd Earl of Derwentwater).

98 Bruce Wood remarks upon the potential humor for a contemporary court audience of the fact that much of Paisible's playing in the earlier masque would have accompanied Venus's lascivious vocal lines: see Bruce Wood, ed., *John Blow: Venus and Adonis* (Purcell Society Edition, Companion Series 2; London: Stainer and Bell, 2008), xx.

138 *"Their greatest gallantry imaginable"*

aesthetic priorities at the English court. While certain courtly genres, such as sung New Year's and Birthday odes,[99] non-dramatic balls,[100] and even French ballets[101] persisted, there is no evidence of "recreational" theatrical performances—whether plays, masques, or chamber operas like *Venus* and *Dido*—taking place at court after 1688. The absence of these forms is not altogether surprising: William and Mary presided over a more modestly proportioned and less playful court, whose priorities diverged to a considerable extent from those of Charles and James, both politically and with respect to the allocation of financial resources. With the removal of Queen Mary of Modena and the increasing irrelevance of Catherine of Braganza (who left England for Portugal in March 1692), the post-Revolutionary court had no guiding figure to act as impresario, or at least inspiration, for such productions. Perhaps even more significant is the demographic change that had been underway at court since the late 1670s. The princely thespians Mary and Anne had successively grown up and moved on to more serious, adult pastimes; the most prominent of Charles II's dancing children, James, Duke of Monmouth, had been executed in 1685 for his rebellion against the newly enthroned James II; and with the marriage of Lady Mary Tudor to Viscount Radcliffe in 1687, the last of a generation of royal offspring completed the apprenticeship in courtly arts in which recreational dramatic presentations assumed such an important place.[102] Nor was there, in the closing years of the Stuart era, any new influx of high-born youth to fill the resulting void. The infant Prince of Wales, James Francis Edward, had gone into French exile in December 1688, one day short of the half-year anniversary of his birth, while the illegitimate children of James II by Arabella Churchill and Catherine Sedley were quickly shuffled away,[103] leaving only a single royal scion, William Henry, Duke of Gloucester, born to Princess Anne in July 1689, to be schooled in court theatrics. The young duke, however, pursued a

---

99 But not, interestingly, the sub-genre known as the "welcome song"; see Andrew R. Walkling, "Reading the Restoration Court Ode" (in progress).

100 Several balls can be identified as having taken place in the Hall Theatre on 4 November, William III's birthday, between the Revolution and the destruction by fire of Whitehall Palace in January 1698: see LC5/148, pp. 267 and 293 and WORK5/43, ff. 67^v–68^r (1689; *Register*, nos. 1350, 1349); WORK5/45, f. 97^r (1691; *Register*, no. 1402); WORK5/46, f. 91^r (1693; *Register*, no. 1458); LC5/151, p. 388 and WORK5/47, 93^r (1694; *Register*, nos. 1479, 1480); and LC5/152, p. 36 and WORK5/49, f. 96^r (1697; *Register*, nos. 1569, 1570).

101 The prime example is the ballet *Le Palais des Plaisirs*, performed for William III and the French ambassador at Kensington on 13 May 1698, about which Jennifer Thorp is currently preparing an article.

102 Lady Mary seems to have appeared in a leading role on the stage one more time on 12 December 1687, when Goodwin Wharton recorded having seen "ye play cheefly concerning my Lady Rattliff one of ye Kings dowghters": British Library, Add. MS 20007, p. 60, quoted in R. Jordan, "Some Restoration Playgoers," *Theatre Notebook* 35 (1981): 51–57, p. 55. It is not clear where this unnamed play took place; given Wharton's paranoia and belligerent behavior (discussed by Jordan), it seems unlikely that he would have attended a production at court.

103 These included Churchill's children Henrietta (born 1667), James (born 1670), Henry (born 1673), and Arabella (born 1674), all surnamed FitzJames, and Sedley's daughter Catherine Darnley (born c.1681). Henrietta married Henry, 1st Baron Waldegrave, in November 1683, while James, Henry, and Arabella all went into exile after their father's overthrow.

different path: inspired by his military-minded uncle and namesake, he assembled a youthful company of would-be soldiers who performed mock battles in his London residence and at St. George's Hall, Windsor.[104] These events, which the duke's sometime attendant and biographer Jenkin Lewis tellingly terms "his plays,"[105] became the theatrical form of choice for this sole surviving royal child actor and his companions—who, from an initial group of twenty-two "boys of Kensington" in 1693, ultimately came to number over ninety, including the sons of several courtiers.[106] As Matthew Kilburn reports, "Gloucester's 'army' became an accepted part of court ceremonial during his lifetime, particularly on royal birthdays and protestant festivals such as the anniversary of the birth of Elizabeth I."[107] The duke's untimely death in 1700, at the age of eleven, brought even this novel practice to an end; no child heir would again grace the British royal household until the arrival in England of the future George II's daughters Anne (b. 1709), Amelia (b. 1711), and Caroline (b. 1713) in October 1714. This demographic shift, in conjunction with changing social and cultural practices both at court and in the expanding public arena, spelled the end of the Restoration masquing tradition and permanently changed both the generic and the performative expectations associated with epideictic drama.

104 Jenkin Lewis, ed. Philip Hayes, *Memoirs of Prince William Henry, Duke of Glocester, From his Birth, July the 24th, 1689, to October, 1697* (London: Philip Hayes *et al.*, 1789), 50–51: "In little attempts towards acting plays in the family, for his entertainment, the Duke would act the part of a Prince himself, prettily and gracefully. But above all delights, was his acting as in battle, and sieges; and we were to carry on our intrenchments as regularly as though they were real. ... We every night had the ceremony of beating up the Tatta-ta-too, and the Word, and Patrole, as in *garrison*; which latter was sometimes an excellent piece of diversion." For descriptions of battles staged in St. George's Hall, see pp. 60–62 and 91; the latter of these took place in June 1696, shortly before the duke's seventh birthday.

105 *Ibid.*, 66: "I ... repeated stories from history to divert and assist him in his plays." These stories included those "of Alexander and Cæsar, and such renowned heroes of old" (p. 9).

106 *Ibid.*, 9 and 14. This is not to suggest that youthful amateur theatrical activity did not persist in other venues: see for example Matthew Prior's "*PROLOGUE, spoken by Lord* BUCKHURST, *at* Westminster-*School, at a Representation of Mr.* DRYDEN's *CLEOMENES,* The Spartan HERO. *At* CHRISTMAS, 1695" in Adrian Drift, ed., *Miscellaneous Works Of his late Excellency Matthew Prior, Esq;* (Dublin: G. Risk, G. Ewing, W. Smith, and G. Faulkner, 1739), 18–20. Lionel Sackville, Lord Buckhurst (later 7th Earl and 1st Duke of Dorset), who was a member of Gloucester's make-believe regiment, celebrated his eighth birthday just a few weeks after the 1695–96 Christmas holiday. Van Lennep, ed., *The London Stage* (1: 456 and clxxxiv) erroneously identifies the speaker of the prologue as "Lord Bathurst," *i.e.* Allen Bathurst, who became Baron Bathurst of Battlesden in 1712. (Bathurst, born in November 1684, was coincidentally also a companion of Gloucester.)

107 Matthew Kilburn, "William, Prince, duke of Gloucester (1689–1700)," *Oxford Dictionary of National Biography*, Oxford University Press, 2004; online edition, January 2008 [http://www. oxforddnb.com/view/article/29454, accessed 29 February 2012]. For a celebration of the youthful company's exploits, see John Blow's song entitled "The Duke of *Gloucesters* March," printed as a single songsheet by Thomas Cross in the 1690s ("Joyful Cuckoldom," no. 57; "Old Songs," no. 1) and in *Wit and Mirth: or Pills to Purge Melancholy ... Vol. IV* (London: "Sold by the Booksellers of *London* and *Westminster*," 1706; John Young, 1707, 1709), 192; rpt. in *Wit and Mirth: or Pills to Purge Melancholy ... The Sixth and Last Vol.* (London: J[acob] Tonson, 1720), 47.

Part II

"For such uses as the King shall direct"

Through-composed opera, foreign musicians, and the Royall Academy of Musick

4 Operatic experiments of the 1650s

It is perhaps characteristic of the complicated development of musical drama in seventeenth-century England that what is for modern audiences the most readily recognizable manifestation of the form—through-composed opera incorporating both tuneful air and recitative—emerges as the most uncertain, the most ephemeral, and the most contested generic category in the seminal period under discussion in the present book. We have explored, in the Introduction, the range of issues surrounding the definition and use of the term "opera" in England during this period, and have noted the ways in which the English perception of opera was influenced by a variety of genres and styles. We might also take into account the widely acknowledged influence, both direct and indirect, of Italian and French practice on the developing notion of opera, and its constituent parts, in England during the first half of the century. What this discussion reveals is that, apart from the presence of music, no single feature can be regarded as indispensable to the establishment of an operatic form in England, although certain essential qualities may be seen to predominate within the larger categories we have established.

The category to be examined here is, by definition, entirely dependent upon one of those qualities: through-composition. Yet even the act of establishing such a category feels like a kind of begging of the question: if the through-composed dramatic works of seventeenth-century England constitute such a disparate group, what justification is there for conceiving of them as a group at all? Is this no more than an implicit recognition of the formal and teleological biases of conventional opera scholarship? As I hope to show in the discussion that follows, through-composed opera does hold an important and distinct place in the history of musical drama in the Restoration—and, moreover, that place has only tangentially to do with the exceptional 1680s masque experiments *Venus and Adonis* and *Dido and Aeneas*, treated in Chapter 3. A proper understanding of its status requires a multi-faceted approach, incorporating questions of genre, textual analysis, and, perhaps most fundamentally, administrative/performance history. The establishment of this generic and historical-analytical category can be grounded in two strands of argument that may be characterized, respectively, as definitional and functional. The first involves charting the larger trends and thematics of through-composed opera as it was received and understood in Restoration England: this approach serves to reveal the essential externality, the perceived foreignness of the form. The second, functional, argument considers how the development of musical

144 *"For such uses as the King shall direct"*

drama, broadly conceived, in this period is affected by the specific features—what we might call the corollaries—of through-composed opera, via both their presence and their absence. There are several such corollaries to through-composition: some are largely inevitable, such as the use of the recitative style and the need to employ performers with a set of specialized musical and dramatic skills; others seem to have been culturally, or perhaps pragmatically, determined, as in the expectation of scenic (but at least initially *not* machine) spectacle, and the precept of political utility. In all instances, these corollaries deserve our attention, and can help us to make sense of the applicability of through-composed opera to other forms, including dramatick opera (the subject of my next study).

Of all the corollaries of through-composition, probably the most self-evident, and certainly the most commonly cited, is recitative. As it was to the Florentine Camerata and the Italian monodists at the end of the sixteenth century, recitative is the holy grail both for English composers of the Stuart era and for modern scholars seeking, however fruitlessly, to pinpoint the moment at which opera first emerged on the London stage. The supposed quantum leap that allowed dramatic dialogue and plot to be articulated in song was undoubtedly slow in coming to England: apart from Ben Jonson's ambiguously configured private masque *Lovers Made Men* of 1617, in which, allegedly, *"the whole masque was sung, after the Italian manner, stilo recitativo,"*[1] there is no known instance of recitative being used to construct a through-composed English theatrical work prior to mid-century. The 1650s, however, saw a sudden blossoming of interest in the form, represented by Richard Flecknoe's *Ariadne Deserted by Theseus* (1654) and Sir William Davenant's *The Siege of Rhodes* (1656) and *The History of Sir Francis Drake* (1659). Both *Ariadne Deserted* and *The Siege of Rhodes* were prefaced with theoretical disquisitions which, although neither explicitly invokes the term "opera," sought to advance the concept of through-composed drama founded on recitative. The former is described on its title page as "A Dramatick Piece Apted for Recitative Musick," while the latter was "Made a Representation by the Art of Prospective [*sic*] in Scenes, And the Story sung in *Recitative* Musick." In neither case does the actual music survive, but Eugene Haun and James Winn have profitably explored the texts of *Ariadne* and *Rhodes*, respectively, showing how effectively they function as libretti designed for musical settings that combine recitative and air.[2] Notwithstanding Flecknoe's ostentatious (if manifestly second-hand) invocation of the famous Italian composer

---

1 Stephen Orgel, ed., *Ben Jonson: The Complete Masques* (New Haven: Yale University Press, 1969), 257 (lines 16–17). A number of scholars have contended that this phrase, which first appeared only in Jonson's *Works* of 1640, should not be construed as indicating the use of any genuine recitative style in *Lovers Made Men* (a.k.a. *The Masque of Lethe*); however, see the well-considered argument in favor of a literal reading of the statement in Peter Walls, *Music in the English Courtly Masque, 1604–1640* (Oxford: Clarendon Press, 1996), 86–103.

2 Eugene Haun, *But Hark! More Harmony: The Libretti of Restoration Opera in English* (Ypsilanti: Eastern Michigan University Press, 1971), 42–49; James Winn, "Heroic Song: A Proposal for a Revised History of English Theater and Opera, 1656–1711," *Eighteenth-Century Studies* 30 (1996–97): 113–37, pp. 116–19. For a different but useful perspective on the nature of *The Siege of*

Operatic experiments of the 1650s   145

"*Claudio Montanendo*" and his pivotal role in the revival of ancient musical propriety, "conjoyning in one body again the scattered limbs of *Orpheus* (*Musick & Poetry*),"[3] the advent of through-composed dramatic works at this time in England owes less *per se* to the flourishing operatic tradition on the Continent than to a growing body of extended non-theatrical recitative-based pieces appearing at home, including the Italianate solo songs "Hero's Complaint to Leander" ("Nor com'st thou yet") by Nicholas Lanier and "Ariadne's Lament" ("Theseus, O Theseus") by Henry Lawes, as well as a number of declamatory pastoral dialogues by various composers, mostly dating from the 1630s and '40s.[4] These experiments, themselves highly dramatic in nature, certainly paved the way for the emergence of full-fledged stage works incorporating recitative, and the particular timing of the development may, as Eugene Haun has suggested, be in part attributable to the resumption of songbook publishing in England in 1652–53 under the auspices of John Playford.[5]

It is worth observing that the presence/use of recitative in a theatrical work is not actually a necessary condition for that work to be through-composed: certain court masques of the 1630s, such as Ben Jonson's *Love's Triumph through Callipolis* and *Chloridia* (both 1631), Aurelian Townshend's *Tempe Restored* (1632), and Davenant's *Luminalia* (1638) and *Salmacida Spolia* (1640), as well as the latter's Inns of Court masque *The Triumphs of the Prince d'Amour* (1636), seem to have consisted entirely of songs and instrumental dance tunes but without any connecting dialogue (either spoken *or* sung). The Caroline court masque is, however, an exceptional theatrical form whose conventions do not readily translate into the dramatic sphere; moreover, several of these works do lapse briefly into speeches in their antimasques, the very point at which the performance could be considered most "dramatic" in a conventional sense. On the other hand, neither is

---

Rhodes's recitative, see Ian Spink, *Henry Lawes: Cavalier Songwriter* (Oxford: Oxford University Press, 2000), 110–11.

3 Richard Fleckno[e], *Ariadne Deserted by Thesevs, And Found and Courted by Bacchus* (London: n. pub., 1654), sig. A5^r.

4 See Ian Spink, *English Song: Dowland to Purcell* (London: B. T. Batsford, 1974; rpt. 1986), 46–53. A particularly remarkable use of recitative singing to integrate pastoralism with politics can be found in the celebration of the marriage of Thomas Belasyse, 2nd Viscount Fauconberg, with Oliver Cromwell's daughter Mary, which took place at Hampton Court on 18 November 1657. No musical settings survive, but the event prompted not only a pair of pastoral dialogues by Andrew Marvell ("*Two Songs at the Marriage of the Lord* Fauconberg *and the Lady* Mary Cromwell," in Andrew Marvell, *Miscellaneous Poems* [London: Robert Boulter, 1681], 135–39), but also a lost poem by Sir William Davenant, an "*Epithalamium upon the marriage of the Lady Mary daughter to his Highnesse, wth the Lord Viscount Ffalconbridge, to bee sung in recitative musick*" listed among the contents of his presumably never-published collection "*Severall poems upon severall occasions*," which was registered with the Stationers' Company on 7 December 1657 (*Stationers' Register*, 2: 157). It should be noted that Davenant also imagined that his epic poem *Gondibert* might be sung in some form of recitative: see *The Preface to Gondibert* (Paris: Matthieu Guillemot, 1650), 45–46.

5 Haun, 4. Lawes's "Theseus, O Theseus" claims pride of place on the opening seven pages of the composer's *Ayres and Dialogues, For One, Two, and Three Voyces ... The First Booke* (London: John Playford, 1653).

146   *"For such uses as the King shall direct"*

the mere appearance of recitative sufficient to establish through-composition, as is demonstrated by the range of pre- and immediately post-1660 theatrical works in which extended recitative passages appear to coexist with songs and spoken dialogue. Examples include Jonson's *The Vision of Delight* (1617), Townshend's *Albion's Triumph* (1632), Flecknoe's *The Marriage of Oceanus and Britannia* (1659), Sir Robert Stapylton's *The Slighted Maid* and *The Step-Mother* (February and October 1663, respectively), and, most notably—because it is the only large-scale example whose music actually survives—the 1659 version of James Shirley's *Cupid and Death*.[6] While most of these works do not even advance pretensions to full musical status, they exist alongside and in relation to the limited repertoire of through-composed pieces from this early period that, in at least some cases, we may begin to think of as "operatic" (see Table 4.1).

The foregoing discussion, of course, does not tell the whole story of how opera was perceived by English observers in this period. While recitative, as a corollary of through-composition, remains an essential component of any attempt to characterize the form, it is noteworthy how frequently we encounter, in the early documents, a formula that explicitly pairs the musical with the visual elements of these staged representations: as Thomas Blount's *Glossographia*, first published in 1656, puts it, opera is "performed by Voyces in that way, which the Italians term *Recitative*, being likewise adorned with Scenes by Perspective."[7] Blount's definition echoes an earlier, private observation made by John Evelyn,[8] and anticipates Davenant's descriptions of *The Siege of Rhodes* and its two successor

---

6   The original version (*Cvpid and Death. A Masque. As it was Presented before his Excellencie, The Embassadour of Portugal, Upon the 26. of March, 1653* [London: J. Crook and J. Baker, 1653]) is almost identical, textually speaking, to that of 1659 (for which there are two issues of the playbook: *Cupid and Death, A Private Entertainment, represented with Scenes & Musick, Vocall & Instrumentall* and *Cvpid and Death, A Private Entertainment, represented with Scenes, Variety of Dancing, and Musick, Both Vocall & Instrumentall* [London: John Crooke and John Playford, 1659]); Matthew Locke's autograph score, containing his own music and that of Christopher Gibbons, is in British Library, Add. MS 17799. For a comprehensive discussion of this work, see Robert Thompson and Andrew R. Walkling, eds., *Cupid and Death* (Musica Britannica 2, revised edition: London: Stainer and Bell, in progress).

7   T[homas] B[lount], *Glossographia: or a Dictionary Interpreting all such Hard Words ... as are now used in our refined English Tongue* (London: Humphrey Moseley, 1656), sig. Ee1[v]. As Haun (p. 26) notes, Blount's volume had been advertised as "in the Presse" as early as 1653.

8   Evelyn, *Diary*, 2 (1620–1649): 449–50 (June 1645): "we went to the Opera, which are Comedies [& other plays] represented in Recitative Music by the most excellent Musitians vocal & Instrumental, together with variety of Seeanes painted & contrived with no lesse art of Perspective, and Machines, for flying in the aire, & other wonderfull motions." The performance Evelyn saw, of Giovanni Rovetta and Maiolino Bisaccioni's *Ercole in Lidia* at the Teatro Novissimo, may actually have taken place c.22–27 May (New Style), since Evelyn identifies the time as "Ascension Weeke" (see p. 451). Compare Sir John Reresby's description, recounting his stay in Venice during Carnival in 1657, of "operas, which are usually tragedies, sung in music, and much advantaged by variety of scenes and machines" (*The Travels and Memoirs of Sir John Reresby, Bart.* [London: Edward Jeffery *et al.*, 1813], 67); the original manuscript, "very probably written by his own hand, which Mr. Hodges purchased out of the Library of Mr. Topham Beauclerk" (p. v), is not known to be extant.

Table 4.1 Theatrical works known or believed to deploy through-composition or to contain substantial recitative passages, 1600–73

YEAR	WORK	AUTHOR	COMPOSER(S)	RELEVANT FEATURES	MUSICAL SOURCE(S) OF EXTANT RECITATIVE PASSAGES
1617	*The Vision of Delight*	Ben Jonson	Nicholas Lanier	1 or more recitative passages[a]	*lost*
1617	*Lovers Made Men*	Ben Jonson	Nicholas Lanier	**THROUGH-COMPOSED**[b]	*lost*
1632	*Albion's Triumph*	Aurelian Townshend	?	1 "song"[c]	*lost*
1654	*Ariadne Deserted by Theseus*	Richard Flecknoe	Richard Flecknoe	**THROUGH-COMPOSED**	*lost*
1656	*The Siege of Rhodes*	Sir William Davenant	Henry Lawes (*entries 1, 5*)* Henry Cooke (*entries 2, 3*) Matthew Locke (*entry 4*)	**THROUGH-COMPOSED**	*lost*
1659	*The History of Sir Francis Drake*	Sir William Davenant	Matthew Locke (?+others)	**THROUGH-COMPOSED**	*lost*
1659	*The Marriage of Oceanus and Britannia*	Richard Flecknoe	Richard Flecknoe	4 passages labeled "Recitative"(?+others)	*lost*
1659	*Cupid and Death* [original version 1653]	James Shirley	Matthew Locke*	2 antimasque episodes; grand masque	British Library, Add. MS 17799
1663	*The Slighted Maid*	Sir Robert Stapylton	John Banister	1 "ode", 2 masques	*lost*
1663	*The Step-Mother*	Sir Robert Stapylton	Matthew Locke	1 dialogue, 2 masques	*lost*
1663	*Pompey*	Katherine Philips	John Banister*	1 act song	Christ Church, Oxford, Mus. 350; British Library, Add. MS 33234
1667	Italian opera [not performed]	Giovanni Battista Draghi	Giovanni Battista Draghi	**THROUGH-COMPOSED**	*lost*
1673	*The Empress of Morocco*	Elkanah Settle	Matthew Locke	1 masque	Christ Church, Oxford, Mus. 692

N.B. Davenant's *The First Day's Entertainment at Rutland House* and *The Cruelty of the Spaniards in Peru* contain no recitative (see Table 4.2).

Key:
〜〜〜〜 = delineates scope of Table 4.2
* = other composer(s) known to have been involved, but not with recitative passages

[a] Delight (?and others) "spake in song (*stylo recitativo*)."
[b] *"the whole Maske was sung (after the Italian manner) Stylo recitativo."*
[c] Mercury sings second song "*In voce Recitativa.*"

148   *"For such uses as the King shall direct"*

productions, *The Cruelty of the Spaniards in Peru* (1658) and *The History of Sir Francis Drake* (1659).[9] Thus it may be apt to characterize opera as an essentially "technological" genre, combining a newly emerging musical technology (recitative) with the theatrical technology of scenic spectacle.[10] This qualification helps to elucidate the form's connection to the earlier court masque: like the masque, opera was a heightened theatrical form whose stock-in-trade was the elicitation of wonder in its viewers. Yet in the case of opera these technologies were, in a sense, lent a greater degree of democratization: the lofty declamatory speech/song style of the masque was simplified, both linguistically and musically, into the more conversational—yet nonetheless still rhetorically elevated—recitative, while the costly scenes and machines found in the court productions were reduced to more affordable stationary wings embellished with changeable shutters and supplemented by an occasional scene of relieve. (Machines, in Davenant's case at least, were eliminated entirely.) In both the literary and the visual realm, the form was marked not only by a less abstruse rhetoric, but by an emphasis on linear narrative and dramatic characterization—as seen even in Davenant's oddly formal and non-dialogic *Cruelty of the Spaniards*. To this inventory of opera's "technology," we might add one other feature also very much present in the masque: the use of theatrical representation to articulate a political and social philosophy and thereby to exert some degree of ideological control over the spectators (and, by extension, over those who might later read the texts or hear about the performances at second hand).[11] While not perhaps "technical" in a conventional sense, this component, like its scenic and musical counterparts, required considerable deftness and skill

---

9 See *The Siege of Rhodes Made a Representation by the Art of Prospective in Scenes, And the Story sung in Recitative Musick. At the back part of Rutland-House in the upper end of Aldersgate-Street, London* (London: Henry Herringman, 1656 [2 states]; 2nd ed., "... *At the Cock-Pit in Drury Lane*" 1659); *The Cruelty of the Spaniards in Peru. Exprest by Instrumentall and Vocall Musick, and by Art of Perspective in Scenes, &c. Represented daily at the Cockpit in Drury-Lane, at Three after noone punctually* (London: Henry Herringman, 1658); and *The History of S' Francis Drake. Exprest by Instrumentall and Vocall Musick, and by Art of Perspective in Scenes, &c. The First Part. Represented daily at the Cockpit in Drury-Lane at Three Afternoon Punctually* (London: Henry Herringman, 1659[/60]). Having witnessed a performance of (probably) *Sir Francis Drake* on 5 May 1659, John Evelyn echoed Davenant's formulation, describing the work as "a new ~~Italian~~ Opera after the *Italian* way in *Recitative Music & Sceanes*, much inferior to the Italian composure & magnificence" (*Diary*, 3 [1650–1672]: 229).

10 See Leslie Hotson, *The Commonwealth and Restoration Stage* (Cambridge, MA: Harvard University Press, 1928; rpt. New York: Russell and Russell, 1962), 134–36 for a discussion of the academy set up by Sir Balthazar Gerbier in Bethnal Green in 1649 (later relocated to Whitefriars) whose myriad subjects of instruction included the "*Mathematick*" discipline of "*Architecture*, both that for *Building*, and that for *Magnificent Houses*, and in particular the *Secret Motions of Sceanes*" (quotation from *Mercurius Pragmaticus* 25 [12–19 September 1648]: sig. K[k]1ʳ).

11 For a discussion of this component with relation to pre-1660 operatic entertainments, see Susan Wiseman, *Drama and Politics in the English Civil War* (Cambridge: Cambridge University Press, 1998), chapters 5 and 6, as well as Chad Thomas, "Negotiating the Interregnum: The Political Works of Davenant and Tatham," *1650–1850: Ideas, Æsthetics, and Inquiries in the Early Modern Era* 10 (2004): 225–44.

Operatic experiments of the 1650s 149

in the execution as it sought to superimpose its constructed version of reality onto the normal perceptual frame of its audience.

Sir William Davenant's four "operatic" works of 1656–59 certainly illustrate the features just rehearsed. Davenant was nothing if not an experimenter, and these theatrical pieces served as a proving ground for his efforts to reshape the now moribund court masque form into something both valuable and entertaining to his patrons. We have long since progressed beyond the somewhat perverse notion, originally advanced by Edward Dent, probably on the basis of a misreading of a remark made by John Dryden in 1672, that Davenant's deployment of through-composition was no more than a ruse, designed to circumvent the terms of the 1642 Parliamentary order for the closing of the playhouses.[12] Rather, a series of actions and statements by the playwright offer a picture of him seeking to utilize the elevated discourse of musical speech and scenic spectacle for political/moral ends, specifically in the service of the regime. These include his original securing of a license to erect "a Theatre or Playhouse, with necessary tireing and retiring Rooms and other places convenient … wherein Plays, musical Entertainments, Scenes or other the like Presentments, may be presented" in 1639,[13] his publication of *A Proposition for Advancement of Moralitie By a new*

---

12 Edward J. Dent, *Foundations of English Opera: A Study of Musical Drama in England During the Seventeenth Century* (Cambridge: Cambridge University Press, 1928; rpt. New York: Da Capo Press, 1965), 65 and 97: "The plain fact was that D'Avenant was not really attempting to start English opera as a primary object of his efforts. His first desire was to get the theatres re-opened and plays (naturally, his own) performed"; "As soon as the theatres were placed on a firm footing [after 1660], there was no more need to disguise plays under the title of 'moral representations.'" Despite being often cited in support of Dent's contention, Dryden's statement actually makes no such claim: "*It being forbidden* [Davenant] *in the Rebellious times to act Tragedies and Comedies, because they contain'd some matter of Scandal to those good people, who could more easily dispossess their lawful Sovereign than endure a wanton jeast; he was forc'd to turn his thoughts another way: and to introduce the examples of moral vertue, writ in verse, and perform'd in* Recitative Musique. … [A]*t his Majesties return*[,] … *growing bolder, as being now own'd by a publick Authority, he review'd his* Siege of Rhodes, *and caus'd it to be acted as a just* Drama" (John Dryden, *The Conquest of Granada by the Spaniards* [London: Henry Herringman, 1672], sig. a2ᵛ). Dent takes his supposition even further, arguing (pp. 65–68) that *Rhodes* was not only conceived but originally written as a full-length spoken play, and then cut down to function, initially, as a libretto. For a judicious discussion of the problems with Dent's contentions, see Haun, 64–69.

13 Patent of 20 March 1639, transcribed in Robert Sanderson, *Foedera, Conventiones, Literæ, Et Cujuscunque Generis Acta Publica … Tomus XX* (London: J[acob] Tonson, 1735), 377–78; see also the docquet in SP38/18, under the date of 25 March (*Calendar of State Papers, Domestic 1638–39*: 604). This initial foray into theatre management encountered stiff opposition from residents of the Fleet Street neighborhood and from Davenant's potential competitors in the business, and he was forced to abandon his plans by October: see Folger Shakespeare Library, MS Z.c.22 (39). For a discussion of these events see John Freehafer, "Brome, Suckling, and Davenant's Theater Project of 1639," *Texas Studies in Language and Literature* 10 (1968): 367–83. W. J. Lawrence, in "The Origin of the English Picture-Stage" (in W. J. Lawrence, *The Elizabethan Playhouse and Other Studies* [2 vols.: Stratford-upon-Avon: Shakespeare Head Press, 1912–13; rpt. New York: Russell & Russell, 1963], 2: 121–47, p. 127) concludes from the wording of the

150   *"For such uses as the King shall direct"*

way of Entertainment of the People in 1653,[14] his issuance of a manuscript proposal to Secretary of State John Thurloe in early 1656,[15] and his presentation of a debate "Against, *and* For Publique Entertainment *by* Moral Representations" in *The First Day's Entertainment at Rutland House*, first performed on 23 May 1656.[16] Davenant clearly knew what he was doing: his 1656 proposal pointedly emphasizes the economic and social benefits to be gained from "pleasant assemblies, which are severall wayes occasion'd in all great cities, not only in times of peace, for transmitting the wealth of the gentry to retaylers and mechanicks, but allsoe in seasons of hazard, because States should never seeme dejected, nor the People be permitted to be sad."[17] In anticipation of the project, he seems to have shopped carefully for a suitable venue: in the 1656 proposal, bemoaning London's loss of high-income consumers and patrons, he could already observe with some exactitude that "thirteene houses of the nobility are let or offer'd to hire," and his selection of Rutland House, the sequestrated former home of Cecily Manners, the Roman Catholic Dowager Countess of Rutland (d. 1654) was obviously strategic, located as it was in "Cripplegate Liberty," a small patch of autonomous territory adjacent to Charterhouse Yard, situated just up Aldersgate Street and literally steps beyond the boundary that circumscribed the limits of the City of London authorities.[18] Once his plans had been approved by the Protectorate government, Davenant assembled a top-shelf team that included John Webb, the pupil and artistic heir of Inigo Jones, as scene designer, and a group of composers, singers, and instrumentalists who represented what one scholar has labeled "the cream of the musical Establishment."[19] Initially at least, his admission charge of 5s was commensurate with this, although after moving to the Cockpit Theatre in Drury

---

patent that "D'Avenant fully intended to give evening concerts as well as occasional performances of opera."

14 (London: n. pub., "1654" [but actually published 1653]): see James R. Jacob and Timothy Raylor, "Opera and Obedience: Thomas Hobbes and *A Proposition for Advancement of Moralitie* by Sir William Davenant," *The Seventeenth Century* 6 (1991): 205–50 (for the date, see p. 241).

15 Bodleian Library, Oxford, MS Rawlinson A. 46, ff. 293–94, endorsed "Some Observations concerning the People of this Nation": see C. H. Firth, "Sir William Davenant and the Revival of the Drama during the Protectorate," *English Historical Review* 18 (1903): 319–21. Firth notes (p. 319) that while the undated document "is bound up with papers relating to January 1656–7 ... the probable date of it is the early part of 1656, for it obviously preceded the opening of Davenant's entertainments." Dennis Arundell, in *The Critic at the Opera* (London: Ernest Benn, 1957; rpt. New York: Da Capo Press, 1980), 60, seems to infer a 1657 date.

16 *The First Days Entertainment at Rutland-House, By Declamations and Musick: After the manner of the Ancients* (London: H[enry] Herringman, "1657" [recte 1656]), 2. For the spelling of this source, see the Introduction, n. 20, above.

17 See Firth, 320.

18 There may also have been a more direct personal connection, since Davenant had written an elegy on the death of Cicely's husband Francis Manners, 6th Earl of Rutland, in Decmber 1632: see W[illiam] Davenant, *Madagascar; with Other Poems* (London: Thomas Walkl[e]y, 1638), 108–10.

19 John Protheroe, "Not so Much an Opera ... A Restoration Problem Examined," *The Musical Times* 106 (1965): 666–68, p. 666. Davenant himself described them as "the most transcendent

Operatic experiments of the 1650s 151

Lane in 1657 or 1658 he strove for greater affordability, assuring his more impecunious prospective auditors that "*Notwithstanding the great expence necessary to Scenes, and other ornaments in this Entertainment, there is a good provision made of places for a shilling.*"[20]

Davenant's pragmatism can also be seen in his highly flexible generic commitments: his initial gambit, the appropriately titled *First Days Entertainment at Rutland-House, By Declamations and Musick: After the manner of the Ancients* can hardly be called dramatic at all, consisting as it did of orations presented in the form of two classically inspired debates, framed by several illustrative musical pieces for instrumental consort and a pair of strophic songs with choruses.[21] Its chief purpose was twofold: first, to advance the playwright's philosophical and utilitarian arguments on behalf of what he termed "Moral Representations," a goal enacted in the work's first debate, between Diogenes "*the Cynick*" and Aristophanes "*the Poet*" (p. 2). The second debate seems to have been intended to underscore the political and social motivations of Davenant's project. In the printed text, this consists of a rather superfluous discussion "*concerning the præeminence of* Paris *and* London" (p. 45),[22] but there is evidence that the topic may have emerged out of a menu of ideas for disputations in Davenant's mind. A contemporary report on the production, written by an unidentified attendee following the premiere of 23 May 1656, promises that "other Declamations wilbee ready" after ten days of performances,[23] and several weeks earlier the poet Abraham Cowley had written a letter to an unnamed correspondent requesting on behalf of Davenant that the recipient "take upon yow ye trouble of writing one Pro and Con upon what Theme yow please, or (if yow like it) upon this (The praeminence of a single or married life, under what persons yow shall Judge most proper)."[24]

---

of *England* in that Art, and perhaps not unequal to the best Masters abroad" (*The Siege of Rhodes* [1656], sig. A3^r).

20 *The Cruelty of the Spaniards*, 27. This concessionary pricing scheme may have been born of necessity: an unidentified observer of the premiere of *The First Day's Entertainment* in 1656 (SP18/128/108; see n. 23, below) noted that "[t]he expectation was of 400 persons, but there appeared not aboue 150 auditors."

21 Dent describes it (p. 54) as "little more than what nowadays would be called a 'lecture-recital in costume.'" According to a contemporary report submitted to the Protectorate government (see n. 23, below), Davenant had advertised the performance with "Bills" announcing "The Entertainment by Musick and Declarations after the manner of the Ancients." The instrumental music appears to have been the work of George Hudson and Henry Cooke, while the songs were composed by Henry Lawes and Charles Coleman (see Table 4.5 nn. † and ‡, and Table 4.6).

22 It is this dialogue that Samuel Pepys read aloud "with great mirth" to his ailing wife Elisabeth (who was of French extraction) on 7 February 1664: see *Diary*, 5: 40 (Pepys's copy of the text is still in his library at Magdalene College, Cambridge, PL 2347).

23 SP18/128/108, endorsed "June 1656" (*Calendar of State Papers, Domestic 1655–56*: 396; an accurate transcription of the document is printed in Hotson, *The Commonwealth and Restoration Stage*, 150).

24 Letter dated 3 April 1656: Princeton University Library, Taylor MSS, RTC01, Box 5, Folder 29, verso (quoted, with a number of inaccuracies, in Eric Walter White, *A History of English Opera* [London: Faber and Faber, 1983], 66).

152 *"For such uses as the King shall direct"*

Thus, *The First Day's Entertainment* seems initially to have been conceived as a sort of modular piece, into which debates on topics of perceived importance could be inserted as desired—thereby effectively creating a "Second Day's" and "Third Day's Entertainment," and so on.[25] Not all of these debates may have been political *per se*, but it is interesting to note that Cowley's letter describes "[t]he subiects for ye first day" as "1. For and against Morall Representations in ye persons of Diogenes and Aristophanes; 2. For and against ye right of ye Spaniards to ye West Indies, in ye persons of a Spaniard and an Indian, wth Musique and Songs afterward agreeable to ye matter & persons." The invocation of Spain and the West Indies is apt—indeed, more so than the London/Paris debate—given that in 1656 England, in alliance with the French, was in the thick of a war against Spain brought on in part by Oliver Cromwell's "Western Design" to deprive the Spaniards of territory in the Caribbean, thus weakening the Iberian stranglehold on much of the New World. This topic would seem to have been a particular priority for Davenant: in his proposal of early 1656 to deploy opera in the service of the Protectorate regime, he suggested that "[i]f morall representations may be allow'd … the first arguments may consist of the Spaniards' barbarous conquests in the West Indies and of their severall cruelties there exercis'd upon the subjects of this nation: of which some use may be made."[26] While not ultimately incorporated into *The First Day's Entertainment*, this theme found its way into Davenant's later operas *The Cruelty of the Spaniards in Peru* and *The History of Sir Francis Drake*, which, although they focus instead on the fate of the Inca land empire in Central and South America, clearly function as political propaganda in support of the ongoing Anglo-Spanish conflict.[27]

The blatantly propagandistic character of *Peru* and *Drake* is entirely predictable, given the statements made in Davenant's proposals and, if less overtly, in the tenor of *The First Day's Entertainment*. Less clear is why the playwright chose instead to follow up his exordium with a different sort of production entirely.

---

25 Davenant may have had plans for other types of Classically inspired declamations as well: see the "*essay for the new theater, representing the preparacon of the Athenians for the reception of Phocion after hee had gained a victory*" announced as part of the unpublished "*Severall poems upon severall occasions*" (see n. 4, above), as well as the lost octavo "Satyricall declamations at the Opera" listed in William London's *A Catalogue of New Books* (London: Luke Fawn and Francis Tyton, 1660), sig. C2^v, which is almost certainly the same as the "Satyrical Declamations, by Sir *William Davenant* Knight" advertised two years earlier in *Mercurius Politicus* 416 (13–20 May 1658): 538.

26 See Firth, 321.

27 See Sir Henry Herbert's sour observation, recorded in 1662, that Davenant "exercised the Office of Master of the Reuells to Oliuer the Tyrant, And wrote the first and second parte of *Peru* … Wherein hee sett of the Justice of Oliuers Actinges by Comparison with the Spaniards And Endeauoured thereby To make Oliuers Crueltyes appeare Mercyes, in Respect of the Spanish Crueltyes" (N. W. Bawcutt, ed., *The Control and Censorship of Caroline Drama: The Records of Sir Henry Herbert, Master of the Revels 1623–73* [Oxford: Clarendon Press, 1996], 264 (no. R38). Herbert's "first and second parte" presumably refers to *Peru* and *Drake*, rather than the mooted sequels to the latter (for which see below). For a good discussion of the former work and its political contexts and implications, see Janet Clare, "The Production and Reception of Davenant's *Cruelty of the Spaniards in Peru*," *Modern Language Review* 89 (1994): 832–41; as Clare points out (pp. 834–35), "Davenant's representation of the defeat of the Spanish and the collaboration of the colonized Indians with the English enacts the objectives, but not the outcome, of the Western campaign."

Operatic experiments of the 1650s 153

Nothing in *The First Day's Entertainment* could be seen necessarily to point to *The Siege of Rhodes* as an obvious next step: while the opening debate invokes "the Ornaments of a publique *Opera*, Musick and Scenes" (p. 36), nowhere in the text are recitative or through-composition specifically mentioned. *Rhodes*, on the other hand, is heavily invested in its status as a through-composed piece, as can be seen in Davenant's rather detailed discussion of recitative and musical text-setting in the printed preface. Moreover, the work is not explicitly propagandistic: set in the 1520s, in a distant location of scant importance to seventeenth-century English overseas policy, it offers little in the way of nationalistic rhetoric apart from presenting, at the beginning of the Fifth Entry, "a general Assault given to the Town; the greatest fury of the Army being discern'd at the English Station" (p. 29).[28] Instead, it serves as a historical backdrop for a heroic tale designed, in Davenant's formulation, "to advance the Characters of Vertue in the shapes of Valor and conjugal Love" (sig. A3^v) by depicting the bravery and honor of the lead characters, Alphonso and Ianthe, under pressure from military assault and the invidious effects of jealousy. This quality, which led subsequent commentators from Dryden onwards to see in *Rhodes* the origin of the Restoration rhymed heroic tragedy, has caused it to be viewed as the pivotal work in Davenant's Protectorate tetralogy, rather than as the anomaly it actually represents. Davenant's operatic theorizing notwithstanding, *Rhodes* sits uncomfortably within any contemporary definition of opera, whether English or Continental. Unlike the original academic-courtly Italian form, it eschews the gods and supernatural forces of Classical mythology, not to mention other features common to both that genre and the English court masque (with which Davenant was eminently familiar), including dancing and spectacular machine effects.[29] With its intimate setting, its tortured heroes, ethical dilemmas, grandiloquent rhetorical flights, and its absorption into the sweep of great historical events, *Rhodes* is fundamentally of a piece with the Baroque *Trauerspiel* described by Walter Benjamin, rather than with Classically derived tragedy and its musical offspring, opera. The fact that *Rhodes* was quickly transformed into a spoken play (with an altered cast of characters and an added Second Part) after the Restoration says less about Davenant's supposed desire to outsmart the Cromwellian authorities with an artificially conceived musical setting than it does about how this mutation in the original plan for "Moral Representations" set to music pointed out a new, and perhaps unexpected, way of proceeding.

Davenant's seemingly experimental and evolutionary process may help to explain the perplexing jumble of styles seen in his four Protectorate-era

---

28 This feature appears to have represented a coordinated effort: John Webb's design for the shutter representing the scene (Devonshire Collection, Chatsworth) is labeled "The Towne generally assaulted especially at the English Bulwarke."

29 As Marie-Claude Canova-Green observes, "Il est remarquable que ces premiers essais d'opéras ne semblent s'inspirer ni des livrets d'opéras italiens, les seuls modèles alors existants, ni des ballets de cour français de la Régence, bien que son long séjour à Paris ait sans doute permis à Davenant de se familiariser avec les uns comme avec les autres" ("Le Relais Français dans l'Implantation de l'Opera en Angleterre (1660–1685)," in Christopher Smith and Elfrieda Dubois, eds., *France et Grande-Bretagne de la Chute de Charles Ier à celle de Jacques II (1649–1688)* [Norwich: Society for Seventeenth-Century French Studies, 1990], 239–48, p. 240).

154   *"For such uses as the King shall direct"*

"operas."[30] The most peculiar of these is *The Cruelty of the Spaniards in Peru*, which offers a narrative structure, but couched within a highly formalized pattern of six entries that are devoid of actual dramatic dialogue.[31] As in *The First Day's Entertainment*, form is the defining characteristic; indeed, as Table 4.2 shows, *Peru* grows directly out of the generic makeup of *Entertainment*, relying primarily on speeches directed at the audience, illustrative songs, and symphonies. The theatrical element consists not of dialogue (in recitative or otherwise), but rather in the addition of specifically visual ingredients: scenery, dances, and tumbling/acrobatics.[32] Since it is also a relatively small step substantively from the oratorical debate on the Spanish right to the West Indies originally mooted for *The First Day's Entertainment* to the speech-driven moralizing presentation that is *Peru*,[33] it may be that the latter work's eccentric structure and generic qualities provide evidence that Davenant had already written it by 1656, while his "operatic" vision was still under development.[34] Having discerned the need for something different—perhaps less bluntly political—to draw in audiences, the playwright might have shelved *Peru*, along with the missing West Indies debate, and only pulled it out two years later, when—with the Spanish war still raging, albeit now mostly in the Netherlands rather than across the Atlantic—he found a need for a new operatic entertainment to keep his project moving forward.[35]

In this rendition of events, the real point of arrival in Davenant's operatic trajectory is *The History of Sir Francis Drake*. *Drake* represents a kind of fine-tuning of the playwright's double-pronged approach: like *Peru*, it is contemporary and propagandistic, but at the same time it incorporates the essential features of

---

30 For a fascinating and entertaining exploration of the qualities of Davenant's "apparitional" theatre of the 1650s, see Kevin L. Cope, "The Glory that WAS Rome—and Grenada [*sic*], and Rhodes, and Tenochtitlan: Pleasurable Conquests, Supernatural Liaisons, and Apparitional Drama in Interregnum Entertainments," *Studies in the Literary Imagination* 32/2 (Fall 1999): 1–17.

31 Each entry follows the same pattern of events: 1. an instrumental symphony to accompany the appearance of the scene; 2. a narrative speech (in verse) by the Priest of the Sun; 3. a gymnastic feat performed by the Priest's "attendant"; 4. a strophic song (with chorus); 5. a preparatory tune while the dancers enter; and 6. a character dance. The final entry, which concludes with "the grand Dance," adds an extra tune/dance before the song.

32 Comparing it to the more conventionally theatrical *Siege of Rhodes*, Dennis Arundell (*The Critic at the Opera*, 61) opines that *Peru* "seems more dramatic—or anyway more theatrically exciting—than the more naturalistic [*Rhodes*]. It is all full of atmosphere."

33 Clare (p. 834) remarks upon the shift from the West Indies to Peru, although it is worth observing that the setting of *Sir Francis Drake*—whose action appears to be adumbrated in the sixth entry of *The Cruelty of the Spaniards*—is specifically the Isthmus of Panama, rather than modern-day Peru proper. Davenant's locational vagueness with regard to the New World is perhaps more easily excused when we recall that Sir Robert Howard's *The Indian Queen* (1664) centers upon the inter-American conflict between Incas and Aztecs, a geographic and historical impossibility.

34 Davenant may have been influenced by the publication of John Phillips's translation of Bartolomé de Las Casas's *The Teares of the Indians* (London: Nath[aniel] Brook, 1656), whose dedication and preface passionately urge Lord Protector Cromwell and the English people in general to rise up in response to "*Spanish Cruelties*" (sig. A5ᵛ) against the natives and "*revenge the Blood of that innocent People*" (sig. b3ᵛ).

35 Susan Wiseman (*Drama and Politics in the English Civil War*, 145) suggests that *Peru* "may have been intended for earlier performance but delayed by the Hispaniola expedition [which failed disastrously in early 1655] only to become viable again after the defeat of the Spanish at Santa Cruz in 1657."

Table 4.2 Generic features in (and performance venues for) the "operatic" productions of Davenant, compared with works by Flecknoe, Jordan, and Shirley, 1654–59

PRODUCTION	Performed	Published	RUTLAND HOUSE	COCKPIT	Scenes	Machines	Speeches	Recitative (Through-Composed)	Songs	Symphonies	Dance	Acrobatics
Ariadne Deserted by Theseus (FLECKNOE)	—?	1654			§				X	X	X	
Cupid his Coronation (JORDAN)	1654	——		"at the Spittle diverse tymes"	‖		X		X	X	X	
Fancy's Festivals (JORDAN)	1654–57?	1657			‖		X		X	X	X	
The First Day's Entertainment at Rutland House (DAVENANT)	1656	"1657"*	X				X		X	X		
The Siege of Rhodes (DAVENANT)	1656–59?	1656, 1659	X	X	X			X	X	X		
The Cruelty of the Spaniards in Peru (DAVENANT)	1658–59?	1658		X	X		X		X	X	X	X
The History of Sir Francis Drake (DAVENANT)	1659?	1659[/60]		X	X			X	X	X	X	
The Marriage of Oceanus and Britannia (FLECKNOE)	—?	1659			X	X[a]	X	†	X	X	X	X
Cupid and Death (SHIRLEY)	1659**	1659**		"att the Military Ground in Leicester ffields"	X	X[b]	X	‡	X	X	X	[?][c]

Key/Notes:

* Actually published 22 November 1656: see the copy in the Thomason Collection, British Library (shelfmark: E.1648.(2.)).

** 2nd version; first performance/edition (probably without recitative), 1653.

§ Scenic backdrop, "*The Landscapt, or Prospect of a Desart Isle … with a Ship afar off sailing from thence*" (p. 1), but no scene changes indicated.

‖ "*The Scene*" (rear shutter?) drawn on multiple occasions to reveal seated masquers, who "*descend*" to the stage to dance (and, in one instance in *Fancy's Festivals*, speak lines).

† Four distinct passages labeled "Recitative" (pp. 4–6 [interrupted by a chorus], 14–15, 18–20, 26–27); work is not through-composed.

‡ Three recitative passages (pp. 15–17, 19–21, 22–27); music is in British Library, Add. MS 17799; work is not through-composed.

---

[a] Oceanus enters "*mounted on a Chariot compos'd of a great Scollop shell, drawn by two Seahorses in swimming posture; the chariot gliding on the wheels of watermils*" (pp. 3–4, 17 ["*as before*"]).

[b] Cupid "discover'd flying in the Aire" (p. 15); Mercury "seen descending upon a Cloud" (p. 22). *N.B.* these effects also used in the 1653 production.

[c] Possible acrobatic display by "apes" in the 5th antimasque entry? See Thompson and Walkling, eds., *Cupid and Death*.

Rhodes: active characters presenting a historically situated story through dramatic dialogue—which is cast in recitative, thus making the work (with its songs and instrumental music) through-composed.[36] *Drake* retains much of *Peru's*

36 It is worth observing that, unlike *The First Day's Entertainment* (which featured Edward Coleman's wife and "a nother wooman" according to the report in SP18/128/108) and *Rhodes* (in which Mrs. Coleman famously sang the part of Ianthe), Davenant's last two "operatic" works contain exclusively male characters. Moreover, as Dennis Arundell points out (*The Critic at the Opera*, 69),

156   *"For such uses as the King shall direct"*

meta-theatrical disposition by including character dances (although the gymnastic tumbling is eliminated), and by avoiding any serious dramatic conflict: the title character, supremely confident, marches through the landscape, instructing his son in the finer points of virtue, checking the unheroic excesses of his overzealous associates, and brilliantly managing his troops in preparation for the culminating battle against the Spanish. Yet Davenant's final operatic effort, despite the complete absence of love, jealousy, treason, doubt, or even a worthy military adversary, admits of a degree of the dramatic force seen in *Rhodes*: it is more elevated, more serious than *Peru*, and seeks to build tension, particularly in the striking *grand guignol* scene in the fifth entry, which discovers a bound and "dishevel'd" Spanish bride, taken prisoner by Drake's Symeron allies (p. 27).[37] At the same time, in contrast to the earnest *Trauerspiel*-like heroics of *Rhodes*, *Drake*'s heroism is suitably attenuated, subordinated to the principal goal of providing its audience with splendid entertainment. Thus, while still lacking both mythological content and machine spectacle, *Drake* most accurately exemplifies the European-wide evolution of masque and ballet into opera.[38] Davenant must have recognized the greater suitability of this work to operatic treatment: while *Rhodes* was converted (expanded and altered) into a spoken play in 1661,[39] *Drake* was joined with *Peru* (possibly in the same year, but certainly by 1663) to form two musical acts of the five-act pastiche *The Play-House to be Let*.[40] Yet questions persist: how do we explain Davenant's decision to create and present in 1656 a work (*Rhodes*) whose style and content have so little to do with either what came before or what succeeded it within his larger "project"? And why, having at last arrived at an acceptable model in *Drake*, did he subsequently abandon through-composed opera altogether after the Restoration? There is circumstantial evidence to suggest that, had the Restoration, with its changed theatrical priorities, not occurred, Davenant might have continued to traffic in through-sung operas: *Drake*'s title page enticingly describes that work as "*The First Part*," implying possible plans

---

in contrast to *Rhodes*'s complement of seven singers, *Drake* calls for "no less than fifteen soloists, of whom five were principals, as well as a male chorus and the usual dancers"; he labels *Drake* "an opera on the grand scale" (p. 70). Arundell's explanation focuses on the company's move from the restricted space of Rutland House to the larger Cockpit between *Rhodes* and *Peru*, but it is important to recall that *Rhodes*, with its female lead and its small cast, continued to be played at the Cockpit alongside its larger, all-male, more political Spanish siblings.

37   Compare the essentially non-dramatic *grand guignol* in the fifth entry of *Peru*, where the Spaniards are shown torturing the Indians and English and practicing cannibalism. The "Symerons," or Cimarrones, were African slaves brought to Panama by the Spanish, who then escaped and led an independent existence fighting against their former masters: see Philip Nichols, *Sir Francis Drake Revived* (London: Nicholas Bourne, 165[2]), 7 (earlier editions had been published in 1626 and 1628).

38   See the assessment of John Evelyn, quoted in n. 9, above.

39   See Protheroe, "Not so Much an Opera" (n. 19, above).

40   "THE Play-house to be Let," in *The Works of Sʳ William Davenant Kᵗ* (London: Henry Herringman, 1673), section 2 (dated 1672), pp. 67–119.

Operatic experiments of the 1650s   157

for further dramatic treatments of Sir Francis's circumnavigation of the globe, the attack on Cadiz, and/or the defeat of the Spanish Armada; moreover, in May 1659 the playwright registered a forthcoming "booke called *The second part of the Seige of Rhodes, made a representacon by the Art of Prospective in scenes & the story sung in recitative musicke*,"[41] whose provocative title leaves open the question of its relationship to the post-1660 spoken sequel to the original opera.[42] Yet even these two tantalizing hints seem to point in contradictory directions, at least with regard to Davenant's political and artistic intentions. The most we can say is that, despite his efforts over four years and as many productions, he never succeeded in establishing a clear operatic pattern for his successors to follow, and it is therefore less surprising, under the circumstances, that these works ultimately had little subsequent influence, at least in the realm of musical drama.

Davenant was not the only figure looking to experiment with operatic form during the Protectorate. Richard Flecknoe's *Ariadne Deserted by Theseus*, which appeared in print two years before *The Siege of Rhodes*, shares many generic features with the latter, as can be seen in Table 4.2.[43] Yet Flecknoe's approach differs in significant ways. First, while Davenant strove to make his productions available to the general public,[44] Flecknoe seems to have pursued his equivalent creative goals with more exalted ambitions in mind. At the very outset of his preface to *Ariadne Deserted*, he avers that the music of princes, "as their Persons, ... should be elevated above the Vulgar, and made not only to delight the ear, but also their understandings; not patcht up with Songs of different subjects, but all of one piece" (sig. A3^r). This, of course, implies considerations of structure and subject matter but also, crucially, recitative. Yet where Davenant, having worked out the principle that "frequent alterations of measure [in the poetry] ... are necessary to *Recitative* Musick for variation of *Ayres*" (*Rhodes*, sig. A3^v), handed off the technical accomplishment of the music itself to his team of composers (Henry

---

41 *Stationers' Register*, 2: 225 (dated 30 May).

42 A further complicating factor is found in John Evelyn's remark (*Diary*, 3: 309) that on 9 January 1662 he "saw acted the <2>d part of the Seige of *Rhodes*: ... it was in *recitativa* Musique." This confusing detail is generally dismissed as a product of Evelyn's notorious unreliability in this portion of his (actually retrospective) "diary"—indeed, Evelyn's editor suspects that the last part of the phrase "is probably a later addition to the text" (p. 309 n. 1). The likelihood of there having been a through-sung performance of either part of *The Siege of Rhodes* in 1662 is slim, but could Evelyn have been remembering a pre-1660 performance of *Rhodes, Part 2* for which no other evidence survives?

43 For a detailed exploration of *Ariadne Deserted* and Flecknoe's contribution to opera, see Haun, 35–49.

44 As Janet Clare has observed (p. 834), Davenant's thinking did undergo some change: in 1653's *A Proposition for Advancement of Moralitie*, "he had argued the moral and socially educative advantages for the lower classes of a reformed stage. In the letter to Thurloe [of 1656] he changes tack, emphasizing that the clientele he now proposes to attract is the gentry."

158 *"For such uses as the King shall direct"*

Lawes, Henry Cooke, and Matthew Locke),[45] Flecknoe seems to have aspired to being sole master—both librettist and composer—of his (admittedly modest) *Gesamtkunstwerk*. His discussion of the difference between Italian and English as languages appropriate for musical setting, particularly in recitative, far outpaces Davenant's less sophisticated reflections, and even leads him to an implied critique of the musical coterie on which Davenant would soon draw:

> I cannot but note their want of judgment, who have endevoured to imitate at all parts in our language the Italian Recitative Musick, not considering, that the Musick of all Nations is cast in the mould of their language, whence there being great difference betwixt their verbosity, and our concised speech, it consequently follows, that the difference should also be betwixt their Musick and Poetry, and ours. (sig. A6^v–A7^r)

In the absence of Flecknoe's actual music, we have no way to assess his claim to compositional innovation. What is clear, however, is that his forms and practice derived their inspiration from the Italian. Flecknoe's sole surviving song, the four-voice homophonic "Go, Phoebus, go" (which reads like a piece written for some unidentified court masque) shows clear Italian influences, particularly in its cadences.[46] *Ariadne Deserted* lacks a French-inspired balletic component— as does *Rhodes*—but unlike Davenant, Flecknoe compensates for the absence of that potentially emotive feature by deliberately harnessing the recitative music to express the passions of his characters. This is particularly true of the heroine: at her first appearance on stage, Ariadne "*expresses ..., in recitative Musick, The Confusion of her Thoughts, and her distracted passions*" (p. 1); shortly thereafter, "*she starts up, and first expresses her Rage and Anger, next her pitifull Lamentations and Grief*" (p. 3); while later "*she falls into a passion of sighing, weeping, and lamenting*" (p. 6). To be fair, we have no music from *The Siege of Rhodes* to compare with this theatrical display of emotion in song. Henry Lawes was certainly capable of such effect, as witness his "Theseus, O Theseus" (treating precisely the same subject matter as Flecknoe), and Matthew Locke would also prove himself up to the task with the laments of Nature and the Chamberlain in the fourth and fifth entries of *Cupid and Death* in 1659. But Davenant's highly dramatic libretto is quite long for a piece set entirely to music, and one suspects that there would have been little latitude for pregnant pauses, emotive text repetition, or drawn-out musical sighing. The text of *Ariadne Deserted*, on the other

---

45 See, moreover, Cooke's boastful remark to Samuel Pepys in 1667 "that he was fain to direct Sir W Davenant in the breaking of his verses into such and such lengths, according as would be fit for music, and how he used to swear at Davenant and command him that way when W. Davenant would be angry, and find fault with this or that note" (*Diary*, 8: 59).

46 *The Musical Companion, In Two Books* (London: John Playford, 1673), 206–7.

Operatic experiments of the 1650s   159

hand, is both considerably shorter and more dramatically static, with a Classically derived story line of exceptional simplicity: the first half of the libretto is given over to Ariadne's lament and the condoling responses of the elements; this is followed by the entry of the Bacchantes, whereupon Bacchus, having discovered the abandoned lady, wonders at her beauty and her sorrow and makes his court to her; the formerly voluble Ariadne then utters a single abbreviated couplet indicating her assent to the wine-god's advances, and the work concludes with a brief expostulation by Bacchus followed by a choral triumph. The interest lies not in any exposition or narrative *per se*, but rather in the textual and musical articulation of the already-familiar characters.[47] *Ariadne Deserted* thus represents an important link to the early seventeenth-century Continental practice of operatic through-composition: with its mythological story and its use of music to express the characters' emotional states, Flecknoe's work is considerably closer to the original Italian model than anything Davenant produced.

There is, we should note, no certain evidence that Flecknoe ever actually did compose the music for *Ariadne Deserted*, even though in the libretto he twice promises its imminent publication.[48] There is similarly no record of any performance of the piece: the extant text does not appear to be a programme libretto, and indeed Flecknoe had a history of printing his work privately for circulation among friends and acquaintants. Moreover, he had none of the official connections or production resources available to Davenant. Our suspicions are further raised by the wording on the title page of Flecknoe's second operatic text, published in 1659. *The Marriage of Oceanus and Britannia* is described as "AN Allegoricall Fiction, really declaring ENGLANDS Riches, Glory, and Puissance by SEA. *To be represented in Musick, Dances, and proper Scenes.*"[49] The use of the future-tense phrase "*To be represented*" suggests the possibility that this work may also never have seen performance, but was simply a prospectus for an unrealized theatrical project.[50] Regardless, it offers an interesting perspective on how the

---

47 Haun (p. 49) is fulsome in his praise of *Ariadne Deserted*: "so obvious is its superiority as an opera libretto to *The Siege* [*of Rhodes*] that there is no comparison. ... Not until the composition of *Dido and AEneas* was there to be another libretto in English so skilfully written."

48 Sig. A2[r–v] (Dedication to Mary Stuart [*née* Villiers], Duchess of Richmond and Lennox): "*permit me, I beseech your Grace ... to present this model of my Recitative Musick to your fair Hands, as I shall shortly my Musick it self, to your admirable faculty of judging and understanding it*"; sig. A7[v] (Preface): "Of the composition of the *Musick*, I shall defer to speak, untill the publishing of it, as shortly I intend to do with a Treatise of the Air of *Musick*, and of this in particular, that as no composition seems more easy to the ignorant than it, so none is more hard to those who understand it."

49 Richard Fleckno[e], *The Mariage of Oceanus and Brittania* (n. p.: n. pub., 1659), title page.

50 Printing plays on speculation appears to have been a regular practice for Flecknoe: see for example *Erminia. Or, the fair and vertuous Lady* (London: n. pub., 1661), sig. A3[r]: "*To the onely few, The Best and Noblest.* I Promis'd you a Play, and to avoid farther importunity) behold it here. I cod not promise you it shud be Acted, (for having no interest in the Stage, I leave that to those who have;)

160 *"For such uses as the King shall direct"*

poet's operatic sensibilities were developing, perhaps as inspired by Davenant's productions, which Flecknoe likely would have attended, and probably read as well. The sole surviving copy of the text, at the Huntington Library, lacks all of signature A except the title page, so we cannot be sure what kind of prefatory theoretical disquisition Flecknoe might have supplied,[51] but *Oceanus and Britannia* clearly represents a departure from *Ariadne Deserted*, and seems to reflect the intervening influence of *The Cruelty of the Spaniards in Peru* and possibly also *The History of Sir Francis Drake*. As Table 4.2 shows, it is actually the only work that unambiguously incorporates every generic element, including a two-part acrobatic/gymnastic episode reminiscent of the feats seen in *Peru*,[52] and even introducing a simple machine effect in Oceanus's wheeled "*Chariot ... drawn by two Seahorses*" (p. 4). What is most striking about this work, however, is that it defies the convention established by *Ariadne Deserted* and in Davenant's four productions that recitative and spoken dialogue are mutually exclusive. Rather, *Oceanus and Britannia* returns to the earlier masque convention (as seen, for example, in *The Vision of Delight* and *Albion's Triumph*) in which recitative is one among several discrete but equivalent forms of song-like expression, rather than the comprehensive musical binding agent of through-composed opera. In two instances (pp. 4, 14), such passages are described somewhat ambivalently as "The Song or Recitative"; two others are given more particular designations.[53] While the word "Recitative" only appears four times (in Parts 1–3), other passages would appear to invite or imply recitative setting. There are also numerous strophic songs, including two labeled "Air or Canzzonet" and a ballad set to the tune "Packington's Pound," as well as choruses (some injected into the recitative passages, as in *Ariadne Deserted*), dances, and instrumental symphonies for the opening of each scene. At the same time, each of the work's five parts commences with a speech, in the style of *Peru*. Thus, we see in *Oceanus and Britannia* a

---

you may think it a preposterous way to Print it before it be Acted." The author of the anonymous tragedy *Emilia* (London: n. pub., 1672), probably also Flecknoe, similarly informs his readers (also "*the Onely Few*") that "I Print not the *Play* before it is Acted, to make it more *Publick*, but onely more *Legible* for those who are to judge of it; who, if they like it in this *Undress*, will much more in its *Theatrical Habit*" (sig. A2[r]).

51 The collation of this octavo pamphlet is [A][1], B–C[8], D[6]: hence, the title page could have been printed, along with a half-title page, as part of sig. D. However, Flecknoe seems normally to have relished such authorial statements, as can be seen in *Ariadne Deserted*, as well as in his more conventional play *Love's Dominion, A Dramatique Piece, Full of Excellent Moralitie; Written as a Pattern for the Reformed Stage* (London: n. pub., 1654).

52 In the 3rd Part (p. 21): "The Introduction. / To the dauncing on the Ropes, / *Castor and Pollux in Grecian military habits, with bright shining stars in their fore heads appearing & dauncing i'th clouds, in which the ropes are conceald*"; a brief speech by Oceanus; "*Hear the Tumblers are introduct like the Phocii or Seacalves, Dauncing and tumbling ridiculously their antique measure.*" *Peru*, it should be noted, also has a rope-dancing episode, featuring two apes (only one of whom dances on the rope), at the end of the First Entry.

53 "The Recitative, In the soft *Lydian* strain" (p. 18); "The Recitative, Directed to the English Marriners and Souldiers" (p. 26).

Operatic experiments of the 1650s   161

comprehensive amalgamation of the earlier forms, one that points the way not towards a putative tradition of through-composed opera, but rather to a "mixed" form—inspired by the principles of court masque, but equally applicable to a narrative theatrical mode—in which recitative exists side-by-side with a wide variety of vocal and instrumental music and, crucially, spoken dialogue.

The same appears to be true of the other theatrical piece of this period in which recitative plays a significant role, James Shirley's *Cupid and Death*, first presented in 1653 and revived in 1659. In adapting what is believed to have been originally a primarily spoken play interspersed with short punctuating songs and dances into a more comprehensively musical work, Matthew Locke opted not to pursue the path of through-composition that he had honed in *Rhodes* and possibly in *Drake*. Instead, he left untouched the spoken dialogue of the work's first three ("domestic") antimasque entries, and devoted his compositional attentions to the fourth and fifth ("emblematic") entries and the main masque itself. In particular, the fifth entry, featuring the Chamberlain's antics involving two apes, Death, and a satyr, alternates spoken text with recitative passages and short bursts of tuneful arioso, mimicking the fragmented manner of an antimasque-style dance.[54] While the fourth entry and the main masque are actually through-composed, the overall effect of *Cupid and Death* is that of a spoken dramatic entertainment, in which recitative is used primarily to heighten the discourse of immortals.[55] It is not clear whether the revised *Cupid and Death* pre- or post-dated the appearance of *Oceanus and Britannia*: in terms of generic features, they are quite similar.[56] What is evident, however, is that the trend in musical theatre seems to have been away from full-blown through-composition, and towards a more flexible model—a development that Davenant seems implicitly to have acknowledged when he expanded and reconfigured *The Siege of Rhodes* into a spoken drama after the Restoration. As we shall see presently, it is this "mixed" model, and not the brief efflorescence of through-composition seen in *Ariadne Deserted*, *Rhodes*, and *Drake*, that informs the ongoing English experiments with recitative in the 1660s.

* * *

In the context outlined above, *The Siege of Rhodes* appears a doubly anomalous case: neither does it fit comfortably, in generic or political terms, among Davenant's other three Protectorate "operatic" entertainments, nor is it indicative of the broader direction in which musical drama was moving in the waning years of the Interregnum. One wonders, then, why it has remained the subject of such exceptional scholarly interest. A possible explanation may lie in its fortuitous

---

54 For a discussion of the varying recitative styles deployed in this work, see Thompson and Walkling, eds., *Cupid and Death*.

55 The title characters themselves are dancers, and have only negligible spoken/sung lines.

56 *Cupid and Death* may even have included acrobatic feats, performed by the apes in the fifth antimasque entry (in both the 1653 and 1659 versions): see Thompson and Walkling, eds., *Cupid and Death*.

162 *"For such uses as the King shall direct"*

exemplification of the other essential feature of "operatic" entertainments, namely scenic ornament. On the evidence of its printed text, *Rhodes* is not much different from the majority of its contemporaries: like *Peru* and *Drake*, it offered a purpose-designed "frontispiece" or proscenium arch and included a number of scene changes. Similar scenic variation is also evident in *Oceanus and Britannia* and *Cupid and Death* (both of which added modest machine effects, something not adopted in Davenant's entirely non-mythological pieces), as well as in Thomas Jordan's mostly spoken masques *Cupid his Coronation* (1654) and *Fancy's Festivals* (1657), which are also considered in Table 4.2.[57] This in itself represents a significant novelty for the English public theatre, and *Rhodes* can justly claim the distinction of having been the first to offer scenic spectacle to a paying audience.[58] But what particularly sets *Rhodes* apart is the chance survival of John Webb's designs for the scenery, which John Orrell has persuasively demonstrated to be for the production's appearance at the Cockpit Theatre in Drury Lane, probably in 1658 or 1659, although some version of the same designs was almost certainly used at Rutland House in 1656 as well.[59] There are eight, or perhaps nine, in all, including a plan and a section of the stage, an elevation of the proscenium and wings, and designs for three sets of shutters and two scenes of relieve.[60] Because

57 Both appear to have used a pair of shutters at the rear of the stage to conceal and reveal the various masquers: see Bodleian Library, Oxford, MS Rawlinson B. 165, ff. 107^r–113^v, ff. 108^v, 109^r, 109^v, [112^r,] and 112^v (see also W. H. Lindgren III, "An Introduction to and Edition of *Cupid his Coronation*," *Neuphilologische Mitteilungen* 76 [1975]: 108–29), and Thomas Jordan, *Fancy's Festivals: A Masque* (London: by Tho[mas] Wilson, 1657), sigs. B1^v, B2^v, B4^r, C3^r, C4^r, D2^r, D2^v, and D4^r. *Cupid his Coronation* sported "a Frontispiece formed piramidically, beautified with the figures of Peace on the Right hand Plenty on the left, and Love more eminently placed in the medium" (f. 108^r).

58 Both productions of *Cupid and Death* appear to have been non-public affairs: the 1653 performance was "Presented before his Excellencie, The Embassadour of Portugal, Upon the 26. of *March*, 1653," while the 1659 performance is simply described as "A Private Entertainment." The same is true of *Cupid his Coronation* ("Presented wth good Approbation at the Spittle diverse tymes by Masters and yong Ladyes y^t were theyre Scholers") and *Fancy's Festivals* ("privately presented by many civil persons of quality"). The publicly presented *First Day's Entertainment* did not include scenery. *Ariadne Deserted by Theseus*, which may not have been performed at all, appears to rely solely upon a painted backdrop, representing "*The Landscapt, or Prospect of a Desart Isle ... with a Ship afar off sailing from thence*" (p. 1).

59 John Orrell, *The Theatres of Inigo Jones and John Webb* (Cambridge: Cambridge University Press, 1985), 67–77. Orrell suggests that Davenant deliberately had the scenes designed in the first instance in anticipation of a later move to the Cockpit, "for whose stage the Rutland House arrangements were in truth a mockup" (p. 73).

60 The plan and section are in British Library, Lansdowne MS 1171, ff. 11^v and 12^r; the remainder are in the Devonshire Collection, Chatsworth. For reproductions of the first three enumerated here, see Orrell, *Theatres*, 69–70 (plates 10 and 11); for the elevation and the five scene designs, see Roy Strong, *Festival Designs by Inigo Jones: An Exhibition of Drawings for Scenery and Costumes for the Court Masques of James I and Charles I* ([Washington, DC]: International Exhibitions Foundation, 1967), plates 107–12; and for all eight, Southern, *Changeable Scenery* (see n. 76 below), plates 10, 11, and 25 (*a–f*). Southern also constructed a model from the plans, images of which can be seen in his plates 12–15; I am grateful to Hyeyun Chin for creating a similar model for me in 2009. Orrell has suggested (see *Theatres*, p. 198 n. 70) that another drawing by Webb in

Operatic experiments of the 1650s   163

of their rarity,[61] these designs have received a tremendous amount of attention in the scholarly literature.

Three points need to be made regarding the *Rhodes* scenery. First, however much he may have sought to emphasize the spectacular, Davenant was operating in a very constricted space. In his prefatory address to the printed playbook, he famously and somewhat whimsically conceded that his scenes were

> confin'd to eleven foot in height, and about fifteen in depth, including the places of passage reserv'd for the Musick. This is so narrow an allowance for the Fleet of *Solyman* the Magnificent, his Army, the Island of *Rhodes*, and the varieties attending the Siege of the City; that I fear you will think, we invite you to such a contracted Trifle as that of the *Cæsars* carv'd upon a Nut.[62]

The Cockpit stage (erected in a theatre that had not originally been designed for scenic effects) was only slightly larger, at eighteen feet deep and, seemingly, with the same height and width (the latter being 22′ 4″, but with the frontispiece supports stepped in slightly in order to accommodate the impingement of the Cockpit's gallery posts[63]). There appears to have been no thrust stage, but the three feet of depth gained by the move to the Cockpit may have induced Davenant to add the dancing (and gymnastics) to *Peru* and *Drake*.[64] Second, partly in response to these space restrictions, the *Rhodes* scenes deploy extremely rudimentary stage technology. The three pairs of perspective rock-face wings were stationary, and thus—in the absence of any machine effects—the only scenic movement occurred through the drawing of shutters at the back of the stage. Webb's stage designs show a grooved frame built to accommodate the three pairs of shutters ("Rhodes" seen from a distance; "The Towne beseiged"; "The Towne generally assaulted"), behind which are spaces for the installation of the two scenes of relieve (showing Solyman's throne and the Turkish army drawn up in battle formation on the slopes of Mount Filerimos), which could be revealed by opening all three of the shutter

---

the Devonshire Collection represents a preliminary design for *Rhodes*'s stationary cliff-like wings: see Stephen Orgel and Roy Strong, *Inigo Jones: The Theatre of the Stuart Court* (2 vols.: London: Sotheby Parke Bernet; Berkeley: University of California Press, 1973), 2: 810 (cat. no. 464).

61 See below for a discussion of the only comparable set of designs from the second half of the seventeenth century, produced by Webb for the production of Roger Boyle, Earl of Orrery's *Mustapha, the Son of Solyman the Magnificent*—interestingly, a kind of sequel to Davenant's two parts of *The Siege of Rhodes*.

62 Sig. A2ᵛ. Despite having written several masques for the Caroline court, Davenant must have been accustomed to the problems of working in a small theatrical space: his 1639 patent permitted the creation of "a Theatre or Playhouse, with necessary tireing and retiring Rooms and other places convenient, containing in the whole forty yards square at the most" (*Foedera*, 20: 378). This would translate to a space of 360 square feet: something like 18′ x 20′ or 15′ x 24′, an incredibly small amount, particularly if it really was "in the whole."

63 See Orrell, *Theatres*, 72–74.

64 Indeed, this may account for the fact that *Peru*, which I have suggested may have been written before *Rhodes*, was shelved while Davenant was still presenting his work at Rutland House.

164   *"For such uses as the King shall direct"*

pairs. Presumably, no more than two scenekeepers—to pull the shutters (each 4½' wide x 7½' high) and to replace the pieces of the relieve scenes while the shutters were closed—would have been necessary to run the entire show.[65] Yet even this limited repertoire of effects was sufficient to allow Davenant to puff the production's deployment of "the Art of Prospective in Scenes," and we may assume the same to be true of *Peru* and *Drake*, which would have used the same stage configuration with different shutters and relieves, a different proscenium arch, and perhaps different stationary wings as well.[66]

Third, we should consider the question of how the *Rhodes* shutter and relieve backdrops were actually used as a component of the drama in which they appeared. Despite its relatively simple attributes, the scenery clearly formed an important part of Davenant's schema for the production. Each of the five "entries" (*i.e.* acts) of the opera opens with the appearance of a new, previously unseen scenic vista, always "prepar'd by Instrumental Musick" (see Table 4.3).[67]

Beginning with the Third Entry, medial scene changes are introduced, so that every entry except the First concludes with the scene introduced in the Second Entry, showing Rhodes "*beleaguer'd at Sea and Land*" (p. 7). The scenes that initiate the Third and Fourth Entries are both scenes of relieve rather than shutters, and the latter of these relieve scenes (showing "the Prospect of Mount *Philermus*" with Solyman's army "in the Plain below, drawn up in *Battalia*" [p. 22]) returns briefly in the Fifth Entry, the only entry in which the scenery is changed twice. Several conclusions emerge from an examination of the patterns revealed in Table 4.3. First, the pivotal scenic vista is the one I have labeled "S2," the shutter showing Rhodes beleaguered, which appears four times in the opera. The first shutter ("S1"), which depicts "a far off, the true Prospect of the City RHODES, when it was in prosperous estate" (p. 2) accompanies only the protatic First Entry, in which the sole dramatic action centers on the Christians' reaction to the impending attack of the Turkish forces. It is only in the Second Entry that the epitasis emerges, with the first appearance both of Solyman (*i.e.* the Ottoman Sultan Suleiman the Magnificent) and of the play's

---

65 These qualifications may provide us with a better means to understanding the attenuated scenic element in the court production of *The Empress of Morocco* of 1673.

66 Orrell (*Theatres*, p. 74) argues that the frontispiece for *Peru* would have consisted of a rounded arch, higher than the "low frontispiece" of *Rhodes*, and therefore necessitating the removal of the music room (supposed to be situated above the stage, at least at Rutland House) to some other location in the larger Cockpit Theatre. This is, however, not a necessary conclusion from the description of the *Peru* frontispiece, which simply says that "A*N Arch is discern'd rais'd upon stone of Rustick work; upon the top of which is written, in an Antique Shield*, PERU; *and two Antique Shields are fix't a little lower on the sides* …" (sig. A2ʳ; see also *The History of Sʳ Francis Drake*, sig. A2ʳ, where "*This Frontispiece was the same which belong'd to the late Representation; and it was convenient to continue it, our Argument being in the same Country*"): while the *Peru/ Drake* frontispiece may have been slightly arched, with the side shields "*fix't a little lower*," there is no evidence that it represented any substantial structural difference from that used for *Rhodes*.

67 Note Davenant's remark in his published prefatory address that the producers had "oblig'd our selves to the variety of Five changes[,] according to the Ancient Drammatick distinctions made for time" (sig. A2ʳ).

Operatic experiments of the 1650s 165

Table 4.3 Musical, scenic, and plot structure in *The Siege of Rhodes*

ENTRY	DISCRETE MUSIC- AL COMPONENT	SCENE (S = shutter; R = relieve)	CHARACTER GROUP (1656/1659)	ADDITIONS ("Pt. 1", 1661)
First Entry (pp. 2–6)[a]	Instrumental music	S1. Prospect of Rhodes		
			CHRISTIANS	+ IANTHE IN SICILY
	Chorus: soldiers			
Second Entry (pp. 7–13)	Instrumental music	S2a. Rhodes beleaguered		
	(Alphonso song + chorus)		CHRISTIANS	
			TURKS	
	Chorus: women			
Third Entry [A] (pp. 14–16)	Instrumental music	R1. *Solyman's throne*		
			TURKS	
[B] (pp. 16–21)		S2b. Rhodes beleaguered		
	Chorus: men and women		CHRISTIANS	+ TURKS (ROXOLANA)[b]
Fourth Entry [A] (pp. 22–23)	Instrumental music	R2a. *Mount Philermus*		
			TURKS	
[B] (pp. 24–28)		S2c. Rhodes beleaguered		
	Chorus: wives		CHRISTIANS	+ TURKS (ROXOLANA)
Fifth Entry [A] (pp. 29–3[5])	Instrumental music	S3. General assault	*"French scenes"*	
			TURKS 5	
			CHRISTIANS 2	
			TURKS 2	
[B] (pp. 3[5]–36)		R2b. *Mount Philermus*		
			TURKS	
[C] (pp. 36–40)		S2d. Rhodes beleaguered		
			CHRISTIANS[c]	+ TURKS (ROXOLANA)
	Chorus: soldiers			

[a] Page numbers from 1656 edition.
[b] Davenant, *Works* (1673), section 2, p. 14: "*The Scene changes to* Solymans *Camp.*"
[c] Four speeches (total 18 lines) for Alphonso and Ianthe added, probably in 1661.

love-interest, the virtuous Christian woman Ianthe. This entry provides us with the opera's only scenic anomaly, in which every action on both sides of the opera's strict religious/military divide—a conversation between the Grand Master Villerius and his Admiral, followed by a (unique) strophic song sung by the Sicilian Duke Alphonso;[68] the appearance of Solyman and his General, Pirrhus; and the arrival before Solyman of Mustapha with the captive Ianthe (to whom Solyman grants safe conduct to Rhodes)—occurs in front of this schematic view, which shows the city walls to the left, with enemy cannons and a battle camp opposing them on

---

68 Dent (p. 73) reasonably suggests that this song may have been sung to a ballad tune, and that the "*Chorus*" (*Rhodes*, 9) that follows a few lines later after a brief intervening conversation between two other characters would have reprised the same tune.

166 *"For such uses as the King shall direct"*

the right. Yet the expansive schematism of this scene is subsequently diminished: beginning with the Third Entry, it becomes—despite being incongruously situated *outside* the walls of Rhodes—the exclusive province of the Christian characters, that is, the Rhodians themselves. The Turks, on the other hand, are associated with the opera's pair of relieve scenes: in the Third Entry, "a Royal Pavilion ... representing *Solymans* Imperial Throne" (p. 14: "R1" in Table 4.3), the production's only interior scene, and in the Fourth and Fifth Entries, the "Prospect of Mount *Philermus*" already mentioned ("R2"). Thus, throughout the last three entries of the opera, the two relieve scenes with their Turkish characters establish a regular counterpoint with the Christian characters' appearances before the "Rhodes beleaguered" shutter (S2). The single exception to this comes at the beginning of the Fifth Entry when a new shutter representing "a general Assault given to the Town" (p. 29; "S3") serves as a backdrop—as we might expect in a battle situation—for a series of rapid interchanges between and among the Turkish and Christian character groups.[69]

Artistically speaking, Davenant and Webb's scenic schema is masterful in its combination of well-worn theatrical custom and exceptional novelty. For an audience at least some of whom had never witnessed changeable scenery before, it offers a sequence of visual revelations spread across the entire span of the opera. The performance opens with a conventional prospect of the city, an aerial view with the sea in the foreground (S1), which Webb seems to have based loosely on Erhard Reuwich's woodcut depiction in Bernhard von Breydenbach's extremely popular *Peregrinationes in Terram Sanctam*, first published in 1486, or possibly on images from either Giovanni Francesco Camocio's *Isole famose porti, fortezze, e terre maritime* of 1571–72 or Giuseppe Rosaccio's *Viaggio da Venetia, a Costantinopoli* of 1598 (see Figure 4.1).[70]

This vista is akin to the kind of static backdrop with which theatregoers would have been familiar from earlier stage practice. After the First Entry, however, the "backdrop" is revealed to the audience as a shutter, which divides, while music plays (both to manifest a sense of wonder and to cover any sound made by the sliding frames), to reveal the more theatrically apt scene of Rhodes beleaguered (S2), where the opera's action gathers momentum. With both Christians and Turks appearing in front of this new stage set, the audience is lulled into a sense of

---

69 This portion of the entry could be said to break down into a total of nine "French scenes," seven of which involve the three Turkish characters as they successively rush on and off the stage in the confusion of the battle: see Table 4.3.

70 Bernhard von Breydenbach, *Peregrinationes in Terram Sanctam* (Mainz: [Pierre Schöffer and] Erhard Reuwich, 1486 *et seq.*), ff. 21ᵛ–22ʳ; [Giovanni Francesco Camocio], *Isole famose porti, fortezze, e terre maritime sottoposte alla Serᵐᵃ Sigʳⁱᵃ di Venetia, ad altri Principi Christiani, et al Sigᵒʳ Turco nouamēte poste in luce* (Venice: "alla libraria del segno di S. Marco," [1571–72]), unfoliated; Giuseppe Rosaccio, *Viaggio da Venetia, a Costantinopoli per Mare, e per Terra, & insieme quello di Terra Santa* (Venice: Giacomo Franco, 1598), f. 48ᵛ. As Figure 4.1 demonstrates, it is unlikely that Webb relied upon the view engraved by Eberhard Kieser for Daniel Meisner, *Thesaurus Philo-politicus. Das ist: Politisches Schatzkästlein güter Herzen unnd bestendiger Freünd* (Frankfurt am Main: Eberhard Kieser, 1623 *et seq.*), H41 (the image shown here is from the 1638 edition).

Operatic experiments of the 1650s 167

comfort with this new degree of mixed mimetic and symbolic theatricality in the scenery. Yet as the Third Entry begins, the spectacle proceeds to the next level: with music again playing, the shutters open to reveal the first scene of relieve, an astonishing masque-like effect made all the more impressive by the fact that it moves the action from an exterior to an interior setting. The subsequent closing of the S2 shutters (this time without musical accompaniment) would seem to be anti-climactic in this case, but it also signals both a change of location and a change of characters, thus setting in motion the Christian/Turkish counterpoint that continues through the next two entries. Even so, at the beginning of the Fourth Entry there is yet another astonishing novelty, as the shutter is drawn to reveal a *different* scene of relieve (R2), a visual signifier of the besieging Turks' freedom of movement through the landscape, as against the confinement of the Rhodian Christians—a factor that is underscored when we return again to S2 in the middle of the Fourth Entry. In the Fifth Entry, with its catastasis and catastrophe, the rhythm of the scene changes accelerates, and the scenic element itself becomes yet more complex as a new, third shutter (S3) is introduced for the first time, highlighting the confusion of battle as the Turks assault the city and the Christians valiantly defend it. In its depiction of "the greatest fury ... being discern'd at the English Station" (p. 29), this shutter scene introduces an additional, propagandistic element to which the audience has not hitherto been witness. From this point, the scenic action winds down, with a return to R2 for the final Turkish scene, followed by the closing once again of S2 for the conclusion with the Christians. Thus, until the final part of the 5th Entry, the scenic ante is constantly being raised and the audience kept slightly off balance as it awaits the next visual revelation: even the second appearance of R2 is a surprise, given that the general assault shutter (S3) would have closed over the baseline S2 shutter at the beginning of the entry, so that the audience, accustomed by now to a consistent back-and-forth alternation between S2 and other scenes, would have expected to see S2 again when S3 opens, but are instead treated to a recapitulation of the relieve scene from the previous entry.

Alongside this environment of constant imbalance and expectation, however, the scenery provides a second, contrary element of consistency and predictable dramatic exposition.[71] Except in the anomalous Second Entry (which occurs as the opera's scenic counterpoint is still gaining momentum) and the Fifth Entry's intricate battle sequence, the scenery is conspicuously used to differentiate the Christian and Turk-ish characters—not only by means of the distinct scenes themselves, but even by the *type* of scene (shutter for the Christians, relieves for the Turks), thus providing the audience with subtle guidance as to which group they are watching at any given

---

71 The analysis that follows is largely performance-oriented; for a penetrating literary reading of *Rhodes*, focusing on how the play "presents an uncanny similarity or replicatory re-presentation of the west to itself" through a process whereby the "reassuringly different 'other'" represented by the Turks "shows evidence of increased affinity to the Rhodians" over the course of Parts 1 and 2, see Susan J. Wiseman, "'History Digested': Opera and Colonialism in the 1650s," in Thomas Healy and Jonathan Sawday, eds., *Literature and the English Civil War* (Cambridge: Cambridge University Press, 1990), 189–204, pp. 198–201.

(a)

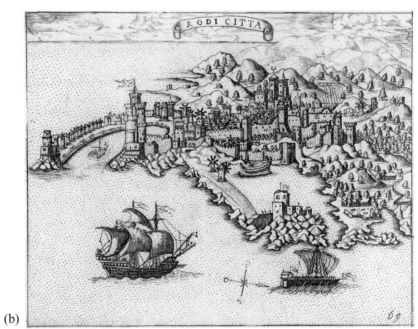
(b)

(c)

Figure 4.1 Comparison of views of Rhodes from (a) von Breydenbach, *Peregrinationes in Terram Sanctam* (1486) (Wikimedia Commons [https://commons.wikimedia.org/wiki/File:Breydenbach_Rodis_1486.jpg]); (b) Camocio, *Isole famose porti* (1571–72) (By permission of the Folger Shakespeare Library [G1015 .C3 1574 Cage, pl. 69]); (c) Rosaccio, *Viaggio da Venetia, a Costantinopoli* (1598) (Houghton Library, Harvard University [Asia 9215.98*]); (d) Meisner/Kieser, *Thesaurus Philo-politicus* (1623/1638) (Wikimedia Commons [https://commons.wikimedia.org/wiki/File:Rodis_in_Orient_1638.jpg]); and (e) Webb, design for first scene from *The Siege of Rhodes* (1656) (© Devonshire Collection, Chatsworth. Reproduced by permission of Chatsworth Settlement Trustees)

170 *"For such uses as the King shall direct"*

moment.[72] At the same time, with four of the five scenes displaying some exterior view of the city (accentuated by the word "RHODES" prominently inscribed on the shield at the center of the frontispiece's frieze), the opera's viewers are left in no doubt as to the general setting of the drama's action. What is perhaps most striking about the designers' effort to offer a consistent visual theme throughout is the fact that three of Webb's five scenes—two shutters and one relieve—effectively offer only slightly different perspectives on an identical view, in which we see the walls of the city, the curve of the island's eastern coastline, and the (somewhat inaccurately situated) slopes of Mount Filerimos to the southwest (see Figure 4.2).[73]

Indeed, apart from changes in the perceived height of the viewer,[74] the difference in perspective is determined purely by movement along a single axis, running roughly northwest to southeast.[75] This overlapping referential frame draws the audience even further into the illusion of actually being present in Rhodes to witness the momentous events of the siege: even the general assault scene (S3) requires little more than a 90° turn to the left (*i.e.* from a southeasterly to a northeasterly perspective) as the view focuses in on the chaos at the English-manned bulwark. All of these features would have contributed significantly to the intensity of the audience's theatrical experience, and it is a sign of the producers' skill that such an effect could be accomplished without resorting to any kind of elaborate stage machinery. In his cramped, eleven-foot-high space in Rutland House, and later at the Cockpit, Davenant proved that what mattered was not the expensive and complex spectacle of machines, but merely the creative use of scenic backdrops to illuminate and embellish the dramatic story.

Besides its sophisticated use of visual effect, Davenant and Webb's design is noteworthy for its extraordinary technical elegance. The persistent counterpoint, as seen in Table 4.3, between S2 and the other scenes, and between shutters and relieves, demanded careful coordination on the part of both the designers and the

---

72 Such an effect may have been all the more essential because of *Rhodes*'s through-sung delivery, where the details and broader thrust of the text may not always have been perfectly clear to the audience. Compare Dent's discussion (p. 74) of the scenery for *Peru*, as described in Davenant's playbook, which he characterizes as "evidently intended not to serve a dramatic purpose, much less to be decorative .... It was intended as a series of pictures to give information as complete and detailed as circumstances permitted, and as an illustration of actualities such as later generations would have represented by a panorama, a lantern-lecture, or a cinematograph performance."

73 Note that the description of R2 explicitly mentions that this view of Mount Filerimos shows "Artificers appearing at work about that Castle which was there, with wonderful expedition, erected by *Solyman*" (p. 22). This construction clearly appears in Webb's drawing (see the detail in Figure 4.2), although of course it is no longer visible when we return to S2 in the latter part of the Fourth and Fifth Entries.

74 S1 has a horizon line at about 4' 10" above the highest point in the plane of the gently raked stage; in S2 the horizon line is at 5' 4¾". R2 shows no horizon, and is in any case more difficult to assess because it is a relieve scene; however, on the design as drawn, the implied line is at approximately 4' 3" above the same point on the stage (taking into account the four-inch differential in base height between Webb's shutter and relieve designs: see Orrell, *Theatres*, 70).

75 For S1, that axis skews somewhat to the north or even northeast, although of course we must take into account considerable distortion in Webb's imaginative aerial rendition of the city.

1st Entry: **S1** (CHRISTIANS)

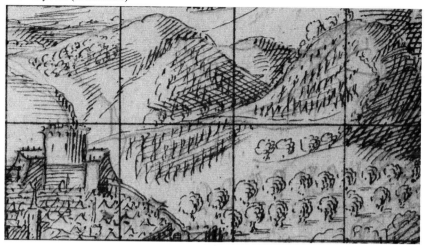

2nd–5th Entries: **S2** (CHRISTIANS)

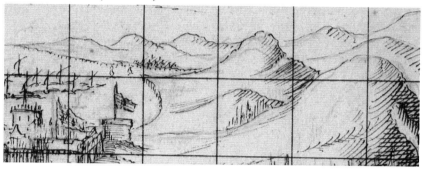

4th–5th Entries: **R2** (TURKS)

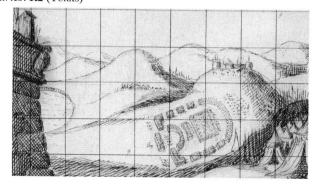

Figure 4.2 Comparative details: Rhodes city wall, the coastline, and Mount Filerimos in three of John Webb's designs for *The Siege of Rhodes* (© Devonshire Collection, Chatsworth. Reproduced by permission of Chatsworth Settlement Trustees)

172 *"For such uses as the King shall direct"*

operators of the scenery. Webb's design for the theatre itself, which has been discussed in detail by Richard Southern,[76] included a shutter frame with three sets of grooves (top and bottom) and four upright guides on both sides, to accommodate the three pairs of shutters. Away from the frame, on either side of the stage, was some kind of wide vertical backstop, designed to keep the inner edges of the shutters safely between the upright guides of the frame when the scenes were drawn back into their open (*i.e.* unused) position. (Had the shutters been removable, only two sets of grooves would have been necessary, rather than the three shown in Webb's drawings.) Thus, on each side of the stage, the three shutter halves that slid in and out to change the scene were kept securely in the frame at all times, whether open or closed, and hence in close proximity to one another, separated by nothing more than the width of one of the boards that formed the upright guides. At most points during the performance, either a single pair of shutters would be closed to reveal the scene painted thereon to the audience, or all three pairs would be opened to expose the scene of relieve beyond. If we assume that the production would have employed only two scenekeepers (one on each side of the stage) and, moreover, that the scenekeepers would never attempt to move two shutters together simultaneously, the physical configuration of the shutters and relieve space logically dictates certain inevitable rules, most fundamentally the extremely limited utility of the shutters in the middle groove (which we shall call "groove B"). Sandwiched as they were between the shutters located downstage ("groove A") and upstage ("groove C"), the middle set of shutters could never be closed or opened from offstage while the other two pairs were open, and thus could never be deployed to reveal or hide the scene of relieve behind: only the shutters in grooves A and C (accessible, respectively, from the front and back of the frame) could be opened (or closed) while the other two sets were open. Thus, the shutters in B could only be used to reveal (in the case of C) or be revealed behind (in the case of A) another pair of shutters. As Table 4.3 demonstrates, the only shutter scene in the opera that neither follows nor precedes a relieve scene is that shown in the First Entry (S1), and hence this pair must have been situated in the B position. S2 and S3, both of which open at various points to reveal the relieve space, would thus seem to be interchangeably assignable to grooves A and C. However, placing S2 in the A position has two slight disadvantages. First, it requires that, in order to effect the constant closing and opening of S2, the scenekeepers be positioned downstage of the frame and shutter assembly throughout much of the performance, rather than in the far more convenient upstage location. Second, situating S2 in front of, rather than behind, S1 necessitates a considerable amount of extra work for the scenekeepers, who would need first to close two pairs of shutters (A/B or C/B) before the opera began and then immediately reopen either A or C, just to get B set, and then at the end of the First Entry close the A shutters to reveal S2 and subsequently open the B shutters (S1) from behind, in order to get them out of the way; similar

---

76 Richard Southern, *Changeable Scenery: Its Origin and Development in the British Theatre* (London: Faber and Faber, 1952) 48–54 (and also 59–72, *passim*).

Operatic experiments of the 1650s 173

agility would be required in the latter part of the Fourth Entry, when S3, located in groove C, would need to be closed behind S2 (in groove A), in order to be revealed by the opening of S2 as the Fifth Entry got underway. Nothing about this arrangement would have been ideal; rather, as the "baseline" scene, S2 would most logically be situated in groove C, at the back of the frame. These shutters could be already closed along with the S1 shutters in groove B when the curtain was drawn up at the commencement of the performance, allowing the S1 shutters to be subsequently pulled aside to reveal the preset S2 scene at the beginning of the Second Entry. Moreover, the shift towards the end of the opera would be made simpler by the fact that S3 (properly in groove A) could be closed *in front of* S2 as the Fifth Entry began, and—in preparation for the later appearance of the relieve—S2 could then be quietly *opened* behind it (rather than the less preferable *closing* of a hidden scene, as in the other model), as the entry progressed. Thus, despite the seeming complexity of the foregoing analysis, a careful assessment of the technical limitations and opportunities faced by the producers of *The Siege of Rhodes* suggests a single best configuration for the positioning of the three shutters; this configuration is presented in graphic form in Diagram 4.1.[77]

The scenic element of *The Siege of Rhodes* offers an unparalleled opportunity to explore the technical aspects of late-seventeenth-century English staging practices. It is only unfortunate that *Rhodes* represents such an exceptional case: literally the first instance of changeable scenery to be presented in the public theatre, it is, as we have seen, far simpler in its conception and execution than the vast majority of works that followed. Nevertheless, its very simplicity enables us to dissect it in detail, in the process observing how Davenant constructed his work, to a significant degree, around the scenic element and the possibilities, as well as the limitations, it presented. As Richard Southern has observed, "Davenant as a playwright paid an unprecedented attention to scenery, even regarding it (as his title-page suggests) as part of the essential vehicle and medium of his drama."[78] Yet we have already remarked upon *Rhodes*'s anomalous status among that body of work that contemporaries might have concurred in designating "opera," including Davenant's other Protectorate productions, and Flecknoe's *Ariadne Deserted*, or perhaps even his *Oceanus and Britannia*. This, I have suggested, may have something to do with Davenant's decision, as early as 1661, to strip *Rhodes* of its innovative recitative component and present it thereafter as a spoken play punctuated by a few strophic songs, thereby effectively abandoning the field of opera and moving in another generic direction entirely. If we consider the other seemingly essential element of the operatic form, "the Art of Prospective in Scenes," the case

---

77 Interestingly, the relevant photograph of Richard Southern's model of Webb's set (*Changeable Scenery*, plate 13) depicts the shutters in an untenable arrangement, with S2 in groove C, but S1 in groove A and S3, impossibly, in groove B. The only way this configuration could be made to work would be if the shutters in grooves B and C (in this case, S3 and S2, respectively) were opened *simultaneously* to reveal the scene of relieve in the middle of the Fifth Entry, an operation that would seem excessively cumbersome, and hence unlikely.

78 Southern, *Changeable Scenery*, 111.

	1st Entry	2nd Entry	3rd Entry *A*	3rd Entry *B*	4th Entry *A*	4th Entry *B*	5th Entry *A*	5th Entry *B*	5th Entry *C*
Relieve Space	*R1*	*R1*	R1	>R1 CHANGED TO R2>	R2	*R2*	*R2*	R2	*R2*
Groove C (S2: *beleaguered***)**	**CCCCC**	**CCCCC**	**=O« »O=**	**»CCCCC«**	**=O« »O=**	**»CCCCC«**	**~O«**(*during scene*)**»O~**	**=O O=**	**»CCCCC«**
Groove B (S1: *prospect***)**	**CCCCC**	**=O« »O=**	**=O O=**	**=O O=**	**=O O=**	**=O O=**	**=O O=**	**=O O=**	**=O O=**
Groove A (S3: *assault***)**	**=O O=**	**=O O=**	**=O O=**	**=O O=**	**=O O=**	**=O O=**	**»CCCCC«**	**=O« »O=**	**=O O=**
Acting Space (*N.B.* not to scale)	W W W W W W	W W W W W W	W W W W W W	W W W W W W	W W W W W W	W W W W W W	W W W W W W	W W W W W W	W W W W W W

Diagram 4.1 Stage configuration and coordination of scene changes in *The Siege of Rhodes*

Operatic experiments of the 1650s 175

is more ambiguous. Davenant remained a principal champion of scenic spectacle on the public stage, so much so that his theatre at Lincoln's Inn Fields came to be known by contemporaries like Samuel Pepys as "the Opera"[79]—despite presenting works that, for the most part, featured little or no music, let alone extended passages of recitative. Davenant's new theatre opened in June 1661 with performances of *Rhodes*, now supplemented with a full-length second part that continued the story told in the pre-Restoration production and that appears to have played alongside its precursor on alternating days.[80] The "first part" was also changed in significant ways, chiefly by the addition of a plot line involving Solyman's jealous wife, Roxolana, whose presence necessitated the creation of other, subsidiary new characters as well.[81] The addition to the first part of *Rhodes* of this new dramatic thread allowed Davenant to fill out the story line in order to compensate for the loss of the earlier musical setting, as well as to set up the dramatic tension in Part 2, where Roxolana's character is further developed. As Table 4.3 shows, scenes involving Roxolana are inserted at the end of each of the last three "entries" (a designation Davenant retained, albeit only for the first part, in the Restoration version of the play). In addition, a new expository scene featuring Ianthe and her two attendants, Melosile and Madina—set in Sicily, where Ianthe plans to sell her jewels and sail to Rhodes to support the war effort—is added to the conclusion of the First Entry. Only the Second Entry is left untouched by Davenant's alterations—although it should be noted that the addition of the new scenes elsewhere actually has no effect on any pre-existing portions of the text.[82]

79 See for example Pepys, *Diary*, 2: 155 (15 August 1661): "to the Opera, which begins again today with *The Witts* [by Davenant, 1634], never acted yet with Scenes; and the King and Duke and Duchesse was there …; and indeed, it is a most excellent play—and admirable Scenes." For another instance of this use of the term, see the letter of Elizabeth Bodvile to Christopher Hatton (later 2nd Baron and 1st Viscount Hatton), possibly July 1661, in Edward Maunde Thompson, ed., *Correspondence of the Family of Hatton Being Chiefly Letters Addressed to Christopher First Viscount Hatton A.D. 1601–1704* (2 vols.: Camden Society, n. s., 22–23; London: Camden Society, 1878), 1: 21: "One Munday I was at the new aprer, and I chancd to sett next to Mr. Lane, hoe told mee a black cap and a staf was a better sight then that was, and many other things which would but troubell you to reed."

80 The revised play was published as *The Siege of Rhodes: The First and Second Part; As they were lately Represented at His Highness the Duke of York's Theatre in Lincolns-Inn Fields. The first Part being lately enlarg'd* (London: Henry Herringman, 1663). For questions about whether the second part of *Rhodes* might also have had a pre-Restoration, operatic existence, see p. 157, above.

81 *Pace* Dent (pp. 65–66), it is not Roxolana's jealousy of Ianthe, but rather that of Alphonso, that occasions the chorus at the end of the Fourth Entry (*Rhodes*, 28: "THis cursed Jealousie, what is't?"). Dent adduces this faulty assertion as evidence for his largely discredited conclusion that *Rhodes* was originally conceived as a full-length spoken play (see n. 12, above).

82 Roxolana is accompanied in her three scenes by the newly added characters Rustan, Haly, and two female attendants. In the scenes in the Third and Fourth Entries, Pirrhus serves as her link to the pre-existing Turkish characters; in the Fifth, Solyman himself appears in order to reconcile with her. The minor role of Haly, a "Eunuch Bassa" who enters only in the Fourth Entry scene (but reappears in several scenes in Part 2), is the one famously botched by the Duke's Company's longtime prompter, John Downes (see n. 94, below).

176   *"For such uses as the King shall direct"*

What is perhaps most surprising about these additions is that, assuming the 1663 playbook is a reliable witness, Davenant appears to have made no alterations to the scenic structure to accommodate his changes to the script. Thus, Ianthe's scene in Sicily takes place, quite incongruously, before the shutter showing the prospect of Rhodes (S1), while all three of Roxolana's appearances, coming as they do at the ends of the last three entries, disrupt the formerly elegant pattern by occurring in front of the Christian backdrop of Rhodes beleaguered (S2). Indeed, with this change, the S2 shutter becomes the indiscriminate province of both Christians and Turks in all four of the entries in which it appears, leaving the Christian party substantially diminished within the visual as well as the textual compass of the play.[83]

This odd situation, in which the scene changes of the post-1660 *Rhodes*, as reflected in the 1663 playbook, seem to have little to do with actual shifts in the location of the action between the separate Christian and Turkish camps, has been noted and discussed at some length by Richard Southern.[84] Reasoning that, given Davenant's strong interest in scenery, "when a new edition of his play, marking the occasion of a fresh presentation, bears the same scene-descriptions, then this argues the retention of the same design of scenery" (p. 111), Southern explores the implications of Davenant's seeming abandonment of the principles we have been observing. His conclusion, that "Davenant did not introduce scenery as an illusionistic setting but, instead, thought out a quite profound conception of it as an accompaniment to the exposition of the plot used in a sort of counterpoint" (p. 114), is provocative, and may have as-yet unrealized implications for our understanding of the playwright's ongoing work with the Duke of York's Company at Lincoln's Inn Fields throughout the 1660s. At the same time, however, Southern appears to lose sight of the importance of Davenant's original conception of the work, and hence the possibility that the scenic incongruities of the later version may be less a brilliant and sophisticated innovation than an *ad hoc* attempt to preserve what he could of the tightly woven scenic fabric of the opera *Rhodes* was initially envisioned to be. It is perhaps significant that in *The Siege of Rhodes, Part 2*, as Southern demonstrates, the use of scenery shows no sign of this "profound conception," but rather returns in nearly every instance to the logical format seen in the early, pre-Restoration version of Part 1.[85]

---

83 See, however, the version published in the posthumous *Works of S*ʳ *William Davenant K*ᵗ (1673, see n. 40, above), section 2 (dated 1672), where the introduction of Roxolana's first scene, at the end of the Third Entry, p. 14, is marked "*The Scene changes to* Solymans *Camp.*" This direction is almost certainly an editorial intervention made by someone who recognized and sought, somewhat diffidently, to address the problem with Roxolana's scenes we have been discussing: if "Solymans *Camp*" is meant to refer to the pavilion relieve scene (R1), such a change would of course be an impossibility, since the scene of Mount Filerimos (R2) must follow immediately as the Third Entry begins. It is worth noting in this context that the last recorded performance of the first part of *Rhodes* took place on 21 May 1667 (see LC5/139, p. 125 and Pepys, *Diary*, 8: 225), further evidence that the 1673 edition is not meant to reflect any actual production change.

84 Southern, *Changeable Scenery*, 109–23.

85 Twice in Part 2, in Acts 4 (pp. 33–36) and 5 (pp. 51–54), both Christians and Turks appear before what is probably the familiar "Rhodes beleaguered" shutter scene (S2). There is also, as in Part 1, a

Operatic experiments of the 1650s 177

From this we may reasonably conclude that Davenant's chief concern in presenting the revised, two-part version of *Rhodes* was less fundamentally about the scenic spectacle as such, and more aimed at highlighting the dramatic qualities of storytelling and acting technique. The importance of the shift from a production "Made a Representation by the Art of Prospective in Scenes, And the Story sung in *Recitative* Musick" (1656 and 1659 title pages) to one simply "Represented" (1663 and 1673 title pages) cannot be overstated. Despite the retention of certain elements, such as the sung choruses in Part 1 and the original scenic logic (and spectacle) carried forward into the new Part 2, the things that had clearly made *Rhodes* an opera in the 1650s had become only secondary considerations by 1661, as a new vision for the production, and for the Restoration theatre itself, gradually emerged. There can be little doubt, for example, that the replacement of singers like Henry Cooke, Matthew Locke, and Edward and Catherine Coleman, who must not have been particularly effective actors,[86] with such high-caliber professional thespians as Thomas and Mary Betterton, Henry Harris, and Hester Davenport[87] represents a tectonic shift in the show's conception, to say nothing of its appearance to the eyes and ears of its audience. Both Samuel Pepys and John Evelyn make this clear in their identification of two of the leading actresses in the Duke's Company with the parts they played in *Rhodes*: Mary (*née* Saunderson) Betterton is consistently nicknamed "Ianthe"[88] and Hester Davenport "Roxolana,"[89]

---

battle scene, which opens Act 5 with "a Prospect of *Rhodes* by night, and the Grand Masters Palace on Fire" (p. 48). Like the analogous scene in Part 1, this can be broken down into a number of rapid-fire "French scene" groupings (2 Turkish; 1 Christian; 3 Turkish). This is also, interestingly, the only place in Part 2 of *Rhodes* where any music is called for: see n. 104, below.

86 See Samuel Pepys's observation, recorded on 31 October 1665, that Catherine Coleman "won't owne that ever she did get any of [her part of Ianthe] without book, in order to the stage" (*Diary*, 6: 284). I have yet to see an adequate explanation for the doubling of many of the singers' parts (see Table 4.4), as indicated in the cancellans leaf (sig. [G1]) found in some copies of the 1656 playbook: see Ann-Mari Hedbäck, "The Printing of *The Siege of Rhodes*," *Studia Neophilologica* 45 (1973): 68–79, p. 71.

87 "All Parts," John Downes assures us (*Roscius Anglicanus* [London: H(enry) Playford, 1708], 21), were "Justly and Excellently Perform'd; it continu'd Acting 12 Days without Interruption with great Applause."

88 Pepys, *Diary*, 3 (1662): 58, 209, 233, 273; 5 (1664): 34, 224, 240; 6 (1665): 73. In the last of these entries, Pepys refers to "Ianthe" playing in *Mustapha*, even though Mrs. Betterton here assumed the role of Roxolana (see below). On only two occasions in his diary does Pepys (who sometimes calls Mrs. Betterton "my Ianthe") refer to her simply as "Baterton[…']s wife": see 5: 335 and 7 (1666): 347.

89 Pepys, *Diary*, 3: 32, 58, 86, 273; Evelyn, *Diary*, 3: 309 ("the faire & famous Comœdian call'd *Roxalana* for that part she acted"). Pepys's specificity in this regard can be seen, for example, in his entry of 10 May 1662 (3: 86), where he records having seen "the second part of *Seige* [*sic*] *of Rhodes*, but it is not so well done as when Roxalana was there"; see also British Library, Add. MS 34217, f. 31ᵛ (see n. 93, below): "the Siege of Rhodes all say / It is an everlasting Play / Though they wonder now Roxalana is gon / What shift it makes to hold out so long." Mrs. Davenport had left the stage to become the mistress of the Earl of Oxford, to be replaced by Mary Norton; see Pepys's clearer reference (and change of heart) on 27 December 1662 (3: 295) to "the new Roxalana; which doth it rather better in all respects, for person, voice and judgment, then the first Roxalane."

178 *"For such uses as the King shall direct"*

while John Downes's recollections appear to have been affected by this factor when, years later, he mistakenly recorded that the part of Roxolana in the Earl of Orrery's *Mustapha* of 1665 was originally taken by Mrs. Davenport, who had left off acting in early 1662, when in fact it had been played by Mrs. Betterton (whom Pepys was at the time still calling "Ianthe").[90] With the theatres secured after the Restoration, Davenant seems to have moved rapidly away from any substantive engagement with operatic form (and indeed with all aspects of his earlier "moral" project[91]), focusing instead on the dramatic potential of heroic tragicomedy. For this new trajectory, the first part of *The Siege of Rhodes*, even with the addition of the Roxolana storyline, was actually little more than a jumping-off point. Part 2 appears to have been much more popular: performances of this portion are known to have continued throughout 1661 and 1662, whereas no certain record exists of any performances of the first part between its initial run in July 1661 and an isolated appearance in May 1667.[92] Moreover, a scurrilous verse satire of 1662 puckishly observes that "when the second part tooke, but for Bully / The ffirst did not satisfie soe fully."[93] The meaning of "Bully" is unclear: it may be an error for "Solly" (*i.e.* Solyman, played by Betterton), or perhaps an unkind reference to "Haly," the prompter John Downes's theatrical Waterloo.[94] In addition to this, the Duke's Company followed up on their success in 1665 with

---

90 *Roscius Anglicanus*, 26.

91 In July 1661, Davenant also took legal steps to distance himself from the group of "adventurers" who had invested in his operatic endeavor in 1656, claiming that he could not cooperate with their efforts to recover their claimed financial losses on the grounds that the Duke's Company was an entirely unrelated operation: see C10/99/21 (*Register*, no. 81), discussed in Hotson, *The Commonwealth and Restoration Stage*, 139–40.

92 For the performance on 21 May 1667 at Lincoln's Inn Fields, attended by Charles II and his mistress Barbara Villiers, Countess of Castlemaine, see LC5/139, p. 125 (*Register*, no. 456) and Pepys, *Diary*, 8: 225. This is not to suggest that Part 1 was unquestionably not performed during this period: the records of the king's attendance at performances by the Duke's Company only begin in October 1666, and thus it was probably before this time that Davenant wrote his "*EPILOGUE to the King at* Whitehall, *at the Acting the Siege of* Rhodes" (*The Works of S*ʳ *William Davenant K*ᵗ, section 1, p. 340). This, of course, could be for a presentation of either or both parts of the play (the Epilogue also includes a reference to the plot of *Mustapha*, thus suggesting a date of c.1665–66). However, see also the Prologue to John Wilson's comedy *The Cheats*, first presented in mid-March 1663, which promises "*No tedious Sieges to the Musick-room*" (Wilson, *The Cheats* [London: G. Bedell, T. Collins, and Cha(rles) Adams, 1664], sig. *A4*ʳ), a reference that would have little applicability to a stand-alone performance of Part 2, which contained almost no music.

93 British Library, Add. MS 34217, f. 31ᵛ (?June/July 1662; see *Register*, no. 138). The full poem is printed in Hotson, *The Commonwealth and Restoration Stage*, 246–47.

94 Downes, *Roscius Anglicanus*, 34: "*I must not forget my self, being Listed for an Actor in Sir* William Davenant'*s Company in* Lincolns-Inn-Fields: *The very first Day of opening the House there, with the Siege of* Rhodes, *being to Act* Haly; *(The King, Duke of* York, *and all the Nobility in the House, and the first time the King was in a Publick Theatre) The sight of that* August *presence, spoil'd me for an Actor.*" Downes, who assumed the position of prompter the following year, may be exaggerating slightly about the precipitous end to his stage career: "*The very first Day*" of the new *Rhodes* production is believed to have been 28 June 1661, but on 2 July Samuel Pepys witnessed a performance of Part 2, with Charles II and his aunt Elizabeth in the audience, which he described as "well acted, all but the Eunuches, who was so much out that he was hissed off the stage" (*Diary*, 2: 131). See the brief discussion of this discrepancy in Judith Milhous and Robert D. Hume's edition of *Roscius Anglicanus* (London: The Society for Theatre Research, 1987), 73 n. 215.

Operatic experiments of the 1650s 179

a kind of sequel to *Rhodes*, Roger Boyle, 1st Earl of Orrery's *Tragedy of Mustapha, The Son of Solyman the Magnificent*.[95] Orrery's play is set two decades after the action of *Rhodes*, in Hungary, early in the reign of the then-infant King John II (János Zsigmond Zápolya), and although the Christian characters are entirely different, a number of the most important Turkish characters are carried over from Davenant's *Rhodes* plays, including Solyman, Roxolana, Pirrhus, Rustan, and Haly.[96] Table 4.4 shows the progression of these "Solyman" plays over the twenty years from 1656 to 1676, indicating both the placement of roles and the actors by whom they were performed, and incorporating a third play, Elkanah Settle's *Ibrahim the Illustrious Bassa*, presented in 1676.[97]

As we can see, in all of these plays the main "romantic" parts were given to leading actors, regardless of their previous assignments: Mary Betterton (Ianthe in *Rhodes*) became Roxolana in the new play, while Henry Harris, the former Alphonso, was now Solyman's son Mustapha; in 1676, the part of Roxolana passed to Mary Lee, while Mary Betterton adopted Mary Davis's former role of Isabella, Queen of Hungary, Harris played the part of Ulama, "*the Sophies Son and Heir of* Persia," and William Smith (who had not appeared in *Rhodes*) traded his role as Zanger, Solyman's younger son, for that of *Ibrahim*'s title character. Yet one part remained constant: in both Orrery's and Settle's plays, Thomas Betterton continued his reign as Solyman the Magnificent, thus providing a tangible, and presumably memorable, link between all the productions.[98] John Protheroe was the first to suggest that the chalk-on-paper drawing by John Greenhill (d. May 1676) at Kingston Lacy, Dorset, previously called "Thomas Betterton as Bajazet" was in fact a representation of Betterton "as Solyman in *The Siege of Rhodes*, as produced in 1661 and frequently revived in following seasons."[99] Given Betterton's continuance in that role in *Mustapha* and *Ibrahim*, the identification could profitably be expanded to include the later plays—indeed, the actor's development of the role over the course of all four plays may have served as justification for the creation of Greenhill's drawing in the first place.[100] *Mustapha*, in particular,

---

95 Printed in Orrery's *The History of Henry the Fifth. And the Tragedy of Mustapha, Son of Solyman the Magnificent* (London: H[enry] Herringman, 1668), [53]–124.

96 The title character, one of Solyman's competing sons, is not to be confused with *Rhodes*'s "Mustapha Bassa." The name of Solyman's other son, Zanger, also occurs in *Rhodes*, used in passing for an offstage military figure (pp. 30, "39" [*recte* 35]; *cf.* p. 14: "Zangiban").

97 Elkanah Settle, *Ibrahim the Illustrious Bassa* (London: W[illiam] Cademan, 1677).

98 However, see Pepys, *Diary*, 9: 62–63 (11 February 1668): "I never saw such good acting of any creature as Smith's part of Zanger; and I do also, though it was excellently acted by [*blank*], do yet want Betterton mightily."

99 Protheroe, "Not so Much an Opera" (see n. 19, above), 667 (italics reversed). This identification is repeated in information provided by the National Trust, present owner of the house and portrait.

100 Excepting, it seems from Pepys's remark quoted in n. 98, above, in 1668. Betterton's costume appears already to have been famous in 1663, when a stage Puritan, announced as one of the contenders for the summer lease in *The Playhouse to be Let*, aspires to "hire the Turband, Scepter, and / Throne of our *Solyman* the Magnificent; and reign / This long Vacation over all the dominions / In *Portugall-Row*" (*i.e.* at the Lincoln's Inn Fields Theatre): see Davenant, "THE Playhouse to be Let" (see n. 40, above), 74.

Table 4.4 Performers in the Duke's Company's "Solyman" plays, 1656–76

	CHARACTER	RHODES (opera) (1656, 1658?–59)	RHODES 1 & 2 (1661–62 [?Jan.])	RHODES 1 & 2[a] (1662 [?May]–63)	MUSTAPHA[b] (1665–68)	IBRAHIM[c] (1676)
TURKS	Solyman the Magnificent	Henry Cooke	Thomas Betterton	Thomas Betterton	Thomas Betterton[d]	Thomas Betterton
	Pirrhus, Vizier Bassa	John Harding/ Alfonso Marsh (Sr.)	[unidentified]	[unidentified]	?Henry Norris/ John Richards[e]	
	Mustapha, Bassa	Henry Purcell (Sr.)/ Thomas Blagrave	[unidentified]	[unidentified]		
	Rustan, [Vizier] Bassa			[unidentified]	Samuel Sandford	__[f]
	Haly, Eunuch Bassa		John Downes[g] / [unidentified]	[unidentified]	Philip Cademan	
	Achmat, Eunuch Bassa				James Nokes	
	Mustapha, Solyman's son				Henry Harris*	
	Zanger, Solyman's son				William Smith	
	Ibrahim, the Vizier Bassa					William Smith
	Ulama, the Sophy's Son and heir of Persia					Henry Harris*
	Morat, Bassa					Matthew Medbourne
	Muphti				__[h]	Thomas Gillow
	Roxolana, wife to Solyman		Hester Davenport	Mary Norton	Mary Betterton*[i]	Mary Lee
	Zarma, Roxolana's woman		[unidentified]	[unidentified]	Jane Long	
	Mirza/Mirva, Roxolana's woman		[unidentified]	[unidentified]	__ Norris	Margaret Hughes
	4 Pages/Ladies attending Roxolana		[(Pages) unidentified]	[(Pages) unidentified]	[(Ladies) unidentified]	[(Ladies) unidentified]
	Asteria, Solyman's daughter					Elizabeth Currer
	[Solyman's guards, mutes, pages, etc.]				[unidentified][j]	[unidentified][k]
CHRISTIANS	Villerius, Grand Master of Rhodes	Gregory Thorndell/ Dubartus Hunt	Thomas Lilleston	Thomas Lilleston[l]		
	Admiral of Rhodes	Matthew Locke/ Peter Rymon	Nicholas Blagden	?[unidentified][m]		
	High Marshal of Rhodes[n]		[unidentified]	[unidentified]		
	Alphonso, a Sicilian Duke	Edward Coleman/ Roger Hill	Henry Harris	Henry Harris		
	Ianthe, wife to Alphonso	Catherine Coleman	Mary (Saunderson) Betterton[o]	Mary Betterton		
	Melosile, Ianthe's woman		[unidentified]	[unidentified]		
	Madina, Ianthe's woman		[unidentified]	[unidentified]		
	King of Hungary, an infant				[unidentified]	
	Cardinal of Veradium				John Young	
	Thuricus, Hungarian Lord				Matthew Medbourne	
	Viche, Hungarian Lord				Edward Angel	
	Isabella, Queen of Hungary				Mary Davis[p]	Mary Betterton*
	Cleora, Queen of Hungary's woman				Anne Gibbs Shadwell	
	Chorus (*Rhodes*, Part 1 only)	[unidentified]	[unidentified]	[unidentified]		

Key:
* = had played a different character in *The Siege of Rhodes*

---

[a] Revival (cast unknown) of Part 1 recorded, 21 May 1667; revival (cast unknown) of Part 2 recorded, 24 February 1677.

[b] Performed in the Hall Theatre, Whitehall, on 18 October and ?5 November 1666. Revival (cast unknown) recorded, 6 October 1686.

[c] Also said to have been performed at Newhall (Boreham, Essex), under the auspices of Elizabeth (*née* Cavendish) Monck, Duchess of Albemarle (see Elkanah Settle, *Ibrahim the Illustrious Bassa* (London: for W[illiam] Cademan, 1677), sig. A2[v].

[d] Betterton did not perform in 1668 revival (see Pepys, *Diary*, 9: 63 [11 February 1668]), on account of an extended illness (see Pepys, *Diary*, 8: 482 and 521 [16 October and 6 November 1667], and 9: 256 [6 July 1668]).

[e] 1668 playbook (sig. [P1][v]): Norris; John Downes: Richards (*Roscius Anglicanus* [London: H(enry) Playford, 1708], 25–26).

[f] Mentioned in text (p. 12).

[g] Downes abandoned acting permanently after a few performances (see *Roscius Anglicanus*, 34).

[h] Mentioned in text (pp. 118–19).

[i] Downes, *Roscius Anglicanus*, 26, reports that the part was later taken "by one Mrs. *Wiseman*."

[j] P. 124 (closing scene): "*Enter* [to Solyman and Roxolana] Zarma, *four of* Roxolana's *Ladies*, Achmat, Haly, *the three Attendants of* Mustapha *and* Zanger, *eight of the Guard, and six Pages. The number on the Stage being now twenty four* [*i.e.* 26?]."

[k] Includes "Dorea" (p. 12).

[l] Lilleston probably left the stage in the summer of 1664; this part may subsequently have been performed by the actor/violinist John Singleton (see Holman, *Fiddlers*, 335).

[m] Blagden associated with the King's Company? from 1662.

[n] Four-line speech in First Entry of *Rhodes*, Part 1 reassigned from Villerius to High Marshal in 1663 edition (p. 5); otherwise only appears in Part 2.

[o] Married to Thomas Betterton, 24 December 1662.

[p] Role allegedly taught to Elizabeth Barry by the Earl of Rochester and performed in 1675 (see Thomas Betterton, *The History of the English Stage, from the Restauration to the Present Time* [London: E(dmund) Curll, 1741], 15–17).

182   *"For such uses as the King shall direct"*

joined *Rhodes* as a signally successful venture for the Duke's Company: John Downes reports that "[a]ll the *P*arts being new Cloath'd with new Scenes, Sir *William*'s great Care of having it perfect and exactly perform'd, it produc'd to himself and Company vast *Profit*."[101] The play, which premiered on 3 April 1665, was successfully performed at least once in the Hall Theatre at Whitehall during the plague closures of the following year,[102] and the "new Scenes" were designed by John Webb: four drawings survive in the Devonshire Collection at Chatsworth, making *Mustapha* the only identifiable Restoration play besides *Rhodes* for which such designs are extant.[103]

* * *

As sequels to the original *Siege of Rhodes*, Davenant's *Rhodes, Part 2*, Orrery's *Mustapha*, and Settle's *Ibrahim* are indicative of the specific character of the move away from opera post-1660. The emphasis on scenic spectacle remained— indeed, was consolidated and expanded, as was the case generally in the new patent theatres. But, as we have seen, the musical aspect seems to have disappeared almost entirely. This is true not only of the recitative component, which Davenant appears to have eliminated even from the revised version of *Rhodes, Part 1*, but also of the elements he must have retained for that play only, that is, the songs and

---

101 *Roscius Anglicanus*, 26 (Downes does not mention *Ibrahim*). The characters of the "Solyman" plays remained memorable to Restoration audiences for a considerable time: see for example the exchange between Petulant and Witwoud in William Congreve's *The Way of the World* (London: Jacob Tonson, 1700), 12, in which Witwould helpfully interprets Petulant's vague reference to "What-dee call-'ems" to mean "Empresses, my Dear— ... Sultana Queens," to which Petulant replies, "Ay, *Roxolana*'s."

102 For the initial 1665 run at Lincoln's Inn Fields, see Pepys, *Diary*, 6: 73 (3 April) and Evelyn, *Diary*, 3: 405 (6 April); for the court presentation on 18 October 1666, see Evelyn, 3: 465–66 and Pepys, 7: 329. Boswell (282) speculates that *Mustapha* may have been acted at court a second time on or about 5 November 1666: see LC5/139, p. 125 (undated entry in warrant for royal payment for performances, but with "Mustopha at Court" possibly just misplaced from the top of the list, where the performance of 18 October is not mentioned) and LC5/138, p. 366 (*Register*, no. 351: order dated 31 October for provision of supplies "for his Maties Comedians vpon ye Night they Act at Court," although neither the night nor the play is specified); for the 5th as the particular date of a play performance at court, see Pepys, *Diary*, 7: 358. Both of the patent theatres were closed by proclamation between 5 June 1665 and approximately 29 November 1666; *Mustapha* appeared again at Lincoln's Inn Fields on 5 January 1667 (see Pepys, *Diary*, 8: 5).

103 The surviving designs—seemingly drawn up for the Hall Theatre—consist of two shutters and two scenes of relieve, several features of which are strongly reminiscent of the *Rhodes* designs; one of the drawings (for Act 2, scene 2) has a flap with an alternative design underneath. For reproductions, see William Smith Clark II, ed., *The Dramatic Works of Roger Boyle Earl of Orrery* (2 vols.: Cambridge, MA: Harvard University Press, 1937), frontispiece and facing 1: 244, 246, 268, and 280; and Richard Barber, *Samuel Pepys Esqre* (London: G. Bell and Sons [for National Portrait Gallery], 1970), 41 (cat. 70). Modified versions of Webb's *Mustapha* scenes appear to have been deployed at Lincoln's Inn Fields as well: these were so successful, or perhaps so costly, that they subsequently reappeared in other plays, including Orrery's comedy *Guzman*, performed in April 1669 (see Southern, *Changeable Scenery*, 144–45)—which is not known to have been given at court.

Operatic experiments of the 1650s 183

the "Instrumental Musick" that feature so prominently at the end and beginning, respectively, of each entry. The subsequent two plays differ from their precursor in containing no songs, and while Part 2 of *Rhodes* includes instrumental music in one scene,[104] *Mustapha* has none whatsoever.[105] (*Ibrahim*, performed a number of years later at Dorset Garden, has a song in Act 3.) This is a far cry from Davenant's "operatic" practice, and points up the relevance to the earlier form of a third essential component, namely, non-vocal airs. Indeed, any assessment of the importance of music in operatic works of the preceding decade must reach beyond the issue of recitative and consider the instrumental element as well: how, broadly speaking, was instrumental music deployed in those works of the 1650s that contemporaries considered "operatic"? There are two basic categories of instrumental music in the seventeenth-century English theatre: "symphonies"—that is, music intended to set a mood in the drama or to cover such mechanical actions as scene changes or the raising of the curtain—and music for dancing. Both of these categories may include generic airs as well as more programmatic or "character" music. Because such music is signaled not by the poetic dialogue printed in the playbook, but rather by the more haphazard medium of stage directions, we are in even less of a position to evaluate its character, let alone its very prevalence, than we are with recitative.

The problems that must be confronted in this area can be illustrated by looking briefly at two works. The first of these is *Ariadne Deserted by Theseus*: we have already observed that Flecknoe's opera, despite its stated emphasis on "Recitative Musick," is distinctly lacking in the areas of scenic spectacle and dance, and it may indeed be that the production was not intended to incorporate dancing (that is, if it was ever performed—or, for that matter, if Flecknoe ever actually composed the music).[106] In three instances, however, the text clearly indicates cues for what we might describe as programmatic music. At the beginning of the drama, Ariadne is "*awaked out of sleep, by sad (but delicate) Musick, (supposed the harmony of the celestial minds)*" (p. 1), and music also plays a role in the all-important turn of the story: the final exposition of Ariadne's lament comes "*after sad Musick*" (p. 6), and is immediately followed by "*lively, and sprightly Musick ... heard afar off, by degrees approaching the Place*" (pp. 6–7) as the Bacchantes "*appear, in Ovant Triumph, with their* Timbrels, Systrums, Thyrseses, *and other Ensigns of* Bacchus Orgyes" (p. 7). It is hard to know what Flecknoe's idea of "*sad Musick*" might have been, but in the third case we can imagine that this "*lively, and sprightly*"

---

104 In the chaotic opening scene of Act 5 (see n. 85, above), after the Christians exit, "A Symphony expressing a Battail is play'd awhile" (p. 50), and at the end of the scene "*A Symphany sounds a Battail again*" (p. 51).

105 This, of course, does not mean that it would not have had a conventional "theatre suite." The extant seven-movement suite labeled "Mustapha" in British Library, Add. MS 24889, ff. 7[r–v] may be associated with the revival of the play performed on 6 October 1686: see Curtis A. Price, *Music in the Restoration Theatre* (Studies in Musicology, 4; Ann Arbor: UMI Research Press, 1979), 203–4.

106 But *cf. The Marriage of Oceanus and Britannia*, whose playbook calls for five (unspecified) symphonies and six dances (plus one episode of rope dancing/tumbling).

184 *"For such uses as the King shall direct"*

Bacchic music, accompanied by the onstage percussive sounds of timbrels and sistra, might have deployed shawms and those other late-Renaissance wind instruments sometimes designated "hautboys."[107]

A rather different picture emerges from the second work to be considered, Shirley's *Cupid and Death*. In the case of this part-spoken work, the complete musical setting by Christopher Gibbons and Matthew Locke for the 1659 production has survived, which allows us to compare the witness of the printed playbook with what was actually performed in the theatre.[108] The *Cupid* playbook mentions a total of seven dances, and, with one possible exception, all are accounted for with appropriate music.[109] It also calls for a single machine symphony, "a solemn Musick" to be played at the commencement of the main masque while "*Mercury* [is] seen descending upon a Cloud" (p. 22). Yet the manuscript score contains two other symphonies as well. One is "for the Curtayne" (f. 4ʳ) at the beginning of the work, which begins (appropriately) with a theme featuring rising scales, followed by a short jig-like tune for the appearance of the Host ("*a jolly sprightly old man*" [p. 1]), and concluding with a broad flourish in $\frac{3}{2}$, possibly as the Chamberlain enters to initiate the dialogue. The other symphony is played while "the Scene changes, where the slayne Louerˢ Appeare on Thrones" (f. 29ᵛ) in Elizium, representing the final discovery of the masquers. Neither of these essential movements is mentioned in the playbook.[110] Of far greater significance, though, is the fact that the printed text is entirely silent regarding the existence of the twenty-one other instrumental "ayres," organized into mostly three-movement suites, that punctuate much of the action in *Cupid*'s five antimasque entries. Most were composed by Locke, and thus are believed to have been added, along with the recitative passages, for the 1659 performance (whose playbook closely follows that of 1653). However, some five or six, gathered together in two suites in the middle of the second and fourth entries, are by Gibbons, and hence may be associated with the masque's earlier production. All these suites may be similar in character to the lost music called for in *The Siege of Rhodes*, where each of the six entries is "prepar'd by Instrumental Musick," or cued in the rather more specific references in Davenant's other three operatic texts. Few if any of Gibbons and Locke's instrumental movements can be described as programmatic in the sense of conveying some discernable quality of the unfolding drama; more to the point, anyone who has heard or witnessed a performance of *Cupid and Death* can attest to the work's dense musicality and to the essential role of the airs in establishing a more expansive

---

107 Note the correlation of the production of Perrin and Cambert's *Ariane* in 1674 with the introduction of the new French oboe into England, to be discussed below.

108 British Library, Add. MS 17799; see Thompson and Walkling, eds., *Cupid and Death* (n. 6, above).

109 This includes three courtly dances, each consisting of between one and three connected movements, and three antimasque or rustic dances. The seventh cue may be for an improvised solo lute movement: "*Enter a Lover playing upon a Lute, Courting his Mistris; they dance*" (p. 15 in the 1659 playbook), or it may have been covered by the preceding suite of airs (see below). For more details concerning the dances, see Thompson and Walkling, eds., Table VI.

110 In the latter instance, the playbook notes the scene change (p. 26), but says nothing about music.

Operatic experiments of the 1650s   185

pacing throughout, both features that would be substantially different were it not for this important sonic element.

A survey of Davenant's Protectorate operatic works (see Table 4.5) reveals a rich palette of instrumental airs, especially in the cases of *Peru* and *Drake*.

Besides the various unidentifiable "Flourishes," "Consorts," "Ayres," "Symphanies," and "Instrumental Musick," there are a number of formal dance-type movements, including an almain, three courantes, a pavan, and two sarabands (one of which is actually danced, "with Castanietos"[111]), as well as a danced jig. But we also find, particularly among the danced movements, several programmatic and character pieces, such as "a Trumpet-Ayre," "a Mimick Dance," "a martiall Dance," and "a halting Dance" in *Peru*, plus ayres in both *Peru* and *Drake* that are described using such adjectives as "Rustick," "dolfull," "warlike," "martiall," "mournfull," and "wild." Whether or not Davenant's composers deployed anything actually akin to, for example, a *battalia* style is impossible to determine with the limited evidence we have, but the range of descriptors used suggests a tremendous variety and even sophistication in the instrumental music for these theatrical works—far more varied and sophisticated, it might be hazarded, than that for *Cupid and Death*. Such a panoply of instrumental forms indicates another avenue for exploring opera's "technologies" as Davenant and his musical collaborators understood them. Like recitative and scenic spectacle, these airs would have contributed substantively to the works' theatricality and dramatic force—as, indeed, would the physical dances that in some cases accompanied them. How compelling the instrumental music actually was in performance is another matter, of course. Not all assessments were complimentary: the author of a ballad denigrating the 1658 production of *Peru* snickered,

> Neither must I here forget
> The Musick, how it was set,
> [Bate] two Ayers and an half and [by] *Jove*,
> All the rest was such a Gig,
> Like the squeaking of a Pig,
> Or Cats when they're making their Love.[112]

Whatever their reception might have been, both instrumental music and dance appear to have played some part in distinguishing opera from other, less musical dramatic forms, and thus surely need—despite the near-complete lack of either musical or choreographical data—to be taken into consideration in any attempt to understand what opera in the 1650s was and how it worked.

How much instrumental music actually does survive from Davenant's operas is an open question: there may be any number of airs and dances lurking incognito in

---

111 *The Marriage of Oceanus and Britannia* also contains a "daunce with Castanietes" (p. 34).

112 "*A* BALLAD *against the* OPERA, *call'd, The Cruelty of the* Spaniards *in* PERU, *Writ by Sir* W. D'Avenant," in *The Third Part of Miscellany Poems* (London: Jacob Tonson, 1716), 323–25, p. 324, with emendations taken from Bodleian Library, Ashmole MS 36, ff. 163–64.

186   *"For such uses as the King shall direct"*

the vast printed and manuscript repertory that covers this period, although in most cases the inadequate nature of the tune titles likely precludes our ever ferreting them out. There are, however, a few instances of tunes whose names are provocatively relevant, and thus may represent fragments of the larger works. Two are of particular interest, in part because they persisted in the published sources right through to the first quarter of the eighteenth century: one, entitled "The Apes Dance," may have something to do with the "Rustick Ayre" at the end of the 1st Entry of *Peru*, to which a pair of apes perform at rope-dancing,[113] while another, known as "The Simerons" (or "Symerons") "Dance" (or "Jigg"), can only refer to the African ex-slave allies of the English forces in *Drake*, four of whom "*dance a Morisco for joy*" near the conclusion of the 2nd Entry.[114] Both are attributed in at least one source to Matthew Locke, and thus argue for that composer's continued participation in Davenant's venture after his onstage appearance as the Admiral in *Rhodes*. A table showing the appearances of a number of instrumental tunes related to musical dramatic productions of the 1650s and early 1660s can be found in Appendix C; as the "Key to titles used to identify the tunes" provided there demonstrates, the titles of these tunes were by no means consistent over time, and it is helpful to be aware of the ways in which earlier associations were forgotten, or at least blurred. Sometime in the late 1680s, The Simerons Dance was renamed, coming to be known among the country dancing community as "Lady of Pleasure";[115] The Apes Dance was also retitled, but more interestingly, as "THe *Opera*," a name it retained (often in tandem with the older simian reference) until about 1725.[116] As the table in Appendix C reveals, there are at least three other tunes that appear in the 1670 first edition of *Apollo's Banquet* and carry the word "opera" in their titles: "THe *Opera* Tune by Mr. *Lock*," "THe *Opera* Dance," and "THe *Opera* Jigg."[117] Whether these tunes also originated in one of

---

113 *Peru*, 6: "a Rope descends out of the Clowds, and is stretcht to a stifness by an Engine, whilst a Rustick Ayre is play'd, to which two Apes from opposite sides of the Wood come out, listen, return; and, coming out again, begin to dance, then, after a while, one of them leaps up to the Rope, and there dances to the same Ayre, whilst the other moves to his measures below[.] Then both retire into the Wood. The Rope ascends." The apes dance again in the 6th Entry (pp. 25–26), but here they are accompanied by a Spaniard and a baboon.

114 *Drake*, 13. Two of the Simerons reappear in the "Grand Dance" at the end (p. 37), where they join a number of other characters from the opera.

115 See Appendix C; the last reference to the Simerons is found in the 1690 edition of *Apollo's Banquet*; however, the first appearance of the "Lady of Pleasure" title is in the 1687 *Apollo's Banquet*, which prints the tune twice under both the old and the new name (nos. 25 and 88). The tune was also printed under the title "PRince *Rupert's* welcome" in *Musick's Recreation on the Viol Lyra-Way* ("*The Second Edition*," but actually the 3rd or 4th) in 1682.

116 See in particular *Musick's Recreation on the Viol Lyra-Way*, "*The Second Edition*" (1682), which calls it "THE Apes Dance in the *Opera*." The dance instructions printed in the successive editions of *The Dancing Master* (1675–c.1725) reappear, without the music, in a slightly modified form in *A New Academy of Complements; or, The Lover's Secretary ... The Fourth Edition* (London: C. Bates and A. Bettesworth, 1715), 156 and 158.

117 Nos. 46–48; the first appears in two other sources simply as a "*Gavott*," while the second can be found in one of those sources, still adjacent to its companion piece, as "A *New Dance*."

Table 4.5 Instrumental music in the "operatic" productions of Sir William Davenant, 1656–59

PRODUCTION/LOCATION	MUSICAL ELEMENT (*dances italicized*)*	PAGE
The First Day's Entertainment at Rutland House	COMPOSERS: Henry Cooke, George Hudson	
→Prologue	a Flourish of Musick… the Curtains are Drawn	sig. A3ʳ
→Diogenes	A Consort … adapted to the sullen Disposition of Diogenes… the Curtains are suddenly open'd	1
→Aristophanes	A Consort … befitting the pleasant Disposition of Aristophanes	21
†→Parisian	A Consort … after the French Composition … the Curtains are suddenly open'd	44
→Londoner	a Consort … imitating the Waites of London	65
‡ after Epilogue]	a Flourish of loud Musick… the Curtain is clos'd	sig. [G2]ᵛ
The Siege of Rhodes	COMPOSERS: Charles Coleman, George Hudson	
→1st Entry	The Entry is prepar'd by Instrumental Musick	3
→2nd Entry	The Entry is … prepar'd by Instrumental Musick	7
→3rd Entry	The Entry is … prepar'd by Instrumental Musick	14
→4th Entry	The Entry is … prepar'd by Instrumental Musick	22
→5th Entry	The Entry is … prepar'd by Instrumental Musick	29
The Cruelty of the Spaniards in Peru	COMPOSER(S): Matthew Locke, ?+others	
→1st Entry	Instrumentall Musick	1
	a Symphany (being a wild Ayre sutable to the Region) … prepar[es] the Scene	
{THE SOMERSET (p. 4)} end of 1st Entry]	a Rustick Ayre … to which two Apes … come out	6
	[Apes] dance … to the same Ayre =The Apes Dance?	
→2nd Entry	Alman	6
	Corante	
	a Trumpet-Ayre changes the Scene	
{THE SEA-HORSE (p. 8)} end of 2nd Entry]	a dolfull Ayre	10
	two Indians[:] a Mimick Dance	
→3rd Entry	A Symphany, consisting of four Tunes prepares the change of the Scene	10
{THE SPRING (p. 13)} end of 3rd Entry]	a warlike Ayre	14
	a martiall Dance … by four Peruvians, arm'd with Glaves	

(*Continued*)

→4th Entry	A Symphany consisting of four Tunes `prepares the change of the Scene`	15
{THE SELF-SPRING (p. 17)}　　　　end of 4th Entry]	a Sarabrand … whilst two Spaniards enter	18
	[Spaniards] afterwards dance with Castanietos	
→5th Entry	A Dolefull Pavin … `to prepares the change of the Scene`	19
{THE PORPOISE (p. 21)}　　　　end of 5th Entry]	a mournfull Ayre	22–23
	three Peruvians [and] an insulting Spaniard[:] a halting Dance	
→6th Entry	A Symphony `prepares the last change of the Scene`	23
{THE DOUBLE SOMERSET (p. 25)}	a wild Ayre … (differing from that in the First Entry)	25–26
after 6th speech/acrobatic feat	a Spaniard … loaden with Ingots [etc.] … makes his footing to the tune of the Instruments [; afterwards] Two Apes … dance to the Ayre[:] a great Baboon … joynes with them in the Dance [etc.]	
end of 6th Entry]	an Ayre, consisting of three Tunes	27
	the grand Dance[: 3 Indians; 3 English; a Spaniard] who … in his gestures expresse[s] pride and sullennesse towards the Indians, and payes a lowly homage to the English, who often salute him with their feet, which salutation he returns with a more lowly gravity; whilst … English and … Indians … salute and shake hands, in signe of their future amity	
The History of Sir Francis Drake	COMPOSER(S): Matthew Locke, ?+others	
→1st Entry	`THE preparation of the opening of the Scene[:]` Prelude	2–3
	Corante	
	`the Curtain rises` … to an Ascending Ayre	
	a Martiall Saraband	
after Mariners' chorus	Two Marriners … dance to a Rustick Ayre	5
→2nd Entry	A Symphony variously humour'd `prepares the change of the Scene`	8
before Mariners' final chorus	Four Simerons … dance a Morisco　　　　**=The Simerons Dance?**	13
→3rd Entry	`THe change of the Scene is prepar'd by` a Symphony, consisting of a Martiall Ayre	13
before Peruvian's final song	Five Peruvians … Dance to a Rustick Ayr	16
during Peruvian's final song	they Dance again in a Round	
→4th Entry	A Wilde Ayre, by way of Symphony `prepares the change of the Scene`	18
end of 4th Entry]	two Land-souldiers and … two Sea-men dance a Jigg	23

→ 5th Entry		Entry is prepar'd by an Ayr and …	
		Corante	23
	end of 5th Entry]	*Bridegroom danc[es] with Castanietos, to express … joy … whilst the Father [of the Bride] moves to his measures, denoting … fright*	30
→ 6th Entry		Entry is prepar'd with a Martiall Ayre	31
	end of 6th Entry]	*The Grand Dance[: 2 Land-souldiers; 2 Sea-men; 2 Symerons; a Peruvian] intimating mutuall desires of amity*	37

Key:

{} = acrobatic feat performed by the Priest of the Sun's Attendant, always immediately following Priest's speech

---

* Italicization in original quotations is ignored.

† First song (pp. 42–43) performed immediately prior: "Did ever war so cease" (by Henry Lawes).

‡ Second song (pp. 84–85) performed prior to Epilogue: "London is smother'd with sulph'rous fires" (by Charles Coleman).

190   *"For such uses as the King shall direct"*

the pre-Restoration productions, or simply use the term, as we know Pepys and others did, to designate Davenant's company at Lincoln's Inn Fields after mid-1661, cannot be ascertained; the dancing operatic apes would themselves have reappeared at the new theatre when *Peru* was incorporated into *The Play-House to be Let*, probably in 1663. Once again, *Cupid and Death*, also considered in Appendix C, offers a useful point of comparison: only one of its many instrumental movements, the "Antick Dance" from Locke's suite of airs at the beginning of the second antimasque entry, shows up in multiple printed sources, although several others appear once each (and one appears twice). Moreover, while in many cases Locke is identified as the composer, the publications make no mention whatsoever of *Cupid* as the original source of the tunes; thus, we only know this fact because of the providential survival of the full score. One other noteworthy tune, which has received scant attention on account of the rarity of its source, is that entitled "Iantha," which appears in the supplement to the ?1662 printing of the third edition of John Playford's *The Dancing Master*.[118] This binary fourteen-bar duple-time piece in G minor, which is given in Example 4.1, is characterized by dotted rhythms and repeated quarter notes on the second and third beats, and its stress pattern of 3–4–3[119]/4–3–3–3 suggests the metrical irregularity of the *Rhodes* poetic text. On the other hand, there is no obvious place in the opera where the tune actually fits the text, and thus it is difficult to imagine that it could have been sung, either by Ianthe or by anyone else. Perhaps it was originally an instrumental tune, although of course *Rhodes* has few of these, and no dances at all (see Table 4.5). Ultimately, our tentative identification of this tune as a prospective survival from *Rhodes* relies on the serendipitous title; there are potentially many other tunes in these sources that may derive from Davenant's operas, but with their more generic names, they will probably never be revealed as such.

The implied comparison between Davenant's works and *Cupid and Death*, noted above, raises an important question about the creative forces behind the music in these theatrical productions. Davenant's operas were a substantial undertaking that required, at least in the instances for which we have reliable information, a whole cadre of composers, rather than just one or two. Yet the surviving evidence suggests a curiously flexible approach to the allocation of responsibilities (see Table 4.6). We know too little about *Peru* and *Drake* to draw any firm conclusions, apart from the fact that Matthew Locke, who had composed the vocal music for the Fourth Entry of *Rhodes*, seems to have contributed dance tunes (The Apes Dance; The Simerons Dance) to the later productions. Locke, the junior member of the *Rhodes* team, was apparently not involved in *The First Day's*

---

118 *The Dancing Master* (London: John Playford, ?1662 [title page missing]), [1]41 (section 2 ["*The TUNES of the French Dances and other New* TUNES *for the* TREBLE-VIOLIN"], no. 26). The only known copy of this print is in the Glasgow University Library, Special Collections Department (shelfmark Q.c.85). This tune should not be confused with another "Iantha" (later "Ianthia"), which first appeared in 1706 in the 13th edition of *The Dancing Master* (p. 364; p. 352 in all subsequent editions).

119 This could also be 3–4–4, depending upon how one reads the slurring in the descending eighth-note scale at the end of the first half of the piece.

Operatic experiments of the 1650s 191

Example 4.1 "Iantha," from *The Dancing Master*, ?1662

Entertainment, the most musically undemanding of the four productions, but the other four *Rhodes* composers all were, albeit in a somewhat different configuration. Two of them seem to have been consistent in the duties they undertook: Henry Lawes, the leading vocal composer of his day, wrote one of the two songs for *The First Day's Entertainment* and composed the opening and closing entries of *Rhodes*; George Hudson, who later became Composer to the Twenty-Four Violins at Charles II's court and is not known ever to have written any songs, provided instrumental music for both productions. But Charles Coleman (probably the eldest of the five, and an established vocal composer) moved from writing a song for *The First Day's Entertainment* to composing instrumental music for *Rhodes*, while Henry Cooke, whose body of secular vocal music is otherwise quite limited,[120] turned from instrumental composition in the earlier production to vocal in the later, supplying *Rhodes* with settings for the Second and Third Entries. Both Cooke and Locke, of course, were also performers in the opera (see Table 4.4), which may have prompted their assumption of responsibility for three-fifths of the vocal music, including a great deal of recitative—a style of which Charles Coleman is not known to have been a particularly active practitioner. Nevertheless, Coleman is now recognized as a composer of rare dramatic talent: Ian Spink even goes so far as to suggest that "had the times been other than they were he might have been the founding father of English Opera."[121] Why he would have shifted his attention to the fairly restricted instrumental component of *Rhodes* is not clear.

One explanation for some of these changes may lie in the evident differences in musical performance circumstances between *First Day's* and *Rhodes*: the musicians for the former, according to the contemporary account of the production, were located "aboue in a loouer hole railed about and couered wth Sarcenetts to conceale them,"[122] whereas, as Dennis Arundell has observed, *Rhodes*, with its proscenium arch and perspective scenery as well as its presumed need for close coordination between instrumentalists and singers, appears to have required the

---

120 Four of Cooke's six surviving secular songs appear together as a group in *Catch that Catch Can: or the Musical Companion* (London: J[ohn] Playford, 1667), 201–12.
121 Spink, *English Song* (see n. 4, above), 118. On p. 117, Spink discusses Coleman's "Wake, my Adonis" (?early 1640s), describing the "remarkable ... range of tragic feeling it displays" and concluding that "for its time it may only be compared with Lanier's *Hero and Leander*, though it is much shorter and the style rather different."
122 SP18/128/108.

192   *"For such uses as the King shall direct"*

Table 4.6 Composers for the "operatic" productions of Sir William Davenant, 1656–59

	Charles Coleman (>1600–1664)	*Henry Lawes* (1596–1662)	*George Hudson* (c.1610/20–1672)	*Henry Cooke* (c.1615–1672)	*Matthew Locke* (1621/2–1677)
*First Day's**	**v**[a]	**v**[b]	**i**	**i**	—
*Rhodes***	**i**	**v**[c]	**i**	**v**[d]	**v**[e]
Peru	?	?	?	?	**i** (+v?)
Drake	?	?	?	?	**i** (+v?)

Key:
i = composed instrumental music
v = composed vocal music

Notes:
* Playbook, sig. [G3][r]: "*The* Vocal *and* Instrumental Musick *was compos'd by Doctor* Charles Coleman, *Capt.* Henry Cook, *Mr* Henry Lawes, *and Mr* George Hudson"; SP18/128/108: "The first song was made by Hen: Lawes y[e] other by D[r] Coleman who were the Composers."
** Playbook, sig. [G1][r]: "The Composition of *Vocal Musick* was perform'd / The *First Entry* by Mr. *Henry Lawes*. / [The] *Second Entry* [by] Capt. *Henry Cook*. / [The] *Thurd Entry* [by] Capt. *Henry Cook*. / [The] *Fourth Entry* [by] Mr. *Matthew Lock*. / [The] *Fifth Entry* [by] Mr. *Henry Lawes*. / The *Instrumental Musick* was compos'd by D[r] *Charles Coleman*, and M[r] *George Hudson*."

---

[a] **One song only** ("London is smother'd with sulph'rous fires").
[b] **One song only** ("Did ever war so cease").
[c] **Entries 1** (incl. "Come ye termagant Turks"†) **and 5** (incl. "With a fine merry gale"‡).
[d] **Entries 2** (incl. "How bravely fought the fiery French", "Let us live, live! for being dead") **and 3** (incl. "Ye wives all that are").
[e] **Entry 4** (incl. "This cursed jealousy, what is't?"§).

---

† Text of song also found in *Windsor Drollery* (1671/1671/1672) and *The Academy of Complements With Many New Additions* (1684).
‡ Text of song also found in Bodleian Library, MS Rawlinson F. 214, f. 79[v].
§ Text of song also found in Folger Shakespeare Library, MS V.a.308, f. 104[r] ("From The game of love, or cards for the year 1687").

placement of its band directly in front of the stage.[123] That band, we should note, seems to have consisted of only six performers, and thus would not have occupied a great deal of space in either location.[124] In any event, it is likely that *Peru* and *Drake* also employed multiple (if not all) members of the aforementioned compositional group, and moreover that, given these works' quite different musical demands, Davenant's composers would have been obliged to persist in the same eclectic vein as they had for the two earlier productions.

123 *The Critic at the Opera*, 56–57. Arundell also observes (p. 56) a possible difference between the traverse curtains for *The First Day's Entertainment*, which are "drawn open" and "clos'd" throughout the performance (sig. *A3*[r] and pp. 1, 41, 44, 83, 86, and [90]), and the single rising curtain for *The Siege of Rhodes*, which is "drawn up" at the beginning of the work and only "let fall" at the very end (pp. 2 and 40).
124 The list given on the cancellans sig. [G1][v] (see n. 86, above) names Thomas Baltzar, John Banister, Humphrey Madge (all violinists), Thomas Bates (bass viol), Christopher Gibbons (keyboards), and William Webb (generally known as a singer, but may have played bass viol).

5 Foreign musicians at the Restoration court, 1660–73

Our identification of a coherent set of musical and technical principles that can be applied to the theatrical productions of the Protectorate makes it all the more curious that the rich tradition of dramatic music established, in particular, in Davenant's operatic venture is so little in evidence in the years immediately after the Restoration. While the notion of English opera may have persisted in the public consciousness, the three leading London impresarios of the early 1660s—Davenant, Thomas Killigrew, and George Jolly—devoted their attention to the performance of straight plays in which (as we have seen in the cases of *Rhodes, Part 2* and *Mustapha*) music had little if any currency. Indeed, after the production of *The History of Sir Francis Drake*, a full quarter of a century was to elapse before through-sung opera in English would be heard again on the London stage. This fact would appear to fly in the face of inclusive language used in those all-important documents that established the institutions of the post-Restoration theatre, namely, the licenses and patents that created at first three, and then ultimately two, companies whose virtual monopoly over the performance of "legitimate" theatre would remain in force in England for over 300 years.[1] That language is exemplified in the formal patents issued to Killigrew on 25 April 1662 and to Davenant on 15 January 1663, as well as that given to one William Legge on 31 March 1664 for the erection of the jointly controlled "Nursery" for the training up of young actors: all three stipulate that theatres may be erected "wherein tragedies, comedies, plays, operas, music, scenes, and all other entertainments of the stage whatsoever may be showed and presented."[2] Indeed, the provocative reference to "operas" recurs in a number of

---

1 The terms of the 1660 arrangement, codified in the Licensing Act of 1737 (10 Geo. II, cap. 28) and its successor, the Theatres Act of 1843 (6 & 7 Vict., cap. 68), were finally repealed with the passage of the Theatres Act of 1968 (1968, cap. 54).

2 This passage, as quoted from Davenant's patent, is virtually identical in both Killigrew's and Legge's (which, additionally, rehearses the formula from the two earlier patents and that of Jolly). The Killigrew and Davenant patents both subsequently repeat altered or abbreviated versions of the list—again, in the same sequence and with the same elements in the two documents: "tragedies, comedies, plays, operas, and other performances of the stage"; "plays and entertainments of the stage of all sorts"; "plays, scenes, and entertainments"; "plays and entertainments of the stage as aforesaid"; "comedies, tragedies, plays, or entertainments of the stage." The first two of

194   *"For such uses as the King shall direct"*

these documents, from Davenant's original drafts, prepared in 1660, proposing the establishment of a theatrical duopoly and the suppression of all competition, to the licenses granted to George Jolly in 1660 and 1663, along with various restatements of the terms of Jolly's original license as late as 1667. Yet as the comparison offered in Table 5.1 reveals, the invocation of opera was probably intended to be no more than formulaic: the crucial documents—the draft monopoly proposal and the joint "privilege" of 1660 in favor of Killigrew and Davenant, the 1660 license to Jolly, and the three formal patents of 1662–64 (these items are presented in "small caps" in the table)—all proceed in the same fashion, listing tragedies, comedies, plays, and operas, before diverging slightly to encompass Jolly's farces and to add the after-thought of music and scenes to the later patents. Jolly's secondary licenses permitting him to perform in the provinces are more haphazard (one mentions opera, while the other does not), and of particular interest is Davenant's elaboration of the term in his draft ban of 1660 to "Operas by Recitative Musick." But the incorporation of the words "musick" and "scenes," which cannot, strictly speaking, be described as generic categories in themselves, is telling. These components, once essential to the definition of the operatic form, were now the province of the theatres generally, to be exploited as needed in "all ... entertainments of the stage whatsoever."

The decisive move away from an "operatic" conception of the theatre after 1660, while certainly an important step in the development of Restoration drama, is less significant for the history of English opera itself. Given the patent companies' enthusiastic embrace of stage spectacle, it is surprising how far the position of music seems to have declined with the establishment of the new order. This is by no means to suggest that music disappeared entirely from the public theatres: there are plenty of unidentified instrumental tunes and even full-blown theatre suites from the 1660s, not to mention song texts (with no associated music) in numerous plays. But it is instructive to observe how little hard evidence of musical activity in the theatres actually survives from the first decade of Charles II's reign. Peter Holman's largely comprehensive catalogue of "Attributed music for plays in the commercial theatre, 1660–1669" lists a mere twenty plays from this period for which any clearly ascribable music is extant.[3] In eleven cases these are single songs (two of the plays have a pair of songs each, for a total of thirteen songs), while in another six instances Holman finds instrumental music (four dance movements and possibly two full suites). Beyond this, there are a few atypical cases: the 1663/64 production of *Macbeth* (a song and a dance by Matthew Locke appear to survive, as does an older musical setting by Robert Johnson that was probably reused) and the 1667 Dryden/Davenant adaptation of *The Tempest*,[4]

---

these repetitions also appear in the Legge patent. Davenant's original copy of his patent is in the Rosenbach Museum, Philadelphia (cat. no. 2003.0070); for additional references, see Table 5.1.

3 Holman, *Fiddlers*, 356–58 (Table 14.1). Holman's list includes a song by John Banister, for Sedley's *The Mulberry Garden*, that does not survive.

4 This consists of four songs by John Banister and possibly one by Pelham Humfrey. The 1667 *Tempest* production also included music, all of which is lost, for four dances and for a masque of devils.

Table 5.1 Comparison of generic formulae in theatre patents and related documents of the 1660s

Document	Date	Opening phrase	Main genres	Secondary genres	Farces	Closing clause
DAVENANT/KILLIGREW DRAFT MONOPOLY[a]	1660 19 July	"the representations of	Tragedys, Comedys, Playes, Operas,			and all other entertainments of that nature "
Davenant (?/Killigrew) draft ban[b]	1660 20 August	"to desist and forbeare the performing, acting and shewing any	Comedies, Tragedies,	Operas by or any Representation by Dancing, or Scenes, Musick, *→		[*]or any Plays, or other Entertainments of the Stage whatsoever "
KILLIGREW/DAVENANT PRIVILEGE[c]	1660 21 August	"the representation of	tragydies, comedyes, playes, operas,			and all other entertainments of that nature "
KILLIGREW PATENT[d]	1662 25 April	"[may be shown and presented]	tragedies, comedies, plays, operas,	musick, scenes,		and all other entertainment of the stage whatsoever [←†] "
DAVENANT PATENT[e]	1663 15 January	"[may be showed and presented]	tragedies, comedies, plays, operas,	music, scenes,		and all other entertainments of the stage whatsoever[←†] "
LEGGE NURSERY PATENT[f]	1664 31 March	"[may be shewed and presented]	tragedies, Comedies, Playes, Operas,	Musique, Sceanes,		and all other Entertainments of the stage whatsoever[←†] "
Beeston Salisbury Court license[g]	1660 ?late June	"†[may bee Acted]	Comedies tragedies	trage Comedies, Pastoralls, and Interludes		[←†] "
JOLLY LICENSE[h]	1660 24 Dec'ber	"the representation of	Tragedies, Comedies, Plaies, Operas,		Farces	and all other entertainments of that nature "
Jolly revocation/exchange (restatement of 1660 license)[i]	1662 30 Dec'ber	"the representation of	Tragedyes Comedyes Playes Operas		& ffarces	
Jolly non-London license (Master of the Revels)[j]	1663 1 January	"to act	Comedies Tragedies	Trage-Comedies pastoralls and enterludes		throughout Eng: "
Jolly non-London license (King)[k]	1663 29 January	"to exercise such	playes Opperas	Maskes Showes Scenes	&	& all other presentations of ffarcesy[e] Stage w[h]soever "
Jolly revocation (restatement of 1660 license)[l]	1667 24 April	"y[e] representation of	Tragedyes, Comedes, Playes, Operas		Farces	& all other Entertainments of that nature "

Sources:

[a] SP29/8/1 (Register, no. 8).
[b] SP29/10/169 (Register, no. 18).
[c] British Library, Add. MS 19256, f. 47 (Register, no. 19).
[d] C66/3013/20; Killigrew's own copy is in the Theatre Museum, Victoria and Albert Museum, London (on loan from Drury Lane Theatre) (Register, no. 131).
[e] C66/3009/3; Davenant's own copy is in the Rosenbach Museum, Philadelphia, cat. no. 2003.0070 (Register, no. 186).
[f] C66/3054/5; British Library, Add. Charter 17753 (Register, no. 277).
[g] British Library, Add. MS 19256, f. 100 (Register, no. 6).
[h] SP29/24/37 (Register, no. 51).
[i] British Library, Add. Charter 9297 (Register, no. 179).
[j] SP44/48, pp. 6a–7 (Register, no. 183).
[k] SP44/9, pp. 247–50 (Register, no. 188).
[l] SP29/77/39; SP29/198/39; SP44/23, pp. 438–39 (Register, no. 381).

196 *"For such uses as the King shall direct"*

plus three unusual works, all from 1663, in which recitative music played some significant part. Of this last category we can say very little, since the actual music survives from just one of the three, Katherine Philips's *Pompey*—and only one of the four extant songs in this play, John Banister's "From lasting and unclouded day" has any recitative component.[5] The other two plays in question were both written by the courtier and amateur Classicist Sir Robert Stapylton: *The Slighted Maid*, for which *"The Instrumental, Vocal, and Recitative Musick, was composed by Mr. Banister,"*[6] and *The Step-Mother*, whose music, according to precisely the same formula, *"was compos'd by Mr. Lock."*[7] These undoubtedly are, and were, fascinating works: Dennis Arundell has even termed *The Slighted Maid* "the missing link ... between masque and opera."[8] However, the loss of the music, as in so many other instances, precludes our arriving at a fuller understanding of how the musical element of the plays functioned.[9]

Taken as a whole, this catalogue implies a somewhat limited role for music generally on the early Restoration stage, although we must always bear in mind that our knowledge of the utilization of music—and in particular of instrumental music and its direct corollary, dance—is necessarily hampered by the very poor quality of the evidence.[10] Even bearing in mind these limitations, we might regard 1663 as something of a high-water mark: in this year, audiences could go to Lincoln's Inn Fields and see *The Slighted Maid* (in February and May), *The Play-House to be Let* (in August), and *The Step-Mother* (in October), all of which featured to some degree the operatic elements of recitative singing, scenic spectacle, and

---

5 Banister's song is preserved in British Library, Add. MS 33234, f. 30ᵛ and Christ Church, Oxford, Mus. 350, pp. 93–97. For a discussion of the play and its music see Price, *Music in the Restoration Theatre*, 62–64 and 262 nn. 34–43. I am most grateful to Alan A. Luhring who, a number of years ago, kindly sent me copies of his transcriptions of the *Pompey* songs.

6 *The Slighted Maid, A Comedy* (London: Thomas Dring, 1663), sig. A4ᵛ.

7 *The Step-Mother, A Tragi-Comedy* (London: Timothy Twyford, 1664), sig. A4ᵛ.

8 Arundell, *The Critic at the Opera*, 75–87 (quotation from p. 87). See also Curtis Alexander Price, *Henry Purcell and the London Stage* (Cambridge: Cambridge University Press, 1984), 7–9.

9 Interestingly, both *Pompey* and *The Step-Mother* have connections to Davenant's post-operatic *The Play-House to be Let*: see William Van Lennep, ed., *The London Stage[,] 1660–1800[:] A Calendar of Plays, Entertainments & Afterpieces Together with Casts, Box-Receipts and Contemporary Comment Compiled from the Playbills, Newspapers and Theatrical Diaries of the Period[,] Part 1: 1660–1700* (Carbondale: Southern Illinois University Press, 1965), 67. At some point in the 1660s Davenant revised his old comedy *The Wits*, adding a "Catch ... sung, and acted ... in Recitative Burlesque" to Act 5: see *The Works of Sʳ William Davenant Kᵗ*, section 2, pp. 214–15; the passage does not appear in the edition of 1636, reprinted in 1665. The alterations may have been added around 1667, when Samuel Pepys saw the play "now corrected and enlarged" (*Diary*, 8: 171 [18 April]).

10 For example, scholars have generally concluded that most plays of the period *were* supplied with largely non-programmatic theatre suites, to be played before the show and between each act—even though few examples from the early decades of the Restoration, even of unassignable suites, actually survive. See for example Peter Holman, ed., *Matthew Locke: The Rare Theatrical: New York Public Library, Drexel MS 3976* (Music for London Entertainment 1660–1800, Series A Volume 4; London: Stainer and Bell, 1989).

Foreign musicians at the Restoration court 197

theatrical dancing to instrumental music. Yet even in the case of *The Play-House to be Let*, with its third-act reprise of Davenant's *History of Sir Francis Drake*, the interest in the larger structures and aesthetic of through-composition, so ably fostered by Davenant only a few years before, had clearly dissipated.[11] Why this change occurred is a difficult question to answer: the theatre proprietors' estimation of audience preference may be a factor; or perhaps the sudden exodus of talent into Charles II's court musical establishment in 1660 forced their hand. But two other considerations may also be relevant. The first is a generational shift among the leading English musicians that occurred in the early years of the 1660s. By 1664, the two senior members of Davenant's operatic compositional team (Coleman and Lawes, both of whom were already in their 60s at the time of the Restoration) were dead; Nicholas Lanier, the creator of "Hero's Complaint to Leander," died two years later, at the age of 77. With Hudson and Cooke immersed in their new duties at court, the composition of theatrical music was taken up by a younger generation, which appears to have been dominated by three figures, all of whom are known to have been involved in the early performances of *Rhodes*: Matthew Locke (b. 1621/2) had composed the Fourth Entry and sung the role of the Admiral; John Banister (b. 1624/5) had played in the six-man instrumental ensemble; and Alfonso Marsh (b. 1626/7) had shared the role of Pirrhus. Yet apart from the music for *The Slighted Maid* and *The Step-Mother*, and Banister's song for Philips's *Pompey* (also from 1663, although it is not known where, or precisely when, this play was produced), there is little evidence for even a limited use of recitative in theatre music during the early years of Charles II's reign. Marsh is primarily known for his tuneful, strophic songs, and while both Locke and Banister were at the forefront of musical creativity and experimentation at court, producing odes, new types of anthem (both forms also pioneered by Henry Cooke), and ensemble settings for novel instrumental configurations, their surviving theatre music shows little of the sophistication being exercised in the courtly realm. Holman's table, admittedly less an indicator of what was actually happening than of what has chanced to survive, lists mostly straightforward songs and dance tunes; the most extravagant items are John Banister's suite of instrumental airs for *The Indian Queen*, performed in January 1664,[12] and the music believed

---

11 The Musician who presents *Drake* within the play offers an articulate justification of recitative ("In Tragedy, the language of the Stage / Is rais'd above the common dialect; / Our passions rising with the height of Verse; / And Vocal Musick adds new wings to all / The flights of Poetry"), but the aspirational nature of his disquisition is revealed when he concedes to the Player that "'tis not in custom" (Davenant, "THE Play-house to be Let," 72). We might note that even as Davenant had increased the amount of recitative music, scenes, and dancing in his productions in the waning years of the Protectorate, Richard Flecknoe appears to have been moving in the other direction, seemingly abandoning his model of through-composition, as introduced in *Ariadne Deserted by Theseus* for the more mixed style displayed in *The Marriage of Oceanus and Britannia*.

12 For an edition of Banister's suite, fragments of which survive in a variety of mostly manuscript sources, see Margaret Laurie and Andrew Pinnock, eds., *The Indian Queen* (Purcell Society, 19; London: Novello, 1994), Appendix D (pp. xxxi, 149–54, and 176–77).

198 *"For such uses as the King shall direct"*

to have been written by Locke for Davenant's *Macbeth* adaptation of 1663 or 1664 (despite the fact that very little of this music actually exists).[13] Even Banister's songs for the 1667 production of *The Tempest*, including his celebrated echo duet "Go thy way," are notable for their harmonic, structural, and textural simplicity, and only gain in stature by their later incorporation into the more complex musical fabric of the play's 1674 revival as a dramatick opera.

A second consideration relating to the disappearance of through-composed English opera in the 1660s is the manifest preference of Charles II for musicians, and music, of foreign extraction. The diligence of a number of scholars has progressively unearthed more and better information about the activities of foreign musicians in Restoration England.[14] A good deal of our knowledge is dependent on anecdotal evidence, for example in the observations of Samuel Pepys; with respect to those musicians who served at court, there is some official documentation, but it is remarkable how fragmentary this is, particularly when compared with the detailed records of the native ensembles, such as the Twenty-Four Violins. Even at an early stage, Charles II and his officers appear to have distinguished between English musicians, who were granted regular places in the royal musical establishment, and foreigners, who served more informally within the household.[15] This distinction, and its effects on the documentary record, become clear in the case of the ensemble known as "the King's Italian Musicians," which was active at court throughout much of the 1660s and early into the following decade. For the entire ten-year period between 1663 and 1673, fewer than twenty-five documents or entries in accounts exist that record the functioning of this group of musicians. Of these, only nine involve actual records pertaining to the general makeup of the ensemble and payments to its various members; two of these are undated, but probably come from around 1664–66, when the group was first being set up. In addition to these nine items, there are two undated petitions requesting the release of unspecified arrearages. Four other documents are associated with

---

13 For a discussion and transcription of the *Macbeth* tunes, see Amanda Eubanks Winkler, ed., *Music for* Macbeth (Middleton, WI: A-R Editions, 2004), vii–viii, 1–3, and 97–98.

14 See W. J. Lawrence, "Foreign Singers and Musicians at the Court of Charles II," *The Musical Quarterly* 9 (1923): 217–25; J. A. Westrup, "Foreign Musicians in Stuart England," *The Musical Quarterly* 27 (1941): 70–89; and, more specifically, Margaret Mabbett, "Italian Musicians in Restoration England (1660–90)," *Music and Letters* 67 (1986): 237–47. The French musicians are briefly discussed in Holman, *Fiddlers*, 290–91.

15 A good example of the latter is the guitarist Francesco Corbetta, who arrived in England in 1661 and was appointed "Groom of the privy chamber to the Queen," a position he later exchanged for that of "Page of the backstairs to the King" (SP29/142/50 [undated petition, filed under "c.1665," but probably from late 1666 or 1667: *Calendar of State Papers, Domestic* 1665–66: 143; Ashbee, 8: 337]). For more on Corbetta, see my in-progress article "Francesco Corbetta in England, 1661–c.1677"; this discussion, along with much of what follows in the next four paragraphs, constitutes the bulk of a long-deferred article that was originally announced under the title "Some Further Notes on Italian Musicians in Restoration England" (see Andrew R. Walkling, "Masque and Politics at the Restoration Court: John Crowne's *Calisto*," *Early Music* 24 [1996]: 27–62, p. 61 n. 93).

the comings and goings of the musicians to and from the Continent, while another four record gifts of gold chains and medals from the king. There are also five miscellaneous documents that shed a small amount of light on the group's personnel and quotidian activities. This scant official record is supplemented by several illuminating entries by diarists, in particular Pepys. Armed with these scraps of information, it is possible to piece together an incomplete and speculative, but nonetheless useful, portrait that has important implications for our understanding of opera, such as it was, in the first decade of the Restoration.

The Italian ensemble appears to have had its origin sometime around the winter of 1663–64, after Vincenzo Albrici and his brother Bartolomeo left the Saxon Electoral Court at Dresden[16] and traveled to England, where they submitted a proposal to Charles II for the formation of an ensemble consisting of eight members, including five singers ("The Woman," "The Eunuch," contralto, tenor, and bass), a "Poete," and the brothers themselves as composers.[17] Each was to receive an annual salary of £200, except the woman, who would get £300—all impressive figures by any measure.[18] Vincenzo Albrici, who would eventually become the group's leader, might be the "learned, and Civvill ... Musicien" sent to Henry Bennet, Baron (and later Earl of) Arlington by Sir Bernard Gascoigne from Turin

16 For more on Vincenzo Albrici's career, see Carl-Allan Moberg, "Vincenzo Albrici (1631–1696): Eine Biographische Skizze mit Besonderer Berücksichtigung seiner Schwedischen Zeit," in Anna Amalie Abert and Wilhelm Pfannkuch, eds., *Festschrift Friedrich Blume zum 70. Geburtstag* (Kassel: Bärenreiter, 1963), 235–46. According to Mary E. Frandsen ("Albrici, Vincenzo," *Grove Music Online*, Oxford University Press [http://www.oxfordmusiconline.com/subscriber/article/grove/music/00480, accessed 22 July 2012]), the Albrici brothers left Dresden in August 1663.

17 SP29/66/30 (in Italian, apparently from the Albricis themselves ["noi"]). This document, undated and probably misfiled (see *Calendar of State Papers, Domestic* 1661–62: 613; Ashbee, 8: 174–75), appears in the archive alongside a second, also undated, document, SP29/66/31, which summarizes the terms of the proposal in English. (See Mabbett, 238 for a translation of the former, and her Appendix, nos. 2 and 3 for transcriptions of both.) A third document containing a summary statement of salaries, SP44/23, p. 29 (*Calendar of State Papers, Domestic* 1665–66: 281; Ashbee, 8: 174), is closely related to SP29/66/31; it is dated 1 March 1666, which may provide some guidance as to the date of the latter document as well. In a document of 1653 associated with the Swedish court (transcribed in Einar Sundström, "Notiser om Drottning Kristinas Italienska Musiker," *Svensk Tidskrift för Musikforskning* 43 [1961]: 297–309, pp. 308–9), Vincenzo is listed as "Organista e Compositore," while Bartolomeo is described as a "soprano non Castrato" (see n. 34, below, for Bartolomeo's later appointment as a singer in James II's Roman Catholic Chapel Royal). Depending on when Vincenzo and Bartolomeo arrived in England, they may have been accompanied by the instrument builder Girolamo Zenti, who had been with them in Stockholm the previous decade. Zenti, who was described in the Swedish document as "ottimo mastro di Clavicembali ed Organi," was granted an annual salary of £50 by Charles II on 27 January 1664 (SP29/91/55; SP44/16, p. 19 [*Calendar of State Papers, Domestic* 1663–64: 455; Ashbee, 8: 166]), but then left England almost immediately (SP44/16, p. 21 ["Pass for Girolamo Zinti, the King's virginal maker, to Italy," 29 January 1664: *Calendar of State Papers, Domestic* 1663–64: 458; Ashbee, 8: 166]) and never returned, having died in Paris sometime before the fall of 1666. For his replacement, Andrea Testa, see n. 48, below.

18 Charles II's Master of the Music was paid a £200 salary as well, but the other "English" performers received far less.

200   "For such uses as the King shall direct"

in late 1663 or early 1664,[19] and he and his brother may have commenced their tenure as Charles II's court servants at the beginning of April 1664.[20] In any case, they were certainly in England by early 1665, when they were issued passes "to go abroad and return," presumably to recruit personnel.[21] The three singers that they must have secured on their trip—the Croatian-born tenor Giovanni Sebenico; the Bolognese Matteo Battaglia (a countertenor?); and Pietro Cefalo (a castrato?)—were formally appointed into the king's service as of 1 April 1666.[22] At precisely this moment, Bartolomeo Albrici was dispatched abroad again on his own, "to return shortly, bringing back some companions for his Majesty's use."[23] It may be at this time that he engaged three or four other members of the group—his sister Leonora; the bass Pietro Reggio; a second castrato, Hilario Suarez; and perhaps the keyboardist, librettist, and composer Giovanni Battista Draghi—none of whose actual names are recorded in any documents until much later, if at all.[24]

---

19 SP29/99/26, p. 3 (letter of [31 May/]7 June 1664: *Calendar of State Papers, Domestic* 1663–64: 607; Ashbee, 8: 168; for a partial transcription, see Mabbett, Appendix, no. 4).

20 In April 1666, Sir John Shaw was reimbursed out of the Privy Purse for £600 "for ye Italian Musick" (Bodleian Library, Malone MS 44, f. 101^v). This amount could constitute salary payments of £300 each for Vincenzo and Bartolomeo, hence covering a year and a half (*i.e.* six quarters) for each brother. Sometime after June 1666, another document (see n. 22, below) records the need to pay not only the three new members of the ensemble for their first quarter of service, but also the Albrici brothers for arrears going back to 1 October 1665; thus, calculating back an additional year and a half from that date, we arrive at 1 April 1664. Shaw actually received an additional 1% "for charges of returning 600"; in quoting this entry, Ashbee (8: 175) seems to misread it as referring to "charges of returning" to England after the recruiting trip abroad.

21 SP29/116/22 (25 March 1665: *Calendar of State Papers, Domestic* 1664–65: 273; Ashbee, 8: 170 [misdated and miscited as volume "106"]).

22 See SP29/160/155 (c. June 1666: *Calendar of State Papers, Domestic* 1665–66: 484; Ashbee, 8: 175): "Peter Cefalo, Mathew Battaglia, John Sebenico Were received in his Majesties Service the 1 day of Aprill 1666; there is due unto them a quarter to all the three at fifty pound a quarter, which is 150 pound." The document goes on to state that the Albrici brothers, whose appointment probably began much earlier (see n. 20, above), are each owed "3 quarters a piece beginning the 1 day of October 1665, till the last of June 1666 At fifty pound a quarter: some [*i.e.* sum] £300." Note also the proximity of the appointment date of the three newcomers to the establishment list(s) of 1 March 1666, discussed in n. 17, above.

23 SP29/152/59 (31 March 1666: *Calendar of State Papers, Domestic* 1665–66: 326; Ashbee, 8: 175).

24 Leonora Albrici is first identified simply as Bartolomeo's sister in a Privy Purse account entry for April 1668, but her name is given in a warrant for gold chains and medals for the three Albrici siblings the following month (see discussion below); Suarez and Draghi's names only appear for the first time in a petition of 18 November 1679. Reggio (d. 1685) is a particular puzzle: his name is never explicitly mentioned in connection with the Italian ensemble, and thus his employment in that group is purely speculative. Moreover, he is commonly believed to be the "slovenly and ugly fellow, Seignor Pedro" who joined music meetings at the home of Samuel Pepys on three Friday afternoons in the summer of 1664, before the Albricis had even begun to assemble their musical team (see Pepys, *Diary*, 5: 217 [22 July], 226 [29 July], and 239 [12 August]). It should be observed that Pepys (who classified him as an "idle master," and quickly sought to be rid of him) never actually identifies "Seignor Pedro" as Reggio; moreover, he makes no mention of his erstwhile musical companion when he describes seeing the Italians sing two and a half years later (see n. 27, below), leading us to wonder whether the long-established identification of "Seignor Pedro"

Foreign musicians at the Restoration court   201

Both Reggio and Suarez had been associated with the Albrici brothers at the court of Queen Christina of Sweden in the early 1650s, and so Bartolomeo's chief aim must have been to round out the group with collaborators who were already well known to him.[25] Suarez appears to have been added as an afterthought—only one "Eunuch" is called for in the Albricis' original proposal—but the concentration of treble voices was clearly an important feature of the ensemble: by January 1667, with the nine-person group now complete, John Evelyn could report hearing "rare *Italian* voices, 2 *Eunuchs* & one Woman, in his Majesties greene Chamber next his Cabinet,"[26] while a few weeks later Pepys, attending a gathering at the home of his colleague William, Viscount Brouncker, described

> the music, that is to say, Seignor Vincentio, who is the maister Composer, and six more, where of two Eunuches ... and one woman, very well dressed and handsome enough but would not be kissed, as Mr. Killigrew, who brought the company in, did acquaint us. They sent two Harpsicons before; and by and by, after tuning them, they begun; and I confess, very good music they made[.][27]

Beyond these notices, few other actual instances of performances by the Italians in their capacity as "his Majesty's Italian Musicians" are known:[28] they appear to have

---

with Reggio is even tenable. Reggio is thus doubly obscured: no document ever actually connects him with the king's Italian ensemble, and at the same time Pepys (who would show a distinct interest in Reggio's music later on, during the 1680s) is the only known witness to his supposed presence in London prior to 1674, when his song "Arise ye subterranean winds" was performed in *The Tempest*. For a summary of what little we do know about Reggio, whose whereabouts between 1657 and the mid-1670s are otherwise a complete mystery, see Gloria Rose, "Pietro Reggio—A Wandering Musician," *Music and Letters* 46 (1965): 207–16.

25 Leonora had probably been in Stockholm as well, since the Albrici patriarch, Domenico, was also associated with Queen Christina's court. For details on the harpsichord builders/technicians Girolamo Zenti and Andrea Testa, who had also been in Stockholm with the Albricis, see nn. 17, above and 48, below.

26 Evelyn, *Diary*, 3: 474 (24 January 1667).

27 Pepys, *Diary*, 8: 64–65 (16 February 1667). Pepys qualified his assessment of the music, however, comparing it without favor to "what I have heard in English," and the singing of the castrati to that of English women "and men also, as Crispe of the Wardrobe." The "Harpsicons" were probably played by Draghi and Bartolomeo Albrici, both of whom were known as keyboardists rather than singers—see Pepys's remark of a few days earlier (*ibid.*, 55) that Draghi "pretends not to voice, though it be good but not excellent." In 1675, Bartolomeo would be paid £10 for "Ext[raordinary] attendance" as the main keyboardist in the production of *Calisto*: see LC5/141, p. 197 (27 May 1675: Ashbee, 1: 150); he would later become well known to John Evelyn as one of "the most renouned Masters" (20 November 1679: *Diary*, 4: 186) and as harpsichord teacher to his daughter Mary (7 February 1682 and 14 March 1685: *ibid.*, 271, 421, and 428); see also the letter from Lady Mary (*née* Sheldon) Tuke to Mary Evelyn of 13 June 1683 in British Library, Add. MS 78435, ff. 79^r–80^v, f. 79^v: "this in short is all I can say at y^s time Singnor Bartholomis by chance came in now, & will charge him self y^s letter shall be diliuer'd to Morrow to you."

28 The Italians (or at least the males of that group) performed a parallel service as singers in the Roman Catholic chapel of Queen Catherine of Braganza, where Samuel Pepys heard them on four successive Easter Sundays (1666–69), and on two other Sundays as well: see *Diary*, 7: 87 and 99,

202   *"For such uses as the King shall direct"*

sung from barges on the Thames in July 1666 and on 28 September 1668,[29] but the majority of their secular, court duties probably involved intimate, private performances in the royal apartments, such as the one Evelyn happens to have witnessed.

The makeup of the ensemble did not remain fixed: early in 1668 Vincenzo Albrici appears to have left England (he was back in Dresden by April 1669 at the latest) and Sebenico was named Master in his stead on 22 April 1668.[30] The resulting decrease in the group's membership was not remedied until more than two years later, when one Symon Cotterau was appointed on 9 July 1670, under the sponsorship of Francis, Baron Newport (later 1st Earl of Bradford), Comptroller of the Household.[31] By 1673, however, the changing political climate in England was having its effect on this group of Roman Catholic musicians, and both Cefalo and Sebenico left the country permanently during that year.[32] Draghi may have taken over from Sebenico as Master—he was described as such by Thomas Shadwell in 1675[33]—and the Italians who remained were soon shifted entirely to the protected chapel establishments of Queen Catherine of Braganza (to which they had already been devoting some measure of their time and effort)

8: 154 and 427, 9: 126 and 515. For an important account of the Queen's Chapel, incorporating information on the Italians, see Peter Leech, "Musicians in the Catholic Chapel of Catherine of Braganza, 1662–92," *Early Music* 29 (2001): 570–87.

29 For the former, see the Privy Purse payment to Thomas Killigrew of £1 12s "w[c]h he p[d] to watermen y[t] carried the Italian Musick" (Bodleian Library, Malone MS 44, f. 102[v] [Ashbee, 8: 176]); the latter is recorded by Pepys (*Diary*, 9: 322). One wonders whether the 1668 performance might have had some connection with the drastic court retrenchment scheme, which was due to take effect the following day (Michaelmas, the first day of the new fiscal year; see C. D. Chandaman, *The English Public Revenue, 1660–1688* [Oxford: Clarendon Press, 1975], 218–19). As Mabbett observes (p. 239 n. 13), Pepys's praise on this occasion for "one voice that alone did appear considerable, and that was Seignor Joanni" is probably a reference to the tenor and recently appointed Master of the ensemble Sebenico (and not, as the editors of Pepys suggest [p. 322 n. 2], to Draghi, who was not a singer by profession). Pepys's editors commit a similar oversimplification in interpreting the entry for 2 November 1666 (7: 352, n. 4), when the diarist heard "that the King's Italian here is about setting three parts for Trumpets and shall teach some to sound them," as a possible reference to Draghi, rather than the more likely Vincenzo Albrici.

30 See SP29/239/33; SP29/239/33A; and SP44/30, p. 28 (*Calendar of State Papers, Domestic 1667–68*: 364; Ashbee, 8: 187), Sebenico's undated petition for "the place of Master of y[e] Italian Musick ... as well for your Majestyes Chamber or Cabinett as of her Majestyes Chappell and Cabinett," with the endorsement naming him to both positions.

31 LC3/73, p. 103 (Rough Establishment Book, 1660–70: Ashbee, 1: 222, confusingly conflating entries from two separate Establishment Books; see n. 49, below). This entry, listing Cotterau as "Italian Musition ... in ordinary for y[e] private Musique," also gives Sebenico's name, presumably because he was Master at the time.

32 SP44/40, p. 28 (for Cefalo, April 1673: *Calendar of State Papers, Domestic 1673*: 194; Ashbee, 8: 212) and SP44/40, p. 73 (for Sebenico, 5 July 1673: *Calendar of State Papers, Domestic 1673*: 425; Ashbee, 8: 213). Sebenico is described in the latter as "an Italian and Master of his Majesties Italian Musick here, who having served faithfully eight yeares desired leave to returne into his owne Countrey and there to remaine." His departure seems to have been greeted with equanimity: four days before the pass was issued, he was granted a gold chain and medal as a gift from the king (see below).

33 Thomas Shadwell, *Psyche: A Tragedy, Acted at the Duke's Theatre* (London: Henry Herringman, 1675), sig. (*b*)1[v]: "*All the Instrumental Musick (which is not mingled with the Vocal) was composed by that Great Master, Seignior Gio: Baptista Draghi, Master of the Italian Musick to the King.*"

Foreign musicians at the Restoration court   203

and Mary of Modena, the newly arrived Duchess of York.[34] Even before 1673, though, the fluctuations in personnel among the Italians may have been considerably greater than the surviving documents would seem initially to indicate. One clue to this process can be found in the series of warrants ordering the Jewel House to prepare gold livery chains and medals for several members of the Italian ensemble at various times. The issuance of these costly sartorial mementoes was a common practice in Renaissance and early modern Europe,[35] but Charles II seems to have reserved the distinction especially for Italians: at least five, and possibly

34 In subsequent years, Draghi would serve both court and public patrons as a composer, while Bartolomeo Albrici, as we have seen, provided extraordinary service in *Calisto*. Several of the Italians seem to have been active as private tutors in London and elsewhere, and to have performed in concerts at private homes (for Bartolomeo, see n. 27, above; for Reggio, see Evelyn, *Diary*, 220–21 [23 September 1680], 384–85 [25 July 1684], 421, 427, and 428 [all 14 March 1685]; for Draghi, *ibid.*, 384–85 [25 July 1684], 404 [28 January 1685], and 422 [14 March 1685]). Sometime before 18 November 1679, Draghi, Suarez, Bartolomeo Albrici, and Francesco Galli (of the Duchess of York's Chapel) submitted a petition requesting payment of their wages, which were by now four years in arrears, "they having at his Majesties desire left the Service of forraine Princes, & being now forced to goe away, being prosecuted as Roman Catholiques" (SP44/55, pp. 52–53 [*Calendar of State Papers, Domestic* 1679–80: 284; Ashbee, 8: 237; for a transcription, see Mabbett, Appendix, no. 9]). While Charles II was reported to have responded favorably to the petition, it is unclear whether or not the Italians actually left England at this time, as was being threatened: Suarez was paid £100 out of the Secret Service account sometime between 10 May and 7 June 1680 (Bodleian Library, MS Rawlinson D. 872, p. 12 [for a transcription of this manuscript, see John Yonge Akerman, *Moneys Received and Paid for Secret Services of Charles II and James II* (Camden Society, 52; London: Camden Society, 1851); reference at p. 14] and T48/14, p. 12 [not in Ashbee]), and Draghi was definitely present in London in 1682, when he wrote songs for two Duke's Company productions; he may be the "John Baptiste ... born beyond the seas" who received a grant of denization on 4 December 1681 (SP44/67, f. 4^r [Ashbee, 8: 243]). Galli may have been the harpsichord player "Signor *Francisco* ..., esteem'd on⟨e⟩ of the most excellent masters in Europe on that Instrument" who was heard by John Evelyn on 2 December 1674 (*Diary*, 4: 49) and again on 27 January 1682 (*ibid.*, 270). With regard to the "prosecution" of the musicians, see the "information" of c.1679, reporting that "Bartheleme Albrici, Italian traveller, Roman Catholic, lives in Elizabeth Noure's house in Panton Street" (SP29/442/77 [*Calendar of State Papers, Domestic* Addenda: 479; not in Ashbee]). In 1687, some two and a half years into the reign of James II, Bartolomeo was appointed as a "Gregorian" singer in the new Roman Catholic Chapel Royal; when the Chapel establishment was reconfigured in 1688, he was reappointed as a Gregorian "& to supply at the Organ" alongside the main organist, Draghi, and his salary was increased from £40 to £50 to match the amount previously paid all the other Gregorians (see documents cited in Chapter 7, n. 45, below). Sometime between 3 July and 2 October 1688, Sidney, Baron Godolphin (then Treasury Commissioner and Chamberlain to Queen Mary of Modena) was reimbursed from the Secret Service account for £50 "he payd to Stephano[?] Albrici" (Bodleian Library, MS Rawlinson D. 872, p. 167; T48/14, p. 167 [Ashbee, 5: 275]; see also Akerman, 209). Baron Godolphin may have been employed to front money to some of the foreign Chapel singers: sometime between 18 October 1687 and 10 January 1688 he had been reimbursed for £400 "he payd the Italian Singers by his ... Ma^{ts} order" (Bodleian Library, MS Rawlinson D. 872, p. 140; T48/14, p. 140 [Ashbee, 5: 274]; see also Akerman, 174); this amount would have been sufficient to cover the annual salaries of the three principal Italians in the Chapel: Innocenzo Fede (£200 *p.a.*), Antonio Maria Grandi (£100 *p.a.*), and [?]Giuseppe Sansoni (£100 *p.a.*).

35 See Sir John Hawkins, *A General History of the Science and Practice of Music* (5 vols.: London: T. Payne and Son, 1776), 3: 372 n. *: "A golden medal and chain was the usual gratuity of princes to men of eminence in any of the faculties, more especially law, physic, poetry, and music. ... It

204   *"For such uses as the King shall direct"*

as many as seven, of the nine members of his musical ensemble would ultimately receive one, and medals also appear to have been given to a celebrated Italian puppeteer in 1662 and to the king's favorite *commedia dell'arte* performer Tiberio Fiorilli and five of his associates in 1673 (see Table 5.2).

Two noteworthy facts emerge from the data presented in Table 5.2. First, the value of the medals varied considerably: mostly, they increased over time, but the £70 medal presented to the departing Master, Sebenico, in July 1673 stands in provocative contrast to the (reportedly) £50 one given to the famous Fiorilli two months later, and may say something about the esteem in which Sebenico was held.[36] Second, in several cases, the granting of the medal seems to have been a valedictory gesture: both Sebenico and Fiorilli received theirs very shortly before departing the country, and that given to Matteo Battaglia in July 1670 appears to be associated with the arrival of Symon Cotterau, who may have been engaged as Battaglia's replacement (see below). The three medals given to the Albrici siblings in May 1668 are somewhat harder to interpret. We do know that Vincenzo left the English monarch's employment at around that time (although Sebenico was already applying for Vincenzo's "now vacant" post the previous month). But does this mean that Bartolomeo and Leonora also abandoned England in 1668, perhaps carrying with them the gift for their brother, who had already taken his leave?[37] It may be noteworthy that sometime in April the two of them were paid a half-year of their respective pensions out of the Privy Purse, perhaps to settle their account.[38] Moreover, Bartolomeo and Leonora's purported departure would help to explain their absence from the Establishment Book lists of 1669–70 (see below) and why, in May 1671, a warrant was issued for the two siblings' reappointment "as an additional establishment to his Majesty's Italian musicians," with Leonora's salary reduced to £200 to match her brother's.[39] Later, describing herself as

---

seems that the medal and chain once bestowed as a testimony of princely favour, was ever after a part of the dress of the person thus honoured, at least on public occasions."

36 In Fiorilli's case, a total of six medals were given at once, and one (possibly female?) member of the company also received "Twenty Ounces of White plate" (see Table 5.2, n. ‡).

37 W. J. Lawrence drew the same conclusion in 1923: see "Foreign Singers," 222. The later order, in June, for a pair of slightly costlier medals for "the two Italian musicians" is an added confusion: could they have been intended for the two castrati (figures who, by common custom, were seldom explicitly referred to by name)? The problem is that both Suarez and Cefalo (who, I have suggested, was the other "eunuch") were both back in England again within a few years (see Table 5.2 n. †, and nn. 49, below and 32, above [for Cefalo] and 34, above [for Suarez]). Whether or not the "Eunuch (who it seems is a Frenchman, but long bred in Italy)" heard by Pepys in a performance of *The Faithful Shepherdess* at the Bridges Street Theatre on 10, 12, and 14 October 1668 (*Diary*, 9: 326–27 and 329) was Suarez, as Mabbett (p. 239) suggests, is uncertain; see Lawrence's persuasive argument ("Foreign Singers," 223–24) that it was the visiting celebrity Baldassare Ferri.

38 Bodleian Library, MS Malone 44, f. 106^v (not in Ashbee): "Sig^r Altrice & his Sister half a Y^{rs} Pention." Although their name is misspelled here, the £250 paid is exactly the sum of half Bartolomeo's £200 salary plus half Leonora's more generous £300 allotment.

39 SP44/34, p. 96 (25 May 1671: *Calendar of State Papers, Domestic* 1671: 272; Ashbee, 8: 207). Mabbett (p. 240) appears to agree, at least in broad terms, with this conclusion. Why Leonora and Bartolomeo would have returned to England in the spring of 1671 is not clear, but it may be significant that Giovanni Sebenico was issued a pass "to go on business to his own country and

Foreign musicians at the Restoration court   205

Table 5.2 Gold chains and medals issued to Italian performers by Charles II, 1662–73

Date	Value	Recipient(s)	Other Relevant Information
6 November 1662[a]	*£25*	*"Signor Bologna alias Pollicinella"**	*no details known***
5 May 1668[b]	£30 ea.	Vincenzo, Bartolomeo, Leonora Albrici	**April**: Bartolomeo & Leonora paid ½-year's salary; **before 22 April**: Sebenico petitions for Vincenzo's position as Master
27 June 1668[c]	£36 ea.	"the two Italians"†	—
8 July 1670[d]	£40	Matteo Battaglia	**9 July**: Symon Cotterau entered in Establishment Book
1 July 1673[e]	£70	Giovanni Sebenico	**5 July**: pass to leave England
4 September 1673[f]	*£50? (ea.?)*	*Tiberio Fiorilli, alias "Scaramouche"; ?Domenico Biancolelli, alias "Arlequin"; 4 other members of the company‡*	***10 September***: *pass to leave England*[g]; ***12 September***: *order for export of Italian comedians' goods*[h]

Key:
italic type = theatrical performers
roman type = musical performers

Notes:
  * Pietro Gimonde of Bologna: see George Speaight, *The History of the English Puppet Theatre* (2nd ed.: Carbondale: Southern Illinois University Press, 1990), 346.
 ** Had performed at court on 8 October (see Pepys, *Diary*, 3: 216); no subsequent record of his presence in England.
  † Possibly the "eunuchs" Hilario Suarez and Pietro Cefalo? But Cefalo was known to be in England, 15 March 1669 or 1670 and April 1673, and Suarez was in England and in the royal service for at least four years prior to November 1679.
  ‡ Another document (LC5/140, p. 329 [12 September 1673: *Register*, no. 801]) orders delivery to Fiorilli of "Twenty Ounces of White plate as a guift from his Majestie unto one of his Company."

Sources:
[a] LC5/107, f. 93[r] (*Register*, no. 173).
[b] LC5/139, p. 215; LC5/12, p. 137; LC5/107, f. 127[r] (Ashbee, 1: 84).
[c] LC5/139, p. 217; LC5/12, p. 138; LC5/107, f. 127[v] (Ashbee, 1: 85).
[d] LC5/12, p. 160; LC5/107, f. 142[r] (Ashbee, 1: 99).
[e] LC5/140, p. 283; LC5/107, f. 166[r] (Ashbee, 1: 127).
[f] LC5/140, p. 328 (*Register*, no. 797); see also letter of Sir Thomas Player to Sir Joseph Williamson, 9 September 1673: "a medall … is prepareing … for Scaramucci of 50*l*" (SP29/337/21 [*Calendar of State Papers, Domestic* 1673: 539; not in *Register*], transcribed in W. D. Christie, ed., *Letters Addressed from London To Sir Joseph Williamson While Plenipotentiary at the Congress of Cologne In the Years 1673 and 1674* [2 vols.: Camden Society, n. s., 8–9; London: Camden Society, 1874], 2: 16).
[g] SP44/40, p. 105 (*Calendar of State Papers, Domestic* 1673: 540; not in *Register*).
[h] PRO30/32/49 (properly "T54/4"), p. 26 (*Calendar of Treasury Books* 4: 392; *Register*, no. 800).

return" on 28 October 1670 (SP104/12, p. 346 [*Calendar of State Papers, Domestic* 1670: 501; not in Ashbee]). One wonders whether all three might have been back in England by February 1671, in time for the performance of *The Queen's Masque*, which included Carissimi's chorus "Amanti, che dite, che fate?" (see Chapter 1).

206 *"For such uses as the King shall direct"*

"a poore Maid, stranger, & in no good health, which bringeth me very scarce of money," Leonora submitted on her own and Bartolomeo's behalf a pair of petitions for arrears, claiming in one of them (believed to be addressed to the Earl of Arlington) that "after that, by your L^d^ps grace We were againe received in the service of His Matie, we have allwayes been in our pay a quarter of a year behind the other Italian Musitians."[40] It is less certain that Matteo Battaglia left England after receiving his gold chain and medal: he may instead have shifted his attention entirely to the queen's Roman Catholic chapel in 1670, and thus "departed" from the main group. Already in April 1669, he is recorded as "maestro" of the chapel Italians, presumably having received that post in preference to Sebenico (who had petitioned for it the year before but may only have become Master of the secular group, despite an initial endorsement in his favor for both positions).[41] It is possible that Battaglia may have married Leonora Albrici between 1674 and 1676,[42] and he must have continued to hold a position of responsibility, as he is named as the recipient of the first of two quite substantial payments, totaling £800, made from the Secret Service accounts in the autumn of 1677.[43] Ultimately, however, he too decamped, perhaps taking Leonora with him: by March 1679 he

40 SP29/281A/3; SP29/281A/3/I (*Calendar of State Papers, Domestic* 1670: 611; Ashbee, 8: 207). The petition is undated, but is certainly misfiled: Leonora avers that "Now we are creditors of three quarters ended at March last, & the other Italian Musitians onely of two," implying that the petition would have had to be written at least ten months after their May 1671 reappointment, and certainly during the months of April, May, and June, before the conclusion of the ensuing quarter. My own inclination would be to assign it to 1673: in 1672, the arrearage would have constituted 100% of what they were owed, making the claim of being "allwayes ... in our pay a quarter of a year behind" since May 1671 somewhat nonsensical, and by 1674 the ensemble may already have been disbanded, and Leonora out of a job (see p. 220, below).

41 The description comes from Lorenzo Magalotti, who attended the Queen's Chapel on Easter Eve (10/20 April) 1669 in the company of Cosimo III, Grand Duke of Tuscany: see Anna Maria Crinò, ed., *Un Principe di Toscana in Inghilterra e in Irlanda nel 1669: Relazione Ufficiale del Viaggio de Cosimo de' Medici Tratta dal «Giornale» de L. Magalotti, con gli Acquerelli Palatini* (Temi e Testi 13: Rome: Edizioni di Storia e Letteratura, 1968), 50. Peter Leech ("Musicians in the Catholic Chapel of Catherine of Braganza," 579) cites a second document from a member of the Tuscan entourage, British Library, Add. MS 16504 that also mentions Battaglia by name, albeit not explicitly as Master.

42 See the order to the customs commissioners to "deliver, Customs free, a seizure of three dozen of Roman gloves, lately brought in the *John and Mary* hoy from Dort, belonging to Signora Eleanora Battalia and seized by John Tombes, tide surveyor London port" in PRO30/32/38 [properly "T11/3"], p. 250 (5 December 1676: *Calendar of Treasury Books* 5: 393; not in Ashbee).

43 PRO30/32/5, p. 91 (4 September 1677: *Calendar of Treasury Books* 5: 1333; Ashbee, 5: 271) and PRO30/32/5, p. 133 (27 November 1677: *Calendar of Treasury Books* 5: 1335; not in Ashbee). The first is for £300 to "Mr. Battaylea, an Italian musician"; the second, for £500 is simply described as "to the Etalians." The latter entry, of course, does not explicitly refer to the recipients as musicians, but the only foreign actors in London at the time were French, and in any case the payment did not consist of actual money, but rather a "tally" received by the Treasury from the farmers of the hearth tax and immediately "Delivered ... to the Etalians" for possible redemption in the Exchequer—and thus would certainly not have been given to a group of visitors from abroad.

was in Düsseldorf in the employ of the Duke of Jülich and Berg, son of the Count Palatine of Neuburg, from whose court he had originally come to England over a dozen years before.[44]

The uncertainty over the nature and purpose of the payment made, at least in part, to Battaglia in 1677 is symptomatic of the perplexing character of the data that survives regarding salary disbursements to all of the Italians. As so often happened at the Restoration court, the royal largesse operated more in theory than in practice, and so the already defective record is rendered more obscure by the constant round of remunerative delays and uncertainties that were a part of life for royal servants throughout Charles II's reign. This can be seen in an undated petition, possibly from around 1666, in which the musicians plead for the granting of a line of credit with an unnamed London banker, so as not "to have to disturb Your Majesty every quarter for … payment."[45] Without an identifiable date, we can say nothing about the outcome in this instance, but a few fleeting records of disbursements out of the Privy Purse do survive. We have already noted the payment for a half-year's "Pention" (£250) to Bartolomeo and Leonora Albrici in April 1668. An earlier payment in February 1667 of £375 to "ye Italian Musick in full of their Pention to Xmas last"[46] calculates out correctly at one quarter's pension each for Leonora (at £75 per quarter) and six others (at £50 each per quarter). If this really involved covering the arrearages "in full," then perhaps Charles II was not too badly behind at that moment—although we have no information as to any payments due or issued to the remaining two members of the nine-person group. Another entry in the Privy Purse accounts, from February 1669, is more ambiguous: this payment of £1000 "To Sr Joh^n Shaw for m—^{n}"[47] could, of course, be for just about anything. But the amount is quite large in comparison to most of the entries in the account, and Sir John Shaw had also been the conduit for a payment of £600 "for ye Italian Musick" in April 1666 (see n. 20, above). If the three Albrici siblings had in fact left England in the spring of 1668, there might indeed have been five Italian musicians in need of a year's payment at £200 apiece

---

44 The newly minted Duke, Johann Wilhelm II, had been in England in 1675 as "Prince of Neuburg" (see Evelyn, *Diary*, 4: 65), where he had danced in Charles II's birthday ball on 29 May (see Chapter 1 and Table 1.1). Both father and son would later succeed to the position of Elector Palatine. See Alfred Einstein, "Italienische Musiker am Hofe der Neuburger Wittelsbacher," *Sammelbände der Internationalen Musikgesellschaft* 9 (1908): 336–424, pp. 367 and 385. No record survives of any pass permitting travel abroad for Battaglia, as indeed for any of the three Albricis subsequent to Vincenzo and Bartolomeo's initial recruitment trips in the mid-1660s.

45 SP29/187/65 (?1666: *Calendar of State Papers, Domestic* 1666–67: 418; Ashbee, 8: 179); for a transcription and translation, see Mabbett, Appendix, no. 6, whose translation I quote here. Both the *Calendar of State Papers, Domestic* and Ashbee read the phrase "quella provviggione, che s'hà degnato d'assegnarci per il pane Quotidiano" as referring specifically to money for the musicians' "diet," when in fact it appears simply to be a circumlocutory phrase for their salaries, in keeping with the flowery rhetoric of the rest of the petition. See Pepys's observation (*Diary*, 8: 56, discussed below) that the Italians were given "200*l* a year apiece …, but badly paid."

46 Bodleian Library, MS Malone 44, f. 103^v (February 1667: Ashbee, 8: 179).

47 *Ibid.*, f. 109^r (February 1669: not in Ashbee).

208 *"For such uses as the King shall direct"*

once the following Christmas had come and gone—and with the parallel French ensemble (to be discussed presently) disbanded by this time, there would be no need for the distinguishing adjective "Italian" in the Privy Purse account entry. This is, of course, heaping speculation upon speculation, and it further raises the important question of where the other payments to the Italians—ultimately thousands of pounds' worth, even if we consider only the inaccurate establishment estimate of £1700 *per annum* originally floated by the Albrici brothers in the mid-1660s—would have come from. Clearly, even with the expansive net I have sought to cast here, the entries we have reviewed by no means make up the full story of how, when, and how much the Italians were actually remunerated for their services.

Such a problem starkly illustrates the multiple deficiencies of the documentary record, particularly with regard to those obscure corners of the Restoration court musical establishment that did not fall under the "regular" course of administration and finance, and thus appear only as fleeting glimpses among the material calendared in Andrew Ashbee's monumental *Records of English Court Music*. Much about the operation of Charles II's foreign musical groups is lost to us because their activities and payments were mostly not processed through official channels, and thus except in rare instances—for example the registering of petitions, or the issuance of gold chains and medals, or of passports—were not memorialized in the kinds of documents that would have been preserved over the centuries in the standard departmental archives. We are extraordinarily fortunate to have uncovered the very revealing Privy Purse accounts of February 1666–June 1669 in Bodleian Library, Malone MS 44, but even here we must not allow ourselves to become overly complacent, since this document is an eighteenth-century transcription, and there is good reason to suspect that the transcription may in fact be selective and hence incomplete for the period it purports to cover. What the surviving documentary scraps *do* reveal, even in their radically incomplete state, are certain patterns that can allow us to piece together contextual information that may then be corroborated by anecdotal evidence from other, non-official sources. With respect to Charles II's Italian musicians, I have thus far sought to elucidate patterns relating to such matters as personnel and the timing of various changes in the composition and fortunes of the ensemble. But there is another, crucial facet of their existence and activities that is revealed by the recurring appearance in documents relating to them of the name of Thomas Killigrew. Killigrew is listed in the Privy Purse accounts as having paid the "watermen y^t carried the Italian Musick" in July 1666 (see n. 29, above), and as receiving £10 "for a Harpsicall" in November 1667.[48] As we have seen, it was he who presented the Italian ensemble

---

48 *Ibid.*, f. 106^r (Ashbee, 8: 183). This entry should be considered in the context of another associate of the Italian cohort, the harpsichord maker Andrea Testa. Testa had originally come to England sometime between 1664 and 1666 as a replacement for Girolamo Zenti, his former master at the Swedish court (for Testa as Zenti's assistant, see Sundström, "Notiser om Drottning Kristinas Italienska Musiker," 304, where he is called "Festa"). He was twice paid out of the Privy Purse

Foreign musicians at the Restoration court 209

in February 1667 to the group of enthusiasts that included Samuel Pepys; moreover, his name also appears as court sponsor in a somewhat perplexing Establishment Book entry of 1669 or 1670 that lists Sebenico and Cefalo.[49] Killigrew was, of course, the proprietor of the King's Company, but unlike his collaborator and competitor Davenant he was also a Groom of the Bedchamber to Charles II,[50] and thus had connections at court. Even in the scanty documentary record just rehearsed, Killigrew emerges, seemingly in consequence of this positioning, as an important liaison or power broker of some sort where the Italian musicians were concerned. His own connections to Italy were well established: he had served as Charles II's diplomatic resident in Venice from 1650 to 1652, and Pepys learned in February 1667 that he had traveled "eight or ten times ... to Rome to hear good music; so much he loves it, though he never did sing or play a note."[51] According to Pepys, it was Killigrew who took credit for "gather[ing] nine Italians from several Courts in Christendome to come to make a consort for the King"; indeed, one or more of his Roman journeys may have explicitly involved some recruitment, possibly in conjunction with the initial arrival of the Albrici brothers in 1663 or 1664, or with their own subsequent trips abroad.

What is especially significant about Pepys's reports of his encounters with Killigrew is the light it sheds on what seems to have been the impresario's chief aim in assembling the Italian ensemble in the first place: the production of operas in London. This project, about which the official documents are entirely silent, may have its roots in an effort authorized by Charles II during the heady early

---

"for [mending] ye Virginalls": £28 in December 1666 (Bodleian Library, Malone MS 44, f. 103^r [Ashbee, 8: 178, misdated November]) and £30 in July 1668 (*ibid.*, f. 107^v [Ashbee, 8: 190]), and sometime around 1667 or 1668 he submitted a petition requesting a pension "out of yor Ma^{ts} privy purse ... & that he may have yor Ma^{ts} expresse order or warrant in usuall forme to that effect" (SP29/233/143 [*Calendar of State Papers, Domestic* 1667–68: 201; Ashbee, 8: 184]; see also Mabbett, Appendix, no. 7). It is from this document that we learn that Zenti, upon departing England in early 1664, and prior to "dieing at Parris in ye French King's service," had sent Testa "(as one fitly qualified) to supply his place."

49 LC3/25, p. 55, headed "Italian musitians" (Rough Establishment Book of 1666, but entry dated "March 15 1669": Ashbee, 1: 222). It is not clear what this entry is meant to signify, and why it does not mention any other Italians, such as Suarez, Draghi, or Reggio. Battaglia, as we have seen, may already have been in the process of transferring over full-time to the Queen's Chapel at this point; Henry Cart de Lafontaine (*The King's Musick: A Transcript of Records Relating to Music and Musicians (1460–1700)* [London: Novello and Company, 1909], 222) interprets the date of the entry as 15 March 1669/70, which would put it closer to the parallel entry in LC3/73, p. 103 (dated 9 July 1670: see n. 31, above), that appears to record the appointment of Symon Cotterau, seemingly in Battaglia's stead.

50 Appointed 2 February 1661: see LC3/24, f. 3^r. From August 1660, Killigrew also held the reversion to the office of Master of the Revels (see C66/2591 [not in *Register*], and the now-lost document catalogued as *Register*, no. 276), to which position he succeeded in May 1673 (see LC3/24, f. 18^r [*Register*, nos. 5 and 774] and *London Gazette* 778 [1–5 May 1673], verso, and 780 [8–12 May 1673], verso). In addition, he held posts as a Chamberlain to Catherine of Braganza and as Charles II's Court Jester: see Martin W. Walsh, "Killigrew's Cap and Bells," *Theatre Notebook* 38 (1984): 99–105.

51 Pepys, *Diary*, 8: 56 (12 February 1667: *Register*, no. 369).

210　*"For such uses as the King shall direct"*

days of the Restoration. Less than five months after coming to the throne, and only two after the initial granting of theatrical warrants to Killigrew and Davenant, the king issued a license to Giulio Gentileschi "per rappresentare nella Città di Londra opere musicali, con machine mutationi di scene et altre apparenze."[52] Gentileschi was, at least in theory, well placed for such an effort: as the son of the Caroline court painter Orazio Gentileschi, he had been active in English artistic circles prior to the Civil War, albeit not always under optimal circumstances. He knew Nicholas Lanier (with whom he and his brother had famously clashed in Italy in the autumn of 1627 and the spring of 1628[53]), and would probably have had at least some acquaintance with Killigrew, who was more than a dozen years his junior, during the late 1630s.[54] Charles II's license (written entirely in Italian) authorizes Gentileschi "condurre d'Italia in Inghilterra una Compagnia di Musici"—whose members would have received "il titolo de nostri ser[v]i," presumably along the lines of the English patent company actors—and to build a suitable theatre for his planned performances. According to the terms of the license, Gentileschi would retain an exclusive right for five years to mount such productions, or to assign that privilege to someone else at his discretion.[55] In fact, there is no record of his actually returning to London in 1660 at all, and no opera company materialized. This is not entirely surprising: Gentileschi, who thirty years earlier as a young man in Genoa had been described as "un procuratore per affairi,"[56] was more a hatcher of schemes than a begetter of results, a person of no known musical or theatrical expertise whose impulsive nature would have ill suited him to accomplish the intricate arrangements of personnel, technology, artistry, and (most importantly) finance necessary to plant a Venetian-style public

---

52　SP29/19/16 (22 October 1660: *Calendar of State Papers, Domestic* 1660–61: 319; *Register*, no. 38), quoted in Ashbee, 8: 140, Boswell, 114–15, and Mabbett, Appendix, no. 1 (with translation).

53　Michael I. Wilson, *Nicholas Lanier: Master of the King's Musick* (Aldershot: Scolar Press, 1994), 116–18, 127–28, and 156–59; see also Gabriele Finaldi and Jeremy Wood, "Orazio Gentileschi at the Court of Charles I," in Keith Christiansen and Judith W. Mann, eds., *Orazio and Artemisia Gentileschi* (New York: Metropolitan Museum of Art and New Haven: Yale University Press, 2001), 223–31, p. 225, and W. Noel Sainsbury, "Artists' Quarrels in Charles I.'s Reign," *Notes and Queries* 20 (2nd ser., no. 8, 1859): 121–22. On 19 January 1629, Gentileschi was in England, where he was arrested for attacking his father's rival Sir Balthazar Gerbier in the Strand (SP13/133/29, ff. 54–55).

54　By the Spring of 1641, Gentileschi and his brother Francesco were in Lisbon, where they engaged in an ill-fated scheme to provide the newly established Portuguese king João IV with mass-produced light field artillery for use in his "War of Restoration" against the Spanish. By the summer of 1647, Francesco was in prison in Lisbon, awaiting trial before the Inquisition, while Giulio had moved on to Modena, where he promoted the weapons technology to Duke Francesco I: see Angelo Angelucci, *Documenti Inediti per la Storia delle Armi da Fuoco Italiane* (Turin: G. Cassone, 1869), 1: 398–405 (nos. 106–7).

55　"[S]olo il d° Gentileschi con la sua compagnia, per il spatio di cinque anni uenturi possa fare rappresentare simili opere musicali, et non altri, concedendogli anco il potere sustituire in suo luogo chi gli piacerà, et uorrà con l'istessa facoltà, et autorità à lui concessa."

56　See Mary Newcome, "Orazio Gentileschi in Genoa," in Christiansen and Mann, eds., *Orazio and Artemisia Gentileschi*, 165–71, pp. 168 and 171 n. 32.

Foreign musicians at the Restoration court   211

opera company in London. Whatever his original intentions, we can be fairly sure that by the first part of 1664, with his five-year monopoly due to expire in approximately eighteen months, he had thrown in the towel. Whether he sold off his rights or simply abandoned them may never be ascertained, but it must have been obvious that such a venture could only be attempted successfully by someone who had managerial experience in the theatre, access to performance spaces and a trained workforce (particularly in the technical arena), and connections at court. Obviously, Killigrew fit the bill perfectly. While it is difficult to know exactly how things played out, we can recall that the Albrici brothers may have been in England by April 1664 and continued laboring to build their ensemble over the next two years. Killigrew's part in the plans is revealed in a conversation he had with Pepys at the Bridges Street playhouse on 2 August 1664. William Legge's patent for the creation of a joint "nursery" training theatre to service the two professional acting companies had been issued a few months before,[57] and Killigrew informed Pepys that he was in the process of

> setting up a Nursery; that is, is going to build a house in Moore fields wherein he will have common plays acted. But four operas it shall have in the year, to act six weeks at a time—where we shall have the best Scenes and Machines, the best Musique, and everything as Magnificent as is in Christendome; and to that end hath sent for voices and painters and other persons from Italy.[58]

At this point in time, the Albrici brothers still had their two overseas trips ahead of them, but there can be little doubt that opera was on the agenda from an early date. In their initial proposal to Charles II, Vincenzo and Bartolomeo had effectively offered the king two options: one consisted of a small treble-only vocal ensemble—perhaps a kind of *musica secreta*—but should "sua Maiestà volesse havere ancora questi acciò fosse tutto finito il concerto che se ne potrebbe servire in Cammera *et in teatro* sarebbe bisogno,"[59] Charles should expect to increase the size (and cost) of the group to include contralto, tenor, bass, and, most importantly ("che è il principale"), the poet—that is, an Italian librettist. This, of course, is the group that ultimately materialized; moreover, by 1664 Killigrew's preparations on the technical side were already underway. By the time he talked to Pepys, he had engaged one Italian "scenekeeper," Antonio Brunatti, whose appointment, ostensibly at the Bridges Street Theatre, had commenced the previous month,[60]

---

57 C66/3054/5; British Library, Add. Charter 17753 (31 March 1664: *Register*, no. 277). The previous license for a nursery, held by George Jolly, had been surrendered to Killigrew and Davenant on 30 December 1662 (see Table 5.1) and a warrant was issued revoking Jolly's privilege and authorizing the new nursery plans on 23 July 1663 (SP29/77/38–39 and SP44/15, pp. 117–19 [*Register*, nos. 223 and 224]).

58 Pepys, *Diary*, 5: 230 (*Register*, no. 288).

59 SP29/66/30 (my emphasis).

60 LC3/25, p. 158 (*Register*, no. 201), LC3/73, p. 186 (*Register*, no. 24, citing foliation), and LC3/26, p. 210 (*Register*, nos. 155, 201), all listing Brunatti's appointment as 12 July 1664. The *Register's*

212   *"For such uses as the King shall direct"*

and in March or May of 1665 another, possibly Portuguese, employee named Emanuel Fonseca would be brought in to supplement Brunatti alongside a crew of approximately a dozen English scenekeepers and stagehands.[61]

As we have already seen, the process of assembling the full complement of Italian musicians was a protracted one, and the ensemble was only properly rolled out in late 1666 or early 1667. It was in February of the later year that Pepys first heard them sing (at Lord Brouncker's, under Killigrew's auspices), although he would, upon reflection, pronounce himself "not at all smitten with the music tonight, which I did expect should have been so extraordinary, Tom Killigrew crying it up, and so all the world, above all things in the world."[62] Indeed, the diarist had himself been treated to a full taste of Killigrew's promotional efforts just a few days earlier in the same venue: on 12 February he rode

> with my Lord Brouncker by coach to his house, there to hear some Italian Musique; and here we met Tom Killigrew, Sir Rob. Murray, and the Italian Seignor Baptista—who hath composed a play in Italian for the Opera which T. Killigrew doth intend to have up; and here he did sing one of the acts.[63]

"Seignor Baptista," *i.e.* Giovanni Battista Draghi, was "the poet as well as the Musician," thus providing Charles II and Killigrew with further added value beyond the purely literary role originally envisioned by the Albrici brothers. He also, according to Pepys, sang the act entirely from memory while accompanying himself at the keyboard, and the diarist's expression of amazement at this standard operatic technique is perhaps one sign of how limited the average theatre-going Londoner's experience of through-composed musical drama would have been after 1660.[64] In any case, Killigrew was clearly aiming to remedy that lacuna: informing Pepys that his earlier plans for mounting operas at the Nursery in Moorfields had been "defeated," he announced that he was now looking instead "to have some times of the year these Operas to be performed at the two

---

    handling of these long-term theatrical Establishment Lists is less than satisfactory, but see the helpful digest in John Harold Wilson, "Players' Lists in the Lord Chamberlain's *Registers*," *Theatre Notebook* 18 (1963–64): 25–30.

61 LC3/25, p. 158 and LC3/26, p. 210, both giving a date of 23 May 1665 for Fonseca's appointment. Another entry, in LC3/73, p. 211 (*Register*, no. 24, citing foliation), which lists Fonseca among the "Groomes of the Greate Chamber in Ordinary without ffee and Sceane Keepers in his Majesty's Theatre Royall & stage keepers in Ordinary," is dated 23 March 1665. One of these is almost certainly a copying error, as the two lists agree on every other appointment date involving employees of the King's Company, and thus would not appear to reflect different stages in the appointment process.

62 Pepys, *Diary*, 8: 66.

63 Pepys, *Diary*, 8: 54 (*Register*, no. 369).

64 *Ibid.*, 56–57: "My great wonder is how this man doth do to keep in memory so perfectly the music of that whole Act, both for the voice and for the instrument too—I confess I do admire it. But in Recitativo the sense much helps him, for there is but one proper way of discoursing and giving the accent."

Foreign musicians at the Restoration court 213

present Theatres."[65] Killigrew no doubt hoped that the royal court, beyond simply housing and supporting the Italian musicians within its establishment, would provide significant patronage for his undertaking,[66] and he would have had reason to be optimistic about the venture's artistic prospects. Not only had Draghi already written at least part of an opera, but Giovanni Sebenico might also have proven a useful resource: he would later make a name for himself as an opera composer, presenting the first of his three known operatic compositions at Turin on 6 December 1673, a mere five months after leaving England for the last time.[67] And although Pepys's account of February 1667 makes it clear that Draghi's opera was in Italian,[68] Killigrew's subsequent efforts to further his scheme might possibly have something to do with the still unexplained existence of the singable English version of Francesco Cavalli's 1655 opera *L'Erismena*, the manuscript of which was recently acquired by the Bodleian Library.[69]

If the *L'Erismena* adaptation is in any way relevant to Killigrew's operatic endeavors, the fact of its being in English may indicate some further change of plans as events developed. We have already speculated that not only Vincenzo Albrici but also Bartolomeo and Leonora may have left England in the spring of 1668, and as early as the previous autumn Killigrew seems to have been teaching English actresses to sing in the Italian style: on 9 September 1667 he boasted to Pepys

65 *Ibid.*, 56. The nature of Killigrew's "defeat" seems to be that he never actually succeeded in setting up a nursery theatre in Moorfields after securing the patent in the name of William Legge in March 1664: only in 1667 was a nursery created, in Hatton Garden, northwest of Holborn Bridge. For the complex dealings of Killigrew and Davenant involving George Jolly and his original patent (upon which the authority to create the Nursery was ultimately based), see Hotson, *The Commonwealth and Restoration Stage*, 182–88.

66 He told Pepys "that the Citty Audience was as good as the Court—but now they are most gone" (*Diary*, 8: 56).

67 See Miloš M. Velimirović, "Giovanni Sebenico (Prispevek k Biografiji)," *Muzikološki Zbornik* 1 (1965): 49–58, p. 52. This opera, entitled *L'Atalanta*, must however have been composed entirely in Turin, as the librettist was Bernardino Bianco, the Savoyard Secretary of State, Finance, and Ceremonies.

68 *Diary*, 8: 55: "The words I did not understand, and so know not how they are fitted; but believe very well, and all in the Recitativo very fine ... and the poetry, T. Killigrew and Sir R. Murray, who understood the words, did say was excellent." While the disappearance of Draghi's opera is not surprising, it is curious that no trace of any Italian compositions or texts by him survive apart from the two songs published in Pignani's *Scelta Di Canzonette Italiane* of 1679 (see Chapter 1, n. 155). All of Draghi's later vocal compositions involved setting English texts (including, famously, Dryden's "Song for St. Cecilia's Day" of 1687, his only large-scale work for which the music survives).

69 Now Bodleian Library, MS. Mus. d. 282. For a summary of recent findings about this work, see David Stuart and Greg Skidmore, "Cavalli's *Erismena*," *Early Music* 38 (2010): 482–83. I am grateful to Beth Glixon for corresponding with me about the manuscript, and for informing me of the discovery that the prologue given therein is a translation of the third Venetian prologue of 1655–56. A recording of this English version of the opera (minus the prologue) was made in 1968 by an ensemble including members of the Oakland Symphony, under the direction of Alan Curtis (Vox Records, SVBX 5213).

214   *"For such uses as the King shall direct"*

that he will bring me to the best music in England (of which endeed he is master), and that is two Italians and Mrs. Yates, who he says is come to sing the Italian manner as well as ever he heard any.[70]

Killigrew proceeded to complain that the actress Elizabeth Knepp, whom Pepys had earlier witnessed under training by Draghi,[71] "won't take pains enough" to master the technique, but that he was willing to give her a pass because of her superb acting skills. Moreover, by November 1668 two more Italian scenic engineers had been employed at Bridges Street, possibly to replace Brunatti and Fonseca, who disappear from the records after 1665.[72] Whatever the circumstances, all of these efforts appear to have been insufficient. The reappointment of Bartolomeo and Leonora Albrici in May 1671 may represent a further attempt to advance the plan, but in the end, no actual Italian opera production is known to have materialized in Restoration England,[73] and by 1673 the Italian musical ensemble had been reduced to a rump of three or four performers, all principally associated with the Queen's Chapel and its Latin liturgical repertoire, who supplemented their incomes by offering private tuition to the London public.

If the history of Charles II's Italian musical ensemble is difficult to parse from the surviving documentation, that of his other group, the French musicians, is even more obscure. The king seems to have experimented with several options as the 1660s progressed. A French instrumental ensemble of some sort was in England in November 1660, regarding which no official record survives,[74] and the following year the harpsichordist Jean de La Vollée was appointed to Charles's Private Music.[75] La Vollée might have arrived in England with the instrumentalists, or perhaps with one of the French acting companies who were performing

---

70 Pepys, *Diary*, 8: 430 (not in *Register*). For livery warrants naming the otherwise unknown Mrs. Yates (possibly the wife of the boxkeeper Thomas Yates) among the King's Company actresses, see LC5/61, p. 338 and LC5/138, p. 71 (30 June 1666: *Register*, no. 346) and LC5/138, p. 271 (8 February 1668: *Register*, no. 425); in the latter document, Yates's name has been cancelled.

71 Pepys, *Diary*, 8: 57 (12 February 1667). On two other occasions in 1667, Pepys heard another acquaintance, Mrs. Manuel, "the Jew's wife, formerly a player," sing with "one of the Italian's, her gallant": see *ibid.*, 384 (12 August) and 599 (30 December).

72 The new Italian scenekeepers were Pietro Valentino Cuccino (LC3/25, p. 157 [*Register*, no. 30] and LC3/73, p. 186 [*Register*, no. 24, citing foliation]: appointed 7 November, but subsequently crossed out in both sources, and in the latter marked "dead") and Francesco Franco, known as "Torangiu" or "Torangu" (*ibid.*: appointed 30 November). Torangiu was still in service in the summer of 1670 (LC3/26, p. 207 [*Register*, no. 30]), but is not recorded again thereafter.

73 See below for a discussion of John Evelyn's claim (*Diary*, 4: 30) to have seen "an *Italian Opera* in musique, the first that had ben in *England* of this kind" on 5 January 1674.

74 Pepys, *Diary*, 1: 297–98 (20 November, reporting on events of the previous evening): "the King, Queene, and Princesse at the Cockpitt all night, where Generall Monke treated them; and after supper, a play [Ben Jonson's *The Silent Woman*]—where the King did put a great affront upon Singleton's Musique, he bidding them stop and bade the French Musique play—which my Lord says doth much out-do all ours." Pepys's editors speculate (p. 298 n. 1) that this may have been a visiting group; for the "Singleton–Locke" ensemble, see Holman, *Fiddlers*, 284–86.

75 LC3/73, p. 102 (Ashbee, 1: 220).

tragédies à machines at the Cockpit in the late summer and autumn of 1661.[76] In any case, he seems to have been recruited primarily for service in the Roman Catholic chapel that was being set up in anticipation of Charles II's marriage to Catherine of Braganza. In the Establishment Book entry that provides the date of La Vollée's appointment (18 October 1661), his sponsor is identified as Ludovic Stuart, Seigneur d'Aubigny, who was in line to become the new queen's Chief Almoner and who was responsible for presenting a concert at Arundel House on 11 January 1662 consisting of "excellent Musique, perform'd by the ablest Masters both French & Eng, on *Theorba, Viols, Organs* & Voices as an Exercise against the coming of the *Queene*, as purposly composd for her chapell &c."[77] Although the Queen's Chapel would later be staffed primarily by Portuguese and Italian musicians, there appears to have been a French ensemble—probably incorporating La Vollée—at this early stage, since the king's organ builder John Hingeston was paid for installing three organs in the chapel at St. James's Palace in the spring of 1663, one of which was "for the French music."[78] The identity of the other members of this group is not definitively known, but they may be the same as the six performers (including La Vollée) named in a warrant of 23 July 1663 that ordered their admission as "the King's French musicians";[79] they appear to have been formally sworn in on 19 October.[80] As Peter Holman has shown, all except the "Jouëur de Clavessin" La Vollée must have been singers, although the precise configuration of the voice parts remains somewhat confusing,[81] particu-

---

76 These performances will be discussed in my next book, *English Dramatick Opera, 1661–1706*; see also Colin Visser, "*The Descent of Orpheus* at the Cockpit, Drury Lane," *Theatre Survey* 24 (1983): 35–53, and John Orrell, "Scenes and Machines at the Cockpit, Drury Lane," *Theatre Survey* 26 (1985): 103–19.

77 Evelyn, *Diary*, 3: 310.

78 LC5/137, p. 420 (warrant dated 1 April 1663: Ashbee, 1: 43). This particular organ, possibly the smallest of the three, was transported from Whitehall.

79 SP44/15, p. 116 (*Calendar of State Papers, Domestic* 1663–64: 214; Ashbee, 8: 160).

80 The date is given as part of the entry in the undated Establishment Book, LC3/73, p. 98 (see below). Besides being recorded in the warrant of July 1663, the names of the six musicians can be found together in several other documents, all undated. Four of these are general establishment books/ lists of the Royal Household: LC3/26, pp. 76, 80 (Ashbee, 1: 221); LC3/73, p. 98 (Ashbee, 1: 221); SP29/76/67 (*Calendar of State Papers, Domestic* 1663–64: 201; Ashbee, 8: 167; for a transcription, see E. S. de Beer, "A List of the Department of the Lord Chamberlain of the Household, Autumn, 1663," *Bulletin of the Institute of Historical Research* 19 [1944 for 1941]: 13–24); and E36/231, f. 117ᵛ (Ashbee, 8: 167); the latter two lists are believed to be from 1664. There is also a separate list, headed "Noms des Musiciens francois de sa Maiesté," in which four of the musicians are identified by voice part: SP29/1/67 (*Calendar of State Papers, Domestic* 1660–61: 7; Ashbee, 8: 160). This document, which is almost certainly misfiled among the State Papers of 1660, is accompanied by a six-stanza French poem by Claude des Granges, the bass of the group, appealing for a court position (SP29/1/71 [*Calendar of State Papers, Domestic* 1660–61: 7; Ashbee, 8: 160]; transcribed in Boswell, 165–66). It is noteworthy that every list gives their names in the same order, although this order has no apparent correlation to the hierarchy of their voice parts.

81 Those with identified voice ranges are, from highest to lowest, Nicolas Fleuri (*haute-contre*), Guillaume Sautre (*haute taille*), Elenor[?] Guigaut[?] (*basse taille*), and Claude des Granges (*bass*). There is a good deal of uncertainty regarding the identity of the (presumably male) *basse*

216   *"For such uses as the King shall direct"*

larly with respect to the group's "Maistre," the ambiguously named Ferdinand de Florence.[82] Indeed, the latter individual may be the "Mr. Ferdinando" who had the care of three boys in the Queen's Chapel and was the recipient of materials for their liveries on several occasions between March 1664 and May 1665.[83] What we do not have in the case of these French musicians is any documentation as to their salaries or the payment thereof, their association with prominent courtiers, their personal attributes, the timing of their comings and goings across the Channel, or even their employment at other European courts, either before or after their sojourns in England. But they certainly seem not to have fared as well as their Italian counterparts: already by the end of May 1664, the king's envoy in Turin, Sir Bernard Gascoigne, was urging Lord Arlington to "send away those Francemen that not worth a fiddelstick."[84] Gascoigne, as we have seen, was involved in recruiting Italian musicians, so his bias was natural enough, but Charles II and his surrogates appear to have heeded the advice. Sometime in the winter or spring of 1665, Ferdinand de Florence learned that he was about to be dismissed, and petitioned the king, noting that his relocation to London had occasioned "de grands frais que montent a plus de Six cens Jacobuses" and that he had forfeited "Une des premieres places" at the court of Louis XIV, "laquelle jl à perdue sans esperance d'y pouuoir jamais rentrer n'y de pretendre."[85] Ferdinand's request for "Vne récompense proportionnée aux frais quil a faits et a la pention que le Roy de france luy donnoit lors quil essoit a son seruice" initially met with success, as he appears to have been granted the 600 Jacobuses (a gold coin worth between 22*s* and 25*s* that could be cashed as current in Paris), to be transmitted through Lords Arlington and Aubigny; however, he failed to obtain the money and returned to France empty-handed. A few years later (possibly in 1670) he was back in England petitioning for the promised cash, having in the meantime found "la porte fermée pour moy, au suiet de mon esloignement a toutes sortes de

---

taille singer, whose name is variously given, depending upon how one interprets the cursive minims in the documents, as Elenor/Eleonor/Eldnor and Guigant/Guigaut/Gingant/Gingaut/Guignant.

82 Ferdinand de Florence is identified simply as "Maistre de la Musique," but of the five independent voice parts presumed to have constituted the ensemble, the only one not filled in the list above would have been the treble. Given Ferdinand's apparently Italian origins, one wonders whether he might have been a castrato; see, however, his petitions of 1665 and c.1670 (see nn. 85 and 86, below), in which he explicitly refers to his "famille" and "ma petite famille."

83 LC5/118 and LC5/138, pp. 19–20 (31 March 1664: Ashbee, 1: 53); LC5/118; LC5/138, p. 29 (20 July 1664: Ashbee, 1: 55); LC5/118 (9 October 1664: Ashbee, 1: 58); LC5/118; LC5/138, p. 53 (16 May 1665: Ashbee, 1: 63). Ferdinand de Florence had also been recruited by Lord d'Aubigny, as he indicated in his 1665 petition (see n. 85, below)—although, curiously, he claims therein to have been approached by d'Aubigny while in London (perhaps as a visitor, with the French instrumentalists?) in 1660.

84 SP29/99/26 (see n. 19, above).

85 SP29/113/117 (*Calendar of State Papers, Domestic* 1664–65: 227; not in Ashbee). This petition is tentatively dated "? February 1665," but we should note that "Mr. Ferdinando" continued to be in charge of the three singing boys in the Queen's Chapel until at least the middle of May.

Foreign musicians at the Restoration court 217

decentes hospitalitez."[86] The fate of his appeal is unknown, as is that concerning the remainder of the group, who also found themselves terminated from the royal service, perhaps in early 1668, and who petitioned "pour avoir le moyen de s'en aller" from England.[87] The disbandment of the ensemble is probably related to the household retrenchment scheme of 1668 (see n. 29, above), which initially threatened to affect all of the king's musicians, although the English performers, including the Chapel Royal singers and the Twenty-Four Violins, were ultimately granted a reprieve. Out of the remaining original members of the French group, only the bass, Claude des Granges, survived: he appears to have been absorbed into the main musical establishment in early 1668 as, somewhat incongruously, a singer associated with the violin band.[88] Jean de La Vollée also stayed on in England—he received a grant of denization in 1673[89]—but there is no further record of him holding an appointment at court.

This is essentially all that we know for certain about Charles II's French ensemble of the 1660s. But there is one additional piece of information that it is crucial to take into consideration. Scholars have long been perplexed by an Establishment Book entry dated 31 March 1665 in which one "Mon[s] [Louis] Grabu" is named as "Composer in his Ma[ties] Musique," under the sponsorship of George Villiers, 2nd Duke of Buckingham.[90] Grabu is of course a well known, if often severely maligned, figure in Restoration musical history, whose full biography I have explored elsewhere.[91] His earliest appearance in England has traditionally been dated to 2 April 1665, when he was married in the Queen's Chapel at St. James's Palace (where, as we have seen, the French ensemble—soon to be divested of its leader, Ferdinand de Florence—may have been in service).[92]

---

86 SP29/281A/225 (*Calendar of State Papers, Domestic* 1670: 637; Ashbee, 8: 205–6). As with so many such petitions, the date is uncertain; could Ferdinand have been in England in February 1671, at the time of *The Queen's Masque*? (See Chapter 1 for a discussion of the possible French component of this entertainment.)

87 SP29/137/135 (undated [?March ?c.1668]: *Calendar of State Papers, Domestic* 1667–68: 318; Ashbee, 8: 192).

88 LC5/14, p. 44 (Ashbee, 1: 108), warrant dated 18 September 1671, retroactively establishing an appointment for des Granges effective 25 March 1668, at £100 *p.a.*, "during his Majesty's pleasure"; see also the subsequent warrants for payment, both dated November 1671: SP38/25/151 (Ashbee, 8: 210) and SO3/16, p. 471 (Ashbee, 5: 60). Early in 1669, des Granges was listed among the musicians explicitly exempted from the retrenchment (SP29/255/87 [5 February 1669: *Calendar of State Papers, Domestic* 1668–69: 183; Ashbee, 8: 191] and LC5/12, p. 230 and British Library, Egerton MS 2159, ff. 12[r] and 13[r] [21 February 1669: Ashbee, 1: 88]), and he subsequently appears in establishment lists of 1668–69 (LC3/25, p. 57 [Ashbee, 1: 227]) and 1671 (LC3/27, p. 71 rev. [Ashbee, 1: 229]). For a further discussion of des Granges's career, see pp. 271–76, below.

89 SP44/36, p. 205; SP38/25/339; SO3/16, p. 623 (May 1673: *Calendar of State Papers, Domestic* 1673: 238; Ashbee, 5: 62, 8: 212).

90 LC3/73, p. 98 (31 March 1665: Ashbee, 1: 221).

91 Andrew R. Walkling, "The Ups and Downs of Louis Grabu" (in progress).

92 James Cyril M. Weale, ed., *Registers of the Catholic Chapels Royal and the Portuguese Embassy Chapel 1662–1829* (Catholic Record Society, 38; London: Catholic Record Society, 1941), 1 [Marriages]: 4.

218 *"For such uses as the King shall direct"*

Just under a year later, Grabu would burst unexpectedly onto the English musical scene, being named Master of the King's Music in place of the deceased Nicholas Lanier, with effect from 25 March 1666.[93] The Catalan-born, French-trained musician's elevation would be something of a surprise if indeed he had no prior connection with the royal musical establishment, but the 1665 entry, in which he is explicitly described as a "Composer" (a position he never held during his subsequent tenure as Master of the Music) suggests some earlier appointment, probably with the French ensemble. Like his Italian counterparts Vincenzo and Bartolomeo Albrici, who are clearly designated "Nostri [*i.e.* the king's] in arte Musicâ Compositores" in their pass for foreign travel issued on 25 March 1665 (see n. 21, above), Grabu may have taken up compositional and even organizational duties with the French performers, just as their original *maître* was about to get the sack. Ultimately, of course, Grabu left this shadowy musical existence behind and moved quickly into the spotlight of the "English chamb^r Musick in Ordinary to his Ma^{te}."[94] His appointment to the chief post in the royal musical establishment can tell us something about Charles II's priorities, which are known to have inclined toward French music and French musical institutions and practice: Grabu, we should note, was admired in his time not for his skills as a composer or a performer, but for his ability to instill a Lullian professionalism in the musicians under his direction, a quality that would have complemented the English king's desire to mimic the practices of his French cousin, Louis XIV.[95] Moreover, two of Charles's most promising English musicians were sent abroad for training in the 1660s: the violinist John Banister in 1661–62[96] and the singer Pelham Humfrey from late 1664 or early 1665 until October 1667.[97] Both men were also composers, and alongside Matthew Locke contributed substantially to the development of theatrical music (including recitative) in England during the 1660s and '70s.

93 Lanier died shortly before 24 February 1666, when he was buried. Although Grabu's appointment was paid as from 25 March, he was not actually sworn into the position until June or perhaps even November 1666, and only received his formal patent in the spring of 1667: see Walkling, "Ups and Downs."

94 LC5/138, p. 367 (24 November 1666: Ashbee, 1: 74).

95 See for example Pepys, *Diary*, 8: 458 (1 October 1667) and 9: 163 (15 April 1668), discussed in Walkling, "Ups and Downs."

96 See the discussion in Holman, *Fiddlers*, 291–92.

97 See Peter Dennison, *Pelham Humfrey* (Oxford Studies of Composers; Oxford: Oxford University Press, 1986), 6, and Edward F. Rimbault, ed., *The Old Cheque-Book, or Book of Remembrance, of the Chapel Royal, From 1561 to 1744* (Camden Society, n. s., 3; London: Camden Society, 1872), 213.

6 The Royall Academy of Musick, 1673–75

The centrality, from 1666, of Louis Grabu to the largest and most important component of the royal musical establishment—not to mention the special consideration afforded to Claude des Granges after 1668—may be read as both a symptom and a cause of the seeming lack of genuine enthusiasm for imported through-composed opera in the early years of the Restoration. Prior to 1669, there was no such thing as French opera, and so Charles II's interest in Gallic music could have had little or nothing to do with opera *per se*.[1] In the meantime, the expertise of the Italians was for the most part segregated into specialized domains, such as the Queen's Chapel and the ongoing (but ultimately unsuccessful) schemes that Thomas Killigrew was hatching out at the periphery of the court. Beginning in around 1673, however, there was a significant shift that saw a new surge of interest in operatic production and performance. This shift was at least partly political in origin, emanating from a complex of issues concerning religion and the royal succession that would ultimately flare up most prominently in the "Exclusion Crisis" at the end of the decade, and would exacerbate the concerns that led to the "Glorious Revolution" ten years thereafter. Three political events can be considered to be of special importance to the reintroduction of opera into England, as well as to broader developments in court cultural production at this time:[2] the passage of the Test Act (25 Car. II, cap. 2), which required that all civil and military officers and servants of the royal household formally abjure Roman Catholic loyalties and practices by the end of Trinity term (8 July) 1673 or face draconian legal sanctions; the consequent open acknowledgement of his Catholicism by Charles's brother and heir James, Duke of York, who declined to receive communion at Anglican services on Easter 1673 and resigned his post as Lord High Admiral in

---

1 For the early history of operatic performances in France, which were fundamentally Italian in character, see Neal Zaslaw, "The First Opera in Paris: A Study in the Politics of Art," in John Hajdu Heyer, ed., *Jean-Baptiste Lully and the Music of the French Baroque* (Cambridge: Cambridge University Press, 1989), 7–23.

2 I hope to make the political concerns of the Restoration court, as manifested in cultural production, the subject of a future book, provisionally entitled *Instruments of Absolutism: Restoration Court Culture and the Epideictic Mode*.

220   *"For such uses as the King shall direct"*

June; and the widowered duke's decision to remarry later that same year with the proviso that any spouse he chose must share his adherence to the Roman faith.

The first of these events dramatically curtailed Charles II's ability to retain royal servants of his choosing, including musical personnel: several English Roman Catholics were deprived of their positions in the months that followed,[3] and nearly all French and Italian musicians who held offices by royal patent were also obliged to surrender their offices—including, ultimately, the Master of the Music, Louis Grabu, who appears to have hung on into 1674 before being forced to resign.[4] The second event, while less directly relevant to court musicians in the short term, had important long-term repercussions, since the controversy over his brother's religion and the resultant political consequences were probably instrumental in Charles II's move toward a cultural policy that was more overtly absolutist and, in particular, French in orientation. This, combined with the more immediate impact of the Duke of York's search for a new, Catholic wife overseas helped to create what can best be described as a paradox: at precisely the moment Charles II was seeking to emulate Continental, mostly Catholic cultural practices and to mount a grand celebration for the first royal wedding in more than a decade, which would in turn necessitate the employment of a new cadre of foreign performers, many of whom could now more readily be recruited from leading European courts, the king's ability to surround himself with precisely those servants who could actualize his ambitions was severely restricted by parliamentary edict.

The court's response to this problem seems to have emerged gradually, but the initial phase of that response was dictated by fast-moving events. Having considered several candidates during the summer of 1673, the Duke of York settled upon Maria Beatrice d'Este, daughter of the late Duke Alfonso IV of Modena and his wife Laura Martinozzi (a niece of Cardinal Jules Mazarin and now, as dowager duchess, regent on behalf of her teenaged son), as his bride. The marriage—which, when it came to be known of, would prove deeply unpopular with the English people and in particular with Charles II's already much-antagonized

---

3 See Ashbee, *passim, e.g.* 1: 137–38, 151, 184; 8: 340; see also Holman, *Fiddlers*, 299. An Order in Council forbidding all Roman Catholics from "His Maties Royall p^rsence or ... His Palace or ... ye place where his court shalbe" was drawn up on 14 November, to take effect as of the 18th (see LC5/141, p. 25, quoted in Ashbee, 1: 131), although it was only published on the 20th; a similar order was issued on 3 February 1675. For comment, see *Calendar of State Papers, Venetian* 38 (1673–75): 183. Charles subsequently banned Roman Catholics from St. James's Palace (home of the Duke of York) as well, "declaring that the whole is dependent on Whitehall" (*ibid.*, 193).

4 See Walkling, "Ups and Downs." The provisions of the 1673 Test Act did not cover Catherine of Braganza's household, and thus her chapel establishment became the professional refuge of the likes of Bartolomeo Albrici, Matteo Battaglia, and Giovanni Battista Draghi. However, the 1678 Test Act (30 Car. II, stat. 2, cap. 1), which went into effect as of 1 December of that year, explicitly exempted only those of the queen's servants who were "Naturall borne Subject[s] of the King of Portugall ... not exceeding Nine in number at any one time," thus forcing the Italians out of royal service. It may be this personnel shakeup that provoked the petition of 1679 from Draghi, Suarez, Bartolomeo Albrici, and Galli (SP44/55, pp. 52–53: see Chapter 5, n. 34, above).

Parliament[5]—was celebrated by proxy in Modena on 20/30 September, the Duke of York being represented by his Groom of the Stool, Henry Mordaunt, 2nd Earl of Peterborough. The event was accompanied by a Te Deum and several masquerades and theatrical entertainments,[6] following which, a few days afterwards, the new bride set off for England accompanied by her mother the duchess, her brother Prince Rinaldo, and a retinue of attendants. After a delay in Paris on account of illness,[7] she and her party left that city on 13/23 November, and arrived at Dover on the 21st, whereupon the marriage was confirmed by the Bishop of Oxford and consummated that same night.[8]

James's selection of the fifteen-year-old Maria (commonly known to British historians as "Mary of Modena") was of greater geopolitical significance than might at first appear, since the match became, from its earliest stages, a pet project of the French king Louis XIV. According to Giovanni Giacomo Corniani, the Venetian Resident at Florence, Louis had "committed himself … deeply in this business,"[9] and his agents had acted as intermediaries in the negotiations that made it possible.[10] Indeed, when Mary passed through Paris in October and November 1673, it was announced that she would "be treated by [him] as a daughter of France and she will begin to enjoy the benefits from the very first moment that she enters that country and for the whole time she will be defrayed at the Court" of the French king.[11] Subsequent accounts of Mary's treatment in Paris confirm this: she was housed in state at Fontainebleau, "where she is lodged in the royal palace, being served by the officials of the crown," and then at the Arsenal in

---

5 When Parliament resumed its session on 20 October 1673, the Commons, knowing that a 1–2-week prorogation was imminent, dispensed with prayers and immediately voted an address to the king "That the intended Marriage of his Royal Highness with the Dutchess of Modena be not consummated; and that he may not be married to any Person, but of the Protestant Religion" (*Journals of the House of Commons*, 9: 281). Only after further such addresses were made in November (*ibid.*, 283–85) did the king inform them—no doubt not without some satisfaction—that the marriage had already taken place (*ibid.*, 285–86).

6 *Calendar of State Papers, Venetian* 38: 131, 135. It was nonetheless a hurried affair, owing to the opposition of the Papal authorities in Rome, who noted that James had not officially declared himself a Catholic, "yet as the duchess [Laura] had obtained the opinion of several theologians …, and being pressed on by the repeated protests of the English ambassador, who let it be understood that he must either have the total conclusion or he would leave, she gave orders for everything to be carried out" (p. 135). The Venetian ambassador at Rome noted (p. 131) that "the nuptials of the princess were performed by the hands of the parish priest, as the bishop was unwilling to take part."

7 *Ibid.*, 172.

8 *Ibid.*, 181.

9 *Ibid.*, 119.

10 Louis even sent an ambassador to the Pope in order to overcome the serious opposition to the marriage in Rome. As the Venetian ambassador in that city reported, the French envoy "represented that the House of Este being under the protection of the Most Christian crown, the duchess of Modena had employed him to inform his Holiness that they had celebrated the marriage between the princess, her daughter and the duke of Jorch [*i.e.* York] and remarked on the benefit which would result to the Catholic Church from having that princess in England" (*ibid.*, 142).

11 *Ibid.*, 134.

222 *"For such uses as the King shall direct"*

Paris, where she remained "for some days";[12] she was granted "the entry to royal audiences and will have the honour of a seat equal to the queen";[13] the king and queen sent their own coaches to collect her for her initial reception at court, while Louis himself called at her apartments the following day;[14] and on her journey to Calais she was attended "by the royal coaches and officials of the court."[15]

Clearly, the connection between the Italian princess and soon-to-be English duchess and Europe's most powerful monarch was meant to be prominently on display in these events. But Mary's journey through France may have had other consequences as well—less high-profile politically speaking, but nonetheless of tremendous relevance to Restoration cultural practices and to Charles II's desire, noted above, to politicize those practices in specific ways. It is evident that the king and his ministers saw the arrival of the new Duchess of York as an opportunity to reshape the court's cultural landscape both by exploiting the growing sophistication of English theatrical resources and, in particular, by adopting the latest French musical trends. Chief among these trends, of course, was the recent French innovation of opera, which combined the through-composition inherited from the earlier Italian style with an emphasis on the spectacular elements of scenic and machine technology, musical grandeur embodied in both choral and instrumental performance, and, perhaps most importantly, dance. In effect, this novel form breathed new vitality into the older spectacular European theatrical traditions of which the "classic" English court masque constituted an important example, and it is thus small wonder that Charles II immediately seized upon this significant new opportunity.

His task was made easier by the arrival in London, sometime in the latter months of 1673, of a gaggle of skilled French performers. These included the composer and harpsichordist Robert Cambert (recently ousted from the *Académie Royale des Opéra* through the machinations of Jean-Baptiste Lully); as many as six dancers, several of whom had already gained considerable fame in Paris; possibly a number of singers; and four wind players specializing in the "flute douce" (*i.e.* French recorder) and "hautbois" (*i.e.* French Baroque oboe), both instruments hitherto unknown in England.[16] The precise timing and circumstances of their

---

12 *Ibid.*, 160–61.

13 *Ibid.*, 154. According to the Venetian ambassador in Paris, this was in exchange for the treatment accorded Charles II's sister (Louis XIV's sister-in-law) when she traveled to England in 1670 in order to negotiate the Treaty of Dover.

14 *Ibid.*, 167. On the earlier occasion, "The king despatched his first gentleman of the Bedchamber and desired that she should be served by the officials of the crown with sumptuous furnishings of dwelling place and table."

15 *Ibid.*, 180; see also p. 168.

16 See David Lasocki, "Professional Recorder Playing in England, 1500–1740, II: 1640–1740," *Early Music* 10 (1982): 182–91 and *idem*, "The French Hautboy in England, 1673–1730," *Early Music* 16 (1988): 339–57. The identities of the four wind players, [?Jean] Boutet, Maxent de Bresmes, Pierre Guiton, and Jacques Paisible, are only first revealed in documents relating to the 1675 production of *Calisto*: LC5/141, p. 547 (*Register*, no. 888; Ashbee, 1: 146) and LC5/141, p. 197 (*Register*, no. 920; Ashbee, 1: 150). Guiton and Paisible are also listed in LC9/274, p. 312 (included in *Register*, no. 909; not in Ashbee), as is "a hoyboy"—probably de Bresmes who, like

advent are not entirely clear, and may not have been directly related to Mary's appearance in November. On 22 August 1673, in a letter prematurely reporting that "[t]he match with Modena is looked upon as broke," James Vernon also informed the future Secretary of State Sir Joseph Williamson (currently abroad representing England at peace talks in Cologne) that

> the Duke's house [*i.e.* Dorset Garden] are preparing an Opera and great machines. They will have dansers out of France, and St. André comes over with them, who is to have a pension of the King, and a patent of master of the compositions for ballets[.][17]

Vernon, who is referring here to the celebrated French dancer Adrien Merger de Saint-André, would certainly have been in the know. He was private secretary to the Duke of Monmouth, alongside whom Saint-André had danced in a special production of Lully's *Les Fêtes de l'Amour et de Bacchus* presented before Louis XIV in Paris in 1672,[18] and Monmouth had important connections to Dorset Garden and specifically to the dramatick opera that ultimately emerged in 1675, Thomas Shadwell and Matthew Locke's *Psyche*.[19] Saint-André probably arrived in England in late November 1673, when the promised pension of £150, paid out of the king's Secret Service account, began to accrue.[20]

Guiton and Paisible, was paid £5 for his services in the masque, whereas Boutet received only £3 (see LC5/141, p. 197 and Walkling, "Masque and Politics at the Restoration Court: John Crowne's *Calisto*" [see Chapter 5, n. 15, above], 34 [Table 2], 45–46, and 61 n. 90). Information on the pre-1673 activities of de Bresmes and Guiton can be found in Andrew Ashbee and David Lasocki, comps. (assisted by Peter Holman and Fiona Kisby), *A Biographical Dictionary of English Court Musicians, 1485–1714* (2 vols.: Aldershot: Ashgate, 1998), 1: 187 and 527–28.

17 SP29/336/273 (*Calendar of State Papers, Domestic* 1673: 505; *Register*, no. 794), transcribed in W. D. Christie, ed., *Letters Addressed from London to Sir Joseph Williamson while Plenipotentiary at the Congress of Cologne in the Years 1673 and 1674* (2 vols.: Camden Society, n. s., 8–9; London: Camden Society, 1874), 1: 180–81.

18 See *La Gazette d'Amsterdam* 1673/8 *bis* (23 February 1673): 2: "Monsieur fut Dimanche voir l'Opera; Il s'y rencontra un nombre infini de Seigneurs, & entr'autres Monsieur le Duc de Monmouth, Monsr. le Grand, & le Marquis de Villeroy, qui y dancerent publiquement"; Jean-Laurent Lecerf de La Viéville de Fresneuse, *Comparaison de la Musique Italienne, et de la Musique Françoise* (2nd ed.; Brussels: François Foppens, 1705), 2: 173: "il y eût une representation singuliere & glorieuse ..., en ce que M^r le Grand, M^r le Duc de Monmouth, M^r le Duc de Villeroy & M^r le Marquis de Rassen voulurent bien y danser avec quatre de ses Danseurs, un jour que le Roy y étoit"; and [Maupoint], *Bibloteque des Theatres* (Paris: Laurent-François Prault, 1733), 134: "cet Opera fut représenté depuis le quinze Novembré 1672. jusqu'en Juillet de l'année suivante[.] Dans une des représentations que le Roy honora de sa présence, M. le Grand, Messieurs les Ducs de Montmouth, de Villeroy & M. le Marquis de Rassen danserent une entrée, avec les sieurs Beauchamps, Saint-André, Favier l'aîné & la Pierre."

19 See the discussion in Walkling, *English Dramatick Opera*.

20 T48/30 ("A Charge of all Moneys received for secrett service at his Ma^{ts} Excheq^r by Sr Stephen Fox in two yeares—from Midsommer 1673 to Midsom:^{r} 1675 as alsoe an Accompt of what have been paid severall Persons, and Uses in the said two yeares"), p. 4, recording £237 10s disbursed to Saint-André "for a yeare & 7/mo" under the heading "Paid quarterly Payments to persons for w^{ch}

224 *"For such uses as the King shall direct"*

With regard to the flute/oboe players, David Lasocki has suggested that they arrived in the company of Cambert, who seems to have left Paris soon after 9/19 August 1673, the date on which he assigned power of attorney to his wife Marie Du Moustier.[21] This would place their appearance considerably earlier than the importation of Saint-André and the other dancers mentioned by Vernon, and even prior to the sealing of the Modena match, and John Buttrey has argued that Cambert was actually dispatched to England under the auspices of Louis XIV to be installed in the retinue of Louise de Kéroualle, newly elevated as Duchess of Portsmouth and Charles II's chief mistress.[22] Cambert's role, Buttrey suggests, was to promote French-style culture (and its attendant grandeur) at the duchess's household, a favorite haunt of the English king, and incidentally to report back to his masters in Paris any political goings-on therein. As we shall see, Cambert may also have been considered a kind of adjunct to the court musical establishment, and the band of four recorder/oboe players appear to have been absorbed into the court altogether, albeit in ways that were designed to confound investigators, both then and now. In any case, what cannot be doubted is that the turmoil in the Parisian theatrical and musical world, which broke out in full force in March 1672 when Lully appropriated the royal *privilège* to perform operatic works formerly held by Cambert's collaborator, the poet Pierre Perrin, forced a number of

---

particular Privy Seals did passe." For a single quarterly payment of £37 10*s*, made on 25 March 1675, see British Library, Add. MS 28080, f. 14^{r-v} ("Accompt of Secrett Service from the end of Decemb: 1674—to the 10th of June 1675"), verso; the annual figure of £150 also appears in British Library, Egerton MS 3352, ff. 167^r–168^v, f. 167^r (dated May 1674 in a modern annotation and summarized, as "Leeds MSS, Packet 16," in Andrew Browning, *Thomas Osborne, Earl of Danby and Duke of Leeds 1632–1712* [3 vols.: Glasgow: Jackson, Son & Co., 1951], 3: 48). Note also the warrant of 27 March 1675, ordering the Customs Commissioners to "deliver to Monsieur de St. Andre for his own private use six pieces of tapestry in two bundles and a looking glass, the said bundles of tapestry being old hangings brought over in the packet boat from Calais to Dover and from Dover to London" (PRO30/32/50 [properly "T54/5"], pp. 304–5 [*Calendar of Treasury Books* 4: 714]).

21 See André Tessier, "Robert Cambert à Londres," *La Revue Musicale* 9 (1927–28): 101–22, p. 108, and W. H. Grattan Flood, "Quelques Précisions Nouvelles sur Cambert et Grabu à Londres," *ibid.*, 351–61, pp. 352–53. Cambert's wife and daughter must have joined him in London later on (see Chapter 7, n. 65, below). According to an entry in Archives Nationales, Paris, LL 80, Cambert was not replaced as organist of the Chapitre de Saint-Honoré until 3 September 1674, more than a year later. In considering this delay, the nineteenth-century opera historians "Nuitter" and "Thoinan" suggest that the canons, "incertains de la durée du séjour de leur organiste à l'étranger, et en considération de ses bon services, ont bien pu attendre une année avant de lui donner un successeur définitif" (see Ch. Nuitter [Charles Louis Étienne Truinet] and Er. Thoinan [Antoine Ernest Roquet], *Les Origines de L'Opéra Français d'après les Minutes des Notaires, les Registres de la Conciergerie et les Documents Originaux Conservés aux Archives Nationales, a la Comédie Française et dans Diverses Collections Publiques et Particulières* [Paris: Librarie Plon, 1886], 304).

22 John Buttrey, "New Light on Robert Cambert in London, and his *Ballet et Musique*," *Early Music* 23 (1995): 198–220. It is perhaps noteworthy, in terms of Buttrey's thesis, that Cambert's departure from France in late August 1673 closely follows the official grant of denization to Louise, which had been effectuated prior to the 11th of that month, providing legal sanction to her long-term residence in England and paving the way for her creation as Duchess on the 19th.

The Royall Academy of Musick, 1673–75   225

performers to seek out new opportunities, and this development certainly worked to the benefit of theatre-loving Londoners, not least among them Charles II.[23]

Whatever may have been the initial impetus for the French performers' arrival in England in the autumn of 1673, there can be little doubt that their appearance had a marked effect on the nature of court entertainments immediately after the advent of the new Duchess of York. We have little definitive evidence regarding the precise features or timing of those entertainments that were put on during the earliest phase of this important transition, but some telling details emerge from accounts of the court's activities recorded by the Venetian ambassador, Girolamo Alberti. Alberti's chief concern was with court protocol, and the sojourn of Mary's mother the Duchess and regent of Modena and her brother Prince Rinaldo in London, which lasted from mid-November 1673 until the end of December, gave him plenty to report. In stark contrast to the treatment received by the Modenese party at the hands of the French king, as well as the English court's own intention to host an unprecedented series of lavish entertainments to celebrate the match,[24] the visit was plagued with ceremonial difficulties. As a minor Italian potentate, Duchess Laura felt herself to be of a higher social degree than the English nobility,[25] and the Venetian ambassador's reports expatiate endlessly on the question of who was allowed to sit rather than stand in the presence of the English royal family, and how the various European envoys, afraid of committing a breach of protocol, declined to pay formal respects to the Modenese

---

23 For example, Louis XIV's grant of the Théâtre du Palais-Royal for Lully's exclusive use in April 1673 forced out both Molière's *Troupe du Roy* and Tiberio Fiorilli's *Comédie-Italienne*, who had previously been sharing the venue. Fiorilli's troupe took advantage of this state of affairs to make an extended trip to England, which began with their arrival on or about 21 April (see PRO30/32/48 [properly "T54/3"], p. 360 [*Calendar of Treasury Books* 4: 127; *Register*, no. 771]) and ended around 10–12 September (see SP44/40, p. 105 [*Calendar of State Papers, Domestic* 1673: 540; not in *Register*] and PRO30/32/49 [properly "T54/4"], p. 26 [*Calendar of Treasury Books* 4: 392; *Register*, no. 800]), after the players had received substantial gifts from Charles II (noted in Table 5.2, above). Upon their return to Paris, the Italians were again installed alongside the *Troupe du Roy*, this time in the new theatre at the Hôtel de Guénégaud: see John S. Powell, *Music and Theatre in France, 1600–1680* (Oxford: Oxford University Press, 2000), 62–63.

24 A number of preparations were being made in the Hall Theatre at this time: see the payment for "mending the matts of the staires & degrees in the Theater" sometime in December 1673 (WORK5/21, f. 89^v [*Register*, no. 815]) and the succession of documents ordering the provision of velvet-covered armchairs for the king and queen and a "Curtaine of blewe, redd, and white ... to fall downe before the Stage" issued between 24 November 1673 (just as Mary and her retinue were arriving in London) and 25 March 1674 (immediately prior to the transplantation of the opera *Ariane* to Drury Lane) (*Register*, nos. 814, 818, 828, and 833 [for full references, see n. 119, below]; bills for the materials can be found in LC9/274, pp. 61, 77, and 107). There is also an order of 30 June 1674 for the delivery of "One Canopie of State of Crymson Velvett trymed with Gold & Silver fringes with two Greate Chaires & two Cushions suiteable for the Theatre. Two Cushions & a Carpett of Aurora Damaske trymed with silke fringe for ye same" (LC5/86, p. 26 [*Register*, no. 849]).

25 *Calendar of State Papers, Venetian* 38: 188 (report of 12/22 December): "she observed audibly that [the English duchesses] might well allow her to take precedence seeing they were subjects born, whereas she, in her own territories, raised money without parliament."

226   *"For such uses as the King shall direct"*

duchess and her son.[26] Discussing the issue in his report for 12/22 December, the ambassador provides an important piece of information about court theatricals as well:

> Preparations had been made for a ballet at the Court with musical interludes in French, and the performance was fixed for last Tuesday evening [*i.e.* 9 December] when everything was suddenly postponed. This was due to a punctilio of the English duchesses. Not being conceded the tabouret opposite the queen they refuse even to be present when the duchess of Modena is seated thereon.[27]

The ambassador further noted that "The ballet will be performed none the less," but subsequently offered no additional information about when, or whether, it ultimately appeared.[28] The reference here to a "ballet" (presumably translated by the twentieth-century English editor Allen B. Hinds from the Italian *"ballo"*) appears to be the first indication we have of a French theatrical entertainment sponsored by and performed at the Restoration court. Another such entertainment was not long in coming: by 26 December, according to the Venetian ambassador, the elder Duchess and Prince Rinaldo had tired of the constant slights they were receiving at court, not to mention the anti-Catholic hostility of the English population more generally, and decided to embark for Italy on 30 December, before the Christmas festivities had concluded.[29] On 2/12 January 1674, he reported that

> The duchess of York was in tears when she took leave of her mother and has been so since, so much so that with her eyes swollen and her health

---

26 See *e.g. ibid.*, 186 (report of 5/15 December): "With regard to ceremonial the queen went to visit the duchess mother who sat on the tabouret. This honour is not accorded to any of the English duchesses, who avoid such rencounters. The mother also sits at the side of the duke's table on a chair like that of their royal Highnesses. The ambassadors have not yet paid their respects in her own apartment, although the French one offered to do so once for all.
   "Prince Rinaldo does not appear at the duke's table, being served in his own apartment. He still scruples to allow the English peers to place themselves on his right when they visit him, after having disputed the title of 'Excellency,' so that now no one approaches him. They do not choose to follow the example of Lord Stafford, who, as the prince's apartment is in St. James's palace, considers it the house of the duke of York and not of the prince, to whom he says he conceded the right hand in the house of a third person."

27 *Ibid.*, 188; the report continues: "This agrees with their quitting the queen's chamber when the duchess of Modena seats herself. Accordingly she does not frequent it ... ."

28 *Ibid.*; the ambassador's report further notes that "the duchess[es?] will be present under protest that in that place there is no precedence. As a fact there is not, for every one is seated, except those within the queen's circle, beyond which the duchesses very often place themselves." The delayed production is probably the same as that anticipated in a letter of 8 December by Bianca Barbazzi, one of Mary's Italian maids: British Library, Add. MS 53816, ff. 114–16 (not seen; cited in James Anderson Winn, *Queen Anne: Patroness of Arts* [Oxford: Oxford University Press, 2014], 18 and 648 n. 58).

29 *Calendar of State Papers, Venetian* 38: 194 (report of 5 January 1674, New Style).

disordered, she was in no state to attend the Court ballet last evening [*i.e.* Thursday, 1 January], and so it was postponed.[30]

It might be tempting to speculate that this "Court ballet" was the same as the one originally cancelled on 9 December—although a delay of over three weeks between scheduled performances would seem unlikely under the circumstances. What must in any case be acknowledged is a noticeably increased emphasis on the part of Charles II's court on the presentation of theatrical entertainments, in particular those incorporating music, dance, and other forms of spectacle. As early as 6 December, less than two weeks after her arrival in London, Mary was treated to a performance of *The Empress of Morocco* at Dorset Garden.[31] As we have seen in Chapter 2, Elkanah Settle's notorious play had probably been premiered at court in March or April of that year, and is believed to have opened for its initial public run in June or July. At this very early point in her career as Duchess of York, Mary's command of the English language must have been rudimentary at best, and we can surmise that the production's main appeal for her would have been its noteworthy (albeit not especially sophisticated) sets and Matthew Locke's striking musical masque. The subsequent "ballet ... with musical interludes in French" would presumably have held greater interest, and would have showcased the talents of the recently arrived Continental performers: not only the dancers and wind-players, but also French singers, who may have presented works from Cambert's repertoire. No evidence has yet come to light regarding the identities of any such singers—as we have seen, all of the former members of Charles II's French ensemble except Jean de La Vollée (harpsichordist), Louis Grabu (erstwhile composer), and Claude des Granges (bass) were long gone by this time. However, as I will argue below, des Granges did remain an active member of the court musical establishment throughout this period, and we should also take account the presence of the elderly French countertenor Anthony Robert, a longtime servant of the late Queen Henrietta Maria and by this time a member of Charles II's ensemble of Lutes and Voices.[32] It is possible that, despite the Francocentric nature of the performances, some of the Italian or Portuguese sing-

---

30 *Ibid.*, 197.

31 Henry W. Robinson and Walter Adams, eds., *The Diary of Robert Hooke M.A., M.D., F.R.S. 1672–1680* (London: Taylor and Francis, 1935; rpt. London: Wykeham Publications, 1968), 73; Hooke himself records paying 1*s* 6*d* to see the show.

32 Robert (born c.1597) had first arrived in England in 1626. From 1661 he was Master of the Music to Henrietta Maria (until her death in 1669), and also a member of Charles II's Lutes and Voices; as we have noted in Chapter 2, he is credited with having taught dancing to numerous members of the royal family. He is exceptional for having remained unmolested as a paid and liveried member of the royal musical establishment after the passage of the Test Act. This could have been on account of his advanced age, but in 1675 he was still well enough to appear in *Calisto* (see Walkling, "Masque and Politics," 34 and 37 [Table 2 and n. 8]), and he was later employed as a singing master to Princesses Mary and Anne (see Walkling, "Professional Actors as Royal Drama Coaches, 1674–81" [in progress]), prior to his death in 1679. For an accounting of Robert's career, see the article in Ashbee and Lasocki, *Biographical Dictionary* (see n. 16, above), 2: 963–64.

228 *"For such uses as the King shall direct"*

ers remaining in Catherine of Braganza's chapel establishment were pressed into service: as we shall see, the "Italian Musition" Symon Cotterau seems to have been involved prior to his untimely death in January 1674. But there may well have been actual singers from Paris too: Jean-Baptiste Lully's prohibition on the use of musical forces in any theatre beyond his privileged *Académie Royale de Musique* (the most draconian version had been promulgated on 22 April 1673, following Molière's sudden death and the closure of the *Troupe du Roy*'s *Le Malade Imaginaire* in February—and only five days before the opening of Lully's first full-fledged opera *Cadmus et Hermione*) left not only dancers and instrumentalists in the lurch, but singers as well. It is important to bear in mind that, as will be shown below, what documentation we do have for the presence of any French performers at the English court in early 1674 is entirely circumstantial, and thus the absence of a reference to French singers in the archival record should by no means be taken as evidence that there were none in London at the time.

With regard to two of the French productions put on in the winter of 1674, we are fortunate at least to have printed texts that give us a good idea of what these performances looked like, as well as a few documentary scraps that tell us something about the circumstances under which they were presented. Much of this has been summarized previously, particularly in a 1984 article by Pierre Danchin,[33] with important additional information provided in subsequent studies by Christina Bashford and John Buttrey.[34] However, a number of misconceptions persist, and the discussion that follows seeks to elucidate what we can know, or at least surmise, about court-sponsored French musical theatre in the mid-1670s from the surviving evidence, while at the same time drawing attention to certain questions for which satisfactory answers have yet to emerge.

The earliest of the French operatic productions for which a text is extant is the pastoral *Ballet et Musique pour le Divertissement du Roy de la Grande Bretagne*,[35] apparently a collaboration between the composer Cambert,[36] the

---

33 Pierre Danchin, "The Foundation of the Royal Academy of Music in 1674 and Pierre Perrin's *Ariane*," *Theatre Survey* 25 (1984): 55–67. See also the earlier studies by Tessier and Grattan Flood, cited in n. 21, above.

34 Christina Bashford, "Perrin and Cambert's 'Ariane, ou le Mariage de Bacchus' Re-Examined," *Music and Letters* 72 (1991): 1–26; for Buttrey's article, see n. 22, above.

35 ([London]: "aux dépens de l'Autheur … par Thomas Nieucombe," 1674). The only copy of this print whose whereabouts are presently known was formerly in the collection of the Royal Academy of Dancing and is now at the British Library (shelfmark C.194.a.203). However, it may be that the copy once in the collection of Godfrey E. P. Arkwright, described by Lawrence ("Foreign Singers," 225) and Grattan Flood (p. 358), and sold by Sotheby's to Otto Haas at the Arkwright sale (13 February 1939, lot 65), is a different one: where the British Library copy has the printed subscription "*S. BRE.* …" at the end of the libretto (sig. [E]2^v), Grattan Flood describes Arkwright's copy as being signed by "M. de Bream" (*i.e.* the French wind player Maxent de Bresmes), who is evidently further described in the copy as "musicien français de la chapelle royale de violons et hautbois." This mistaken identification is probably a manuscript endorsement; in any case, there is no trace of it in the British Library copy.

36 See Buttrey, "New Light on Robert Cambert," 212 for a transcription of Cambert's only surviving air from the *Ballet*, found in Westminster Abbey Library, MS CG27, p. 49.

dancer and choreographer Jean Favier the elder,[37] and the itinerant novelist and adventurer Sébastien Bremond.[38] Favier, who had already made his mark on the Parisian stage, must have been among the group of "dansers out of France" who accompanied Saint-André, while Bremond arrived in England under his own auspices, as he later recounted in an entertaining manuscript autobiography now in the Bibliothèque Nationale, Paris.[39] *Ballet et Musique* is a fairly modest work: the action takes place "devant la Porte de la Maison d'Iris" (p. 7), no scenic or machine technology of any kind is deployed, and there are not even any explicit act or scene divisions, although the linear, episodic story breaks down into approximately eight sections in which different types of characters and opinions concerning the love of Daphnis for Iris are presented.[40] The work begins with a prologue praising Charles II *"que Regnés dans l'Empire de l'Onde"* and *"de que les Mal-heureux / Peuvent tout esperer, & ne doivent, rien craindre"* (pp. 3–4); however, this is delivered not by mythological or allegorical figures, but rather by Iris and Daphnis themselves, the latter of whom promises to entertain the king *"Par le reçit [sic] de [m]on Amour"* (p. 4). Apart from whatever choral forces may have been required, the production could be mounted with a fairly restricted cast, made up of four male and two female singers: Daphnis, who is present throughout; three other men who could appear as "desbauchés" in the second scene (pp. 7–13) and as a trio of shepherds in the fourth (pp. 15–17), and who could also divide up the later solo roles of a satyr (pp. 17–23), a shepherd (pp. 21–24), and Daphnis's friend Tircis (pp. 25–28); Iris, who sings only in the Prologue and the final scene, and thus could double as a gypsy girl (pp. 13–15); and a shepherdess who joins the conversation at several junctures (pp. 5–6, 19, 21, and 24).[41] Intervening dances would allow time for those singers performing multiple roles to change costumes, and the dancers themselves would have been very busy both onstage and off, appearing successively as hunters (p. 7), drunkards (p. 9), gypsies and basques (p. 13), shepherds and shepherdesses (p. 15), and satyrs (p. 17). Curiously, after "LEs Bergers & les Satyres dancent ensemble" (p. 22), all dancing ceases and the performance continues on a purely vocal basis through three more episodes/scenes

37 Favier later became a well-known dancer in Paris, and devised one of the first systems of dance notation: see Rebecca Harris-Warrick and Carol G. Marsh, *Musical Theatre at the Court of Louis XIV: Le Mariage de la Grosse Cathos* (Cambridge: Cambridge University Press, 1994). I am grateful to Drs. Harris-Warrick and Marsh for originally drawing my attention to the *Ballet et Musique* libretto a number of years ago.

38 For information on Bremond, see Edwin P. Grobe, "S. Bre., French Librettist at the Court of Charles II," *Theatre Notebook* 9 (1954–55): 20–21, and *idem*, "Sébastien Bremond: His Life and His Works" (Indiana University, Ph.D. dissertation, 1954).

39 Bibliothèque Nationale, Paris, MS N. acq. fr. 9185, ff. 19–25: "Récit des Avantures de M. de Brémond par lui mesme a M. de Lagny."

40 For a useful discussion and summary of the libretto, see Buttrey, "New Light on Robert Cambert," 213–19.

41 As Bremond explains in his statement printed at the end of the libretto (sig. [E]2^{r-v}), "le peu d'Acteurs qu'on a trouvé capables de bien chanter, Vous doit faire excuser le peu d'incidens qu'il y a, & la contrainte dont il à fallu se servir par tout."

230   *"For such uses as the King shall direct"*

(Daphnis interacts with a shepherdess and shepherd, with Tircis, and finally with Iris, leading to the celebratory choral conclusion).

Bremond makes clear, both in his autobiography and in an address to the reader appended to the printed libretto, that *Ballet et Musique* was presented for the celebrations surrounding the Modena match, although the two accounts differ in some essential details. In the former source, Bremond writes that Charles II "me fit dire de faire un opéra pour ce mariage," a task that he avers was quickly accomplished,[42] whereas in the latter he was supposedly approached by Cambert and Favier, who had already formulated a "dessein de donner une petite demy-heure de Divertissement meslé de Musique & de Dance" for the king.[43] According to Bremond, it was only later that Cambert decided to associate this entertainment with the Duke of York's marriage, for which "on estendit seulement un peu La Matiere" (sig. [E]2^r) at the last minute. As John Buttrey sensibly points out, this might account for the work's somewhat lopsided structure, although why Favier and his colleagues could not have added more dances to the closing section of the piece is not immediately clear. With regard to the text, Bremond himself admits to appropriating "trente où quarante vers ... d'un autre Autheur," which "Ceux qui s'y connoissent un peu ... rendront Justice à qui il appartient" (sig. [E]2^v). Buttrey suggests that this may be the lengthy solo for Iris in the last scene, possibly borrowed wholesale by Cambert from some (now unknown) earlier work for which he had already composed the music.[44] All in all, Buttrey observes, the inspiration for *Ballet et Musique* lies not in the conventional French *ballet de cour*; rather, this "quite substantial all-sung pastorale" follows the pattern of Cambert and Perrin's 1659 *Pastorale d'Issy*, often regarded as a forerunner of French opera.[45] This quality would seem to argue more forcefully for Cambert having taken a pivotal role in the project; indeed, despite being a novelist of some distinction (several of his works were later published in England, both in French and in translation), Bremond was a mere novice when it came to writing operatic libretti—which may also help to explain the slightly disorganized and dramatically unadventurous quality of *Ballet et Musique*'s text.

We know nothing of how the work was received by Charles II and his court; as we shall see, there was a much larger project afoot at the time, and apart from one non-specific order dated 14 January 1674 for the delivery of supplies "for his

---

42 Bibliothèque Nationale, MS N. acq. fr. 9185, f. 23^v: "je parvins ... à être connu du Roy et de S. A. le Duc d'Yorck, qui s'étant marié en secondes noces avec la Princesse de Modène S. M. me fit dire de faire un opéra pour ce mariage. Cela fut bientôt expédié et bon ou méchant qu'il fût il ne laissa pas que de plaire." This is part of a larger extract quoted and helpfully translated in Danchin, 56–57.

43 *Ballet et Musique*, sig. [E]2^r.

44 Buttrey, 212. In a move later to be emulated by Thomas Shadwell in his dramatick opera *Psyche*, Bremond also points out that "on aura pû voir les Paroles du premier Air dans un Livre intitulé *L'Amoureux Africain*. Mais l'Autheur de ce Livre, estant le mesme qui à composé ce petit Ouvrage, il à cru estre en droit de s'en pyuvoit servir, où il voudroit" (sig. [E]2^v).

45 *Ibid.*, 210 and 220 n. 30.

Ma^ts Comædians each night they Act at Court,"[46] there are no surviving official records or contemporary newsletter accounts that can be shown for certain to refer to the *Ballet et Musique* performance(s). However, Bremond himself provides an extraordinarily detailed account of one facet of the production: his fateful altercation with the musician Symon Cotterau, whom we have already witnessed joining the ranks of Charles II's Italian musicians in July 1670.[47] According to Bremond's vivid anecdote, Cotterau (whom Bremond colorfully describes as "homme assés brutal et fanfarron de profession"[48]) approached Bremond in the theatre immediately before the performance and violently seized from him one of the finely bound copies of the programme libretto that were to be distributed as souvenirs to the royal family, who had not yet arrived for the show. Bremond's fury at this "action de cette insolence de la part d'un musicien aux yeux de toute la Cour" (f. 24^r) found its outlet the following day when he encountered Cotterau in Covent Garden and mortally wounded the musician in a duel; he was arrested and, when Cotterau died five days later, bound over for murder. At his trial he pleaded benefit of clergy and was recommitted for six months but then, according to his account, released the day after his sentencing through the intervention of Charles II himself. Bremond's reprieve came on 7 March 1674, as recorded in a surviving docquet of the king's order,[49] and if he was accurate in recounting that his time in prison, from Cotterau's death until the trial, was five weeks, this, when added to the five days Cotterau took to expire, would appear to place the performance of *Ballet et Musique* on or about 25 January (a Sunday).[50] Yet we need to treat this calculation with caution: Bremond's account was written many years later (and, moreover, by a man accustomed to transforming personal experiences into riveting stories), so that some of the details may have been incorrectly recalled or glossed over. In fact, there is a surviving record of Bremond's trial:[51] this official document informs us that the writer was indeed convicted of the lesser charge of manslaughter and that he escaped forfeiture of his goods and chattels, and it confirms that he pled benefit of clergy by the usual method of demonstrating his ability to read.[52] It also supplies the previously unknown fact that Bremond was not alone in being tried for Cotterau's murder: alongside him in the dock was his collaborator in *Ballet et Musique*, the dancer Jean Favier—who, unlike Bremond, was found innocent of

---

46 LC5/140, p. 407 (*Register*, no. 824).

47 LC3/73, p. 103 (see p. 202, above).

48 BN, MS N. acq. fr. 9185, ff. 23^v–24^r (see *Register*, no. 826).

49 SP44/28, f. 108^r (*Calendar of State Papers, Domestic* 1673–75: 193; not in *Register*): "Warrant for the release of Sebastian Bremont, convicted of manslaughter at the Old Bailey, who having benefit of clergy was burnt in the hand and re-committed for six months."

50 See Danchin, 57; Grobe ("S. Bre.," p. 21) mistakenly calculates that the performance took place "in the first week of February."

51 London Metropolitan Archives, MJ/GB/B/009, item 174, p. 6: "Sebastian Bremond p murdro Smionis Catereau."

52 *Ibid.*: "pose non cuł de murdro cuł hom: tant ca: nł pe łi le C̄r̄e."

232   *"For such uses as the King shall direct"*

all charges.[53] However, two discrepancies with the author's narrative also emerge, providing evidence that Bremond is not offering a complete and accurate account: Bremond was remanded for nine, rather than six, months[54] and, although the court's record lacks a precise date, its placement among other documents in the volume seems to indicate that the proceedings occurred sometime around 25 February, over a week before the prisoner's release by royal warrant. This information allows us, while still relying on Bremond's rather vague five-week calculation, to move the potential date of the *Ballet et Musique* performance back to approximately 16 January, right around the time of the order to provide necessaries "for his Ma[ts] Comædians" mentioned above.

What *Ballet et Musique* and the known circumstances surrounding its production offer in particular is a preliminary glimpse of the active, if occasionally fractious, community of foreign performers working in London around the beginning of 1674. Although only Cambert and Favier are identified by name, we can be fairly confident that a medium-sized group of French singers, most if not all of the six dancers, and Cambert's four wind-music colleagues were probably all involved. Bremond himself would have been somewhat peripheral to this group, artistically speaking, but the fact that he was in the company of Favier in Covent Garden on the day Cotterau was mortally wounded is noteworthy. It is the unfortunate Cotterau who seems to have been the outsider: he had come to England some three and a half years earlier and under different circumstances, as an "Italian Musition"—this despite his seemingly French name and hence origin. Bremond informs us that Cotterau "étoit de l'Opera" (f. 23[v]), apparently an indication that he was among the performers in *Ballet et Musique* (which Bremond has just called "un opéra"), but whether or not he had one of the four solo roles remains unclear. If he did, the show would probably have had to be cancelled after the first night, assuming additional performances were intended. Yet without knowing anything for certain about the number and quality of any imported French singers we cannot determine how Cotterau—or for that matter Claude des Granges or Anthony Robert, who were also available for such duties—would have stacked up when the production was cast, nor how this somewhat disparate group would have coalesced under the pressure from the English court to create a *corps* of French operatic/ballet performers.

The question of how many French singers were actually in London at this time is rendered more uncertain by the fact that *Ballet et Musique* was really just a precursor of a much more extravagant production that may already have been in the works by the beginning of 1674. This is the well known if rather perplexing *Ariane, ou le Mariage de Bacchus*, originally written by Perrin and Cambert in 1659

---

53   *Ibid.*: "Joħes ffavie[*hole in MS*]"; "pose non cut nec se retrZ." See also the entry on p. 7, all of which is struck out: "1 . Joħes ffavier de poch\ sti\ Martin[*hole*]in[*hole*]"; "ven\ x Com\." This note appears to identify Favier as a resident of the parish of St. Martin-in-the-Fields, which included Covent Garden, where, according to Bremond, the duel with Cotterau took place.
54   *Ibid.*: "rem\ 9 mens."

following the success of the *Pastorale d'Issy*, and later revised and expanded in anticipation of a performance in Paris by the *Académie Royale des Opéra* that never occurred. As Christina Bashford has demonstrated, this revised version would have been available for Cambert to bring along with him to London, the only necessary change of any substance being the creation of a new allegorical prologue referring to the Duke of York's marriage and praising Charles II, in place of that lauding Louis XIV.[55] Yet in spite of being almost completely written and composed prior to Cambert's arrival in England, *Ariane* would have needed substantial preparation time, given both the work's technical demands and the number of performers required. Although the opera was first presented to the public at the newly opened Drury Lane Theatre at the end of March 1674, the majority of rehearsals seem to have taken place in the Hall Theatre at Whitehall, while Drury Lane was still being fitted up for use. We do not know precisely when rehearsals for *Ariane* began: three documents from December 1673 and January 1674 refer to the existence of one or more unspecified "operas," but their implications remain a subject of contestation. The earliest of these references comes from a petition of Richard Vokins, Yeoman of the Wax Chandry, who incurred the wrath of Charles II's Board of the Greencloth for having set up expensive wax candles without authorization "at the practizing for an Opera for his Maj^{tie} at Whitehall" during December, an infraction for which he had been summarily stripped of his responsibilities.[56] Later, the carpenters of the Office of Works were remunerated for a variety of activities carried out during the month of January, including "giving attendance seu'all nights when the Danceing and Operas were practissed."[57] Finally, there is John Evelyn's well-known diary entry in which he reports that on 5 January 1674, "I saw an *Italian Opera* in musique, the first that had ben in *England* of this kind."[58]

With regard to the first two references, there is certainly some latitude for interpretation. The phrase "an Opera *for his Maj[es]tie*" (my emphasis) in Vokins's petition might be taken to imply a production intended specifically for a royal rather than a public audience, and thus the hapless chandler's infraction in December is just as likely to have been committed at a rehearsal of *Ballet et Musique*— or indeed of some other work, perhaps one of the postponed ballets mentioned

---

55 Bashford, "Perrin and Cambert's 'Ariane, ou le Mariage de Bacchus' Re-Examined" (see n. 34, above). Bashford sensibly speculates (p. 21) that Sébastien Bremond might have been commissioned to write the Prologue's French text, as well as to make some minor alterations to Perrin's original. It is interesting to note that, in contrast to *Ariane*, the English-language version of Cavalli's *L'Erismena* did not feature a newly written prologue, instead recycling the third prologue written for performances in Venice (see Chapter 5, n. 69, above), which, of course, makes no mention whatsoever of Charles II.

56 LS13/171, p. 298 (*Register*, no. 830). The petition, dated 18 March 1674, is transcribed in Boswell, 94. Vokins would later be restored and would continue in the office until the abolition of the Chandry in 1702.

57 WORK5/21, f. 97^v (*Register*, no. 822).

58 Evelyn, *Diary*, 4: 30.

234   *"For such uses as the King shall direct"*

above—as one for *Ariane*. In the case of the payment to the carpenters, the document's language, which mentions "Danceing and Operas," seems to indicate their presence at more than one production, possibly both *Ballet et Musique* in its final stages as well as early (or ongoing) rehearsals for *Ariane*. On the other hand, we have already seen that *Ballet et Musique* is devoid of scenic effects, and thus may not even have required the carpenters' attendance, either for rehearsals or for the performance.[59] With regard to the phrasing's confusing plurality, we should recall that the application of the Italian term *opera* to any French through-sung balletic performance would have been very much a novelty in England in early 1674, and hence "Danceing and Operas" could be a clumsily formulated designation for the preparations surrounding a single work.

This latter consideration is perhaps also applicable to the third reference, from John Evelyn's diary. Scholars have made much of this tantalizingly fleeting notice of a supposed Italian production, despite the absence of corroborating evidence in any contemporary source. Some have seized on the curious English-translation score of Cavalli's *L'Erismena* discussed above, with the result that the score itself has now been assigned, on no good grounds, a tentative date of "c.1674."[60] It is of course possible that, in deference to the Modenese visitors, an actual opera in Italian was put together in London in late 1673 and performed during the Christmas season revelries (albeit only after the abrupt departure of Duchess Laura and Prince Rinaldo on 30 December). The Modenese were themselves probably more familiar and more comfortable with the well-established Italian operatic form than with the new French one, and would later employ the medium to allegorize English political events at the time of the Duke of Monmouth's rebellion against James II and his Modenese consort in 1685.[61] But several of the key figures among the Italian ensemble of the 1660s—Vincenzo Albrici, Sebenico, and Cefalo—had already left the country (the latter two quite recently), and in contrast to the admittedly spotty documentation regarding the French influx, there is no evidence at all that any new Italian operatic performers were stepping ashore in England at the time. Evelyn's diary entry is certainly mysterious, but three considerations may help us to make sense of it, in the absence of real proof that an Italian opera was performed. First, we have already remarked in Chapter 1 on what Arthur Scouten aptly labels "the perils of Evelyn," namely, the often overlooked

---

59 Indeed, if *Ariane*, in which scenic spectacle was a significant element, was simultaneously in rehearsal in the Hall Theatre (hence requiring the presence of the carpenters), this may help to account for *Ballet et Musique*'s purely static *mise en scène*.

60 The English score, we should note, most closely resembles that found in Biblioteca Marciana, Venice, Cod. It. IV.417, which is associated with the original version of *L'Erismena* produced throughout Italy in the 1650s and 1660s, and does not incorporate revisions made by Cavalli and others in 1670 and afterwards: see Harold Powers, "L'Erismena travestita," in Harold Powers, ed., *Studies in Music History: Essays for Oliver Strunk* (Princeton: Princeton University Press, 1968), 259–324.

61 See S[teven] E. Plank, "Monmouth in Italy: *L'Ambitione Debellata*," *The Musical Times* 132 (1991): 280–84.

The Royall Academy of Musick, 1673–75   235

fact that the early years of the diarist's famous *Kalendarium* were actually compiled retrospectively from a mass of notes, and thus often suffer from lapses of recollection and faulty details. Yet even if we ignore the potential for fatal inaccuracy and grant that Evelyn did indeed witness some remarkable theatrical event on 5 January 1674, the phrase "*Italian Opera* in musique" needs to be treated with caution. Evelyn was conversant with the Italian operatic form, having seen a performance of Rovetta and Bisaccioni's *Ercole in Lidia* in Venice in 1645.[62] At the same time, he seems to have felt comfortable deploying the label "Italian" to describe operas of any kind, including a performance of one of Davenant's works that he attended in 1659. For this event (one of the last times a through-composed drama was presented in England prior to 1674), Evelyn qualified his characterization, initially calling the work an "*Italian Opera*," but then altering the entry to "*Opera* after the *Italian* way in *Recitative Music & Sceanes*."[63] In making this change, he inadvertently reveals what, specifically, he considered "Italian" about opera in the first place—a definition encompassing both through-composition and spectacle that we, too, have been applying throughout the present discussion, and which would have been perfectly apposite to the French *Ariane*. Indeed, as a form that was hitherto entirely unknown to Evelyn, this through-composed French entertainment with both machines and significant amounts of dancing, "the first that had ben in *England* of this kind," would reasonably have necessitated the explanatory designation "*Italian Opera*," in which the adjective "Italian" simply functions as part of a compound generic descriptor that not only includes what we would regard as the essential term "opera," but also adds the helpful elucidation "in musique." Of course, there is the problem that neither *Ariane* nor any other French opera is known to have been performed on the date of Evelyn's report. In considering this objection, we should recall that the noted virtuoso and polymath, no doubt like many of his London contemporaries who unfortunately did *not* keep records of their daily activities, seems to have availed himself of access to open rehearsals of several important Restoration court theatrical events. He may have seen a preliminary "performance" of *The Queen's Masque* on or about 9 February 1671,[64] and is known to have attended rehearsals of *Calisto* on at least two occasions in December 1674.[65] Although once in a while Evelyn was present at an actual performance at court (as, for example in the case of *Mustapha* in October 1666, which he attended under some duress[66]), for the most part he was a peripheral figure as regards the elite clientele who populated these grand events, and

---

62 Evelyn, *Diary*, 2: 449–50 (see Chapter 4, n. 8, above).

63 *Ibid.*, 3: 229 (see Chapter 4, n. 9, above). Although Evelyn does not specify which of Davenant's operas he saw on this date, *The History of Sir Francis Drake* is the most likely candidate. Note also how Evelyn, in describing *Calisto* in 1675, refers to it as "a Comedie" on one occasion and as "the *Pastoral*" on another (see Introduction).

64 *Ibid.*, 569–70 (see Chapter 1).

65 *Ibid.*, 4: 49–51 (see Chapter 2).

66 *Ibid.*, 3: 465–66 (see Chapter 4, n. 102, above): "I was invited to see this Tragedie, exceedingly well writ, by my Lord Chamberlain, though in my mind, I did not approve of any such passe time,

236   *"For such uses as the King shall direct"*

seems (somewhat hypocritically) to have used rehearsals to satiate his boundless curiosity while remaining disapprovingly aloof from the panoply and ado of the proceedings themselves. Thus, it is entirely possible that the *"Italian Opera in musique"* Evelyn witnessed at the beginning of January was an early rehearsal of *Ariane*, a work whose novelty would have appealed to the diarist even more than that of an actual Italian production.[67]

The initial planning and rehearsal stages of *Ariane* remain largely a blank to us, although some useful points can be distilled from later documentation. First, the Hall Theatre at Whitehall seems to have been regarded as both an acceptable and indeed a necessary venue for rehearsals prior to the production's move to Drury Lane. We can glean this fact from an order of 27 March 1674, three days before the opera's opening, notifying the Surveyor General, Sir Christopher Wren, of

> His Ma[ts] pleasure that you cause to bee deliuered unto Mons[r] Grabu or to such as he shall appoynt such of the Scenes remayning in the Theatre at Whitehall as shalbe usefull for the french Opera at the Theatre in Bridges street and the said M[r] Grabu is to returne them againe safely after foureteene dayes tyme into the Theatre at Whitehall[.][68]

The Drury Lane Theatre was, of course, still under construction until shortly before this order: the King's Company only inaugurated the new house on Thursday the 26th with a revival of John Fletcher's *The Beggar's Bush*, before quickly making way for the French opera with its transplanted scenery. There is, we should observe, no evidence to support the suggestion put forward by W. J. Lawrence that *Ariane* may have been performed as a finished work at Whitehall before it appeared at Drury Lane.[69] For one thing, the specification of "such of the Scenes remayning in the Theatre at Whitehall as shalbe usefull for the french

---

in a season of such Judgements & Calamitie." See also Evelyn's attendance at several court balls of the 1660s and 1670s, summarized in Table 1.2.

67 W. J. Lawrence goes a step further, proposing in his article "Early French Players in England" (in *idem, The Elizabethan Playhouse and Other Studies* [2 vols.: Stratford-upon-Avon: Shakespeare Head Press, 1912–13; rpt. New York: Russell & Russell, 1963], 1: 125–56, p. 144) that what Evelyn saw was a performance of Shadwell and Locke's *Psyche*—an unlikely supposition, given not only that *Psyche* is manifestly *not* through-composed, but also that its premiere was still more than a year in the future. Dent, applying Lawrence's erroneous reasoning as to the dating of *Psyche* (p. 108), splits the difference, arguing that Evelyn could be referring to either work, since "he evidently means by an 'Italian opera' not an opera in the Italian language, or by an Italian composer, but simply a dramatic performance set to music, or, as the English expression of the day was, 'a vocal representation.'"

68 LC5/140, p. 456 (*Register*, no. 834; Ashbee, 1: 135).

69 W. J. Lawrence, "A Restoration Opera Problem," *The Times Literary Supplement* 1443 (26 September 1929): 737. Lawrence's supposition is refuted by Boswell (pp. 111–12), but returns in Richard Luckett, "Exotick but Rational Entertainments: The English Dramatick Operas," in Marie Axton and Raymond Williams, eds., *English Drama: Forms and Development: Essays in Honour of Muriel Clara Bradbrook* (Cambridge: Cambridge University Press, 1977), 123–41, p. 129.

The Royall Academy of Musick, 1673–75   237

Opera" implies that Grabu had been invited to choose a number of preexisting scenes from stock just at the moment when the production was entering its final preparatory stages. In addition, *Ariane* was an opera, not a court ballet like *Ballet et Musique*, and no full-fledged, fully staged opera is known to have been presented at court during the Restoration period. These considerations, along with the fact that Charles II attended the Drury Lane premiere on Monday, 30 March,[70] all seem to suggest that *Ariane* was designed from the start as a public presentation.

There can be no doubt that the production of *Ariane* was intended to be a major event, whose performances appear to have continued into April, well beyond the original two-week window stipulated in the order for the loan of scenery from Whitehall. Moreover, there is no reason to believe, as has sometimes been asserted, that this ambitious endeavor was a failure, artistically or otherwise.[71] Despite a possible hiatus during Holy Week, which lasted from the 12th to the 19th, performances were still going on after Easter, when the Florentine ambassador Giovanni Salvetti reported that

> their Majesties have spent the greater part of [Easter Week] in devotions, in seeing English comedies or hearing the French operas performed to music. These last are a novelty in this realm and have aroused everyone's curiosity to see them.[72]

Salvetti's consistent use of the plural even seems to imply that *Ariane* was not the only French opera being performed at Drury Lane at this time, possibly confirming Claude-François Ménestrier's otherwise baffling assertion, made only a few years after the event, that other works by Cambert were also presented in London under the composer's aegis.[73] In any case, the arousal of widespread curiosity among the London public, noted by Salvetti, would seem to justify the exceptional length of the French opera or operas' run: with the six days between Palm Sunday and Easter excluded, the production could still have enjoyed as many as fourteen

---

70 LC5/141, p. 73 (*Register*, no. 879).

71 See for example Holman, *Fiddlers*, 298.

72 Report of Friday, 24 April/4 May: British Library, Add. MS 27962 V, f. 245ᵛ (*Register*, no. 836): translation from John Orrell, "A New Witness of the Restoration Stage, 1670–1680," *Theatre Research International* n. s., 2 (1976–77): 86–97, p. 91.

73 Claude-François Ménestrier, S. J., *Des Représentations en Musique Ancienne et Modernes* (Paris: R. Guignard, 1681), 248: "C'est de ce royaume [*i.e.* France] que ces représentations [*i.e.* operas] on passé en Angleterre. Le sieur Cambert, qui les avoit commencées en France, les porta en ce pays-là, et fit voir plusieurs fois la *Pomone, les Peines et les Plaisirs de l'Amour* et quelques autres pièces qu'il avoit fait jouer à Paris quelques années auparavant." The phrase "quelques autres pièces" would, of course, include both *Ariane* and *Ballet et Musique*. Ménestrier's assertion is subsequently cited in Lecerf de La Viéville, *Comparaison de la Musique Italienne, et de la Musique Françoise* (see n. 18, above), 2: 177. Note also W. J. Lawrence's observation in "Early French Players in England" (see n. 67, above), 145, that "[i]f the season lasted a fortnight or three weeks, as the entries in the Lord Chamberlain's Accounts indicate, more than one opera must have been performed."

238 *"For such uses as the King shall direct"*

or fifteen playing days, a substantial quantity for any Restoration show. There is, moreover, reason to believe that an even longer engagement was expected, but that the production had to be cut short prematurely after a brawl on Wednesday, 22 April when, as Salvetti described it, "the leader of the French troupe, who had been made prisoner for debt, was forcibly liberated by his fellows from the hands of the justice, two of whose officers were wounded."[74] Salvetti's further remark that "This is so great a crime in the realm that those from the said troupe who are taken cannot escape the gallows unless they obtain a special pardon from his Majesty under the great seal of England" underscores the obvious impracticability of continuing the opera's performances in the short term, and the King's Company immediately returned to their playhouse with an "English comed[y]," a revival of John Dryden's *Marriage A-la-Mode*, on the 23rd. By the following Monday, the 27th, Thomas Killigrew, now back in charge of the theatre, was ordered to return to Sir Christopher Wren "the scenes belonging to his Ma[ts] Theatre at Whitehall which were formerly deliuered to M[r] Grabu for the ~~seruice~~ use of the ffrench opera in Bridges street,"[75] thus bringing the French operatic experiment at Drury Lane definitively to a close.

The circumstance of the King's Company amidst all this activity is uncertain. There is no evidence that (as has occasionally been suggested or implied) the company's core performers had anything at all to do with the operatic production, although some non-acting staff, such as scenekeepers and musicians, may have been retained for service in the theatre. Thus, upon opening their brand new house with *The Beggar's Bush* on 26 March, the actors appear to have been obliged immediately to decamp again, and were only able to return nearly a month later— seemingly on very short notice—after the opera performers unexpectedly found themselves entangled with the law. Although no evidence for this survives, it is possible that during the enforced hiatus the King's Men may have resumed acting at Lincoln's Inn Fields, where they had been temporarily housed following the fire that destroyed the Bridges Street Theatre in January 1672. In any case, their supplantation by the French opera, however short-lived, was undoubtedly a bitter pill, causing the playwright and company shareholder John Dryden to write a grumpy prologue for the *Beggar's Bush* performance in which he (speaking for the entire company, as ventriloquized by the actor Michael Mohun) bemoaned not only the stiff competition offered by the Duke's players, who were at the time preparing to mount the much anticipated operatic rendition of *The Tempest* in their splendid new theatre at Dorset Garden, but also the impending arrival of the French troupe at Drury Lane:

> 'Twere Folly now a stately Pile to raise,
> To build a Play-House while You throw down Plays.
> Whilst Scenes, Machines, and empty *Opera's* reign,

---

74 British Library, Add. MS 27962 V, f. 245[v], as translated in Orrell, "A New Witness," 91.
75 LC5/140, p. 471 (*Register*, no. 838; Ashbee, 1: 137).

And for the Pencil You the Pen disdain.
While Troops of famisht *Frenchmen* hither drive,
And laugh at those upon whose Alms they live:
...
Well please your selves, but sure 'tis understood,
That *French* Machines have ne'r done *England* good:
I wou'd not prophesie our Houses Fate:
But while vain Shows and Scenes you over-rate,
'Tis to be fear'd—
That as a Fire the former House o'rethrew,
Machines and Tempests will destroy the new.[76]

The double-barrelled salvo against both the extravagant *Tempest* production in preparation at Dorset Garden and the through-composed opera about to commandeer the King's Company's own theatre is made even more explicit in a manuscript version of Dryden's prologue in which the final line's "Machines and Tempests" becomes a more jarring trochee-initiated "Tempests and Operas."[77] In an effort to hit home the hapless company's complaint, Dryden renewed his attack in the epilogue to the same play, criticizing the Duke's Company's alleged dependence on "worn Plays and Fustian Stuff / Of Rhyme" in preference to true wit, posing an alternative in their own offering of high-quality revivals written by "Abler Men" than themselves, and closing with a final jab at the *Ariane* production:

If they shou'd fail, for last recruits we breed
A Troop of frisking Monsieurs to succeed:
(You know the *French* sure cards at time of need.)[78]

This *cri de coeur* encapsulates the dilemma in which the King's Company found itself: having labored for two years to recoup the loss of their ruined playhouse and erect a replacement at considerable expense, they were prevented from occupying it—and hence from competing effectively with their ambitious and better-equipped rivals—by the interposition of a troupe of singing and dancing Frenchmen, whose novelty and court sponsorship threatened a potentially indefinite usurpation.

Indeed, one might wonder why, if Charles II had the power to impose an extravagant court-sponsored operatic production on one of the two newly constructed

---

76 John Dryden, "A Prologue spoken at the Opening of the NEW HOUSE, *Mar.* 26. 1674," in *Miscellany Poems ... By the most Eminent Hands* (London: Jacob Tonson, 1684), 286–89, pp. 288–89.
77 Huntington Library, Ellesmere MS 8923; see Helene Maxwell Hooker, "Dryden's and Shadwell's *Tempest*," *Huntington Library Quarterly* 6 (1942–43): 224–28. Curiously, Hooker makes no mention of the phrase's obvious applicability to *Ariane*, arguing instead (p. 227) that "Whereas the 'Machines and tempests' of the printed versions is suggestive but ambiguous, the manuscript reading, 'Tempests and Operas,' seems clearly a reference to the operatic *Tempest*."
78 Dryden, *Miscellany Poems*, 289–91, p. 291.

240   *"For such uses as the King shall direct"*

theatres, he chose Drury Lane rather than the state-of-the-art Dorset Garden. There is no reason to believe that the monarch's influence over his namesake company differed in any way from that over the players semantically associated with his brother the duke—one might even assume that the well-placed Killigrew (who succeeded to the position of Master of the Revels on 1 May 1673[79]) would have been better positioned than his rivals to dissuade or otherwise prevent the king from arbitrarily undermining a fragile commercial venture in favor of a royal pet project. Although it could be argued that the respective locations of the two playhouses might have been a factor—Drury Lane was situated near Covent Garden, within the large Westminster parish of St. Martin-in-the-Fields (where, as we have seen, at least one of the French dancers, Jean Favier, was resident), while Dorset Garden lay within the boundaries of the City of London, whose authorities were rather less tolerant of court-sponsored Popish spectacles[80]—some other, more compelling consideration must also have been in play.

The answer lies, I believe, in the process through which the King's Company attempted to regain its footing after the devastating 1672 fire by constructing a new permanent theatre to house their operations. The conflagration of 25 January 1672, which destroyed not only the nine-year-old Bridges Street Theatre but also a considerable number of private residences in the neighborhood, was a widely noted catastrophe,[81] and while the players were fortunate in being able within a short time to occupy the recently abandoned playhouse in Lincoln's Inn Fields (originally fitted up in 1661 under Davenant's direction for the Duke's Company,

---

79 See Chapter 5, n. 50, above.
80 See Matthew Sylvester, ed., *Reliquiæ Baxterianæ: or, Mr. Richard Baxters Narrative of the Most Memorable Passages of his Life and Times* (London: T. Parkhurst, J. Robinson, J. Lawrence, and J. Dunton, 1696), pt. 3, 89: "This Year [*i.e.* 1671] a new Play-House being built in *Salisbury-Court* in *Fleet-Street*, called the *Duke of York's*, the Lord Mayor (as is said) desired of the King, that it might not be; the Youth of the City being already so corrupted by Sensual Pleasures; but he obtained not his desire."
81 See Alfred J. Horwood, "The Manuscripts of the Right Honourable the Earl of Mount Edgcumbe, Mount Edgcumbe, co. Cornwall," in *Second Report of the Royal Commission on Historical Manuscripts* (London: Her Majesty's Stationery Office, 1874), 20–24, p. 22 (*Register*, no. 669); British Library, Add. MS 40860, f. 23^v (Diary of Arthur Annesley, 1st Earl of Anglesey: see J. J. Cartwright, "A Manuscript Belonging to Lieutenant-General Lyttelton Annesley," in *Historical Manuscripts Commission, Thirteenth Report, Appendix, Part VI: The Manuscripts of Sir William Fitzherbert, Bart., and Others* [London: Her Majesty's Stationery Office, 1893], 261–78, p. 270); newsletter sent to Sir Richard Bulstrode, 26 January 1672: Harry Ransom Humanities Center, University of Texas at Austin, PFORZ-MS-0609, p. 4 (see [Alphonse Wyatt Thibaudeau], ed., *The Collection of Autograph Letters and Historical Documents Formed by Alfred Morrison (Second Series, 1882–1893): The Bulstrode Papers, Volume I (1667–1675)* [1 vol. only: (London: Strangeways and Sons), 1897], 217); Sylvester, ed., *Reliquiæ Baxterianæ*, pt. 3, 89–90; see also the printed broadside poem *On the Unhappy Conflagration of the Theatre Royal* (*Register*, no. 670). According to the Florentine ambassador Giovanni Salvetti, the fire "would have done much more damage if the presence of the King and the Duke of York had not prevented it, in respect of their keeping good order and commanding the demolition of divers houses to prevent the spread of the flames" (British Library, Add. MS 27962 T, f. 269^r, as translated in Orrell, "A New Witness," 90).

The Royall Academy of Musick, 1673–75   241

who had only recently moved to Dorset Garden), their loss was significant enough to require external support. Plans were rapidly put on foot to rebuild the Bridges Street Theatre newer and better:[82] as early as 9 February the Florentine ambassador could report that materials were being assembled, and that Charles II had pledged £2000 (with another £1500 promised by Barbara Villiers, Duchess of Cleveland).[83] The company's leaders were well aware that Charles had personally (albeit retroactively) contributed £1000 toward the building of Dorset Garden in November 1671, and thus they might reasonably have expected such royal largesse in their own more desperate case.[84] But whether or not the king's gift (of which no other record survives) was indeed paid promptly and in full, the considerable expense would have demanded other extraordinary sources of revenue, as well as sacrifices from every member of the company.[85] As costs mounted, so did the attendant anxieties, and in an undated petition the players were compelled to advise the king that they had "become very much in debt." Lamenting that "they cannot be able to finish their said house and stock themselves with cloathes and Scenes for the acting therein but must of necessity sink under the burthen of soe great a charge unlesse supported by yor Maties most gratious aid and assistance," the company begged that Charles might "be gratiously pleased to order that they be forth with paid the arrears due from yor Matie whereby they may be enabled to sett the Painters at worke."[86] The reference to painters implies that the construction process was by this time fairly well advanced, which would seem to place the petition sometime in 1673. Although the money for "the arrears due"

82 See John Dryden's "*Prologue to Witt without money: being the first Play acted after the Fire*" in *Westminster Drollery, the Second Part / The Last, and now Only, Compleat Collection, of the Newest and Choisest Songs and Poems* (London: William Gilbert and Thomas Sawbridge, 1672), 8–9 and *Covent Garden Drolery* (London: James Magnes, 1672), 11: "*But as our new-built City rises higher, / So from old* Theaters *may new aspire, / Since Fate contrives magnificence by fire.*"

83 British Library, Add. MS 27962 T, f. 277$^{r–v}$, as translated in Orrell, "A New Witness," 90 (*Register*, no. 673).

84 Newsletter from John Starkey to Sir Willoughby Aston, Bart., 18 November 1671: British Library, Add. MS 36916, f. 233^r (*Register*, no. 657).

85 A series of plays acted solely by the women of the company in or around June suggests that the males may have been pressed into service in the demolition and/or reconstruction effort. Wealthier members of the company advanced money for the building of the scenehouse, which was paid off gradually in subsequent years: see in particular the agreement with Nicholas Burt, dated 20 March 1674 (Houghton Library, Harvard University, ppfMS Thr 389 (2); transcribed in J. Payne Collier, "Dryden, Killigrew, and the First Company which Acted at Drury Lane Theatre," *The Shakespeare Society's Papers* 4 [1849]: 147–55 [see *Register*, nos. 735 and 831]), and the other agreements of the same date referenced in C6/221/48 (see *Register*, nos. 831 and 992). Thomas Killigrew took out a series of disastrous loans on the security of his patent, a move that tied the company up in legal proceedings for years afterwards: see Judith Milhous and Robert D. Hume, "Charles Killigrew's 'Abstract of Title to the Playhouse'[:] British Library Add. MS 20,726, Fols. 1–14," *Theatre History Studies* 6 (1986): 56–71, and *Register*, nos. 786, 788, 817, 951, 966, 967, 1126, 1161, 1219, and 1240.

86 SP29/183/72 (mistakenly filed with papers of 1666: see *Calendar of State Papers, Domestic 1666–67*: 383, and *Register*, no. 803); the document is printed and discussed in W. J. Lawrence, "The Players' Petition to Charles II," *The Athenæum* 3938 (18 April 1903): 508.

242   *"For such uses as the King shall direct"*

from the king for his attendance at plays would not actually be forthcoming until much later,[87] Charles may have helped his actors in other ways: sometime late in 1672 a "king's brief" was issued, soliciting donations from around the country to assist in the rebuilding of the playhouse and its devastated neighborhood, the full loss of which was listed as £11,488 2s 6d.[88] As a result of this brief, which would have been circulated by the central religious authorities and announced by parish clergy to their congregations during Sunday services, small sums of money were collected in parish churches throughout late 1672 and much of 1673: Table 6.1 provides an undoubtedly incomplete list of parishes where collections are known to have been taken.[89] Although it has previously been observed by some scholars that the wording of the entries in several parish registers seems to assign the funds to the reconstruction of adjoining residences rather than the playhouse itself,[90] other entries clearly label the money as having been collected "for the Theater Royal," and thus would seem to evince a specific obligation handed down from the highest levels, almost certainly at the king's instigation.[91]

Obviously, it was in Charles's interest to help the company get back on its feet, but his assistance may have come at a price. If the monarch's own money and influence were being expended to erect the new theatre, it would stand to reason that he might leverage these contributions to secure temporary use of the facility for the court-sponsored French troupe, perhaps with an eye to an ongoing sharing

---

87 A note in the Treasury Minutes for 3 October 1673 records that the company was "to have a Warrant drawne for £650 due to them from his Majesty" (British Library, Add. MS 28077 [properly "T29/ [4a]"], p. 33 [*Calendar of Treasury Books* 4: 198; *Register*, no. 806]), but it was not until 30 April 1674 that a series of eight warrants was issued for a total of £1930, ostensibly for plays seen by the king from 12 December 1666 to 9 June 1673 (LC5/140, pp. 473–74 [*Register*, no. 839]), and these arrears were not actually paid off in full until 1676 or 1677 (AO1/400/103; see Boswell, 296–97 for a comprehensive listing of the relevant documents).

88 Wyndham Anstis Bewes, *Church Briefs: or Royal Warrants for Collections for Charitable Objects* (London: Adam and Charles Black, 1896), 284.

89 The dating of several of these is uncertain, although consultation of the original documents might yield further information. In two instances, Table 6.1 suggests revised dates for entries (Holy Trinity, Exeter [Devon] and Caversham, Oxfordshire [in Berkshire since 1911]) that would otherwise be inexplicable outliers from the chronological cluster of entries that falls primarily between November 1672 and August 1673: see Table 6.1, notes c and f for explanations.

90 See for example T. N. Brushfield, "Church Brief for a London Theatre," *Notes and Queries* 94 (8th ser., no. 10, 1896): 299; Orrell, "A New Witness," 91; note to *Register*, no. 789 (p. 153).

91 As evidence of the unusual nature of this request, we can consider the somewhat shocked reaction of nineteenth-century commentators to the notion that post-worship announcements might be devoted to soliciting money to rebuild a theatre: see George Miles Cooper, "Berwick Parochial Records," *Sussex Archaeological Collections* 6 (1853): 223–43, p. 242 ("it would now be thought a strange proceeding to raise money by church-brief for the rebuilding of a playhouse"), and John Southerden Burn, *Registrum Ecclesiae Parochialis, The History of Parish Registers in England* (London: Edward Suter, 1829), 143 n. 1 ("a *modern* congregation would be astounded to hear the clergyman read, at the close of the morning prayers, a brief for the rebuilding the Opera-House, or Drury Lane Theatre").

Table 6.1 Church collections on king's brief for the Theatre Royal and neighboring properties, 1672–74

Date	Location		Amount	Stated Purpose	Reference
16 November 1672	Wem, Salop		18s 3d	"for 38 of the inhabitants of Russell Street in the County of Middlesex in St. Martin's of ye field wch fire begain in ye house called ye theater Rial"	*N&Q* 94: 299
1 December 1672	St. Margaret's, Westminster	*	£20 9s 2d	"Towards the Great Loss by ffyer near Russell street in the parish of St. Martins in the ffeilds in ye County of Middlesex"	*N&Q* 94: 299[g]
22 February 1673	Torpenhow, Cumberland	*	2s 5d	"For the inhabitants of Russell Street, Westminster"[f]	*TCWAAS* 3: 39
17 March [?1673[a]]	Holy Trinity, Exeter		13s 3d	"for houses burnt in St. Martyn in ye fields"	*N&Q* 94: 299
6 April 1673	Maresfield, Sussex	*	1s 6d	"for the Inhabitants of Russell Street, St. Martin's Lane, Middlesex"	*SAC* 21: 215
27 April 1673	Symondsbury, Dorset		2s 0d	"for the Theater Royal in London being burnt"[h]	*N&Q* 94: 58[h]
27 April 1673	Wellow, Wilts/Hants[d]	*	2s 2¼d	"for ye Inhabitants of Russell Streete in ye p^{ish} of St Martins in Middlesex"	*Wellow*, 247
4 May 1673	Stretford, Lancs		2s 2d	"for a voyalant Fire in the theatree royall in the parrish of Martin in the fileds in the Covnty of Middle sexe"	*N&Q* 51: 385
11 May 1673	Langley Burrell, Wilts		2s 7d	"for releife, &c., in Russell Street in S. Martin's in the fields"	*WANHM* 36: 454
18 May 1673	Chapel-en-le-Frith, Derbys	*	3s 8d	"for Royal Theatre, nr. Brussel Street, St. Martin-in-the-Field, London"	*N&Q* 94: 7
25 May [?1673[b]]	Caversham, Oxon		6s 0d	"Towards the Losse by Fire at the Theatre Royall in London"	*Register*, no. 690
28 May 1673	St. Nicholas's, Durham	*	14s 6d	"Upon a Brefe that came from London"	*Pittington*, 233
27 July 1673	Purley, Berks		1s 5d	"for ye fire neare ye Theatre Royall in St Martins in ye fields"	*Register*, no. 789
24 August 1673	Clent, Staffs/Worcs[e]	*	4s 9d	"for a fire in [Russel Streete] in ye Parish of S. Martyn in ye ffields in ye cou'ty of Middlesex"	*N&Q* 52: 448
19 October 1673	Ruscombe, Berks		2d	"for the Theator Royall"	*BBOAJ* 19: 24
4 January 1674	Cranbrook, Kent	*	4s 1d	"For losses occasioned by a fire which began at the house called the Theatre Royal, near Russell Street, in the parish of St. Martin's in the field, London"	*AC* 14: 209[i]
1672 or 1673 (*undated*)	Preshute, Wilts		3s 6d	"for the Theatre Royal"	*WANHM* 30: 115

(*Continued*)

1673 (*undated*)	Berwick, Sussex	*	2s 0d	"for the Theater Royall in London"	*SAC* 6: 242
1673 (*undated*)[c]	Holbeach, Lincs		12s 1d	"for the Theater Royall and the residue of the property that was burnt at the same time in London"	*N&Q* 94: 299
1673 (*undated*)	Loughborough, Leics	*	?	"for rebuilding the Theatre Royal in London"	*N&Q* 94: 7[j]

Key:
* = catalogued in Wyndham Anstis Bewes, *Church Briefs: or Royal Warrants for Collections for Charitable Objects* (London: Adam and Charles Black, 1896), 284

Key to references:
AC: W. Tarbutt, "Briefs in the Parish of Cranbrook," *Archæologia Cantiana: Being Transactions of the Kent Archæological Society* 14 (1882): 206–22.

BBOAJ: Anon., "A List of Briefs in the Parish Register Book of Ruscombe, and in the Book of Churchwardens' Accounts," *Berks, Bucks, and Oxon Archæological Journal* n. s. 19 (1913–14): 24–26.

N&Q:
- John E. Bailey, "Church Collections in the Seventeenth Century," *Notes and Queries* 51 (5th ser., no. 3, 1875): 385.
- "Vigorn," "Collections upon Briefs, 1672–1705," *Notes and Queries* 52 (5th ser., no. 4, 1875): 447–49; see also Cornelius Walford, "Kings' Briefs: Their Purposes and History," *Transactions of the Royal Historical Society* 10 (1882): 1–74, Appendix 1 (pp. 61ff.).
- T. N. Brushfield, "Church Brief for a London Theatre," *Notes and Queries* 94 (8th ser., no. 10, 1896): 7.
- W. F. Prideaux, "Church Brief for a London Theatre," *Notes and Queries* 94 (8th ser., no. 10, 1896): 58.
- T. N. Brushfield, "Church Brief for a London Theatre," *Notes and Queries* 94 (8th ser., no. 10, 1896): 299.

Pittington: James Barmby, ed., *Churchwardens' Accounts of Pittington and Other Parishes in the Diocese of Durham* (Surtees Society, no. 84; Durham: Andrews & Co., 1888).

Register: Judith Milhous and Robert D. Hume, comps. and eds., *A Register of English Theatrical Documents 1660–1737* (2 vols.: Carbondale: Southern Illinois University Press, 1991), citing documents in Berkshire Record Office, D/P 93/1/1 (Purley) and 162/1/1 (Caversham).

SAC:
- George Miles Cooper, "Berwick Parochial Records," *Sussex Archaeological Collections* 6 (1853): 223–43.
- Edward Turner, "Briefs," *Sussex Archaeological Collections* 21 (1869): 207–17.

TCWAAS: C. H. Gem, "Torpenhow Church," *Transactions of the Cumberland and Westmorland Antiquarian & Archæological Society* 3 (1876–77): 34–42.

WANHM:
- E. Ll. Gwillim, "Notes from the Register Books of the Parish of Preshute during the 17th Century," *The Wiltshire Archæological and Natural History Magazine* 30 (1898–99): 100–16.
- A. B. Mynors, "A List of Briefs from the Register Books of Langley Burrell," *The Wiltshire Archæological and Natural History Magazine* 36 (1910): 448–63.

Wellow: Charles W. Empson, *Index to the Registers of Baptisms, Marriages, & Burials of the Parish of Wellow, in the Counties of Southampton and Wiltshire* (London: Eyre and Spottiswoode, 1889).

---

[a] N&Q cites year as "1673/4"; original MS not seen.

[b] *Register* suggests year as 1672: "This item is the last in a list of six charitable collections, the others all definitely dated 1672."

[c] "delivered in at the Visitation 1673."

[d] Parish straddled county boundary until 1895.

[e] Exclave of Staffordshire (until 1844), but within Diocese of Worcester.

[f] Note also collection "for one John Smith of the same place," 15 December 1672 (2*s* 7*d*).

[g] See also John Edward Smith, *Bygone Briefs: An Essay to Which are Appended Copies of Some of the Documents Referred To, and a Schedule of More than a Thousand Briefs Laid in the Parish of St. Margaret, Westminster, Between the Years 1644 and 1793* (London: Wightman & Co., 1896), 74.

[h] See transcription in Folger Shakespeare Library, MS Y.d.23 (185v) and British Library, General Reference Collection 11826.r/s (R[ichard] J[ohn] Smith, "A collection of material towards an history of the English Stage"), 169.

[i] See also G. E. Hubbard, *The Old Book of Wye: Being a Record of a Kentish Country Parish from the Time of Henry the Eighth to that of Charles the Second* (Derby: Pilgrim Press, 1951), 136.

[j] See also John Southerden Burn, *Registrum Ecclesiae Parochialis, The History of Parish Registers in England* (London: Edward Suter, 1829), 143.

246 *"For such uses as the King shall direct"*

arrangement,[92] or until a proper opera house (which Drury Lane manifestly was not) could be constructed. Caught in a Faustian bargain, the King's Company would have had little choice but to comply. As compensation, Charles seems to have become a regular patron of Drury Lane, attending the inaugural presentation of *The Beggar's Bush* on 26 March (where he would have heard Dryden's bitter prologue and epilogue), the short-notice performance of *Marriage A-la-Mode* on 23 April immediately after the debacle that put a stop to the opera, and three more productions in May—not to mention the 30 March opening of *Ariane* itself, for which, curiously, it was the King's Company who were paid the customary £10 fee.[93] By contrast, the king attended no performances at Dorset Garden between 18 March (at which point Drury Lane had not yet opened) and the beginning of November, even waiting until the middle of the latter month to view the Duke's Company's spectacular new rendition of *The Tempest*, despite that production having premiered months earlier, at the end of April.[94] Thus, the king's players appear to have received at least some favorable treatment in exchange for having to endure temporary dispossession by the French opera.[95]

With regard to the opera itself, it is clear not only that the production was meant to be extravagant, but also that a good deal of care was taken to emphasize that fact. The ample preparations already outlined bespeak the visual and technical splendor of the production, which included, besides six different scenic vistas (one for each act, plus a separate one for the Prologue), a moving nautical chariot consisting of *"a Great Shel as it were of Mother of Pearl"* and pulled by airborne zephyrs, which was probably used twice over the course of the Prologue;[96] a pair of flying chariots in 1.vi;[97] three, or perhaps four, flying effects in various

---

92 The sharing of theatres by more than one company was a well-established practice in Paris, where Molière's *Troupe du Roy* and Fiorilli's *Comédie-Italienne* shared the Petit-Bourbon, Palais-Royal, and Guénégaud Theatres between 1658 and 1680. This arrangement, we should note, ended in acrimony in 1679–80: see Jan Clarke, *The Guénégaud Theatre in Paris (1673–1680), Volume 3: The Demise of the Machine Play* (Lewiston, NY: Edwin Mellen Press, 2007), 188–201. We might also consider Thomas Killigrew's plan, as reported by Samuel Pepys in February 1667, "to have some times of the year [Italian] Operas to be performed at the two present Theatres" (see pp. 212–13, above).

93 LC5/141, p. 73 (*Register*, no. 879); inexplicably, Charles was not charged double for an operatic performance, as was the case with the later productions of the Duke's and United Companies. The May productions at Drury Lane were James Shirley's *The Changes* (the 11th), John Dryden's *The Indian Emperor* (the 12th), and the premiere of Nathaniel Lee's *The Tragedy of Nero* (the 16th).

94 LC5/141, p. 216 (*Register*, no. 924), recording that Charles saw *The Tempest* three times in November (the 17th, 18th, and 28th), paying the double price of £20 in each instance.

95 On the other hand, it was the Duke's Company who were summoned to attend the king at Windsor in the summer of 1674, where they were paid £74 for an unknown number of performances: see C8/299/134 (*Register*, no. 999) and the report of the Florentine ambassador Salvetti in British Library, Add. MS 27962 V, f. 278ᵛ (*Register*, no. 856; see Orrell, "A New Witness," 92–93).

96 *Ariadne* (see n. 104, below), sigs. B1ᵛ (carrying the three nymphs Thames, Seine, and Tiber) and B3ʳ (where the nymph Po *"appears born as the former"*). The zephyrs are only mentioned in the French version: "ces *Nimphes* portées sur une Conque de Nacre, & tirées par des *Zephirs* volans, abbordent sur le Rivage, & chantent le *Prologue*" (*Ariane*, sig. A4ᵛ).

97 "*Whilst they are singing,* Mars *appears in the Clouds riding on a Chariot, speaking to* Bellona *who rides on another*" (p. 8).

The Royall Academy of Musick, 1673–75 247

places, each involving as many as three characters (at least one of these effects also deployed a trap door);[98] "*A huge Sea-Monster*" in the second *intermède* who "*vomits out of his Jawes several Sea-gods, and plunges into the Sea*";[99] and an impressive descending and ascending palace with an elaborate throne and special lighting effects for the final apotheosis scene.[100] Such a display must have taxed the new Drury Lane Theatre to its technological limits, and was likely impossible to rehearse properly in the less well equipped Hall Theatre.[101] It may be noteworthy that as early as September 1673 the Lord Chamberlain ordered "John Guipponi Groome of the Chamber in ord[inary] wth out ffee in quality of machenist to attend the Theatre Royall."[102] Guipponi had been appointed machinist at the lavishly outfitted Dorset Garden Theatre in April 1671, seven months before that venue had opened for performances.[103] Now, on orders from the court, he appears to have been transferred to Drury Lane in order to help get that theatre up and running, both as regards its general functioning and with respect to the elaborate opera that may or may not already have been anticipated at that point.

Ariane's extravagance was further trumpeted in the two programme libretti available for sale at the performances, both of which were produced by the king's printer Thomas Newcombe (who had also printed the *Ballet et Musique* libretto for Bremond).[104] One of the libretti provides Perrin's original sung text, while the other offers a translation made, according to a prefatory address "To the Reader,"

---

98 1.vii (p. 9): "*Three Furies breaking forth from beneath, flee up into the Aire to meet* Mars *and* Bellona, *upon which they all come down*"; 2.vii (p. 21): "*The Fury with her burning Torch in her hand flies up into the Aire, with Dragons following her*"; and 3.v (p. 29): "*Apollo and Diana fly down from one side, and Hercules from the other side of the Theatre to meet Mars and Bellona.*" See also 3.iii (p. 26): "*Little Cupids fluttering about* Bacchus, *do charm him with chaines of Flowers.*"

99 P. 22.

100 5.vii (pp. 49–50, 52): "*A glittering Palace comes down from Heaven, on the middle of which is seen a Royal Throne; over the Throne hangs a Crown made of seven Precious Stones, the Crown suspended by four little* Cupids *flying.* Venus *with the three Graces sits on the Throne with Bands of Symphonists about her. During the Symphony, the Palace and Throne descend slowly upon the Theatre*"; "*The seven Gems which compos'd her Crown, are inflam'd of a sudden, and chang'd into so many bright Stars, known in Heaven by the name of* Ariadnes *Hair*"; as the opera concludes, "*Clowns dance to the sound of voices and Instruments all the while the Palace is drawing up.*" In the 4th *intermède* there is a minor machine effect in which "*a small Cloud comes down from above that steals* [the Satyrs'] *Bottle up into Heaven*" (p. 42).

101 Boswell (p. 111) remarks that the Hall Theatre could never have accommodated the flying palace in the opera's final scene.

102 See LC3/27, p. 98, entry dated 27 September (see *Register*, no. 628, where the full implications of this entry are not made clear).

103 LC3/26, p. 210, entry dated 10 April (*Register*, no. 155 [see also no. 201]).

104 *Ariane, Ou Le Mariage de Bacchus Opera: Compose Par le Sieur P. P. Et Mis en Musique par le Sieur Grabut, Maitre de la Musique Du Roi. Represente par L'Academie Roiale de Musique, Au Theatre-Roial* ("Londres": par Thomas Nieucomb, 1673[/]4) and *Ariadne, Or, The Marriage of Bacchus An Opera, Or A Vocal Representation First Compos'd by Monsieur P. P. Now put into Musick by Monsieur Grabut, Master of His Majesties Musick. And Acted by the Royall Academy Of Musick, At the Theatre-Royal in Covent-Garden* (London: by Tho[mas] Newcombe, 1673[/]4). The dual date "1673/4" on both title pages clearly indicates that they were printed

248   *"For such uses as the King shall direct"*

for the satisfaction of those, who being unacquainted with the *French* Tongue, and who being Spectators, would find themselves necessitated to see the most pressing of their *Senses* go away from the *Theater* ungratified, by their not understanding the Subject that brought them thither.[105]

In fact, this *"Traduction"* can best be described as a loose verse paraphrase of the original—one that, indeed, demanded considerable poetic effort on the part of the translator.

In addition, both versions of the libretto feature an elegant fold-out frontispiece (possibly a visual response to the lavish *Empress of Morocco* playbook of 1673) in which is purportedly offered a view of the theatre with a scene from the opera's prologue in progress (see Figure 6.1). This engraved print, which raises a number of questions about the nature of the performance, depicts the allegorical characters Thames, Seine, and Tiber gesturing and singing together while a quintet of zephyrs cavort in mid-air and sprinkle some sort of powder over a large seashell-chariot drawn by a pair of dolphins, astride which two other zephyrs or cupids ride. In the background is a prospect of the Thames, with a small covered barge and another barely discernable boat with five occupants being rowed in front of a panoramic vista of London Bridge situated beneath a cloud-filled sky. The sides of the acting space are delineated by a pair of regular architectural façades or screens of a strongly Palladian character. Each is two stories high and consists of five or possibly six bays; atop their cornices are ranged Classical statues positioned at regular intervals, each situated above one of the structure's two-stage pilasters. Although these façades are depicted as single, solid masses, it is almost certain that they would have consisted of a sequence of moveable side-wings—probably perspective flats—since the opera features five additional scenic vistas in the subsequent acts. The stage is framed by a frontispiece of austerely classical form, consisting of two pairs of fluted Corinthian piers supporting a solid recessed entablature ornately adorned with repeating decorative motifs, but lacking figurative elements, apart from a pair of crossed palms surmounted by crowns on the frieze above each pier. By contrast, the stage front and the plinth-like panels supporting the proscenium arch are decorated with paintings or carvings showing theatrical masks, musical instruments, sheets of paper or fabric, and backgrounds of delicate foliage. The stage projects only slightly, in a shallow oval curve, beyond the plane of the arch, and there appear to be no proscenium entrance doors or balconies like those seen in the William Dolle engravings of Dorset Garden published with *The Empress of Morocco* the previous year.

---

before the old-style "new year" began on 25 March, and hence before the production opened on the 30th. It is also noteworthy that the front matter of each libretto flows continuously into the numbered pages of the main text (in the French version, p. 1 is on sig. B3^r; in the English version, it is on sig. B4^r), rather than being confined to signature A, as was normally the case with playbooks, whose front matter was printed last, after the main text had been produced and the production had concluded. A notation on the title page of the Bodleian Library's copy of the English version of the libretto indicates that it was purchased for 5*d*.

105 *Ariadne*, sig. A4^r.

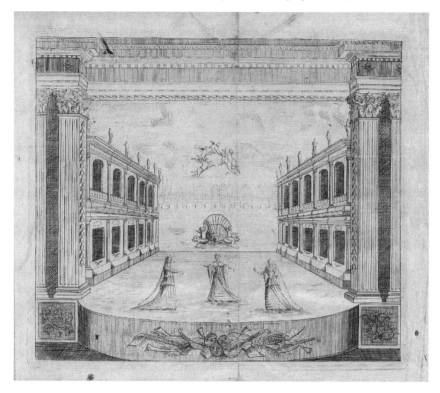

Figure 6.1 Anonymous engraved fold-out frontispiece from the *Ariane/Ariadne* programme libretti, showing a scene from the Prologue with Thames, Tiber, and Seine singing (Houghton Library, Harvard University [38576.42])

It is unclear what actual stage is being shown in this image: the title pages of both libretti clearly mention the location of the production as (in the words of the English version) "the *THEATRE-ROYAL* in *Covent-Garden*," and we might therefore expect the brand-new Drury Lane venue to be featured in the depiction. Indeed, scholars have noted similarities between the *Ariane* engraving and a drawing by Sir Christopher Wren of a longitudinal section of a theatre, thought by some to represent a plan for the rebuilt Drury Lane:[106] both images show heavy Corinthian pilasters and a semi-oval stage front. On the other hand, the Wren plan clearly depicts elements that are not found in the *Ariane* view, including a large apron stage flanked by pairs of proscenium entrance doors, plinths at stage level supporting the pilasters, and a different design for the entablature in which the corona is embellished with prominent block modillions. One explanation, of course, is that, with the opera in rehearsals at Whitehall and with Drury Lane still under construction, the artist was compelled to engage in an act of imagination,

---

106 All Souls College, Oxford, Wren Collection, 2: 81. See the brief discussion in Boswell, 111–12.

250 *"For such uses as the King shall direct"*

attempting to show the production on the Drury Lane stage before the theatre itself had been completely built. The engraving, we should note, is almost certainly not a depiction of the Hall Theatre at Whitehall (whose carved figure of Fame surmounting the proscenium arch had been newly refurbished by Robert Streeter for *The Queen's Masque* in 1671[107]), and thus Drury Lane is the most likely candidate; yet without any definitive view or plan of that theatre against which to compare this unique image, it is impossible to ascertain precisely what the engraving is intended to represent.

This is by no means the only puzzle posed by the *Ariane* production and its surviving documentation. Questions also remain about the personnel who presented the opera and the administrative and organizational structure under which such performances were able to take place. Both of the printed libretti sold to audience members at Drury Lane in March 1674 unequivocally describe the collective body of musicians and dancers involved in the opera as a distinct theatrical company called the "Royall Academy of Musick."[108] This institution, so prominently identified both on the libretti's two title pages and as the corporate author of their fulsome dedications to the king,[109] appears in no other contemporary document, and hence remains one of the most intractable mysteries associated with Charles II's efforts to establish French-style opera in England in the mid-1670s. There can be little doubt that the aim of the Royall Academy was to advance Charles's political agenda by mounting spectacular through-composed musical-theatrical entertainments modeled on those recently introduced at the court of Louis XIV. As with the grand pastoral inventions of Perrin, Cambert, and their associates in Paris, and especially the magnificent *tragédies en musique* of Lully and Quinault, the principal goal of *Ariane* and its possible successor entertainments at Drury Lane was to celebrate the power and majesty of the king through words, music, dance, and lavish spectacle while flaunting the intellectual, creative, and financial resources at the crown's disposal. The propagandistic value of these stunning performances would of course be enhanced by the fact that (again in keeping with Parisian practice) they were offered up to the general public through performances at London's newest public theatre. The encomiastic language and tone commonly associated with French opera is most evident in *Ariane*'s prologue, where Charles is extolled by the nymph Tyber as a "Monarch ever Great and Good," who

> By Wholsom, Just, and gentle Laws,
> In calm his Restor'd Empire awes;
> Whilst his Dreadful Navies, controul

---

107 See Chapter 1, n. 129.

108 See the respective title pages of *Ariadne* and *Ariane*: "ACTED by the Royall Academy OF MUSICK"/"REPRESENTE PAR L'ACADEMIE ROIALE DE MUSIQUE." Throughout this book, I use the spelling "Royall Academy of Musick" (without quotation marks) in order to differentiate this institution from the much more well-known Royal Academy of Music established in London in 1719.

109 See *Ariadne*, sig. A3ᵛ and *Ariane*, sig. A3ʳ: "*Your Royal Academy of Musick*"/"*Votre Accademie de Musique.*"

The Royall Academy of Musick, 1673–75   251

And rule both Seas, from Pole to Pole;
Making Commerce and Arts flourish at home,
As in my *Cæsars*-times they did in *Rome*.[110]

At the same time, the printed dedication mixes adulatory rhetoric with a more functional discussion of the rationale for and aspirations of the king's newly created opera company. Following a description of Charles's achievement in bringing peace to his nation through the recent conclusion of the Third Anglo-Dutch Naval War, the dedication proceeds:

> *But, SIR, all these high Prerogatives; all these choice Blisses She* [*i.e.* England] *does injoy, seem'd little in Your Royal Eyes: Your Vast Mind was not yet fully satisfied, in having by Your Invincible Force made her Triumph over her Fierce and Audacious Enemies, bringing them (in spight of their Obstinacy) to Beg Peace at Your Royal Hands, and by that happy Peace, fild the hearts of Your People with Joy and Satisfaction: You would compleat the Splendor and Magnificence of Your Imperial Seat, by establishing within her stately VValls Your* Academy *of* Opera's, *the fairest and most charming of all Publick Showes; You have made this Queen of Cities to become also the Center, the Source of Love, Pleasures, and Gallantry; raising her present Glory and Pomp to a Pitch, capable rather of creating Envy and Emulation in the Proudest of her* Neighbours, *than being any more jealous of them for their Greatness and Magnificence.*[111]

One of the most striking aspects of this dedicatory epistle is the categorical implication that *Ariane* is merely the inaugural production of what is anticipated to become a permanent fixture in the London theatrical world. Although the author is quick to concede that "*Your Majesty will doubtless find these* First Representations *of Your Opera very defective,*" Charles is urged to

> *pardon its faults, and consider that the* Academy *that executes the same is yet an Infant, a new-born Beauty, whose* Features *and* Lineaments *are scarce come to their shape and proportion; but, cannot fail growing to*

---

110 *Ariadne*, sig. B2ʳ. Compare the original French text (*Ariane*, sig. B1ʳ): "*le plus sage des Rois,* / *Fait observer jcy la Justice & les Lois*[;] / *Sans troubler ton Repos, met la Terre en allarmes,* / *Porte sur les deux Mers la Terreur de ses Armes;* / *Fait Triompher le Commerce & les Arts,* / *Et ramêne en ces Lieux l'heureux tems des Cesars.*"

111 *Ariadne*, sig. A2ᵛ–A3ʳ. The last phrase, with its rather confusing syntax, represents a somewhat misplaced attempt to embellish the French version (*Ariane*, sig. A2ᵛ): "vous accomplissez l'ouurage de sa grandeur; vous la comblez d'honneur & de joie, & la mettéz en estat de ne rien envier deformais à ses voysins les plus galans, de plaisant & de magnifique." The English paragraph quoted here is the portion of the dedication that is least faithful to its French analogue, being considerably longer and more complex than the original in its encomiastic diction.

252   *"For such uses as the King shall direct"*

> *Perfection in her due time and age, provided You daign own her for Your Creature, and afford her Your Royal Care and Protection*[.][112]

If such indulgence is forthcoming, the dedication promises, the new Academy may in time *"contribute to Your Diversion, and ... gather together Your Palms, Your Laurels, and Your Royal Mirtles, into VVreaths and Garlands of Triumph to Crown Your Sacred Head."*[113]

This exuberant rhetoric bespeaks plans on a grand scale for an established opera company in England, formed (like its consecutive French counterparts, Perrin's *Académie Royale des Opéra* of 1669 and Lully's *Académie Royale de Musique* of 1672) with a considerable degree of royal approbation and material support. In theory, the Royall Academy could trace its roots back to the exclusive license granted by Charles II to Giulio Gentileschi in 1660, whose rights seem to have passed to Thomas Killigrew in the mid-1660s and may have been extracted from that impresario as part of the arrangements for funding the rebuilding at Drury Lane. But while the court had provided some limited backing to Killigrew's earlier efforts to establish an opera company in London, its involvement seems to have gone much farther in 1673–74. Ample evidence of this can be seen in the wide range of factors we have already discussed: the importation of French singers, dancers, and instrumentalists; the employment of the Hall Theatre for rehearsals and the officially sanctioned loan of "such ... Scenes ... as shalbe usefull for the french Opera";[114] the appropriation of the Drury Lane Theatre and the displacement of its rightful occupants for the space of four weeks; the production of the two extravagant programme libretti by the king's printer; the allowance of the appellation "Royall" and of the effusive dedication to Charles; and even such seemingly peripheral actions as the transfer of John Guipponi from Dorset Garden to Drury Lane in September 1673, the provision of new costumes for the royal violinists in February or March 1674 (see n. 119, below), and the release of Sébastien Bremond from prison in early March of that year.

Perhaps most significant is the apparent centrality of Louis Grabu to the whole enterprise. Grabu's role in the *Ariane* production has been especially perplexing to scholars: we might well suppose that Robert Cambert had a hand in the creation of the Royall Academy, given his solid credentials in that field. Yet Cambert's name actually appears nowhere in the court records in late 1673 or early 1674; rather, it is Grabu who consistently surfaces in the few documents that shed light on the opera company's activities—for example, the order of 27 March to the Office of Works that the Whitehall scenery "bee deliuered unto Mons[r] Grabu or to such as he shall appoynt." Grabu was at this time still Master of the Music—seemingly clinging to his post in defiance of the dictates of the Test Act, although his tenure would not endure much longer—and his administrative role in the royal musical

---

112 *Ariadne*, sig. A3[r].
113 *Ariadne*, sig. A3[r–v].
114 LC5/140, p. 456 (see n. 68, above).

establishment must have carried over to the new opera company in some significant way. Indeed, as I have speculated elsewhere, "il maestro di questa Truppa francese," whose forcible liberation brought about the abrupt cessation of the operatic season at Drury Lane on 22 April, was quite possibly none other than Grabu himself, whose substantial debt of over £430 to the London mercer Walter Lapp may have arisen from a personal outlay on the musician's part for costumes for *Ariane*.[115] Grabu would have been ideally situated to be the leader of the Royall Academy, given his French training and his intimate knowledge of the workings of Charles II's musical establishment: if the English king genuinely wished to have an operatic company in London whose chief purpose would be, like its sister institution in France, "*to contribute to Your Diversion, and [to] gather together Your Palms, Your Laurels, ...*" and so on—*i.e.*, to serve as an instrument of propaganda for royal policy, and hence an unofficial cultural arm of the court—Grabu, working in tandem with the opera specialist Cambert, was certainly in a position to deliver.

The nature of the partnership between Grabu and Cambert, however, remains perplexing in one important respect: on the title pages of the two programme libretti for *Ariane*, the opera is confusingly described as having been "*First Compos'd by Monsieur* P. P. Now put into MUSICK by Monsieur *Grabut*, Master of His Majesties *MUSICK*."[116] This odd claim, whose perfunctory mention of Perrin and complete exclusion of Cambert has the effect of elevating Grabu to the role of prime creative mover, is puzzling, given what we know of the circumstances. Much of the opera's music had been written by Cambert before his coming to England: some for the original and considerably shorter pastoral version of 1659, and (it is generally believed) the remainder in about 1671–72 when, as Christina Bashford has shown, Perrin himself penned most of the revisions and additions to the text, apart from the new prologue, that would show up in London two years later. The possibility remains that Cambert did not have time to finish setting the new portions of *Ariane* prior to Louis XIV's closing of the *Académie Royale des Opéra* on 1 April 1672, and simply handed the task off to Grabu in England a year and a half later, while he himself turned his attention to composing Bremond's *Ballet et Musique* libretto. Such an arrangement would perhaps justify the claim advanced on the *Ariane/Ariadne* title pages; otherwise, it is difficult to understand why Cambert, who was present and active in musical circles at the Restoration court at the time of *Ariane*'s performance, and must surely have been involved in the production in some way, would have allowed Grabu—who may even have been a former student of his—to take full credit for the opera's composition.[117]

---

115 Walkling, "Ups and Downs."

116 Compare the French version: "COMPOSE PAR LE SIEUR *P. P.* ET Mis en *Musique* par le Sieur *Grabut*, Maitre de la MUSIQUE DU ROI."

117 Bashford (p. 22) concludes that "the score performed at Drury Lane in 1674 is likely to have been a hybrid, in which music by Cambert was sung and played alongside music by Grabu." Prior to Bashford's discovery, some had reasoned (erroneously, as it turns out) that since the words found in the London version of the opera but not in Perrin's 1659 pastoral were created in England,

254   *"For such uses as the King shall direct"*

The performance of *Ariane* (and perhaps other works as well) by a named theatrical troupe under the likely direction of a prominent figure in the court musical world raises additional questions about the forces deployed at Drury Lane in March and April 1674. As we have already observed, the actors of the King's Company probably had nothing to do with the Royall Academy of Musick. On the other hand, certain support personnel, including scenekeepers and musicians, may have remained at their posts while the actors went out on furlough. We have noted the Lord Chamberlain's order for the transfer of the machinist John (*i.e.* Giovanni?) Guipponi from Dorset Garden while Drury Lane was still under construction, and *Ariane* would certainly have necessitated a full complement of the King's Company's regular machinists and scenekeepers, possibly including the Italians Antonio Brunatti and Francesco Franco ("Torangiu"), who may still have been in England at this time (see Chapter 5, nn. 60 and 72, above). A large band of violins would also have been required, and since it was Charles II's string players who normally staffed the public theatres in any case (and Louis Grabu was certainly capable of training these English players to perform in the French style), we can assume that they were involved in the opera as well.[118] Indeed, the festivities surrounding the Modena match in late 1673 and early 1674 seem to have generated a series of documents (some of them cancelled and postponed for unknown reasons) ordering special costumes for the king's violinists to wear.[119] These "Habitts of seuerall coloured rich Taffataes ... like Indian Gownes but not soe full[,] with short sleeues to the Elbow and trymmed with Tinsell about the neck and bottome and at the sleeves after the fashion," embellished with headdresses

---

Grabu would naturally have overseen the entire process, composing new music for the newly written text. Bashford's argument puts such speculation to rest, but has inadvertently spawned the more radical suggestion that Grabu could have reset the entire opera from scratch. This seems unlikely, particularly given that Cambert would probably have been regarded by everyone involved (including Grabu, who was not known for his egotism) as the superior composer.

118 Interestingly, Cambert's music may have been scored in four, rather than the expected five, parts: see his (incomplete) published editions of *Pomone* (Paris: Christophe Ballard, 1671) and *Les Peines et Les Plaisirs de l'Amour* (*idem*, 1672), both reprinted in facsimile (Geneva: Minkoff, 1980).

119 These orders to the Great Wardrobe were issued on 24 November 1673 (LC5/64, f. 81^v [*cancelled*]; LC5/140, p. 373 [*cancelled*, and with date altered to 18 December]: *Register*, no. 814); 18 December 1673 (LC5/140, p. 386 [*cancelled*]: *Register*, no. 818); 17/18 February 1674 (LC5/64, f. 83^r; LC5/120; LC5/140, p. 436: *Register*, no. 828; Ashbee, 1: 133); and 25 March (LC5/64, f. 88^r; LC5/120: *Register*, no. 833; Ashbee, 1: 135). (All four include additional orders for armchairs for the king and queen and a curtain for the Hall Theatre stage: see n. 24, above.) With regard to the gowns, see the note dated 25 February 1674 in LC3/27, p. 145 (see Ashbee, 1: 133), which identifies one William Watkins as "Indian Gowne maker in Ordinary to His Maties Roabes." Bills for the materials and construction of the costumes are in LC9/111 and LC9/274, pp. 42 and 52, while LC9/111, f. 19^r and LC9/260, f. 35^r list a payment of £6 to the mercer Walter Lapp—from whom Louis Grabu may have obtained credit for materials used in *Ariane*—for supplying the Great Wardrobe with a new set of twenty-four garlands "pro Music dn̄i Regis in Theatro apud Whitehall."

The Royall Academy of Musick, 1673–75   255

consisting of "Garlands of seuerall coloured floures"[120] had been in use since the mid-1660s, when the king's twenty-four violins were first loaned out to the two patent theatres for service on a regular basis.[121] The renewal of these costumes at the time of the *Ariane* production[122] suggests an effort to burnish the image of the court's musical forces in the public eye—both in the French opera and, later, in *The Tempest* at Dorset Garden, where all twenty-four of the violins famously played together as a single, massive ensemble.[123]

Even with this deployment of pre-existing forces, however, the opera would undoubtedly have necessitated the use of specialist, foreign performers, including instrumentalists, singers, and dancers capable of rendering the latest French styles and, crucially, presenting a through-sung work written entirely in the French language.[124] We have already discussed the appearance of some of these performers in England in late 1673 and their likely participation in the court presentation of *Ballet et Musique* in January 1674—although *Ariane*, with its large cast of gods, bacchantes, and shepherds, would have required even more singers (both male and female) than had its smaller-scale precursor. There can be little doubt that the four French flute/oboe players [?Jean] Boutet, Maxent de Bresmes, Pierre Guiton, and Jacques (James) Paisible, were integral to the *Ariane* performances— in which they seem even to have appeared onstage in costume[125]—despite the fact that their names are only known from documents of the following year, recording

120 LC5/138, p. 46; LC5/61, p. 224; LC5/119 (18 March 1665: *Register*, no. 315; Ashbee, 1: 61); the bill for taffeta (£79 5*s* 7*d* for 92⅜ ells) is in LC9/108. This order and the related one of 20 March cited in n. 121, below, may be associated with the premiere of Orrery's *Mustapha* at Lincoln's Inn Fields on 3 April 1665 (see pp. 38 and 178–82 for a discussion of the importance of this play).

121 LC5/138, p. 45; LC5/61, p. 225; LC5/119 (20 March 1665: *Register*, no. 316; Ashbee, 1: 61), ordering "Habitts of seuerall coloured Silkes for foure and Twenty violins[,] twelue of them being for his Maties service in the Theatre Royall and the other twelue Habitts for His Maties service in His Highnesse the Duke of Yorkes Theatre" (see the original order of 20 December 1664 assigning nine of the violinists to play at Bridges Street "whensoever Mr Thomas Killigrew shall desire them" [LC5/138, p. 429: *Register*, no. 299; Ashbee, 1: 59]). The earliest known date for the appearance of the royal violinists in costume is 25 January 1664, for which Killigrew received from the Great Wardrobe "the value of forty pounds in silkes for to cloath the Musick for the play called the Indian Queene to bee acted before their Maties" (LC5/138, p. 15: *Register*, no. 268; not in Ashbee).

122 Fresh sets of these costumes had been made up in early 1669 (see LC5/62, f. 52^v; LC5/63, p. 13; and LC5/119 [18 January 1669: *Register*, no. 477; Ashbee, 1: 87]), and the violinists would be attired in new gowns again for *Calisto* in 1675 (see LC5/141, p. 553 and LC5/64, f. 120^r [26 January 1675: *Register*, no. 893; not in Ashbee—but see Ashbee, 1: 147, erroneously identifying a press to hold *Calisto* stage costumes described in an order of 28 January (also LC5/141, p. 553: *Register*, no. 897) as "for the habits for the violins"]).

123 This will be discussed more fully in Walkling, *English Dramatick Opera* (in progress).

124 Note the reminder to purchasers of the English version of the libretto (*Ariadne*, sig. A4^r) that it represented "a meer Translation, and nothing else," as well as the Florentine ambassador's reference to "the French troupe" ("questa Truppa francese"; see p. 238, above).

125 *Ariadne*, 1: "*Several Hoboyes belonging to* Bacchus, *coming out of the Portico*" are joined by singers and dancers who "*joyn Concert with the Instruments.*"

256 *"For such uses as the King shall direct"*

their participation in the court masque *Calisto*.[126] And by the same logic, we can speculate that some of the French singers known to have appeared in *Calisto*—not just the established English court servants Claude des Granges and Anthony Robert, but also the imported performers Bury, Letelier, Panine (or "Danier"?), and Pierre Beaupuis—may originally have been engaged for the *Ariane* production.[127] Beaupuis, a bass, might even have performed the role of Bacchus: he was well established in Parisian musical circles, and seems to have been involved with Perrin and Cambert's *Académie Royale des Opéra*, where he could have learned this or some other role in preparation for the abortive Paris performance. Beaupuis's circumstances suggest that Cambert may have been directly responsible for bringing him to England, sometime in the autumn of 1673. He is last seen singing in Paris in a production of two tragedies with musical and danced *intermèdes*, presented at a school for young gentleman in the Faubourg Saint-Germain between 11 and 23 September (New Style),[128] and was probably back in France by late 1675 or early 1676, when he sang in Lully and Quinault's opera *Atys*, and when his voice part first emerges in the "French notebooks" of Marc-Antoine Charpentier, who composed for Beaupuis's new masters, the Guise family.[129]

We are fortunate to have somewhat more information about one category of performers who appeared in *Ariane*: the dancers. Neither the *Ariane* libretti nor that for *Ballet et Musique* provides any details regarding the identities or number of dancers deployed in the two productions, although we can be fairly certain that both Saint-André and Favier were part of a larger group of French dancers who appeared in both, and who may already have begun rehearsals for *Ariane* when *Ballet et Musique* was presented in mid-January. It seems that these dancers were also preparing to appear in productions of the King's Company, perhaps as part of the arrangement by which the Royall Academy of Musick had been allowed to co-opt the Drury Lane Theatre.[130] A lengthy note entered into one of

---

126 See n. 16, above. With regard to their role in *Ariane*, see Holman, *Fiddlers*, 344. In Sir George Etherege's 1676 play *The Man of Mode*, Act 2, scene 1, the character Medley asks Emilia, "What, you are of the number of the Ladies whose Ears are grown so delicate since our Operas, you can be charm'd with nothing But Flute doux, and French Hoboys[?]" (*The Man of Mode, or Sᵣ Fopling Flutter* [London: Henry Herringman, 1676], 21).

127 See documents cited in n. 135, below.

128 See *Sedecias et Zenobie, Tragedies, Qui seront representées, dans la Maison de Monsievr Filz, au Fau-bourg S. Germain ...* (Paris: Pierre Esclassan, 1673), 10 and 22.

129 See Philippe Quinault, *Atys, Tragedie en Mvsiqve. Ornée d'Entrées de Ballet, de Machines, & de Changements de Theatre. Representée devant Sa Majesté à Saint Germain en Laye, le dixiéme jour de Janvier 1676* (Paris: Christophe Ballard, 1676), sig. *2ʳ and pp. 25, 32, 49, and 67. Beaupuis, it should be noted, did *not* appear in the opera *Thésée* the previous year, when *Calisto* would have been in rehearsals. For the Charpentier information, see Patricia Ranum's biographical sketch of Beaupuis at http://ranumspanat.com/beaupuis_loulie.html (last accessed 3 May 2016), which unfortunately contains multiple errors of fact and interpretation.

130 There is a possibility that the French oboists were also pressed into service at Drury Lane, albeit somewhat later: see pp. 265–66, below.

The Royall Academy of Musick, 1673–75   257

the Lord Chamberlain's Warrant Books and dated 2 May 1674,[131] only ten days after the premature closing of the opera, records a dispute over two separate agreements by which "the ffrench Danceing Masters should dance at ye Kings Theatre." One, made between Grabu and the King's Company shareholder John Lacy, provided for a fee of 10*s* per day "for everyday they did dance," while the other, between Killigrew, Lacy, the actor/manager Charles Hart and "ye six dancers" themselves, promised a potentially more lucrative 5*s* per day "whether they did dance or not." These conflicting sets of terms appear to indicate a progression—the precise timing of which is uncertain—from specific payments for piecework, originally negotiated with Grabu as director of the Royall Academy of Musick and hence the dancers' supervisor, to a more permanent retainer-type arrangement in which the dancers seem to have been regarded as regularly contracted members of the King's Company. In the event, this latter arrangement threatened to come apart when the dancers, perhaps at the urging of Grabu, cited a clause in the original patents issued to Killigrew and Davenant forbidding the poaching of performers between the companies "without leaue or a discharge giuen by ye house where they were first entertained." Apparently the dancers, having rehearsed for their King's Company appearance "for two monethes together" and been provided with costumes at the company's expense, refused at the last minute to accept payment (and, we may presume, to perform their dances) and disavowed ever having acceded to the new contract, citing their preexisting relationship with Grabu "which did not leaue them at Liberty to make any ... binding agreem^t" with Killigrew and his associates. In response, the King's Company managers, "utterly deny[ing]" the dancers' claim that this potential conflict had been raised in the course of the negotiations, proffered "two Wittnesses ready to take theire Oathes" as to the validity of the contract and alleged that Grabu had been "often at theire practising, & knew theire Clothes were makeing & shewed noe dislike." This last fact, interpreted as demonstrating Grabu's implicit acknowledgement of the revised agreement, seems to have settled the matter in the minds of the court arbitrators, although the resulting solution may actually have represented a compromise of sorts. On 6 May, precisely two weeks after the closure of the opera, the Lord Chamberlain Henry Jermyn, 1st Earl of Saint Albans, ordered four of the six dancers to "attend Mr Killegrew ... & observe & performe his Comands ... and not to depart that service without leave."[132]

The document recording the order of 6 May is crucially important, because it explicitly identifies its four subjects as "Mr Pecurr M^r Le Temps Mr Sheuan and M^r D'muraile ffrench Dancers in the late Opera." The handling of French orthography by Restoration scribes was creative at best, and the problem is actually

131 LC5/140, p. [533] (index page: "NOPQ") (*Register*, no. 840; Ashbee, 3: 253–54; 5: 67).

132 LC5/140, p. 472; LC5/190, f. 84^r (6 May 1674: *Register*, no. 841; Ashbee, 1: 137). This was followed on 16 May by a blanket restatement of the official policy prohibiting the theatre companies from enticing performers away from one another: see LC5/15, p. 2 and LC7/1, p. 3 (*Register*, no. 842).

258   *"For such uses as the King shall direct"*

exacerbated by the rudimentary familiarity with the language that they did possess. Modern interpreters might be better served had the scribes known no French at all, and thus not attempted educated guesses that are frequently incorrect and hence misleading. However, scholars have been able to identify these four dancers as Guillaume-Louis Pecour, ?Anne-Louis Lestang (known as "le Jeune" or "le Cadet"), [?] Jouan, and Romain Dumirail, all of whom had been active in Paris prior to 1674.[133] Table 6.2 provides references to some biographical data on these dancers, and suggests that the troupe who performed in *Ariane* (as we have seen, the original document outlining the contract dispute refers to "ye sixe dancers") probably also included the group's presumed leader, Saint-André, as well as Jean Favier, the choreographer of *Ballet et Musique*. We cannot say for certain why these latter two are not mentioned in the subsequent order, although Saint-André, for one, may have been assigned to other duties: as we have noted, he had originally come to England to work on the Duke's Company's operatic productions, and he is the only one of the dancers known to have had a formal association with Charles II's court, in the form of his £150 annual pension as "master of the compositions for ballets" (to use the phrase coined by James Vernon). In any case, this new state of affairs must have been in place only for a short time. Favier and Pecour probably left England in the latter half of 1674: they danced in the premiere of Lully and Quinault's opera *Thésée* at Saint-Germain-en-Laye in January of the following year.[134] Jouan, about whom far less is known, may have departed with them. Dumirail, Lestang, and Saint-André, on the other hand, appear to have stayed on in London, where all three performed in *Calisto* in February and April 1675. In this instance, we are fortunate to have several documents enumerating the personnel for Crowne and Staggins's masque, in which are found the names of these three French dancers (in a delightful variety of eccentric spellings, as Table 6.2 demonstrates).[135]

133 See for example *Sedecias et Zenobie*, 5, 7, 9, 10, 12, 18, 21, 22, and 24 (Pecour); and 21, 22, and 24 (Lestang). Additional information is cited in Table 6.2, nn. § (Jouan) and ‡ (Pecour/Dumirail/Lestang).

134 See Philippe Quinault, *Thesée* [*sic*] *Tragedie en Mvsiqve. Ornée d'Entrées de Ballet, De Machines, & de Changements de Theatre. Representée devant Sa Majesté à Saint Germain en Laye, le dixiéme jour de Ianvier 1675* (Paris: Christophe Ballard, 1675), 42, 58, and 75 (Favier); 16, 42, 58, and 75 (Pecour). This *livret* also refers to Lestang (sig. [π3]^v and pp. 26, 42, and 58), but this may have been a brother, father, or son of the dancer who came to London: see for example Marie-Françoise Christout, *Le Ballet de Cour de Louis XIV, 1643–1672: Mises en Scène* (Vie Musicale en France sous les Rois Bourbons, 12; Paris: A. et J. Picard, 1967), 126 nn. 13 and 15 ("Lestang aîné et cadet" in *Xerxes*, 1660), n. 22 and 127 n. 27 ("Lestang frères" in *Ballet de l'Impatience*, 1661). Subsequent references to the name Lestang in ballet *livrets* do not distinguish between l'aîné and le cadet.

135 See LC5/141, pp. 197 (*Register*, no. 920; Ashbee, 1: 150) and 548 (*Register*, no. 888; Ashbee, 1: 146), and LC9/274, pp. 311–12 (comprehended in *Register*, no. 909), all digested in Walkling, "Masque and Politics," 34 (Table 2). Saint-André is missing from LC5/141, p. 197 (an order dated 27 May 1675 for payments to individual performers), probably because his appearance was covered under the terms of his generous court pension.

Table 6.2 French dancers employed in *Ariane* and *Calisto*, 1674–75

6 May 1674[a] *Ariane*	Jan./Feb. 1675[b] *Calisto* [A]	27 May 1675[c] *Calisto* [B]	29 Mar. 1675[d] *Calisto* [C]	5–6 Mar. 1675[e] apprehension	IDENTITY	FRENCH PERF'CES	DATES	*Biographical Dictionary* *	I.E.D. **
[?][f]					JEAN FAVIER (L'AÎNÉ) †	*p ch* *T A*	1648–?1719	——	——
Sheuan[g]					—— JOUAN §		*fl.* 1666–1674	*[13: 301]*	——
Pecurr					GUILLAUME-LOUIS PECOUR‡	*p* *sz T A*	*c.* 1653–1729	11: 247	5: 128–29
D'muraile	Muraile	Dunnraille	Timirall	[*not apprehended*]	ROMAIN DUMIRAIL ‡	*P* *A*	*fl.* 1674–1716	4: 501	
Le Temps	Letang	Lestant	Lettang	[*not apprehended*]	?ANNE-LOUIS LESTANG (LE JEUNE) ‡	*p* *sz°* *A*	d. 1737	9: 257	4: 152
[*?not reassigned*]	St. Andre	[*not paid through normal channels*][i]	St Andrea	[*not apprehended*]	ADRIEN MERGER DE SAINT-ANDRÉ ‡	*p ch*	1635–1716	13: 171–72	5: 489–90
	Berto	Berteau	Birto	Berteau	[*unknown*][j]		——	*[2: 66]*	——
	Delisle	De Lisle	Deliel	De Lisle	[*unknown*]		——	*[4: 297]*	
	Herriette	Harriette	Aratt	Huriet	—— HENRIETTE	*sz*	——	*[7: 278]*	
	Le Duke	le Duc	Duke	Le Duke	—— LE DUC[k]	*p* *sz*	——	*[9: 19]*[p]	
	Le Roy	Le Roy	La Roy	Le Roy	LE ROI	*sz*	——	*[9: 247]*	
	——	Clarke	——	——	[?"LE CLERC"][l]		?	*[3: 300]*	——
(ENGLISH DANCERS IN CALISTO)[h]	*Dyer*	*Dyer*	*Degar*		?BENJAMIN OR JOHN DYER		?	4: 530	——
	Isaack	*Isaack*	*Isack*		—— ISAAC[m]		*fl.* ?1631–1716	8: 103–4	3: 521–23
	Motley	*Mottley*	*Matlee*		[*unknown*][n]		——	*[10: 344]*	
	Smyth	*Smyth*	*Smith*		?JOHN SMYTH		*fl.* 1675–?1699	14: 190	——

(Continued)

Key to sources:

* Philip H. Highfill, Jr., Kalman A. Burnim, and Edward A. Langhans, *A Biographical Dictionary of Actors, Actresses, Musicians, Dancers, Managers & Other Stage Personnel in London, 1660–1800* (16 vols.: Carbondale: Southern Illinois University Press, 1973–93). (**N.B. Entries from this source referenced in brackets and italics rely solely on the data given in the present table.**)

** Selma Jeanne Cohen *et al.*, eds., *International Encyclopedia of Dance* (6 vols.: New York: Oxford University Press, 1998).

† See Rebecca Harris-Warrick and Carol G. Marsh, *Musical Theatre at the Court of Louis XIV: Le Mariage de la Grosse Cathos* (Cambridge: Cambridge University Press, 1994), 21–29.

§ See Marie-Françoise Christout, *Le Ballet de Cour de Louis XIV, 1643–1672: Mises en Scène* (Vie Musicale en France sous les Rois Bourbons, 12; Paris: A. et J. Picard, 1967), 131 nn. 122, 134; 132 n. 139; and 133 nn. 166, 176.

‡ See Jérôme de La Gorce (trans. Margaret M. McGowan), "Guillaume-Louis Pecour: A Biographical Essay," *Dance Research* 8/2 (Autumn 1990): 3–26 (includes references to Dumirail [pp. 6, 9, 17, 18], Lestang [5, 6–8, 10, 18], and Saint-André [10]).

Key to recorded appearances in French performances, 1671–76:

(*N.B.* dancers in Lully's *Alceste*, 19 January 1674, not identified in any source.)

p = danced in premiere of Molière and Lully's *Psyché*, 17 January 1671 (N. S.): see Molière, *Psiché Tragi-Comédie, et Ballet. Dansé devant sa Majesté au mois de Ianvier 1671* (Paris: Robert Ballard, 1671), *passim*

ch = danced in premiere of Lully's *Cadmus et Hermione*, 27 April 1673 (N. S.): see François Parfaict, *Dictionnaire des Theatres de Paris* (7 vols.: Paris: Rozet, 1767), 2: 3

sz = danced in *intermèdes* of *Sédécias* and *Zénobie* at the school for young gentlemen operated by Jean-Marie Filz in Faubourg Saint-Germain, 11–23 September 1673 (N. S.): see Anon., *Sedecias et Zenobie, Tragedies, Qui seront représentées, dans la Maison de Monsievr Filz, au Fau-bourg S. Germain, ruë de Seve, le Lundy 11. le Ieudy 14. & Samedy 16. Septembre: et Les mêmes jours de la Semaine suivante* (Paris: Pierre Esclassan, 1673), *passim*

T = danced in court premiere of Lully's *Thésée*, 10 January 1675 (N. S.): see Philippe Quinault, *Thesée Tragedie en Mvsiqve. Ornée d'Entrées de Ballet, De Machines, & de Changements de Theatre. Representée devant Sa Majesté à Saint Germain en Laye, le dixième jour de Ianvier 1675* (Paris: Christophe Ballard, 1675), *passim*

A = danced in court premiere of Lully's *Atys*, 10 January 1676 (N. S.): see Philippe Quinault, *Atys, Tragedie en Mvsiqve. Ornée d'Entrées de Ballet, de Machines, & de Changements de Theatre. Representée devant Sa Majesté à Saint Germain en Laye, le dixiéme jour de Janvier 1676* (Paris: Christophe Ballard, 1676), *passim*

---

[a] *"ffrench Dancers in the late Opera" assigned to dance for King's Company*: LC5/140, p. 472; LC5/190, f. 84[r] (*Register*, no. 841; Ashbee, 1: 137).

[b] *List of performers*: LC5/141, p. 548 (*Register*, no. 888; Ashbee, 1: 146).

[c] *Warrant for payment (listing French dancers separately from English)*: LC5/141, p. 197 (*Register*, no. 920; Ashbee, 1: 150).

[d] *Bill for shoes*: LC9/274, pp. 311–12 (comprehended in *Register*, no. 909; not in Ashbee).

[e] *Apprehended for unspecified reasons, then released*: LC5/190, f. 118[r–v] (*Register*, nos. 911, 912; not in Ashbee).

[f] Choreographer of *Ballet et Musique* (?January 1674); probably also one of "y[e] six dancers" assumed to have danced in *Ariane* (see LC5/140, p. 533 [2 May 1674: *Register*, no. 840; Ashbee, 5: 67]).

[g] Erroneously transcribed as "Shenan" in all previous modern sources (Nicoll, Boswell, *Register*, Ashbee, etc.); the possible identification of this dancer with Jouan is suggested in Moira Goff, "Shadwell, Saint-André, and the 'Curious Dancing' in *Psyche*" in David Wilson, ed., *The Restoration of Charles II: Public Order, Theatre and Dance* (Cambridge: Early Dance Circle, 2002), 32 n. 47.

[h] See also PRO30/32/46 (properly "T53/[0b]"), p. 203: warrant for payment of £100 "without Account unto John (Joseph) [*sic*] Preist … in reward for Service by him performed at the late Ballet at Whitehall" (16 September 1675: *Calendar of Treasury Books* 4: 815; *Register*, no. 933). For the actual disbursement, see E403/1786, p. 22 (12 October 1675).

[i] See T48/30 ("A Charge …"), p. 4; British Library, Add. MS 28080, f. 14^v; and British Library, Egerton MS 3352, f. 167^r.

[j] "George Birto, gentleman" of the parish of St. Paul's, Covent Garden, indicted for recusancy, 15 December 1678: see John Cordy Jeaffreson, ed., *Middlesex County Records* (4 vols.: London: Middlesex County Records Society, 1892), 4: 100.

[k] "Mr Le Duck in James Street" included in "A List of Dancing Masters and Musicians Papists" presented to the Privy Council on 5 October 1681 (see Lilian Gibbens, "Roman Catholic Tradesmen in London, 1681," *Catholic Ancestor* 8 [2000]: 58–62, p. 59).

[l] Attribution (suggested by *Biographical Dictionary*) is extremely speculative; alternatively, this entry could refer to John Clarke, Groom of the Revels (d. 1701; see *Biographical Dictionary*, 3: 303–4), or possibly Joseph Clark, contortionist (d. ?1696; see *Biographical Dictionary*, 3: 298–99).

[m] "Mr Isaac in Duke Street" included in "A List of Dancing Masters and Musicians Papists." 1681 (see note k, above).

[n] Possibly the "Morby" who was apprehended with Smyth and three other English dancing masters on 19 November 1674 (LC5/190, f. 106^v [*Register*, no. 878; not in Ashbee]).

[o] The Lestang who danced in *Sédécias* and *Zénobie* may have been Anne-Louis Lestang's elder brother, who also appeared in *Cadmus et Hermione* and *Thésée*.

[p] *Biographical Dictionary* suggests identity as Lewis Laduke (d. 1680).

262 *"For such uses as the King shall direct"*

Listed with them are five others not known to have been associated with the *Ballet et Musique* and *Ariane* productions of the previous year. Three of these—Henriette, Le Duc, and Le Roi—can be shown to have danced previously in Paris,[136] while the other two—Berteau and De Lisle—remain unidentified in the French sources.[137] Curiously, the five dancers just named were all arrested for an unknown cause on 5 March 1675 and brought before Lord Chamberlain Arlington "to answer to such things as shalbe objected against them."[138] This was during the time when the revised version of *Calisto* was being rehearsed in preparation for its opening on 22 April, and it may be that the dancers had attempted to abandon the long-running production; in any case, having presumably satisfied Arlington, they were released from custody the following day after "paying theire ffees."[139] It remains a mystery why only the five newcomers were arrested, while the more well-established Dumirail, Lestang, and Saint-André seem not to have been involved in the dispute. Perhaps their prior arrangements (Dumirail and Lestang's with Killigrew, Saint-André's with the court and the Duke's Company) had the effect of checking their desire to misbehave—or it may be that they held a different status from the five recent arrivals, on account of their association with the Royall Academy of Musick. The documents relating to the French dancers in England during 1674 and 1675—the existence of which proceeds as much from happenstance as from any kind of comprehensive effort by the court to keep a record of their activities—raise as many questions as they answer, and it is important to tread cautiously in interpreting these ephemeral scraps of information.

The *Calisto* production of 1675, and particularly the presence therein of French performers, including dancers, singers, and flute/oboe players known or believed to have appeared in *Ariane* the year before, implicitly poses a larger set of questions about the fate of the Royall Academy of Musick. Although there can be little doubt that the much publicized French opera production collapsed in disarray in the wake of the brawl of 22 April 1674, this should not necessarily be taken as evidence that the Academy itself was immediately disbanded as an organization,

---

136 See *Sedecias et Zenobie*, 9, 12, 19, 22, and 23 (Henriette); 7, 9, 10, 12, 18, 21, 22, and 24 (Le Duc); and 7, 9, 10, 12, 18, 19, and 24 (Le Roy). Le Roy may also have danced in *Ballet des Ballets* at Saint-Germain-en-Laye in 1671 (along with Favier, Saint-André, and Lestang): see [Molière], *Ballet des Ballets, Dansé devant Sa Majesté en son Chasteau de S. Germain en Laye au mois de Decembre 1671* (Paris: Robert Ballard, 1671), 22 and 37.

137 For a possible reference to Berteau in London in December 1678, see Table 6.2, note j. As Table 6.2 shows, one of the *Calisto* documents (LC5/141, p. 197, from which Saint-André's name is absent) seems to include a "Mr Clarke" in the list of French dancers. This "Clarke" appears nowhere else in the records pertaining to the *Calisto* production, and might in fact be a miscategorized reference to John Clarke, Groom of the Revels since 24 October 1671 (and, from 24 April 1678, Whitehall theatrekeeper). A less likely explanation might be that he was the contortionist Joseph Clark (d. ?1696), although nothing in the text of *Calisto* can be read as indicating the appearance of such a figure.

138 LC5/190, f. 118^r (*Register*, no. 911; not in Ashbee).

139 *Ibid.*, f. 118^v (*Register*, no. 912; not in Ashbee).

The Royall Academy of Musick, 1673–75   263

however informal it may have been from the start.[140] As we have seen, the dancers' contract dispute with Killigrew and his associates in May presupposed the continued existence of a legally established third theatrical company, a point underscored by the fact of the Lord Chamberlain's intervention in the matter. In the event, the remaining *Ariane* dancers—Lestang, Dumirail, and ultimately Saint-André—drifted back to France,[141] although the fate of the five newcomers seen in *Calisto* is less clear.[142] But the dancers' continued presence in England, along with musicians such as the singer Beaupuis, through at least 1675 suggests an ongoing demand for French performers that must have had official backing at some level, even if the Royall Academy itself—whose name appears nowhere apart from the *Ariane/Ariadne* libretti—ultimately ceased to exist.

140 A number of scholars (*e.g.* Orrell, "A New Witness," 92; Danchin, 64) have misinterpreted an order of 1 June 1674 that the Customs Commissioners permit the export of "52 parcells of goods in Coffers or Ballots belonging to the French Comedians" (PRO30/32/49 [properly "T54/4"], p. 312 [*Calendar of Treasury Books* 4: 533; *Register*, no. 844]) as referring to departing members of the Royall Academy. These "French Comedians," however, had nothing to do with the opera performers: they had arrived in England in December 1672 (see PRO30/32/48 [properly "T54/3"], pp. 213, 230, 237 [17 December 1672, 1 January 1673, 9 January 1673: *Calendar of Treasury Books* 4: 14, 24, 29; *Register*, nos. 743, 752, 753]), lodged themselves at York House on The Strand, and in May 1673 were dispatched to Germany in the train of the peace envoys Sir Leoline Jenkins and Sir Joseph Williamson (PRO30/32/48, p. 376 [1 May 1673: *Calendar of Treasury Books* 4: 127; *Register*, no. 773]). The players probably did not return to England with the envoys in April 1674, but their goods, having originally been exported under diplomatic provisions, would have had to pass back through English customs before being returned to their owners, presumably now in France.

141 Lestang and Dumirail appeared (alongside Favier and Pecour) in the court premiere of Lully and Quinault's *Atys* at Saint-Germain-en-Laye in January 1676: see Quinault, *Atys* (see n. 129, above), 14 and 25 (Dumirail); sig. *2ᵛ and pp. 14, 32, and 50 (Lestang). The record of Saint-André's £150 annual pension ends at Midsummer 1675, but this is because of the patchy survival of Secret Service accounts: for later evidence of his presence in London, see Etherege, *The Man of Mode*, 64 (Act 4, scene i), where the title character describes himself as "fit for / Nothing but low dancing now, a Corant, a Boreè, [*sic*] / Or a Minnuét: but St. *Andrè* [*sic*] tells me, if I / Will but be regular[,] in one Month I shall rise agen." Saint-André was back in Paris by June 1680 at the very latest, when he was listed among the members of the *Académie Royale de Danse*: see *Le Mercure Galant*, June 1680, 266.

142 Both Berteau and Le Duc appear to have stayed on in England until at least 1678 and 1681, respectively: see Table 6.2, notes j and k.

7   French musicians at court, 1675–89

The problem in attempting to understand the history of French music and musicians in England during the 1670s and beyond is that documentation for the supposed relationship between the Restoration court and expatriate French performers is sorely lacking, not just for the crucial year and a half between late 1673 and early 1675 explored in the previous chapter, but even more so in the post-*Calisto* period. During the ensuing three years, and indeed for a long time thereafter, we catch only fleeting glimpses of the activities of men like Cambert, Grabu, and the French wind players, even though we know that they remained in England throughout this time. Only Grabu appears frequently in the court records, and this is because he spent a good portion of 1676 and 1677 tied up in litigation over his debts—possibly acquired, as we have observed, in the service of the *Ariane* production.[1] Yet none of this should necessarily be taken to indicate that these individuals were not still actively pursuing their careers as musicians, or that their association with the court was simply terminated in deference to the strictures of the Test Act.

A prime instance of the continuation of French musical activity within the court's orbit can be seen in the work of Robert Cambert, who stayed on in England despite the probable demise of the Royall Academy of Musick in the spring of 1674 and the departure of several of its members during the ensuing year. Notwithstanding Pierre Des Maizeaux's later characterization of him as "Sur-Intendant de la Musique de Charles II,"[2] Cambert appears never to have held a *bona fide* court appointment: as we have already noted, John Buttrey has plausibly argued that he was based not in the royal music itself, but rather in the household of Charles II's chief mistress, the Duchess of Portsmouth, from whence the musician—who, according to Lecerf, had attracted "*des marques d'amitié & des bienfaits considérables du Roi d'Angleterre & des plus grands Seigneurs de la Cour*"[3]—would have been available to the royal court on an informal basis as

---

1 See p. 253, above.
2 Pierre Des Maizeaux, revised (1709) version of "La Vie de Monsieur de Saint-Evremond. A Monsieur Bayle," printed in *Oeuvres Meslées de M*. *de Saint-Evremond ... Seconde Edition* (see n. 82, below), 1: XLV (sig. I3^r).
3 Lecerf de La Viéville, *Comparaison de la Musique Italienne, et de la Musique Françoise* (see Chapter 6, n. 18, above), 2: 177.

need dictated. His sole appearance in the English court records is in an order of Saturday, 4 July 1674, commanding twelve of the royal violinists to meet in the Hall Theatre "on Wednesday morning next by seaven of the clock, to practise after such manner as Monsr Combert shall enform them," in preparation for a performance before the king at Windsor the following Saturday, the 11th.[4] This otherwise unidentified event most likely involved a presentation of the composer's own music, presumably a sizeable program or work (albeit probably not a fullblown opera, as has occasionally been suggested) that demanded forces in excess of the complement of voices, harpsichord, and flutes/oboes (and dancers?) that the resident French performers would have been capable of providing on their own at that time.

Cambert reemerges in 1676, when the Duchess of Portsmouth's apartments played host to one of the more intriguing episodes relating to Charles II's continuing engagement with French operatic forms and practice. This was the six-week visit to England of three of Louis XIV's opera singers, Gillet, Godonesche, and La Forest, between late May and early July, the circumstances and events of which have been explored by John Buttrey in some detail.[5] The singers performed scenes from all of the then-existing Lully *tragédies en musique*—*Cadmus et Hermione* (1673), *Alceste* (1674), *Thésée* (1675), and *Atys* (1676), accompanied by Cambert on the harpsichord. A particular favorite of the English king's seems to have been *Atys*'s celebrated third-act *sommeil* scene, which Charles II is reported to have heard four times in as many days, and which may have been repeated for him on other occasions as well.[6] This scene, notably, requires at least two French "flute" players, and on 29 June the French ambassador Honoré Courtin remarked that Cambert had indeed been joined by "les flustes; il y a ici deux françois que en joüent parfaittement bien."[7] The French wind players, at least some of whom had originally arrived in England in the company of Cambert, seem to have become a well established fixture in London by this time: Courtin later reported the presence at one of Portsmouth's *soirées* of "cinq ou six hommes qui jouent fort bien de la fluste,"[8] and this same group may have appeared on London's public stage earlier that year in a performance of Ben Jonson's *Volpone*—possibly the one given at Drury Lane on 17 February, with Charles II in attendance—for which "a Consort

---

4 LC3/25, p. 246; LC5/15, p. 16 (*Register*, no. 851; Ashbee, 1: 140); the court was in residence at Windsor from May to September 1674.

5 Buttrey, "New Light on Robert Cambert" (see Chapter 6, n. 22, above), citing reports of the French ambassador Courtin in Archives du Ministère des Affaires Étrangères, Paris, Correspondance Politique: Angleterre 118–19. All three had sung in *Atys* in January 1676 (see Quinault, *Atys*, sig. **4^v and pp. 25, 31, 32, and 49); Gillet and Godonesche had also appeared in *Thésée* in January 1675 (see Quinault, *Thesée*, sig. [π3]^r and pp. 13, 16, 42, and 74).

6 See Archives du Ministère des Affaires Étrangères, Correspondance Politique: Angleterre 119, f. 21^r.

7 *Ibid.*

8 *Ibid.*, f. 38^r (6 July). By 1676, some of this number may have consisted of Englishmen trained by the French players: Holman (*Fiddlers*, 420) mentions John Banister II and Robert King, as well as a new Frenchman, one François La Riche, in relation to James II's Private Music after 1685; the same may be true of the "six hautbois" who appeared in *Rare en Tout* in 1677 (see below).

266 *"For such uses as the King shall direct"*

of Hautboyes were added to the Musick."[9] We already know that four such players had been featured in *Calisto* in 1675, and had probably also appeared in *Ariane* in 1674, although only the *Calisto* documents offer precise numbers and names. One of these, [?Jean] Boutet, appears to have left England not long after *Calisto*,[10] but the other three stayed on, at least for a time. The names of two of them, Maxent de Bresmes and Pierre Guiton, are found in a list of June 1678 where they are identified as "Frenchmen [who] serve his Majesty as musicians in the Chapel Royal."[11] No mention of them is made in any other documents, so we are unable to ascertain when or why this change of status was effected, nor what ultimately became of the pair: they may have left England in the exodus of 1678–79 associated with the Popish Plot scare, in which many other foreign Roman Catholics found themselves caught up.[12] However, it is entirely reasonable to imagine that they would have formed part of the secular ensemble heard at the Duchess of Portsmouth's and possibly at Drury Lane in 1676.

The disparate circumstances under which Cambert and the two aforementioned wind players seem to have been retained on the fringes of the royal court should cause us to reconsider the status of Charles II's most important, and presumably most valuable, French musician. Scholars have tended to look with bemused pity on the plight of Louis Grabu in the latter part of the 1670s, pointing out the undeniable facts established in the archival record: the unfortunate man was deprived of the Mastership in 1674, had become mired in legal troubles by early 1676, was reduced to petitioning the crown for a substantial amount of back wages in 1677, and would flee the country with his wife and three children

---

9 See the discussion in Holman, *Fiddlers*, 344–45. For the manuscript "Prologue at the Fox, when a Consort of Hautboyes were added to the Musick," see Robert Gale Noyes, "A Manuscript Restoration Prologue for *Volpone*," *Modern Language Notes* 52 (1937): 198–200; for the 1676 performance, which is only speculatively associated with this prologue, see LC5/142, p. 52 (*Register*, no. 1014).

10 In any case, Boutet seems to have been the least valued member of the original quartet: see Chapter 6, n. 16, above.

11 LC5/143, p. 106 (8 June 1678: Ashbee, 1: 179); no record of any payments to them is known. Given the way the 1678 entry is phrased, there is no reason to assume that the third person on this list, the mysteriously named "Cir Felix alias La Montagu Cir," was necessarily a wind player at all.

12 These included the violin virtuoso Nicola Matteis (pass issued 29 November 1678: SP44/334, p. 577 [*Calendar of State Papers, Domestic* 1678: 615]); Sébastien Bremond (pass issued 20 December 1678: SP44/334, p. 594 [*Calendar of State Papers, Domestic* 1678: 619]); Louis Grabu (pass issued 31 March 1679: SP44/51, p. 207 [*Calendar of State Papers, Domestic* 1679–80: 338; Ashbee, 8: 235]); and Claude des Granges (pass issued 15 May 1679: SP44/51, p. 240 [*Calendar of State Papers, Domestic* 1679–80: 338; Ashbee, 8: 340]). Bremond had been indicted for recusancy (possibly alongside the *Calisto* dancer Berteau) only five days prior to the issuance of his pass: see John Cordy Jeaffreson, ed., *Middlesex County Records* (4 vols.: London: Middlesex County Records Society, 1892), 4: 100. See n. 43, below, for the suggestion that des Granges may not actually have departed at all; his situation is instructive in the consideration of several other Roman Catholic musicians—specifically Giovanni Battista Draghi, Hilario Suarez, Bartolomeo Albrici, and Francesco Galli—who claimed to be leaving the country at this time, but then reappear in London in later years: see Chapter 5, n. 34, above.

in the late winter of 1679.[13] Yet it is likely that Grabu's loss of his court employment stemmed from the political exigencies of the Test Act, not from any artistic or managerial failings on his part: indeed, the normally intractable royal bureaucracy actually seems to have gone out of its way to accommodate him just prior to his dismissal, releasing large sums of his arrears over a relatively short span of time, and the submission of his petition three and a half years later provoked a similar flurry of activity.[14] Moreover, it is important to recall that much of the documentation pertaining to Grabu's activities at court prior to 1674 arises directly out of his exercise of the quotidian administrative responsibilities associated with his official position. When viewed in the light of Cambert's circumstance and that of the two aforementioned French wind players, Grabu's near-absence from post-1674 court records relating to music is not especially surprising, and is thus inadmissible as evidence that he was not engaged in regular musical activities, even as he grappled with his more well-documented legal and financial woes.

There are two salient facts relating to Grabu's musical career in the period between 1674 and 1679. The first is a court document of 17 January 1677, ordering twelve of the king's violins "to attend to practise Monsr Grabues Musick."[15] Unfortunately, we have no information as to what was performed—or, for that matter, when or where such a performance was supposed to occur—but this order, particularly as it mirrors that involving Cambert two and a half years earlier, would seem to indicate Grabu's continued presence at court, not only as composer of the music in question, but quite possibly as the director of its rehearsal and performance as well.[16] Moreover, the officially dispossessed musician, supposedly forbidden by the Test Act even to come into the presence of his former employer, seems to have gained the king's ear, however briefly, at around the same time. In his petition of 5 May 1677, Grabu reminds Charles that he had "a few dayes since gratiously pleased to declare" a willingness to pay the ex-Master's arrears in exchange for the surrender of his lifetime patent for the Mastership, which had been issued under the Great Seal ten years previously.[17] Although the king's promise remained unfulfilled (and Grabu wisely held on to the patent for another decade), both the circumstances under which this deal appears to have been struck and the almost instantaneous burst of administrative

---

13 Discussion forthcoming in Walkling, "Ups and Downs."
14 Walkling, "Ups and Downs."
15 LC5/141, p. 521 (17 January 1677: Ashbee, 1: 168); four of these violinists—Jeffrey Ayleworth, John Gamble, Thomas Greeting, and John Myer—were also among those who had been assigned to play for Cambert in 1674.
16 There is a remote possibility that the work presented on this occasion was Grabu's *Pastoralle*, which was not published until 1684, but portions of which turn up in manuscripts in France dating from the early 1680s: see Walkling, "Ups and Downs."
17 LC5/142, p. 56 (Ashbee, 1: 170–71); this petition and its outcome will be discussed in Walkling, "Ups and Downs." For Grabu's original patent, dated 17 April 1667, see E403/2463, f. 120^v and C66/3093/13 (Ashbee, 5: 55).

268   *"For such uses as the King shall direct"*

activity that it produced suggest that, as late as 1677, Grabu could still command a degree of special consideration at court. The second fact pertaining to Grabu's musical activities is composite: a number of songs and instrumental works dating from 1678, the majority of which are associated with plays, suggest that sometime around the beginning of this year the musician embarked on a new career writing theatrical music, probably for the Duke's Company at Dorset Garden.[18] This is noteworthy not only because it appears to signal a new direction in Grabu's career at this time, but also because it could be taken to imply that prior to 1678 Grabu was *not* available for such tasks, and hence may have remained active at court, despite ostensibly having been terminated in the autumn of 1674.

One benefit of the suggestion that Louis Grabu may have continued to play a role in the Restoration court's musical life during the years 1675–77 is that it permits a reexamination of the role of Grabu's successor, Nicholas Staggins. Staggins's elevation to the Mastership of the Music at Michaelmas 1674 represents a curious choice on the part of the court authorities (and, hence, of Charles II himself). Although his father Isaac Staggins was a longtime member of the musical establishment, having held various positions since 1660, young Nicholas, whose date of birth is unknown, had only joined the bands of violins and (English) winds in late 1670, and there is no evidence of his having attained any special distinction prior to his assumption of Grabu's duties. In certain respects, his profile is similar to that of Grabu himself during the time of the latter's tenure as Master: his compositional output was modest (Staggins was, in fact, only officially appointed to a position as Composer in 1682), and he was probably regarded more for his organizational and managerial skills than for his musical virtuosity. Not enough of Staggins's music for *Calisto* survives to allow us to make an informed judgment of his abilities in the realm of through-composed theatrical music, but it is perhaps telling that he is not known to have carried out a similar assignment again until 1693, when he composed the first of three royal birthday odes for William III.[19] Whatever his special talents, Staggins would certainly have stood to profit from the advice, and perhaps even the assistance, of his dispossessed predecessor, who brought the advantage of some eight years' experience in the position. But Grabu's

---

18 Walkling, "Ups and Downs." Grabu is known to have composed vocal music for Shadwell's *The History of Timon of Athens* (January 1678) and D'Urfey's *Squire Oldsapp* (June 1678), and a seven-movement theatre suite for Dryden and Lee's *Oedipus* (September 1678), all of which were put on by the Duke's Company. He also wrote the song "One night while all the village slept" from Lee's *Mithridates*, a King's Company production, but which, I have argued in Chapter 3, was probably originally written for a court performance by Princess Anne and her companions, possibly presented on 8 February 1678. In addition, five instrumental tunes by Grabu were published in 1678 and 1679, and there are three unassigned theatre suites by him that may also date from this period. Apart from three instrumental dance tunes first published in 1672, these works constitute the earliest surviving datable exemplars of Grabu's compositional output.

19 All three odes are to texts by Nahum Tate: "Sound a call, the Tritons sing" (1693), "Spring, where are thy flow'ry treasures?" (1694), and "Summon to the cheerful plain" (1697). Only a single musical fragment from one of these odes (that of 1693) is known to survive.

French musicians at court, 1675–89 269

expertise may have carried even more value to the court as a whole, since much of the time during which he is presumed to have been available for service (albeit off the books, and hence invisible to us) coincides with a crucial period between 1676 and 1678 when Staggins was away on an extended overseas journey at the king's behest.[20]

We do not know for certain when Staggins embarked on this trip, nor precisely when he returned. He seems to have been involved in a rush of preparations in January and February 1676: on 27 January a payment of £93 2*s* was warranted, covering various copying and possibly compositional activities dating back to May 1675,[21] and on 26 February a pass was issued for him "to go and remain in Italy and other foreign parts for a year, with his servants."[22] By 18 March he had successfully collected a year's back wages for his positions as Master of the Music and wind player,[23] and on the 27th he appointed his father Isaac as "his true and lawful attorney."[24] The elder Staggins subsequently received payments intended for his son over the next couple of years,[25] and Nicholas only reappears for certain in these documents when he collected his livery payments in person on 8 July 1678.[26] By this time, he had probably been back in England for several months, as another full year's wages for the Mastership and the wind position were specially

---

20 In a 1695 petition for back wages, Staggins averred that he had traveled to "France ... Italy, & other Forein Parts, to capacitate & make my self fit for ye Service of His Late Ma^ty K^g Charles ye Second" (3 June 1695: Bodleian Library, Oxford, MS Rawlinson C. 421, f. 199^r [Ashbee, 5: 91–92, giving date 5 June]).

21 LC5/141, p. 346 (Ashbee, 1: 155–56, giving a date of "(January 27)"). This sum was actually paid, by the Treasurer of the Chamber, sometime after Michaelmas 1676, when it was attached to two earlier payments in arrears to Staggins, amounting to a total of £133 2*s*: see AO1/400/103 (Ashbee, 5: 147), where the date of the 1676 warrant is recorded as "the 27th of Febry." Earlier, on 7 February, Staggins had belatedly been paid £221 to be distributed "without account" to the musicians who had appeared in *Calisto* nearly a year before: see PRO30/32/43 [properly "T52/5"], p. 51 and PRO30/32/46 [properly "T53/[0b]"], p. 290 (*Calendar of Treasury Books* 5: 123; Ashbee, 8: 223).

22 SP44/334, p. 136 (*Calendar of State Papers, Domestic 1675–76*: 581; Ashbee, 8: 224).

23 £246 10*s* 10*d*, warranted on 4 March (PRO30/32/46, p. 304 [*Calendar of Treasury Books* 5: 146; Ashbee, 8: 224]), minuted on the 13th (PRO30/32/33 [properly "T29/5"], p. 129 [*Calendar of Treasury Books* 5: 28; Ashbee, 8: 224]) and collected from the Exchequer on the 18th (E403/1786, p. 184 [Ashbee, 5: 201]). Staggins had originally petitioned for the money prior to 1 February (PRO30/32/33, pp. 104–5 [*Calendar of Treasury Books* 5: 10; Ashbee, 8: 223]); an order of 17 July for the payment of a number of musicians, including Staggins, expressly notes that he "had a payment lately made to him by the King's commandment to provide for his journey into France" (PRO30/32/46, p. 399 [*Calendar of Treasury Books* 5: 274; Ashbee, 8: 226]).

24 LC9/341, p. 42 and LC9/258, f. 97^v (Ashbee, 1: 158). The letter of attorney was only registered, however, on 31 August, when "Mr. Stagins" (possibly Isaac) paid £3 19*s* to cover this and several other transactions: see LC9/376iii, tag 159, "An accompt of Moneys Received for Debenters," f. [4]^r (Ashbee, 1: 292).

25 For instances where Isaac Staggins is identified as payee, see LC9/199i, ff. [18]^v and [19]^r and LC3/40, pp. 27 and 31 (Ashbee, 1: 252), and AO1/400/103 (Ashbee, 5: 146; see Table 7.1).

26 LC9/199ii, f. 18^v and LC3/40, p. 38 (Ashbee, 1: 253). Peter Holman mistakenly deduces (*Fiddlers*, 303) that "Staggins apparently returned sometime between 30 November 1678, when Charles Coleman II signed for two of his liveries, and 18 February 1678/9, when the Lord Chamberlain once again began to address orders and warrants to him."

270 *"For such uses as the King shall direct"*

warranted on 6 May of that year and paid within three weeks,[27] with an additional half year's worth, ordered as part of a general payment to a number of musicians the preceding December, released to him in late June.[28] Indeed, on 25 June 1678 Henry Savile wrote to John Wilmot, 2nd Earl of Rochester, that Staggins "is come over [*i.e.* from abroad] with great credit and many new aires. His Majesty has allready constituted him lord paramount over all the musick."[29] Scholars have not adequately addressed the question of who oversaw the King's Music during its titular Master's long absence. A document of 22 May 1677 ordering the Twenty-Four Violins to rehearse for the king's impending birthday celebration (to be discussed below) is addressed "To M[r] Staggins Master of his Ma[ties] Musick & in his absence to M[r] Lock who Officiate[s] for him,"[30] but the by-now venerable Matthew Locke, who would be dead by early August of the same year, would not have been ideally suited to assume the full range of administrative responsibilities attached to the Mastership. It is thus possible that Grabu could have stepped back into some sort of leadership role at this time—either when Staggins departed, or after Locke's death—only giving way upon Staggins's return to England armed with new experience, knowledge, and credentials, and Charles II's making him "lord paramount over all the musick." Indeed, the timing of Staggins's return and rise to a new ascendancy coincides roughly with the likely end of Louis Grabu's shadowy relationship with the court, as evidenced by the commencement of his career as a theatre composer.

If Grabu did indeed have some behind-the-scenes role to play in the activities of the royal musical establishment during Staggins's absence overseas, it would constitute yet another stage in the court's ongoing endeavor to maintain a presence for French music, despite the best efforts of an increasingly xenophobic Parliament and political nation. These efforts included the attempt to institutionalize French through-composed opera in the Royall Academy of Musick in 1674;

---

27 PRO30/32/47 [properly "T53/[0c]"], p. 250 and PRO30/32/35 [properly "T27/4"], p. 251 (*Calendar of Treasury Books* 5: 983; Ashbee, 8: 233, giving "0*d*" for 10*d*). The sum was collected (by whom is not recorded) on 27 May: see E403/1791, p. 75 (Ashbee, 5: 205).

28 This amount was included in a warrant of 22 December 1677 ordering payments to a large number of musicians: PRO30/32/35, p. 194 (*Calendar of Treasury Books* 5: 824; Ashbee, 8: 232). Staggins's money was collected on 25 June: see E403/1791, p. 132 (Ashbee, 5: 205). Note that Staggins's separate position as a member of the violin band was paid directly by the Treasurer of the Chamber rather than the Exchequer, and thus is documented differently.

29 S. C. Lomas, *Calendar of the Manuscripts of the Marquis of Bath Preserved at Longleat, Wiltshire. Vol. II* (Dublin: His Majesty's Stationery Office, 1907), 165 and John Harold Wilson, ed., *The Rochester–Savile Letters, 1671–1680* (Columbus: Ohio State University Press, 1941), 61–62, p. 61. Savile continues, "Hee may raigne there like Great Turke and cutt whose catts-gutts hee please if the harmony bee not to his liking. With what moderation hee will use this absolute power, I leave it to fate and the immortall gods to determine." For possible evidence of Staggins's increased authority over the twenty-four violins, see LC5/143, p. 272 (18 February 1679: Ashbee, 1: 182; *Register*, no. 1080) and LC5/144, p. 146 (22 November 1681: Ashbee, 1: 196; *Register*, no. 1143).

30 LC5/142, p. 38 (see n. 69, below).

to create a hybrid form, staffed with a combination of English and French performers, in *Calisto* in 1675; and, in 1676–77, to revert to more modest projects while still maintaining Cambert and Grabu in a semi-official capacity. The compositional and organizational undertakings of these two men, as we have seen, could be actualized in a variety of ways: French singers temporarily imported from abroad; French wind players kept in reserve through extraordinary appointments at the periphery of the court and deployed as needed; English members of the Twenty-Four Violins pressed into service on special occasions. But Charles II (and, by extension, his adjuncts) seem to have had recourse to another source of French musical talent as well. Whereas the particular status and activities of Grabu, Cambert, de Bresmes, and Guiton are largely shrouded in mystery, there is evidence that the Restoration court also supported an organized, core ensemble of French singers and wind players, whose services would thus have been available on a more regular basis. This small but consequential group of French performers appears to have been maintained in defiance of the Test Act, through the deployment of a series of evasive maneuvers, including deliberate financial sleight-of-hand. It seems to have begun as an effort to retain the French bass singer Claude des Granges within the musical establishment, but was subsequently expanded over the course of the later 1670s to encompass two flute/oboe players, Jacques Paisible and Francis (*i.e.* François?) Mariens, and two additional singers, Jacques Arnould and Louis Brunot.[31] Although the court's notorious fiscal insolvency would ultimately complicate matters for these performers, their position in Charles II's musical establishment, at least on paper, appears to have persisted right up until the time of the king's death in 1685, and in all but one case to have resulted in further employment in the next reign.

We have already noted the special treatment accorded Claude des Granges, who alone among the French ensemble of the 1660s survived the retrenchment of 1668. His unusual position as "one of his Majesty's French musicians in ordinary being established among the violins for singing the bass"[32] took effect as of Lady Day 1668, although it was not formally created until the autumn of 1671, whereupon he was quickly paid 2¼ years' worth of the arrears on his substantial annual salary of £100.[33] Two subsequent payments show his continuance in this capacity: in 1672–73 he received a further £100 (covering his service for the year ending at

---

31 We should also note the continued, if anomalous, presence of the aged countertenor Anthony Robert in Charles II's ensemble of Lutes and Voices (see Chapter 6, n. 32, above).

32 LC5/14, p. 44 (see Chapter 5, n. 88, above).

33 AO1/397/90, f. 5ʳ (Ashbee, 5: 130); specific payments are undated, but this Audit Office summary covers the period from Michaelmas 1671 to Michaelmas 1672. The article on des Granges in Ashbee and Lasocki, *Biographical Dictionary* (see Chapter 6, n. 16, above) erroneously states (1: 506) that "No notice of payments has been discovered, so he was probably paid from the privy purse"; this mistake appears to stem from the fact that citations to the relevant entries in Ashbee (5: 130, 133, and 137) have unaccountably been omitted from the indices: see Ashbee, 5: 319 and 9: 142.

272   *"For such uses as the King shall direct"*

Midsummer 1671),[34] and sometime after Michaelmas 1673 he collected another large sum: £200, amounting to his entire arrears up to Midsummer 1673, the last quarter day prior to the enforcement of the Test Act.[35] Immediately thereafter, des Granges vanishes from the court accounts—as well we might expect given the circumstances. But on 10 May 1675, Charles II issued a Signet Warrant retroactively authorizing a regular annual payment, commencing at Midsummer 1673, of £100, the same amount that des Granges had been receiving prior to that date.[36] This document—issued, perhaps not coincidentally, less than two weeks after the final performance of *Calisto*, in which des Granges had been a participant—stipulated that the money be paid to the Master of the Music, Staggins, "without account, for such uses as the King shall direct." The disposition of the sequence of payments resulting from this order is summarized as *"Series 1"* in Table 7.1; their deliberately mysterious character—the unspecified "uses" are never identified, and no recipient other than Staggins is ever named in association with any of their disbursements—suggests a clandestine effort on the court's part to circumvent the strictures of the Test Act in order to retain the services of an essential musical figure, and it therefore seems likely that the payments were intended as a way of continuing des Granges's salary.[37]

The probable identification of these payments as being for des Granges would help to explain several other references to the singer in post-1673 court documents. It is noteworthy, for example, that he was one of only two French performers in *Calisto* (the other was the dancer Saint-André) who did not receive a special fee in exchange for their services.[38] Des Granges is believed to have fled England with other Roman Catholics in 1679,[39] but was back in the royal service with "a new Certificate" in early 1681;[40] thereafter, he surfaces in two orders for single quarterly payments of £25 each, issued on 15 July 1682 and 2 December 1684,[41] and his name is listed in an account of arrears owed to Charles II's servants as of Midsummer 1684.[42] In the latter document, des Granges is said to be due £650 for the six and a half years dating back to Christmas 1677, precisely the

---

34 AO1/398/94, f. 4ʳ (Ashbee, 5: 133).

35 AO1/398/95, f. 4ᵛ (Ashbee, 5: 137); des Granges is not known, however, to have received any of the livery payments that were normally issued to royal servants.

36 SP44/334, p. 61 (*Calendar of State Papers, Domestic 1675–76*: 113; Ashbee, 8: 219); see Table 7.1, note a.

37 Peter Holman (*Fiddlers*, 298) seems to believe that the original order represents a payment intended for Staggins himself, and that the Englishman may in consequence have assumed the duties of the Mastership of the Music from Grabu as of Midsummer 1673, a responsibility for which the money served as recompense. This is almost certainly a misreading of the document, particularly given the continuation of the payments into the late 1670s, when Staggins was well ensconced (and suitably remunerated) as Master in his own right.

38 See Walkling, "Masque and Politics," 34–36 (Table 2), 38, and 51–52 (including Table 6).

39 See nn. 12, above, and 43, below.

40 LC3/28, p. 102 (entry in establishment book, giving date of 10 March "1680": Ashbee, 1: 231).

41 See Table 7.1, notes f and g.

42 British Library, Add. MS 51320, f. 70ᵛ. I am very grateful to Andrew Ashbee, who discovered this document after the publication of his *Records of English Court Music* series, for kindly providing me with a digest of its contents before I had the opportunity to go and see it myself.

French musicians at court, 1675–89   273

point at which the payments to Staggins appear to have dried up.[43] Ultimately, his tenacity was rewarded following the accession of James II: sometime between 27 December 1685 and 22 March 1686 he received an advance of £50 from the Secret Service account "to be repayd out of his Wages" (*i.e.* possibly on the security of his arrears),[44] and by July 1687, he had been appointed as one of the group of ten "Gregorians" in James's Roman Catholic Chapel Royal (see Table 7.1, "*Series 5*" and "*Series 6*").[45] Armed with this information, it is therefore possible to trace a near-continuous association of Claude des Granges with the Restoration court from 1663 to the Revolution of 1688–89, encompassing more than a quarter-century of service.[46]

The initial experiment in illicit payments to an otherwise proscribed French musician from Midsummer 1673 appears to have inspired Charles II to expand this program as the decade wore on. On 25 February 1676, just as Nicholas

---

43 The £650 figure raises several questions. First, it seems to include the £25 payment, covering the first quarter of 1678, that may have been ordered on 15 July 1682 (see Table 7.1, note f), and is recorded as having already been paid (to Staggins, as usual) sometime between Michaelmas 1682 and Michaelmas 1683 (AO1/403/119 [Ashbee, 5: 162]). Second, the continuous accrual of arrears would appear to contradict the evidence of des Granges having obtained a pass to travel with his wife, niece, and maidservant to "parts beyond seas" on 15 May 1679 (SP44/51, p. 240; see n. 12, above), and his supposed return to England nearly two years later. It is of course possible that des Granges's pass—whose issuance may have been precipitated by the death of his elderly colleague Anthony Robert on 9 May 1679—was never used, and that the musician simply stayed on in London through the height of the "Exclusion Crisis," and hence continued to accumulate salary. In any event, des Granges seems to have been in financial difficulty toward the end of Charles II's reign: on 31 May 1683 he was ordered to be arrested at the suit of one Thomas Blackwell (LC5/191, f. 114ᵛ [Ashbee, 1: 206]). There is, moreover, no evidence that his remaining arrears were ever paid, even after James II's accession.

44 Bodleian Library, MS Rawlinson D. 872, p. 100; T48/14, p. 100 (Ashbee, 5: 273); see also Akerman, 125 (see Chapter 5, n. 34, above).

45 Des Granges's colleagues among the Gregorians included Bartolomeo Albrici (see Chapter 5, n. 34, above) and Jacques Arnould (see p. 279, below). For the first Chapel Royal establishment, dated 5 July 1687 and retroactive to Lady Day 1687, see T52/12, p. 211 (*Calendar of Treasury Books* 8: 1442; Ashbee, 8: 271) and LS13/255, p. 53 (Ashbee, 5: 84); for the second establishment, dated 20 March 1688 and retroactive to Christmas 1687 (which reduced the number of Gregorians to eight), see T52/12, pp. 430–31 (*Calendar of Treasury Books* 8: 1823; Ashbee, 8: 277) and LS13/255, p. 59 (Ashbee, 5: 86–87). By a royal warrant issued on 5 August 1687, the Chapel musicians were exempted from deductions normally assessed for the payment of salaries (LS13/255, p. 53 [Ashbee, 5: 85]). In the summer of 1687 they traveled with the king to Windsor, ultimately returning to London on 11 October, whereupon they were compensated for their lodging costs (LC5/148, pp. 54–56 [19 December 1687: Ashbee, 2: 16–17]); they returned to Windsor with the king, from 24 July–20 September 1688, following which they again received a travel allowance (LC5/148, p. 341 [20 October 1688: Ashbee, 2: 21]). For a detailed study of this institution, see Peter Leech, "Music and Musicians in the Catholic Chapel of James II at Whitehall, 1686–1688," *Early Music* 39 (2011): 379–400.

46 After James II's overthrow, des Granges seems to have remained in London until his death in 1692: his will is in London Metropolitan Archives (Archdeaconry Court of Middlesex), DL/AM/PW/1691/28 (summarized in Ashbee and Lasocki, *Biographical Dictionary of English Court Musicians* [see Chapter 6, n. 16, above], 1: 507); for probate, dated 8 March, see E406/51, p. 19 (Ashbee, 5: 90).

Table 7.1 Court payments to certain French musicians, 1668–89

PERIOD/DATE OF ACTUAL PAYMENT (Michaelmas–Michaelmas, unless otherwise specified)	Series 1 (£100 per annum)[a] Claude des Granges (French Singer)						Series 2 (£200 per annum)[b] French Recorders						Series 3 (£200 per annum)[c] French Singers					
	QUARTERS/ AMOUNTS PAID					NAMED PAYEE/ (DISTRIBUTION)	QUARTERS/ AMOUNTS PAID					NAMED PAYEE(S)/ (DISTRIBUTION)	QUARTERS/ AMOUNTS PAID					NAMED PAYEES/ (DISTRIBUTION)
	Year	A	B	C	D		Year	A	B	C	D		Year	A	B	C	D	
1671–1672 AO1/397/90, f. 5ʳ (Ashbee, 5: 130)	1668	~	£25	£25	£25	des Granges												
	1669	£25	£25	£25	£25													
1672–1673 AO1/398/94, f. 4ʳ (Ashbee, 5: 133)	1670	£25	£25	£25	£25	des Granges												
1673–1674 AO1/398/95, f. 4ʳ (Ashbee, 5: 137)	1671	£25	£25	£25	£25	des Granges												
	1672	£25	£25	£25	£25													
1674–1675 AO1/399/97 (Ashbee, 5: 140)	1673	£25	£25	£25	£25	Staggins (at king's direction)												
1675–1676 AO1/399/100 (Ashbee, 5: 143)	1674	£25	£25	£25	£25	Staggins (at king's direction)	1676	£50	£50	£50		Staggins (at king's direction)						
1676–1677 AO1/400/103 (Ashbee, 5: 146)	1675	£25		£25	£25	Staggins* (at king's direction)	1677	£50	£50	£50	£50	Staggins* (at king's direction / "for the French musicians")[d]						
1677–1678 AO1/401/106 (Ashbee, 5: 150)	1676		£25	£25	£25	Staggins (at king's direction)												
1678–1679 AO1/401/109 (Ashbee, 5: 153)	1677	£25	£25	£25		Staggins (at king's direction)												
1679–1680 AO1/402/112 (Ashbee, 5: 156)					£25	Staggins (at king's direction)	1677				[£50] £37½	Staggins (at king's direction)						
[no payment recorded]							1677				£12½	Paisible[e] [order 14 Aug. 1684]						

1680–1681 [AO1/402/115: *no relevant payments recorded*]						
1681–1682 [AO1/403/118: *no relevant payments recorded*]						
[payment status uncertain]		*des Granges*[f] [order: 15 Jul. 1682]		*Paisible*[f] [order: 15 Jul. 1682]		
[no payments recorded]	1678	*des Granges*[g] [order: 2 Dec. 1684] £25?	£25	"*the musicians*"[h] [order: 2 Aug. 1678]	1678	£50 £50 £50
1682–1683 AO1/403/119 (Ashbee, 5: 162)		Staggins (at king's direction) £25?				
1683–1684 [AO1/404/121: *no relevant payments recorded*]						

			Mariens; Paisible (£25 each/qtr., then £8⅓ each/qtr.†)			Arnould; Brunot (£25 each/qtr., then £8⅓ each/qtr.†)
	[no record of actual arrears payments to des Granges[i]]	1678			1678	
1679		1679	[£50] £50	£50	1679	£50 £50 £50
1680		1680	[£50] £16⅔	£16⅔ £16⅔	1680	£16⅔ £16⅔ £16⅔
1681		1681	[£50] £16⅔	£16⅔ £16⅔	1681	£16⅔ £16⅔ £16⅔
1682		1682	[£50] £16⅔	£16⅔ £16⅔	1682	£16⅔ £16⅔ £16⅔
1683		1683	[£50] £16⅔	£16⅔ £16⅔	1683	£16⅔ £16⅔ £16⅔
1684		1684	£16⅔	£16⅔ £16⅔	1684	£16⅔ £16⅔ £16⅔

10 February 1688
E403/1810, p. 176 (Ashbee, 2: 214)

[SETTLEMENT OF ARREARS: payment "for 6½ years from Midsummer 1678 to Christmas 1684 at £100 a year [each], payable from the loan on French linen and tobacco"]

1678	[£25] £25	[£25] —	[£25] —
1679	[£25] —	[£25] —	[£25] —
1680	[£25] —	[£25] —	[£25] —
1681	[£25] —	[£25] —	[£25] —
1682	[£25] —	[£25] —	[£25] —
1683	[£25] —	[£25] —	[£25] —
1684	[£25] —	[£25] —	

* Paid to Isaac Staggins as assignee of Nicholas Staggins.

† All arrears discounted by ⅔ from Midsummer 1679.

(Continued)

Period/Date of Actual Payment (Michaelmas–Michaelmas, unless otherwise specified)	Series 4 (£40 each *per annum*)[k] James II Private Music					
	Quarters/ Amounts Paid					Named Payees/ (Distribution)
	Year	A	B	C	D	
1684–1685 AO1/404/124 (Ashbee, 5: 165; 2: 136)	1685	~	£20			Mariens; Paisible (£10 ea./qtr.)
1685–1686 AO1/405/127 (Ashbee, 2: 136)				£20	£20	Mariens; Paisible (£10 ea./qtr.)
	1686	£20	£20			
1686–1687 AO1/405/130 (Ashbee, 2: 137)				£20	£20	Mariens; Paisible (£10 ea./qtr.)
	1687	£20	£20			
1687–1688 AO1/406/133 (Ashbee, 2: 139)				£20	£20	Mariens; Paisible (£10 ea./qtr.)
	1688	£20	£20			
[*gap in records, Christmas 1688–Midsummer 1692*][l]				*£20*	*£20*	Mariens; Paisible (£10 ea./qtr.)
	1689	*£20*	~	~	~	

Series 5 (£50 each *per annum*: 1687 **BCD** [*N.B.* bulk payments for 1687 **BC** recorded in LS1/30 (Ashbee, 5: 232)]) James II Roman Catholic Chapel Royal (First Establishment)[m]

Includes:
"Mr La Grange" (Gregorian)
"Mr Arnould" (Gregorian)
"Mr Peasible" (Instrumentalist)

Series 6 (£50 each *per annum*: 1688 **ABCD**/1689 **A** [*N.B.* no record of actual payments]) James II Roman Catholic Chapel Royal (Second Establishment)[n]

Includes:
"Mr Legrange" (Gregorian)
"Mr Arnould" (Gregorian)
"Mr Peasable" (Instrumentalist)

Key:
~ = no appointment in effect for this quarter
[£_] = included in list of arrears, Midsummer 1684, owed to "Claudius de Grange at 100ᵗ per Annu⁾ from Christmas 1677 to Midsomer 1684 for six yeares and a Half [£]650/0/0" and to Nicholas Staggins for "the ffrench Recorders at 200ᵗ per Annu⁾ from Michmas 1677 to Midsomer 1684 for six yeares and three Quarters [£]1350/0/0" (British Library, Add. MS 51320, f. 70ᵛ)

Key to quarters:
A = Lady Day (26 December–25 March)
B = Midsummer (26 March–24 June [Feast of St. John the Baptist])
C = Michaelmas (25 June–29 September)
D = Christmas (30 September–25 December)

[a] **Initiating documents:**
- **Appointment of des Granges as "one of his Majesty's French musicians in ordinary … among the violins for singing the bass":**
  Warrant to Clerk of the Signet, 18 September 1671: LC5/14, p. 44 (Ashbee, 1: 108).
  Signet warrant, November 1671: SO3/16, p. 471 and SP38/25/151 (Ashbee, 5: 60 and 8: 210).
- **Initiation of payments through Staggins "without account, for such uses as the king shall direct":**
  Signet warrant, 10 May 1675: SP44/334, p. 61 (CSPD 1675–76: 113; Ashbee, 8: 219).

[b] **Initiating documents:**
Minute of Privy Seal warrant, 25 February 1676: SP44/334, p. 136 (*CSPD* 1675–76: 578; Ashbee, 8: 223–24).
Royal warrant, 24 May 1676: PRO30/32/43 (properly "T52/5"), pp. 149–50 (*CTB* 5: 293; Ashbee, 8: 227).
Docquet entry, 21 July 1676: PRO30/32/13, p. 83 (*ibid.*).
Letters dormant of Privy Seal, 31 July 1676: PRO30/32/43 (properly "T52/5"), p. 254 (*ibid.*).

[c] **Initiating document:**
Royal warrant "[to pay the] Treasurer of the Chamber £400 a year for 4 French musicians," 11 July 1678: PRO30/32/54, p. 100 (*CTB* 5: 1461; Ashbee, 8: 233 [erroneously giving "£200"]).

[d] **Order:**
Money warrant, 24 April 1677 ("for 1 year from Christmas last"): PRO30/32/47 (properly "T53/[0c]"), p. 60 (*CTB* 5: 605; Ashbee, 8: 228).
Auditor of receipt to pay Treasurer of the Chamber £200 for Staggins "for the French musicians," ?7 July 1677: PRO30/32/35 (properly "T27/4"), p. 114 (*CTB* 5: 682; Ashbee, 8: 230).

[e] **Order:**
Treasurer of the Chamber to pay £12 10s to "Mr. Peaceable": T61/2, p. 395 (*CTB* 7: 1287; Ashbee, 8: 258).

[f] **Order:**
Treasurer of the Chamber to pay £25 "to Dr. Staggins on £200 being intended for Mr. Peaceable" and £25 "to Claudius de Grange": T61/2, p. 163 (*CTB* 7: 543–44; Ashbee, 8: 246–47).

[g] **Order:**
Treasurer of the Chamber to pay £25 "to Claudius de Grange": T61/3, p. 23 (*CTB* 7: 1420; Ashbee, 8: 260).

[h] **Order:**
"Charles Bertie to the Auditor of Receipt, to pay £200 for the musicians": PRO30/32/35 (properly "T27/4"), p. 295 (*CTB* 5: 1079; Ashbee, 8: 234).

[i] *N.B.* "Claudius des granges His Maties Servant in ye Quality of Musitian in Ordinary to His Matie with Fee; a new Certificate," 10 March 168[1]: LC3/28, p. 102 (Ashbee, 1: 231).

[j] **Order:**
Treasury Commissioners "to issue to Francis Mariens, James Peasable, James Arnau and Lewis Brunot, four of his late Majesty's private musick, the sum of £1133 6s 8d pursuant to a warrant signed by their Lordships for this purpose from the imposition on tobacco and sugar," 9 February 1688: E403/3086, f. 65^v (Ashbee, 2: 205).

[k] **Initiating documents:**
Establishment list issued "At Windsor castle: By His Maties Command to my Ld. Chamberlaine," 31 August 1685: LC3/30, p. 101 (Ashbee, 2: 122).
Lord Chamberlain's warrant to swear musicians, 31 August 1685: LC5/146, p. 18 (Ashbee, 2: 2–3).
Royal warrant, 21 October 1685: LC3/30 (Ashbee, 2: 5).
Warrant, 21 October 1685: SP44/336, pp. 256–57 (*CSPD* 1685: 360; Ashbee, 8: 262–63).

[l] **Document:**
List of payments in arrears, 25 March 1689: LC9/389 (Ashbee, 2: 23–24) [*N.B.* amounts in italics (1688–89) are presumed: no actual order for, or record of, payment exists].

[m] **Initiating document:**
Chapel Royal establishment, 5 July 1687: T52/12, p. 211 (*CTB* 8: 1442; Ashbee, 8: 271) and LS13/255, p. 53 (Ashbee, 5: 84).
Additional document: Royal warrant: Chapel musicians to be paid without deductions, 5 August 1687: LS13/255, p. 53 (Ashbee, 5: 85).

[n] **Initiating document:**
Chapel Royal establishment, 20 March 1688: T52/12, pp. 430–31 (*CTB* 8: 1823; Ashbee, 8: 277) and LS13/255, p. 59 (Ashbee, 5: 86–87).

278   *"For such uses as the King shall direct"*

Staggins was undertaking preparations for his overseas journey, a second payment stream was established, this time of £200 *per annum*, commencing from Christmas 1675, and again described as being "for certain uses directed by the King, and to be received ... without account."[47] A third stream, also of £200 *per annum*, and backdated to Christmas 1677, seems to have been initiated on 11 July 1678, not long after Staggins's return (see below). The earlier of these two new streams, digested in Table 7.1 as *"Series 2,"* is particularly illuminating. Like the parallel annual disbursements of £100 that I have argued were intended for des Granges, these were also channeled through Staggins as Master of the Music,[48] but in this case their real purpose gradually emerges as the documents progress. In July 1677, a marginal note identifies the funds as being "for the French musicians,"[49] and in July 1682 a small amount of money set aside for payment to Staggins is unequivocally listed as being "on £200 being intended for Mr. Peaceable,"[50] *i e.* the French flute/oboe player Jacques Paisible, who had come to England in 1673 as the junior member of the ensemble that also included de Bresmes and Guiton. By Michaelmas 1680, the payments had fallen nearly three years into arrears and, like those intended for des Granges, would be further disrupted by the Restoration court's mounting fiscal insolvency. Despite a few sporadic orders issued in 1678, 1682, and 1684 for payment of various, mostly fractional, sums, the Midsummer 1684 statement of arrears already mentioned acknowledges a substantial debt of £1350, stretching back more than six years, owed to "Dr Nicholas Staggins for the ffrench Recorders."[51] Most of that amount,

---

47   SP44/334, p. 136 (*Calendar of State Papers, Domestic* 1675–76: 578; Ashbee, 8: 223–24); for additional documents setting up this payment stream, see Table 7.1, note b.

48   As Table 7.1 shows, during Nicholas Staggins's absence abroad, at least some of the payments in both *"Series 1"* and *"Series 2"* were collected from the Treasurer of the Chamber by his father Isaac.

49   PRO30/32/35, p. 114 (see Table 7.1, note d).

50   T61/2, p. 163 (see Table 7.1, note f).

51   British Library, Add. MS 51320, f. 70^v: "To Dr Nicholas Staggins for the ffrench Recorders at 200^{li} per Annu$^)$ from Mic̄hmas 1677 to Midsomer 1684 for six yeares and three Quarters [£]1350/0/0." As Table 7.1 reveals, some questions remain about the dates and amounts of the arrears recorded in this entry: according to AO1/402/112, £37 10s (or three-quarters of the usual £50 quarterly payment) had already been disbursed for the last quarter (Michaelmas to Christmas) of 1677 sometime prior to Michaelmas 1680, and hence this quarter should not have been listed—at least not in full—among the arrears outstanding as of Midsummer 1684. On the other hand, the remaining £12 10s does appear belatedly to have been released in August 1684, after the creation of the list (see T61/2, p. 395 [see Table 7.1, note e], identifying "Mr. Peaceable" as the recipient)—although no record survives of either Staggins or Paisible having actually received the money. The situation regarding the following two quarters, constituting the first half of 1678, is also perplexing: the requisite sum of £100 would seem to be included in an order of 2 August 1678 "to the Auditor of Receipt, to pay £200 for the musicians" (see n. 60, below for an explanation of this amount), but part of the same £100 sum appears to be covered by £25 ordered to be paid by the Treasurer of the Chamber "to Dr. Staggins on £200 [*i.e. per annum*, and by this time significantly in arrears] being intended for Mr. Peaceable" (see n. 50, above) some four years later, on 15 July 1682. Again, there is no record as to when this £25, presumably representing Paisible's personal share of one quarter's payment (which apparently had not been paid to him in the wake of the August 1678 order), was actually disbursed. The accounting of outstanding arrears given at the time of the final settlement

French musicians at court, 1675–89   279

plus a bit more, was still outstanding in 1688, when James II finally arranged to clear his late brother's books, albeit at a hefty discount.[52] By this time, with the political and social upheavals of the early 1680s now well in the past—and with the new monarch openly disregarding the provisions of the Test Act—Paisible was comfortably in possession of two court appointments, one in the Private Music and one in the Roman Catholic Chapel Royal (see Table 7.1, "*Series 4*" and "*Series 5*"/"*Series 6*," respectively).[53] Joining him in the former ensemble was another wind player, one Francis Mariens, who is sometimes listed in the documents simply as "Monsieur Mario."[54] Mariens emerges as a close associate of Paisible, alongside whom he is explicitly named in the 1688 order for payment of Charles II's arrears. It appears, therefore, that the £200 annual payment just discussed may have been divided equally between Paisible and Mariens, and although the latter's presence in England can only be documented with certainty as far back as Midsummer 1678 (the commencement of the arrears with which his name is connected), he may already have been Paisible's colleague as early

---

in 1688 (see nn. 52 and 56, below) reaches back only to Midsummer 1678, implying that the full £100 covering the first two quarters of 1678 was indeed paid out at some unknown date, most likely between 15 July 1682 and the death of Charles II. Note that the atypical order to provide £25 to Paisible specifically may have come as a result of the musician having survived the wreck of *HMS Gloucester* on 6 May 1682.

52 By royal command, all salary arrears from Midsummer 1679 to Christmas 1684 (the last payable "quarter day" of Charles II's life) were cleared at the drastically reduced rate of £33 6s 8d per £100 owed: see for example the statement in T54/11, pp. 387–88 (22 November 1686: *Calendar of Treasury Books* 8: 1017).

53 On 14 April 1685, Paisible was provided with a habit to wear at James's coronation (T27/9, p. 56 [*Calendar of Treasury Books* 8: 130; Ashbee, 8: 261, misdated to July]), although his name does not appear in Francis Sandford's *The History of the Coronation of the Most High, Most Mighty, and Most Excellent Monarch, James II* ([London]: Thomas Newcomb, 1687), the official record of the event. He was formally sworn into the Private Music on 22 October 1685 (LC9/342, pre-numbered pages, "Musitians," p. [2] [Ashbee, 2: 5]). It should be noted that James II offered his servants considerably lower wages than had his more profligate brother—Paisible's main court salary, for example, was reduced from £100 to £40 *per annum*—but this reduction was balanced by a much greater regularity, and hence reliability, of actual payment. Paisible's supplementary role in the Chapel (for which he received an additional £50 *per annum*), and the question of what instrument(s) he played there, are briefly discussed in Leech, "Music and Musicians in the Catholic Chapel of James II" (see n. 45, above), 386. During each of the four summers of James's short reign, he was among those who accompanied the king to Windsor—initially as a member of the Private Music, but from 1687 in his capacity as an attendant in the Chapel: see LC5/147, p. 10 (12 November 1685, including riding charges to Hampton Court: Ashbee, 2: 6); LC5/147, p. 221 (9 November 1686: Ashbee, 2: 12); and the documents cited in n. 45, above.

54 See the documents cited in Table 7.1, note k. Mariens was sworn into the Private Music on 10 September 1685 (LC9/342, pre-numbered pages, "Musitians," p. [9] [Ashbee, 2: 3]), and was paid riding charges for his attendance at Windsor in the summer of 1688 (LC5/148, p. 316 [20 October 1688: Ashbee, 2: 21]). Earlier that year, on 10 March, Mariens witnessed a document assigning the wages of his fellow musician François La Riche to a creditor (LC9/342, f. 25ʳ [Ashbee, 2: 18]).

280　*"For such uses as the King shall direct"*

as Christmas 1675, when this series of payments was first established.[55] Perhaps he had been engaged as a replacement for [?Jean] Boutet who, as we have seen, disappears from the records after the *Calisto* production.

The retrenched arrears payment of 1688, we should note, actually lumps together four French members "of his late Majesty's private musick," each of whom were owed £100 *per annum* from Midsummer 1678.[56] The other two, identified as "James Arnau" and "Lewis Brunot," were probably not wind players, despite being coupled with Paisible and Mariens in the 1688 documents: they are almost certainly the "Mr Arnoul in St James" and "Mr Brunet singing mast^r in Vere Street" named in "A List of Dancing Masters and Musicians Papists" included in a larger "Lyste of Several Papists" presented to the Privy Council on 5 October 1681.[57] No further details are known of Brunot/Brunet, but James Arnau/Arnoul can be identified with the Mr. Arnould who sang with Claude des Granges and Bartolomeo Albrici among the "Gregorians" in James II's Roman Catholic Chapel Royal in 1687 and 1688.[58] Unlike his Gregorian colleagues, he appears to have followed the ill-fated king into exile in France, where he would later (in 1701) describe himself as "Jacques Arnould, ordinaire de la musique du Roi d'Angleterre."[59] Evidently, these two singers, Arnould and Brunot, also formed a part of Charles II's surreptitious French musical establishment, and their appointments—possibly effected, as we have seen, in conjunction with the return of Nicholas Staggins from abroad—may have officially begun as early as Christmas 1677 (see Table 7.1, "*Series 3*"), since a royal warrant issued on 11 July 1678 orders the Treasurer of the Chamber to pay "£400 a year for 4 French musicians."[60]

55　He and Paisible might thus have been the "deux françois que ... joüent parfaittement bien" mentioned by the French ambassador in June 1676 (see p. 265, above).

56　E403/3086, f. 65^v (see Table 7.1, note j) and E403/1810, p. 176.

57　Lilian Gibbens, "Roman Catholic Tradesmen in London, 1681," *Catholic Ancestor* 8 (2000): 58–62, p. 59 (giving "Bere Street" for "Vere Street"). I have been unable to locate the original document, but see PC2/69, p. 365 for a minute of the list's presentation to the Council. The list transcribed by Gibbens is the same one that also mentions the *Calisto* dancers Le Duc and Isaac (see Table 6.2, notes k and m), as well as several other court-associated musicians, including "Mr Robert [*i.e.* the son of the late singer Anthony Robert] his wife his mother & all his family"; "Mr Gorey at Charing Crosse" (Jeremy Gohory, dancing master to Catherine of Braganza and Princesses Mary and Anne); and "Both Launays in Hart's Street that teach to play upon Guitarr" (Henry Deloney and Mr. Delloney or Delawney: see Walkling, "Masque and Politics," 35 [Table 2 and nn. 21–22]).

58　For Arnould's appointment in the Chapel Royal, see the documents cited in n. 45, above.

59　Document (not found) cited in Edward T. Corp, "The Exiled Court of James II and James III: A Centre of Italian Music in France, 1689–1712," *Journal of the Royal Musical Association* 120 (1995): 216–31, p. 221 n. 29; the reference given by Corp (British Library, Add. MS 12592) is incorrect.

60　PRO30/32/54, p. 100 (*Calendar of Treasury Books* 5: 1461; Ashbee, 8: 233); see Table 7.1, note c. This would explain why the Auditor of Receipt was commanded to pay £200 "for the musicians" (PRO30/32/35, p. 295 [see Table 7.1, note h]) on 2 August of that year, rather than the £100 that would have been owed to Paisible and Mariens alone for the first two quarters of 1678. There is, interestingly, no sign of Arnould and Brunot in the 1684 list of arrears in British Library, Add. MS 51320, ff. 69^r–71^v (see n. 51, above).

The discovery of the off-the-books salary payments to five French musicians digested in Table 7.1 is highly significant because it provides a context for understanding the general lack of documentation regarding the activities of these figures at court in the latter years of the 1670s and the first half of the 1680s. While only limited details of specific musical events survive—for example those directed by Cambert in July 1674 and the early summer of 1676, and by Grabu in January 1677—our knowledge that such performers were consistently present at court and that a core group of them seem to have been drawing regular, albeit clandestine and technically illegal, salaries allows us to infer their frequent participation in music-making there, both as members of a small, perhaps exclusively French, ensemble and as an added component in the event of more ambitious orchestral endeavors.

This new understanding of the place of French musical activity at court in the aftermath of the Royall Academy of Musick and the *Calisto* production raises questions about the nature of the music itself. This is difficult territory, given the extremely limited quantity of through-composed music that survives from any of the court and court-sponsored productions of the period. Just as we possess only a few identifiable dances from Sir William Davenant's operas of the 1650s, and nothing at all of Richard Flecknoe's fascinating works of the same period, or of Giovanni Battista Draghi's abortive Italian opera of c.1667,[61] so the musical remains dating from the 1670s present a similarly paltry assemblage. Nothing at all of *Ariane* is known to survive in any French or English sources, and, consequently, we are left with only some disembodied scraps of Staggins's music for *Calisto*,[62] and a single melody by Cambert for *Ballet et Musique*, fortuitously unearthed by John Buttrey.[63] It therefore remains exceedingly difficult to assess the nature of through-composed court theatrical music in the 1670s—a predicament not much different from that afflicting the 1650s and 1660s, despite the considerable expansion of activity in this area during this later decade. Of course, certain imported works can be at least partially reconstructed: Cambert's *Pomone*, if it was presented by the Royall Academy of Musick at Drury Lane in April 1674, and the Lully episodes heard at the Duchess of Portsmouth's in 1676 are both examples.[64] But this still leaves us with a deafening silence in place of the tunes, rhythms, and harmonies that we would ideally wish to have available for examination. Only in the 1680s, as will be shown presently, is it possible to find the intact musical scores that permit a full analysis of through-composition in Restoration England.

In the absence of any such compositions for the period immediately prior to the 1680s, we can at least consider the known activities of the composers themselves. Certainly, the evidence already discussed suggests that both Cambert and

---

61 *Cupid and Death* is, of course, the notable exception.
62 See Walkling, "Masque and Politics," 31–32; Holman, *Fiddlers*, 369–73; and Chapter 2, n. 67, above.
63 See Chapter 6, n. 36, above.
64 See n. 16, above, for the suggestion that the performance directed by Grabu in January or February 1677 might have been his *Pastoralle* (published 1684).

282 *"For such uses as the King shall direct"*

Grabu may have continued to compose music for Charles II's court throughout the mid-1670s. Grabu, as we have seen, might have carried out administrative duties as well, particularly between Staggins's departure in 1676 and his return in 1678, and this may have created a need for further assistance in the compositional realm. Such a requirement would have been exacerbated in February or March 1677, when Cambert died under mysterious circumstances that have never been satisfactorily explained.[65] The chief beneficiary of the resulting vacancy seems to have been Jacques Paisible, who emerges at this time as not merely an instrumentalist, but a composer as well.[66] In October 1677, for example, we find him carrying a personal letter from the Earl of Rochester in Oxfordshire to Rochester's friend Henry Savile at court, in which Rochester requests that Savile "take care of" Paisible, "that the King may hear his Tunes, when he is easie and private, because I am sure they will divert him extreamly."[67] Savile replied soon after, informing the Earl that "I obeyed your commands to His Majesty who has heard with very great delight Paisible's new compositions."[68] In fact, Paisible had already made his mark at court earlier that same year when he commandeered the full complement of Charles II's Twenty-Four Violins (twice as many as had previously been made available to Cambert and Grabu) to rehearse "such Musick as is to be in ye ffrench Comedy to be acted before his Matie on ye Nyne & twentieth of May instant," the king's birthday celebration.[69]

---

65 Cambert's obituary was published in *Le Mercure Galant*, April 1677: 15–18; curiously, his widow Marie Du Moustier and their daughter Marianne seem to have stayed on in England for nearly two years after the tragedy, being granted a pass to depart for France on 1 December 1678 (SP44/51, p. 95 [*Calendar of State Papers, Domestic* 1678: 615]). For an exploration of the questions surrounding Cambert's demise, see Albert I. Borowitz, "Lully and the Death of Cambert," *The Music Review* 35 (1974): 231–39, an article that has since been reprinted in multiple venues: see Borowitz, *A Gallery of Sinister Perspectives: Ten Crimes and a Scandal* (Kent, OH: Kent State University Press, 1982), 51–61; "Crimes Gone By: Collected Essays of Albert Borowitz 1966–2005," special issue of *Legal Studies Forum* 29 (2005): 899–910; and Borowitz, *Musical Mysteries from Mozart to John Lennon* (Kent, OH: Kent State University Press, 2010), 3–15.

66 Claude des Granges is also known to have possessed compositional skills: two Latin motets by him survive from the early or mid-1660s (see Leech, "Musicians in the Catholic Chapel of Catherine of Braganza," 577), and sometime during the 1670s he appears to have written music, now lost, for an English song, "With a damn'd sullen fate let's no longer conspire," the words for which were printed in Thomas Duffett, *New Poems, Songs, Prologues and Epilogues* (London: Nicholas Woolfe, 1676) and "P. W.," *New Songs, and Poems, A-la-mode both at Covrt, and Theaters, Now Extant* (idem, 1677), 45–46, and also appear in Beinecke Library, Yale University, Osborn fb107, p. 67 ("Song 133").

67 Letter of John Wilmot, 2nd Earl of Rochester to Henry Savile, [October 1677], as printed in *Familiar Letters: Written by the Right Honourable John late Earl of Rochester, And several other Persons of Honour and Quality* (2 vols.: London: Sam[uel] Briscoe, 1697), 1: 40–43, p. 42, and Wilson, ed., *The Rochester–Savile Letters* (see n. 29, above), 46–47. Rochester continues by wishing that Charles II may "*ever* have *Harmony* in his *Mind*, as this Fellow will pour it into his *Ears*."

68 Letter of Savile to Rochester, 1 November 1677: see Lomas, *Calendar of the Manuscripts of the Marquis of Bath ... Vol. II* (see n. 29, above), 158–59, p. 159, and Wilson, ed., *The Rochester–Savile Letters*, 48–49, p. 49.

69 LC5/142, p. 38 (22 May 1677: *Register*, no. 1010; Ashbee, 1: 171–72).

The piece in question was the part-sung, part-spoken, masque-like entertainment *Rare en Tout*, which we have explored in Chapter 3. The five professional singers required for this French "opera" probably comprised three men—possibly including Claude des Granges and Anthony Robert (Arnould and Brunot had presumably not yet arrived)—and two women, while the necessary dancers may have been either English or French, "occupational" or "recreational" (and might have been choreographed by Saint-André, assuming he was still in London at the time). Of particular interest is the "son de six hautbois" supposed to appear in the production's first, maritime *intermède*[70]: this ensemble may have included de Bresmes, Guiton, Mariens, and probably Paisible himself, and should be compared with the "cinq ou six hommes qui jouent fort bien de la fluste" heard by Ambassador Courtin the previous year, not to mention the "Consort of Hautboyes" thought to have appeared in *Volpone* at Drury Lane at around the same time. We have noted in Chapter 3 the unfavorable reception accorded *Rare en Tout* by both Ambassador Courtin and John Verney. Yet in contrast to Courtin's purely negative assessment,[71] Verney felt, at least, that "the dances and voices was pretty well performed,"[72] implying perhaps that Paisible's contribution—quite possibly his debut as a composer—may have represented a worthy effort. As is the case with so many other works from this decade, none of the *Rare en Tout* music is known for certain to be extant, and indeed only a scattering of pieces by Paisible actually survives from the 1670s and 1680s at all,[73] so it is difficult to assess the overall quality of his output during this period, or even to know precisely how prolific a court composer he actually was.

---

70 Anne de La Roche-Guilhen, *Rare en Tout: Comedie Meslée de Musique Et de Balets Represantée devant Sa Majesté Sur le Theatre Royal De Whitehall* ("Londres": Jacques Magnes and Richard Bentley, 1677), 9.

71 Archives du Ministère des Affaires Étrangères, Correspondance Politique: Angleterre 123, f. 266^v: "La Comédie estoit détestable, et la Musique ne valoit pas mieux."

72 Alfred J. Horwood, "The Manuscripts of Sir Harry Verney, Bart., at Claydon House, Co. Bucks.," in Historical Manuscripts Commission, *Seventh Report of the Royal Commission on Historical Manuscripts. Part I. Report and Appendix* (London: Her Majesty's Stationery Office, 1879), 433–509, p. 469.

73 For a possible suite for *Rare en Tout*, see Chapter 3, n. 33, above. Paisible's earliest surviving tune that can be definitively dated is "A new Theater Tune By Mr Peasable," first published in the 1678 edition of Thomas Greeting's *The Pleasant Companion* (London: J[ohn] Playford), no. 68. Several tunes by him were published in the 1679 collection *A Vade Mecum For the Lovers of Musick* (London: John Hudgebut), 10, 22, 23, 27, and 36; the two on p. 27 also appear in a ten-movement instrumental suite for an unknown play identified simply as "Pleasure" in Royal College of Music, London, MS 1172, ff. 41^r–42^v and 43^r, which has thus been tentatively dated c.1679. Paisible's eight-movement suite for Thomas Shadwell's *Timon of Athens*, found in British Library, Add. MSS 39565/30839/39566–67, ff. 37^v–38^v, British Library, Add. MS 35043, ff. 66^v–67^r and 37^r, Royal College of Music, London, MS 1144i/ii, ff. 54^r–55^r/74^r–75^r, and Christ Church, Oxford, Mus. 482, ff. 16^v–17^v (bass part only), may have been written for the 1678 premiere of that play (for which Grabu provided vocal music), although the manuscripts themselves all date from the 1690s. (For a fragmentary overture to *Timon of Athens* that could perhaps be by Paisible, see Curtis Alexander Price, *Henry Purcell and the London Stage* [Cambridge: Cambridge University Press, 1984], 94 n. 96.) A set of "Brauls" (*i.e.* branles) is attributed to Paisible in *Apollo's Banquet ... The 5th Edition* (London: Henry Playford, 1687), pt. 2, no. 72. Paisible is also listed as the composer of two English songs from this period: "Could man his wish obtain" was published in 1683 in *Choice*

284 *"For such uses as the King shall direct"*

Paisible's involvement in *Rare en Tout* is important in another respect as well, because it provides the earliest evidence of his association with a group of music-loving French expatriates, operating on the periphery of the royal court, who engaged in their own experiments with through-composed opera. At the center of this society was Hortense Mancini, Duchess Mazarin, whose dramatic appearance in England in December 1675 had caused something of an uproar, both in London social circles and in the notoriously susceptible loins of Charles II.[74] In the end, Mazarin succumbed only briefly to the lure of becoming a royal mistress, despite the considerable efforts of a group of courtiers who wished to supplant the well ensconced Duchess of Portsmouth in the king's affections.[75] Among these courtiers (whose anti-Portsmouth maneuvers were really directed against that duchess's ally, the Lord Treasurer Thomas Osborne, Earl of Danby) was Lord Chamberlain Arlington, whose daughter Isabella, Duchess of Grafton, was, I have argued in Chapter 3, not only the dedicatee but quite possibly the central onstage character of *Rare en Tout*. The young duchess would herself subsequently become part of the Mazarin circle, which also included her tutor/companion Anne de La Roche-Guilhen, *Rare en Tout*'s librettist. But the pivotal creative and intellectual figure of Mazarin's circle was her devoted admirer Charles de Marguetel de Saint-Denis, Seigneur de Saint-Évremond, the polymathic essayist, critic, poet, and dramatist who resided in London throughout the last thirty years of his life. As we have noted in Chapter 3, Saint-Évremond was himself a particular friend of Arlington, appears to have been the (slightly furtive) organizer of the *Rare en Tout* production,[76] and certainly had more than a passing association with La Roche, whose talents he acknowledged more than once in his writings. Beyond this, Saint-Évremond had a strong interest in musical drama and opera: according

---

Ayres and Songs ... The Fourth Book (London: John Playford), 5, and was reprinted as a broadside ballad (described as *"Play'd and Sung at the King's Play-House"*; at least three different versions of the print survive); the instrumental tune can be found in Greeting, *The Pleasant Companion* (1682ff.), no. 71; *Musick's Recreation on The Viol, Lyra-way* (London: J[ohn] Playford, 1682), pt. 2, no. 11 (p. 64); Humphry Salter, *The Genteel Companion* (London: Richard Hunt and Humphry Salter, 1683), no. 21; *The Delightful Companion ... Second Edition* (London: John Playford and John Carr, 1686), no. 34; and *Apollo's Banquet ... The 5th Edition*, pt. 1, no. 70; the un-notated text of the song appears in *A New Collection of the Choicest Songs* (London: D. Brown and T. Benskin, 1682), sig. D1v. A second song, "Such a damn'd fatigue fools do make of wooing," described as *"made to an excellent Tune of Mr. Peasable's,"* is in Thomas D'Urfey, *Choice New Songs Never Before Printed* (London: Joseph Hindmarsh, 1684), 8–9; the text alone is reprinted in *A Compleat Collection of Mr. D'Urfey's Songs and Odes* (London: Joseph Hindmarsh, 1687), 89–90. The remainder of Paisible's extant corpus dates from the 1690s and beyond.

74 Among many illuminating scholarly explorations of the Duchess Mazarin and her arrival in London, see in particular Susan Shifrin, "'Subdued by a Famous Roman Dame': Picturing Foreignness, Notoriety, and Prerogative in the Portraits of Hortense Mancini, Duchess Mazarin," in Julia Marciari Alexander and Catharine MacLeod, eds., *Politics, Transgression, and Representation at the Court of Charles II* (New Haven: Yale University Press, 2007), 141–74.

75 See the discussion in Buttrey, "New Light on Robert Cambert," 201–5.

76 We can recall Courtin's statement that "Tout cela tombe sur St. Evremont qui en paroissoit le directeur. Il fait ce qu'il peut pour se défendre de cette qualité" (Archives du Ministère des Affaires Étrangères, Correspondance Politique: Angleterre 123, f. 267r).

French musicians at court, 1675–89   285

to his early biographer Pierre Des Maizeaux, "il ne manquoit aucun Concert, ni aucun Divertissement de cette nature-là."[77] This interest manifested itself in a variety of literary and performative projects, ranging from his satirical play *Les Opéra* (?1676),[78] to his sponsorship of *Rare en Tout* (1677), to his critical essay "Sur les Opera, a Monsieur de Bouquinquant" (c.1678).[79] Saint-Évremond's evident familiarity with Cambert's work suggests that he may have been on intimate terms with the composer, or at the very least that he had attended the Royall Academy of Musick's production(s) in 1674; his knowledge of the Lully/Quinault *tragédies en musique* must have been arrived at more indirectly, through reports from friends in Paris or access to manuscript or published scores, and perhaps attendance at the 1676 *soirées* mentioned above.[80]

In any event, during the last twenty-five years of his life, Saint-Évremond also wrote a number of his own through-sung dramatic works, which appear to have been performed by members of the Mazarin circle in the intimate setting of the duchess's apartments (see Table 7.2).[81] The earliest of these, a pastoral *Idylle en Musique*, was presented sometime around 1678 as a kind of experiment in the operatic form, and the discussions it provoked led him "quelques jours après" to write the above-mentioned essay "Sur les Opera," which he addressed to the Duke of Buckingham, who had been present at the performance in the Duchess Mazarin's lodgings.[82] Consisting of four scenes sung by three shepherds,

---

77 Pierre Des Maizeaux and Israel Silvestre, eds., *Oeuvres Meslées de M^r. de Saint-Evremond, Publiées sur les Manuscrits de l'Auteur* (2 vols.: London: Jacob Tonson, 1705), 1: sig. c4^r.

78 First published in 1705 (*Oeuvres Meslées*, 2: 111–80). For a modern facsimile edition with commentary, see Robert Finch and Eugène Joliat, eds., *Saint-Evremond: Les Opéra* (Geneva: Droz, 1979).

79 First published in French in 1684 (*Œuvres Meslées. Tome XI* [Paris: Claude Barbin], 77–124), and in two separate English translations in 1685–87: *Mixt Essays Upon Tragedies, Comedies, Italian Comedies, English Comedies, and Opera's* (London: Timothy Goodwin, 1685 [*Register*, no. 1262]; rpt. 1687), 19–28; and Ferrand Spence, *Miscellanea: or Various Discourses ... By the Sieur de Saint Euvremont* (London: Sam[uel] Holford, 1686), 41–62. For a modern edition, see René Ternois, ed., *Saint-Évremond: Œuvres en Prose* (4 vols.: Paris: Marcel Didier, 1962–69), 3: 129–64.

80 See for example Saint-Évremond's letter to his friend Anne Hervart, Master of Requests at the French court, dated 4 February [?1676], responding to the latter's thoughts on the subject (René Ternois, ed., *Saint-Évremond: Lettres* [2 vols.: Paris: Marcel Didier, 1967–68], 1: 217–19, p. 218). Note also Saint-Évremond's letter to Ralph Montagu, 1st Earl of Montagu, written in 1700, in which he observes that the advent of Arcangelo Corelli's music "nous doivent faire mépriser la chaconne de [Lully and Campistron's *Acis et*] *Galatée* et la logistille [*i.e.* the fifth-act fairy scene] de *Roland*" (*ibid.*, 2: 385).

81 For a detailed exploration of these entertainments, see Susan Shifrin and Andrew R. Walkling, "'Idylle en Musique': Performative Hybridity and the Duchess Mazarin as Visual, Textual, and Musical Icon," in Susan Shifrin, ed., *"The Wandering Life I Led": Essays on Hortense Mancini, Duchess Mazarin and Early Modern Women's Border-Crossings* (Newcastle upon Tyne: Cambridge Scholars Publishing, 2009), 48–99. Mazarin's various living quarters are enumerated in this volume's Appendix A, pp. 193–98.

82 See the revised version of Pierre Des Maizeaux, "La Vie de Monsieur de Saint-Evremond. A Monsieur Bayle," printed in Des Maizeaux and Silvestre, eds., *Oeuvres Meslées de M^r. de Saint-Evremond, Publiées sur les Manuscrits de l'Auteur. Seconde Edition Reveüe Corregée & Augmentée* (3 vols.: London: Jacob Tonson, 1709), 1: XLIV (sig. I2^v): describing Saint-Évremond's authorship of

286   *"For such uses as the King shall direct"*

embellished with an overture and ritornelli for violins and "Flûtes," Saint-Évremond's *Idylle* explicitly follows the lead of the court masque genre (including *Rare en Tout*) by having one of the characters refer pointedly to Mazarin ("*Hortence* toute aimable en ses moindres discours / Avec ceux qui peuvent lui plaire"[83]), thus drawing the duchess's offstage persona into the otherwise fictional realm of the theatrical presentation. Later entertainments would go even farther, bringing the duchess and members of her household directly onto the stage, effectively dissolving the distinction between dramatic artifice and the similarly theatricalized reality of Mazarin's *précieuse* courtly-domestic environment. No original music survives for any of these works, but it appears that their composition represented a joint effort between the dilettante Saint-Évremond and one or more professional "assistants"—chief among whom, according to Pierre Des Maizeaux, was Paisible.[84] Indeed, the association between the two men appears to have been long-lasting, successfully bridging the musician's temporary self-imposed exile at the Jacobite court at Saint-Germain-en-Laye between 1689 and early 1693.[85] Paisible's return to Williamite England (a move

---

his essays on Italian, English, and French comedy, Des Maizeaux goes on to record that "M. de St. Evremond fit dans ce tems-là une IDYLLE, dont il composa lui-même la Musique. Cette Piece fut chantée chez Madame de Mazarin, où il se trouva plusieurs personnes de distinction. La Conversation roula ensuite sur les Comedies en Musique, & particulierement sur les Opera, qui faisoient alors tant de bruit en France. M. de St. Evremond ne parla pas fort avantageusement de ces sortes de Compositions; mais n'ayant pas eû le tems de dire tout ce qu'il en pensoit, il écrivit quelques jours après un Discours sur ce sujet, qu'il adressa au Duc de Buckingham, qui avoit été de cette Conversation."

83   *Oeuvres Meslées* (1705), 2: 204; this piece was first published in fragmentary form in 1694 (see Table 7.2). A second, undatable *Idylle en Musique* believed to be by Saint-Évremond was first published in 1706 in the collection *Mélange Curieux des Meilleures Pieces Attribuées à Mr. De Saint-Evremond, et de Plusieurs Autres Ouvrages Rares ou Nouveaux* (2 vols.: Amsterdam: Pierre Mortier, 1706), 2: 296–302. For yet another work with very similar characteristics, and hence possibly also written by Saint-Évremond, see *L'Innocente*[:] *Idile en Musique*, printed in Lecerf de La Viéville, *Comparaison de la Musique Italienne, et de la Musique Françoise* (see Chapter 6, n. 18, above), 2: 42–59.

84   In the "Preface" first published with the 1705 *Oeuvres Meslées* (1: sig. c4^r), Des Maizeaux simply says that "Il est vrai que pour les Ouvertures, les Basses continues, les Chœurs, & toute la Symphonie, il les donnoit à faire à quelque Musicien habile"; however, in "La Vie de ... Saint-Evremond," he elaborates upon this last phrase, saying, "il la donnoit à faire à Mr. *Paisible*, ou à quelque autre habile Musicien" (quoted from the original version, first printed in *Mélange Curieux* [1706], 1: 93 [sig. d11^r]; see also *Oeuvres Meslées ... Seconde Edition* [1709], 1: LXIX [sig. M3^r]).

85   Paisible seems to have waited until some months after the "Glorious Revolution" to join his exiled former master in France. On 25 March 1689, he appeared on a list as being owed £30 of arrears on his £40 annual salary in the regular musical establishment (LC9/389 [Ashbee, 2: 23]), and in late June or July, the visiting Dutch virtuoso Christiaan Huygens recorded being "At the meetingh of musick, ou l'on chantoit des pieces des Opera Francoises," and that "Le Paisible y jouoit de la Flute admirablement bien" (Christiaan Huygens [ed. J. A. Vollgraff], *Oeuvres Complètes. Tome XXII. Supplément à la Correspondance. Varia. Biographie. Catalogue de Vente* [The Hague: Martinus Nijhoff, 1950], 744–45). For Paisible's presence at Saint-Germain-en-Laye, see Corp, "The Exiled Court of James II and James III" (see n. 59, above), 220. Sometime around the middle of the 1690s, in one of his many playful letters to Mazarin, Saint-Évremond reported the successful outcome of a quest to locate Paisible in London, and went on to describe his quarry as "ce grand et paresseux Musicien ... avec des manieres que

rendered less difficult by the fact that he had been made a "Free Denizen" of the country on 16 December 1687[86]) saw the musician building a formidable new career as a composer and performer, on both wind and stringed instruments, in the London theatres, and serving as a household musician to the future Queen Anne[87] and subsequently to her husband Prince George of Denmark.[88] Yet he might well have continued to assist his old friend in his ongoing musical experiments,[89] and may even have contributed to the rather more vulgar scenes written by Saint-Évremond in the last years of his life for his new heartthrob, the Marquise de La Perrine, and perhaps to the eccentric entertainment "Le Colier," a confrontation between gods and lapdogs written for a "*Mr. de* la Devese" (see Table 7.2) that seems to require scenery and even a flying apparatus for one of the characters.[90]

The bulk of Saint-Évremond's "operatic" output was probably written in the 1690s, and thus falls outside the immediate scope of the present study; however,

---

sentent un homme bien nourri … et des termes qu'il peut avoir appris dans sa petite bibliotheque" (Ternois, ed., *Saint-Évremond: Lettres*, 2: 230).

86 See W[illia]m Durrant Cooper, ed., *Lists of Foreign Protestants, and Aliens, Resident in England 1618–1688. From Returns in the State Paper Office* [Camden Society, 82; London: Camden Society, 1862], 53); however, Paisible and his wife Mary Davis were obliged to seek retroactive formal sanction for their repatriation following the passage in December 1697 of the "Act against Corresponding with the Late King James and his Adherents" (9 Gul. III, cap. 1), which set a deadline of 1 February 1698 by which "any Person who since the … Eleventh Day of December in the Yeare of our Lord One thousand six hundred eighty eight went into France or any of the French Kings Dominions without License first had from His Majesty" was obliged to "obtaine His Maj[ties] Licence [under the Privy Seal] for his or her staying here," or face prosecution for treason. For the couple's eleventh-hour license, dated 31 January 1698, see SP44/351, p. 37 (*Calendar of State Papers, Domestic* 1698: 61); it is listed, along with many others, in House of Lords, London, MS 1900a (15 February 1703: Cuthbert Headlam and J. B. Hotham, *The Manuscripts of the House of Lords, Volume V (New Series)* [London: His Majesty's Stationery Office, 1910; rpt. 1965], 206).

87 Edward Chamberlayne, *Angliæ Notitia: or, the Present State of England … The Nineteenth Edition* (London: R. Chiswell *et al.*, 1700), 519 (Ashbee, 5: 291): "Musician, Mr. *Tho.* Paisible, 50*l.*"

88 See T52/24, pp. 86 and 122 (23 June and 8 August 1709: *Calendar of Treasury Books* 23: 223, 299; Ashbee, 8: 309, 310). A very comprehensive biography of Paisible, focusing in particular on his post-1693 activities, can be found in Ashbee and Lasocki, *Biographical Dictionary* (see Chapter 6, n. 16, above), 2: 852–66.

89 The two works dated "c.1692" in Table 7.2 (*Scene en Musique* and *Scene de Bassette*) would seem to have been written prior to Paisible's return from exile in 1693. However, it should be pointed out that the dates given in the table represent no more than approximations: for a discussion of their rationale, see Shifrin and Walkling, 70 n. 40.

90 Saint-Évremond appears to have had an interest in scenic technology: on 22 July 1710, William Pinkethman's summer company in Greenwich mounted a revival of Aphra Behn's *The Emperor of the Moon* in which was featured "a New Invention first Contriv'd by Monsieur St. Everimont, which Represents a Suit[e] of Hangings, which in an Instant is Transform'd to Men and Women" (see *Daily Courant* 2729, verso). This effect, from Act 2 scene 3, had been a part of the play since its premiere in 1687, but Saint-Évremond's "new" device appears not to have been used in the original production: see Aphra Behn, *The Emperor of the Moon: A Farce* (London: Joseph Knight and Francis Saunders, 1687), 27–29; 2nd ed. (1688), 22–24.

Table 7.2 Pastoral and domestic operatic episodes of the Sieur de Saint-Évremond, c.1678–1703

Date	Episode	Characters: Pastoral	Characters: London	Mentioned in Text	Paris 1694 (12mo) [C. Barbin]	Paris 1697a (12mo) [Libraires]	Paris 1700 (8vo) [v/ Barbin]	London 1705 (4o) [J. Tonson]	Amsterdam 1706 (12mo) [P. Mortier]	London 1708 (12mo) [P./I. Vaillant]	London 1709 (4o) [J. Tonson]	London 1711 (8vo) [J. Tonson]	London 1714 (12mo) [J. Tonson]
c.1678	*Idylle en Musique* [I] * (OVERTURE + 4 SCENES)	Lisis,b Tircis, Damonc		HORTENCEd	5: 142–63	5: 117–36		2: 197–209			2: 309–21	4: 1–13	3: 314–28
[uncertain]	*Idylle en Musique* [II] (4 SCENES)	Tircis, CALISTE, Damon, CLORIS		Guidone					2: 296–302	2: 205–11		7: 285–92	7: 312–19
c.1685	*Parodie d'une Scene de l'Opera de Roland* †		ORIANE, MABILE,f [MAZARIN] [ROCHESTER] Morin,g La Forêth	Germain,i Saissac,j Sir Roger,k HEWES,l STRAMFORD,m Douvre,n Feversham°	5: 94–101	5: 74–80		2: 385–88			3: 41–44	4: 257–60	4: 192–97
c.1688	*Les Noces d'Isabelle*		ISABELLE,p Old Poet, [ISABELLA] [Saint-Evremond] Young Musician,q Milonior [Painble] [Milon]					2: 499–503			3: 155–59	5: 49–54	4: 365–70
c.1692	*Scene en Musique*	Lisis, JULIE, Damon, Philandre, CALISTE						2: 567–69			3: 223–25	5: 236–39	5: 42–46
c.1692	*Scene de Bassette*		MAZARIN, MIDDLETON,s Villiers,t Bowcher,u Mustaphav	GRAFTON,w LICHFIELD,x KILDAIR,y MASSONz				2: 553–56			3: 209–12	5: 120–24	5: 21–26
c.1693	*Prologue en Musique* (OVERTURE + 2 SCENES) ‡	Lisis, Tircis, Damon,c *lovers, friends*	Composer, MAZARIN [?Saint-Evremond]	Bowcheru			273–79	2: 604–10			3: 260–66	5: 280–87	5: 96–104
c.1696	*Le Consert de Chelsey* §	Lisis,b Damon, *singers*aa	HORTENCEd					2: 688–91			3: 344–47	5: 392–95	5: 232–36
c.1699 –1703 [for Mme. de La Perrine] ‖	*Les Grateuses*		BETHE,bb Author, *friends*, [Saint-Evremond] GRATEUSES	Montandrecc					2: 305–7	2: 214–16		7: 295–97	7: 322–25
c.1699 –1703 [for Mme. de La Perrine] ‖	*La Jeune Veuve Refugiée*		WIDOW, Friend [LA PERRINE] [Saint-Evremond]	Pibrac,dd L'Abbé,ee BETHÉbb					2: 307–11	2: 216–20		7: 298–302	7: 326–30
c.1699 –1703 ["*Par Mr. de la Devese*"] ¶	*Le Colier*	THEMIS, Cupid	BELETTE,ff Fripon,gg Celadon [Mr. de C.]	CELINDE [Mlle. de R.]					2: 312–16	2: 221–25		7: 302–6	7: 331–36

Key:
Characters—typeface indicates: Male Characters; FEMALE CHARACTERS; *identified choral groups*; ALL-FEMALE CHORAL GROUPS
* = in 1694 and 1697 editions, published as "*Fragment d'une Idylle,*" with first scene missing
† = …*Sur les Joüeuses de Bassete de la Banque de Madame Mazarin*—first part parodies Quinault/Lully, *Roland* (premiered 8 January 1685 at Versailles; performed at the Paris Opéra beginning 8 or 9 March 1685), act 2, scene 1. Also appears in Bibliothèque Nationale, Paris, MS fonds français 15263, ff. 403–6

‡ = in 1700 edition (*Nouvelles Oeuvres Meslées de Monsieur de Saint-Evremont* [chez la Veuve de Claude Barbin]), published as "*Fragment d'une Idylle*," as a single scene and with multiple textual variants

§ = ...*Sur le bruit que avoit couru de la Mort de Monsieur le Duc Mazarin*—Duchess Mazarin living at No. 4, Paradise Row, Chelsea, 1693–99 (actual rumors of the death of her husband have not been discovered)

|| = ——— (*née* Monginot), Marquise de La Perrine

¶ = ?Abel Rotholp de La Devèse

[a] Published as fifth volume of Paris, 1692 four-volume duodecimo edition. Entire five-volume set also reprinted as Paris, 1697b [*C. Barbin*].

[b] "*un Dessus.*" (*Le Consert de Chelsey* [1705], 688).

[c] "*qui fait la Basse.*" (*Idylle en Musique* [1705], 205).

[d] Hortense Mancini, Duchess Mazarin (1645–1699).

[e] Servant of the Duc de Monpensier.

[f] Henrietta (1645/6–1687) (daughter of Richard Boyle, 1st Earl of Burlington), wife of Laurence Hyde, 1st Earl of Rochester (second creation).

[g] "Tailleur" (gambling "banker") of the Duchess Mazarin.

[h] Servant of the Duchess Mazarin (*speaks one partial line only*).

[i] ?Sir John Germaine, 1st Baronet Germaine (1650–1718) ?or Henry Jermyn (see below, note n).

[j] Louis-Guillaume, Comte de Clermont-Lodève, Marquis de Sessac, Vicomte de Lautrec, Vicomte de Nebouzan, Baron de Castelnau-Caumont, Seigneur de Venez, Seigneur de Boussagues, Seigneur de Beaulieu (c.1632–1705). Married 1698 to Jeanne, daughter of Louis, Duc de Luynes.

[k] ?Sir Roger Strickland (c.1640–1717).

[l] ?Margaret Hughes (?–1719) (actress), mistress and heir of Prince Rupert of the Palatinate.

[m] Elizabeth (c.1657–1687) (daughter of Sir Daniel Harvey), wife of Thomas Grey, 2nd Earl of Stamford.

[n] Henry Jermyn (c.1636–1708), created Baron Dover on 13 May 1685.

[o] Louis de Duras, 2nd Earl of Feversham (1640–1709).

[p] Spanish servant of the Duchess Mazarin.

[q] Jacques (James) Paisible, flute/hautboy player and composer (?1656–1721).

[r] Chaplain to the Duchess Mazarin. (But compare "Elizabeth Milon, waiting gentlewoman to the Duchess of Mazarin," granted a pass to go to France, 5 Dec. 1678 [*Calendar of State Papers, Domestic* 1678: 616]).

[s] Jane (Needham), Mrs. Charles Myddelton (c.1646–c.1692).

[t] Francis ("Frank") Villiers (?–1694), younger son of George Villiers, 4th Viscount Grandison; "one of the Tellers of the Exchequer" from February 1685.

[u] "Bocher" in 1700 edition. Unidentified "tailleur" (gambling "banker") of the Duchess Mazarin—possibly identified with Morin (see above, note g)?

[v] Servant ("*Petit Turc*") of the Duchess Mazarin (*silent*).

[w] Isabella (1667–1723) *suo jure* Countess of Arlington (daughter of Henry Bennet, 1st Earl of Arlington), wife of Henry FitzRoy, 1st Duke of Grafton (son of Charles II and Barbara Villiers).

[x] Charlotte Fitzroy (1664–1718) (daughter of Charles II and Barbara Villiers), wife of Edward Henry Lee, 1st Earl of Lichfield (second creation).

[y] Elizabeth (1665–1758) (daughter of Richard Jones, 1st Earl of Ranelagh), wife of John Fitzgerald, 18th Earl of Kildare.

[z] Unidentified.

[aa] "*Le Bas dessus.*"; "*Une Basse.*"; "*Une Haute-contre.*"

[bb] "Betty," servant of the Marquise de La Perrine.

[cc] François de la Rochefoucauld, Marquis de Montandre (1672–1739).

[dd] Guy Du Faur, Seigneur de Pibrac (1529–1584).

[ee] Anthony L'Abbé (c.1680–c.1737), French dancing master.

[ff] Dog belonging to Mr. de Lab[bé?].

[gg] Dog belonging to Mlle. de R./"Celinde," lover of Mr. de C./"Celadon."

290   *"For such uses as the King shall direct"*

two works believed to date from the 1680s offer further insight into the nature of these pieces. The *Parodie D'une Scene De l'Opera de Roland, Sur le Joüeurs & Joüeuses de Bassete de la Banque de Madame Mazarin* presents a "domestic" scene involving the Duchess Mazarin and her friend Henrietta (*née* Boyle) Hyde, Countess of Rochester, the subject of which is the two ladies' love of the popular card-game Basset.[91] Both Mazarin and Rochester appear to have actually sung in the episode themselves, as did their favorite "tailleur" (gambling banker) Morin. The duchess's servant La Forêt also makes a cameo appearance, and the women refer in their conversation to several of their real-world associates, who may have been in the audience at the performance. The bulk of the episode consists of a travesty of Act 2, scene 1 of Lully and Quinault's *tragédie en musique, Roland*, which had premiered at Versailles on 8 January 1685 and began a lengthy run in Paris two months later. The tone of the work is satirical, parodying the original opera's magical grove with its Fountain of Love, and replacing Quinault's heroic characters Angélique and Témire with the two gambling, gossiping noblewomen, who appear under the assumed names of "Oriane" and "Mabile."[92] The *Parodie D'une Scene De ... Roland* displays yet again both Saint-Évremond's interest in and his critical attitude toward through-composed opera, but it also represents the domestication of the form, in terms of content as well as setting. The same is true of his other pre-1690s entertainment, *Les Noces d'Isabelle*, which probably dates from around 1688. This witty interlude posits a bigamous marriage between the Duchess Mazarin's Spanish serving-woman Isabella (not to be confused with the similarly named Duchess of Grafton) and two previously competing gentlemen, "un vieux poete" and "un jeune musicien." The poet, who describes himself as "Vieillard caduc proche du trépas,"[93] is almost certainly Saint-Évremond himself, while the young musician is explicitly addressed by the episode's fourth character (Mazarin's chaplain Milon, who performs the dual "marriages") as "*Paisible*"—a marginal note in the early-eighteenth-century editions explicates the name as "*Fameux Musicien*."[94] Paisible's starring role in this *divertissement* would have obviated his fulfilling his customary duties as an instrumentalist, but at least two of his wind-playing colleagues may have been in attendance, as the text indicates not only successive ritornelli for "*Les Violons*" and "*Les Flutes*" but also, at the very end of the piece, one for "*Les Violons & les Hautbois*" (p. 503).

---

91 Like the *Idylle en Musique*, this episode first appeared in print in 1694 (see Table 7.2), but it was probably written not long after *Roland*'s premiere in 1685, once Saint-Évremond had had a chance to look at a copy of the score, which was published in Paris by Christophe Ballard that same year.

92 Shifrin and Walkling, 74–77; as Shifrin and I have shown, Saint-Évremond was at pains to invert the hierarchy of the scene's two characters (in the original, Témire was the companion of the heroine Angélique, Queen of Cathay) so as to give the Duchess Mazarin both the leading role and the less demanding vocal line.

93 *Oeuvres Meslées* (1705), 2: 500.

94 *Ibid.*, 502: "Parlez, Vieillard, parlez, *Paisible*, / Goûterez-vous un bonheur si sensible." Note that in real life Paisible would already have been married at this time to the actress/singer Mary Davis (see p. 137, above).

8 Through-composed drama in the 1680s

The foregoing discussion does not mean to suggest that Jacques Paisible was transformed into the (or even a) leading composer of operatic music at court in the late 1670s. In fact, as we have observed in Chapter 3, the onset of the Popish Plot scare and the subsequent "Exclusion Crisis" in the latter part of 1678 effectively put a stop to a wide range of court entertainments, including "recreational" plays, balls, and masques, to say nothing of French-inspired through-composed productions. Many French and Italian musicians and other artistic figures joined the general exodus of foreign-born Roman Catholics; those who lingered faced legal persecution, or at the very least, like Saint-Évremond (who "ne pouvant retourner en son pais"), were forced to register their places of abode with the authorities.[1] It is surprising, in fact, to find evidence that at least four of Charles II's five remaining French musicians—Paisible, Mariens, Arnould, and Brunot—seem to have stayed on in England through the crisis, despite the inhospitable circumstances.[2] Perhaps they clung to a hope of collecting their mounting arrears. By the time the anti-Popish and anti-court fever subsided in the early 1680s, the musical and theatrical landscape had changed: Grabu was gone; Matthew Locke and John Banister, who had driven the emergence of dramatick opera on the public stage, were both dead; the relationship between the king's musical establishment and the patent theatres had become more tenuous;[3] and the tastes of the court were moving away from the unabashedly French forms that had characterized the 1670s. This last development, I have suggested, came about as a consequence of the resurgence of royal absolutism in the wake of Charles II's hard-won victory

---

1 For Saint-Évremond and his Flemish valet Gaspard Girrard, see Cooper, ed., *Lists of Foreign Protestants, and Aliens*, 28.

2 For the questions surrounding des Granges's movements, see Chapter 7, n. 43, above. The evidence presented above and in Table 7.1 puts to rest Peter Holman's speculation that the French wind players were absent from England between 1682, when Henry Purcell wrote parts for them in the welcome song "What shall be done in behalf of the man?," and 1686, when wind parts reappeared in the welcome song "Ye tuneful muses": see Holman, *Henry Purcell* (Oxford Studies of Composers; Oxford: Oxford University Press, 1994), 157.

3 Holman, *Fiddlers*, 354–55.

292   *"For such uses as the King shall direct"*

over his political opponents, and it affected every area of the arts at court.[4] With respect to musical drama, simply employing French musicians to perform operatic works in French was no longer desirable in this new environment. Instead, the dividing line between native English styles and those originating on the Continent (specifically French and Italian) was beginning to blur, and new hybridized forms were emerging as a result. The earliest example, of course, is *Venus and Adonis*, which we have already discussed in Chapter 3. The fact that John Blow (who is not known to have written any other operatic works, either before or afterwards) could create a through-composed piece in English, but with a number of French courtly features, such as a Lullian overture, *galant* dances, and a *précieuse* pastoral atmosphere, says much about the transformation of through-composed drama since the era of Davenant and Flecknoe. Of special interest is the highly embellished "Tune for Flutes" at the end of the Prologue, a duet for recorders that, in the earliest surviving manuscript score, appears with a plethora of ornament signs written above the upper melody line.[5] *Venus and Adonis* features additional obbligato passages for solo recorder in the first act and a brief mournful duet in the third,[6] but this particular movement, which functions as a kind of act tune for the Prologue, is clearly intended as a virtuoso showpiece, quite possibly for Paisible and Mariens: as Peter Holman has observed, the ornaments are graces, consisting of "shakes" and "beats," rather than the florid "divisions" characteristic of traditional English ornamental practice.[7]

As I have suggested in Chapter 3, *Venus and Adonis* represents an effort to respond to the altered performance circumstances of the early 1680s, as can be seen by its diminutive scale, its emphasis on musical rather than theatrical sophistication, and its use of Anglophone performers in place of the largely French forces deployed in such works as *Ballet et Musique*, *Ariane*, and even *Rare en Tout*. Moreover, despite its apparent revival in an academic setting at Oxford at some later date, it seems not to have been originally intended as a high-profile exercise in dramatic innovation, or to shake up the generic structures of court masque. Our view of *Venus* as a notable work is determined by a few specific qualities: the survival of the fully intact score; the reputation of Blow as a court musician and a composer in other genres; and, perhaps most of all, the masque's presumed affiliation with Tate and Purcell's *Dido and Aeneas*. But these are all

---

4 Andrew R. Walkling, "'Big with new events and some unheard success': Absolutism and Creativity at the Restoration Court," in Rebecca Herissone and Alan Howard, eds., *Concepts of Creativity in Seventeenth-Century England* (Woodbridge: Boydell Press, 2013), 15–34.

5 Bruce Wood, who describes the ornaments as "unusual in English music of this period," observes that they appear to have been added to the score by a performer, not by the original copyist, John Walter: see Bruce Wood, ed., *John Blow: Venus and Adonis* (Purcell Society Edition, Companion Series 2; London: Stainer and Bell, 2008), xxi–xxii and 125.

6 See the discussion of these passages in *ibid.*, xx: Wood considers those in Act 1 to be an afterthought, noting their relatively awkward character and the presumed chronology of their copying.

7 Holman, *Fiddlers*, 375; see also his transcription of the upper line with its ornament marks on p. 376 (Ex. 15.2).

Through-composed drama in the 1680s 293

traits that depend primarily on hindsight, and there is no evidence that *Venus* was regarded by contemporaries as an exceptional novelty, however much the very notion of through-composition may have seemed exotic to those outside of the Mazarin/Saint-Évremond circle. What would have been novel, of course, was the need to produce an all-sung work deploying almost exclusively English performers—the first time such a thing would have been attempted since *The History of Sir Francis Drake* in 1659 (assuming that the English-language version of Cavalli's *L'Erismena* never saw the stage). The selection of musicians must have been an important part of the process. Blow and his producer(s) would naturally have used court-trained instrumentalists from the Twenty-Four Violins and the Private Music, who would have acquired experience in this kind of playing during the 1670s.[8] And the dances must have been relatively easy to cast: with the exception of the dance for a shepherd and shepherdess in the Prologue and the character-oriented "Dance by a Huntsman" at the end of the first act, the remaining dances—all in Act 2—could be performed by courtiers and "little Cupids."[9] Yet apart from the indispensable "Moll" Davis (who may have been the most experienced operatic singer left in England at the time[10]) and her royal daughter, the singers were probably recruited from the Chapel Royal. Several of these men had appeared in *Calisto* at court (alongside Davis), and in the dramatick operas *The Tempest* and probably *Psyche* at Dorset Garden, in the mid-1670s. Given their experience with long-form and declamatory singing in anthems and court odes, they would have been well suited to perform in *Venus and Adonis*. Indeed, scholars are generally agreed that the Chapel singer James Hart is likely to have sung the male title role,[11] and also that Blow, as Master of the Children of the Chapel, would have cast the Little Cupids out the ranks of his youthful charges.

One point worth noting about *Venus and Adonis* is that, despite its being through-sung, the bulk of the work actually contains very little that could properly be called recitative. Instead, Blow deploys a technique in which passages

---

8 As Holman points out (*ibid.*; see also Wood, ed., *Venus and Adonis*, xx–xxi), the *Venus* score appears to differentiate between a full string band—which performed the overture, act tunes, and dances, and may have accompanied the four-part choruses in the Prologue and Act 3—and a bass-heavy continuo group of bowed and plucked stringed instruments for the sung solo and duet passages, supplemented with two solo violins and the abovementioned two recorders for occasional ritornelli or obbligato lines. This division, which seems to have originated in *Calisto* (see Holman, *Fiddlers*, 367–68) would have accorded well with the court's own built-in distinction between the Violin Band and the Private Music.

9 The extended suite of dances "for ye Graces" at the end of the act is immediately preceded by a "Cho[rus] of ye Graces," but it is unlikely that the three singers—a soprano, a countertenor, and a bass—would also have performed the dances. According to an annotation in British Library, Add. MS 22100, f. 123^r, the dance for Cupid (*i.e.* intended to be performed by Lady Mary Tudor) at the end of the Prologue "was ommitted."

10 It is entirely possible that Davis may have sung some of the female pastoral parts ("Caliste," "Cloris," or "Julie": see Table 7.2) in Saint-Évremond's operatic episodes, particularly after her marriage to Paisible in 1686.

11 See for example Wood, ed., *Venus and Adonis*, xv.

294   *"For such uses as the King shall direct"*

designed to advance the plot through dialogue—all of them performed by Cupid, Venus, and Adonis—begin with very brief recitative-like gestures but then lapse almost immediately (usually after only 2–4 bars) into a more strictly rhythmic and melodic arioso. The sole exception is the emotionally charged exchange between the two lovers that constitutes much of Act 3. Thus *Venus*, a through-composed "operatic" piece, essentially lacks the two chief "technologies" of opera, namely, recitative and scenic spectacle, that had been incorporated into the English definition of the form in the 1650s. This is not true, we should note, of *Dido and Aeneas*, which makes use of both features in a limited way, and *Venus* therefore needs to be understood as being explicitly outside the norm of Restoration musical works: an experiment in multiple respects, whose broader impact on the revival and development of an English through-composed operatic form remains uncertain at best.

That revival was, nevertheless, not long in coming—although at least initially it represented a compromise of sorts between the old courtly aspirations of the 1670s and the impetus toward generic innovation that was emerging in the new decade. As early as August 1683, Charles II had formulated plans "to p[er] forme an Opera in like manner of y^t of ffrance," and had dispatched the United Company's manager Thomas Betterton and a few of his compatriots to Paris "to fetch y^t designe."[12] The recent death of Queen Marie-Thérèse may have encouraged the king and his ministers—in particular the Secretary of State Robert Spencer, Earl of Sunderland, who seems to have coordinated the plans—to believe that during the period of official mourning the *Académie Royale de Musique*, or at least some portion thereof, might be available to mount a production in London. The record of the ensuing negotiations has been cited numerous times, and I will be exploring it in detail elsewhere;[13] what ultimately transpired was not the importation of a new group of French performers, but instead the return of Louis Grabu, who had been disappointed in his efforts to gain preferment at the court of *Le Roi Soleil*. In exchange for agreeing "to endeauour to represent something at least like an Opera in England for his Majestyes diuersion," Grabu was offered royal protection and financial incentives, including a renewal of his old appointment as a house composer for the patent theatres, and was said to be "very willing and ready to go ouer."[14] He was certainly in England by late January 1684, as his music for the Earl of Rochester's play *Valentinian* appeared in the United Company's premiere of that work at court on 11 February (Shrove Monday); he subsequently composed other theatre pieces, including a suite for Thomas Southerne's *The Disappointment*, which opened sometime in April, and in June he announced the publication of his French *Pastoralle* in a handsomely engraved folio edition

12 Folger Shakespeare Library, MS L.c.1417 (14 August 1683), p. 1 (*Register*, no. 1213).

13 Walkling, "Ups and Downs."

14 Letter of Richard Graham, 1st Viscount Preston to James, Duke of York, 12/22 September 1683: British Library, Add. MS 63759, f. 48^r, calendared in Alfred J. Horwood, "The Manuscripts of Sir Frederick Graham, Bart., at Netherby Hall, co. Cumberland," in Historical Manuscripts Commission, *Seventh Report of the Royal Commission on Historical Manuscripts. Part I. Report and Appendix* (London: Her Majesty's Stationery Office, 1879), 261–428, p. 288 (*Register*, no. 1216).

Through-composed drama in the 1680s   295

dedicated to Cambert's old patron, the Duchess of Portsmouth.[15] But his principal task was far more extensive: the "something at least like an Opera" became the most elaborate experiment in English through-composition prior to the eighteenth century: the musical, scenic, and allegorical extravaganza *Albion and Albanius*.

Albion and Albanius affords us a unique opportunity to study a work for which both a significant amount of information regarding performance circumstances and contemporary reaction, *and* a complete musical score, survive. Of all the operatic and masque-like works presented in England between the 1650s and 1690— including the dramatick operas to be discussed in my next book[16]—only *Calisto* offers more contextual documentation, and only *Cupid and Death* and *Venus and Adonis* are preserved in as musically comprehensive a form. Moreover, latterly *Albion and Albanius* has received some attention from scholars—particularly Bryan White, whose Ph.D. dissertation has produced, among other things, a much welcomed modern edited score[17]—although there remains much that can be said about this extraordinary work. In the present context, it is necessary briefly to survey *Albion*'s creation and performance circumstances—issues that are intimately tied up with structural and generic considerations—and to touch upon the contemporary responses that the opera provoked.

The history of *Albion*'s genesis is complex, and our understanding of it depends upon the statements of the opera's librettist, John Dryden, who is notorious for habitually manipulating precisely such statements for his own personal and political ends.[18] It appears that Dryden's original intention was to write a dramatick opera, drawing upon the foundational national myth of King Arthur. This work was to be prefaced with a through-sung prologue praising Charles II through an allegorical rendition of the restoration of the monarchy in 1660.[19] However, because of some unspecified "intervening accidents" that "deferr'd the performance of the main design," Dryden changed course, choosing instead "to turn the

---

15 See Walkling, "Ups and Downs"; the advertisements for *Pastoralle* appeared in *London Gazette* 1940 (19–23 June 1684) and 1947 (14–17 July 1684), both verso. Although neither the advertisements nor the print itself explicitly say so, the publication also included Grabu's *Valentinian* music: see Peter Holman, "'*Valentinian*,' Rochester and Louis Grabu," in John Caldwell, Edward Olleson, and Susan Wollenberg, eds., *The Well Enchanting Skill: Music, Poetry, and Drama in The Culture of the Renaissance: Essays in Honour of F. W. Sternfeld* (Oxford: Clarendon Press, 1990), 127–41.

16 We might compare *Psyche*, whose performance circumstances are somewhat obscure and whose printed score lacks much of the work's instrumental music.

17 Bryan Douglas White, "Louis Grabu and his Opera *Albion and Albanius*" (2 vols.: Ph.D. dissertation, University of Wales, Bangor, 1999) and Bryan White, ed., *Louis Grabu: Albion and Albanius* (Purcell Society Edition, Companion Series 1; London: Stainer and Bell, 2007).

18 See Steven N. Zwicker, *Politics and Language in Dryden's Poetry: The Arts of Disguise* (Princeton: Princeton University Press, 1984).

19 I am very dubious about the oft-repeated notion, originally articulated by Margaret Laurie, that this work was commissioned "to celebrate the twenty-fifth anniversary of the Restoration" (A. Margaret Laurie, ed., *King Arthur* [The Works of Henry Purcell, 26; London: Novello (Purcell Society), 1971], vii). There is little evidence that such quadranscentennial observances, so popular in our own day, were ever part of seventeenth-century commemorative culture.

296   *"For such uses as the King shall direct"*

intended Prologue into an Entertainment by it self, ... by adding two acts more to what I had already Written."[20] The timing of this decision is not clear, although it appears that Grabu had already composed much of the music for this prologue that, with some minor but crucial alterations, was transformed into Act 1 of the new through-sung opera. In any case, as Edward Saslow has argued, Dryden's text for the complete opera was likely ready by April 1684,[21] and at least part of Grabu's score may have been written by the end of May, when Charles II celebrated his birthday by being "Entertained with m^r drydens new play the subject of which is the last new Plott."[22] This dry-run performance, possibly of just the third act, which deals with the Rye House Plot of March–April 1683, seems to have been followed by other semi-public rehearsals at court: Dryden later averred that the king *"had been pleas'd twice or thrice to command, that it shou'd be practis'd, before him, especially the first and third Acts of it,"*[23] and by the beginning of 1685, with the work's public premiere impending, Edward Bedingfield, a correspondent of the theatre aficionado Katherine Manners, Countess of Rutland, reported that the piece, "soe well performed at the repetition that has been made before his Majesty at the Duchess of Portsmouth's, pleaseth mightly."[24]

This pattern of rehearsals at Whitehall (possibly in multiple venues there) for an opera that was ultimately destined for the public stage puts us in mind of the preparations for *Ariane* eleven years earlier. As we have seen, Cambert and Grabu's project of 1673–74 benefited from court support in the form of rehearsal space while the Drury Lane Theatre was under construction and from leverage in gaining access to that theatre once it opened, and perhaps received additional logistical assistance along the way. Ultimately, however, the Royall Academy of Musick seems to have been treated as an autonomous entity, equivalent to the established patent companies. Only Grabu, Cambert, des Granges, Robert, and Saint-André are known to have held regular, paid court or court-associated

---

20 John Dryden, *Albion and Albanius: an Opera. Perform'd at the Queens Theatre, in Dorset Garden* (London: Jacob Tonson, 1685), sig. (b)2^r; see Earl Miner, George R. Guffey, and Franklin B. Zimmerman, eds., *The Works of John Dryden ... Volume XV* (Berkeley: University of California Press, 1976; hereafter cited as "Dryden, *Works*, 15"), 10–11.

21 Edward L. Saslow, "Dryden in 1684," *Modern Philology* 72 (1974–75): 248–55, p. 251. April 1684 is when Dryden began work on his translation of Louis Maimbourg's *History of the League*, a project undertaken at the "expresse command" of Charles II (see *Stationers' Register*, 3: 232).

22 Folger Shakespeare Library, MS L.c.1542 (29 May 1684), p. 1. For a discussion of this notice, see James Anderson Winn, *John Dryden and His World* (New Haven: Yale University Press, 1987), 394 and 608 n. 35.

23 Dryden, *Albion and Albanius*, sig. (b)2^v; see Dryden, *Works*, 15: 12. See also Dryden's statement in the Dedication to *King Arthur* in 1691 that "the Opera of *Albion and Albanius*, was often practis'd before [Charles] at *Whitehal*, and encourag'd by His Royal Approbation" (John Dryden, *King Arthur: or, The British Worthy* [London: Jacob Tonson, 1691], sig. A1^r; see Vinton A. Dearing, ed., *The Works of John Dryden ... Volume XVI* [Berkeley: University of California Press, 1996], 3).

24 Letter of Edward Bedingfield to the Countess of Rutland, 1 January [1685]: H. C. Maxwell Lyte, *The Manuscripts of His Grace the Duke of Rutland, K. G., Preserved at Belvoir Castle. Vol. II* (Historical Manuscripts Commission, Twelfth Report, Appendix, Part V; London: Her Majesty's Stationery Office, 1889), 85 (*Register*, no. 1250).

Through-composed drama in the 1680s   297

appointments prior to Christmas 1675 (when the payments to Paisible and, probably, Mariens commenced), and we know that the French dancers, in any case, were subject to Grabu's oversight, and to the rules governing regular actors. Moreover, there is a good chance that Grabu, as the company's presumed manager, was forced to borrow a substantial sum of money on his own recognizance to mount the production, money that probably came from the London mercer Walter Lapp. *Albion and Albanius* poses a similar case: despite some court assistance and approbation, the United Company shouldered the primary responsibility for the vast financial outlay this extravagant venture required. As Edward Bedingfield noted, "the rates proposed will not take soe well, for they have set the boxes at a guyny a place, and the Pitt at halfe. They advance 4,000*l*. on the opera, and therefore must tax high to reimburse themselves."[25] James II was himself obliged to pay £30 at the premiere, double the prevailing rate for "The King and Queene & a Box for ye Maydes of Hono^r."[26]

Yet notwithstanding the similarities between the productions of *Ariane* and *Albion and Albanius*, some of the circumstances surrounding the latter reflect changes that had occurred since the 1670s. Most obviously, *Albion* was sung in English, and hence performed by English musicians, thus eliminating the need for anything like a Royall Academy of Musick with its imported talent. Moreover, the altered political climate of the 1680s prompted a quite different approach from that taken during the preceding decade. With Charles II now firmly in command of the unfettered monarchical power he had long coveted, the performative assertion of his authority in *Albion* could aspire to a degree of magnificence not seen in England since the court masques of the 1630s. Indeed, *Albion and Albanius* represents the acme of that potent pairing of spectacular musical and scenic "technologies" that we have been tracing since the mid-1650s: the extravagant, machine-laden production (which this time appeared in the fully rigged Dorset Garden Theatre) introduces a veritable empyrean of principal divinities who descend one after the other to comfort and encourage their terrestrial counterparts amidst significant quantities of dancing and a richly varied palette of musical components ranging from recitative to strophic song to imposing symphonies and grand choruses, the scope of which had hitherto been virtually unknown in England. The opera's overall effect may even be said to have been heightened when Charles II's death in early February 1685 obliged Dryden and Grabu to insert a scene of the late

25 *Ibid.* The proposed ticket prices mentioned by Bedingfield represent increases by factors of 4.2 for the pit and 5.25 for the boxes over normal admission costs (2*s* 6*d* and 4*s*, respectively). For a discussion of what the ticket prices and the length of the show's run would have had to be in order for the United Company to have earned back its investment, see Judith Milhous, "The Multimedia Spectacular on the Restoration Stage," in Shirley Strum Kenny, ed., *British Theatre and the Other Arts, 1660–1800* (Washington: The Folger Shakespeare Library [Associated University Presses], 1984), 41–66, pp. 55–56 and associated endnotes.

26 LC5/147, p. 68 (*Register*, no. 1275). We have noted that Charles II paid only £10 in 1674 to attend *Ariane*, albeit probably without his consort or her maids (interestingly, this amount was paid to the King's Company, not the Royall Academy of Musick: see n. 49, below).

298 *"For such uses as the King shall direct"*

monarch's apotheosis just prior to the final celebratory chorus. Not only did this allow for the introduction of yet another fantastic machine and a new conclave of gods, but it also empowered Dryden to assert Charles's earlier approbation of the work as having *"establish'd the Reputation of it, above censure, and made it in a manner Sacred."*[27] Beyond all this, however, what is exceptional about the opera is not only its magnificence or its flagrantly triumphalist rhetoric, but its very substance as a work of musical theatre. *Albion*'s generic uniqueness is grounded in Dryden's innovative handling of allegorical material—a feature that highlights the poet's creative response to the propagandistic requirements of the English court—and, secondarily, to Grabu's musical elaboration of his collaborator's inventive vision. Thus, in a multiplicity of ways, *Albion* transcended the bounds of opera as it had been practiced in England heretofore.

The premiere of *Albion and Albanius*, in the new monarch's presence, on 3 June 1685 must therefore have been a remarkable event on many levels. This fact was not lost on the one genuinely evaluative commentator of whom we are aware, the translator Ferrand Spence, who roundly praised the work and its production,

> not only for the amussitated [*i.e.* well-executed] *management of the* subject-matter, *and the* ingenious *contrivance of the* versification, *but for the* great *and* God-like *Argument, for the* Heroique *design of it's* Instruction, *for the* admirable *and* sumptuous *performance in the* sweetness *of the* Musick, *in the* Harmonique *Movements and Postures, in the* richness *of the* Habits, *and the* Beauty *of the* Machines *and* Decorations, [which] *we may* oppose *in* competition *with any* thing, *that ever* Paris *or* Venice *it self did yet see.*[28]

Conceding both the United Company's "immense *charges in* carrying *it on*" (sig. c5ᵛ) and some immediate doubts as to "*whether our* English *voices are so* fine *and* fit *for things of this* nature" (sig. d3ᵛ), Spence pleaded the novelty of the venture, "*as yet in a* State *of* Probation" (sig. d1ᵛ), "*remembring, that* things *cannot at first* receive *their* ultimate *perfection,* qui non est hodiè, cras magis aptus erit" (sig. d3ᵛ–d4ʳ), and remarking that "*this* portion *of the* Stage's *diversion being but a* Novice *in our* Theatre, *and having just* receiv'd *the* Royal Approbation *and* encouragement, ... *it would be* unmannerly *to let any thing* slip *the* Press, *that so much as* indirectly *strikes at the* design" (sig. c5ʳ⁻ᵛ). Spence should by no means be considered an unbiased appraiser of *Albion and Albanius*, but he understood what the work was trying to accomplish both artistically and politically, and how through-composed opera, with its unique ability to augment the wit of the verbal text with the sensual extravagances of music and spectacle such that "*all the* powers *of our* Souls, *be* adequately *fill'd with* Pleasure, *and be* rapt *up into an* Eternal *Enjoyment*" (sig. c10ʳ⁻ᵛ), was ideally suited to achieve this goal.

---

27 Dryden, *Albion and Albanius*, sig. (b)2ᵛ; see Dryden, *Works*, 15: 12. Dryden continues, "*'Tis therefore humbly and Religiously dedicated to his Memory.*"

28 Spence, *Miscellanea* (see Chapter 7, n. 79, above), sig. d1ʳ⁻ᵛ.

Through-composed drama in the 1680s 299

Spence's sympathetic treatment notwithstanding, the majority of published comments on *Albion and Albanius* were rather less complimentary. The anonymous manuscript satire "A Journal from Parnassus," believed to have been written in 1687 or early 1688, depicts Dryden's longtime rival Thomas Shadwell cursing the laureate's "last dull Opera," that

> ... with Rainbows, Flutes, & Peacock's Tails
> The needy bankrupt Players has undone,
> In hopes that where the blund'ering [*sic*] Poet fails,
> The Painter or the Fidler would attone:
> But all in vain! the gaudy Project miss'd,
> And whilst the Furies sung, the Audience hiss'd.[29]

Subsequently, Dryden is made to admit that he has discovered no appropriate method for the writing of an opera, "which has been the great (if not the only) reason why I have not been so successful ... as ... some of my Italian Freinds" (p. 34), and later the United Company actors themselves appear in order to complain that "Opera's have ruined our Stock & ... Farces [presumably a reference to Aphra Behn's extravagant 1687 "machine farce" *The Emperor of the Moon*, to which Grabu also contributed music] our Credit" (p. 55).

Two other contemporary sources focus their censure on *Albion*'s supposedly nonsensical qualities: Dryden's persistent detractor Gerard Langbaine approvingly quotes an anonymous squib in which it is satirically asserted that "*some have sworn, (th' Intrigue so od[d] is laid) / That* Bayes [*i.e.* Dryden] *and He* [Grabu] *mistook each others Trade*[:] / Grabut *the Lines, and He the Musick made*,"[30] while an undated "EPILOGUE. Spoken to the University of Oxon. By Mrs. *COOK*"[31] combines a jab at *Albion* with a sly paraphrase of the opening of Dryden's poem *Absalom and Achitophel*, lamenting that,

> IN these our Pious times, when writing Plays
> Was thought a Sin,———
> And nothing Sanctify'd but *Opera*'s[,]
> When to *Pindarick* Farce, true Sense gave place,
> And Musick yielded to *Grabugh*'s Grimace,

---

29 Hugh MacDonald, ed., *A Journal from Parnassus* (London: Oxford University Press for P. J. Dobell, 1937), 8–9.

30 Gerard Langbaine, *An Account of the English Dramatick Poets* (Oxford: George West and Henry Clements, 1691), 152. This amusing critique may in part have been inspired by Dryden's own statement in his Prologue that Grabu, in writing the music, had "so exactly express'd my Sence, in all places, where I intended to move the Passions, that he seems to have enter'd into my thoughts, and to have been the Poet as well as the Composer" (Dryden, *Albion and Albanius*, sig. (b)1ᵛ; see Dryden, *Works*, 15: 8).

31 *Poems on Affairs of State: From Oliver Cromwell, To this present time ... Part III* ([London]: n. pub., 1698), 173–76; the quoted passage is on p. 173. Since Dryden is still referred to as "Laureat," this epilogue must have been delivered sometime between June 1685 and the end of 1688; later in the poem, there is an apparent reference to Aphra Behn, who died in April 1689.

300   *"For such uses as the King shall direct"*

the haughty laureate will now no longer deign to write mere prologues for university performances. There may also be a reference to *Albion and Albanius* intended in the 1688 broadside poem *An Epistle to Mr. Dryden*, often attributed to Thomas Rymer. The poem, which appears to have been written around the time of William of Orange's invasion, and which combines an attack on James II's policies with a last-ditch plea to Dryden to consider changing his allegiance, begins:

> *DRYDEN*, thy Wit has catterwauld too long,
> Now *Lero*, *Lero*, is the only Song.
> What Singing, Dancing, Interludes of late
> Stuff, and set off our goodly Farce of State?[32]

The seeming implication of these lines is that the high-flying performativity that contemporaries associated with the opera has now devolved into raucous chants of the popular song "Liliburlero," which famously pervaded the cultural sensibility of the "Glorious Revolution." After a couple of mocking references to James II's officials, the poet continues, inquiring,

> … was e'er seen the like, in Prose or Metre,
> To this mad Play, or work of Father *P[etre]*?
> At Court no longer Punchionello takes,
> Each Scene, Part, Cue, mishapen to the *Mac*'s.
> Such Plot, and the Catastrophe is such,
> We must be either *Irish* all, or *Dutch*.

This intentionally oblique passage is difficult to parse with precision, but it is nonetheless clear that Dryden's efforts to hitch his star to the new operatic fashion, particularly in light of his now hypocritical evisceration of Thomas Shadwell ("the *Mac*") a decade earlier in his poem *Mac Flecknoe*, provided considerable fodder for his critics.

All of the above-mentioned attacks, we should note, are fundamentally grounded in one way or another in broader invectives against Dryden, a divisive

---

32 *An Epistle to Mr. Dryden* (n. p.: n. pub., [1688]); some copies of the print bear the subscription "*Exeter*, Nov. 5. 1688." The poem was subsequently reprinted in *A Collection of the Newest and Most Ingenious Poems, Songs, Catches, &c. Against Popery* (London: n. pub., "1689" [but the Bodleian Library copy is annotated "Published in Lond. in the latter end of Dec. 1688"]), 4–5; *A Supplement to the Collection of Miscellany Poems Against Popery & Slavery* (London: n. pub., 1689), 33–37; *Poems on Affairs of State, The Second Part* (London: n. pub., 1697), 103–6; and *State-Poems* (n. p.: n. pub., 1697), 143–46. In the latter three versions, the printing of the name "*Wem*" (referring to the Lord Chief Justice and Lord Chancellor George Jeffreys, 1st Baron Jeffreys of Wem) at the beginning of line 7 as "*W–m*" has misled Frank Ellis into reading the reference as to William, Prince of Orange, and thence to conclude that the poem's opening refers to the loud celebrations that broke out in the streets of London once the future king had arrived in the city: see Frank H. Ellis, "The Glorious Revolution as Farce," in Robert P. Maccubbin and Martha Hamilton-Phillips, eds., *The Age of William III & Mary II: Power, Politics, and Patronage 1688–1702* (Williamsburg, VA: The College of William and Mary, 1989), 333–39, pp. 333–34.

Through-composed drama in the 1680s 301

figure at the best of times, who sparked even more bitter controversy after his conversion to Roman Catholicism in about 1685 and his publication of *The Hind and the Panther* in 1687. But the most comprehensive, and ultimately most effective, assault on *Albion and Albanius* can be found in the oft-quoted anonymous poem entitled "*The Raree-show, from Father* Hopkins."[33] This scathing condemnation may have been written during the brief period when the opera was in production,[34] although it is not known to have appeared in print until some thirty years later.[35] The ten-stanza poem, which was intended to be sung to Grabu's lyrical "Minuet" for two Nereids in Act 3 of *Albion*,[36] is packed with topical references. Alongside the expected denigration of Dryden's poetry ("such stuff we want Patience"), his "dull Ear" for music and even his "dull Prefaces," as well as the undiscerning nature of the audience, the poem repeatedly alludes to the disastrous financial loss borne by the United Company. While it allows that Thomas Betterton's

33 This is how the title appears in the two printed sources (see n. 35, below), but "From Father Hopkins" actually constitutes the first three words of the poem; hence, the title may be a slightly corrupted version of something like "The Raree-show: 'From Father Hopkins ....'" The reference to "Father Hopkins" appears to represent an effort to associate Dryden's supposedly doggerel verse with that of John Hopkins, co-author of the mid-sixteenth-century English metrical psalter, with a nod to the song's original text, "From the low palace of our Father Ocean ...." The term "raree show" was widely used in the seventeenth century to refer to a peep-show or other lowbrow carnivalesque entertainment.

34 There is no mention of the show's premature closure on 13 June; on the other hand, the poem's ninth stanza does mention Grabu's scheme to collect "Angels" as subscriptions for his planned publication of the opera's score, which was first advertised on the 11th (see n. 39, below). The angel, we should note, was a disused gold coin of the early seventeenth century roughly equivalent in value to the half-guinea required of subscribers by the advertisement as an up-front 50% payment; in a second advertisement at the end of July this concession was removed, prospective subscribers now being obliged to pay the entire one-guinea cost at the outset. The fact that the poem refers to angels rather than the metrically equivalent "guineas" suggests that it must at least have been written and circulated prior to this change in the subscription terms.

35 *Wit and Mirth or, Pills to Purge Melancholy ... Vol. V* (London: John Young, 1714), 111–12; rpt. in *Wit and Mirth: or Pills to Purge Melancholy ... The Sixth and Last Vol.* (London: J[acob] Tonson, 1720), 245–46. The text also appears in Bodleian Library, Oxford, MS Firth c.16, pp. 96–97. This manuscript has been identified as a commonplace book copied for and by Aphra Behn; on pp. 101–2, the first seven lines of the poem are copied again, this time in Behn's own hand, and then cancelled, presumably after Behn realized that the text had already been entered into the volume. For a discussion of this manuscript, see Mary Ann O'Donnell, "A Verse Miscellany of Aphra Behn: Bodleian Library MS Firth c.16," *English Manuscript Studies, 1100–1700* 2 (1990): 189–227. I am very grateful to Mary Ann O'Donnell for her generosity in discussing this manuscript with me, sharing her notes, and providing me with facsimiles of the relevant pages.

36 See Bodleian Library, MS Firth c.16, p. 101 (the incomplete, canceled copy of the poem), which Behn has titled "Bays his Blind side, or Satyricall Remarks upon a late Raré show vulgerly calld an Opera And sett to the only tollerable good tune in the whole worke." In the two editions of *Wit and Mirth*, the upper line of the tune is printed without accompaniment: it contains three negligible variants from Grabu's printed score of 1687 (p. 244), involving the subtraction or addition of *appoggiatura*-like preparations (measures 3, 7, and 15), and a more significant variant in the raising of the third note in measure 13 from a c'' to a $c\#''$, thereby changing the implied harmony from an F-major triad to a more interesting first-inversion D-minor[7] chord.

302   *"For such uses as the King shall direct"*

"Decorations, / And the Machines were well written we knew," such extravagant theatrical effects, including "Rain-bows and Peacocks," were not sufficient to compensate for the opera's other failings.[37] As a result, the comic player and company shareholder Cave Underhill is left swearing at his apparent £200 loss and asking, "Who thought infallible *Tom* [Betterton] could have blunder'd[?]," while the actors William Smith (Betterton's co-manager), James Nokes (also a shareholder), and Anthony Leigh, all humorously described as "in a Feaver with railing, / Curse Poet, Painter, and Monsieur *Grabeau*" for their misfortune. Grabu, indeed, has long been considered the primary butt of this squib: each of the first six stanzas closes with a repetition of his name, hilariously rhymed with the words "view," "true," "knew," "do," and "spew," and readers are treated to comical images of the poor composer being variously subjected to curses, plagues, and "thrashing" (once the joke has worn thin, however, the final four stanzas move on to other rhymes and hence matters, such as reminding the ultra-royalist Dryden of his hypocrisy in having memorialized Oliver Cromwell early in his career[38]). But apart from the derisive characterization of his efforts as "little better" than Dryden's execrable poetry, Grabu's reputation emerges from this brutal volley of criticism mostly unscathed. Only in the penultimate stanza is his substantive contribution to the project directly addressed: acknowledging the composer's plans, announced to the public in June and July 1685,[39] to publish a full score by subscription scheme, the poem advises him to "Print thy dull Notes" ("dull" being this poet's preferred term of opprobrium) but, implausibly, to abandon the hefty proposed charge of a half-guinea up front (with an equivalent amount to be paid upon completion of the volume) in favor of "a round Shilling." Having cut Grabu's grand ambitions down to size, the poem returns in its final stanza to Dryden, taunting him one last time with the sly suggestion that only the incorporation of this doggerel mock-song into *Albion and Albanius* at "the next performing" will prevent a precipitous decline in the show's astronomical ticket prices.

The combined effect of the abovementioned satires—in particular "*The Raree-show, from Father* Hopkins"—has been to foster a perception of *Albion*

---

37 One of the show's few redeeming elements appears to have been the unidentified dancer "*Lane*," who, the poem's author informs us, has obtained "no Applause for thy Capers, / Tho' all without thee would make a Man spew; / And a Month hence will not pay for the Tapers." Perhaps Lane performed the role of the solo devil in Act 2 scene 1, apparently the only solo dance in the opera. The first line in this stanza of "*The Raree-show*" is the only one in the printed version of the poem that does not scan properly; Bodleian Library, MS Firth c.16, which is generally far more corrupt than the printed version, supplies a logical emendation: "Lane thou hast had no Applaues [*sic*] for thy Capers" (p. 96).

38 Dryden is urged to "Stick to thy Talent of bold Panegyricks, / And still remember the breathing the Vein," a sardonic reference to his rather strained metaphorical likening of Cromwell to a physician who "fought to end our fighting and assay'd / To stanch the blood by breathing of the vein" in his *Heroic Stanzas Consecrated to the Glorious Memory of His Most Serene and Renowned Highness, Oliver, Late Lord Protector* (1658), stanza 12.

39 *London Gazette* 2042 (11–15 June 1685) and 2055 (27–30 July 1685), both verso; for a discussion of the production of Grabu's score, see Walkling, "Ups and Downs."

Through-composed drama in the 1680s 303

and Albanius as not merely a commercial failure, but an object of derision. Yet there is no real evidence that the opera was an artistic, or even a critical, flop. Its most adverse outcome was certainly financial, and this fact seems to be implicitly acknowledged in the two most comprehensive critiques, "*The Raree-show*" and "A Journal from Parnassus": in the latter of these, the players decry "the insupportable Loss they had sustain'd from [Dryden's] & Mr Grabu's late Compositions," which they assert to have been "as fatal as the most malignant Conjunction among the Planets."[40] In point of fact, the production's closure and the United Company's consequent fiscal woes probably really were just a product of unforeseeable bad luck. After a nearly two-year process of planning and preparation, including the last-minute response to the untimely death of Charles II, the opera had the ill fortune to reach the stage only eight days before the invasion and rebellion against James II spearheaded by that onetime court dancing sensation, James, Duke of Monmouth. Monmouth landed at Lyme Regis on 11 June, and by the 13th news of the uprising had reached London. As we might imagine, this acute political crisis dealt a death-blow to *Albion and Albanius*: as John Downes later recalled, "The Nation being in a great Consternation, it was perform'd but Six times, which not Answering half THE Charge they were at, Involv'd the Company very much in Debt."[41] From the crown's perspective, on the other hand, the timing of the opera could not have been better. Instead of being presented immediately after James II's coronation, which took place on 23 April (St. George's Day),[42] it had been held back in order to adorn the session of James's new parliament—the first in more than four years, and a product of the aggressive campaign of the early 1680s to remodel corporate charters and ensure a reliably loyal legislative body. Parliament convened on 19 May, and *Albion* opened just over two weeks later, once the essential business of securing the new king's revenue for life had been attended to. The opera's laudatory rhetoric and performative magnificence was well suited to the occasion, and while the immediate crisis of Monmouth's Rebellion forced the closure of the production, historians have long observed that the existential threat to the regime that the rebellion seemingly posed was swiftly neutralized, not only militarily at Sedgemoor, but in an outpouring of loyalty and support for James II, both in Parliament and in the country at large. Thus, *Albion and Albanius*, whatever its flaws, seems to have caught—and perhaps, in some small way, even helped to shape—the mood of the nation at a critical juncture.

Dryden and Grabu's ill-fated extravaganza was not the last through-composed opera to be performed publicly in England before the collapse of James II's regime. In 1686 the new monarch accomplished what his brother had been unable to, bringing a ready-made French company to London for a production of

---

40 *A Journal from Parnassus*, 57.

41 *Roscius Anglicanus*, 40.

42 The theatres reopened after the period of mourning following Charles II's death on Monday, 27 April. The order for the reopening had been issued on the 20th (the day after Easter): LC5/145, p. 185 (*Register*, no. 1255).

304   *"For such uses as the King shall direct"*

Lully and Quinault's opera *Cadmus et Hermione* at one of the public theatres, most likely Dorset Garden.[43] The royal party attended the opening on Thursday, 11 February, paying £25 (as opposed to the usual £15) for two boxes,[44] although Peregrine Bertie, writing to the theatre-loving Countess of Rutland, reported that "the musicke was indeed very fine, but all the dresses the most wretched I ever saw."[45] According to Bertie, the opera "was acted by none but French." Given that Lully's *Armide* was premiering concurrently at the Paris Opéra (it had opened six days earlier, on 15 February, New Style), the London production must have been mounted by a touring company, perhaps the same one that appeared in Amsterdam the following year, offering performances of *Amadis* (opened 26 February), *Cadmus et Hermione* (opened 17 May), and *Atys* (opened 9 August).[46] *Cadmus* was, of course, something of a chestnut by 1686: Quinault and Lully's first operatic collaboration had premiered in Paris more than a dozen years earlier, in April 1673. But it would have been a good candidate for a London revival, since its prologue was only generally allegorical, with no explicit mention of *Le Roi Soleil*, and thus could be indiscriminately applied to James II without any significant alterations.[47] It is even possible that Louis Grabu might have been involved in this project, perhaps assuming the kind of supervisory role that he is known to have had in 1673–74 with regard to the Royall Academy of Musick.[48] However, this is only one of many things that we do not know about the production: it is surprising to find a near-complete absence of documentation, whether orders to the customs officers to import the players' goods; records of payments from the court, or by or to the United Company;[49] contemporary newsletter reports about the performers'

---

43 See W. J. Lawrence, "The French Opera in London: A Riddle of 1686," *The Times Literary Supplement* 1782 (28 March 1936): 268. Lawrence identifies the opera as *Cadmus* on the basis of a satirical reference in the prologue to Thomas Jevon's machine farce *The Devil of a Wife*, which opened at Dorset Garden on 4 March 1686: see *The Devil of a Wife, Or A Comical Transformation* (London: J[ohn] Eaglesfield, 1686), sig. (a2)ʳ.

44 LC5/147, p. 125 and LC5/16, p. 124 (*Register*, no. 1280) and AO1/405/130.

45 Letter of Peregrine Bertie to the Countess of Rutland, 11 February 1686: *The Manuscripts of His Grace the Duke of Rutland ... Vol. II* (see n. 24, above), 104. Bertie had already twice noted the imminent appearance of the opera in similar letters of 23 and 28 January (p. 102), the former intimating a premiere during the week of 25 January, the latter announcing a two-week delay. The Countess had herself been a "recreational" actress in the 1670s (albeit not at court), and seems to have had considerable interest in theatre gossip: see Van Lennep, ed., *The London Stage*, 1: 248 and references cited on p. ccxlvi.

46 J. Fransen, *Les Comédiens Français en Hollande au XVIIᵉ et au XVIIIᵉ Siècles* (Bibliothèque de la Revue de Littérature Comparée, 25; Paris: Honoré Champion, 1925), 170–71.

47 See Quinault's explication of the allegory (*Cadmus et Hermione* [Paris: Christophe Ballard, 1673], sig. A1ʳ): "LE ROY s'est mis au dessus des loüanges ordinaires, & ... pour former quelque idée de la grandeur & de l'éclat de sa Gloire, il a falu s'élever jusques à la Divinité mesme de la lumiere qui est le Corps de sa Devise."

48 Walkling, "Ups and Downs."

49 It is interesting to note that, as with *Ariane* in 1674, it was the patent company, not the French players, who received payment for the royal attendance at the performance. This is presumably because, even as the foreigners temporarily occupied the building, it was the patentees who remained liable for both building rent (a combined £10 for each acting day, regardless of which theatre was being

Through-composed drama in the 1680s 305

activities, either onstage or off; a printed programme libretto—nearly all of the usual sources of information are unaccountably silent.[50]

Two phenomena are noteworthy with regard to the 1686 performance(s) of *Cadmus et Hermione*. First, the production represented a return to a more conventional wholesale appropriation of French through-composed opera, and the seeming abandonment of efforts to fashion a hybrid, native form.[51] Whether this revitalization of the model established in the 1670s was a consequence of James II's particular brand of francophilia or a more *ad hoc* response to the United Company's unwillingness or inability to underwrite further costly experiments, it appears that the spark of creative adaptation exhibited in *Albion and Albanius* had, in the public sphere at least, gone out. Second, *Cadmus* has the distinction of effectively closing the book on the development of through-composed opera in England for the better part of a generation. The 1690s would become the great age of dramatick opera, a decade in which the quest to define a national style of musical theatre continued, but without the explicit pressure or guidance from the royal court that had driven efforts to establish through-composed opera since the issuance of Giulio Gentileschi's patent in 1660. Given the latent antagonism to through-composition and the political implications thereof embodied in dramatick opera of the mid-1670s, as well as the seeming disappearance of that mixed form in the following decade, it is hardly surprising that the part-sung/part-spoken genre would reemerge after the "Glorious Revolution," both as a kind of political statement in itself, and as a means of empowering the patent actors, who had previously seen themselves summarily displaced in favor of singers whenever a high-profile court theatrical project was afoot. Dramatick opera relied first and foremost upon the talents of the actors, sequestering the musical forces into a discrete realm of pastoral diversions, conjurations, machine effects, and interpolated masques. Singers were by no means inconsequential to this venture: as Curtis Price showed long ago, the public's thirst for song-and-dance entertainments prompted ever more brazen resorts to "musical excess" within the dramatick opera form as the seventeenth century yielded to the eighteenth.[52] But the musical "technology"

---

used) and ground rent (£130 annually for Dorset Garden): see Judith Milhous, "United Company Finances, 1682–1692," *Theatre Research International* 7 (1981–82): 37–53, p. 42.

50 Lawrence, for example, is left to imply, on the most speculative grounds, that Lully's erstwhile scene painter Jacques Rousseau, a Huguenot who had fled to England after Louis XIV's revocation of the Edict of Nantes in October 1685, *might* have assisted with the production ("The French Opera in London", 268).

51 This circumstance, however, hardly justifies Franklin Zimmerman's claim (in an overstated paraphrase of W. J. Lawrence) that the *Cadmus* production was designed "to make up for the dismal failure of ... *Albion and Albanius*": see Franklin B. Zimmerman, *Henry Purcell, 1659–1695: His Life and Times* (London: Macmillan; New York: St. Martin's Press, 1967), 135; (2nd, revised edition: Philadelphia: University of Pennsylvania Press, 1983), 132; *cf.* Lawrence, "The French Opera in London," 268: "it may be that in this way Grabut [*sic*] made some compensation for the disappointment he had caused."

52 Price, *Music in the Restoration Theatre*, 93–110; for a thorough discussion of this development and its contexts after the death of Henry Purcell, see Kathryn Lowerre, *Music and Musicians on the London Stage, 1695–1705* (Farnham: Ashgate, 2009).

306   *"For such uses as the King shall direct"*

of opera—most importantly, recitative as a means of dramatic expression and plot advancement—was largely absent from this orgy of spectacle. Further experimentation in recitative technique was thus deferred, and it was only later that English recitative found a more enduring voice through a wholesale adoption of the Italian *secco* style. As late as 1711, Joseph Addison could observe in *The Spectator* that

> THERE is nothing that has more startled our *English* Audience, than the *Italian Recitativo* at its first Entrance upon the Stage. People were wonderfully surprized to hear Generals singing the Word of Command, and Ladies delivering Messages in Musick.[53]

Addison, it should be noted, found the supposed innovation "much more just than tha[t] which prevailed in our *English* Opera[,] ... The Transition from an Air to Recitative Musick being more natural, than the passing from a Song to plain and ordinary Speaking, which was the common Method in *Purcell*'s Operas" (pp. 158–59). But he also expressed concern that Italian recitative, having been designed to reflect the accents and patterns of Italian speech, was not ideally adapted to the English mode of expression. Concluding that "the Recitative Musick in every Language, should be as different as the Tone or Accent of each Language; for otherwise, what may properly express a Passion in one Language, will not do it in another" (p. 159), Addison opined "that an *English* Composer should not follow the *Italian* Recitative too servilely, but make use of many gentle Deviations from it, in Compliance with his own Native Language" (p. 160), thereby allowing "the *Italian* Opera to lend our *English* Musick as much as may grace and soften it, but never entirely to annihilate and destroy it. Let the Infusion be as strong as you please, but still let the Subject Matter of it be *English*" (p. 161).

It is interesting to observe that in expressing his view that "A Composer should fit his Musick to the Genius of the People" (p. 161) when writing for the stage, Addison does not seem to have been aware of any of the examples he might have adduced to illustrate or investigate the point: *The Siege of Rhodes* or *The History of Sir Francis Drake*; *Ariadne Deserted by Theseus*; the extended recitative passages in *The Marriage of Oceanus and Britannia*, *Cupid and Death*, or *Calisto*; *Venus and Adonis* or *Dido and Aeneas*; or, most obviously, *Albion and Albanius*, printed copies of whose score would have been readily to hand. Rather, his citation of the dramatick operas of Purcell as a counter-example to the "more just" practice of through-composition reveals how thoroughly that mixed form had come to serve as an expression of the English "Genius," thereby implying that through-composition, and the recitative "technology" that made it possible, were alien qualities that either had never made an appearance in English dramatic music, or had been tried but proved unsuccessful. As we have seen, the most valid aspect of this otherwise false assumption is the tremendous breadth of experimentation with

---

53 *The Spectator* 29 (3 April 1711), quoted from *The Spectator. Vol. 1* (London: S[amuel] Buckley and J[acob] Tonson, 1712), 158.

the form carried out over the course of some three and a half decades, from the middle of the 1650s to the end of the 1680s. Some of these experiments, it is true, went nowhere, but others represent important developments, with respect to both musical style and the web of (mostly court) patronage and politics out of which they arose. It is perhaps ironic that through-composed opera, a form so closely identified with the court throughout the Restoration period, would ultimately only find a secure footing as an inherently public genre in the oligarchical eighteenth century. Yet this should not entirely surprise us, since, with its exploitation of complex "technologies" in the realms of expression and production, the artistically sophisticated and fiscally costly form is designed in any era to embody the tastes and values of a dominant political, social, and cultural elite.

Appendix A

Transcription of National Archives, London, AO1/2053/28, ff. 4^v–5^r (costumes for 1667 court ball)

Masquerading:

Habitts for danceing omitted in the yeare: 1667. vizt

ffor iiij^r Habitts with other ffurniture for representing a Courtier an English gentl: a yeoman and a Plowman	£14.03.00
ffor ii^e ffantasticke Habitts of blew Bayes. wth laced Capps & vizards	6.10.00
ffor iiij^{re} vests & iiij^r pe of blew breeches wth other ffurniture	35.12.00
Habitts for iiij^r Scaramouches of blacke bayes with shoes	7.00.00
ffor makeing of vj^x Roman Habitts of white Tinsell with blacke bugle Lace	52.10.00
A Roman Roabe. Bases. breeches. & buskins for M^r ffelton	39.00.12
A deepe blew Cuth Coate & Hose. Orenge color wastcoate. scarlet Ratteene Hose laced with gimp laces and other ffurniture	35.13.03
One suite wth other ffurniture for the Earle of Rochester	32.00.00
A yellow Tinsell Coate & Hose shammer'd wth tinsell Lace. & other ffurniture	37.13.06
A scarlet Pudesoy Coat shammerd with siluer and gold Lace	66.05.06
A Robe & doublet of Cloth of gold with other ffurniture	11.18.06
A greene taffaty Rapeene. & wide knee breeches shamer'd all ouer wth other ffurniture	12.06.06
A scarlet Morello Mohaire Coat & breetches shamerd all ouer wth Gold and silver Lace	16.15.00
Habitts for vj^x Egiptian men and one Egiptian Woeman	14.00.00
A pinke Color Lutestring Coate wth Ringraves shamer'd all ouer with siluer Lace with other ffurniture	104.04.06
A blacke veluet Coat shamer'd wth white Ermin spotted & other ffurniture	27.19.09
A Cherry colour sattin Vest and sarsnet breeches. the sleeues shamer'd wth iij^{ee} Rowes of Pearle. and other ffurniture	12.02.00
A Roman Habitt wth Scollops and other ffurniture	18.04.06
Makeing a purple Cloth suit embrodered a fflannill wast coate, altring two Coates & Ringraves wth other ffurniture for Mis Gwinn	10.07.00
Makeing a sad color fflower'd veluet Coat breeches & Causus embrodred with gold & siluer Lace and other ffurniture	36.18.00
A Turcks Habitt wth a sky color vest. a Coat of spotted Plush, the vest laced wth gold Lace and other ffurniture	50.05.06
	£641 9s 6d

Appendix B

Letters relating to Lord Sunderland's court ballet, 1686

SATURDAY, 26 DECEMBER 1685
Peregrine Bertie to Katherine Manners, Countess of Rutland

(HMC *Rutland* 2[1]: 99)
"...there will be a ball, if not a masque, at my Lord Sunderland's."

THURDAY, 31 DECEMBER 1685
Peregrine Bertie to Katherine Manners, Countess of Rutland

(HMC *Rutland* 2: 100)
"To-night is [a masque] att my Lord Sunderland's, but the masque[r?]s will not bee entertained till after supper."

THURSDAY, 28 JANUARY 1686
Peregrine Bertie to Katherine Manners, Countess of Rutland

(HMC *Rutland* 2: 102)
"Last Tuesday was a masque at the Duke of Northumberland's. [I hear] the company was but very ordinary. The weeke following will be a very noble one att my Lord Sunderland's. Noe body is to be there but those who are invited, and all in masquerade."

TUESDAY, 2 FEBRUARY 1686
Peregrine Bertie to Katherine Manners, Countess of Rutland

(HMC *Rutland* 2: 102–3)
"The grate ball or masque att Court is, I believe, put quite of, my Lady Anne Spencer being ill of the small-pox, and my Lady Derby going into the country, and my Lady Brandon desiring to be excused. There was to be in all twelve couple, each woman after a severall country fashion, and the men to have the habits of the same country as their partners, the Duke of Northumberland and my Lady

---

1 H. C. Maxwell Lyte, *The Manuscripts of His Grace the Duke of Rutland, K.G., Preserved at Belvoir Castle. Vol. II* (Historical Manuscripts Commission, Twelfth Report, Appendix, Part V; London: Her Majesty's Stationery Office, 1889).

312 *Appendix B*

[**p. 103**] Grafton, Spaniards; my Lord Manchester and my Lady Derby Grecians; my Lord Dumblain and Mis Fox, Moores; my Lord Litchfield and my Lady Walgrave, Shepherds. I have not yet heard the others habits, but they were all given them by the Queen. I jest now heare of a great misfortune which has happened this morning, and will certainly put of the ball; 'tis that the Duke of Grafton and Jacke Talbot have fought this morning in Chelsey Fields about some words that passed last night. …"

SATURDAY, 6 FEBRUARY
Peregrine Bertie to Katherine Manners, Countess of Rutland

(HMC *Rutland* 2: 103–4)

"The greate ball att Court goes on still and others are sent to to dance in their places who desired to bee excused, and those who are prevented by the unfortunate quarrell between the Duke of Grafton and Mr. Talbot."

[**p. 104**] "When the ball at Court is over, I will be sure to send your Ladyship an account of all the habits."

[SATURDAY, 6] FEBRUARY
Charles Bertie to Katherine Manners, Countess of Rutland

(HMC *Rutland* 2: 106)

"On Munday night the maides of honour with the young Lords performe a balle before the Queen at Whitehall."

MONDAY, 15 FEBRUARY
[Peformance]

ASH WEDNESDAY, 17 FEBRUARY
Peregrine Bertie to Katherine Manners, Countess of Rutland

(HMC *Rutland* 2: 104)

"I … must beg your Ladyship's pardon for not giving you an account of the masque att Court this post. My Lord Grey was with mee jest now and tells mee it was not fine at all, and that everybody was displeased with it."

THURSDAY, 18 FEBRUARY
John Povey to Sir Robert Southwell (transcript, 19th cent.?)

(British Library, Add. MS 28569, f. 60^{r-v} [partially quoted in *The London Stage*, 1: 347])

"Sir, The enclosed had been sent last post, had it not been detained late by a play at Court, which ended our Carnival. The night before, the King and Queen, were entertained by the Lord President, at a ball or masque, in Lady Portsmouth's lodgings. The Masquers were twelve couple, whose habits were of several nations, and prescribed by a picture sent to each of them, from the Queen, and the least habit cost above a hundred pounds, and some above three hundred pounds,

Appendix B   313

besides jewels of which Mrs Fox, and some others had above thirty thousand pounds value each.

At this splendid entertainment, the spectators were fewer, than there are generally Courtiers in the drawing-roome on a Sunday night none being permitted but by a ticket which was granted with [**f. 60v**] that difficulty that Sir John Bedloe [*i.e.* Bellew]'s son, of Ireland, having been at the charge of three hundred pounds, for supplying the place of the Lord Scarsdale who had strained his leg, against the time, could not prevaile for a ticket, for his mother, or any relation to enter by, and the Earl of Oxford, Lord Cornbury and others of less quality, found the like difficulty. All was doubtless very splendid within, but not half so much talked off as others of less note: the reason of which is plaine."

SATURDAY, 20 FEBRUARY
James Fraser to Sir Robert Southwell

(Folger Shakespeare Library, MS V.b.287 [5], pp. 1–2)

"On Monday night last My lord President Entertain'd their Maties, & R. highnesses wth a very noble and magnificent Ball, where 11 couple[s] danced aray'd in all the glory & riches of the Indies. if one were to have sought for diamonds or perles that night, no place in London could have afforded any but what was to be seen in the dutchess of portsmouth lodgings for there the divertisement & Entertainment was. the mascaraders were all differently drest, some appearing in a greek, a 2^d in a Roman, 3^d in an Hungarian 4th like the Great Sultan, a 5th like a mauritanian a 6th like a Masilian, a 7th resembling a peruvian, 8th like a shepheard, 9th like a polonian, 10th like a plain Country man, & an 11th like a venetian dress. The supper was very sumptuous and methodicall, at one Table their Maties, R. Highness & all the Ladys whose quality entitles them to that honour, were placed, & it held about 20. at the 2^d in another room sat all the Mascaraders that danced, at the 3^d were all the noblemen, persons of quality, Ambassadors & forraign ministers. The order that [**p. 2**] was every where observed in the whole conduct and contrivance of the Entertainment was no less remarkable than the charges great. none was permitted to come that had not a Ticket, and for every Ticket there was a place at the Ball, by wch means there was neither supernumerary persons nor places."

SATURDAY, 20 FEBRUARY
Lady Lucy Bright to Katherine Manners, Countess of Rutland

(HMC *Rutland* 2: 105)

"I presume your Ladyship has had a full account of my Lady Sunderland's fine masquerade and all the several habits, so that I need not in this repeate them, but must own it pleased me to hear that the King said Lord Manchester was the best habitted and most gracefull dress off any, and now 'tis said that att Easter the Queen will have them all meet again in the great Hall where everybody may see them, for this, I hear, has disobliged very many people."

Appendix C

Instrumental music associated with early operas and masques found in contemporary printed collections, 1662–c.1725

The following table charts the occurrences of tunes associated with operas and masques of the 1650s in a number of post-1660 musical publications. It provides the locations of the tunes in each source, identifies (with superscripted abbreviations) the various names given to the tunes in different sources, and indicates (with underlining) instances in which a source explicitly names Matthew Locke as a tune's composer. The left-hand column gives abbreviations representing the titles of the publications (see the key for full titles) with their dates of publication; the superscripted figures in this column represent edition numbers.

| | ?Rhodes 1656 | Peru 1658 | Drake 1659 | ? | | | Cupid and Death 1659† | | | | | | | | |
	Iantha	The Apes Dance	The Simerons Dance	The Opera Tune	The Opera Dance	The Opera Jig	[Jig] (1st entry)	Ayre (2nd entry)	Antick Dance (2nd entry)	Ayre (3rd entry)	Saraband (3rd entry)	Ayre (5th entry)	Ayre (Masque)	Corant (Masque)	Saraband (Masque)
CMA 1662		no. 271^A	no. 279^{Sd}					no. 280	no. 281			no. 275	no. 276	no. 277	no. 278
DM$^{[3c]}$?1662	no. 26 (p. [1]41)	no. 35^A (p. [1]44)													
DM$^{[3d]}$ 1665		no. 15^A (p. [1]38)	no. 33^{Sd} (p. [1]44)	no. 80^g (p. [1]59)	no. 81nd (p. [1]59)				no. 34 (p. [1]45)						
AB^1 1670		no. 93^A	no. 51^{Sj}	no. 46^{OT}	no. 47^{OD}	no. 48^{OJ}			no. 52						
AB^2 1678		no. 36^A	no. 31^{Sj}				§2, no. 30		no. 32						
AB^5 1687		no. 29°	nos. 25^{Sj}, 88^{LP}						no. 28						
AB^6 1690		no. 17°	no. 14^{Sj}												
AB^7 1693															
MH$^{[1]}$ 1663		no. 52^A	no. 38^{Sd}						no. 39						
MH$^{[2]}$ 1678		no. 52^A	no. 38^{Sd}						no. 39	no. 66	no. 67	no. 68			
MDC 1666		no. 55^A													
MRV$^{[2i]}$ 1669			no. 12^{Sd}												
MRV$^{[2ii]}$ 1682		no. 16^{AO}	no. 8^{PRW}												
TC 1677				p. 11^g											
DM^5 1675		p. 159°													
DM^6 1679		p. 159°													
DM^7 1686		p. 159^{OA}													
DM^{nas} [1688]			p. 3^{LP}												
DM^8 1690		p. 145^{OA}	p. 197^{LP}												
DM$^{9-18}$ 1695–c.1725		p. 87^{OA}	p. 133^{LP}												
CCDM 1718		p. 99^{OA}	p. 146^{LP}												

†Full score in British Library, Add. MS 17799.

Key to publications: (*N.B.* asterisked items contain harmonizations; all others are melody-line only)

CMA	*Courtly Masquing Ayres*
DM	*The Dancing Master*
	(*N.B.* editions "3a" [1654–56] and "3b" [1657] not extant; 4th ed. [1670] contains no relevant tunes; edition "nas" [?1688] issued as "*A new Additional Sheet to the DANCING-MASTER*," supplementary to 7th ed.)
AB	*Apollo's Banquet*
	(*N.B.* 3rd ed. [1682] and 4th ed. [1684] not extant.)
MH	*Musick's Handmaid[e]*
MDC	*Musick's Delight on the Cithren*
MRV	*Musick's Recreation on the Viol Lyra-Way*
	(*N.B.* 1st ed. [1661] contains no relevant tunes.)
TC	*Tripla Concordia*
CCDM	*The Compleat Country Dancing-Master*

Key to titles used to identify the tunes: (*N.B.* minor variations of punctuation/typography ignored)

A	"THe Apes Dance." (1662–78)
O	"THe *Opera*." (1675–90)
AO	"THE Apes Dance in the *Opera*." (1682)
OA	"The *Opera, or* The Apes Dance." (1686–c.1725)
Sd	"THe Simerons Dance." (1662–78)
Sj	"THe *Simerons* Jigg." (1670–90)
PRW	"PRince *Rupert's* welcome." (1682)
LP	"Lady of Pleasure." (1687–c.1725)
g	"A *Gavott*." (1665)/"Gavat." (1677)
OT	"THe *Opera* Tune by Mr. *Lock*." (1670)
nd	"A *New Dance*." (1665)
OD	"THe *Opera* Dance." (1670)
OJ	"THe *Opera* Jigg." (1670)

Select bibliography

Pre-1800 sources

B., A., *Synopsis of Vocal Musick* (London: Dorman Newman, 1680).

Le Ballet de la Paix Dance en presence de Monseigneur le President de Bordeaux Ambassadeur Extraordinaire de Roy de France en Angleterre (n. p.: n. pub., 1660).

B[lount], T[homas], *Glossographia: or a Dictionary Interpreting all such Hard Words ... as are now used in our refined English Tongue* (London: Humphrey Moseley, 1656).

Boyle, Roger, Earl of Orrery, *The History of Henry the Fifth. And the Tragedy of Mustapha, Son of Solyman the Magnificent* (London: H[enry] Herringman, 1668).

Bre[mond], S[ébastien], *Ballet et Musique pour le Divertissement du Roy de la Grande Bretagne* ([London]: "aux dépens de l'Autheur ... par Thomas Nieucombe," 1674).

Brougham, Henry *et al.*, comp., *Biographia Britannica: or, the Lives of the Most Eminent Persons Who have Flourished in Great Britain and Ireland, From the Earliest Ages, Down to the Present Times* (6 vols.: London: W. Innys *et al.*, 1747–66).

Catch that Catch Can: or the Musical Companion (London: J[ohn] Playford, 1667).

Chamberlayne, Edward, *Angliœ Notitia: or The Present State of England* (London: John Martyn, 1669–79; R. Littlebury, R. Scott, and G. Wells, 1682; further editions, 1684–1704).

Choice Songs and Ayres for One Voyce ... The First Book (London: John Playford and John Ford, 1673).

A Collection of the State Papers of John Thurloe, Esq. (London: for the Executor of Fletcher Gyles, *et al.*, 1742).

Crowne, John, *The Prologue to Calistho, with the Chorus's Between the Acts* (London: n. pub., 1675).

———, *Calisto: Or, The Chaste Nimph. The Late Masque at Court, As it was frequently Presented there, By several Persons of Great Quality. With the Prologue, and the Songs Betwixt the Acts* (London: James Magnes and Richard Bentley, 1675).

The Dancing Master (London: John Playford, ?1662).

[Davenant, Sir William], *A Proposition for Advancement of Moralitie By a new way of Entertainment of the People* (London: n. pub., "1654" [*recte* 1653]).

———, *The First Days Entertainment at Rutland-House, By Declamations and Musick: After the manner of the Ancients* (London: H[enry] Herringman, "1657" [*recte* 1656]).

———, *The Siege of Rhodes Made a Representation by the Art of Prospective in Scenes, And the Story sung in Recitative Musick. At the back part of Rutland-House in the upper end of Aldersgate-Street, London* (London: Henry Herringman, 1656 [2 states]).

320 *Select bibliography*

———, *The Cruelty of the Spaniards in Peru. Exprest by Instrumentall and Vocall Musick, and by Art of Perspective in Scenes, &c. Represented daily at the Cockpit in Drury-Lane, at Three after noone punctually* (London: Henry Herringman, 1658).

———, *The Siege of Rhodes Made a Representation by the Art of Prospective in Scenes, And the Story sung in Recitative Musick. At the Cock-Pit in Drury Lane* (London: Henry Herringman, 1659).

———, *The History of Sr Francis Drake. Exprest by Instrumentall and Vocall Musick, and by Art of Perspective in Scenes, &c. The First Part. Represented daily at the Cockpit in Drury-Lane at Three Afternoon Punctually* (London: Henry Herringman, 1659[/60]).

———, *The Siege of Rhodes: The First and Second Part; As they were lately Represented at His Highness the Duke of York's Theatre in Lincolns-Inn Fields. The first Part being lately enlarg'd* (London: Henry Herringman, 1663).

———, *The Works of Sr William Davenant K^t* (London: Henry Herringman, 1673).

———, "THE Play-house to be Let," in *The Works of Sr William Davenant K^t* (London: Henry Herringman, 1673), section 2, pp. 67–119.

——— and John Dryden, *The Tempest, Or the Enchanted Island* (London: Henry Herringman, 1674).

Downes, John, *Roscius Anglicanus, or an Historical Review of the Stage* (London: H[enry] Playford, 1708).

Dryden, John, *The Indian Emperour, or, The Conquest of Mexico by the Spaniards. Being the Sequel of the Indian Queen* (London: H[enry] Herringman, 1667).

———, *Tyrannick Love, or the Royal Martyr* (London: H[enry] Herringman, 1670).

———, *The Conquest of Granada by the Spaniards* (London: Henry Herringman, 1672).

———, "A Prologue spoken at the Opening of the NEW HOUSE, *Mar.* 26. 1674," in *Miscellany Poems ... By the most Eminent Hands* (London: Jacob Tonson, 1684), 286–89.

———, *Albion and Albanius: an Opera. Perform'd at the Queens Theatre, in Dorset Garden* (London: for Jacob Tonson, 1685).

———, *Amphitryon; Or, The Two Socia's* (London: J[acob] Tonson and M. Tonson, 1690).

———, *King Arthur: Or, The British Worthy. A Dramatick Opera* (London: Jacob Tonson, 1691).

Duffett, Thomas, *Beauties Triumph; A Masque. Presented by the Scholars of Mr. Jeffery Banister, And Mr. James Hart, At their New Boarding-School for Young Ladies and Gentlewomen, kept in that House which was formerly Sir Arthur Gorges, At Chelsey* (London: n. pub., 1676).

———, *New Poems, Songs, Prologues and Epilogues* (London: Nicholas Woolfe, 1676).

——— (attr. "P. W."), *New Songs, and Poems, A-la-mode both at Covrt, and Theaters, Now Extant* (London: Nicholas Woolfe, 1677).

"Epilogue, *spoken by the Lady* Mary Mordont, *before the King and Queen, at Court, to the faithfull Shepheardess*," in *Covent Garden Drolery* (London: James Magnes, 1672), 86.

"Epilogue *spoken by the Lady* Mary Mordant, *before the King and Queen, at Court, to the faithfull Shepheardess*," in *Covent Garden Drolery ... The Second Impression, with Additions* (London: James Magnes, 1672), 86.

E[velyn], J[ohn], *The State of France, as it Stood in the IXth Yeer of this Present Monarch, Lewis XIIII* (London: G. Bedell and T. Collins, 1652).

Flecknoe, Richard, *Love's Dominion* (London: n. pub., 1654).

———, *Ariadne Deserted by Thesevs, and Found and Courted by Bacchus. A Dramatick Piece Apted for Recitative Musick* (London: n. pub., 1654).

Select bibliography 321

————, *The Mariage of Oceanus and Brittania. An Allegoricall Fiction, really declaring Englands Riches, Glory, and Puissance by Sea. To be represented in Musick, Dances, and proper Scenes* (n. p.: n. pub., 1659).

Fletcher, John, *The Faithfull Shepherdesse ... The Fifth Edition* (London: G. Bedell and T. Collins, 1665).

Grabu, Louis, *Albion and Albanius: An Opera. or, Representation in Musick* (London: for the Author and William Nott, 1687).

Hamilton, Anthony, trans. Abel Boyer, *Memoirs of the Life of Count de Grammont: Containing, in Particular, the Amorous Intrigues of the Court of England in the Reign of King Charles II* (London: J. Round *et al.*, 1714).

Hawkins, Sir John, *A General History of the Science and Practice of Music* (5 vols.: London: T. Payne and Son, 1776).

Howell, James, *The Nvptialls of Pelevs and Thetis. Consisting of a Mask and a Comedy, [F]or the The [sic] Great Royall Ball, Acted lately in Paris six times By The King in Person. The Duke of Anjou. The Duke of Yorke. with divers other Noble men. Also By The Princess Royall Henrette [sic] Marie. The Princess of Conty. The Dutchess of Roqvelaure. The Dutchess of Crequy. with many other Ladies of Honour* (London: Henry Herringman, 1654).

Jordan, Thomas, *Fancy's Festivals: A Masque* (London: by Tho[mas] Wilson, 1657).

Langbaine, Gerard, *An Account of the English Dramatick Poets* (Oxford: George West and Henry Clements, 1691).

La Roche-Guilhen, Anne de, *Rare en Tout: Comedie Meslée de Musique Et de Balets Represantée devant Sa Majesté Sur le Theatre Royal De Whitehall* ("Londres": Jacques Magnes and Richard Bentley, 1677).

Lawes, Henry, *Ayres and Dialogues, For One, Two, and Three Voyces ... The First Booke* (London: John Playford, 1653).

Lecerf de La Viéville de Fresneuse, Jean-Laurent, *Comparaison de la Musique Italienne, et de la Musique Françoise* (2nd ed.; Brussels: François Foppens, 1705).

Lee, Nathaniel, *Mithridates, King of Pontus* (London: James Magnes and Rich[ard] Bentley, 1678).

Lewis, Jenkin, ed. Philip Hayes, *Memoirs of Prince William Henry, Duke of Glocester, From his Birth, July the 24th, 1689, to October, 1697* (London: Philip Hayes *et al.*, 1789).

Locke, Matthew, *The English Opera; or The Vocal Musick in Psyche, with the Instrumental Therein Intermix'd To which is Adjoyned The Instrumental Musick in the Tempest* (London: "by *T. Ratcliff*, and *N. Thompson* for the Author, and are to be Sold by *John Carr*," 1675).

Ménestrier, Claude-François, *Des Représentations en Musique Ancienne et Modernes* (Paris: R. Guignard, 1681).

Monconys, Balthasar de, *Iovrnal des Voyages de Monsievr de Monconys* (3 vols.: Lyon: Horace Boissat and George Remeus, 1665–66).

The Musical Companion, In Two Books (London: John Playford, 1673).

Musick's Recreation on the Viol Lyra-Way, "*The Second Edition*" (London: J[ohn] Playford, 1682).

Musicks Hand-maid: New Lessons and Instructions for the Virginals or Harpsychord (London: J[ohn] Playford, 1678).

P[errin], P[ierre], *Ariane, Ou Le Mariage de Bacchus Opera: Compose Par le Sieur P. P. Et Mis en Musique par le Sieur Grabut, Maitre de la Musique Du Roi. Represente par*

322 *Select bibliography*

L'Academie Roiale de Musique, Au Theatre-Roial ("Londres": par Thomas Nieucomb, 1673[/]4).

———, trans. Anon., *Ariadne, Or, The Marriage of Bacchus An Opera, Or A Vocal Representation First Compos'd by Monsieur P. P. Now put into Musick by Monsieur Grabut, Master of His Majesties Musick. And Acted by the Royall Academy Of Musick, At the Theatre-Royal in Covent-Garden* (London: by Tho[mas] Newcombe, 1673[/]4).

Pignani, Girolamo, *Scelta Di Canzonette Italiane de Piu Autori* (London: by A. Godbid and J[ohn] Playford, 1679).

"*A Prologue spoken at Court to the Emperess of* Morocco," "*Spoken by the Lady* Elizabeth Howard," and "*Another Prologue spoke at Court to the Emperess of* Morocco," in *A Collection of Poems Written upon Several Occasions By Several Persons* (London: Tho[mas] Collins, John Ford, and Will[iam] Cademan, 1673), "178" [*recte* 168]–"179" [*recte* 169], 170–171, and "182" [*recte* 172]–174.

"Prologue *to* Horace, *spoken by the Dutches of* Munmouth, *at Court,*" in *Covent Garden Drolery* (London: James Magnes, 1672), 80–81.

"*Prologue to* Horace, *spoken by the Dutchess of* Munmouth *at Court,*" in *Covent Garden Drolery ... The Second Impression, with Additions* (London: James Magnes, 1672), 80–81.

Purcell, Henry, *The Vocal and Instrumental Musick of the Prophetess, or the History of Dioclesian* (London: "by *J.* Heptinstall, for the Author, and ... *John Carr,*" 1691).

Quinault, Philippe, *Thesée Tragedie en Mvsiqve. Ornée d'Entrées de Ballet, De Machines, & de Changements de Theatre. Representée devant Sa Majesté à Saint Germain en Laye, le dixiéme jour de Ianvier 1675* (Paris: Christophe Ballard, 1675).

———, *Atys, Tragedie en Mvsiqve. Ornée d'Entrées de Ballet, de Machines, & de Changements de Theatre. Representée devant Sa Majesté à Saint Germain en Laye, le dixiéme jour de Janvier 1676* (Paris: Christophe Ballard, 1676).

Raymond, Jo[hn], *An Itinerary Contayning a Voyage, Made through Italy, in the Yeare 1646, and 1647* (London: Humphrey Moseley, 1648).

Saint-Évremond, Charles de Marguetel de Saint-Denis, Seigneur de, trans. Anon., *Mixt Essays Upon Tragedies, Comedies, Italian Comedies, English Comedies, and Opera's* (London: Timothy Goodwin, 1685; rpt. 1687), 19–28.

———, trans. Ferrand Spence, *Miscellanea: or Various Discourses ... By the Sieur de Saint Euvremont* (London: Sam[uel] Holford, 1686), 41–62.

———, trans. Anon., *The Works of M^r de St. Evremont. In II. Volumes. Translated from the French* (London: Awnsham and John Churchill, 1700), 521–28.

———, ed. Pierre Des Maizeaux and Israel Silvestre, *Oeuvres Meslées de M^r. de Saint-Evremond, Publiées sur les Manuscrits de l'Auteur* (2 vols.: London: Jacob Tonson, 1705).

———, *Mélange Curieux des Meilleures Pieces Attribuées à Mr. De Saint-Evremond, et de Plusieurs Autres Ouvrages Rares ou Nouveaux* (2 vols.: Amsterdam: Pierre Mortier, 1706).

———, ed. Pierre Des Maizeaux and Israel Silvestre, *Oeuvres Meslées de M^r. de Saint-Evremond, Publiées sur les Manuscrits de l'Auteur. Seconde Edition Reveüe Corregée & Augmentée* (3 vols.: London: Jacob Tonson, 1709).

Sedecias et Zenobie, Tragedies, Qui seront representées, dans la Maison de Monsievr Filz, au Fau-bourg S. Germain (Paris: Pierre Esclassan, 1673).

Select Ayres and Dialogues For One, Two, and Three Voyces (London: John Playford, 1659; rpt. as the first part of *The Treasury of Musick,* 1669).

Settle, Elkanah, *The Empress of Morocco. A Tragedy. With Sculptures. As it is Acted at the Duke's Theatre* (London: William Cademan, 1673).

———, *Ibrahim the Illustrious Bassa* (London: W[illiam] Cademan, 1677).

Shadwell, Thomas, *Psyche: A Tragedy, Acted at the Duke's Theatre* (London: Henry Herringman, 1675).

S[hirley], J[ames], *Cvpid and Death. A Masque. As it was Presented before his Excellencie, The Embassadour of Portugal, Upon the 26. of March, 1653* (London: J. Crook and J. Baker, 1653).

———, *Cupid and Death, A Private Entertainment, represented with Scenes & Musick, Vocall & Instrumentall* (London: John Crooke and John Playford, 1659).

———, *Cvpid and Death, A Private Entertainment, represented with Scenes, Variety of Dancing, and Musick, Both Vocall & Instrumentall* (London: John Crooke and John Playford, 1659).

Stapylton, Sir Robert, *The Slighted Maid, A Comedy* (London: Thomas Dring, 1663).

———, *The Step-Mother, A Tragi-Comedy* (London: Timothy Twyford, 1664).

Waller, Edmund, "Prologue to the Lady Actors," in *idem, The Second Part of Mr. Waller's Poems* (London: Tho[mas] Bennet, 1690), 53–54.

———, "Prologue to the Lady Actors," in *idem, The Maid's Tragedy Altered. With some other Pieces* (London: Jacob Tonson, 1690), 50–51.

Westminster-Drollery. Or, A Choice Collection of the Newest Songs & Poems Both at Court and Theaters, By a Person of Quality (London: H[enry] Brome, 1671 ["Never before publish'd"]; 1671 ["*With Additions*"; 3 separate issues]; 1672 ["*With Additions*"]; 1674 ["*The third Edition, with many more Additions*"]).

Whitelocke, Bulstrode, *Memorials of the English Affairs* (London: Nathaniel Ponder, 1682).

———, *Memorials of the English Affairs ... With Many Additions Never Before Printed* (London: J[acob] Tonson, 1732).

Wilson, John, *Cheerfull Ayres or Ballads First Composed for one Single Voice and Since Set for Three Voices* (Oxford: Ric[hard] Davis, 1660).

Post-1800 sources

Akerman, John Yonge, *Moneys Received and Paid for Secret Services of Charles II and James II* (Camden Society, 52; London: Camden Society, 1851).

Armytage, George J., ed., *Allegations for Marriage Licences Issued by the Vicar-General of the Archbishop of Canterbury, July 1679 to June 1687* (Harleian Society, 30; London: [Harleian Society], 1890).

Arthur, Harold, Viscount Dillon, "Some Familiar Letters of Charles II. and James Duke of York Addressed to their Daughter and Niece, the Countess of Litchfield," *Archaeologia* 58 (1902–3): 153–88.

Arundell, Dennis, *The Critic at the Opera* (London: Ernest Benn, 1957; rpt. New York: Da Capo Press, 1980).

Ashbee, Andrew and David Lasocki, comps. (assisted by Peter Holman and Fiona Kisby), *A Biographical Dictionary of English Court Musicians, 1485–1714* (2 vols.: Aldershot: Ashgate, 1998).

Barber, Richard, *Samuel Pepys Esqre* (London: G. Bell and Sons [for National Portrait Gallery], 1970).

Barclay, Andrew, "Charles II's Failed Restoration: Administrative Reform Below Stairs, 1660–4," in Eveline Cruickshanks, ed., *The Stuart Courts* (Stroud: Sutton Publishing, 2000), 158–70.

324   *Select bibliography*

Bashford, Christina, "Perrin and Cambert's 'Ariane, ou le Mariage de Bacchus' Re-Examined," *Music and Letters* 72 (1991): 1–26.

Bathurst, Benjamin, ed., *Letters of Two Queens* (London: R. Holden, 1924).

Bawcutt, N. W., ed., *The Control and Censorship of Caroline Drama: The Records of Sir Henry Herbert, Master of the Revels 1623–73* (Oxford: Clarendon Press, 1996).

Beal, Peter, *In Praise of Scribes: Manuscripts and their Makers in Seventeenth-Century England* (Oxford: Clarendon Press, 1998).

Bennett, J. A., *The Manuscripts of S. H. Le Fleming, Esq., of Rydal Hall* (Historical Manuscripts Commission, Twelfth Report, Appendix, Part VII; London: Her Majesty's Stationery Office, 1890).

Bray, William, ed., *Diary and Correspondence of John Evelyn, F.R.S.* (London: George Routledge and Sons; New York: E. P. Dutton and Co., 1906).

Bulman, William J., "Publicity and Popery on the Restoration Stage: Elkanah Settle's *The Empress of Morocco* in Context," *Journal of British Studies* 51 (2012): 308–39.

Burden, Michael, "Aspects of Purcell's Operas," in *idem*, ed., *Henry Purcell's Operas: The Complete Texts* (Oxford: Oxford University Press, 2000), 3–27.

Buttrey, John M., "The Evolution of English Opera Between 1656 and 1695: A Re-investigation" (Ph.D. dissertation, Cambridge University, 1967).

———, "New Light on Robert Cambert in London, and his *Ballet et Musique*," *Early Music* 23 (1995): 198–220.

C., J. D., "Christmas at the Court of Charles the Second," *Notes and Queries* 18 (2nd ser., no. 6, 1858): 517–20.

Cameron, Kenneth M., "The Monmouth and Portsmouth Troupes," *Theatre Notebook* 17 (1962–63): 89–94.

Canova-Green, Marie-Claude, "Le Relais Français dans l'Implantation de l'Opera en Angleterre (1660–1685)," in Christopher Smith and Elfrieda Dubois, eds., *France et Grande-Bretagne de la Chute de Charles Ier à celle de Jacques II (1649–1688)* (Norwich: Society for Seventeenth-Century French Studies, 1990), 239–48.

Chan, Mary and Jamie C. Kassler, eds., *Roger North's The Musicall Grammarian 1728* (Cambridge: Cambridge University Press, 1990).

Christiansen, Keith and Judith W. Mann, eds., *Orazio and Artemisia Gentileschi* (New York: Metropolitan Museum of Art and New Haven: Yale University Press, 2001).

Christie, W. D., ed., *Letters Addressed from London to Sir Joseph Williamson while Plenipotentiary at the Congress of Cologne in the Years 1673 and 1674* (2 vols.: Camden Society, n. s., 8–9; London: Camden Society, 1874).

Clare, Janet, "The Production and Reception of Davenant's *Cruelty of the Spaniards in Peru*," *Modern Language Review* 89 (1994): 832–41.

Clark, William Smith II, ed., *The Dramatic Works of Roger Boyle Earl of Orrery* (2 vols.: Cambridge, MA: Harvard University Press, 1937).

Cooper, W[illia]m Durrant, ed., *Lists of Foreign Protestants, and Aliens, Resident in England 1618–1688. From Returns in the State Paper Office* (Camden Society, 82; London: Camden Society, 1862).

Corp, Edward T., "The Exiled Court of James II and James III: A Centre of Italian Music in France, 1689–1712," *Journal of the Royal Musical Association* 120 (1995): 216–31.

Danchin, Pierre, "The Foundation of the Royal Academy of Music in 1674 and Pierre Perrin's *Ariane*," *Theatre Survey* 25 (1984): 55–67.

De Beer, Esmond S., "King Charles II's Own Fashion: An Episode in Anglo-French Relations 1666–1670," *Journal of the Warburg Institute* 2 (1938–39): 105–15.

Select bibliography 325

De Marly, Diana, "King Charles II's Own Fashion: The Theatrical Origins of the English Vest," *Journal of the Warburg and Courtauld Institutes* 37 (1974): 378–82.

———, "Musicians' Costumes in the Restoration Theatre," *Early Music* 5 (1977): 507–15.

Dennison, Peter, *Pelham Humfrey* (Oxford Studies of Composers; Oxford: Oxford University Press, 1986).

Dent, Edward J., *Foundations of English Opera: A Study of Musical Drama in England During the Seventeenth Century* (Cambridge: Cambridge University Press, 1928; rpt. New York: Da Capo Press, 1965).

Elliott, George Percy, ed., "Diary of Dr. Edward Lake, … Chaplain and Tutor to the Princesses Mary and Anne, … in the Years 1677–1678" (1846), in *The Camden Miscellany* 1 (Camden Society, 39; London: Camden Society, 1847), sig. [3]A1r–[3]D4v (pp. 1–32).

Eubanks Winkler, Amanda, ed., *Music for* Macbeth (Middleton, WI: A-R Editions, 2004).

Evelyn, John, ed. Harriet Sampson, *The Life of Mrs. Godolphin* (London: Oxford University Press, 1939).

Firth, C. H., "Sir William Davenant and the Revival of the Drama during the Protectorate," *English Historical Review* 18 (1903): 319–21.

Gethner, Perry, ed., *Femmes dramaturges en France (1650–1750)* (Biblio 17, no. 79; Paris: Biblio 17, 1993).

Gibbens, Lilian, "Roman Catholic Tradesmen in London, 1681," *Catholic Ancestor* 8 (2000): 58–62.

Gilman, Todd S., "London Theatre Music, 1660–1719," in Susan J. Owen, ed., *A Companion to Restoration Drama* (Oxford: Blackwell Publishers, 2001), 243–73.

Grattan Flood, W. H., "Quelques Précisions Nouvelles sur Cambert et Grabu à Londres," *La Revue Musicale* 9 (1927–28): 351–61.

Greene, Douglas G., ed., *The Meditations of Lady Elizabeth Delaval Written Between 1662 and 1671* (Surtees Society, 190: Gateshead: Northumberland Press, 1978).

Grobe, Edwin P., "S. Bre., French Librettist at the Court of Charles II," *Theatre Notebook* 9 (1954–55): 20–21.

Ham, Roswell G., "Dryden's Dedication for *The Music of the Prophetesse*, 1691," *Publications of the Modern Language Association* 50 (1935): 1065–75.

Hammond, Paul, "Dryden's *Albion and Albanius*: The Apotheosis of Charles II," in David Lindley, ed., *The Court Masque* (The Revels Plays Companion Library; Manchester: Manchester University Press, 1984), 169–83.

Harris, Frances, *Transformations of Love: The Friendship of John Evelyn and Margaret Godolphin* (Oxford: Oxford University Press, 2002).

Hartmann, Cyril Hughes, *Memoirs of the Comte de Gramont by Anthony Hamilton. A New Translation by Peter Quennell with and Introduction and Commentary by Cyril Hughes Hartmann* (London: George Routledge and Sons, 1930).

Haun, Eugene, *But Hark! More Harmony: The Libretti of Restoration Opera in English* (Ypsilanti: Eastern Michigan University Press, 1971).

Hedbäck, Ann-Mari, "The Printing of *The Siege of Rhodes*," *Studia Neophilologica* 45 (1973): 68–79.

Holland, A. K., *Henry Purcell: The English Musical Tradition* (Harmondsworth: Penguin, 1932; rpt. 1948).

Holman, Peter, ed., *Matthew Locke: The Rare Theatrical: New York Public Library, Drexel MS 3976* (Music for London Entertainment 1660–1800, Series A Volume 4; London: Stainer and Bell, 1989).

———, "'*Valentinian*,' Rochester and Louis Grabu," in John Caldwell, Edward Olleson, and Susan Wollenberg, eds., *The Well Enchanting Skill: Music, Poetry, and Drama in*

326   Select bibliography

The Culture of the Renaissance: Essays in Honour of F. W. Sternfeld (Oxford: Clarendon Press, 1990), 127–41.

———, *Henry Purcell* (Oxford Studies of Composers; Oxford: Oxford University Press, 1994).

Hooker, Helene Maxwell, "Dryden's and Shadwell's *Tempest*," *Huntington Library Quarterly* 6 (1942–43): 224–28.

Horwood, Alfred J., "The Manuscripts of the Right Honourable the Earl of Mount Edgcumbe, Mount Edgcumbe, co. Cornwall," in *Second Report of the Royal Commission on Historical Manuscripts* (London: Her Majesty's Stationery Office, 1874)

———, "The Manuscripts of Sir Frederick Graham, Bart., at Netherby Hall, co. Cumberland," in Historical Manuscripts Commission, *Seventh Report of the Royal Commission on Historical Manuscripts. Part I. Report and Appendix* (London: Her Majesty's Stationery Office, 1879), 261–428.

———, "The Manuscripts of Sir Harry Verney, Bart., at Claydon House, Co. Bucks.," in Historical Manuscripts Commission, *Seventh Report of the Royal Commission on Historical Manuscripts. Part I. Report and Appendix* (London: Her Majesty's Stationery Office, 1879), 433–509.

Hotson, Leslie, *The Commonwealth and Restoration Stage* (Cambridge, MA: Harvard University Press, 1928; rpt. New York: Russell and Russell, 1962).

Hulse, Lynn, "'The King's Entertainment' by the Duke of Newcastle," *Viator: Medieval and Renaissance Studies* 26 (1995): 355–405.

Hume, Robert D., "The Politics of Opera in Late Seventeenth-Century London," *Cambridge Opera Journal* 10 (1998): 15–43.

Jacob, James R. and Timothy Raylor, "Opera and Obedience: Thomas Hobbes and *A Proposition for Advancement of Moralitie* by Sir William Davenant," *The Seventeenth Century* 6 (1991): 205–50.

Jordan, R[ob], "Some Restoration Playgoers," *Theatre Notebook* 35 (1981): 51–57.

———, "An Addendum to *The London Stage 1660–1700*," *Theatre Notebook* 47 (1993): 62–75.

Lafontaine, Henry Cart de, ed., *The King's Musick: A Transcript of Records Relating to Music and Musicians (1460–1700)* (London: Novello and Company, 1909).

Lasocki, David, "Professional Recorder Playing in England, 1500–1740, II: 1640–1740," *Early Music* 10 (1982): 182–91.

———, "The French Hautboy in England, 1673–1730," *Early Music* 16 (1988): 339–57.

Lauder, Sir John, ed. Adam Urquhart and David Laing, *Historical Observes of Memorable Occurrents in Church and State from October 1680 to April 1686* (Bannatyne Club, no. 66: Edinburgh: Thomas Constable, 1840).

Laurie, Alison Margaret, "Purcell's Stage Works" (2 vols.: Ph.D. dissertation, Cambridge University, 1962).

——— and Andrew Pinnock, eds., *The Indian Queen* (Purcell Society, 19; London: Novello, 1994).

Lawrence, W. J., "The Players' Petition to Charles II," *The Athenæum* 3938 (18 April 1903): 508.

———, "Early French Players in England," in *idem, The Elizabethan Playhouse and Other Studies* (2 vols.: Stratford-upon-Avon: Shakespeare Head Press, 1912–13; rpt. New York: Russell & Russell, 1963), 1: 125–56.

———, "Foreign Singers and Musicians at the Court of Charles II," *The Musical Quarterly* 9 (1923): 217–25.

Select bibliography   327

————, "The Origin of the Substantive Theatre Masque," in *idem*, *Pre-Restoration Stage Studies* (Cambridge, MA: Harvard University Press, 1927), 325–39.

————, "A Restoration Opera Problem," *The Times Literary Supplement* 1443 (26 September 1929): 737.

————, "The French Opera in London: A Riddle of 1686," *The Times Literary Supplement* 1782 (28 March 1936): 268.

Leech, Peter, "Musicians in the Catholic Chapel of Catherine of Braganza, 1662–92," *Early Music* 29 (2001): 570–87.

————, "Music and Musicians in the Catholic Chapel of James II at Whitehall, 1686–1688," *Early Music* 39 (2011): 379–400.

Lindgren, W. H. III, "An Introduction to and Edition of *Cupid his Coronation*," *Neuphilologische Mitteilungen* 76 (1975): 108–29.

Lomas, S. C., *Calendar of the Manuscripts of the Marquis of Bath Preserved at Longleat, Wiltshire. Vol. II* (Dublin: His Majesty's Stationery Office, 1907).

Luckett, Richard, "Exotick but Rational Entertainments: The English Dramatick Operas," in Marie Axton and Raymond Williams, eds., *English Drama: Forms and Development: Essays in Honour of Muriel Clara Bradbrook* (Cambridge: Cambridge University Press, 1977), 123–41.

————, "A New Source for 'Venus and Adonis'," *The Musical Times* 130 (1989): 76–79.

Luttrell, Narcissus, *A Brief Historical Relation of State Affairs* (6 vols.: Oxford: Oxford University Press, 1857).

Mabbett, Margaret, "Italian Musicians in Restoration England (1660–90)," *Music and Letters* 67 (1986): 237–47.

MacDonald, Hugh, ed., *A Journal from Parnassus* (London: Oxford University Press for P. J. Dobell, 1937).

McDonald, Jennifer, "Matthew Locke's *The English Opera*, and the Theatre Music of Purcell," *Studies in Music* 15 (1981): 62–75.

Maguire, Nancy Klein, *Regicide and Restoration: English Tragicomedy, 1660–1671* (Cambridge: Cambridge University Press, 1992).

Marsh, Christopher, *Music and Society in Early Modern England* (Cambridge: Cambridge University Press, 2010).

Maxwell Lyte, H. C., *The Manuscripts of His Grace the Duke of Rutland, K. G., Preserved at Belvoir Castle. Vol. II* (Historical Manuscripts Commission, Twelfth Report, Appendix, Part V; London: Her Majesty's Stationery Office, 1889).

Middleton, W. E. Knowles, ed. and trans., *Lorenzo Magalotti at the Court of Charles II: His* Relazione d'Inghilterra *of 1668* (Waterloo, Ont.: Wilfrid Laurier University Press, 1980).

Milhous, Judith, "The Multimedia Spectacular on the Restoration Stage," in Shirley Strum Kenny, ed., *British Theatre and the Other Arts, 1660–1800* (Washington: The Folger Shakespeare Library [Associated University Presses], 1984), 41–66.

———— and Robert D. Hume, "Charles Killigrew's 'Abstract of Title to the Playhouse'[:] British Library Add. MS 20,726, Fols. 1–14," *Theatre History Studies* 6 (1986): 56–71.

————, "Dating Play Premières from Publication Data, 1660–1700," *Harvard Library Bulletin* 22 [1974]: 374–405.

Miner, Earl, George R. Guffey, and Franklin B. Zimmerman, eds., *The Works of John Dryden ... Volume XV* (Berkeley: University of California Press, 1976).

Moberg, Carl-Allan, "Vincenzo Albrici (1631–1696): Eine Biographische Skizze mit Besonderer Berücksichtigung seiner Schwedischen Zeit," in Anna Amalie Abert and

328   Select bibliography

Wilhelm Pfannkuch, eds., *Festschrift Friedrich Blume zum 70. Geburtstag* (Kassel: Bärenreiter, 1963), 235–46.

Nicoll, Allardyce, *A History of Restoration Drama, 1660–1700* (Cambridge: Cambridge University Press, 1923; rev. eds., 1928, 1940; rev. and reissued 1952 as vol. 1 of *A History of English Drama, 1660–1900* [7 vols.: Cambridge: Cambridge University Press], 1952–59, 1973; vol. 1 rpt. 1961, 1965, 1967, 1977, 2009).

Novak, Maximillian E., intro., *The Empress of Morocco and Its Critics* (Augustan Reprint Society, Special Publications 3; Los Angeles: William Andrews Clark Memorial Library, 1968).

O'Donnell, Mary Ann, "A Verse Miscellany of Aphra Behn: Bodleian Library MS Firth c.16," *English Manuscript Studies, 1100–1700* 2 (1990): 189–227.

Orgel, Stephen, ed., *Ben Jonson: The Complete Masques* (New Haven: Yale University Press, 1969).

Orlich, Leopold von, ed., *Briefe aus England über die Zeit von 1674 bis 1678; in Gesandtschafts-Berichten des Ministers Otto von Schwerin des Jüngern an den Großen Kurfürsten Friedrich Wilhelm* (Berlin: G. Reimer, 1837).

Orrell, John, "A New Witness of the Restoration Stage, 1670–1680," *Theatre Research International* n. s., 2 (1976–77): 86–97.

———, *The Theatres of Inigo Jones and John Webb* (Cambridge: Cambridge University Press, 1985).

Pitou, Spire, "A Forgotten Play: La Roche-Guilhen's 'Rare en tout' (1677)," *Modern Language Notes* 72 (1957): 357–59.

Powell, John S., *Music and Theatre in France, 1600–1680* (Oxford: Oxford University Press, 2000).

Price, Curtis A., *Music in the Restoration Theatre* (Studies in Musicology, 4; Ann Arbor: UMI Research Press, 1979).

———, *Henry Purcell and the London Stage* (Cambridge: Cambridge University Press, 1984).

Protheroe, John, "Not so Much an Opera … A Restoration Problem Examined," *The Musical Times* 106 (1965): 666–68.

Rimbault, Edward F., ed., *The Old Cheque-Book, or Book of Remembrance, of the Chapel Royal, From 1561 to 1744* (Camden Society, n. s., 3; London: Camden Society, 1872).

Rose, Gloria, "Pietro Reggio—A Wandering Musician," *Music and Letters* 46 (1965): 207–16.

Saslow, Edward L., "Dryden in 1684," *Modern Philology* 72 (1974–75): 248–55.

Scouten, Arthur H., "The Perils of Evelyn," *Restoration* 16 (1992): 126–28.

Seaton, Ethel, *Literary Relations of England and Scandinavia in the Seventeenth Century* (Oxford: Clarendon Press, 1935; rpt. New York: Benjamin Blom, 1972).

Shifrin, Susan and Andrew R. Walkling, "'Idylle en Musique': Performative Hybridity and the Duchess Mazarin as Visual, Textual, and Musical Icon," in Susan Shifrin, ed., *"The Wandering Life I Led": Essays on Hortense Mancini, Duchess Mazarin and Early Modern Women's Border-Crossings* (Newcastle upon Tyne: Cambridge Scholars Publishing, 2009), 48–99.

Southern, Richard, *Changeable Scenery: Its Origin and Development in the British Theatre* (London: Faber and Faber, 1952).

Spalding, Ruth, ed., *The Diary of Bulstrode Whitelocke 1605–1675* (Records of Social and Economic History, New Series 13; Oxford: Oxford University Press for the British Academy, 1990).

Spink, Ian, *English Song: Dowland to Purcell* (London: B. T. Batsford, 1974; rpt. 1986).

———, *Henry Lawes: Cavalier Songwriter* (Oxford: Oxford University Press, 2000).

Strong, Roy, *Festival Designs by Inigo Jones: An Exhibition of Drawings for Scenery and Costumes for the Court Masques of James I and Charles I* ([Washington, DC]: International Exhibitions Foundation, 1967).

Sundström, Einar, "Notiser om Drottning Kristinas Italienska Musiker," *Svensk Tidskrift för Musikforskning* 43 (1961): 297–309.

Ternois, René, ed., *Saint-Évremond: Lettres* (2 vols.: Paris: Marcel Didier, 1967–68).

Tessier, André, "Robert Cambert à Londres," *La Revue Musicale* 9 (1927–28): 101–22.

[Thibaudeau, Alphonse Wyatt], ed., *The Collection of Autograph Letters and Historical Documents Formed by Alfred Morrison (Second Series, 1882–1893): The Bulstrode Papers, Volume I (1667–1675)* (1 vol. only; [London: Strangeways and Sons], 1897).

Thompson, Robert and Andrew R. Walkling, eds., *Cupid and Death* (Musica Britannica 2, revised edition; London: Stainer and Bell, in progress).

Thorp, Jennifer, "Dance in Late 17th-Century London: Priestly Muddles," *Early Music* 26 (1998): 198–210.

Thurley, Simon, *The Whitehall Palace Plan of 1670* (London: London Topographical Society, 1998).

Tilmouth, Michael, transcr. and ed., *Matthew Locke: Dramatic Music with the Music by Humfrey, Banister, Reggio and Hart for "The Tempest"* (Musica Britannica 51; London: Stainer and Bell, 1986).

Toynbee, Margaret R., "An Early Correspondence of Queen Mary of Modena," *Notes and Queries* 188 (January–June 1945): 90–94, 112–18, and 135–40.

———, "A Further Note on an Early Correspondence of Queen Mary of Modena," *Notes and Queries* 193 (1948): 292–95.

Tuppen, Sandra, "Shrove-Tide Dancing: Balls and Masques at Whitehall under Charles II," *The Court Historian* 15 (2010): 157–69.

Van Lennep, William, "The Smock Alley Players of Dublin," *ELH* 13 (1946): 216–22.

———, ed., *The London Stage[,] 1660–1800[:] A Calendar of Plays, Entertainments & Afterpieces Together with Casts, Box-Receipts and Contemporary Comment Compiled from the Playbills, Newspapers and Theatrical Diaries of the Period[,] Part 1: 1660–1700* (Carbondale: Southern Illinois University Press, 1965).

Velimirović, Miloš M., "Giovanni Sebenico (Prispevek k Biografiji)," *Muzikološki Zbornik* 1 (1965): 49–58.

Walkling, Andrew R., "Masque and Politics at the Restoration Court: John Crowne's *Calisto*," *Early Music* 24 (1996): 27–62.

———, "Court, Culture, and Politics in Restoration England: Charles II, James II, and the Performance of Baroque Monarchy" (2 vols.: Ph.D. dissertation, Cornell University, 1997).

———, "Politics and Theatrical Culture in Restoration England," *History Compass* 5.5 (August 2007): 1500–20.

———, "The Apotheosis of Absolutism and the Interrupted Masque: Theater, Music, and Monarchy in Restoration England," in Julia Marciari Alexander and Catharine MacLeod, eds., *Politics, Transgression, and Representation at the Court of Charles II* (New Haven: Yale University Press, 2007), 193–231.

———, "The Masque of Actaeon and the Antimasque of Mercury: Dance, Dramatic Structure, and Tragic Exposition in *Dido and Aeneas*," *Journal of the American Musicological Society* 63 (2010): 191–242.

———, "Politics, Occasions and Texts," in Rebecca Herissone, ed., *The Ashgate Research Companion to Henry Purcell* (Aldershot: Ashgate, 2012), 201–67.

330 *Select bibliography*

———, "'Big with New Events and Some Unheard Success': Absolutism and Creativity at the Restoration Court," in Rebecca Herissone and Alan Howard, eds., *Concepts of Creativity in Seventeenth-Century England* (Woodbridge: Boydell Press, 2013), 15–34.

———, "The Ups and Downs of Louis Grabu," in progress.

———, "Professional Actors as Royal Drama Coaches, 1674–81," in progress.

Walls, Peter, *Music in the English Courtly Masque, 1604–1640* (Oxford: Clarendon Press, 1996).

Ward, Richard, *The Manuscripts of his Grace the Duke of Portland, Preserved at Welbeck Abbey. Vol. III* (Historical Manuscripts Commission, Fourteenth Report, Appendix, Part II; London: Her Majesty's Stationery Office, 1894).

Weale, James Cyril M., ed., *Registers of the Catholic Chapels Royal and the Portuguese Embassy Chapel 1662–1829* (Catholic Record Society, 38; London: Catholic Record Society, 1941).

Westrup, J. A., "Foreign Musicians in Stuart England," *The Musical Quarterly* 27 (1941): 70–89.

White, Bryan Douglas, "Louis Grabu and his Opera *Albion and Albanius*" (2 vols.: Ph.D. dissertation, University of Wales, Bangor, 1999).

———, ed., *Louis Grabu: Albion and Albanius* (Purcell Society Edition, Companion Series 1; London: Stainer and Bell, 2007).

White, Eric Walter, *The Rise of English Opera* ([New York]: Philosophical Library; London: John Lehmann, 1951; rpt. New York: Da Capo Press, 1972).

———, *A History of English Opera* (London: Faber and Faber, 1983).

———, comp., *A Register of First Performances of English Operas and Semi-Operas from the 16th Century to 1980* (London: The Society for Theatre Research, 1983).

Wilson, John, ed., *Roger North on Music: Being a Selection from his Essays Written During the Years c.1695–1728* (London: Novello, 1959).

Wilson, John Harold, ed., *The Rochester–Savile Letters, 1671–1680* (Columbus: Ohio State University Press, 1941).

———, *All the King's Ladies: Actresses of the Restoration* (Chicago: University of Chicago Press, 1958; rpt. Chicago: Midway Reprints, 1974).

———, "Players' Lists in the Lord Chamberlain's *Registers*," *Theatre Notebook* 18 (1963–64): 25–30.

Winn, James Anderson, *John Dryden and His World* (New Haven: Yale University Press, 1987).

———, *"When Beauty Fires the Blood": Love and the Arts in the Age of Dryden* (Ann Arbor: University of Michigan Press, 1992).

———, "Heroic Song: A Proposal for a Revised History of English Theater and Opera, 1656–1711," *Eighteenth-Century Studies* 30 (1996–97): 113–37.

———, "'A Versifying Maid of Honour': Anne Finch and the Libretto for *Venus and Adonis*," *Review of English Studies* n. s., 59 (2008): 67–85.

———, "John Dryden, Court Theatricals, and the 'Epilogue to the faithfull Shepheardess'," *Restoration* 32/2 (Fall 2008): 45–54.

———, *Queen Anne: Patroness of Arts* (Oxford: Oxford University Press, 2014).

Wiseman, Susan J., "'History Digested': Opera and Colonialism in the 1650s," in Thomas Healy and Jonathan Sawday, eds., *Literature and the English Civil War* (Cambridge: Cambridge University Press, 1990), 189–204.

———, *Drama and Politics in the English Civil War* (Cambridge: Cambridge University Press, 1998).

Wollston, Silas, "New Light on Purcell's Early Overtures," *Early Music* 37 (2009): 647–55.

Wood, Bruce, ed., *John Blow: Venus and Adonis* (Purcell Society Edition, Companion Series 2; London: Stainer and Bell, 2008).

—— and Andrew Pinnock, "'Unscarr'd by turning times'?: The dating of Purcell's Dido and Aeneas," *Early Music* 20 (1992): 372–90.

Yoch, James J., "The Renaissance Dramatization of Temperance: The Italian Revival of Tragicomedy and *The Faithful Shepherdess*," in Nancy Klein Maguire, ed., *Renaissance Tragicomedy: Explorations in Genre and Politics* (New York: AMS Press, 1987), 115–38.

Name index

N.B. Indexing of names of pre-1800 individuals is comprehensive, excepting bibliographical references; only selected post-1800 names are indexed.

Abell, John 57 n. 106
Addison, Joseph 306
Ailesbury, Earl of *see* Bruce, Thomas
Albemarle, Duchess of *see* Cavendish/
  Monck/Montagu, Elizabeth
Albemarle, Duke of *see* Monck, George
Albert de Luynes, Jeanne d' 289
Albert de Luynes, Louis Charles d', Duc
  de Luynes 289
Alberti, Girolamo 60 n. 114, 225
Albrici (?/Battaglia), Leonora
  200, 201 n. 25, 204, 205, 206, 207,
  213, 214
Albrici, Bartolomeo 199, 200, 201,
  203 n. 34, 204, 205, 206, 207, 208, 209,
  211, 212, 213, 214, 218, 220 n. 4,
  266 n. 12, 273 n. 45, 280
Albrici, Domenico 201 n. 25
Albrici, Vincenzo 68 n. 156, 199, 200, 201,
  202, 204, 205, 207, 208, 209, 211, 212,
  213, 218, 234
Alfonso IV, Duke of Modena 212
Allan, John 107
Ambassador, Florentine *see* Salvetti,
  Giovanni
Ambassador, French *see* Bordeaux-
  Neufville, Antoine de; Gaston, Jean
  Baptiste; Colbert, Charles; Courtin,
  Honoré; Barillon d'Amoncourt, Paul
Ambassador, Portuguese *see* Sá e
  Menezes, João Rodrigues de
Ambassador, Swedish *see* Dona, Count
Ambassador, Venetian *see* Alberti,
  Girolamo
Amelia, Princess (b. 1711) 139
Angel, Edward 180
Anglesey, Earl of *see* Annesley, Arthur
Anjou, Duc d' *see* Philippe I

Anne, Princess (b. 1709) 139
Anne, Princess/Anne, Queen 33, 44 n. 57,
  48 n. 78, 53, 72 n. 4, 76, 82 n. 35, 88
  n. 62, 90, 94, 95, 97, 98, 117, 120, 121,
  123, 124, 125, 126, 127, 128, 129 n. 68,
  138, 227 n. 32, 268 n. 18, 280 n. 57,
  287, 313
Annesley, Arthur, 1st Earl of Anglesey 96
  n. 82, 240 n. 81
Apsley, Lady Frances *see* Petre/Apsley
Apsley, Sir Allen 123
Apsley/Bathurst, (Lady) Frances 75, 82,
  120, 121, 124, 126 n. 54
Apsley/Wentworth, (Lady) Isabella 76,
  120–1 n. 36
Arlequin *see* Biancolelli, Domenico
Arlington, Countess of *see* Bennett/Fitzroy,
  Isabella
Arlington, Countess of *see* Nassau-
  Beverweerd, van/Bennet, Isabella
Arlington, Earl of *see* Bennet, Henry
Armyne/Belasyse, Susanna, [1st] Baroness
  Belasyse of Osgodby 125 n. 53, 126
Arnauld, Simon, Seigneur de Pomponne
  113, 119 n. 30
Arnould, Jacques 271, 273 n. 45, 275, 276,
  280, 283, 291
Arran (*i.e.* Aran), Earl of (Irish) *see* Butler,
  Richard
Arran, Earl of (Scottish) *see* Douglas/
  Hamilton, James
Arundell, Dennis 154 n. 32, 155–6 n. 36,
  191, 192 n. 23, 196
Ashbee, Andrew 3, 6, 129 n. 67, 130
  n. 73, 200 n. 20, 200 n. 21, 202 n. 31,
  207 n. 45, 208, 255 n. 122, 270 n. 27,
  271 n. 33, 272 n. 42, 279 n. 53
Ashbury, Joseph 127

334 *Name index*

Aston, Herbert 80 n. 25
Aston, Sir Willoughby 59 n. 114, 79 n. 20,
  241 n. 84
Aubigny, Seigneur d' *see* Stuart, Ludovic
Ayleworth, Jeffrey 267 n. 15

Baillie, Hugh Murray 36 n. 36
Baker, Mistress 133 n. 84
Baltzar, Thomas 192 n. 124
Banister, Jeffery 132–3 n. 83
Banister, John 65, 66, 69, 129 n. 68, 131,
  147, 192 n. 124, 194 n. 3, 194 n. 4, 196,
  197, 198, 218, 291
Banister, John II 265 n. 8
Barbazzi, Bianca 226 n. 28
Barbin, Claude 118, 288, 289
Barckmann, Mrs., Baroness Leijonbergh 33
Barclay Squire, W. 2
Barillon d'Amoncourt, Paul, Marquis de
  Branges 126 n. 56
Barlow, Lucy *see* Walter (Barlow), Lucy
Barry, Elizabeth 125, 181
Bashford, Christina 228, 233, 253,
  254 n. 117
Bates, Thomas 192 n. 124
Bathurst, Allen, Baron Bathurst of
  Battlesden/1st Earl Bathurst 139 n. 106
Bathurst, Benjamin 82 n. 36, 120 n.
  36, 121
Bathurst, Lady Frances *see*
  Apsley/Bathurst
Battaglia, Matteo 200, 204, 205, 206, 207,
  209 n. 49, 220 n. 4
Baxter, Richard 240 n. 80
Bayning, Mary 132 n. 83
Beach, William 87 n. 58
Beal, Peter 79, 80 n. 23, 108 n. 110
Beauchamps, Pierre 90 n. 64, 223 n. 18
Beaupuis, Pierre 256, 263
Bedingfield, Edward 296, 297
Beeston, William 195
Behn, Aphra 287 n. 90, 299, 301 n. 35,
  301 n. 36
Belasyse, Mary *see* Cromwell/Belasyse
Belasyse, Susanna *see* Armyne/Belasyse
Belasyse, Thomas, 2nd Viscount
  Fauconberg/1st Earl Fauconberg
  145 n. 4
Belette (dog) 288–9
Bellew, Sir John, 1st Baron Bellew
  of Duleek 53 n. 101, 55, 313
Bellew, Walter, 2nd Baron Bellew
  of Duleek 53 n. 101, 55, 58, 313
Benjamin, Walter 153

Bennet, Henry, 1st Earl of Arlington 50,
  54, 105, 113, 117, 118, 119, 123, 123–4
  n. 47, 124 n. 49, 125, 128, 130, 131 n.
  77, 199, 206, 216, 257, 262, 269 n. 26,
  284, 289
Bennet, Isabella *see* Nassau-Beverweerd,
  van/Bennet
Bennett, John 45
Bennett/Fitzroy, Isabella, [1st] Countess
  of Euston/[1st] Duchess of Grafton/2nd
  Countess of Arlington 33, 45, 54, 57, 76,
  117, 118, 119, 284, 288–9, 290, 311–12
Berkeley, Charles, 1st Earl of Falmouth
  73 n. 7
Berkeley, Charles, Viscount Dursley/10th
  Baron Berkeley/2nd Earl of Berkeley
  56, 57
Berkeley, George, Viscount Dursley/9th
  Baron Berkeley/1st Earl of Berkeley 33,
  56, 57, 73 n. 7
Berkeley, Mary (Bagot) 73 n. 7
Berkeley, Mary 33, 59 n. 110, 61 n. 122,
  73 n. 7, 75
Berteau 259, 261
Bertie, Charles 277, 312
Bertie, Lady Mary 59 n. 110, 60, 61 n. 122,
  64 n. 138, 65, 66, 77
Bertie, Peregrine 51 n. 94, 52, 53,
  57 n. 104, 57 n. 106, 57 n. 108, 127 n.
  58, 304, 311, 312
Betterton (Saunderson), Mary 95, 96, 177,
  178, 179, 180, 181
Betterton, Thomas 95, 96, 177, 178, 179,
  180, 181, 294, 301, 302
Betty (Marquise de La Perrine's servant)
  288–9
Beverweerd, Charlotte 118
Beverweerd, van, Isabella *see* Nassau-
  Beverweerd, van/Bennet
Bianco, Bernardino 213 n. 67
Biancolelli, Domenico ("Arlequin") 205
Birto, George *see* Berteau
Bisaccioni, Maiolino 146 n. 8, 235
Blackwell, Thomas 273 n. 43
Blagden, Nicholas 180, 181
Blagge, Col. Thomas 97
Blagge, Henrietta Maria 34
Blagge, Margaret 34, 72–3 n. 6, 86 n. 55,
  88 n. 63, 95, 97, 101, 106 n. 100, 107,
  108, 110
Blagrave, Thomas 180
Blanquefort, Marquis de *see* Duras,
  Louis de
Blount, Thomas 146

Name index 335

Blow, John 21, 22, 129, 130, 131, 132, 139 n. 107, 292, 293
Bodvile, Elizabeth 175 n. 79
Bohemia, Queen of *see* Elizabeth
Boothhouse, Samuel 39 n. 49
Bordeaux-Neufville, Antoine de 30
Boswell (Murrie), Eleanore 4, 17 n. 44, 34, 35 n. 30, 38, 48 n. 73, 65 n. 149, 80 n. 27, 82 n. 35, 86, 88, 98, 106, 182 n. 102, 236 n. 69, 247 n. 101
Boutell, Elizabeth 125 n. 52
Boutet, ?Jean 70 n. 164, 222–3 n. 16, 255, 266, 280
Bowcher (Duchess Mazarin's *tailleur*) 288–9
Boyle, Richard, 1st Earl of Burlington 76, 81–2, 110 n. 116, 289
Boyle, Roger, 1st Earl of Orrery 38, 163 n. 61, 178, 179, 182, 255 n. 120
Boyle/Hyde, Henrietta, [1st] Countess of Rochester 288–9, 290
Bradford, Earl of *see* Newport, Francis
Braganza, Catherine of, Queen *see* Catherine of Braganza
Brandenburg, Elector of *see* Friedrich Wilhelm
Brandon, Baron Gerard of *see* Gerard, Charles
Brandon, Baroness Gerard of *see* Civelle, de/Gerard, Jane
Brandon, Duke of *see* Douglas/Hamilton, James
Brandon, Viscount *see* Gerard, Charles
Brandon, Viscountess *see* Mason/Gerard/Brett, Anne
Braybrooke, Baron Griffin of *see* Griffin, Edward
Bremond, Sébastien 229, 230, 231, 232, 233 n. 55, 247, 252, 253, 266 n. 12
Bresmes, Maxent de 222–3 n. 16, 228 n. 35, 255, 266, 271, 278, 283
Breydenbach, Bernhard von 166, 168
Bright, Lady Lucy 58, 313
Brouncker, William, 2nd Viscount Brouncker 201, 212
Browne, Mr. (Clerk of the Coopers' Company) 78 n. 17
Bruce, Thomas, 2nd Earl of Ailesbury 277
Brunatti, Antonio 211, 212, 214, 254
Brunot, Louis 271, 275, 277, 280, 283, 291
Bryaxis 85 n. 46
Buccleuch, Duchess of *see* Scott, Anne
Buccleuch, Duke of *see* Scott, James
Buckhurst, Baron *see* Sackville, Lionel

Buckingham, Duke of *see* Villiers, George
Bulstrode, Sir Richard 41, 50 n. 84, 60 n. 121, 61 n. 123, 74 n. 11, 79 n. 21, 81 n. 32, 96 n. 78, 100 n. 85, 108 n. 113, 126 n. 56, 240 n. 81
Burlington, Earl of *see* Boyle, Richard
Burt, Nicholas 241 n. 85
Bury 256
Buti, Francesco 28
Butler, James, 12th Earl of Ormonde/1st Marquess of Ormonde/1st Duke of Ormonde 50, 54, 61, 97, 113
Butler, Richard, 1st Earl of Arran (*i.e.* Aran, Irish Peerage) 33, 71 n. 1
Butler, Thomas, 6th Earl of Ossory 33, 54, 96, 97
Butler/Stanley, Elizabeth, [9th] Countess of Derby 54, 97, 311, 312
Buttrey, John 224, 228, 230, 264, 265, 281

C., Mr. de 288–9
Cabin, Charles 124 n. 48
Cademan, Philip 180
Cambert, Marianne 282 n. 65
Cambert, Robert 184, 222, 224, 227, 228, 230, 232, 233, 237, 250, 252, 253, 254 n. 117, 254 n. 118, 256, 264, 265, 266, 267, 271, 281, 282, 285, 295, 296
Camocio, Giovanni Francesco 166, 168
Campistron, Jean Galbert de 285 n. 80
Caproli del Violino, Carlo 28
Carissimi, Giacomo 68, 69, 205 n. 39
Carlell, Lodowick 82 n. 36
Carmarthen, Marquess of *see* Osborne, Thomas; Osborne, Peregrine
Caroline, Princess (b. 1713) 139
Cartwright, Sir George 72 n. 3
Castlemaine, Countess of *see* Villiers/Palmer, Barbara
Catherine of Braganza, Queen 30, 31, 32, 33, 34, 38, 39, 40–3, 44, 45, 46, 50, 56, 59, 60, 61 n. 122, 63–4 n. 137, 64, 71, 72, 73, 74 n. 9, 75, 77, 78, 80, 81 n. 30, 88 n. 63, 92, 100, 101, 107 n. 108, 108, 110 n. 116, 117 n. 22, 120, 121–2, 124 n. 47, 125 n. 51, 127, 138, 198 n. 15, 201 n. 28, 202, 206, 209 n. 49, 209 n. 50, 214, 215, 216, 217, 219, 220 n. 4, 225 n. 24, 226, 228, 254 n. 119, 280 n. 57
Catherine, Princess 60 n. 118
Cavalli, Francesco 213, 233 n. 55, 234, 293
Cavendish, William, 1st Duke of Newcastle 29, 30

336   *Name index*

Cavendish, William, 4th Earl of
   Devonshire/1st Duke of Devonshire 44,
   51, 52, 56
Cavendish/Monck/Montagu, Elizabeth,
   [2nd] Duchess of Albemarle/[1st]
   Countess of Montagu/[1st] Duchess of
   Montagu 181
Cefalo, Pietro 200, 202, 204 n. 37, 205,
   209, 234
Cesti, Antonio 68 n. 155
Charles I 27, 35, 36
Charles II 3, 5, 9, 13, 17, 20, 23, 27, 28, 29,
   30, 31, 32 n. 22, 33, 34, 35, 36, 37 n. 37,
   38, 39, 41, 43, 44, 45, 46, 47, 48, 49, 51,
   53, 54, 55, 57, 59, 60 n. 114, 61, 63–4 n.
   137, 64 n. 141, 64 n. 149, 66, 67, 68 n.
   154, 68 n. 156, 71, 72 n. 3, 72 n. 4, 72 n. 5,
   78, 79, 80, 81 n. 30, 83, 85, 86, 92, 93, 97,
   98, 100, 101 n. 90, 102, 108 n. 112, 111,
   112, 113, 114, 115, 116, 117, 118, 119,
   122, 124, 125, 126, 130, 131, 132, 133,
   138, 175 n. 79, 178 n. 92, 178 n. 94, 191,
   194, 195, 197, 198, 199, 200, 202 n. 32,
   203, 204, 205, 207, 208, 209, 210, 211,
   212, 214, 215, 216, 217, 218, 219, 220,
   221 n. 5, 222, 223, 224, 225, 227, 229,
   230, 231, 233, 237, 239, 240, 241, 242,
   246, 250, 251, 252, 253, 254, 258, 264,
   265, 266, 267, 268, 269, 270, 271, 272,
   273, 274, 275, 278, 279, 280, 282, 284,
   289, 291, 294, 295, 296, 297, 298, 303
Chaworth (Lady) Grace *see* Manners/
   Chaworth
Christina, Queen of Sweden 201
Churchill, Arabella 55, 138
Churchill, John, 1st Duke
   of Marlborough 99
Churchill, Sarah *see* Jenyns/Churchill
Cir Felix 266 n. 11
Civelle, de/Gerard, Jane, [1st] Baroness
   Gerard of Brandon/[1st] Countess of
   Macclesfield 31, 33, 35, 56, 311
Clarendon, Earl of *see* Hyde, Henry; Hyde,
   Edward
Clarke 259, 261, 262
Clermont-Lodève, Comte de *see*
   Louis-Guillaume
Cleveland, Duchess of *see* Villiers/Palmer,
   Barbara
Cleveland, Earl of *see* Wentworth, Thomas
Cogan, Henry 82 n. 36
Colbert, Charles, Marquis de Croissy 59,
   60 n. 114
Coleman, Catherine 155 n. 36, 177, 180

Coleman, Charles 27 n. 1, 130 n. 71,
   151 n. 21, 189, 191, 192, 197
Coleman, Charles II 269 n. 26
Coleman, Edward 155 n. 36, 177, 180
Coling, Richard 128
Cominges, Comte de *see* Gaston,
   Jean Baptiste
Compton, George, 4th Earl
   of Northampton 55
Conduitt, John (Master of the Mint)
   78 n. 18
Congreve, William 182 n. 101
Cooke, Henry 130 n. 71, 147, 151 n. 21,
   158, 177, 180, 191, 192, 197
Cooke, Sarah 299
Corbet, Mary 125 n. 52
Corbetta, Francesco 198 n. 15
Corelli, Arcangelo 285 n. 80
Cornbury, Viscount *see* Hyde, Edward
Corneille, Pierre 78
Corniani, Giovanni Giacomo 221
Cornwallis, Charles, 2nd Baron Cornwallis
   of Eye 74 n. 13
Cornwallis, Charles, 3rd Baron Cornwallis
   of Eye 74 n. 13, 101 n. 90
Cornwallis, Henrietta-Maria 74, 75, 81
Cornwallis, Mary 76, 121 n. 36
Cosimo III, Grand Duke of Tuscany 206
Cotterau, Symon 202, 204, 205, 209 n. 49,
   228, 231, 232
Cottington, Elizabeth 80 n. 25
Courtin, Honoré 113, 117, 119, 265, 283,
   284 n. 76
Cowley, Abraham 12 n. 21, 14 n. 35,
   82 n. 36, 151, 152
Coysh, John 78 n. 17
Crachrode, Charles 126 n. 56
Crew, Nathaniel, 3rd Baron Crew (Bishop
   of Oxford) 221
Cromwell, Oliver 145 n. 4, 152, 153,
   154 n. 34, 302
Cromwell/Belasyse, Mary, [2nd]
   Viscountess Fauconberg/[1st] Countess
   Fauconberg 145 n. 4
Crowne, John 20, 22, 75, 77, 85, 89, 90,
   91, 93, 94, 95 n. 76, 96, 100, 101, 102,
   109, 110, 112, 258
Cuccino, Pietro Valentino 214 n. 72
Cummings, W. H. 2
Currer, Elizabeth 180

D'Urfey, Thomas 88 n. 62, 268 n. 18,
   284 n. 73
Dacre, Baron *see* Lennard, Thomas

Name index 337

Dacre, Baroness *see* Palmer
 (Fitzroy)/Lennard, Anne
Danby, Earl of *see* Osborne, Thomas;
 Osborne, Peregrine
Danier *see* Panine
Darnley, Catherine 138 n. 103
Davenant, Charles 16
Davenant, Sir William 5, 9, 11, 12, 13 n.
 32, 14 n. 35, 15, 23, 84 n. 42, 144, 145,
 146, 147, 148, 149, 150, 151, 152, 153,
 154, 155, 156, 157, 158, 159, 160, 161,
 162, 163, 164, 166, 170, 173, 175, 176,
 177, 178, 179, 182, 183, 184, 185, 186,
 187, 190, 192, 193, 194, 195, 196 n. 9,
 197, 198, 209, 210, 211 n. 57, 213 n. 65,
 235, 240, 257, 281, 292
Davenport, Hester 177, 178, 180
Davis, Mary 72 n. 4, 75, 92, 106 n. 103,
 132, 133 n. 85, 135, 136, 137, 179, 180,
 287 n. 86, 290 n. 94, 293
De Lisle 259
De Vic, Anne Charlotte 33
Decies, Viscount *see* Power, Richard;
 Power, John
Defoe, Daniel 47
Deincourt of Sutton, Baron *see* Leke,
 Nicholas; Leke, Robert
Delaval, Lady Elizabeth *see* Livingston/
 Delaval
Delawney, Mr. 280 n. 57
Delloney *see* Delawney, Mr.
Deloney, Henry 280 n. 57
Denham, Sir John 75, 79
Dent, Edward J. 1, 2, 3, 4, 5, 6, 7, 11, 24,
 149, 151 n. 21, 165 n. 68, 170 n. 72, 175
 n. 81, 236 n. 67
Denton, Dr. William 12 n. 28, 101 n. 90
Derby, Countess of *see* Butler/Stanley,
 Elizabeth
Derby, Earl of *see* Stanley, William George
 Richard
Dering, Sir Edward 12 n. 24
Derwentwater, Earl of *see* Radcliffe,
 Edward
Des Maizeaux, Pierre 118 n. 28, 264,
 285, 286
Devonshire, Earl of *see* Cavendish,
 William
Digby/Spencer, Anne, [2nd] Countess of
 Sunderland 53, 313
Dolle, William 86, 87, 248
Dona, Count 79 n. 22
Dorset, Earl of *see* Sackville, Charles;
 Sackville, Lionel

Douglas, James, 2nd Marquess of Douglas
 33
Douglas/Hamilton, James, Earl of
 Arran (Scottish Peerage)/4th Duke of
 Hamilton/1st Duke of Brandon 56
Dover, Baron *see* Jermyn, Henry
Downes, John 175 n. 82, 177 n. 87, 178,
 180, 182, 303
Draghi, Giovanni Battista 68, 147, 200,
 201 n. 27, 202, 203 n. 34, 209 n. 49,
 212, 213, 214, 220 n. 4, 266 n. 12, 281
Drake, Sir Francis 156, 157
Dryden, John 5, 16, 17, 18, 20, 23, 24,
 62 n. 127, 74, 75, 82 n. 36, 82–3 n. 37,
 85, 126, 139 n. 106, 149, 153, 194, 213
 n. 68, 238, 239, 241 n. 82, 240, 268 n.
 18, 295, 296, 297, 298, 299, 300, 301,
 302, 303
Du Faur, Guy, Seigneur de Pibrac 288–9
Du Moustier, Marie 224, 282 n. 65
Dumblane, Viscount *see* Osborne,
 Peregrine
Dumirail, Romain 90, 257, 258, 259, 260,
 262, 263
Duras, Louis de, Marquis de
 Blanquefort/2nd Earl of Feversham 33,
 71 n. 1, 288–9
Dursley, Viscount *see* Berkeley, George;
 Berkeley, Charles
Dyer, Benjamin or John 259

Elizabeth I 139
Elizabeth, Queen of Bohemia/Electress
 Palatine 178 n. 94
Etherege, Sir George 82 n. 36, 125,
 256 n. 126, 263 n. 141
Evelyn, John 6 n. 14, 51–2, 106 n. 100,
 109; witnesses/reports court ball/play/
 masque/concert 12, 30 n. 13, 31, 33, 34,
 37, 40–3, 44–5, 47–9, 60, 62 n. 127, 80,
 81, 100, 107, 108, 109, 110 n. 16,
 182 n. 102, 201–2, 215; witnesses/
 reports public theatrical performance
 13, 146, 148 n. 9, 157 n. 42, 182 n. 102,
 233–6; discusses friends/acquaintances
 110 n. 117, 117, 119 n. 29, 177, 201–2,
 203 n. 34, 203 n. 44
Evelyn, Mary, daughter of John Evelyn
 201 n. 27
Evelyn, Mary, wife of John Evelyn 81

Fairfax, Thomas, Lord 73
Fairfax/Villiers, Mary, [2nd] Duchess
 of Buckingham 33, 59, 61, 73, 75

338 *Name index*

Falmouth, Earl of *see* Berkeley, Charles
Fanshaw, William 98
Fanshawe, Sir Richard 39 n. 49
Fauconberg, Viscount *see* Belasyse,
  Thomas
Fauconberg, Viscountess *see* Cromwell/
  Belasyse, Mary
Favier, Jean 70 n. 64, 223 n. 18, 229, 230,
  231, 232, 240, 256, 258, 262 n. 136,
  263 n. 141
Fede, Innocenzo 203 n. 34
Feltham, Mistress 133 n. 84
Felton, Thomas 33, 48–9 n. 78, 75,
  81 n. 29, 310
Ferdinand, Prince 29 n. 5
Ferdinando, Mr. *see* Ferdinand de Florence
Ferri, Baldassare 83 n. 38, 84, 204 n. 37
Feversham, Earl of *see* Duras, Louis de
Finch, Anne *see* Kingsmill/Finch
Fiorilli, Tiberio ("Scaramouche") 204, 205,
  225 n. 23, 246 n. 92
Fisher, Lady *see* Lane, Jane
Fitzgerald, (Lady) Elizabeth *see* Jones/
  Fitzgerald
Fitzgerald, Catherine, Viscountess
  Grandison of Limerick 96 n. 82, 97
Fitzgerald, Edward *see* Villiers/Fitzgerald,
  Edward
Fitzgerald, John, 18th Earl of Kildare 289
Fitzgerald, Sir John, of Dromana 97
FitzGerald/MacCarthy, Elizabeth, [3rd]
  Viscountess Muskerry/[2nd] Countess
  of Clancarty 34
FitzJames, Arabella 138 n. 103
FitzJames, Henry 138 n. 103
FitzJames, James 138 n. 103
FitzJames/Waldegrave, Henrietta, [1st]
  Baroness Waldegrave 55, 138 n. 103
Fitzroy, George, 1st Duke of
  Northumberland 53, 54, 57, 71 n. 1, 311
Fitzroy, Henry, 1st Earl of Euston/1st Duke
  of Grafton 54, 56, 57, 117, 118 n. 28,
  289, 312
Fitzroy, Isabella *see* Bennett/Fitzroy
Fitzroy/Lee, (Lady) Charlotte, [1st]
  Countess of Lichfield 55, 127, 288–9
Fitzroy/Lennard, Anne *see* Palmer
  (Fitzroy)/Lennard
Flecknoe, Richard xvi, 14, 23, 83 n. 38,
  108 n. 112, 144, 146, 147, 155, 157,
  158, 159, 160, 173, 183, 197 n. 11,
  280, 292
Fletcher, John 75, 81, 82, 84, 85, 236
Fleuri, Nicolas 215 n. 81

Florence, Ferdinand de 216, 217
Fonseca, Emanuel 212, 214
Fortrey, Trevor 126 n. 56
Fortrey, William 126 n. 56
Fountainhall, Lord *see* Lauder, Sir John
Fox, Jane 33, 45, 55, 58, 108, 312, 313
Fox, Sir Stephen 55, 223 n. 20
France, King of *see* Louis XIV
France, Queen of *see* Marie-Thérèse
Francesco I, Duke of Modena 210
Francis of Lorraine, Duke 29 n. 5
Franco, Francesco ("Torangiu")
  214 n. 72, 254
Fraser, Catherine 128 n. 63
Fraser, James 53 n. 100, 57, 58, 108, 313
Fraser, Sir Alexander 97
Fraser/Mordaunt, Carey, [3rd] Countess of
  Peterborough 33, 76, 97, 98, 108 n. 108
Friedrich Wilhelm, Elector of
  Brandenburg/Duke of Prussia 44 n. 57,
  45 n. 61, 101 n. 91
Fripon (dog) 288–9

Galli, Francesco 203 n. 34, 220 n. 4,
  266 n. 12
Gamble, John 267 n. 15
Gascoigne, Sir Bernard 199, 216
Gaston, Jean Baptiste, Comte de Cominges
  35 n. 30
Gentileschi, Francesco 210 n. 54
Gentileschi, Giulio 210, 252, 305
Gentileschi, Orazio 210
George II 139
George of Denmark, Prince/Duke
  of Cumberland 53, 99, 287, 313
Gerard, Charles, 1st Baron Gerard
  of Brandon/1st Earl of Macclesfield
  31, 56
Gerard, Charles, 2nd Baron Gerard of
  Brandon/2nd Viscount Brandon/2nd
  Earl of Macclesfield 56
Gerard, Jane *see* Civelle, de/Gerard,
Gerard/Brett, Anne *see* Mason/Gerard/
  Brett
Gerbier, Sir Balthazar 36 n. 32,
  148 n. 10, 210 n. 53
Germaine, Sir John 288–9
Gethner, Perry 112 n. 1, 114, 115 n. 15
Gibbons, Christopher 146 n. 6, 184, 192
  n. 124
Gillet 265
Gillow, Thomas 180
Gimonde, Pietro ("Pollicinella") 205
Gingant/Gingaut *see* Guigaut

Girrard, Gaspard 291 n. 1
Gloucester, Duke of *see* Henry; William Henry
Glover, Henry 64 n. 142
Godolphin, Sidney, 1st Baron Godolphin/1st Earl of Godolphin 99, 203 n. 34
Godonesche 265
Gohory, Jeremy 280 n. 57
Goodman, Cardell 127 n. 58
Gorges, Sir Arthur 132, 133 n. 83
Grabu, Louis 5, 8, 24, 123 n. 45, 129, 217, 218, 219, 220, 227, 236, 237, 238, 252, 253, 254, 257, 264, 266, 267, 268, 270, 271, 272 n. 37, 281, 282, 283 n. 73, 291, 294, 295 n. 15, 296, 297, 298, 299, 301, 302, 303, 304, 305 n. 51
Grafton, Duchess of *see* Bennett/Fitzroy, Isabella
Grafton, Duke of *see* Fitzroy, Henry
Graham, Richard, 1st Viscount Preston 294 n. 14
Gramont, Countess of *see* Hamilton, Elizabeth
Grandi, Antonio Maria 203 n. 34
Grandison of Limerick, Viscountess *see* Fitzgerald, Catherine
Grandison, Viscount *see* Villiers, George
Granges, Claude des 215 n. 80, 215 n. 81, 217, 219, 227, 232, 256, 266 n. 12, 271, 272, 273, 274, 275, 276, 277, 278, 280, 282 n. 66, 283, 291 n. 2, 296
Greenhill, John 179
Greeting, Thomas 267 n. 15, 283–4 n. 73
Gregory XIII, Pope xiv
Grey, Elizabeth *see* Harvey/Grey
Grey, Ford, 3rd Baron Grey of Warke/1st Earl of Tankerville 73 n. 7
Grey, Thomas, 2nd Earl of Stamford 289
Griffin, Edward, 1st Baron Griffin of Braybrooke 76, 79 n. 21, 81 n. 29
Griffith, Mr. 33
Guidon (Duc de Monpensier's servant) 288–9
Guigaut, Elenor 215–6 n. 81
Guipponi, John 247, 252, 254
Guiton, Pierre 222–3 n. 16, 255, 266, 271, 278, 283
Gwyn, Francis 131
Gwyn, Nell 33, 48, 49, 81, 310

Hamilton, Anthony 32, 34, 53
Hamilton, Duke of *see* Douglas/Hamilton, James

Hamilton, Elizabeth, Countess of Gramont 32
Hamilton, James (b. ?c.1620) 33
Hamilton, James, 3rd Lord Paisley 33, 76, 79 n. 21, 81 n. 29
Hamilton, James, Lord Paisley 76, 79 n. 21, 81 n. 29
Harding, John 180
Harley, Abigail 45
Harris, Frances 88–9 n. 63, 91 n. 70, 92 n. 71, 110 n. 118
Harris, Henry 177, 179, 180
Hart, Charles 257
Hart, James 133 n. 83, 293
Harvey, Sir Daniel 289
Harvey/Grey, Elizabeth, [2nd] Countess of Stamford 288–9
Hatton, Christopher, 2nd Baron Hatton/1st Viscount Hatton 175 n. 79
Haun, Eugene xvi n. 3, 4, 6, 10, 144, 145, 157 n. 43, 159 n. 47
Hawkins, Sir John 66–7 n. 153, 203 n. 35
Henrietta Maria, Queen 27, 28, 29 n. 5, 35 n. 31, 72 n. 5, 85 n. 47, 214 n. 74, 227
Henriette 259, 262
Henriette Anne, Duchesse d'Orléans 28, 35, 222 n. 13
Henry, Earl of Cambridge/Duke of Gloucester 28
Herbert, Henriette *see* Kéroualle/Herbert
Herbert, James 99
Herbert, Lady Catherine *see* Osborne/Herbert
Herbert, Lady Katherine 98
Herbert, Margaret *see* Sawyer/Herbert
Herbert, Philip, 4th Earl of Pembroke/1st Earl of Montgomery 99
Herbert, Philip, 7th Earl of Pembroke and 4th Earl of Montgomery 99
Herbert, Sir Henry 152 n. 27
Herbert, Thomas, 8th Earl of Pembroke and 5th Earl of Montgomery 33, 45 n. 60, 56, 57
Hervart, Anne 10 n. 16, 285 n. 80
Hill, Roger 180
Hinds, Allen B. 226
Hingeston, John 215
Hogarth, William 78 n. 18
Holland, Gervase 61 n. 124
Holman, Peter 34, 65, 69, 90–1 n. 67, 131, 137, 194, 197, 198 n. 14, 214 n. 74, 215, 256 n. 126, 265 n. 8, 266 n. 9, 269 n. 26, 272 n. 37, 291 n. 2, 292, 293 n. 8
Hooke, Robert 51, 227 n. 31

340 *Name index*

Hopkins, John 301 n. 33
Hotson, Leslie 4, 148 n. 10, 178 n. 91
Howard, (Lady) Mary *see* Mordaunt/
  Howard
Howard, Barbara *see* Villiers/Wenman/
  Wentworth/Howard
Howard, Henry, 1st Baron Howard of
  Castle Rising/1st Earl of Norwich/17th
  Earl of Arundel/6th Duke of Norfolk
  86, 87
Howard, Lady Elizabeth 76, 86 n. 52, 87
Howard, Lady Essex 33
Howard, Sir Robert 74, 154 n. 33
Howard, Thomas 76, 81 n. 29
Howard, William, 1st Viscount Stafford/1st
  Baron Stafford 226 n. 26
Howell, James 28 n. 4
Hudson, George 129 n. 69, 151 n. 21, 191,
  192, 197
Hughes, Margaret 83 n. 38, 180, 288–9
Hume, Robert D. 3, 6, 115 n. 17, 178 n. 94
Humfrey, Pelham 66, 68, 74 n. 10, 102,
  129, 130 n. 71, 194 n. 4, 218
Hunt, Dubartus 180
Huygens, Christiaan 286 n. 85
Hyde, Anne, Duchess of York 33, 37 n. 37,
  60, 175 n. 79
Hyde, Edward, Viscount Cornbury/3rd
  Earl of Clarendon 58, 313
Hyde, Henrietta *see* Boyle/Hyde
Hyde, Henry, 2nd Earl of Clarendon 100–1
Hyde, Laurence, 1st Earl of Rochester 289

Inchiquin, Earl of *see* O'Brien, Murrough
Isaac 259, 261, 280 n. 57
Isabella (Duchess Mazarin's servant)
  288–9, 290
Isabella, Princess 121, 125, 126

James I 94
James, Duke of York/James II 17, 20, 23,
  24, 28, 29, 30, 31, 32, 33, 37 n. 37, 42,
  47 n. 69, 48 n. 76, 51, 57, 58, 61, 72, 81,
  92, 93, 97, 100, 107, 121, 126, 127, 129
  n. 68, 131, 137, 138, 175 n. 79, 199 n.
  17, 203 n. 34, 219, 220, 221, 226 n. 26,
  230, 233, 234, 240, 265 n. 8, 273, 276,
  279, 280, 287 n. 86, 294 n. 14, 297, 300,
  303, 304, 305, 312, 313
János Zsigmond Zápolya, King of Hungary
  179
Jeffreys, George, 1st Baron Jeffreys
  of Wem 300 n. 32
Jenkins, Sir Leoline 126 n. 56, 263 n. 140

Jenyns, Richard 97
Jenyns/Churchill, Sarah, [1st] Duchess
  of Marlborough 97
Jermyn, Henry, 1st Baron Jermyn/1st Earl
  of Saint Albans 29, 247, 254, 257, 263
Jermyn, Henry, 3rd Baron Jermyn/1st
  Baron Dover 288–9
Jersey, Earl of *see* Villiers, Sir Edward
João IV, King of Portugal 210 n. 54
Johann Wilhelm II von Wittelsbach, Prince
  of Neuburg, Duke of Jülich and Berg,
  Elector Palatine 33, 207
Jolly, George 193, 194, 195, 211 n. 57,
  213 n. 65
Jones, Inigo 9, 27, 35, 36, 39, 85 n. 47, 150
Jones, Richard, 1st Earl of Ranelagh 289
Jones/Fitzgerald, (Lady) Elizabeth, [18th]
  Countess of Kildare 288–9
Jonson, Ben 9, 27, 58 n. 109, 92, 93, 94,
  144, 145, 146, 147, 214 n. 74, 265
Jordan, Thomas 27 n. 1, 155, 162
Jouan 257, 258, 259, 261
Jülich and Berg, Duke of *see* Johann
  Wilhelm II von Wittelsbach

Kéroualle, Louise de, Duchess of
  Portsmouth/Duchess of Aubigny 42, 52,
  59 n. 110, 61 n. 122, 65 n. 149, 73, 75,
  97, 224, 264, 265–6, 281, 284, 295, 296,
  312, 313
Kéroualle, Sieur de *see* Penancoët,
  Guillaume de
Kéroualle/Herbert, Henriette, [7th]
  Countess of Pembroke and [4th]
  Countess of Montgomery 97, 99
Kieser, Eberhard 166 n. 70, 169
Kilburn, Matthew 139
Kildare, Countess of *see* Jones/Fitzgerald,
  (Lady) Elizabeth
Kildare, Earl of *see* Fitzgerald, John
Killigrew, Thomas 37 n. 37, 193, 194, 195,
  201, 202 n. 29, 208, 209, 210, 211, 212,
  213, 214, 219, 238, 240, 241 n. 85, 246
  n. 92, 252, 255 n. 121, 257, 262, 263
King, Robert 265 n. 8
Kingsmill/Finch, Anne, [5th] Countess
  of Winchilsea 22, 75, 131
Knepp, Elizabeth 214
Knollys, Lady Frances 57 n. 106

L'Abbé, Anthony 288–9
La Devese, Mr. de 287, 288, 289
La Forêst (Duchess Mazarin's servant)
  288–9, 290

Name index 341

La Forest (French singer) 265
La Montagu Cir *see* Cir Felix
La Perrine (Monginot), Marquise de 287, 288, 289
La Pierre 223 n. 18
La Riche, François 265 n. 8, 279 n. 54
La Roche-Guilhen, Anne de 22, 75, 112, 115, 117, 118, 119, 284
La Vollée, Jean de 214, 215, 217, 227
Lacy, John 81, 257
Laduke, Lewis 261
Lafontaine, Henry Cart de 3, 209 n. 49
Lake, Dr. Edward 42, 44, 108 n. 110
Lane (dancer) 302 n. 37
Lane, Jane, Lady Fisher 98
Lane, Mr. (attends *The Siege of Rhodes*, July 1661) 175 n. 79
Lane, Mr. (dancer in *Calisto*) 98
Langbaine, Gerard 80 n. 23, 85 n. 47, 100 n. 86, 299
Lanier, Nicholas 145, 147, 191 n. 121, 197, 210, 218
Lapp, Walter 253, 254 n. 119, 297
Las Casas, Bartolomé de 154 n. 34
Lasocki, David 224, 271 n. 33
Latimer, Viscount *see* Osborne, Thomas
Lauder, Sir John, Lord Fountainhall 127–8
Lawes, Henry 130 n. 71, 145, 147, 151 n. 21, 157–8, 189, 191, 192, 197
Lawrence, W. J. 2, 11, 113, 149–50 n. 13, 204 n. 37, 228 n. 35, 236, 237 n. 73, 304 n. 43, 305 n. 50, 305 n. 51
Lazenby, Phillip 62 n. 128
Le Clerc *see* Clarke
Le Duc 259, 261, 262, 263 n. 142, 280 n. 57
Le Grand, Monsieur 223 n. 18
Le Roi 259, 262
Lee, (Lady) Charlotte *see* Fitzroy/Lee
Lee, Edward Henry, 1st Earl of Lichfield 55, 289
Lee, Mary 179, 180
Lee, Nathaniel 8, 50 n. 86, 75, 82 n. 36, 120, 121, 122, 123 n. 44, 123 n. 45, 127 n. 58, 128, 246 n. 93, 268 n. 18
Lee, Sir Frances Henry 55
Leeds, Duke of *see* Osborne, Thomas; Osborne, Peregrine
Legge, William 193, 194 n. 2, 195, 211, 213 n. 65
Leigh, Anthony 115, 302
Leijonbergh, Baroness *see* Barckmann, Mrs.

Leke, Nicholas, 2nd Baron Deincourt of Sutton/2nd Earl of Scarsdale 98
Leke, Robert, 3rd Baron Deincourt of Sutton/3rd Earl of Scarsdale 53 n. 101, 56, 58, 98, 313
Lennard, Anne *see* Palmer (Fitzroy)/ Lennard
Lennard, Thomas, 15th Baron Dacre/1st Earl of Sussex 99, 101 n. 90
Lennox, Duchess of *see* Stuart, Frances Teresa
Lennox, Duchess of *see* Villiers/Herbert/ Stewart, (Lady) Mary
Leonard, Mr. 98
Lestang, Anne-Louis 90, 257, 258, 259, 260, 261, 262, 263
Letelier 256
Lewes, Mary 99
Lewis, Jenkin 139
Lichfield, Countess of *see* Fitzroy/Lee, (Lady) Charlotte
Lichfield, Earl of *see* Lee, Edward Henry
Lilleston, Thomas 180, 181
Littleton, Lady Anne 57 n. 106
Livingston/Delaval, Lady Elizabeth 74 n. 9
Locke, Matthew 11 n. 19, 12, 21, 22, 84, 85, 87, 113, 129, 146 n. 6, 147, 158, 161, 177, 180, 184, 186, 190, 191, 192, 194, 197, 198, 214 n. 74, 218, 223, 227, 236 n. 67, 270, 291, 315
Long, Jane 180
Lord Chamberlain *see* Montagu, Edward (1660–71); Jermyn, Henry (1671–74); Bennet, Henry (1674–85); Bruce, Thomas (1685)
Lord Steward *see* Butler, James (1660–89)
Louis XIV, King of France 28, 35 n. 30, 69, 93, 118, 126, 209 n. 48, 216, 218, 221, 222, 223, 224, 225, 233, 250, 253, 265, 287 n. 86, 305 n. 50
Louis-Guillaume, Comte de Clermont-Lodève, Marquis de Sessac, Vicomte de Lautrec, Vicomte de Nebouzan, Baron de Castelnau-Caumont, Seigneur de Venez, Seigneur de Boussagues, Seigneur de Beaulieu 288–9
Luckett, Richard 4, 6, 133 n. 84, 136 n. 92
Lully, Jean-Baptiste 10, 52, 69, 90, 91, 218, 222, 223, 224, 225 n. 23, 228, 250, 252, 256, 258, 260, 263 n. 141, 265, 281, 285, 288, 290, 292, 304, 305 n. 50
Luttrell, Narcissus 42, 45 n. 59
Luynes, Duc de *see* Albert de Luynes, Louis Charles d'

342   *Name index*

MacCarthy, Charles, 3rd Viscount
  Muskerry/2nd Earl of Clancarty 34
MacCarthy, Elizabeth *see* FitzGerald/
  MacCarthy
Macclesfield, Countess of *see* Civelle, de/
  Gerard, Jane; Mason/Gerard/Brett, Anne
Macclesfield, Earl of *see* Gerard, Charles
Madge, Humphrey 192 n. 124
Magalotti, Lorenzo 79 n. 20, 206 n. 41
Maguire, Nancy Klein 21 n. 52
Maimbourg, Louis 296 n. 21
Manchester, Earl of *see* Montagu, Edward;
  Montagu, Robert; Montagu, Charles
Mancini, Hortense, Duchess Mazarin 118,
  284–90, 293
Manners, Cecily *see* Tufton/Hungerford/
  Manners
Manners, Francis, Baron Roos of
  Belvoir/6th Earl of Rutland 150 n. 18
Manners, John, Baron Roos of Belvoir/9th
  Earl of Rutland/1st Duke of Rutland
  44 n. 56
Manners, Katherine Wriothesley
  see Noel/Manners
Manners/Chaworth (Lady) Grace, [3rd]
  Viscountess Chaworth 44, 107 n. 108, 108
Manuel, Mrs. 214 n. 71
Maria Beatrice d'Este *see* Mary of Modena
Marie-Thérèse, Queen of France 222, 294
Mariens, Francis 271, 275, 276, 277, 279,
  280, 283, 291, 292, 297
Marlborough, Duchess of *see*
  Jenyns/Churchill, Sarah
Marlborough, Duke of *see* Churchill, John
Marsh, Alfonso (Sr.) 66, 180, 197
Marsh, Christopher 15 n. 37
Martinozzi, Laura, Dowager Duchess
  of Modena 220, 221, 225, 226, 234
Marvell, Andrew 145 n. 4
Mary of Modena, Duchess of York/Queen
  51 n. 93, 53, 58, 96 n. 80, 100 n. 85,
  121, 125, 126, 127 n. 58, 129 n. 68, 131,
  138, 203, 220, 221, 222, 223, 224, 225,
  226, 227, 230, 254, 297, 312, 313
Mary, Princess (sister of Charles II)
  214 n. 74
Mary, Princess/Mary II 33, 44, 72, 73, 76,
  81, 82, 87 n. 55, 88 n. 62, 89, 90, 94, 95,
  97, 98, 100 n. 86, 108 n. 110, 120 n. 34,
  124, 125, 138, 280 n. 57
Mason, Sir Richard 56
Mason/Gerard/Brett, Anne, [2nd]
  Viscountess Brandon/[2nd] Countess
  of Macclesfield 56, 311

Massinger, Philip 82 n. 36
Masson 288–9
Matteis, Nicola 266 n. 12
Maurice, Prince of Orange 119 n. 29
Mazarin, Cardinal Jules 220
Mazarin, Duchess *see* Mancini, Hortense
Medbourne, Matthew 180
Meisner, Daniel 166 n. 70, 169
Ménestrier, Claude-François 237
Milhous, Judith 3, 4, 6, 115 n. 17, 178 n.
  94, 297 n. 25
Milon (Duchess Mazarin's chaplain)
  288–9, 290
Modena, Duchess of *see* Martinozzi,
  Laura
Modena, Duke of *see* Francesco I; Alfonso
  IV
Modena, Mary of *see* Mary of Modena
Modena, Prince of *see* Rinaldo, Prince
Mohun, Michael 238
Molière 69, 90 n. 64, 91, 225 n. 23, 228,
  246 n. 92, 260
Monck, George, 1st Duke of Albemarle
  214 n. 74
Monck/Montagu, Elizabeth *see* Cavendish/
  Monck/Montagu
Monconys, Balthasar de 32, 33, 37, 40
Monginot/La Perrine *see* La Perrine,
  Marquise de
Monmouth, Duchess of *see* Scott, Anne
Monmouth, Duke of *see* Scott, James
Montagu, Charles, 4th Earl of Manchester
  54
Montagu, Edward, 2nd Earl of Manchester
  60, 123 n. 47, 215 n. 80, 235 n. 66
Montagu, Elizabeth *see* Cavendish/Monck/
  Montagu
Montagu, Ralph, 3rd Baron Montagu of
  Boughton/1st Earl of Montagu/1st Duke
  of Montagu 51–2, 285 n. 80
Montagu, Robert, 3rd Earl of Manchester
  54
Montandre, Marquis de *see*
  Rochefoucauld, François de la
Monteverdi, Claudio 145
Montgomery, Countess of *see* Kéroualle/
  Herbert, Henriette; Sawyer/Herbert,
  Margaret
Montgomery, Earl of *see* Herbert, Philip;
  Herbert, Thomas
Morby *see* Motley
Mordaunt, (Lady) Penelope *see* O'Brien/
  Mordaunt
Mordaunt, Carey *see* Fraser/Mordaunt

Name index   343

Mordaunt, Charles, 3rd Earl
  of Peterborough 98, 99, 126
Mordaunt, Henry, 2nd Earl
  of Peterborough 82, 97, 221
Mordaunt/Howard, (Lady) Mary, 7th
  Baroness Mordaunt/[2nd] Countess of
  Norwich/[18th] Countess of Arundel/
  [7th] Duchess of Norfolk 33, 75, 76, 82,
  87 n. 55, 95, 97, 98, 126
Morin (Duchess Mazarin's *tailleur*) 288–9,
  290
Motley 259, 261
Murray, Sir Robert 212, 213 n. 68
Music, Master of the *see* Lanier, Nicholas
  (1660–66); Grabu, Louis (1666–74);
  Staggins, Nicholas (1674–1700)
Muskerry, Viscount *see* MacCarthy,
  Charles
Muskerry, Viscountess *see* FitzGerald/
  MacCarthy, Elizabeth
Mustapha (Duchess Mazarin's servant)
  288–9
Myer, John 267 n. 15

Nassau-Beverweerd, Lodewijk van
  119 n. 29
Nassau-Beverweerd, van/Bennet, Isabella,
  [1st] Countess of Arlington 33,
  119 n. 29, 123–4 n. 47
Neuburg, Prince of *see* Johann Wilhelm II
  von Wittelsbach
Neufville, Antoine de Bordeaux *see*
  Bordeaux-Neufville, Antoine de
Neufville, François de, Marquis de
  Villeroy 223 n. 18
Newcastle, Duke of *see* Cavendish,
  William
Newcombe, Thomas 247
Newdigate, Sir Richard 42, 50 n. 86,
  96 n. 79, 100 n. 85, 294 n. 12, 296 n. 22
Newport, Francis, 2nd Baron Newport/
  Viscount Newport/1st Earl of Bradford
  202
Nichols, Thomas 78 n. 17
Nicoll, Allardyce 3
Noel, Bridget 51 n. 92, 51 n. 93, 52
Noel/Manners, Katherine Wriothesley, Lady
  Roos/[9th] Countess of Rutland/[1st]
  Duchess of Rutland 51 n. 92, 51 n. 93,
  51 n. 94, 52, 53 n. 101, 53 n. 102,
  57 n. 104, 57 n. 106, 57 n. 107, 58,
  59 n. 110, 60, 61 n. 122, 64 n. 138,
  65 n. 148, 65 n. 149, 66 n. 152, 127 n. 58,
  296, 304, 311–13

Nokes, James 180, 302
Norfolk, Duchess of *see*
  Mordaunt/Howard, (Lady) Mary
Norfolk, Duke of *see* Howard, Henry
Norris, Henry 180, 181
Norris, Mrs. 180
North, Roger 66, 67, 68, 69 n. 159
Northampton, Earl of *see* Compton,
  George
Northumberland, Duke of *see* Fitzroy,
  George
Norton, Mary 177 n. 89, 180
Norwich, Earl of *see* Howard, Henry
Noure, Elizabeth 203 n. 34

O'Brien, Capt. Charles 74, 76, 79 n. 21,
  81 n. 29
O'Brien, Murrough, 1st Earl of Inchiquin
  74 n. 12
O'Brien/Mordaunt, (Lady) Penelope, [2nd]
  Countess of Peterborough 126
Oldfield, Mr. (of Soho Square) 56, 57
Oldys, William 96 n. 77
Orange, Prince of *see* Maurice; William
Orléans, Duc d' *see* Philippe I
Orléans, Duchesse d' *see* Henriette Anne
Ormonde, Duke of *see* Butler, James
Orpe, Col. 93, 98
Orrell, John 36 n. 33, 38, 39 n. 44, 162,
  164 n. 66, 263 n. 140
Orrery, Earl of *see* Boyle, Roger
Osborne, Peregrine, Viscount
  Dumblane/2nd Earl of Danby/2nd
  Marquess of Carmarthen/2nd Duke of
  Leeds 51, 53, 55, 98, 99, 312
Osborne, Thomas, 1st Viscount
  Osborne/1st Viscount Latimer/1st
  Earl of Danby/1st Marquess of
  Carmarthen/1st Duke of Leeds
  xvii n. 6, 51, 55, 97, 98, 284
Osborne/Herbert, Lady Catherine 97, 99
Ossory, Earl of *see* Butler, Thomas
"Ossory, Lady" 61 n. 123
Oxford, Bishop of *see* Crew, Nathaniel
Oxford, Earl of *see* Vere, Aubrey de

Paisible, Jacques 22, 113, 115, 118, 119,
  120 n. 33, 137, 222–3 n. 16, 255, 271,
  274, 275, 276, 277, 278, 279, 280 n.
  55, 280 n. 60, 282, 283, 284, 286, 287,
  288–9, 290, 291, 292, 293 n. 10, 297
Paisley, Lord *see* Hamilton, James,
Palatinate, Rupert of the *see* Rupert, Prince
Palatine, Electress *see* Elizabeth

344 *Name index*

Palmer (Fitzroy)/Lennard, Anne, [15th] Baroness Dacre/[1st] Countess of Sussex 97, 98
Palmer, Barbara *see* Villiers/Palmer
Panine 256
Pearse, Elizabeth 78
Pecour, Guillaume-Louis 257, 258, 259, 263 n. 141
Pedro, Seignor 200–1 n. 24
Pembroke, Countess of *see* Kéroualle/ Herbert, Henriette; Sawyer/Herbert, Margaret
Pembroke, Earl of *see* Herbert, Philip; Herbert, Thomas
Penaguião, Conde de *see* Sá e Menezes, João Rodrigues de
Penancoët, Guillaume de, Sieur de Kéroualle 97
Pepys, Elisabeth 151 n. 22
Pepys, Samuel 6 n. 14, 151 n. 22, 190; witnesses/reports court ball/play/ masque/concert 30 n. 13, 31, 32, 33, 34, 37, 39–44, 71 n. 1, 74, 76, 78, 79, 108, 182 n. 102, 202 n. 29, 205, 209, 212, 214 n. 74; witnesses/reports public theatrical performance 81, 83 n. 38, 84, 175, 176 n. 83, 179 n. 98, 181, 182 n. 102, 196 n. 9, 204 n. 37; discusses friends/acquaintances 68 n. 156, 72, 158 n. 45, 177–8, 198, 199, 200 n. 24, 201, 207 n. 45, 209, 211, 212, 213–14, 218 n. 95, 246 n. 92
Perrin, Pierre 184 n. 107, 224, 230, 232, 233 n. 55, 247, 250, 252, 253, 256
Peterborough, Countess of *see* Fraser/ Mordaunt, Carey; O'Brien/Mordaunt, (Lady) Penelope
Peterborough, Earl of *see* Mordaunt, Henry; Mordaunt, Charles
Petre/Apsley, (Lady) Frances 120 n. 34
Philippe I, Duc d'Anjou/Duc d'Orléans 28, 223 n. 18
Philips, Katherine 75, 78, 79, 81, 147, 196, 197,
Phillips, John 154 n. 34
Pibrac, Seigneur de *see* Du Faur, Guy
Pinkethman, William 287 n. 90
Pinnock, Andrew 131
Pitou, Spire 114 n. 10, 120
Player, Sir Thomas 205
Playford, John 145, 190
Pollicinella *see* Gimonde, Pietro
Pomponne, Seigneur de *see* Arnauld, Simon
Portman, Mr. 133 n. 83

Portsmouth, Duchess of *see* Kéroualle, Louise de
Povey, John 53 n. 101, 57, 58, 312
Povey, Thomas 31
Powell, Martin 78 n. 17
Power, John, Viscount Decies/2nd Earl of Tyrone 96 n. 82, 99
Power, Richard, 6th Baron Power/Viscount Decies/1st Earl of Tyrone 99
Preston, Viscount *see* Graham, Richard
Price, Curtis A. 4, 87, 305
Priest, Frances 132, 133 n. 83
Priest, John (Joseph) 261
Priest, Josias 13, 77, 132, 133
Priest, Mistress 133 n. 84
Prunières, Henri 2
Purcell, Henry 1, 2, 4, 5, 17, 18, 129 n. 71, 136, 291, 292, 305 n. 52, 306
Purcell, Henry, Sr. 180
Purcell, Thomas 129

Queen *see* Henrietta Maria; Catherine of Braganza; Mary of Modena; Mary, Princess; Anne, Princess
Quinault, Philippe 52, 91, 250, 256, 258, 263 n. 141, 285, 288, 290, 304

R., Mlle. de 288–9
Radcliffe, Edward, Viscount Radcliffe/2nd Earl of Derwentwater 137 n. 97, 138
Ranelagh, Earl of *see* Jones, Richard
Rassen, Marquis de 223 n. 18
Rawlins, Thomas 82 n. 36
Raymond, John 13
Reggio, Pietro 200, 201, 203 n. 34, 209 n. 49
Reresby, Sir John 146 n. 8
Reuwich, Erhard 166, 168
Rich, Mr. (Sir), Master of the Revels at Lincoln's Inn 59 n. 113
Richards, John 180, 181
Richmond, Duchess of *see* Stuart, Frances Teresa
Richmond, Duchess of *see* Villiers/ Herbert/Stewart, (Lady) Mary
Rider, Richard 104, 105
Rinaldo, Prince 221, 225, 226, 234
Robert, Anthony 72 n. 5, 227, 232, 256, 271 n. 31, 273 n. 43, 280 n. 57, 283, 296
Robert, Anthony II 280 n. 57
Rochefoucauld, François de la, Marquis de Montandre 288–9
Rochester, Countess of *see* Boyle/Hyde, Henrietta

Name index   345

Rochester, Earl of *see* Wilmot, John; Hyde,
   Laurence
Roos of Belvoir, Baron *see* Manners,
   Francis; Manners, John
Roos, Lady *see* Noel/Manners, Katherine
   Wriothesley
Rosaccio, Giuseppe 166, 168
Rossi, Luigi 68 n. 155
Rousseau, Jacques 305 n. 50
Rovetta, Giovanni 146 n. 8, 235
Rubens, Peter Paul 35
Rugge, Thomas 80
Rupert, Prince, Count Palatine of the
   Rhine/Duke of Cumberland 33, 71,
   83 n. 38, 186 n. 115, 289, 317
Russell, Col. John 33
Rutland, Countess of *see* Tufton/
   Hungerford/Manners, Cecily; Noel/
   Manners, Katherine Wriothesley
Rutland, Earl of *see* Manners, Francis;
   Manners, John
Rymer, Thomas 300
Rymon, Peter 180

Sá e Menezes, João Rodrigues de, 3rd
   Conde de Penaguião (Portuguese
   Ambassador) 146 n. 6,
   162 n. 58
Sackville, Charles, 6th Earl of Dorset
   121, 122
Sackville, Lionel, Baron Buckhurst/7th
   Earl of Dorset/1st Duke of Dorset 139
   n. 106
Sadler, Anthony 30
Saint Albans, Earl of *see* Jermyn, Henry
Saint-André, Adrien Merger de 70 n. 164,
   90, 223, 224, 229, 256, 258, 259, 260,
   262, 263, 272, 283, 296
Saint-Évremond, Charles de Marguetel
   de Saint-Denis, Seigneur de 9, 10, 117,
   118, 119, 284–90, 291, 293
Saintsbury, George 17 n. 44
Salvetti, Giovanni 237, 238, 240 n. 81,
   241, 246 n. 95, 255 n. 124
Sandford, Francis 279 n. 53
Sandford, Samuel 180
Sansoni, Giuseppe 203 n. 34
Saslow, Edward 296
Sautre, Guillaume 215 n. 81
Savile, Henry 76, 80, 81 n. 29, 270, 282
Sawyer, Sir Robert 45
Sawyer/Herbert, Margaret, [8th] Countess
   of Pembroke and [5th] Countess of
   Montgomery 33, 45
Scaramouche *see* Fiorilli, Tiberio

Scarsdale, Earl of *see* Leke, Nicholas;
   Leke, Robert
Schwerin the Younger, Otto von 33, 41, 42,
   44 n. 57, 45 n. 61, 100 n. 89, 101 n. 91
Scott, Anne, [1st] Duchess of
   Monmouth/1st Duchess of Buccleuch
   32, 33, 59 n. 110, 61 n. 122, 72, 74, 75,
   78, 79, 80–1, 87 n. 55, 99
Scott, James, 1st Duke of Monmouth/1st
   Duke of Buccleuch 32, 33, 59 n. 110,
   61 n. 122, 71, 72, 73, 74, 75, 79 n. 21,
   80 n. 23, 90 n. 67, 92, 93, 98, 99, 138,
   223, 234, 303
Scouten, Arthur 234
Scrope, Sir Carr 123 n. 45, 125–6
Scudéry, Madeleine de 82 n. 36
Sebenico, Giovanni 200, 202, 204, 205,
   206, 209, 213, 234
Sedley, Catherine 128 n. 63, 138
Sedley, Sir Charles 194 n. 3
Sessac, Marquis de *see* Louis-Guillaume
Settle, Elkanah 21, 22, 75, 85, 86, 87, 88,
   147, 179, 182, 227
Seymour, Charles, 6th Duke of Somerset
   51, 52, 56, 57, 61
Shadwell (Gibbs), Anne 180
Shadwell, Thomas 11, 85–6, 202, 223, 230
   n. 44, 236 n. 67, 268 n. 18, 283 n. 73,
   299, 300
Shaw, Sir John 200 n. 20, 207
Sherwin, William 86 n. 49
Shifrin, Susan 284 n. 74, 285 n. 81,
   287 n. 89, 290 n. 92
Shirley, James 82 n. 36, 146, 147, 155,
   161, 184, 246 n. 93
Shrewsbury, Earl of *see* Talbot, Francis;
   Talbot, Charles
Singleton, John 181, 214 n. 74
Smith, John 245
Smith, Robert 66
Smith, William (actor) 179, 180, 302
Smyth, John 259, 261
Snesby, Richard 61 n. 124
Somerset, Duke of *see* Seymour, Charles
Southern, Richard 162 n. 60, 172, 173, 176
Southerne, Thomas 294
Southwell, Sir Robert 53 n. 100, 53 n. 101,
   57 n. 108, 312, 313
Spence, Ferrand 298, 299
Spencer, Anne *see* Digby/Spencer
Spencer, Lady Anne 56, 311
Spencer, Robert, 2nd Earl of Sunderland
   33, 51 n. 94, 52–7, 73, 101 n. 90, 108,
   114, 117 n. 22, 294, 311, 313
Stafford, Mr. 98

346 *Name index*

Stafford, Viscount *see* Howard, William
Staggins, Isaac 268, 269, 274, 275, 278 n. 48
Staggins, Nicholas 20, 22, 46, 90, 91, 110,
112, 113, 129, 130, 131, 258, 268, 269,
270, 272, 273, 274, 275, 276, 277, 278,
280, 281, 282
Stamford, Countess of *see* Harvey/Grey,
Elizabeth
Stamford, Earl of *see* Grey, Thomas
Stanley, Elizabeth *see* Butler/Stanley
Stanley, William George Richard, 9th Earl
of Derby 54, 99
Stapylton, Sir Robert 146, 147, 196
Starkey, John 59 n. 114, 79 n. 20, 241 n. 84
Stephens, A. 45
Stewart, (Lady) Mary *see* Villiers/Herbert/
Stewart
Stradella, Alessandro 68 n. 155
Streeter, Robert 62 n. 127, 62 n. 128,
62 n. 129, 63, 65, 86, 88 n. 59, 103, 104,
105, 106, 250
Strickland, Sir Roger 288–9
Stuart, Frances Teresa, [3rd] Duchess of
Richmond and [6th] Duchess of Lennox
33, 59 n. 110, 61, 73, 75, 108 n. 112
Stuart, James Francis Edward (Prince
of Wales/"Old Pretender") 138
Stuart, Ludovic, Seigneur d'Aubigny
215, 216
Suarez, Hilario 200, 201, 203 n. 34,
204 n. 37, 205, 209 n. 49, 220 n. 4,
266 n. 12
Suffolk, Countess of *see* Villiers/Wenman/
Wentworth/Howard, Barbara
Suleiman the Magnificent 163, 164, 165,
166, 170 n. 73, 175, 176 n. 83, 178, 179,
180, 181
Summers, Montague 2, 85 n. 47
Sunderland, Countess of *see* Digby/
Spencer, Anne
Sunderland, Earl of *see* Spencer, Robert
Surveyor General *see* Jones, Inigo
(1615–43); Wren, Sir Christopher
(1669–1718)
Sussex, Countess of *see* Palmer
(Fitzroy)/Lennard, Anne
Sussex, Earl of *see* Lennard, Thomas
Sweden, Queen of *see* Christina

Talbot, Charles, 12th Earl of
Shrewsbury/1st Duke of Shrewsbury
32, 33
Talbot, Francis, 11th Earl of Shrewsbury
32, 33

Talbot, John 57, 117 n. 22, 312
Tate, Nahum 2, 5, 136, 268 n. 19, 292
Temple, Anne 33
Testa, Andrea 199 n. 17, 201 n. 25,
208–9 n. 48
Thomason, George 84 n. 43, 155
Thorndell, Gregory 180
Thurloe, John 150, 157 n. 44
Tombes, John 206 n. 42
Torangiu *see* Franco, Francisco
Townshend, Aurelian 145, 146, 147
Trevor, John 98
Trevor, Sir John 98
Tudor, Lady Mary 33, 45, 72 n. 4, 76,
117, 132, 135, 136–7, 137 n. 97, 138,
293 n. 9
Tufte, Edward 7
Tufton/Hungerford/Manners, Cecily, [6th]
Countess of Rutland 150
Tuke (Sheldon), Mary 201 n. 27
Tuppen, Sandra 47, 69, 70, 90 n. 64
Turner, William 92
Tuscany, Grand Duke of *see* Cosimo III
Tyrone, Earl of *see* Power, Richard;
Power, John
Tyrrell, Mr. 81 n. 31

Van Lennep, William 3, 78 n. 16, 81
n. 30, 82 n. 34, 85 n. 47, 101 n. 90,
111 n. 17, 121 n. 39, 123 n. 46, 127
n. 58, 127 n. 60, 139 n. 106, 196 n. 9,
304 n. 45
Vere, Aubrey de, 20th Earl of Oxford 58,
177 n. 89, 313
Verney, Edmund 12 n. 25, 113
Verney, John 12 n. 25, 101 n. 90, 113, 114,
119, 133, 283
Verney, Sir Greville 76, 81 n. 29
Verney, Sir Ralph 12 n. 28, 101 n. 90
Vernon, James 223, 224, 258
Verrio, Antonio 51
Villeroy, Marquis de *see* Neufville,
François de
Villiers, Edward 99
Villiers, Francis 288–9
Villiers, George, 2nd Duke of Buckingham
33, 61, 217, 285, 286 n. 82
Villiers, George, 4th Viscount
Grandison 99
Villiers, Katherine 33
Villiers, Mary *see* Fairfax/Villiers
Villiers, Sir Edward, 1st Earl of Jersey 33
Villiers/Fitzgerald, Edward (son of 4th
Viscount Grandison) 99

Name index 347

Villiers/Herbert/Stewart, (Lady) Mary, [1st] Duchess of Richmond and [4th] Duchess of Lennox 159 n. 48

Villiers/Palmer, Barbara, [1st] Countess of Castlemaine/1st Duchess of Cleveland 31, 33, 53, 54, 55, 57, 61, 65 n. 149, 71 n. 1, 75, 79, 80, 97, 108, 117, 132 n. 83, 178 n. 92, 241, 289

Villiers/Wenman/Wentworth/Howard, Barbara, [3rd] Countess of Suffolk 107

Vokins, Richard 233

Waldegrave, Henrietta *see* FitzJames/ Waldegrave

Waldegrave, Henry, 1st Baron Waldegrave 55, 138 n. 103

Wales, Prince of *see* Charles II; Stuart, James Francis Edward

Waller, Edmund 124, 125 n. 51

Walsingham, Frances 128 n. 63

Walter (Barlow), Lucy 98

Walter, John 135 n. 90, 292 n. 5

Walter, Mary 98

Warke, Baron Grey of *see* Grey, Ford

Waterman, Sir George 63 n. 134

Watkins, William 254 n. 119

Watts, Catherine 126 n. 54, 128 n. 63

Watts, William 65 n. 149

Webb, John 36 n. 33, 37, 38, 39, 40, 62 n. 129, 63–4 n. 137, 88, 106, 111 n. 119, 150

Webb, William 192 n. 124

Wells, John 64 n. 142

Wells, Samuel 62 n. 128

Wells, Winifred 33

Wentworth, Anne 126 n. 56

Wentworth, Lady Henrietta Maria, 6th Baroness Wentworth 82 n. 37, 97, 98

Wentworth, Lady Isabella *see* Apsley/ Wentworth

Wentworth, Thomas, 4th Baron Wentworth/1st Earl of Cleveland 97

Wentworth, Thomas, 5th Baron Wentworth 97

Wharton, Goodwin 138 n. 102

White, Bryan 295

Whitelocke, Bulstrode 12 n. 21

William Henry, Duke of Gloucester 138–9

William, Prince of Orange/William III 33, 44, 48 n. 78, 59 n. 113, 72, 82 n. 36, 99, 108 n. 110, 125, 138, 268, 286, 300

Williamson, Sir Joseph 205, 223, 263 n. 140

Wilmot, John, 2nd Earl of Rochester 33, 48, 86 n. 52, 87 n. 54, 135, 181, 270, 282, 294, 310

Wilson, John (composer) 84

Wilson, John (playwright) 178 n. 92

Winchilsea, Countess of *see* Kingsmill/ Finch, Anne

Winn, James A. 5, 6, 82 n. 35, 82 n. 36, 82 n. 37, 120–1, 131, 144

Wiseman, Mrs. 181

Wiseman, Susan J. 148 n. 11, 154 n. 35, 167 n. 71

Wood, Bruce 131, 137 n. 98, 292 n. 5, 292 n. 6

Wren, Sir Christopher 39, 62 n. 128, 236, 238, 249

Wycherley, William 68

Yarborough, Sir Thomas 34

Yates, Mrs. 214

Yates, Thomas 214 n. 70

Yoch, James 83

York, Duchess of *see* Hyde, Anne; Mary of Modena

York, Duke of *see* James

Young, John 180

Zenti, Girolamo 199 n. 17, 201 n. 25, 208–9 n. 48

Subject index

Academy of John Banister 131

Banqueting House, Whitehall Palace 35, 123 n. 47
Blackfriars, Children of the 83
Bridges Street Theatre 78, 81, 90, 204 n. 37, 211, 214, 236, 238, 240, 241, 255 n. 121

Cockpit Theatre, Drury Lane 148 n. 9, 150–1, 156 n. 36, 162, 163, 164 n. 66, 170, 215
Cockpit-in-Court Theatre, Whitehall Palace 31, 36, 37, 38, 214 n. 74

Dorset Garden Theatre 86, 87, 88, 115, 127 n. 58, 183, 223, 227, 238, 239, 240, 241, 246, 247, 248, 252, 254, 255, 268, 293, 297, 304, 305 n. 49
Drury Lane Theatre 5, 46, 68, 122, 123, 127 n. 58, 195, 225 n. 24, 233, 236, 237, 238, 240, 242 n. 91, 243–4, 246, 247, 249, 250, 252, 253, 254, 256, 265, 266, 281, 283, 296
Duchess of Portsmouth's Company 78
Duke's Company 5, 46, 78, 88, 95, 115, 125, 132, 176, 177, 178, 180, 182, 203, 223, 238, 239, 240–1, 246, 255 n. 121, 258, 262, 268

Hall Theatre, Whitehall Palace 22, 31, 38 n. 40, 39, 40–3, 45, 46, 47, 50 n. 86, 51, 61, 62 n. 127, 62 n. 128, 64 n. 142, 65 n. 144, 67, 86, 87, 88, 100, 103, 109, 110, 113, 115, 123, 131, 135, 138 n. 100, 181, 182, 212 n. 61, 233, 234 n. 59, 236, 250, 252, 254, 262 n. 137, 265
Hatton Garden 213 n. 65
Holyrood Palace 77, 126, 127, 128

Jaffa Cake 18–19

king's brief 242–5
King's Company 5, 16, 31, 46, 50 n. 86, 68, 74, 78, 83, 121, 122, 125 n. 52, 127, 181, 209, 212 n. 61, 214 n. 70, 236, 238, 239, 240–6, 254, 256–7, 260, 268 n. 18, 283 n. 73, 297 n. 26
King's Musick House 131
Kingston Lacy 179

Lincoln's Inn 30, 59
Lincoln's Inn Fields Theatre 175, 176, 178 n. 92, 179 n. 100, 182 n. 102, 182 n. 103, 190, 196, 238, 240, 255 n. 120

Masquing Room, Whitehall Palace 36

Nix v. Hedden 19–20
Nursery 193, 195, 211, 212, 213 n. 65

recitative 9, 10, 13 n. 34, 16, 17, 23, 143, 144–6, 147, 148, 149 n. 12, 153, 154, 155, 157, 158, 159 n. 48, 160, 161, 173, 175, 177, 182, 183, 184, 185, 191, 194, 195, 196, 197, 218, 235, 293, 294, 297, 306
Richmond Palace 27
Royall Academy of Musick 23, 90, 130, 247 n. 104, 250–63, 264, 270, 281, 285, 296, 297, 304
Rutland House 150, 156 n. 36, 162, 163 n. 64, 164 n. 66, 170
Rye House Plot 296

St. James's Palace 81, 84, 85, 123, 125 n. 51, 215, 217, 220 n. 3, 226 n. 26
Shrovetide 20, 31, 33, 37, 40–3, 47, 48, 50, 51, 52, 58, 59, 60, 72, 73, 75–6, 78, 80, 81 n. 33, 86 n. 50, 94 n. 75, 96, 123, 124, 132, 135, 294

350   *Subject index*

United Company 127 n. 58,
   246 n. 93, 294, 297, 298, 299,
   301, 303, 304, 305

velarium 62

Whitehall Palace 27, 31, 32, 34, 35, 36, 37,
   38, 39, 45 n. 59, 46, 47, 52, 61, 81, 88,
   108, 109, 115, 123, 123–4 n. 47, 128,
   131, 138 n. 100, 178 n. 92, 215 n. 78,
   220 n. 3, 233, 236, 237, 238, 249,
   252, 254 n. 119, 261, 262 n. 137, 273,
   296, 312; *see also* Banqueting House;
   Cockpit-in-Court Theatre; Hall Theatre;
   Masquing Room
Windsor Castle 43, 92 n. 71, 120 n. 34,
   121 n. 36, 125, 139, 246 n. 95, 265, 273
   n. 45, 277, 279 n. 53
Works, Office of 39, 45, 50, 69, 103 n. 96,
   104–5, 115, 233, 252

Works index

Acis et Galatée 285 n. 80
Albion and Albanius 5, 7, 15, 16, 17, 18, 23, 24, 295–303, 305, 306
Albion's Triumph 146, 147, 160
Alceste 260, 265
Amadis 304
Ariadne Deserted by Theseus 144, 147, 155, 157, 158, 159, 160, 161, 162 n. 58, 173, 183, 197 n. 11, 306
Ariadne, or the Marriage of Bacchus see *Ariane, ou le Mariage de Bacchus*
Ariane, ou le Mariage de Bacchus 5, 15, 60, 70 n. 164, 90, 110 n. 116, 184 n. 107, 225 n. 24, 232–9, 248–9
Armide 304
Atalanta, L' 213 n. 67
Atys 256, 260, 263 n. 141, 265, 304
Aurengzebe 126, 127

Ballet de l'Impatience 258 n. 134
Ballet et Musique pour le Divertissement du Roy de la Grande Bretagne 16 n. 39, 70 n. 164, 110 n. 116, 228–32, 233, 234, 237, 247, 253, 255, 256, 258, 260, 262, 281, 292
Beggar's Bush, The 236, 238, 246
Bourgeois Gentilhomme, Le 69–70
Britannia Triumphans 35 n. 31

Cadmus et Hermione 52, 228, 260, 261, 265, 304–5
Calisto 5, 12, 15, 17 n. 44, 20, 21, 22, 34, 46, 51, 53 n. 101, 56, 58, 59, 60, 70 n. 104, 72, 73, 75, 76, 81, 82 n. 37, 83, 84, 87 n. 55, 88–111, 112, 113, 114, 116, 117, 120, 123, 124, 125, 127, 128, 129, 132, 133, 134, 135, 137, 201 n. 27, 203 n. 34, 222 n. 16, 227 n. 32, 235, 255 n. 122, 256, 258, 259, 262, 263, 264, 266, 268, 269 n. 21, 271, 272, 280, 281, 293, 295, 306

Changes, The 82 n. 36, 246 n. 93
Cheats, The 178 n. 92
Chloridia 145
Circe 12, 15, 16
Claracilla 37 n. 37
Comical Revenge, The 82 n. 36
Conquest of Granada by the Spaniards, The 62 n. 127, 149 n. 12
Cruelty of the Spaniards in Peru, The 147, 148, 152, 154, 155, 156, 160, 162, 163, 164, 170 n. 72, 185, 186, 187–8, 190, 192, 316
Cupid and Death 7, 146, 147, 155, 158, 161, 162, 184, 185, 190, 281 n. 61, 306, 316
Cupid his Coronation 155, 162
Cutter of Coleman Street 82 n. 36

Dido and Aeneas 2, 3, 5, 15, 16, 20, 21, 24, 136–8, 143, 159 n. 47, 292, 294, 306
Dioclesian see *Prophetess, The*
Disappointment, The 294
Drake, The History of Sir Francis see *History of Sir Francis Drake, The*

Emperor of the Moon, The 287 n. 90, 299
Empress of Morocco, The 21, 22, 24, 75, 85–8, 89, 95, 102, 106, 108 n. 111, 125, 128 n. 62, 133, 134, 135, 147, 164 n. 65, 227, 248
Ercole in Lidia 146–8, 235
Erismena, L' 15, 213, 233 n. 55, 234, 293
Evening's Love, An 82 n. 36

Fâcheux, Les 90 n. 64
Faithful Shepherdess, The 21, 72, 75, 81, 82, 83, 84, 85, 86 n. 50, 87 n. 55, 89, 92, 95, 108, 110 n. 116, 123, 125, 132, 134, 135, 204 n. 37
Fancy's Festivals 155, 162

352 Works index

First Day's Entertainment at Rutland House, The 11, 13 n. 32, 147, 150, 151–2, 153, 154, 155, 162 n. 58, 187, 190–1, 192
Fool Would be a Favorite, The 82 n. 36
French Conjurer, The 115

George Dandin 91
Ghost, or The Woman Wears the Breeches, The 82 n. 36
Grand Divertissement Royal de Versailles, Le 91
Guardian, The see *Cutter of Coleman Street*
Guzman 182 n. 103

History of Sir Francis Drake, The 144, 147, 148, 152, 154–7, 160, 161, 162, 163, 164, 185, 186, 188–9, 190, 192, 193, 197, 235 n. 63, 293, 306, 316
Horace 21, 75, 76, 78–81, 89, 90, 92, 108, 125, 134, 135
Hymenaei 94 n. 75

Ibrahim, or The Illustrious Bassa (novel) 82 n. 36
Ibrahim, the Illustrious Bassa (play) 179, 180, 182, 183
Idylle en Musique 285–6, 288, 290 n. 91
Indian Emperor, The 21, 31 n. 19, 74, 75, 78, 79, 81, 82 n. 36, 89, 92, 108, 133, 134, 135, 246 n. 93
Indian Queen, The 154 n. 33, 197, 255 n. 121

Journal from Parnassus, A 51 n. 91, 299, 303

King and Queen's Entertainment at Richmond, The 27
King Arthur 18, 295

Lord Hay's Masque, The 94 n. 75
Lord Sunderland's court ballet 33, 51 n. 94, 52–8, 73, 108, 114, 117, 311–3
Love in a Tub see *Comical Revenge, The*
Love's Triumph Through Callipolis 145
Lovers Made Men 144, 147
Luminalia 145

Macbeth 194, 198
Maid of Honour, The 82 n. 36
Malade Imaginaire, Le 228

Man of Mode, The 125, 126, 256 n. 126, 263 n. 141
Marriage A-la-Mode 238, 246
Marriage of Oceanus and Britannia, The 146, 147, 155, 159–61, 162, 173, 183 n. 106, 185 n. 111, 197 n. 11, 306
Masque of Augurs 58 n. 109
Masque of Blackness 93–4
Memoirs of the Life of Count de Grammont 32–4, 38, 40, 53, 59
Mithridates 8, 21, 75, 76, 120–8, 132, 133, 134, 135, 268 n. 18
Mulberry Garden, The 194 n. 3
Mustapha, the Son of Solyman the Magnificent 38, 163 n. 61, 177 n. 88, 178, 179, 180, 182, 183, 193, 235, 255 n. 120

Naviganti, I 68, 205 n. 39
Nero, The Tragedy of 246 n. 93
Noces d'Isabelle, Les 288, 290
Nozze di Peleo e di Teti, Le 28–9

Oberon, the Fairy Prince 27
Oedipus 268 n. 18

Palais des Plaisirs, Le 138 n. 101
Parodie d'une Scene de l'Opera de Roland 288, 290
Pastorale d'Issy 230, 233
Pastoralle 267 n. 16, 281 n. 64, 294, 295 n. 15
Peines et Les Plaisirs de l'Amour, Les 237 n. 73, 254 n. 118
Pellegrina, La 90 n. 64
Peru, The Cruelty of the Spaniards in see *Cruelty of the Spaniards in Peru, The*
Play-House to be Let, The 156, 179 n. 100, 190, 196, 197
Pleasure Reconciled to Virtue 27
Pomone 237 n. 73, 254 n. 18, 281
Pompey 147, 196, 197
Prophetess, The 17, 18, 82 n. 36
Proposition for Advancement of Moralitie, A 149–50, 157 n. 44
Psyche 11 n. 19, 12, 15, 91, 132 n. 82, 223, 230 n. 44, 236 n. 67, 293, 295 n. 16
Psyché 260

Queen's Masque, The 8, 34, 53, 59–70, 71, 73, 75, 102, 108, 114, 127, 135, 205 n. 39, 217 n. 86, 235, 250

Works index 353

Rare en Tout 8, 12, 16 n. 39, 21, 22, 56,
75, 112–20, 134, 265 n. 8, 283, 284,
285, 286, 292
Raree-show, from Father Hopkins,
The 301–2, 303
Rebellion, The 82 n. 36
Rhodes, The Siege of see *Siege
of Rhodes, The*
Rival Queens, The 50 n. 86, 127 n. 58
Roland 285 n. 80, 288, 290

Salmacida Spolia 145
Sédécias 256, 258 n. 133, 260, 261,
262 n. 136
Shepherds' Paradise, The 85 n. 47
Siege of Rhodes, The 11, 13, 23, 144, 146,
147, 149 n. 12, 153, 154 n. 32, 155, 156,
157, 158, 159 n. 47, 161–82, 184, 186,
187, 190, 191, 192, 197, 306, 316
Siege of Rhodes, Part 2, The 157,
175, 176, 177, 178, 180, 181, 182,
183, 193
Slighted Maid, The 146, 147, 196,
197
Sophonisba 82 n. 36
Squire Oldsapp 88 n. 62, 268 n. 18

State of Innocence, The 16
Step-Mother, The 146, 147, 196, 197

Tempe Restored 145
Tempest, The 18, 91, 103 n. 98,
132 n. 82, 194, 198, 201 n. 24, 238–9,
246, 255, 293
Thésée 256 n. 129, 258, 260, 261, 265
Timon of Athens, The History of
268 n. 18, 283 n. 73
Triumphs of the Prince d'Amour, The 145

Valentinian 135, 294, 295 n. 15
Venus and Adonis 5, 7, 8, 12–13, 15, 16,
20, 21, 22, 24, 51, 72 n. 4, 75, 83, 117,
131–8, 143, 292–5, 306
Vision of Delight, The 146, 147, 160
Volpone 265–6, 283

Way of the World, The 182 n. 101
Wits, The 175 n. 79, 196 n. 9

Xerxes 258 n. 134

Zénobie 256, 258 n. 133, 260, 261,
262 n. 136